THE GREAT BOOK of WORLD FACTS, LISTS, & QUIZZES

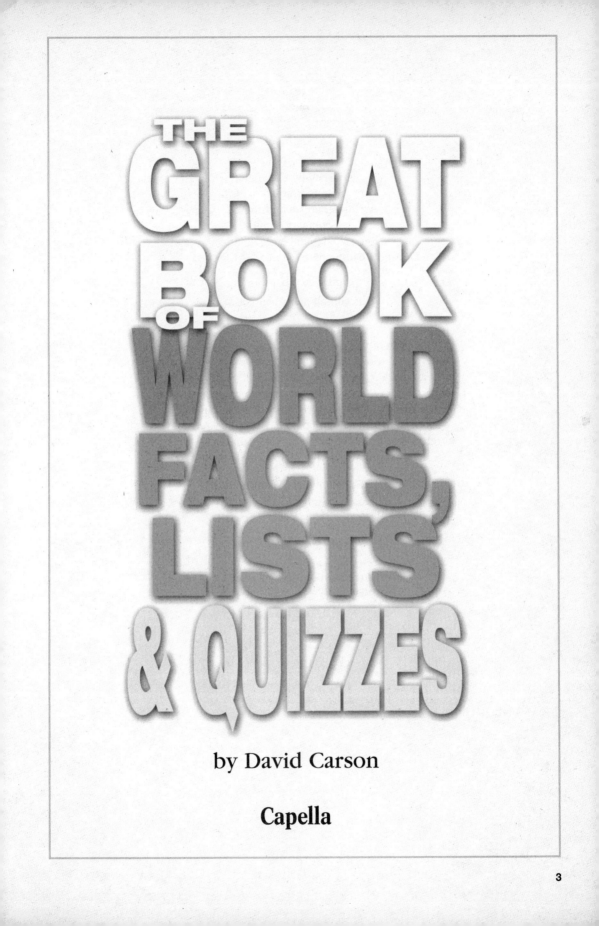

THE GREAT BOOK OF WORLD FACTS, LISTS & QUIZZES

by David Carson

Capella

Published by Capella,
an imprint of
Arcturus Publishing Limited
For Bookmart Limited
Registered Number 2372865
Desford Road, Enderby, Leicester LE9 5AD

ISBN 1-84139-120-9
This edition published 2002

Edited by Paul Whittle
Cover design by Alex Ingr
Book design by Kevin Ancient

Printed in Italy

© Arcturus Publishing Limited
1–7 Shand Street, London SE1 2ES

CONTENTS

1

GEOGRAPHY
&
TRAVEL

Countries of the World

World Capitals

Afghanistan	Kabul, 2,450,000
Albania	Tirana, 300,000
Algeria	Algiers
Andorra	Andorra la Vella, 22,390
Angola	Luanda, 2,000,000
Antigua and Barbuda	St. John's, 21,514; Codrington (capital of Barbuda), est. pop. 1,000
Argentina	Buenos Aires, 13,250,000 (metro. area)
Armenia	Yerevan, 1,226,000
Australia	Canberra, 307,700
Austria	Vienna, 1,600,000
Azerbaijan	Baku, 1,713,300, a port on the Caspian Sea
Bahamas	Nassau, 171,542
Bahrain	Al-Manámah, 140,401
Bangladesh	Dhaka, 9,600,000 (metro. area)
Barbados	Bridgetown, 6,700
Belarus	Mensk (Minsk), 1,666,000
Belgium	Brussels, 949,070 (metro area)
Belize	Belmopan, 5,845
Benin	Porto-Novo (official), 177,660; Cotonou (de facto capital) 33,212
Bhutan	Thimphu (official), 30,340
Bolivia	Sucre, 131,800; Administrative capital and largest city (1997 est.): La Paz, 713,400
Bosnia and Herzegovina	Sarajevo, 387,876 (unofficial)
Botswana	Gaborone, 138,000
Brazil	Brasília, 1,800,000
Brunei Darussalam	Bandar Seri Begawan, 52,300
Bulgaria	Sofia, 1,113,674
Burkina Faso	Ouagadougou, 500,000
Burundi	Bujumbura, 300,000
Cambodia	Phnom Penh, 900,000
Cameroon	Yaoundé
Canada	Ottawa, Ontario
Cape Verde	Praia, 61,797
Central African Republic	Bangui, 706,000

Chad	N'Djamena, 529,555
Chile	Santiago, 5,400,000 (metro. area)
China	Beijing, 8,450,000 (metro. area)
Colombia	Santafé de Bogotá, 7,350,000 (metro. area)
Comoros	Moroni (on Grande Comoro), 23,432
Congo	Brazzaville, 937,580
Congo, Democratic Republic of the	Kinshasa, 6,050,000 (metro. area)
Costa Rica	San José, 315,909
Côte d'Ivoire	Yamoussoukro (official), 120,000; Abidjan (administrative)
Croatia	Zagreb, 930,753
Cuba	Havana, 2,241,000
Cyprus	Lefkosia (Nicosia) (in government-controlled area), 186,400
Czech Republic	Prague, 1,215,771
Denmark	Copenhagen, 1,339,395
Djibouti	Djibouti, 395,000
Dominica	Roseau, 15,853
Dominican Republic	Santo Domingo, 2,100,000
Ecuador	Quito, 1,500,000
Egypt	Cairo, 14,350,000 (metro. area)
El Salvador	San Salvador, 972,810
Equatorial Guinea	Malabo, 30,418
Eritrea	Asmara, 400,000
Estonia	Tallinn, 471,608
Ethiopia	Addis Ababa, 2,200,186
Fiji	Suva (on Viti Levu), 200,000
Finland	Helsinki, 515,765
France	Paris, 10,150,000 (metro. area)
Gabon	Libreville, 419,596
Gambia, The	Banjul, 44,188
Georgia	Tbilisi, 1,279,000
Germany	Berlin (capital since Oct. 3, 1990), 3,471,418
Ghana	Accra
Greece	Athens
Grenada	St. George's, 4,439
Guatemala	Guatemala City, 1,150,452
Guinea	Conakry, 1,508,000
Guinea-Bissau	Bissau, 200,000
Guyana	Georgetown, 248,500
Haiti	Port-au-Prince, 1.5 million
Honduras	Tegucigalpa, 1,500,000
Hungary	Budapest, 2,008,546
Iceland	Reykjavik, 103,036

India	Delhi, 11,500,000 (metro. area)
Indonesia	Jakarta, 12,300,000 (metro. area)
Iran	Teheran, 10,400,000 (metro. area)
Iraq	Baghdad, 4,850,000 (metro. area)
Ireland	Dublin
Israel	Jerusalem, 550,500
Italy	Rome, 2,693,383
Jamaica	Kingston, 104,000
Japan	Tokyo, 34,750,000 (metro. area)
Jordan	Amman, 963,490
Kazakhstan	Astana, 280,200 (formerly Aqmola; capital since 1997)
Kenya	Nairobi, 2,000,000
Kiribati	Tarawa, 25,154
Korea, North	Pyongyang, 2,741,260
Korea, South	Seoul, 19,850,000 (metro. area)
Kuwait	Kuwait, 151,060
Kyrgyzstan	Bishkek (formerly Frunze), 631,000
Laos	Vientiane, 442,000
Latvia	Riga, 874,000
Lebanon	Beirut, 1,100,000
Lesotho	Maseru (1992), 170,000
Liberia	Monrovia, 1,000,000
Libya	Tripoli
Liechtenstein	Vaduz, 5,067
Lithuania	Vilnius, 590,100
Luxembourg	Luxembourg, 75,622
Macedonia	Skopje, 444,229
Madagascar	Antananarivo, 1,000,000
Malawi	Lilongwe, 260,000
Malaysia	Kuala Lumpur, 1,145,000
Maldives	Malé, 62,973
Mali	Bamako, 746,000
Malta	Valletta, 9,183
Marshall Islands	Majuro, 20,000
Mauritania	Nouakchott, 480,000
Mauritius	Port Louis, 134,516
Mexico	Mexico City, 19,750,000 (metro. area)
Micronesia	Palikir
Moldova	Chisinau, 676,700
Monaco	Monaco, 30,400
Mongolia	Ulan Bator, 619,000
Morocco	Rabat, 1,220,000
Mozambique	Maputo, 1,095,300
Myanmar	Rangoon (Yangon)
Namibia	Windhoek, 161,000

Nauru	Yaren, 559
Nepal	Kathmandu, 535,000
The Netherlands	Amsterdam (official), 724,096; The Hague (administrative capital), 445,279
New Zealand	Wellington
Nicaragua	Managua, 974,000
Niger	Niamey, 398,265
Nigeria	Abuja, 339,000
Norway	Oslo, 483,401
Oman	Muscat, 350,000
Pakistan	Islamabad, 201,000
Palau	Koror, 12,299
Palestinian State (proposed)	Undetermined
Panama	Panama City, 450,668
Papua New Guinea	Port Moresby, 250,000
Paraguay	Asunción, 502,426
Peru	Lima, 7,450,000 (metro. area)
The Philippines	Manila, 13,450,000 (metro. area)
Poland	Warsaw, 1,642,700
Portugal	Lisbon, 677,790
Qatar	Doha, 300,000
Romania	Bucharest, 2,351,000
Russia	Moscow, 13,200,000 (metro. area)
Rwanda	Kigali, 232,733
St. Kitts and Nevis	Basseterre (on St. Kitts), 19,000
St. Lucia	Castries, 13,600
St. Vincent and The Grenadines	Kingstown, 15,466
Samoa	Apia, 32,859
San Marino	San Marino, 2,397
São Tomé and Príncipe	São Tomé, 43,420
Saudi Arabia	Riyadh
Senegal	Dakar, 1,729,823
Seychelles	Victoria, 25,000
Sierra Leone	Freetown, 1,300,000
Singapore	Singapore, 3,044,000
Slovakia	Bratislava, 446,600
Slovenia	Ljubljana, 330,000
Solomon Islands	Honiara (on Guadalcanal), 35,288
Somalia	Mogadishu, 900,000
South Africa	Pretoria; Legislative capital: Cape Town; Judicial capital: Bloemfontein. No decision has been made to relocate the seat of government. South Africa is demarcated into nine provinces, consisting of the Gauteng, Northern Province, Mpumalanga, North West, KwaZulu/Natal, Eastern Cape, Western Cape,

	Northern Cape, and Free State. Each province has its own capital
Spain	Madrid, 5,050,000 (metro. area)
Sri Lanka	Colombo (official) 1,994,000; Sri Jayawardenepura Kotte (legislative and judicial), 107,000 (1988 est.)
Sudan	Khartoum, 924,505
Suriname	Paramaribo, 200,970
Swaziland	Mbabane 47,020
Sweden	Stockholm, 703,627
Switzerland	Bern, 129,423
Syria	Damascus, 1,549,932
Taiwan	Taipei, 7,700,000 (metro. area)
Tajikistan	Dushanbe, 524,000
Tanzania	Dar es Salaam (administrative), 1,360,850; Dodoma (official), 45,807 (1978)
Thailand	Bangkok, 7,200,000 (metro. area)
Togo	Lomé, 366,476
Tonga	Nuku'alofa, 34,000
Trinidad and Tobago	Port-of-Spain, 52,451
Tunisia	Tunis, 887,800
Turkey	Ankara, 2,890,025
Turkmenistan	Ashgabat, 518,000
Tuvalu	Funafuti, 3,839
Uganda	Kampala, 773,463
Ukraine	Kyiv (Kiev), 2,637,000
United Arab Emirates	Abu Dhabi, 363,432
United Kingdom	London, 11,800,000 (metro. area)
United States	Washington, DC, 572,059
Uruguay	Montevideo, 1,330,440
Uzbekistan	Tashkent, 2,106,000
Vanuatu	Port Vila, 26,100
Venezuela	Caracas
Vietnam	Hanoi
Western Sahara	El Aaiun (20,010)
Yemen	Sanaá, 972,011
Yugoslavia	Belgrade, 1,168,454
Zambia	Lusaka
Zimbabwe	Harare, 1,184,169

World Currencies

Afghanistan	Afghani
Albania	Lek
Algeria	Dinar
Andorra	French franc and Spanish peseta
Angola	Kwanza
Antigua and Barbuda	East Caribbean dollar
Argentina	Peso
Armenia	Dram
Australia	Australian dollar
Austria	Euro (formerly schilling)
Azerbaijan	Manat
Bahamas	Bahamian dollar
Bahrain	Bahrain dinar
Bangladesh	Taka
Barbados	Barbados dollar
Belarus	Belorussian ruble
Belgium	Euro (formerly Belgian franc)
Belize	Belize dollar
Benin	Franc CFA
Bhutan	Ngultrum
Bolivia	Boliviano
Bosnia and Herzegovina	Dinar
Botswana	Pula
Brazil	Real
Brunei Darussalam	Brunei dollar
Bulgaria	Lev
Burkina Faso	Franc CFA
Burundi	Burundi franc
Cambodia	Riel
Cameroon	Franc CFA
Canada	Canadian dollar
Cape Verde	Cape Verdean escudo
Central African Republic	Franc CFA
Chad	Franc CFA
Chile	Peso
China	Yuan
Colombia	Peso
Comoros	Franc CFA
Congo	Franc CFA
Congo, Democratic Republic of the	Congolese franc
Costa Rica	Colón

Côte d'Ivoire	Franc CFA
Croatia	Kuna (May 1994)
Cuba	Peso
Cyprus	Cyprus pound
Czech Republic	Koruna
Denmark	Krone
Djibouti	Djibouti franc
Dominica	East Caribbean dollar
Dominican Republic	Peso
Ecuador	U.S. dollar
Egypt	Egyptian pound
El Salvador	Colón
Equatorial Guinea	CFA Franc
Eritrea	Nakfa
Estonia	Kroon
Ethiopia	Birr
Fiji	Fiji dollar
Finland	Euro (formerly markka)
France	Euro (formerly French franc)
Gabon	Franc CFA
Gambia, The	Dalasi
Georgia	Lari
Germany	Euro (formerly Deutsche mark)
Ghana	Cedi
Greece	Euro (formerly drachma)
Grenada	East Caribbean dollar
Guatemala	Quetzal
Guinea	Guinean franc
Guinea-Bissau	Guinea-Bissau peso
Guyana	Guyana dollar
Haiti	Gourde
Honduras	Lempira
Hungary	Forint
Iceland	Icelandic króna
India	Rupee
Indonesia	Rupiah
Iran	Rial
Iraq	Iraqi dinar
Ireland	Euro (formerly Irish pound [punt])
Israel	Shekel
Italy	Euro (formerly lira)
Jamaica	Jamaican dollar
Japan	Yen
Jordan	Jordanian dinar

Kazakhstan	Tenge
Kenya	Kenyan shilling
Kiribati	Australian dollar
Korea, North	Won
Korea, South	Won
Kuwait	Kuwaiti dinar
Kyrgyzstan	Som
Laos	Kip
Latvia	Lats
Lebanon	Lebanese pound
Lesotho	Loti
Liberia	Liberian dollar
Libya	Libyan dinar
Liechtenstein	Swiss franc
Lithuania	Litas
Luxembourg	Euro (formerly Luxembourg franc)
Macedonia	Denar
Madagascar	Malagasy franc
Malawi	Kwacha
Malaysia	Ringgit
Maldives	Maldivian Rufiyaa
Mali	Franc CFA
Malta	Maltese lira
Mauritania	Ouguiya
Mauritius	Mauritian rupee
Mexico	Peso
Moldova	Moldovan Lem
Monaco	French franc
Mongolia	Tugrik
Morocco	Dirham
Mozambique	Metical
Myanmar	Kyat
Namibia	Namibian dollars
Nauru	Australian dollar
Nepal	Nepalese rupee
The Netherlands	Euro (formerly guilder)
New Zealand	New Zealand dollar
Nicaragua	Cordoba
Niger	Franc CFA
Nigeria	Naira
Norway	Krone
Oman	Omani rial
Pakistan	Pakistan rupee
Palau	U.S. dollar used
Palestinian State (proposed)	New Israeli shekels, Jordanian dinars, U.S. dollars
Panama	Balboa

Papua New Guinea	Kina
Paraguay	Guaraní
Peru	Nuevo Sol (1991)
The Philippines	Peso
Poland	Zloty
Portugal	Euro (formerly escudo)
Qatar	Qatari riyal
Romania	Leu
Russia	Ruble
Rwanda	Rwanda franc
St. Kitts and Nevis	East Caribbean dollar
St. Lucia	East Caribbean dollar
St. Vincent and The Grenadines	East Caribbean dollar
Samoa	Tala
San Marino	Italian lira
São Tomé and Príncipe	Dobra
Saudi Arabia	Riyal
Senegal	Franc CFA
Seychelles	Seychelles rupee
Sierra Leone	Leone
Singapore	Singapore dollar
Slovakia	Koruna (SKK)
Slovenia	Slovenian tolar
Solomon Islands	Solomon Islands dollar
Somalia	Somali shilling
South Africa	Rand
Spain	Euro (formerly peseta)
Sri Lanka	Sri Lanka rupee
Sudan	Sudanese pound
Suriname	Suriname guilder
Swaziland	Lilangeni
Sweden	Krona
Switzerland	Swiss franc
Syria	Syrian pound
Taiwan	New Taiwan dollar
Tajikistan	Tajik ruble
Tanzania	Tanzanian shilling
Thailand	baht
Togo	Franc CFA
Tonga	Pa'anga
Trinidad and Tobago	Trinidad and Tobago dollar
Tunisia	Tunisian dinar
Turkey	Turkish lira
Turkmenistan	Manat
Tuvalu	Tuvaluan dollar, Australian dollar

Uganda	Ugandan shilling
Ukraine	Hryvnia (since Sept. 2, 1996)
United Arab Emirates	U.A.E. dirham
United Kingdom	Pound sterling (£)
United States	dollar
Uruguay	Peso
Uzbekistan	Uzbekistani som
Vanuatu	Vatu
Vatican City (Holy See)	Italian lira
Venezuela	bolivar
Vietnam	Dong
Western Sahara	Moroccan dirham (DH)
Yemen	Rial
Yugoslavia	Yugoslav new dinar
Zambia	Kwacha
Zimbabwe	Zimbabwean dollar

Languages by Countries

Afghanistan	Pushtu, Dari Persian, other Turkic and minor languages
Albania	Albanian (Tosk is the official dialect), Greek
Algeria	Arabic (official), French, Berber dialects
Andorra	Catalán (official), French, Spanish
Angola	Bantu, Portuguese (official)
Antigua and Barbuda	English
Argentina	Spanish (official), English, Italian, German, French
Armenia	Armenian
Australia	English
Austria	German 98% (small Slovene, Croatian, and Hungarian-speaking minorities)
Azerbaijan	Azerbaijani Turkic, 82%; Russian, 7%; Armenian, 2%
Bahamas	English
Bahrain	Arabic (official), English, Farsi, Urdu
Bangladesh	Bangla (official), English
Barbados	English
Belarus	Belorussian (White Russian)
Belgium	Dutch (Flemish), 57%; French, 32%; bilingual (Brussels), 10%; German, 0.7%
Belize	English (official), Creole, Spanish, Garifuna, Mayan
Benin	French (official), African languages
Bhutan	Dzongkha (official)
Bolivia	Spanish (official), Quechua, Aymara, Guarani
Bosnia and Herzegovina	The language that used to be known as Serbo-Croatian but is now known as Serbian, Croatian, or Bosnian, depending on the speaker's ethnic and political affiliation. It is written in Latin and Cyrillic
Botswana	English (official), Setswana
Brazil	Portuguese
Brunei Darussalam	Malay (official), Chinese, English
Bulgaria	Bulgarian
Burkina Faso	French (official), tribal languages
Burundi	Kirundi and French (official), Swahili
Cambodia	Khmer (official), French, English
Cameroon	French and English (both official); 24 major African language groups
Canada	English, French (both official)
Cape Verde	Portuguese, Criuolo
Central African Republic	French (official), Sangho, Arabic, Hansa, Swahili
Chad	French and Arabic (official), more than 100 tribal languages

Chile	Spanish
China	Chinese, Mandarin, also local dialects
Colombia	Spanish
Comoros	French and Arab (both official), Shaafi Islam (Swahili dialect), Malagasu
Congo	French (official), Lingala, Kikongo, others
Congo, Democratic Republic of the	French (official), Swahili, Lingala, Ishiluba, and Kikongo,others
Costa Rica	Spanish
Côte d'Ivoire	French (official) and African languages (Diaula esp.)
Croatia	What was once known as Serbo-Croatian is now known as Serbian, Croatian, or Bosnian, depending on the speaker's political and ethnic affiliation
Cuba	Spanish
Cyprus	Greek, Turkish (official), English is widely spoken
Czech Republic	Czech; Slovak minority
Denmark	Danish, Faeroese, Greenlandic (an Inuit dialect), small German-speaking minority
Djibouti	Arabic and French (both official), Afar, Somali
Dominica	English (official) and French patois
Dominican Republic	Spanish, English widely spoken
Ecuador	Spanish (official), Quechua
Egypt	Arabic
El Salvador	Spanish
Equatorial Guinea	Spanish (official), French (2nd official), pidgin English, Fang, Bubi, Creole
Eritrea	Afar, Bilen, Kunama, Nara, Arabic, Tobedawi, Saho, Tigre, Tigrinya
Estonia	Estonian (official), Russian, Finnish, English
Ethiopia	Amharic (official), English, Orominga, Tigrigna, over 70 languages spoken
Fiji	Fijian, Hindustani, English (official)
Finland	Finnish, Swedish (both official); small Sami- (Lapp) and Russian-speaking minorities
France	French, declining regional dialects (Provençal, Breton, Alsatian, Corsican)
Gabon	French (official), Fang, Myene, Bateke, Bapounou/Eschira, Bandjabi
Gambia, The	Native tongues, English (official)
Georgia	Georgian (official), 71%; Russian, 9%; Armenian, 7%; Azerbaijani, 6%
Germany	German
Ghana	English (official), Native tongues (Brong Ahafo, Twi, Fanti, Ga, Ewe, Dagbani)
Greece	Greek
Grenada	English

Guatemala	Spanish, Indian languages
Guinea	French (official), native tongues (Malinké, Susu, Fulani)
Guinea-Bissau	Portuguese Criolo, African languages
Guyana	English (official), Amerindian dialects
Haiti	Creole and French (both official)
Honduras	Spanish (official), English widely spoken in business
Hungary	Magyar (Hungarian), 98.2%; other, 1.8%
Iceland	Icelandic
India	Hindi (official), English (official), Bengali, Gujarati, Kashmiri, Malayalam, Marathi, Oriya, Punjabi, Tamil, Telugu, Urdu, Kannada, Assamese, Sanskrit, Sindhi (all recognized by the constitution). Dialects, 1,652
Indonesia	Bahasa Indonesia (official), Dutch, English, and more than 583 languages and dialects
Iran	Farsi (Persian), Azari, Kurdish, Arabic
Iraq	Arabic (official) and Kurdish
Ireland	English, Irish Gaelic
Israel	Hebrew (official), Arabic, English
Italy	Italian; small German-, French-, and Slovene-speaking minorities
Jamaica	English, Jamaican Creole
Japan	Japanese
Jordan	Arabic (official), English
Kazakhstan	Kazak (Qazaq), official language spoken by over 40% of population; Russian, official language spoken by two-thirds of population and used in everyday business
Kenya	English (official), Swahili (national), and several other languages spoken by 25 ethnic groups
Kiribati	English (official), I-Kiribati (Gilbertese)
Korea, North	Korean
Korea, South	Korean
Kuwait	Arabic (official), English
Kyrgyzstan	Kyrgyz (official); Russian is de facto second language of communication
Laos	Lao (official), French, English
Latvia	Latvian
Lebanon	Arabic (official), French, English
Lesotho	English and Sesotho (official); also Zulu and Xhosa
Liberia	English (official) and tribal dialects
Libya	Arabic, Italian and English widely understood in major cities
Liechtenstein	German (official), Alemmanic dialect
Lithuania	Lithuanian (official), Polish, Russian
Luxembourg	Luxermbourgish, French, German

Macedonia	Macedonian, which uses the Cyrillic alphabet, 70%; Albanian, 21%; Turkish, 3%; other, 6%
Madagascar	Malagasy and French (both official)
Malawi	English and Chichewa (both official)
Malaysia	Malay (official), Chinese, Tamil, English
Maldives	Dhivehi (official); Arabic, Hindi, and English are also spoken
Mali	French (official), African languages
Malta	Maltese and English (both official)
Marshall Islands	Both Marshallese and English are official languages. Marshallese is a language in the Malayo-Polynesian family
Mauritania	Arabic (official) and French
Mauritius	English (official), French, Creole, Hindi, Urdu, Hakka, Bojpoori
Mexico	Spanish, Indian languages
Micronesia	English is the official and common language; major indigenous languages are Chukese, Pohnpeian, Yapase, and Kosrean
Moldova	Moldovan (official; virtually the same as Romanian), Russian, Gagauz (a Turkish dialect)
Monaco	French (official), English, Italian, Monégasque
Mongolia	Mongolian, 90%; also Turkic, Russian, and Chinese
Morocco	Arabic (official), French, Berber dialects, Spanish
Mozambique	Portuguese (official), Bantu languages
Myanmar	Burmese, minority languages
Namibia	Afrikaans, German, English (official), several indigenous
Nauru	Nauruan (official) and English
Nepal	Nepali (official), Newari, Bhutia, Maithali
The Netherlands	Dutch, Frisian
New Zealand	English (official), Maori
Nicaragua	Spanish
Niger	French (official); Hausa; Songhai; Arabic
Nigeria	English (official), Hausa, Yoruba, Ibo, and more than 200 others
Norway	Two official forms of Norwegian: Bokmål and Nynorsk
Oman	Arabic (official); also English and Indian languages
Pakistan	Punjabi 48%, Sindhi 12%, Siraiki (a Punjabi variant) 10%, Pashtu 8%, Urdu (official) 8%, Balochi 3%, Hindko 2%, Brahui 1%, English, Burushaski, and others
Palau	Palauan, English (official)
Palestinian State (proposed)	Arabic, Hebrew, English, French
Panama	Spanish (official); many bilingual in English
Papua New Guinea	English, Tok Pisin (a Melanesian Creole English), Hiri

	Motu, and 717 distinct native languages
Paraguay	Spanish (official), Guaraní
Peru	Spanish and Quéchua (both official), Aymara, and other native languages
The Philippines	Filipino (based on Tagalog) and English (both official); regional languages: Tagalog, Ilocano, Cebuano, others
Poland	Polish
Portugal	Portuguese
Qatar	Arabic (official); English is also widely spoken
Romania	Romanian (official); Hungarian- and German-speaking minorities
Russia	Russian, others
Rwanda	Kinyarwanda, French, and English (all official)
St. Lucia	English (official) and patois
St. Vincent and The Grenadines	English (official), French patois
Samoa	Samoan and English
San Marino	Italian
São Tomé and Príncipe	Portuguese
Saudi Arabia	Arabic, English widely spoken
Senegal	French (official); Wolof, Serer, other ethnic dialects
Seychelles	English and French (both official), and Seselwa (a creole)
Sierra Leone	English (official), Mende, Temne, Krio
Singapore	Malay, Chinese (Mandarin), Tamil, English (all official)
Slovakia	Slovak (official), Hungarian
Slovenia	Slovenian; most can also speak Serbo-Croatian
Solomon Islands	English, Solomon Pijin (an English pidgin), over 60 indigenous Melanesian languages
Somalia	Somali (official), Arabic, English, Italian
South Africa	Xhosa and Zulu (official), English, Afrikaans, Ndebele, Sesotho sa Leboa, Sesotho, Swati, Xitsonga, Setswana, Tshivenda
Spain	Castilian Spanish 74% (official), Catalan 17%, Galician 7%, Basque 2%
Sri Lanka	Sinhala (official), Tamil, English
Sudan	Arabic (official), English, tribal dialects
Suriname	Dutch (official), Surinamese (lingua franca), English widely spoken
Swaziland	English and Swazi (official)
Sweden	Swedish
Switzerland	German, French, Italian (all official), Romansch
Syria	Arabic (official), French and English widely understood
Taiwan	Chinese (Mandarin)

Tajikistan	Tajik
Tanzania	Swahili and English (both official), local languages
Thailand	Thai (Siamese), Chinese, English
Togo	French (official), Ewé, Mina (south), Kabyé, Cotocoli (north), and many dialects
Tonga	Tongan (an Austronesian language), English
Trinidad and Tobago	English (official), Hindi, French, Spanish
Tunisia	Arabic (official), French
Turkey	Turkish
Turkmenistan	Turkmen, 72%; Russian, 12%; Uzbek, 9%
Tuvalu	Tuvaluan, English
Uganda	English (official), Swahili, Luganda, Ateso, Luo
Ukraine	Ukrainian
United Arab Emirates	Arabic (official), English as a second language
United Kingdom	English, Welsh, Scots Gaelic
United States	English, sizable Spanish-speaking minority
Uruguay	Spanish
Uzbekistan	Uzbek 74.3%, Russian 14.2%, Tajik 4.4%, other 7.1%
	Vanuatu Bislama (a Melanesian pidgin English), English, French (all 3 official)
Vatican City (Holy See)	Latin, Italian, and various other languages
Venezuela	Spanish (official), various indigenous languages in the remote interior
Vietnam	Vietnamese (official), French, English, Khmer, Chinese
Western Sahara	Hassaniya Arabic, Moroccan Arabic
Yemen	Arabic
Yugoslavia	Serbian 95%, Albanian 5%. What was once known as Serbo-Croatian is now known as Serbian, Croatian, or Bosnian, depending on the speaker's political and ethnic affiliation. It is written in Latin and Cyrillic
Zambia	English (official) and local dialects
Zimbabwe	English (official), Ndebele, Shona (85%)

World Religions

Afghanistan	Islam (Sunni 84%, Shi'ite 15%, other 1%)
Albania	Muslim 70%, Albanian Orthodox 20%, Roman Catholic 10%
Algeria	99% Islam (Sunni)
Andorra	Roman Catholic
Angola	Roman Catholic 47%, Protestant 38%, Indigenous 15%
Antigua and Barbuda	Anglican and Roman Catholic
Argentina	Roman Catholic 92%, Protestant 2%, Jewish 2%, other 4%
Armenia	Armenian Orthodox 94%
Australia	Anglican 26.1%, Roman Catholic 26.0%, other Christian 24.3%
Austria	Roman Catholic 85%, Protestant 6%, other 9%
Azerbaijan	Muslim 87%, Russian Orthodox 5.6%, Armenian Orthodox 2%
Bahamas	Baptist 29%, Anglican 23%, Roman Catholic 22%, others
Bahrain	Islam
Bangladesh	Muslim 83%, Hindu 16%, Buddhist, Christian, other
Barbados	Anglican 40%, Methodist 7%, Pentecostal 8%, Roman Catholic 4%
Belarus	Orthodoxy is predominant
Belgium	Roman Catholic 75%
Belize	Roman Catholic 62%, Protestant 30%
Benin	indigenous 70%, Christian 15%, Islam 15%
Bhutan	Buddhist 75%, Hindu 25%
Bolivia	Roman Catholic 85%
Bosnia and Herzegovina	Slavic Muslim 44%, Orthodox 31%, Catholic 15%, Protestant 4%, other 6%
Botswana	indigenous beliefs 50%, Christian 50%
Brazil	Roman Catholic 90% (nominal)
Brunei Darussalam	Islam (official religion) 67%, Buddhist 12%, Christian 9%, indigenous beliefs and other 12%
Bulgaria	Bulgarian Orthodox 85%, Muslim 13%, Jewish 0.8%, Roman Catholic 0.5%, Uniate Catholic 0.2%, Protestant, Gregorian-Armenian, and other 0.5%
Burkina Faso	Muslim 50%, Christian (mainly Roman Catholic) 10%, indigenous beliefs 40%
Burundi	Roman Catholic 62%, Protestant 5%, indigenous 32%
Cambodia	Theravada Buddhist 95%, others 5%
Cameroon	51% indigenous beliefs, 33% Christian, 16% Muslim

Canada	Roman Catholic 46%, United Church 16%, Anglican 10%
Cape Verde	Roman Catholic fused with indigenous beliefs
Central African Republic	indigenous beliefs 24%, Protestant and Roman Catholic with animist influence 50%, Muslim 15%, other 11%
Chad	Islam 44%, Christian 33%, traditional 23%
Chile	Roman Catholic 89%, Protestant 11%, small Jewish and Muslim populations
China	Officially atheist but traditional religion contains elements of Confucianism, Taoism, Buddhism
Colombia	Roman Catholic 95%
Comoros	Sunni Muslim 86%, Roman Catholic 14%
Congo	Christian 50%, animist 48%, Muslim 2%
Congo, Democratic	Roman Catholic 50%, Protestant 20%, Kimbanguist 10%, Republic of theIslam 10%; syncretic and traditional, 10%
Costa Rica	Roman Catholic 95%
Côte d'Ivoire	indigenous 60%, Islam 23%, Christian 17%
Croatia	Catholic 76.5%, Orthodox 11.1%, Slavic Muslim 1.2%, Protestant 0.4%, others 10.8%
Cuba	at least 85% nominally Roman Catholic before Castro assumed power
Cyprus	Greek Orthodox 78%, Sunni Muslim 18%, Maronite, Armenian, Apostolic, Latin, and others 4%
Czech Republic	atheist 39.8%, Roman Catholic 39.2%, Protestant 4.6%, Orthodox 3%, other 13.4%
Denmark	Evangelical Lutheran 91%, other Protestant and Roman Catholic 2%, other 7%
Djibouti	Muslim 94%, Christian 6%
Dominica	Roman Catholic 77%, Protestant 15%
Dominican Republic	Roman Catholic 90%
Ecuador	Roman Catholic 95%
Egypt	Islam 94%, Christian (mostly Coptic) 6%
El Salvador	Roman Catholic
Equatorial Guinea	Roman Catholic, Protestant, traditional
Eritrea	Islam and Eritrean Orthodox Christianity
Estonia	Lutheran 78%, Orthodox 19%
Ethiopia	Ethiopian Orthodox 35%-40%, Islam 40%-45%, animist 15%-20%, other 5%
Fiji	Christian 52%, Hindu 38%, Islam 8%, other 2%
Finland	Evangelical Lutheran 90%, Greek Orthodox 1.2%, none 9%, other 1%
France	Roman Catholic 81%, Protestant 1.7%, Muslim 6.9%, Jewish 1.3%
Gabon	Catholic 75%, Protestant 20%, Animist 4%

Gambia, The	Islam 90%, Christian 9%, traditional 1%
Georgia	Georgian Orthodox 65%, Russian Orthodox 10%, Armenian Orthodox 8%, Muslim 11%
Germany	Protestant 38%, Roman Catholic 34%, Muslim 1.7%, Unaffiliated or other 26.3%
Ghana	indigenous beliefs 38%, Islam 30%, Christian 24%
Greece	Greek Orthodox 98%, Muslim 1.3%, other 0.7%
Grenada	Roman Catholic 64%, Anglican 21%
Guatemala	Roman Catholic, Protestant, Mayan
Guinea	Islam 85%, indigenous 7%, Christian 8%
Guinea-Bissau	traditional 65%, Islam 30%, Christian 5%
Guyana	Hindu 34%, Protestant 18%, Islam 9%, Roman Catholic 18%, Anglican 16%
Haiti	Roman Catholic 80%, Protestant 16%, Vaudou 95%
Honduras	Roman Catholic 94%, Protestant minority
Hungary	Roman Catholic 67.5%, Protestant 25%, atheist and others 7.5%
Iceland	Church of Iceland (Evangelical Lutheran) 96%, other Protestant and Roman Catholic 3%, none 1%
India	Hindu 82.6%, Islam 11.3%, Christian 2.4%, Sikh 2%, Buddhists 0.71%, Jains 0.48%
Indonesia	Islam 87%, Christian 9%, Hindu 2%, other 2%
Iran	Shi'ite Muslim 95%, Sunni Muslim 4%
Iraq	Muslim 97% (Shi'ite 60%–65%, Sunni 32%–37%), Christian or other 3%
Ireland	Roman Catholic 93%, Anglican 3%, none 1%, unknown 2%, other 1%
Israel	Judaism 82%, Islam 14%, Christian 2%, others 2%
Italy	Roman Catholic 98%, other 2%
Jamaica	Protestant 55.9%, Roman Catholic 5%, other 39.1%
Japan	Shintoist, Buddhist, Christian
Jordan	Islam 92%, Christian 6%, other 2%
Kazakhstan	Muslim, 47%; Russian Orthodox, 44%; Protestant, 2%; other, 7%
Kenya	Protestant, 40%; Roman Catholic, 36%; traditional, 6%; Islam, 16%; others, 2%
Kiribati	Roman Catholic 52.6%, Protestant 40.9%
Korea, North	Buddhism and Confucianism; religious activities almost nonexistent
Korea, South	Christian, 48.2%; Buddhist, 48.8%; Confucianist, 0.8%; Chondogyo (religion of the Heavenly Way), 0.2%; other, 2%
Kuwait	Islam, 85% (Shi'ite 30%, Sunni 45%, other 10%); Christian, Hindu, Parsi, and other, 15%
Kyrgyzstan	Muslim, 75%; Russian Orthodox, 20%; other, 5%

Laos	Buddhist 85%, animist and other 15%
Latvia	Lutheran, Catholic, and Baptist
Lebanon	Islam, 60%; Christian, 40% (17 recognized sects);
Judaism,	negl. (1 sect)
Lesotho	Christian, 80%; indigenous beliefs, Muslim, and Bahai
Liberia	traditional 70%, Christian 10%, Islam 20%
Libya	Islam
Liechtenstein	Roman Catholic, 80%; Protestant, 6.9%; unknown, 5.6%; other, 7.5%
Lithuania	Catholic 85%, others include Lutheran, Russian Orthodox, Protestant, evangelical Christian Baptist, Islam, Judaism
Luxembourg	Roman Catholic 97%, Protestant and Jewish 3%
Macedonia	Eastern Orthodox 67%, Muslim 30%
Madagascar	traditional 52%, Christian 41%, Islam 7%
Malawi	Christian 75%, Islam 20%
Malaysia	Malays (all Muslims), Chinese (predominantly Buddhists), Indians (predominantly Hindus)
Maldives	Islam (Sunni Muslim)
Mali	Islam 90%, traditional 9%, Christian 1%
Malta	Roman Catholic 98%
Marshall Islands	predominantly Christian, mostly Protestant
Mauritania	Islam
Mauritius	Hindu 52%, Christian 28.3%, Islam 16.6%, other 3.1%
Mexico	nominally Roman Catholic 97%, Protestant 3%
Moldova	Eastern Orthodox 98.5%, Jewish 1.5%, Baptist (only about 1,000 members)
Monaco	Roman Catholic 95%
Mongolia	predominantly Tibetan Buddhist; Islam about 4%
Morocco	Islam 98.7%, Christian 1.1%, Jewish 0.2%
Mozambique	traditional 60%, Christian 30%, Islam 10%
Myanmar	Buddhist 89.5%, Christian 4.9%, Muslim 3.8%, Hindu 0.05%, Animist 1.3%
Namibia	Predominantly Christian
Nauru	Protestant 58%, Roman Catholic 24%, Confucian and Taoist 8%
Nepal	Hindu 90%, Buddhist 5%, Islam 3%
The Netherlands	Roman Catholic 34%, Protestant 25%, Muslim 3%, other 2%, unaffiliated 36%
New Zealand	Christian 81%, none or unspecified 18%, Hindu, Confucian, and other 1%
Nicaragua	Roman Catholic 95%, Protestant 5%
Niger	Islam 80%, Animist and Christian 20%
Nigeria	Islam 50%, Christian 40%, indigenous 10%
Norway	Evangelical Lutheran 87.8% (state church), other Protestant and Roman Catholic 3.8%, none 3.2%, unknown 5.2%

Oman	Islam 95%
Pakistan	Islam 97%, Hindu, Christian, Buddhist, Parsi
Palau	Christian. About one-third of the islanders observe Modekngei religion, indigenous to Palau
	Palestinian State (proposed) West Bank: Muslim 75%, Jewish 17%, Christian and other 8%; Gaza Strip: Muslim 98.7%, Christian 0.7%, Jewish 0.6%
Panama	Roman Catholic over 93%, Protestant 6%
Papua New Guinea	over half are Christian, remainder indigenous
Paraguay	Roman Catholic 90%
Peru	Roman Catholic
The Philippines	Roman Catholic 84%, Protestant 10%, Islam 5%, Buddhist and other 3%
Poland	Roman Catholic 95% (about 75% practicing), Russian Orthodox, Protestant, and other 5%
Portugal	Roman Catholic 97%, 1% Protestant, 2% other
Qatar	Islam 95%
Romania	Romanian Orthodox 70%, Roman Catholic 6% (of which 3% are Uniate), Protestant 6%, unaffiliated 18%
Russia	Russian Orthodox, Muslim, others
Rwanda	Roman Catholic 56%, Protestant 18%, Islam 1%, Animist 25%
St. Lucia	Roman Catholic 90%, Protestant 7%, Anglican 3%
St. Vincent and The Grenadines	Anglican 47%, Methodist 28%, Roman Catholic 13%
Samoa	Christian 99.7%
San Marino	Roman Catholic
São Tomé and Príncipe	Roman Catholic, Evangelical Protestant, Seventh-Day Adventist
Saudi Arabia	Islam 100%
Senegal	Islam 92%, indigenous 6%, Christian 2%
Seychelles	Roman Catholic 90%, Anglican 8%
Sierra Leone	Islam 40%, Christian 35%, Indigenous 20%
Singapore	Islam, Christian, Buddhist, Hindu, Taoist
Slovakia	Roman Catholic 60.3%, atheist 9.7%, Protestant 8.4%, Orthodox 4.1%, other 17.5%
Slovenia	Roman Catholic 70.8% (including 2% Uniate), Lutheran 1%, Muslim 1%, other 27.2%
	Solomon Islands Anglican, Roman Catholic, South Seas Evangelical, Seventh-Day Adventist, United (Methodist) Church, other Protestant
Somalia	Islam (Sunni)
South Africa	Christian; Hindu; Islam
Spain	Roman Catholic 99%
Sri Lanka	Buddhist 69%, Hindu 15%, Islam 8%, Christian 8%
Sudan	Islam (Sunni) 70%, indigenous 20%, Christian 5%

Suriname	Protestant 25.2%, Roman Catholic 22.8%, Hindu 27.4%, Islam 19.6%, indigenous about 5%
Swaziland	Christian 60%, indigenous 40%
Sweden	Evangelical Lutheran 94%, Roman Catholic 1.5%, Pentecostal 1%, other 3.5%
Switzerland	Roman Catholic 49%, Protestant 40%, other 5%, no religion 8.3%
Syria	Islam 90%, Christian 10%
Taiwan	Buddhist 4.86 million, Taoist 3.3 million, Protestant 422,000, Catholic 304,000
Tajikistan	Sunni Muslim 80%
Tanzania	Christian 40%, Muslim 33%
Thailand	Buddhist 94.4%, Islam 4%, Hindu 1.1%, Christian 0.5%
Togo	Indigenous beliefs 70%, Christian 20%, Islam 10%
Tonga	Christian; Free Wesleyan Church claims over 30,000 adherents
Trinidad and Tobago	Roman Catholic 33%, Hindu 25%, Anglican 15%, other Christian 14%, Muslim 6%
Tunisia	Islam (Sunni) 98%, Christian 1%, Jewish, less than 1%
Turkey	Islam (mostly Sunni) 98%
Turkmenistan	Muslim 89%, Eastern Orthodox 9%, unknown 2%
Tuvalu	Church of Tuvalu (Congregationalist) 97%
Uganda	Christian 66%, Islam 16%
Ukraine	Orthodox 76%, Ukrainian Catholic (Uniate) 13.5%, Jewish 2.3%, Baptist, Mennonite, Protestant, and Muslim 8.2%
United Arab Emirates	Islam (Sunni 80%, Shi'ite 16%), others 4%
United Kingdom	Church of England (established church), Church of Wales (disestablished), Church of Scotland (established church—Presbyterian), Church of Ireland (disestablished), Roman Catholic, Methodist, Congregational, Baptist, Jewish
United States	Protestant, 61%; Roman Catholic, 25%; Jewish, 2%; other, 5%; none, 7%
Uruguay	Roman Catholic 66%, Protestant 2%, Jewish 2%
Uzbekistan	Muslim (mostly Sunnis) 88%, Eastern Orthodox 9%, other 3%
Vanuatu	Presbyterian 36.7%, Roman Catholic 15%, Anglican 15%, other Christian 10%, indigenous beliefs 7.6%, other 15.7%
Vatican City (Holy See)	Roman Catholic.
Venezuela	Roman Catholic 96%, Protestant 2%
Vietnam	Buddhist, Roman Catholic, Islam, Taoist, Confucian, Animist
Western Sahara	Muslim

Yemen	Islam (Sunni and Shi'ite)
Yugoslavia	Orthodox 65%, Muslim 19%, Roman Catholic 4%, Protestant 1%, other 11%ZambiaChristian 50%-75%, Islam and Hindu 24$-49%, remainder indigenous beliefs
Zimbabwe	Christian 25%, Animist 24%, Syncretic 50%

Great Cities

How much do you know about Alexandria?

QUESTIONS.

1. Once the greatest city of the world, now the second city and chief seaport of Egypt, Alexandria lies on which sea?

2. And on the western edge of the delta of which great river?

3. Alexandria was founded by which great military leader?

4. In what year?

5. Alexander wanted Alexandria to be the greatest seaport in the world, so a magnificent breakwater out into the sea was built. It was named for its length – seven furlongs. What was it called?

6. The breakwater reached out as far an isle, upon which a lighthouse was erected. The lighthouse became one of the Seven Wonders of the Ancient World. What was its name?

7. Under which dynasty, a Macedonian General and his descendants, did Alexandria become the literary and scientific centre of the world?

8. The last and most famous of the Ptolemies died in 30 BC in Alexandria Her name …?

9. In the year 616 AD, Alexandria fell to which marauders?

10. And in 642 AD, to which long-term conquerors?

11. What was the name of the first Christian institution of higher learning, founded in the 2nd century AD?

12. In the western part of Alexandria there are two great temples, the Serapeion and the Poseidonium. To which Gods were they dedicated?

13. What is the name of the mausoleum of Alexander and of the Ptolemies?

14. What is the name of the museum containing a magnificent collection of Greek and Roman antiquities?

15. What is the name of the 15th century fort built on the site of the Pharos lighthouse?

ANSWERS
1. The Mediterranean. 2. The Nile. 3. Alexander the Great. 4. 332 BC. 5. 'The Heptastadium'. 6. Pharos. 7. The Ptolemies. 8. Cleopatra. 9. The Persians. 10. The Arabs. 11. The School of Alexandria. 12. To the Egyptian deity Serapis and the Greek god Poseidon. 13. The 'Soma'. 14. The Alexandria Municipial Museum. 15. Quaitbey Fort.

How much do you know about Amsterdam?

QUESTIONS.

1. Amsterdam lies in the junction of which two rivers?

2. It is divided by canals into how many islands?

3. The islands are connected by how many bridges?

4. With which great Dutch painter is Amsterdam associated in most people's minds?

5. What is the name of the museum which houses one of the largest collections of Dutch and Flemish old masters?

6. And which museum has an extensive collection of modern art works?

7. Which renowned work by Rembrandt shows local gentry dressed as militia?

8. In what year was Amsterdam chartered as a city?

9. In 1369 it became a member of which alliance set up to protect and foster trade?

10. What is the name of Amsterdam's resident symphony orchestra?

11. Amsterdam is home to the headquarters of which international society for the protection of the environment?

12. What has been the heart of Amsterdam for seven centuries?

13. Which houses what monumental building, commenced in 1648?

14. Where is Amsterdam's famous flea market held?

15. Which famous American jazz trumpeter died in Amsterdam in 1989, falling from the window of his hotel room?

ANSWERS
1. The Amstel and the Ij. 2. 90. 3. 400. 4. Rembrandt van Rijn. 5. Rijksmuseum. 6. Stedlijk Museum. 7. 'The Night Watch'. 8. 1300. 9. The Hanseatic League. 10. Concertgebouw Orchestra. 11. Friends of the Earth. 12. The Dam Square. 13. The Royal Palace. 14. In Waterlooplein. 15. Chet Baker.

How much do you know about Athens?

QUESTIONS.

1. Athens is bisected by two small rivers. Name them please?

2. What is the name of the seaport of Athens?

3. What is the centre of Athens called?

4. What is Athens' outstanding natural landmark?

5. What is the name of temple on the Acropolis, now ruined, built to honour the Goddess Athena in the 4th century BC?

6. Through what hall-like structure does one enter the Acropolis?

7. On the north side of the Acropolis are the remains of the 'Gallery of Paintings'. What is it called?

8. The first thing that visitors see as they make their way up from the city to the Acropolis is the remains of another temple, didicated to the goddess of the city. What is it called?

9. Also on the north side are the remains of a temple dedicated to one of Athens' mystical kings. What is it called?

10. This building has a famous porch fronted by statues of six female figures. What are they called?

11. What gift did Athena give to the people of Athens?

12. In 1801, the ruling Ottoman Sultan gave Lord Elgin, the British Ambassador permission to take away "pieces of stones with inscriptions of figures". These "pieces of stone" are still on display in the British Museum. They are called ....?

13. Name the half-man, half-serpent who, according to myth, was the founder of Athens and of Greek Civilisation?

14. What were water-clocks used for in ancient Athens?

15. What was the name of the runner who brought to Athens news of the victory at the Battle of Marathon?

ANSWERS
1. Kifisos and Illisos. 2. Piraeus. 3. Constitutions Square. 4. The Acropolis. 5. The Parthenon. 6. The Propylaea. 7. The Pinakotheke. 8. The Temple of Athena Nike (Winged Victory). 9. The Erechtheum. 10. The Carytids. 11. An olive tree. 12. 'The Elgin Marbles'. 13. Cecrops. 14. To regulate the length of speeches. 15. Pheidippides.

How much do you know about Bangkok?

QUESTIONS.

1. The capital and chief port of Thailand, Bangkok is situated on the delta of which river?

2. What is Bangkok called in Thai?

3. What is the Port area called?

4. And the financial district is centred around ...?

5. For the tourists, a major feature of the city is ...?

6. Bangkok's second municipality is ...?

7. Thon Burr's best known structure is on the waterfront, a temple complex called ... what?

8. Where would you go to see a fine collection of Prehistoric and Bronze Age art and relics?

9. Who was the U.S. entrepreneur and devotee of the Thai way of life who was a resident of Bangkok for many years?

10. The late Jim Thompson's 'Thai House' contains the largest collection of ...?

11. What is Bangkok's oldest temple called?

12. For what was the great Royal Temple Wat Phra Kaeo built?

13. Where would you go to see an exhibition of Thai Boxing?

14. And to see drama, dancing and music?

15. Who is the government of Bangkok administered by ?

ANSWERS
1. The Chao Phraya River. 2. Krung Thep. 3. Khlong Toei. 4. Silom Road. 5. The Floating Markets. 6. Thon Burr. 7. Wat Arun. (Temple of the Dawn). 8. The National Museum. 9. Jim Thompson. 10. 17th Century Thai religious paintings. 11. Wat Po. 12. To house the Emerald Buddha. 13. Ratchadamnoen Stadium or Lumphini Stadium. 14. The Silapakorn National Theatre. 15. A Governor and his deputies.

How much do you know about Barcelona?

QUESTIONS.

1. City, seaport and capital of Barcelona Province and of the Spanish autonomous region of ...?

2. Set between the Pyrenees Mountains and which sea?

3. Different traditions have it that Barcelona was originally founded by either one of two ancient sea-going nations. Can you name either of them?

4. The 'Feria de Barcelona' has been held annually since 1929. In which part of the city?

5. In what building?

6. Every April 23rd there is an important event for the publishing industry. What is it called?

7. What is the centre for drama in the Catalan language?

8. In which auditorium does the Barcelona Symphony Orchestra perform?

9. Major art exhibitions are held in ...?

10. Along which avenue do the people of Barcelona like to take a leisurely stroll?

11. Barcelona boasts two major amusement parks. Can you name either one of them?

12. What is the name of the autonomous Catalan parliament?

13. The old centre of the city is called ...what?

14. The 'Ramblas' is separated from the 'Ensanche' by what monumental plaza?

15. In which other major square can you find a statue to the memory of Christopher Columbus?

ANSWERS
1. Catalonia. 2. The Mediterranean. 3. The Phoenicians or the Carthaginians. 4.
Montjuich. 5. Palacio de las Naciones. 6. The 'Fiesta del Libro'. 7. The Teatro Romea. 8.
The Palacio de la Musica. 9. The Palacio de Pedralbes. 10. Las Ramblas. 11. Tibidabo
or Montjuich. 12. The 'Generalitat'. 13. El Barrio Gotico. 14. Plaza de Cataluna. 15.
Plaza Puerta de la Paz.

How much do you know about Berlin?

QUESTIONS.

1. When did Berlin become the capital of a unified Germany for the first time?

2. And when did it become the capital of a unified Germany for the second time?

3. When was the Berlin Wall built?

4. And when did it come tumbling down?

5. Berlin lies at the confluence point of several rivers, but one in particular is linked with it historically. Which one?

6. The most famous, and probably the important avenue in Berlin runs from the Schloff Platz in the East to Pariser Platz in the West. What is its name?

7. What does the name mean in English?

8. What famous monument is to be found at the western end of the Unter den Linden?

9. What is the name of Berlin's most fashionable avenue?

10. On which street is the Europa Centre, a 22 storey building complex housing offices, restaurants, shops, cinemas, a planetarium and an ice rink?

11. What is the name of the forest which dominates the south western part of the city?

12. And the lake formed by the Havel River is called, what?

13. The Friedrich-Wilhelm University was founded in 1809. Its faculty has include 27 Nobel Prize winners and which famous philosopher?

14. In 1950, which bomb damaged building was razed to the ground to make room for the Marx-Engels Platz?

15. Who was the world famous conductor, resident with the Berlin Philharmonic Orchestra from 1954 to 1989?

ANSWERS
1. 1871. 2. 1990. 3. 1961. 4. 1989. 5. The Spree. 6. Unter den Linden. 7. 'Under the Lime Trees'. 8. The Brandenburg Gate. 9. Kurfurstendamm. 10. Tauentzienstrasse. 11. Grunewald. 12. The Wannsee. 13. G.W.F Hegel. 14. The Hohenzollern Palace. 15. Herbert von Karajan.

How much do you know about Bombay?

QUESTIONS.

1. Bombay is the capital of which Indian state?

2. Besides being India's financial and commercial centre, it is also its principal port, on which sea?

3. What is the city's real name, in Marathi?

4. Bombay harbour is protected from the sea by whichheadland?

5. Entrance into Bombay from the sea, discloses a magnificent panorama, framed by which mountains?

6. The largest of the islands in Bombay harbour is called ...?

7. Visitors come from all over to see what, on the island?

8. The financial section of the city is centred on ...?

9. And the more affluent residential districts are...?

10. What is the name of the great national park in the north of Greater Bombay?

11. What is the name of the site of an ancient Buddhist temple, renowned for its gigantic Buddhist sculptures?

12. What is the name of the city's major museum of art, archaeology and natural history?

13. The well-known author of Midnight's Children and Grimus, among others, hails originally from Bombay. Who is he?

14. Bombay is headquarters to an important Government energy agency What is it called?

15. The Indian film industry is centred on Bombay. What is this industry commonly nicknamed?

ANSWERS
1. Maharashtra. 2. The Arabian Sea. 3. Mumbai. 4. Colaba Point. 5. The Western Ghats. 6. Elephanta Island. 7. 8th and 9th century cave temples. 8. Old Fort Bombay. 9. Malabar Hill, Colaba and Marine Drive. 10. Krishnagir Forest. 11. The Kanheri Caves. 12. The Prince of Wales Museum of Western India. 13. The Jehangir Art Gallery. 14. Indian Atomic Energy Commission. 15. 'Bollywood'.

How much do you know about Budapest?

QUESTIONS.

1. Largest city and capital of Hungary, Budapest lies on which river?

2. The river divides the city into two. How is it separated?

3. If Buda is home to the former Royal Palace, what important building is found in Pest?

4. In the 10th century BC, the Romans established a settlement on the site of Buda. What did they call it?

5. By what fond nickname has Budapest been known to her devotees?

6. What is Budapest's highest natural landmark called?

7. The former Royal Palace is now home to what important institutions?

8. Near to the Palace, the spire of which medieval Gothic Church breaks the skyline?

9. What monument is to be found on Gellert Hill?

10. Budapest's fashionable district is called…?

11. Facing Rose Hill, on an isle in the river, is a mile-long park, with hotels, entertainments etc. What is it called?

12. What is the oldest and best-known of Budapest's eight bridges?

13. What 'healing facilities' attract many visitors?

14. Who established Budapest's Music Academy in 1875?

15. Who was the Budapest-born football player, the star of the Hungarian National team known as the 'Magic Magyars in the 1950's?

ANSWERS
1. The Danube 2. West Bank – Buda; East Bank – Pest 3. Parliament (Orsaghaz) 4. Aquincum 5. 'Queen of the Danube' 6. Janos Hill 7. The National Library; The Historical Musuem and the National Gallery 8. The Church of our Blessed Lady (also Matthieas Church) 9. The Citadel 10. Rose Hill (Rozsa Hill) 11. Margaret's (Margit's) Island 12. Szechenyi Chain Bridge 13. The thermal springs 14. Franz Liszt 15. Ferenc Puskas

How much do you know about Buenos Aires?

QUESTIONS.

1. City, Federal District and Capital of Argentina, Buenos Aires is situated on the shore of which river?

2. Where did settlers first make a settlement in this area?

3. At the north-eastern edge of the enormous flat plain known as …?

4. According to legend, Spanish sailors named the port after their patron saint, who was…?

5. What is the square at the 'heart' of the city called?

6. Which major thoroughfare is reserved for pedestrians?

7. What is the orbital highway called?

8. What do the residents of Buenos Aires call themselves?

9. What is the name of the picturesque section north of the Rio Riachuelo?

10. One of the city's most distinctive features are the fast-moving mini-buses. What are they called?

11. What is the name of the famous thoroughfare, claimed to be the broadest avenue in the world?

12. What is the name of the Government House building facing west up the Avenida de Mayo?

13. The Plaza de Mayo also contains two other distinctive buildings. Can you name them?

14. At the western end of the Ave. de Mayo, we find the Plaza del Congresso and …?

15. What is the name of Buenos Aires' magnificent Opera House?

ANSWERS
1. Rio de la Plata 2. At the mouth of the Rio Riachuelo 3. The 'Pampa 4. Santa Maria del Buen Aire 5. Plaza de Mayo 6. Calle Florida 7. Avenida Generale Paz 8. 'Portenos' 9. 'La Boca' 10. The 'Colectivos' 11. Avenida de 9 Julio 12. Casa Rosada 13. The 'Cabildo' (Town Hall); the Metropolitan Cathedral 14. The National Congress 15. The Colon Theatre

How much do you know about Cairo?

QUESTIONS.

1. Cairo has stood for more than 1,000 years close to the delta of which great African river?

2. A few miles north of Cairo the Nile separates into two branches. What are they called?

3. In North East Cairo there is an obelisk which marks the place where Plato once studied. What is it still called?

4. Which town, now a suburb in the South West of Cairo, was a metropolis in its own right 5,000 years ago?

5. Cairo reached its apogee during which medieval period?

6. Cairo has two major thoroughfares running roughly North – South through the Old Quarters. Their names …?

7. The main thoroughfare through the business and residential quarters is called …what?

8. On the other side of the river from the al-Kurnish is an area of hotels, museums, public gardens, a racetrack, sporting clubs and elegant houses. What is it called?

9. What is the name of the Presidential Palace?

10. Along the eastern and southern edges of Cairo lie extensive cemeteries. What is this area called colloquially?

11. In which of Cairo's many museums are the treasures of Tutankhamen displayed?

12. Which museum specialises in pre-Islamic icons, etc.?

13. Many streets in Cairo are considered to be galleries of architectural master-pieces. The best known is …?

14. What was the subject of the important international conference held in Cairo in 1994?

15. What is the name of the Cairo-born writer, the first Arabic writer to be awarded the Nobel Prize in 1988?

ANSWERS
1. The Nile 2. The Rosetta and the Damietta 3. Heliopolis 4. Memphis 5. The 'Mamluk' era 6. Mu'izz li-Din Allah and Port Said Street 7. Al-Kurnish (the Corniche) 8. The Gezirah 9. Qasra-al-Gumhuriyah 10. The 'City of the Dead' 11. The Egyptian Museum 12. The Coptic Museum 13. Bayn-al-Qasrayn 14. Population and Development 15. Naguib Mahfouz

How much do you know about Chicago?

QUESTIONS.

1. Situated on the south-western shore of which lake?

2. It is crossed by two rivers. Can you name them please?

3. How do foreign ships reach Chicago. By what waterway?

4. How does Chicago rate in terms of size of U.S. cities?

5. What is Chicago called colloquially?

6. What is the centre of the city called, by locals?

7. What are the two distinguished museums which are located in Hyde Park, called?

8. Two other institutions dedicated to learning, dating back to 1856 and 1857 respectively, are to be found in Lincoln Park. Can you name them?

9. What is the name of the institute which houses over 300,000 works of art, plus the Ryersen Library, plus the Burnham Library of Architecture?

10. In 1991 Daniel Barenboim succeeded Georg Solti as musical director of which distinguished orchestra?

11. The Chicago River is connected to the Illinois River by which famous waterway?

12. Prima Ballerina Maria Tallchief formed what ballet company in 1979?

13. Chicago University has its own astronomical observatory. What is its name?

14. Who was appointed first city detective of Chicago in 1850?

15. Chicago can boast not just one but three different lake-front parks. Can you name them please?

ANSWERS
1. Lake Michigan 2. The Chicago and the Calumet 3. The St Lawrence Seaway 4. Third largest 5. The Windy City 6. The Loop 7. The Oriental Institute and the Museum of Science and Industry 8. Chicago Historical Society and Chicago Academy of Sciences 9. The Art Institute of Chicago 10. Chicago Symphony Orchestra 11. The Illinois and Michigan Canal 12. Chicago City Ballet 13. Yerkes Observatory 14. Alan Pinkerton 15. Grant Park; Lincoln Park and Jackson Park

How much do you know about Copenhagen?

QUESTIONS.

1. Copenhagen stands mainly on two islands, one called Amager; the other is…?

2. These islands are at the southern end of what body of water?

3. This is a strait connecting the Baltic Sea and …?

4. In what year did Copenhagen become the capital city?

5. What is the name of the Royal Palace, built in the late 16th century, today a museum?

6. What is the centre of the city called?

7. North-east of Town Hall Square lies the former 'heart of the city'. What is it called?

8. Among the many fine buildings in this square is the Charlottenborg Palace, which today houses …what?

9. The Danish Parliament sits in which fine palace built on the site of the ancient castle of Slotsholmen?

10. One of Europe's most notable botanical gardens belongs to …who, exactly?

11. In these gardens there is statue to a Danish astronomer. His name please?

12. What is the name of Copenhagen's famous amusement park?

13. In which auditorium does the Royal Danish Ballet perform?

14. What is the name of the oldest sports club in the world?

15. What is the name of the church with the famous round tower?

ANSWERS
1. Zealand 2. 'The Sound' 3. The 'Kattegat' 4. 1445 5. Rosenborg 6. Raadhuspladsen (Town Hall Square) 7. Kongens Nytorv (King's New Square) 8. The Royal Academy of Fine Arts 9. Christiansborg 10. Copenhagen University 11. Tycho Brahe 12. The 'Tivoli' 13. The Royal Theatre 14. Copenhagen Rowing Club (Founded 1865) 15. Trinitatis Church

How much do you know about Dublin?

QUESTIONS.

1. Dublin is in which province of Ireland?

2. And stands on which river?

3. It is sheltered on the south side by what?

4. The two houses of the Parliament of the Republic of Ireland are in Dublin. Name them please?

5. Dublin has a very long association with the name 'Guinness'. But in what year did Arthur Guinness found the St. James' Gate Brewery?

6. Dublin has produced many fine writers, four of whom are Nobel Prize Laureates. Can you name any of them?

7. With which of Dublin's theatres was W.B. Yeats most closely connected?

8. What year was Dublin designated 'European City of Culture'?

9. What is the name of the oldest and largest of the city squares?

10. Encircling central Dublin are two canals. Their names, please?

11. What is the name of the University of Dublin?

12. In what year did it receive its charter from Queen Elizabeth 1st?

13. The University is home to a 9th century illuminated religious manuscript. What is its name?

14. To the west there is a great park, containing a zoo; an arboretum; several conservatories and the home of the President of the Republic. What is it called?

15. In what year did Dublin celebrate its millennium?

ANSWERS
1. Leinster 2. The Liffey 3. The Wicklow Mountains 4. The Senate and the House of Representatives 5. 1759 6. W.B Yeats, G.B Shaw, Samuel Becket and Seamus Heaney 7. The Abbey Theatre 8. 1991 9. St Stephens' Green 10. Grand Canal (South) and Royal Canal (North) 11. Trinity College 12. 1592 13. The Book of Kells 14. Phoenix Park 15. 1988

How much do you know about Edinburgh?

QUESTIONS.

1. Edinburgh is on the southern shore of which inlet of the North Sea?

2. What are the hills to the south of the city called?

3. It is about 40 miles north of which river which forms part of the Scottish/English border?

4. Until the new Scottish Parliament's permanent building is completed, where will the Scottish Parliament meet?

5. Where is that located, exactly?

6. Edinburgh was granted its charter in 1329. By whom?

7. In what year did it become the capital?

8. The dominating feature of Edinburgh is what?

9. What is the oldest feature of the Castle, dating back to the 11th century?

10. The main thoroughfare of old Edinburgh is called ...?

11. Which connects the Castle to what other monument?

12. The most fashionable street in Edinburgh is ...what?

13. Everyone has heard of Edinburgh's festival of the Arts. But can you name any of the other international festivals held annually or bi-annually in Edinburgh?

14. In what year was Edinburgh University founded?

15. There are two other universities in Edinburgh; can you name them?

ANSWERS
1. The Firth of Forth 2. The Pentland Hills 3. The River Tweed 4. In the Church of Scotland's General Assembly Hall 5. The Mound, Edinburgh 6. King Robert Bruce 7. 1437 8. Edinburgh Castle, on Castle Rock 9. St Margaret's Chapel 10. The Royal Mile 11. The Palace of Holyroodhouse 12. Princes Street 13. Film and Television Festivals; Jazz Festival; Science and Book Festival 14. 1583 15. Heriot-Watt and Napier

How much do you know about Florence?

QUESTIONS.

1. As what did Florence begin?

2. What is the name of the palatial monument, begun in 1299, which is to be found in the Piazzia della Signoria?

3. Today this building still fulfils an important function. As what?

4. It contains, amongst many others, perhaps the most famous work of sculpture by Michelangelo? What is it called?

5. In the same Piazzia there is an elegant museum built in the late 14th century. What is its name?

6. The museum specialises in masterworks of sculpture. In pride of place is the statue of 'Perseus', by …?

7. Behind the Piazzia della Signoria, and stretching down to the River Arno, another elegant museum begun in 1560. What is it called?

8. Due north of the Piazzia, dominating the skyline, is the dome of which cathedral?

9. Opposite the cathedral stands what other famous building?

10. This has a series of bronze, figured doors, one famous pair of which were made by the most accomplished goldsmith of all time. His name?

11. On the western edge of 'Old Florence' the Dominican order built, beginning in 1279, the church of …?

12. And on the eastern edge, the Franciscans built … ?

13. What is the remarkable building which lies between the Piazza della Signoria and the Cathedral?

14. North of the Cathedral is the former home of the former rulers of Florence. What is it called?

15. Behind the Pitti Palace, south of the Arno River, the hills were transformed into an area of recreation and relaxation. Called …?

ANSWERS
1. A Roman garrison town 2. Palazzo Vecchio 3. The Town Hall of Florence 4. 'David'
5. Loggia dei Lanzi 6. Benvenuto Cellini 7. The Uffizi 8. Santa Maria del Fiore 9. The 'Baptistery' 10. Lorenzo Ghiberti 11. Santa Maria Novella 12. Santa Croce 13. The 'Or San Michele' (The Oratory of St Michael) 14. The Medici Palace 15. The Boboli Gardens

How much do you know about Geneva?

QUESTIONS.

1. Geneva is situated at the western extremity of the largest lake in Central Europe, Lake Geneva, where which river issues from the lake?

2. It commands the natural corridor between which ranges of mountains?

3. The older part of the city stands on the south bank. Can you name two of the residential areas? 4. What is the name of the small isle in the Rhone?

5. What is the district on the north bank, home to many of the city's hotels?

6. The house in which Voltaire lived from 1755 to 1758 has the same name as the district in which it stands. It is …?

7. The most notable of the parks on the south bank is …?

8. The 'haute-ville' or Upper City rests on the city's original hill-site. Its name is…what?

9. And is dominated by which 12th – 13th century church?

10. Geneva has a world-famous botanical research institute. Its name please?

11. What is the name of Geneva's opera house?

12. Geneva also supports a symphony orchestra. Its name?

13. What is Geneva's leading daily newspaper?

14. North of the Rhone is the area where many institutions of world-wide import have their head offices. It is also home to the European section of the United Nations. In what building?

15. At the edge of the lake is the world's highest fountain which many think of as the symbol of Geneva. What is it called?

ANSWERS
1. River Rhone 2. The Alps and the Jura 3. Eaux Vives and Carouge 4. Rousseau's Island 5. Quartier St Gervais 6. Les Delices 7. Le Jardin Anglais 8. Le Plateau de Tranchees 9. St Peter's Cathedral 10. The Conservatory and Botanical Gardens 11. Le Grand Theatre 12. L'Orchestre de la Suisse Romande 13. Le Journal de Geneve 14. Le Palais des Nations 15. Le Jet d'Eau

How much do you know about Hong Kong?

QUESTIONS.

1. Formerly a British dependency, Hong Kong is now officially designated as …what?

2. The region of Hong Kong comprises three main areas. What are they called?

3. What is the name of the river which used to be the natural border between Hong Kong and the Chinese mainland?

4. What is the name of the capital and cultural centre?

5. What is the highest point of Hong Kong?

6. What name is given to the mid-autumn festival?

7. In 1995 the world's first fully interactive media network was established. By which company?

8. Who was the last British Governor of Hong Kong?

9. What date was Hong Kong ceded to Britain?

10. The name of the agreement that was signed?

11. What year was Kowloon and Stonecutters Island ceded to Britain?

12. And what year did Britain sign a 99 year lease for the New Territories?

13. Who, in December 1996, was chosen by the Chinese government to be the Chief Executive of the Hong Kong assembly?

14. On what date did Britain officially hand Hong Kong over to China?

15. Hong Kong's first political party was formed in 1990 by Martin Lee. Its name please?

ANSWERS
1. Chinese Special Administrative Region 2. Hong Kong Island, Kowloon Peninsula and New Territories 3. The Sham Chun 4. Victoria 5. Tai Mo Shan 6. Dragon Boat Festival 7. Hong Kong Telecom 8. Chris Patten 9. 1842 10. The Treaty of Nanking 11. 1860 12. 1898 13. Tung Chee-hwa 14. June 30th 1997 15. United Democrats of Hong Kong

How much do you know about Istanbul?

QUESTIONS.

1. Prior to becoming Istanbul, the city was known as ...?

2. Istanbul covers both sides of a famous waterway. What is the waterway called?

3. What is the narrow inlet of the Bosphorous called which makes Istanbul a seaport?

4. What is the oldest of many old sections of the city called?

5. Stambul is built on the site of an even older city. It's name?

6. What is the name of the largest mosque in Istanbul, built between 1550 and 1557?

7. What is the name of the 6th century Christian church, converted into a mosque in 15th century, now a museum?

8. Which Roman Emperor changed the city's name from Byzantium to Constantinople in 324 AD?

9. Constantinople has been one of the most besieged cities in history. Who laid siege to it in 673-678, and 717-718?

10. And who besieged it in 813 and again in 913?

11. And who occupied it in 1203 and 1204?

12. And who finally took it in 1453 and kept it?

13. However important Istanbul is, it is no longer capital of Turkey, In 1923 that honour was transferred to ...?

14. What is the name of the main residence of the Ottoman Sultans from 1465 to 1853; since 1924 a museum?

15. What is the name of the famous American stage and film director, born in Istanbul in 1909?

ANSWERS
1. Constantinople 2. The Bosphorous Straits 3. The Golden Horn 4. Stambul 5. Byzantium 6. Suleimaniye Mosque 7. Hagia Sophia 8. Constantine the Great 9. The Arabs 10. The Bulgarians 11. The Crusaders 12. The Turks 13. Ankara 14. Topkapi Palace 15. Elia Kazan

How much do you know about Johannesburg?

QUESTIONS.

1. Johannesburg is the capital of which South African province?

2. In what year was it founded?

3. In what year was it chartered as a city?

4. The history of Johannesburg is the history of gold. Who was the miner who first found alluvial gold in the River Jukskei in 1853?

5. And who was the Australian who was the first to find gold in Witwatersrand but failed to exploit his find?

6. What, today, is a very striking feature of the city?

7. The heart of Johannesburg's commercial area is …?

8. And the main shopping artery is …?

9. Most of the original Victorian buildings have gone now, but one exception is to be found on Pritchard Street. What is it called?

10. Few tourists would miss the opportunity to visit the recreation of a Victorian-era mining city called …?

11. And those who like drama make a bee-line for the world-renowned Market Theatre, located in…?

12. To which museum would you go to learn about the history and ethnology of Southern Africa?

13. The University of Witwatersrand started out as …what?

14. What is the name of the site near to Johannesburg where the first evidence of Australopithecus africanus was found?

15. Who was the Johannesburg-born President of South Africa and Nobel Laureate whose reforms led to the end of apartheid?

ANSWERS
1. Gauteng 2. 1886 3. 1928 4. Pieter Jacob Marais 5. George Harrison 6. The great yellow slag heaps, souvenirs of the mining 7. Commissioner Street 8. Eloff Street 9. The Markham Building 10. Gold Reef City 11. The old Produce 12. The Africana Museum 13. The South African School of Mines 14. Sterkfontein 15. F.W de Klerk

How much do you know about Lisbon?

QUESTIONS.

1. Lisbon is situated at the mouth of which great river?

2. What year was the University of Lisbon founded?

3. In what year was the terrible earthquake which almost destroyed Lisbon?

4. What building was put up in 1498 to honour the 15th century navigators who found the sea route to India?

5. The southernmost entry into Lisbon is through …what?

6. Which stands on what street?

7. It is believed that Lisbon was founded by …whom?

8. It was invaded and occupied in the 2nd Century BC, by …?

9. And in the 5th Century AD by …?

10. And occupied from 716 to 1147 AD by …?

11. Lisbon is home to a major international philanthropic foundation set up by a Turkish-born British financier. What is it called?

12. What was the name of the 1st King of Portugal who liberated Lisbon from the Moors in 1147?

13. What is the name of the city opposite Lisbon, on the other side of the Tagus?

14. What is the name of the suspension bridge over the Tagus? (Originally called the Salazas Bridge).

15, What is the name of the Lisbon-born politician who succeeded Mario Soares to become President in 1996?

ANSWERS
1. The Tagus 2. 1288 3. 1755 4. Monastery of Jeronimos 5. The Arco Triumfal 6. Rua Augusta 7. The Phoenicians 8. The Romans 9. The Visigoths 10. The Moors 11. The Gulbenkian Foundation 12. Alfonso 1st 13. Barreiro 14. Ponte de 25 April 15. Jorge Sampaie

How much do you know about London (I) ?

QUESTIONS.

1. London stands at the head of which river estuary?

2. The first known settlement in the Greater London area dates back about how many years?

3. The 'City of London' refers exactly to what?

4. The 'Square Mile' refers to the area upon which In the 1st century AD, the Romans built a settlement. What did they call it?

5. The 'City of London' is governed by what non-political organisation?

6. How long has the 'City' had a Lord Mayor?

7. What is the name of the Lord Mayor's residence since 1753?

8. What is the name of the Central Criminal Courts of the 'City of London'?

9. What was the name of the poor orphan boy who, according to legend, became Lord Mayor of the City of London no fewer than three times?

10. Which famous London church, designed by Sir Christopher Wren, and which survived the 'Blitz' intact stands towards the west of the City?

11. As of the season 2001–02, how many football teams in the English Premiership are based in London?

12. When was the last time a London team won the Premiership, and which team won it?

13. Which early British queen of the Iceni tribe and rebel against the Roman occupiers lies buried under platform 10 at King's Cross station?

14. And which political philosopher lies buried in Highgate Cemetery, in the north of the city?

15. Which play by mystery writer Agatha Christie, the longest-running in the world and now in its 50th year, is still performed nightly at St Martin's Theatre in London?

ANSWERS
1. The Thames. 2. 2,000. 3. The Square Mile. 4. Londinium. 5. The Corporation of the City of London 6. Since before 1200 AD. 7. The Mansion House. 8. The 'Old Bailey'. 9. Dick Whittington. 10. St Paul's Cathedral. 11. Six (Arsenal, Charlton, Chelsea, Fulham, Tottenham, West Ham). 12. Arsenal, in 1998. 13. Boudicca (Boadicea). 14. Karl Marx. 15. The Mousetrap.

How much do you know about London (II) ?

QUESTIONS.

1. The thirty two boroughs surrounding the 'City of London' are called ..... what?

2. What is the correct name of 'the Houses of Parliament'?

3. The homes and offices of the Prime Minister and the Chancellor of the Exchequer are where exactly?

4. To the south-east of the 'City' stands the Tower of London built by .... whom?

5. To the west of the 'City' lie the ancient Inns of Court. There are four. Can you name them?

6. What are the four parks which have been called the 'lungs of London'?

7. What are the famous Royal Botanical gardens called?

8. What is the London home of the Monarch called?

9. London's Metropolitan Police service is housed at ...?

10. In 1998, for the first time, a Mayor was elected to manage the affairs of Greater London. His name is ...?

11. What is the name of the street which used to be, but is now no longer, the home of Britain's national press?

12. The home of the Royal Naval College and the Old Royal Observatory (seat of the prime meridian) are on the river at ... ?

13. In which year was London almost totally destroyed by a fire which broke out in Pudding Lane?

14. A revolution in public transport changed the face of London from 1860 onwards. What was it exactly?

15. Which line was the first to be introduced?

ANSWERS
1. Greater London. 2. The Palace of Westminster. 3. Downing Street. 4. William the Conqueror in the 11th Century. 5. Lincoln's Inn, Middle Temple, Inner Temple and Gray's Inn. 6. Hyde Park, St James's Park, Green Park and Regent's Park. 7. Kew Gardens. 8. Buckingham Palace. 9. Scotland Yard. 10. Ken Livingstone. 11. Fleet Street. 12. Greenwich. 13. 1666. 14. The Underground Railway. 15. The Metropolitan Line, between Paddington and Farringdon St.

How much do you know about Los Angeles ?

QUESTIONS.

1. Los Angeles is located on a hilly plain with mountain ranges to the north and east, and what to the south and west?

2. About one third of the population live in the San Fernando Valley, separated from the rest of L.A. by what?

3. And also by the city's major outdoor recreational park, which is called …?

4. In what year was Los Angeles settled?

5. What was it called at that time?

6. A nearby Native American village, Yang-Na, has been assimilated over the years. It's location is now known as?

7. L.A.'s main growth began after 1876 with the arrival of …what?

8. What are the residents of L.A. known as colloquially?

9. What is the main centre of performing arts called?

10. In which auditorium does the L.A. Philharmonic Orchestra perform during the winter months?

11. Plays, musicals and light opera are performed in …?

12. In good weather concerts and plays are performed in a natural amphitheatre in Hollywood. its name is… ?

13. A unique collection of fossils, formerly housed in the Museum of Natural History has been transferred to the George C. Page Museum of La Brea Discoveries. Where?

14. If you wanted to see a remarkable collection of Native American Art and Artefacts you would go to the Southwest Museum. Where is that?

15. And if you wanted to get a look at L.A. over the years, you would take a walk around …what?

ANSWERS
1. The Pacific Ocean 2. Santa Monica Mountains 3. Griffith Park 4. 1781 5. El Pueblo de Nuestra Senora la Reina de Los Angeles de Porciuncula 6. Elysian Park 7. Southern Pacific Railroad 8. Angelinos 9. The Music Center 10. The Dorothy Chandler Pavilion 11. The Ahmanson Theater 12. The Hollywood Bowl 13. In Hancock Park 14. In Highland Park 15. El Pueblo de Los Angeles State Historical Park

How much do you know about Madrid?

QUESTIONS.

1. What is the name of the river upon which Madrid stands?

2. The traditional centre of Madrid is a crescent shaped square called …?

3. What is the name of the old square built in 1617 where bullfights and executions of heretics took place?

4. What is the name of the great museum, particularly rich in collections of Goya; Velazquez and El Greco?

5. The botanical and zoological gardens are called …?

6. What is the name of the residence of the King?

7. Until the 10th century Madrid was only a Moorish fortress. What was its function?

8. In what year did Philip II move the Spanish court to Madrid?

9. When did it replace Valladolid as the Capital of Spain?

10. What is the traditional nickname of the Madrilenos (the people of Madrid)?

11. Who was the ruler of Spain who lived in Madrid from 1808 until 1812?

12. What was one of the (more complimentary) nicknames given to him by Los Gatos?

13. What is the name of the national parliament?

14. Madrid boasts two fine professional football stadiums. Please name one of them?

15. What is the name of the major bullring?

ANSWERS
1. The Manzanares 2. Puerta del Sol 3. Plaza Mayor 4. The Prado 5. The Buen Retiro Park 6. Zarzuela Palace 7. To protect Toledo 8. 1561 9. 1607 10. Los Gatos (The Cats) 11. Joseph Bonaparte 12. El Rey Plazuelas (King of the Small Squares) 13. El Corte 14. Santiago Bernabeu or Vicente Calderon 15. Monumental de las Ventas

How much do you know about Melbourne?

QUESTIONS.

1. Capital of which Australian state?

2. Situated at the northern end of which bay?

3. Standing at the mouth of which river?

4. Who was the pioneer entrepreneur who purchased 500,000 acres of land at the head of Port Phillip Bay from aboriginal elders in 1835?

5. However Batman was not the founder of Melbourne. That honour went to a settler named …what?

6. Melbourne was chartered as a city in which year?

7. And served as the capital of the commonwealth of Australia until … what year?

8. Can you name the most important gold fields, just outside Melbourne?

9. Near to the city centre there is a development which houses three theatres, a concert hall, an art gallery, etc. What is it called?

10. What is the name of the Art Gallery which features a dramatic stained glass ceiling by the Melbourne artist Leonard French?

11. The Melbourne Concert Hall is home to which orchestra?

12. At which racecourse is the Melbourne Cup run every November?

13. Where do Melbourne's skiers head for at every chance?

14. One of the four 'grand slam' world tennis championships is held in Melbourne annually. Where exactly?

15. The University of Melbourne was founded in 1853. However the city boasts two other, more recently founded, centres of higher education. Can you name them?

ANSWERS
1. Victoria 2. Port Phillip Bay 3. The Yarra River 4. John Batman 5. John Fawkner 6. 1847 7. 1927 8. Ballarat and Bendigo 9. The Victoria Arts Centre 10. The National Gallery of Victoria 11. Melbourne Symphony Orchestra 12. Flemington 13. Mount Buller 14. Flinders' Park 15. The Monash and La Trobe Universities

How much do you know about Mexico City?

QUESTIONS.

1. Mexico City is situated in a valley in which mountains?

2. The centre of Mexico City, historically, is called ...what?

3. This occupies a site formerly occupied by the central square of the Aztec city known as ... ?

4. The Zocalo is flanked on one side by a baroque cathedral begun in 1573 and completed in 1675. What is its name?

5. And by which local government building dating from 1720?

6. And by which federal government building which dates back to 1792?

7. Which boulevard connects the Zocalo with Alameda Park?

8. Mexico City's principal boulevard extends north from the Zocalo to which famous square?

9. And south to which park?

10. What is the name of the residential area?

11. What is the name of the enormous squatter area?

12. In 1994 the World Health Organisation declared that the quality of the air in Mexico City is acceptable on only ...how many days per year?

13. Which institution dominates the educational life of Mexico City (and of Mexico as a whole) ?

14. What is Mexico's most popular religious shrine, found in Mexico City?

15. By what name was the Mexico City born actor and comedian Mario Moreno Reyes better known?

ANSWERS
1. Eastern Sierra Madre 2. The Zocala (Plaza de la Constitution) 3. Tenochtitlan 4. The National Cathedral 5. The Municipal Palace 6. The National Palace 7. Avenida de 5 Mayo 8. Plaza of the Three Cultures 9. Chapultepec Park 10. Pedregal 11. Netzahualcoyotl 12. 20 13. The National Autonomous University of Mexico 14. The Basilica of the Virgin of Guadeloupe 15. Cantinflas

How much do you know about Montevideo?

QUESTIONS.

1. Montevideo stands on the north shore of which river estuary?

2. It was founded in what year?

3. It was founded by the Governor of Buenos Aries in a pre-emptive move against the Portuguese. What was his name?

4. Which highway links Buenos Aries in Argentina to Rio de Janeiro in Brazil, passing through Montevideo, Uruguay?

5. Which 16th century Italian-born explorer gave Rio de la Plata its name, around 1526?

6. What is the name of the Uruguayan national hero whose body rests in its own mausoleum?

7. What was the name give to the final war of liberation from Portugal (1825-1828)?

8. What was the name given to the group of revolutionaries who brought about the liberation?

9. When was the 'Universidad de la Republica' founded?

10. Who was the Montevideo-born statesman credited with transforming Uruguay from an unstable dictatorship into a viable democracy?

11. What is the name of the former seat of National Legislation?

12. What is the name of the very large State enterprise?

13. The head office of which international organisation aimed at establishing the conditions for a Latin American Common Market, is to be found in Montevideo?

14. Where is the Uruguayan national football stadium?

15. What is the name of the Montevideo-born poet whose work, particularly 'Les Chants de Maldoror' was acclaimed posthumously by the European surrealists?

ANSWERS
1. Rio de la Plata 2. 1726 3. Bruno Mauricio de Zabala 4. The Pan American Highway
5. Sebastian Cabot 6. Jose Gervacio Artigas 7. The Cisplatine War 8. The Immortal 33
9. 1849 10. Jose Batile y Ordonez 11. The 'Cabildo' 12. ANCAP (Administracion
Nacional de Combustibles, Alcohol y Portland) 13. Latin American Integration
Association 14. Batile y Ordonez Park 15. Isidore Ducasse

How much do you know about Montreal?

QUESTIONS.

1. The city stands on Montreal Island, at the confluence of two rivers. Name them please?

2. What is the centre of the city called?

3. The city's business activities are centred roughly where?

4. Where are the department stores and major shops to be found?

5. The tall office buildings are concentrated downtown around which boulevard?

6. Which of the city's universities is the oldest, founded 1821?

7. In 1974 the Sir George Williams University and Loyola College were combined to form what?

8. What is the performing arts centre called?

9. Which museum is known for its collection of Canadian art and artefacts?

10. The site of the 1967 International Exhibition on Sainte Helene Island, has been transformed into a recreation and entertainment park, called ...?

11. The "Expos", Montreal's major league professional baseball team play ...where?

12. What is the name of the French style castle, built in 1705, which is today a museum?

13. What is the name of the oldest church in Montreal?

14. What is the ecclesiastical building best viewed from the Place d'Armes called?

15. Who was the first French explorer to set foot on Montreal Island, in 1535?

ANSWERS
1. The St Lawrence and the Ottawa 2. Mount Royal 3. Between Mount Royal and the St Lawrence 4. Around St Catherine St 5. The Rene Levesque Boulevard 6. McGill University 7. Concordia 8. Place des Arts 9. The McCord Museum 10. Parc de Iles 11. Olympic Park 12. Vhateau de Ramezay 13. Notre Dame de Bon Secours 14. St Sulpice Seminary 15. Jacques Cartier

How much do you know about Moscow?

QUESTIONS.

1. Capital, inland port and largest city in Russia, it stands on what river?

2. Apart from the river, Moscow is served by two other large waterways. Can you name them?

3. At the centre of Moscow is the governmental centre of Russia. What is it called?

4. Adjacent to the Kremlin, the site of so many May Day parades, is the …?

5. What is the most imposing structure within the Kremlin?

6. Within the Kremlin walls there are two other notable palaces. What are they called?

7. Among the many ecclesiastical buildings, now used mainly as museums, there are two with five gilded domes each. Their names are …?

8. And one with nine gilded domes, called …?

9. Another landmark of the Kremlin is a bell tower, 98 metres (320 feet) high. What is its name?

10. And on a pedestal nearby, there is … what?

11. And completed in 1961, a huge office building, called…?

12. At one end of Red Square, famous for its unique architecture, stands the Cathedral of whom?

13. Lying to the east of the Kremlin, the ancient commercial section of …what?

14. Descended from a Moscow aristocrat, what was the name of the dynasty which ruled Russia for three centuries?

15. What was the name of Lubyanka Square before it was changed in 1991?

ANSWERS
1. The Moskva 2. The Moskva Canal and the Volga-Don Canal 3. The Kremlin 4. Red Square 5. The Great Kremlin Palace 6. The Granovitaya Palace and the Terem 7. Cathedral of the Assumption and Archangel Cathedral 8. Cathedral of the Anunciation 9. The Tower of Ivan the Great 10. The Tsar's Bell 11. The Palace of Congresses 12. St Basil 13. Kitaigorod 14. Romanov 15. Dzerzhinsky Square

How much do you know about Naples?

QUESTIONS.

1. City in southern Italy, Naples is capital of which region?

2. The city is built on the Bay of Naples, an inlet of which sea?

3. The name of the volcano, visible from the city, is …?

4. What is the name of the 12th century castle built on a rocky islet in the bay, joined to Naples by a causeway?

5. This was previously the site of a villa built by a famous Roman General, whose name was …?

6. On the harbour of Naples itself there is a 13th century castle. What is its name?

7. And on a hill overlooking the city is yet another castle, this one from the 14th century. Its name …?

8. The former Royal Palace (Palazzo Real) built in the 17th century, today houses …what?

9. Near to the Royal Palace is an opera house, one of the largest in Europe. Its name …?

10. The National Museum in Naples houses a vast collection of Greco-Roman paintings and artefacts taken from the remains of which two towns destroyed by Vesuvius?

11. It also houses a very famous single art collection, called …?

12. The most famous church in Naples is …?

13. Which contains the tomb of Naples' patron saint …?

14. But the church renowned for its beautiful interior is …?

15. Where does the name 'Naples' come from?

ANSWERS
1. Campania 2. The Tyrrhenian Sea 3. Vesuvius 4. Castel dell'Ovo 5. Lucullus 6. Castel Nuovo 7. Castel Saint 'Elmo 8. The National Library 9. Teatro San Carlo 10. Pompeii and Herculaneum 11. The Farnese Collection 12. San Gennaro Cathedral 13. St Januarius 14. San Deomenico 15. From its original Greek name 'Neapolis' (New Town)

How much do you know about New York?

QUESTIONS

1. New York is built on a number of islands. How many are there altogether?

2. New York is made up of five boroughs. What are their names?

3. Which is the largest in size?

4. Which is the most densely populated?

5. What is the official residence of the Mayor called?

6. What was the point of entry to New York for many millions of immigrants?

7. Which major thoroughfare bisects New York in a roughly north – south direction for 17 miles?

8. What is the hub of New York's theatre district?

9. New York is home to one of the worlds largest international wildlife conservation parks. What is its name?

10. If the N.Y. Yankees professional baseball team plays at Yankee Stadium, Bronx, where do the N.Y. Mets play?

11. Which late Mayor of New York gave his name to one of the two international airports serving the city?

12. What is the name of New York's financial centre?

13. Which street is synonymous with the advertising industry.

14. When was the construction of the Empire State Building completed?

15. The Metropolitan Opera; The New York Philharmonic; The New York State Theatre; The New York Ballet and The New York City Opera are all to be found in the same group of buildings. What is it called?

ANSWERS
1. 50 2. Queens; Brooklyn; the Bronx; Staten Island; Manhattan 3. Queens 4. Brooklyn
5. Gracie Mansion 6. Ellis Island 7. Broadway 8. Times Square 9. Bronx Zoo 10. Shea
Stadium 11. Harry La Guardia 12. Wall Street 13. Madison Avenue 14. 1931 15.
Lincoln Center for Performing Arts

How much do you know about Oslo?

QUESTIONS.

1. Oslo is situated at the head of Oslo fjord, which gives out onto what body of water?

2. What was Oslo's former name?

3. Who was the founder of Oslo?

4. In what year?

5. In 1624 the city was destroyed. How?

6. It was rebuilt by Christian IV King of Denmark-Norway a little way away from its original site, closer to what fortress?

7. What is the name of the exhibition hall at Skoyen in the west of Oslo?

8. At Okern in the north-east of Oslo important auctions are held. What kind of auctions are they?

9. Where are Oslo's botanical gardens?

10. The 'Framhuset' houses the 'Fram' the famous polar exploration vessel used by two famous explorers. Their names, please?

11. Thor Heyerdahl's famous expedition to the Pacific in 1947 is commemorated by what Oslo building?

12. Many examples of the work of the contemporary Norwegian sculptor Gustav Vigelund are on display where?

13. The University is home to Oslo's most famous concert hall. What is it called?

14. The annual ski-jump competitions are held at …?

15. Thirty miles north of Oslo is the historic village in which the National Assembly voted Norway's constitution in 1814. What is the name of the village?

ANSWERS
1. The Skagerrak 2. Christiana 3. King Harold Hardroode 4. 1050 5. By fire 6. Akerhus
7. Norwegian Trade Fair 8. Fur auctions 9. Toyen, eastern Oslo 10. Nansen and
Amundsen 11. The Kon-Tiki Museum 12. In Frogner Park 13. The 'Aula' 14.
Homenkollen 15. Eidsvoll

How much do you know about Paris?

QUESTIONS

1. What is the name of the river upon which Paris stands?

2. As it flows through Paris, the river contains two islands. Name them please.

3. What is the highest point in Paris?

4. In what period did Paris become the capital of France?

5. Paris contains a famous botanical garden. Its name ?

6. On the Ile de la Cite there is a world famous cathedral, dating back to 1163 A.D. What is it called?

7. In which building can you visit Napoleon's tomb?

8. Who, in the mid 19th century, was responsible for making many changes to the urban landscape?

9. The Eiffel Tower was built for what occasion in 1889?

10. What is the official residence of the President called?

11. By what name were the old central food markets known?

12. Founded about 1257 A.D., the name of the University is?

13. The pre-eminent theatre of France has it's home in Paris. What is it called?

14. In the year 3 B.C. a Celtic tribe, the Parisii, occupied and fortified the Ile de la Cite. What name did they give to it?

15. Who is the patron saint of Paris?

ANSWERS

1. The Seine 2. Ile de la Cite and Ile de St Louis 3. Butte de Montmartre (423 ft above sea level) 4. Late 10th century 5. Les Tuileries 6. Notre Dame 7. Les Invalides 8. Baron George Haussman 9. Paris World Fair 10. Palais de l'Elysee 11. Les Halles 12. The Sorbonne 13. La Comedie Francaise 14. Lutetia 15. St Genevieve

How much do you know about Prague?

QUESTIONS.

1. In which region of the Czech Republic is Prague located?

2. It spreads out on both sides of which river?

3. In which century was there first a settlement here?

4. A 13th century King of Bohemia has given his name to a famous square in Prague, scene of many important historical events. What is it called?

5. Prague has the oldest university in central Europe. Its name is ...?

6. Which was founded ...when?

7. Prague's admirers call it ...what?

8. The Vitava is spanned by many bridges. Which one is the most famous?

9. Who are represented by the figures on the 15th century Town Hall clock, in the Old Town Square?

10. In the square there is also a monument to which 15th century religious reformer?

11. What building dominates the Prague skyline?

12. Next to the castle is the gothic Cathedral of ...?

13. Who is the Prague-born Czech-American tennis player who holds the womens all-time record for singles championships?

14. Who was the Prague-born writer of novels and short stories of an extremely surrealist nature?

15. Which Czech statesman instituted the 'Prague Spring' in 1968, which cost him very dear?

ANSWERS
1. Bohemia 2. The Vitava 3. The 9th century 4. Wenceslas Square 5. Charles University 6. 1348 7. The City of 100 Spires 8. The Charles Bridge 9. The Apostles 10. Jan Hus 11. The Hradcny Castle 12. St Vitus 13. Martina Navratilova 14. Franz Kafka 15. Alexander Dubcek

How much do you know about Rio de Janeiro?

QUESTIONS.

1. What is the affectionate term by which the residents of Rio de Janeiro are known?

2. What are the names of Rio's two most famous beaches?

3. What is Rio's most famous natural landmark?

4. What is Rio's most famous man-made landmark?

5. Who was the French artist who made the statue in 1921?

6. In what year did Portuguese explorers first arrive in the Rio region?

7. In 1992 the United Nations Conference on Environment and Development took place in Rio. What is it better known as?

8. This meeting led to the establishment of a very important document to which many nations have signed up. What document?

9. Who is the Rio-born President of Brazil?

10. What is Rio's famous pre-lenten festival called?

11. The spectacular parades during the festival are made up of members of what particular groups?

12. Who is the famous Rio-born Formula 1 racing driver who contested 204 Grand Prix races in his career?

13. Name the Brazilian national hero and martyr to the cause of independence from Portugal?

14. What is the name of the Rio-born composer, Brazil's foremost composer of the 20th century?

15. Who, as a child played football barefoot on the wasteground of the Bento Ribeiro area of Rio and is now an internationally renowned player?

ANSWERS
1. The Cariocas 2. Copacabana and Ipanema 3. Sugarloaf Mountain 4. Statue of Christ the Redeemer on Corcovado Mountain 5. Paul Landowski 6. 1503 7. The 'Earth Summit' 8. The Convention on Biological Diversity 9. Fernando Henrique 10. 'Mardi Gras' 11. Samba Schools 12. Nelson Piquet 13. Tiradentes 14. Heitor Villa-Lobos 15. Ronaldo

How much do you know about Rome?

QUESTIONS

1. In what year, according to tradition, was Rome built?

2. And by whom?

3. Rome stands on which river?

4. Rome is built on seven hills. Can you name any of them?

5. Rome became the capital of a united Italy in which year?

6. The inner city of Rome is enclosed by what?

7. The geographic centre of Rome is called ...?

8. In this piazza there is a statue of the first king of united Italy. What was his name?

9. One of the finest examples of surviving ancient temples is to be found in Rome. What is it called?

10. And the name of the great amphitheatre, partly ruined?

11. Who designed the National Roman Museum?

12. A famous road connects Rome to southern Italy. What is its name?

13. If you climb the Spanish Steps, to which edifice will you be going?

14. The skyline of Rome is dominated by which great basilica?

15. What is the name of the famous Roman fountain, into which visitors throw coins for good luck?

ANSWERS
1. 753 B.C 2. Romulus and Remus 3. The Tiber 4. Capitoline; Quirinal; Viminal; Esquiline; Caelian; Aventine; Palatine 5. 1871 6. The Aurelian Wall 7. The Piazza Venezia 8. Victor Emmanuel II 9. The Pantheon 10. The Colosseum 11. Michelangelo 12. The Appian Way 13. The Trinita dei Monti Church 14. St Peters 15. The Fountains of Trevi

How much do you know about San Francisco?

QUESTIONS.

1. City in California, U.S.A., located on a peninsular between San Francisco Bay and which ocean?

2. What was it that established San Francisco as the west coast's premier city?

3. Can you name three of San Francisco's most prominent natural landmarks?

4. What is the name of the public rapid transport system of which San Francisco is so proud?

5. Connection to the city from the East Bay towns is made by way of which bridge, a masterpiece of engineering design?

6. And communication to the city from the northern areas of Marin County is made by way of which superb suspension bridge?

7. What is the name of the San Francisco motorway which stops dead, as if cut off by a guillotine?

8. San Francisco is the head office for a number of banks, including one of the worlds very largest. Its name?

9. What is the name of the auditorium in which the San Francisco Symphony Orchestra performs?

10. San Francisco has its own repertory theatre group. What is it called?

11. Which San Francisco museum is renowned for its collection of Jades and Porcelains?

12. And which museum is known for its collection of sculpture by Rodin?

13. What is the name of the dormitory suburb to the south?

14. Where are the most fashionable residential areas?

15. What is the name of the former U.S military base, known for its park-like lawns, which lies to the west of the city?

ANSWERS
1. The Pacific 2. The California Gold Rush (1848-49) 3. Twin Peaks; Mount Sutro; Mount Davidson 4. Bay Area Rapid Transport System (BARTS) 5. The San Francisco–Oakland Bay Bridge 6. The Golden Gate Bridge 7. The Embarcadero Freeway 8. Bank of America 9. The Louise H. Davies Symphony Hall 10. The American Conservatory Theatre 11. The Asian Museum 12. The California Palace of the Legion of Honour 13. San Mateo County 14. Pacific Heights; Nob Hill 15. The Presidio

How much do you know about Stockholm?

QUESTIONS.

1. Situated on Sweden's eastern coast where which body of water joins the Saltsjon and enters the Baltic Sea?

2. Spread over some 20 islands and the adjacent mainland, Stockholm is often referred to as ...what?

3. In what year was Stockholm first mentioned as a town?

4. Its development was largely down to the efforts of which Swedish ruler?

5. The town grew rapidly as the result of a reciprocal trading treaty with which German city?

6. It became the capital of Sweden officially, in what year?

7. And was liberated from Danish control in 1523 by which Swedish King?

8. The original nucleus of the city, the Old Town, is called what in Swedish?

9. The Royal Palace is in which part of Gamla Stan?

10. Another part is Riddar Island, dominated by which church?

11. The third part of Gamla Stan is Helgeands Island, which is the location of what legislative and administrative building?

12. Which of the northern (mainland) districts is the main shopping, business and financial sector?

13. What is the name of the outdoor 'living' museum showing aspects of traditional Swedish life?

14. On the island of Djurgarden is the museum housing the salvaged Swedish warship from 1628. What is it called?

15. Who was the Stockholm-born Prime Minister of Sweden who was assassinated in 1986?

ANSWERS
1. Lake Malaren 2. The Venice of the North 3. 1252 4. Birger Jarl 5. Lubeck 6. 1436 7. Gustav I Vasa 8. Gamla Stan 9. Stads Island 10. Riddarhom Church 11. The House of Parliament 12. Norrmalin 13. Skansen 14. The 'Vasa' Museum 15. Olaf Palme

How much do you know about Sydney?

QUESTIONS.

1. Sydney is the capital not only of Australia but also of which province?

2. It is situated on the southern shore of which Port?

3. What is the name of the river just north of Sydney?

4. And what are the mountains to the west called?

5. Who, in 1788, described Sydney Harbour as 'a noble and capacious harbour, equal if not superior, to any yet known in the world'?

6. In what year was the Sydney Harbour Bridge completed?

7. The Sydney Opera House is surely one of the most easily recognisable buildings in the world. But whereabouts is it situated exactly?

8. What is the name of the Museum of Social History in Queens' Square?

9. What building was formerly on the site now occupied by the New South Wales Conservatorium of Music?

10. What is the address of 'Parliament House', the home of the N.S.W. Legislature?

11. What is the oldest surviving private building in Sydney, built in 1816?

12. Sydney centre is connected to Darling Harbour by what means of transport?

13. Sydney's Museum of Applied Arts and Sciences is housed today in what used to be a power station and tram depot. What is it called?

14. What was used for currency in Sydney until coins were introduced around 1815?

15. Which Sydney suburb is called 'The Cradle of Australia'?

ANSWERS
1. New South Wales 2. Port Jackson 3. Hawkesbury River 4. The Blue Mountains 5. Governor Arthur Phillip 6. 1932 7. Bennelong Point 8. Hyde Park Barracks 9. Government House 10. Macquarie Street 11. Cadman's Cottage 12. A monorail 13. The Powerhouse Museum 14. Rum 15. Parramatta

How much do you know about Tokyo?

QUESTIONS.

1. Located at the head of Tokyo Bay on the Pacific coast of what island?

2. Standing on what river?

3. What was Tokyo called up until 1868?

4. Tokyo is part of Japan's leading manufacturing region. What is the region called?

5. What is at the very heart of the city?

6. What is the major business and entrepreneurial sector called?

7. And the main centre of financial activities is …?

8. In which sector is the Japanese Parliament?

9. And what is the National Parliament called?

10. What is the name of the north-east district, home to many universities, publishers, bookshops, etc.?

11. And whereabouts is the National Museum?

12. The main shopping area with many restaurants, bars, night clubs, etc, is called … what?

13. Lovers of flowers will be drawn to the Meiji Shrine (and perhaps also to Horikiri and Mizumoto) to see …what?

14. And to Ueno Park to see the blossoms of what trees?

15. What is the mass transit system called which circles much of the city?

ANSWERS
1. Honshu Island 2. The Sumida River 3. Edo 4. Keihin Industrial Zone 5. The Imperial Palace 6. The Marunouchi District 7. Around Nihambashi 8. Kasumigaseki 9. The Diet 10. Kanda District 11. In Ueno Park 12. The Ginza 13. The Iris Gardens 14. Cherry trees 15. The Yamanote Loop Railway System

How much do you know about Toronto?

QUESTIONS.

1. Toronto is located on the northern shore of which lake?

2. In what year was it incorporated as a city?

3. What was the name of the first known settlement on the site of Toronto?

4. Which tribe of native North Americans inhabited it at that time?

5. When the University of Toronto was first chartered in 1827 it was known as …what?

6. The University is also home to Connaught Laboratories, which is engaged in the manufacture of …what?

7. The central business area is concentrated around which streets?

8. The central financial district is around …?

9. The city skyline is dominated by the world's tallest self-supporting man-made structure. What is it called?

10. The fashionable boutique shopping area is …?

11. Heading south from this, what do we find?

12. Toronto is home to the world's largest annual exhibition. What is it called?

13. In which modern sports arena do the Toronto professional football and baseball teams play?

14. Which museum has an outstanding collection of Chinese and ancient Egyptian art, and American and Canadian ethnology?

15. What is the name of 'Canada's national newspaper'?

ANSWERS
1. Lake Ontario 2. 1834 3. Teiaiagon 4. The Seneca 5. University of King's College 6. Insulin 7. Bloor; Yonge and Queen Streets 8. King Street and Bay Street 9. The C.N Tower 10. Yorkville–Cumberland 11. The Ontario Parliament 12. The Canadian National Exhibition 13. The 'Skydrome' 14. Royal Ontario 15. Toronto Globe and Mail

How much do you know about Venice?

QUESTIONS.

1. City and seaport in which region of north-east Italy?

2. It is spread over 120 islands formed by 177 canals in the lagoon between the mouths of which two rivers?

3. At the northern extremity of which sea?

4. The city is known colloquially as …what?

5. The islands on which the city stands are interconnected by how many bridges?

6. What is the name of the waterway about 3km long, which divides the city north-west/south east into two portions?

7. Gindecca island in the south, is separated from Venice proper by what …?

8. No cars are allowed, so what is the method of transport preferred by visitors?

9. Venice is rightly famous for its glassware, manufactured mainly on which island?

10. And for its lace, made …where?

11. What is the name of Venice's port which handles the sea-going traffic?

12. What is the heart of Venice called?

13. At the eastern end of the square are the two most imposing buildings in Venice. What are they?

14. The northern and southern sides of the square are occupied by two buildings which, in the time of the Venetian Republic, were the residences of the nine magistrates from amongst whom the Doge was chosen. They are …?

15. The arcades, with the cafes and shops, are built along…what?

ANSWERS
1. Veneto 2. The Po and the Piave 3. The Adriatic 4. 'Queen of the Adriatic' 5. 400 6. The Grand Canal 7. The Gindecca Canal 8. Gondola 9. Murano 10. Burano 11. Marghera 12. St Mark's Square 13. St Mark's Cathedral and the Doge's Palace 14. The 'Procuratie Vecchio' and the 'Procuratie Nuove' 15. The 'Arrio' or 'Fabbrica Nuove'

How much do you know about Vienna?

QUESTIONS.

1. Vienna lies on which famous river?

2. It also lies between two ranges of mountains. Which ones?

3. What is the name of the broad boulevard which in 1857 replaced the walls encircling the inner city?

4. What is the name of the Gothic Cathedral at the centre of the inner city?

5. What is the principal public park called?

6. And where is the Prater situated?

7. The summer palace of the Austria-Hungarian Emperors is called …what?

8. West of Vienna lies the famous forest of …?

9. What is the National Opera House called?

10. Vienna has a strong musical heritage and gives its name to a particular form of music. Which?

11. Which Viennese born composer brought this form to its highest romantic level?

12. What date was the University founded?

13. Until about the first century BC, Vienna was a Celtic settlement. What was its name at that time?

14. In 1278 it passed into the possession of which family?

15. A very important congress took place here from September 1814 until June 1815. Why was it arranged?

ANSWERS
1. The Danube 2. The Alps and the Carpathians 3. The Ringstrasse 4. St Stephens 5. The Prater 6. On an island between the River Danube and the Danube Canal 7. Schonbrunn 8. Wienerwald 9. Staatsoper 10. Viennese Operetta 11. Johann Strauss the Younger 12. 1365 13. Vindobona 14. The Hapsburgs 15. To re-establish territories in Europe after Napoleon's defeat

US States

Alabama

Admission to Statehood: December 14 1819 – 22nd state

State Capital: Montgomery

Nickname: Yellowhammer State

Motto: We dare defend our rights

Area: 51.705 square miles

Population: 4,040,587

Sports Teams: Minor league baseball teams

Famous Alabamians:
Harper Lee, writer; Jesse Owens, athlete; Carl Lewis, athlete; Nat King Cole, musician; Helen Keller, author, educator; Martin Luther King, civil rights activist; Rosa Parks, civil rights activist; Talullah Bankhead, actress

Agriculture:
Poultry and eggs, cattle, nursery stock, peanuts, cotton, vegetables, milk, soybeans

Industry:
Lumber, pulp, paper, electronics, chemicals, textiles, motor tyres, fabricated metals, cement, processed food, oil, plastics, defence and space projects, agriculture

Physical Geography:
Alabama lies in the SE USA, on the Gulf of Mexico. It consists of forested uplands in the northeast, with the rest of the state forming an undulating plain, drained by the Alabama and Tombigbee Rivers

General Information:
Visited by Spanish explorers in the mid-16th century, and later settled by the French, it passed to Britain in 1763 and to the USA in 1783. It was included in the Louisiana Purchase from the French in 1803, and became the 22nd state of the Union in 1819. Alabama was also the location of the Montgomery bus boycotts in 1955-6

Alaska

Admission to Statehood: January 3 1959 – 49th state

State Capital: Juneau

Nickname: Last Frontier

Motto: North to the Future

Area: 591,004 square miles

Population: 620,000 (1991)

Sports Teams: Anchorage Aces (WCHL), Fairbanks Icedogs (AWHL)

Famous Alaskans:
Jack London, author; Ray Mala, actor

Agriculture: Seafood, nursery stock, dairy products, vegetables, livestock

Industry: Oil, gas, timber, fishing, tourism

Physical Geography: The largest state in the US, Alaska lies in the extreme north-west of the North American continent. It is separated from the main body of the USA by Canada. Alaska has coasts in the Arctic Ocean, the Bering Sea and the North Pacific. About one third of Alaska lies in the Arctic Circle.

General Information:
Alaska was first discovered in 1741 by the Russian explorer Vitus Bering. In 1867 it was purchased from Russia for the sum of $2 million dollars, or $3.38 per square mile, making the oil and gas which were then discovered there some of the cheapest ever. Alaska tends to attract the outdoors type of tourist, with some of the main attractions being Mt McKinley, the highest peak in the USA, and the Yukon river, which flows through some of the most spectacular scenery in the world

Arizona

Admission to Statehood: February 14 1912 – 48th state

State Capital: Phoenix

Nickname: Grand Canyon State; Apache State

Motto: God enriches

Area: 114,000 square miles

Population: 5,130,630

Sports Teams: Arizona Cardinals (NFL); Phoenix Suns (NBA)

Famous Arizonans:
Lynda Carter, actress; Cesar Estrada Chavez, labor leader; Cochise, Apache Indian chief; Geronimo, Apache Indian chief; Barry Goldwater, politician; Frank Luke, Jr, WWI fighter ace; Linda Ronstadt, singer; Kerri Strug, gymnast

Agriculture:
Cattle, cotton, dairy products, lettuce, nursery stock, hay

Industry:
Copper and other mining, electric equipment, transportation equipment, machinery, printing and publishing, food processing, electronics, tourism

Physical Geography:
Arizona lies in the southwest USA. The Colorado Plateau, an area of dry plains and escarpments, lies in the northeast, and the Gila and Salt Rivers drain the south and west, an area of desert and valleys.

General Information:
Arizona was acquired from Mexico in 1848 and 1853 (Gadsden Purchase) and became the 48th state of the USA in 1912. Major tourist attractions include the Grand Canyon, Petrified Forest, Hoover Dam, Fort Apache, and the reconstructed London Bridge at Lake Havasu City. Arizona has the largest Indian population in the USA, with more than 14 tribes represented on 19 reservations. The state is divided into 15 counties.

Arkansas

Admission to Statehood: June 25 1836 – 25th state

State Capital: Little Rock

Nickname: The Natural State

Motto: The People Rule

Area: 53,182 square miles

Population: 2,673,400

Sports Teams: Arkansas Riverblades (EHCL); Arkansas Glaciercats (WPHL)

Famous Arkansans:
Maya Angelou, author and poet; Johnny Cash, singer; Eldridge Cleaver, black activist; John Grisham, author; Scott Joplin musician, composer; Alan Ladd, actor; Douglas MacArthur, 5-star general; William Clinton, U.S president (1992–2000)

Agriculture:
Poultry and eggs, soybeans, sorghum, cattle, cotton, rice, hogs, milk

Industry:
Oil production began in 1921; there are major lumbering, petroleum, and gas developments around Smackover and El Dorado and coal deposits in the Arkansas River Valley. The state produces 90% of US bauxite from an area to the S and SW of Little Rock. Manufactures include electronic equipment and wood products, agriculture.

Physical Geography:
Arkansas lies in south central USA, west of the Mississippi River. The north and west is mostly high forested land, with the alluvial plain of the Mississippi in the east, and the the West Gulf coastal plain in the south.

General Information:
Arkansas was explored by the Spanish and French in the 16th and 17th centuries, and formed part of the Louisiana Purchase by the USA in 1803. It became a state in 1836, seceded from the Union in 1861, and was readmitted in 1868. It lies in the S central USA, west of the Mississippi River. It is the birthplace of former President Bill Clinton. Arkansas remains one of the poorest US states.

California

Admission to Statehood: September 9 1850 – 31st state

State Capital: Sacramento

Nickname: Golden State

Motto: I have found it

Area: 163, 707 square miles

Population: 33, 871, 648

Sports Teams: Anaheim Angels (MLB), Anaheim Mighty Ducks (NHL), Golden State Warriors (NBA), LA Avengers (AFL), LA Clippers (NBA), LA Dodgers (MLB), LA Galaxy (MLS), LA Lakers (NBA), LA Kings (NHL), LA Sparks (WNBA), Oakland A's (MLB), Oakland Raiders (NFL), Sacramento Kings (NBA), Sacramento Monarchs (WNBA), San Diego Chargers (NFL), San Diego Padres (MLB), San Francisco Giants (MLB), San Francisco 49'ers (NFL), San Jose Earthquakes (MLS), San Jose SaberCats (AFL), San Jose Sharks (NHL)

Famous Californians: Shirley Temple Black, actress, ambassador; Dave Brubeck, musician; Coolio, rap artist; Leonardo di Caprio, actor; Joe diMaggio, baseball player; Isadora Duncan, dancer; Robert Frost, poet; George Lucas, film director; George S. Patton, general; Robert Redford, actor; Richard Nixon, president

Agriculture: Vegetables, fruits and nuts, dairy products, cattle, nursery stock, grapes

Industry: Electronic components and equipment, aerospace, film production, food processing, petroleum, computers and computer software, tourism

Physical Geography: California is the third largest state in the USA, and lies on the Pacific coast in the west. It consists of a narrow coastal plain with the fertile central valleys of the Sacramento and San Joaquin Rivers. The south is mostly desert, with mountains in the east.

General Information: The California Gold Rush began in 1848, the same year the state was ceded to the USA by Mexico. It is the most prosperous state, its economy based on a wide variety of industry, including the film industry based in Hollywood, and hi-tech industries based in Silicon Valley. The state is also home to a large number of military bases. California attracts a large number of tourists every year, and also has many educational and cultural institutions.

Colorado

Admission to Statehood: August 1 1876 – 38th state

State Capital: Denver

Nickname: Centennial State/Colorful Colorado

Motto: Nothing without Providence

Area: 104 247 square miles

Population: 3 892 644

Sports Teams: Denver Broncos (NFL); Colorado Avalanche (NHL); Denver Nuggets (NBA)

Famous Coloradans:
Lon Chaney, actor; Jack Dempsey, boxer; Douglas Fairbanks, actor

Agriculture:
Cattle, wheat, dairy products, corn, hay

Industry:
Scientific instruments, food processing, transportation equipment, machinery, chemical products, gold and other mining, tourism

Physical Geography:
Colorado is situated in the Midwest of the USA. Eastern dry high plains; hilly to mountainous central plateau;western Rocky Mountains of high ranges alternating with broad valleys and deep narrow canyons.

General Information:
Most of eastern Colorado was acquired by Thomas Jefferson, in the Louisiana Purchase (q.v) of 1803, with the bulk of the remainder acquired from Mexico through the Treaty of Guadalupe Hidalgo in 1848. Colorado was the site of a gold rush in the mid-nineteenth century, and is also a major source of dinosaur fossils. The principal tourist attractions are now the Rocky Mountain National Park, Mesa Verde National Park, and the Great Sand Dunes and Dinosaur National Monuments.

Connecticut

Admission to Statehood: January 9 1788 – 5th state

State Capital:.Hartford

Nickname: Constitution State

Motto: He who transplanted still sustains

Area: 5544 square miles

Population: 3,405,565

Sports Teams: New England Seawolves (AFL)

Famous Nutmeggers:
Benedict Arnold, general; P.T Barnum, showman; John Brown, abolitionist; Charles Goodyear, inventor; Samuel Colt, inventor; Harriet Beecher Stowe, writer; Noah Webster, lexicographer

Agriculture:
Nursery stock, eggs, dairy products, cattle

Industry:
Transportation equipment, machinery, electric equipment, fabricated metal products, chemical products, scientific instruments

Physical Geography:
Western upland, the Berkshires, in the Northwest; narrrow central lowlands; hilly eastern upland.

General Information:
A Puritan settlement in the 17th century, Connecticut was one of the original thirteen states of the Union and ratified the draft US Constitution in 1788.

Delaware

Admission to Statehood: December 7 1787 – 1st state

State Capital: Dover

Nicknames: First State / Diamond State / Blue Hen State/ Small Wonder

Motto: Liberty and Independence

Area: 2489 square miles

Population: 783,600

Sports Teams: No major league teams

Famous Delawareans:
Robert Montgomery Bird, playwright; E.I du Pont, industrialist; Howard Pyle, artist and author; George Read, jurist and signatory of Declaration of Independence

Agriculture:
Poultry, nursery stock, soybeans, dairy products, corn

Industry:
Chemical products, food processing, paper products, rubber and plastic products, scientific instruments, printing and publishing

Physical Geography:
Delaware is situated on the north-east coast of the USA between New Jersey and Maryland, with most of the state lying along the Atlantic coastal plain.

General Information:
Delaware was discovered by Henry Hudson, and settled first by the Dutch and then the Swedes, coming under English control in 1664. Its name derives from Lord de la Warr, who was governor of Virginia in 1610. As the three 'Lower Counties' of Pennsylvania, it enjoyed virtual autonomy under the Quaker Penn family, but in 1776 it achieved independent statehood. It was the first state to ratify the US constitution in 1787.

Florida

Admission to Statehood: March 3 1845 – 27th state

State Capital: Tallahassee

Nickname: The Sunshine State

Motto: In God We Trust

Area: 64,758 square miles

Population: 15,982,378

Sports Teams: Miami Dolphins (NFL); Miami Heat (NBA);Tampa Bay Buccaneers (NFL);Tampa Bay Mutiny (MLS)

Famous Floridans:
Pat Boone, singer; Fay Dunaway, actress; Jim Morrison, singer; Sidney Poitier, actor; Joseph Stilwell, army general

Agriculture:
Citrus, vegetables, nursery stock, cattle, sugarcane, dairy products

Industry:
Tourism, electric equipment, food processing, printing and publishing, transportation equipment, machinery

Physical Geography:
Florida lies in the far SE of the USA, between the Atlantic Ocean and the Gulf of Mexico. It is predominantly a low-lying peninsula with many lakes and rivers.

General Information:
After its discovery by the Spanish, Florida was ceded to the British in 1763 but returned to Spain after the American Revolution. It passed to the USA in 1819, becoming a state in 1845. It was a supporter of the Confederate cause during the US Civil War.Tourism, based on its subtropical climate, is the most important industry, with many popular resorts, such as Miami Beach and Palm Beach, and also Disneyworld.The John F. Kennedy Space Center at Cape Canaveral (known as Cape Kennedy from 1963 to 1973) is also the principal launch site for NASA. Florida also produces some 75% of the USA's citrus fruits.

Georgia

Admission to Statehood: January 2 1788 – 4th state

State Capital: Atlanta

Nickname: Peach State

Motto: Wisdom, justice and moderation

Area: 59,441 square miles

Population: 8, 186, 453

Sports Teams: Atlanta Falcons (NFL); Atlanta Hawks (NBA); Atlanta Thrashers (NHL)

Famous Georgians:
James Bowie, soldier; James Carter, U.S president; Ray Charles, singer; Oliver Hardy, comedian; Martin Luther King, civil rights leader; Gladys Knight, singer; Otis Redding, singer; Alice Walker, writer.

Agriculture:
Poultry and eggs, peanuts, cattle, hogs, dairy products, vegetables

Industry:
Textiles and apparel, transportation equipment, food processing, paper products, chemical products, electric equipment, tourism

Physical Geography:
Georgia lies on the SE coast of the USA, and consists of two physical regions: the Appalachian Mountains in the north and a rolling coastal plain with forests and swamps in the south.

General Information:
Named after King George II, Georgia was the youngest of the original thirteen colonies. Settlement of the state expanded after the American Revolution with the development of agriculture. A supporter of the Confederate cause in the US Civil War, it suffered considerable damage during Gen Sherman's March to the Sea (1864). Although during the 20th century it has experienced many of the problems of the South, such as the decline in the cotton industry and racial unrest, its capital Atlanta is nevertheless the cultural and economic centre of the South-eastern states.

Hawaii

Admission to Statehood: August 21 1959 – 50th state

State Capital: Honolulu

Nickname: Aloha State

Motto: The life of the land is perpetuated in righteousness

Area: 10932 square miles

Population: 1,211,537

Sports Teams: Hawaii has no major league sports teams

Famous Hawaiians:
Konishiki, Sumo wrestler; Tia Carrere, singer and actress; Ellison Onizuka, astronaut;
Don Stroud, actor

Agriculture:
Sugarcane, pineapples, nursery stock, livestock, macadamia nuts

Industry:
Tourism, food processing, apparel, fabricated metal products, stone, clay, and glass
products

Physical Geography:
Hawaii consists of eight main islands, which are the tops of a chain of submerged
volcanic mountains; active volcanoes: Mauna Loa, Kilauea

General Information:
Hawaii was discovered by the British explorer James Cook in 1778. Hawaii
remained a kingdom ruled by several kings until 1894, when it became a republic. It
was annexed by the USA in 1898 and became a territory in 1900. The Japanese
attack on Pearl Harbor (1941) brought the USA into World War II, and Hawaii
became the 50th state in 1959.

Idaho

Admission to Statehood: July 3 1890 – 43rd state

State Capital: Boise

Nickname: Gem State

Motto: It is forever

Area: 83,574 square miles

Population: 1,293,953

Sports Teams: Idaho Steelheads (WCHL)

Famous Idahoans:
Gutzon Borglum, Mt Rushmore sculptor; Carol R. Brink, author; Ezra Pound, poet; Lana Turner, actress

Agriculture:
Cattle, potatoes, dairy products, wheat, sugar beets, barley

Industry:
Food processing, lumber and wood products, machinery, chemical products, paper products, silver and other mining, tourism

Physical Geography:

Snake River plains in the south, central region of mountains, canyons gorges; subalpine northern region

General Information:
First settled in the early nineteenth century, Idaho became a state in 1890. The world's first ski chair lift was opened at Sun Valley in 1936, and the first commercial airmail service in the U.S began in Boise in 1926. Ernest Hemingway died in Ketchum in 1961.

Illinois

Admission to Statehood: December 3 1818 – 21st state

State Capital: Springfield

Nickname: Prairie State

Motto: State Sovereignty, National Union

Area: 57,918 square miles

Population: 12,419,293

Sports Teams: Chicago Bears (NFL); Chicago Bulls (NBA); Chicago Cubs (MLB); Chicago White Sox (MLB)

Famous Illinoisans:
Franklin Pierce Adams, author; Gillian Anderson, actress; Jack Benny, comedian; Ray Bradbury, author; Edgar Rice Burroughs, author; Raymond Chandler, author; Jimmy Connors, tennis champion; Miles Davis, musician; Ernest Hemingway, author; Richard Pryor, comedian; William L. Shirer, author and historian

Agriculture:
Corn, soybeans, hogs, cattle, dairy products, whea

Industry:
Machinery, food processing, electric equipment, chemical products, printing and publishing, fabricated metal products, transportation equipment, petroleum, coal

Physical Geography:
Prairies and fertile plains throughout; open hills in the southern region

General Information:
first discovered by the French in the 17th century, Illinois formed part of the French province of Louisiana until it was ceded to Britain in 1763. It came under US control in 1783, and became a territory in 1809 and a state in 1818. The Illinois and Michigan Canal , built in 1848 joins Lake Michigan to the Mississippi River, ensuring a comprehensive transport network across the eastern states of the US.

Indiana

Admission to Statehood: December 11 1816 – 19th state

State Capital: Indianapolis

Nickname: Hoosier State

Motto: The crossroads of America

Area: 36,420 square miles

Population: 6,080,485

Sports Teams: Indianapolis Colts (NFL); Indiana Pacers (NBA)

Famous Hoosiers:
Hoagy Carmichael, songwriter; Virgil Grissom, astronaut; James Hoffa, labour leader;
David Letterman, TV host; John Cougar Mellencamp, singer/songwriter; J. Danforth
Quayle, US vice-president; Kurt Vonnegut Jr, author; Wilbur Wright, pioneer aviator

Agriculture:
Corn, soybeans, hogs, cattle, dairy products, eggs

Industry:
Steel, electric equipment, transportation equipment, chemical products, petroleum
and coal products, machinery

Physical Geography:
Indiana forms part of the Mississipi Basin, and consists of a hilly southern region,
with fertile plains in the central region, and a flat, heavily glaciated north. The area
along Lake Michigan shore is mostly dunes.

General Information:
originally a French possession, Indiana was ceded to the British in 1763, becoming
part of the US in 1783. It is perhaps best known for the Indianapolis 500 (q.v), a
500-mile race first held in 1911.

Iowa

Admission to Statehood: December 28 1846 – 29th state

State Capital: Des Moines

Nickname: Hawkeye State

Motto: Our liberties we prize and our rights we will maintain

Area: 56,276 square miles

Population: 2,926,324

Sports Teams: Iowa Barnstormers (AFL)

Famous Iowans:
Bix Beiderbecke, jazz musician; Bill Bryson, author; Johnny Carson, TV entertainer;
Herbert Hoover, US president; Glenn Miller, bandleader; James A. Van Allen, space
physicist; John Wayne, actor

Agriculture:
Hogs, corn, soybeans, oats, cattle, dairy products

Industry:
Food processing, machinery, electric equipment, chemical products, printing and
publishing, primary metals

Physical Geography:
Iowa lies in the Midwest of the USA, and is bounded to the east by the Mississipi
River, and to the west by Missouri River. It is a rich and fertile region, rising gently
to the north-west.

General Information:
first explored by the French as early as 1673. Iowa formed part of the Louisiana
Purchase (q.v) in 1803. The state is most famous as the birthplace of President
Herbert Hoover, and the most outstanding landmarks are the Fort Dodge Historical
Museum, and the Effigy Mounds National Monument.

Kansas

Admission to Statehood: January 9 1861 – 34th state

State Capital: Topeka

Nickname: Sunflower State

Motto: To the stars through difficulties

Area: 82,282 square miles

Population: 2,688,418

Sports Teams: Kansas has no major league sports teams.

Famous Kansans:
Fatty Arbuckle, actor; Walter P. Chrysler, car manufacturer; Bob Dole, politician; Amelia Earhart, aviator; Dennis Hopper, actor; Buster Keaton, comedian; Harold Lloyd, actor

Agriculture:
Cattle, wheat, sorghum, soybeans, hogs, corn

Industry:
Transportation equipment, food processing, printing and publishing, chemical products, machinery, apparel, petroleum, mining

Physical Geography:
hilly Osage plains in the east, part of the Great Plains, with a central region of level prairie and hills and high plains in the west.

General Information:
although originally explored by the Spanish, Kansas was ceded to the French in 1682, eventually forming part of the Louisiana Purchase in 1803. Wheat was introduced to the state by the Mennonites in 1874, and Kansas is now the most important wheat-producing area in the US. Kansas is also most famously the home of Dorothy in the 1900 book by Frank L. Baum.

Kentucky

Admission to Statehood: June 1 1792 – 15th state

State Capital: Frankfort

Nickname: Bluegrass State

Motto: United we stand, divided we fall

Area: 40,411 square miles

Population: 4,041,769

Sports Teams: Kentucky has no major league sports teams

Famous Kentuckians:
Muhammad Ali, boxer; Jefferson Davis, president of the Confederacy; Crystal Gayle, singer; Casey Jones, locomotive engineer; Abraham Lincoln, US president; Hunter S. Thompson, writer

Agriculture:
Horses, cattle, tobacco, dairy products, hogs, soybeans, corn

Industry:
Transportation equipment, chemical products, electric equipment, machinery, food processing, tobacco products, coal, tourism

Physical Geography:
Kentucky lies in the central United States, and consists of the Appalachian Mountains in the east, the rounded hills of the Knobs in the north; the Bluegrass plains region, at the heart of the state; wooded rocky hillsides of the Pennroyal; western coal fields; the fertile basins of the Ohio and Mississipi Rivers in the southwest.

General Information:
the Kentucky area was first explored by American hero Daniel Boone in 1769, and was rapidly settled, becoming a state in 1792. Kentucky is most famous for the Kentucky Derby, an annual race for three-year-olds, held at Louisville every year. First held in 1875, it is the oldest horse race in the US.

Louisiana

Admission to Statehood: April 30 1812 – 18th state

State Capital: Baton Rouge

Nickname: Pelican State

Motto: Union, justice and confidence

Area: 51,843 square miles

Population: 4,468,976

Sports Teams: New Orleans Saints (NFL)

Famous Louisianians:
Louis Armstrong, musician; Truman Capote, writer; Fats Domino, musician; Dorothy Lamour, actress; Jerry Lee Lewis, singer; Jelly Roll Morton, jazz musician and composer; Huey Newton, black activist

Agriculture:
Seafood, cotton, soybeans, cattle, sugarcane, poultry and eggs, dairy products, rice

Industry:
Chemical products, petroleum and coal products, food processing, transportation equipment, paper products, tourism

Physical Geography:
Louisiana lies in the southern US, on the Gulf of Mexico. Mostly low-lying, it is dominated by the Mississipi Delta in the south, where the main population centres are located.

General Information:
originally explored by the Spanish, Louisiana changed hands between the French and Spanish, being named after the French king Louis XIV. It was acquired by the US as part of the Louisiana Purchase (q.v) in 1803. Louisiana is the centre of the US jazz scene, which is based mainly in New Orleans, an important US cultural centre. The Mardi Gras festival is held in New Orleans annually.

Maine

Admission to Statehood: March 15 1820 – 23rd state

State Capital: Augusta

Nickname: Pine Tree State

Motto: I direct

Area: 35,387 square miles

Population: 1,274,923

Sports Teams: Maine has no major league sports teams

Famous Mainers:
John Ford, film director; Henry Wadsworth Longfellow, poet; Stephen King, writer; Hiram Maxim, inventor; Marston Morse, mathematician; George Palmer Putnam, publisher

Agriculture:
Seafood, poultry and eggs, potatoes, dairy products, cattle, blueberries, apples

Industry:
Paper, lumber, and wood products, electric equipment, food processing, leather products, textiles, tourism

Physical Geography:
Appalachian Mountains extend through state; western borders have rugged terrain, long sand beaches on southern coast; northern coast mainly rocky promontories, peninsulas, fjords.

General Information:
the area around Maine was claimed by both Britain and France, and became a British possession in 1763. Originally entering the union as part of Massachusetts, Maine became a separate state in 1820. Maine has become famous as the setting for many of the novels of horror author Stephen King, a native of the state.

Maryland

Admission to Statehood: April 28 1788 – 7th state

State Capital: Annapolis

Nickname: Old Line State

Motto: strong deeds, gentle words

Area: 12,407 square miles

Population: 5,296,486

Sports Teams: Baltimore Orioles (MLB); Baltimore Ravens (NFL)

Famous Marylanders:
Spiro T. Agnew, US vice-president; John Wilkes Booth, Lincoln assassin; Philip Glass, composer; Billie Holiday, jazz-blues singer; H.L Mencken, writer; Babe Ruth, baseball player; Upton Sinclair, writer; Leon Uris, writer; Frank Zappa, singer

Agriculture:
Seafood, poultry and eggs, dairy products, nursery stock, cattle, soybeans, corn

Industry:
Electric equipment, food processing, chemical products, printing and publishing, transportation equipment, machinery, primary metals, coal, tourism

Physical Geography:
Maryland is situated on the eastern seaboard of the United States, and consists of two regions, the eastern shore of Atlantic coastal plain, which is split by Chesapeake Bay into a low flat plain in the east and uplands in the west, and an area of higher ground, the Blue Ridge, part of the Alleghenies in the N and W.

General Information:
Maryland is one of the original thirteen colonies of the USA, settled by the English and named after Henrietta Maria, queen of King George I. Maryland landmarks include Harpers Ferry National Historical Park, the Goddard Space Flight Center, and Chesapeake Bay.

Massachusetts

Admission to Statehood: February 6 1788 – 6th state

State Capital: Boston

Nickname: Bay State

Motto: By the sword we seek peace, but peace only under liberty

Area: 10,555 square miles

Population: 6,349,097

Sports Teams: Boston Bruins (NHL); Boston Celtics (NBA); Boston Red Sox (MLB); New England Patriots (NFL); New England Revolution (MLS)

Famous Bay Staters:
John Adams, US president; John Quincy Adams, US president; George Bush, US president; E.E Cummings, poet; Bette Davis, actress; Cecil B. DeMille, film director; Emily Dickinson, poet; Ralph Waldo Emerson, philosopher and poet; Benjamin Franklin, statesman and scientist; Nathaniel Hawthorne, author; John F. Kennedy, US president; Percival Lowell, astronomer; Edgar Allan Poe, writer; Henry David Thoreau, author

Agriculture:
Seafood, nursery stock, dairy products, cranberries, vegetables

Industry:
Machinery, electric equipment, scientific instruments, printing and publishing, tourism

Physical Geography:
Jagged indented coast around Cape Cod; flatland yields to stony upland pastures near central region and gentle hill country in west; land in west is rocky, sandy and not fertile.

General Information:
the site of the landing of the Pilgrim Fathers from the Mayflower in 1620, Massachusetts was one of the original thirteen states. A centre for opposition to British colonial policy leading to the American Revolution and became prominent as a state after 1788. Although Massachusetts has declined in importance as a manufacturing state, it retains its place as a cultural heartland of the USA.

Michigan

Admission to Statehood: January 26 1837 – 26th state

State Capital: Lansing

Nickname: Wolverine State/Great Lakes State

Motto: If you seek a pleasant peninsula, look about you

Area: 96,810 square miles

Population: 9,938,444

Sports Teams: Many, including Detroit Lions (NFL); Detroit Pistons (NBA); Detroit Tigers (MLB)

Famous Michiganians:
Roger Chaffee, astronaut; Francis Ford Coppola, film director; Henry Ford, industrialist; Earvin Magic Johnson, basketball player; Ring Lardner, writer; Diana Ross, singer; Stevie Wonder, singer

Agriculture:
Dairy products, apples, blueberries, cattle, vegetables, hogs, corn, nursery stock, soybeans

Industry:
Motor vehicles and parts, machinery, fabricated metal products, food processing, chemical products, mining, tourism

Physical Geography:
Michigan lies in the north central USA, and is bordered on the east, north and west by the Great Lakes (Superior, Huron, Michigan, Erie and St Clair). It consists mainly of low rolling hills, with more rugged ground in the west of the state.

General Information:
Michigan was first explored by the French in the 17th century, and acquired by the British as part of Canada in 1763. It is a major tourist area, situated as it is amongst the Great Lakes. Detroit is one of the largest automobile manufacturing centres in the world.

Minnesota

Admission to Statehood: May 11 1858 – 32nd state

State Capital: Saint Paul

Nickname: North Star State/Land of 10,000 Lakes

Motto: The star of the north

Area: 86,943 square miles

Population: 4,919,479

Sports Teams: Minnesota Timberwolves (NBA); Minnesota Twins (MLB); Minnesota Vikings (NFL); Minnesota Wild (NHL)

Famous Minnesotans:
Bob Dylan, singer/songwriter; F. Scott Fitzgerald, author; Jean Paul Getty, oil executive; Sinclair Lewis, author; Kate Millett, feminist; Winona Ryder, actress; Charles M. Schultz, cartoonist

Agriculture:
Dairy products, corn, cattle, soybeans, hogs, wheat, turkeys

Industry:
Machinery, food processing, printing and publishing, fabricated metal products, electric equipment, mining, tourism

Physical Geography:
a central hill and lake region covers approximately half the state, with rocky ridges and deep lakes to the northeast, and rolling prairies to the south.

General Information:
Minnesota was acquired from the French as part of the Louisiana Purchase of 1803 (q.v), becoming a state in 1858. The state became a focal point in the 1880s for Scandinavian immigrants, and their influence can still be seen today.

Mississippi

Admission to Statehood: December 10 1817 – 20th state

State Capital:. Jackson

Nickname: Magnolia State

Motto: By valor and arms

Area: 48,434 square miles

Population: 2,844,658

Sports Teams: Mississippi has no major league sports teams.

Famous Mississippians:

Bo Diddley, guitarist; William Faulkner, author; Jim Henson, puppeteer; James Earl Jones, actor; B.B. King, singer, guitarist, composer; Elvis Presley, singer, actor; Muddy Waters, singer, guitarist, composer; Tennessee Williams, playwright; Oprah Winfrey, talk show host; Tammy Wynette, country musician

Agriculture:

Cotton, poultry, cattle, catfish, soybeans, dairy products, rice

Industry:
Apparel, furniture, lumber and wood products, food processing, electrical machinery, transportation equipment

Physical Geography:
Mississippi lies in the south central USA, on the Gulf of Mexico. It consists of the fertile cotton-producing delta between the Yazoo and Mississippi rivers, swamps in the southwest, and generally infertile hills in the east and north-east

General Information:
explored by the Spanish, claimed by the French, Mississippi was ceded to the British in 1763, after which date colonisation began. Mississippi was a centre of cotton production, and also of slavery, fighting on the side of the Confederacy in the US Civil War. Due to a legal technicality, slavery was not officially abolished in the state until 1995.

Missouri

Admission to Statehood: August 10 1821 – 24th state

State Capital: Jefferson City

Nickname: Show Me State

Motto: The welfare of the people shall be the supreme law

Area: 69,709 square miles

Population: 5,595,211

Sports Teams: many, including Kansas City Chiefs (NFL); Kansas City Royals (MLB); St Louis Cardinals (MLB); St Louis Rams (NFL)

Famous Missourians:
Robert Altman, film director; Burt Bacharach, songwriter; Josephine Baker, singer and dancer; Omar Bradley, five-star general; William Burroughs, writer; T.S Eliot, poet; Edwin Hubble, astronomer; Vincent Price, actor; Harry S. Truman, US president; Mark Twain, writer

Agriculture:
Cattle, soybeans, hogs, dairy products, corn, poultry and eggs

Industry:
Transportation equipment, food processing, chemical products, electric equipment, fabricated metal products

Physical Geography:
Rolling hills, open, fertile plains, and well watered prairie north of the Missouri river; south of the river land is rough and hilly with deep, narrow valleys; alluvial plain in the southeast; low elevations in the west

General Information:
Missouri was acquired by the USA as part of the Louisiana Purchase (q.v) from the French in 1803. It is a major producer of tobacco. Notable landmarks include the Ozark National Scenic Riverway, and the Ulysses S. Grant National Historic Site.

Montana

Admission to Statehood: November 8 1889 – 41st state

State Capital:. Helena

Nickname: Treasure State

Motto: Gold and silver

Area: 147,046 square miles

Population: 902,195

Sports Teams: Montana has no major league sports teams

Famous Montanans:
Gary Cooper, actor; Evel Knievel, stunt motorcyclist; Myrna Loy, actress; David Lynch, filmmaker; Rich Hall, comedian

Agriculture:
Cattle, wheat, barley, sugar beets, hay, hogs

Industry:
Mining, lumber and wood products, food processing, tourism

Physical Geography:
Montana is the fourth largest state of the USA, and lies in the extreme north of the country, bordering on Canada. It consists of the Rocky Mountains in the western third of the state, and two-thirds gently rolling northern great plains to the east.

General Information:
Another state acquired as part of the Louisiana Purchase (q.v) of 1803, Montana is also known as 'Big Sky Country', due to the arresting views on offer. The centre of a gold rush in the mid-19th century, Montana was also the site of the infamous Battle of the Little Bighorn (Custer's Last Stand). In recent years Montana has become a lodestone for various right-wing militia movements.

Nebraska

Admission to Statehood: March 1 1867 – 37th state

State Capital: Lincoln

Nickname: Cornhusker state

Motto: Equality before the law

Area: 77,358 square miles

Population: 1,711,263

Sports Teams: Nebraska has no major league sports teams

Famous Nebraskans:
Fred Astaire, dancer; Marlon Brando, actor; Montgomery Clift, actor; Gerald Ford US president; Malcolm X, civil rights activist; Red Cloud, Indian rights activist

Agriculture:
Cattle, corn, hogs, soybeans, wheat, sorghum

Industry:
Food processing, machinery, electric equipment, printing and publishing

Physical Geography:
Nebraska lies in the north central USA, west of the Missouri. Till plains of the central lowland in the eastern third rise to the Great Plains and hill country of the north central and northwest.

General Information:
Also acquired as part of the Louisiana Purchase (q.v), Nebraska was opened up to settlers with the arrival of the railway in 1867, and developed rapidly as a cattle-producing state, and remains one of the leading producers of cattle, along with corn and wheat.

Nevada

Admission to Statehood: October 31 1864 – 36th state

State Capital: Carson City

Nickname: The Silver State

Motto: All for our country

Area: 110,567 square miles

Population: 1,998,257

Sports Teams: Nevada has no major league sports teams

Famous Nevadans:
Andre Agassi, tennis player; Jack Kramer, tennis player; Thelma Pat Nixon, First Lady;
Jack Wilson, Paiute Indian prophet

Agriculture:
Cattle, hay, dairy products, potatoes

Industry:
Tourism, mining, machinery, printing and publishing, food processing, electric
equipment

Physical Geography:
Rugged north-south mountain ranges; southern area is within the Mojave Desert
with the Colorado River Canyon. Nevada is the most arid state in the USA.

General Information:
ceded by Mexico to the USA in 1848, Nevada quickly became the site of a major
gold rush. Today, it is an important tourist centre, and boasts some of the largest
casinos in the world.

New Hampshire

Admission to Statehood: June 21 1788 - 9th

State Capital: Concord

Nickname: Granite State

Motto: Live free or die

Area: 9351 square miles

Population: 1,235,786

Sports Teams: New Hampshire has no major league sports teams

Famous New Hampshirites:
Charles Dana, editor; John Irving, writer; Franklin Pierce, US president; Alan Shepard, astronaut

Agriculture:
Dairy products, nursery stock, cattle, apples, eggs

Industry:
Machinery, electric equipment, rubber and plastic products, tourism

Physical Geography:
New Hampshire lies on the north-east coast of the USA, and consists of Low rolling coast followed by countless hills rising out of a central plateau into the Appalachian Mountains.

General Information:
one of the original thirteen colonies, New Hampshire was first settled by Britain in the early seventeenth century, and became a royal province shortly after. New Hampshire was one of the first states to declare its independence from Britain.

New Jersey

Admission to Statehood: December 18 1787 – 3rd state

State Capital: Trenton

Nickname: Garden State

Motto: Liberty and prosperity

Area: 8722 square miles

Population: 8,414,350

Sports Teams: New Jersey Devils (NHL); MetroStars (MLS); New Jersey Gladiators (AFL); New Jersey Nets (NBA)

Famous New Jerseyites:
Bud Abbott, comedian; Edwin Aldrin, astronaut; Count Basie, band leader; James Fenimore Cooper, author; Lou Costello, comedian; Allen Ginsberg, poet; Philip Roth, author; Frank Sinatra, singer and actor; Bruce Springsteen, musician

Agriculture:
Nursery stock, horses, vegetables, fruits and nuts, seafood, dairy products

Industry:
Chemical products, food processing, electric equipment, printing and publishing, tourism

Physical Geography:
New Jersey lies in the north-east of the US, on the mid-Atlantic coast. The Kittatinny Mountains, part of the Appalachian chain, extend across the north-west of the state, with lower land to the south.

General Information:
New Jersey was one of the original thirteen colonies, first settled in the early seventeenth century by the Dutch, passing into British control later in the century. Although one of the most urbanised states, and a major industrial centre, New Jersey also has a thriving tourist industry based around its forests, beaches, and the mountain regions in the north of the state.

New Mexico

Admission to Statehood: January 6 1912 – 47th state

State Capital: Santa Fe

Nickname: Land of Enchantment

Motto: It grows as it goes

Area: 121,593 square miles

Population: 1,819,046

Sports Teams: New Mexico has no major league sports teams

Famous New Mexicans:
Robert Crichton, author; John Denver, singer; Sid Gutierrez, astronaut; William Hanna, animator; Demi Moore, actress

Agriculture:
Cattle, dairy products, hay, nursery stock, chilies

Industry:
Electric equipment, petroleum and coal products, food processing, printing and publishing, stone, glass, and clay products, tourism

Physical Geography:
New Mexico lies in the southwest of the USA, and is mostly mountainous; 85% of the state is over 4000 feet in elevation. The Great Plains lie to the east, rising to the Rocky Mountains in the centre and high plateau in the west.

General Information:
New Mexico is a comparatively new addition to the USA, being acquired from Mexico in 1848 and 1853. New Mexico is the site of the Carsbad Caverns National Park, and the Gila Cliff Dwellings National Monuments.

New York

Admission to Statehood: July 26 1788 – 11th state

State Capital: Albany

Nickname: Empire State

Motto: Excelsior

Area: 54,475 square miles

Population: 18,976,457

Sports Teams: Buffalo Bills (NFL); Buffalo Destroyers (AFL); Buffalo Sabres (NHL); MetroStars (MLS); New York Dragons (AFL); New York Giants (NFL); New York Islanders (NHL); New York Jets (NFL); New York Knicks (NBA); New York Liberty (WNBA); New York Mets (MLB); New York Rangers (NHL), New York Yankees (MLB)

Famous New Yorkers:
Humphrey Bogart, actor; James Cagney, actor; Maria Callas, soprano; Sammy Davis Jr, actor and singer; Millard Fillmore, US president; Sarah Michelle Gellar, actress; George Gershwin, composer; Jackie Gleason, comedian and actor; Chico, Groucho, Harpo, Zeppo Marx, comdians; Herman Melville, author; Franklin D. Roosevelt, US president; Theodore Roosevelt, US president; Mae West, actress; George Westinghouse Jr, inventor; Walt Whitman, poet

Agriculture:
Dairy products, cattle and other livestock, vegetables, nursery stock, apples

Industry:
Printing and publishing, scientific instruments, electric equipment, machinery, chemical products, tourism

Physical Geography:
New York lies in the northeast of the USA. It is generally an upland region, encompassing the rugged mountains of the northeast Adirondack range, bisected by the Hudson and Mohawk rivers.

General Information:
one of the original colonies, New York was known as New Amsterdam by its first Dutch settlers, until becoming a British colony in the mid-seventeenth century, when it was renamed. New York City is America's largest, (1996 est. pop. 7,380,900). It is the home of many of the USAs most famous landmarks, including the Statue of Liberty, the Empire State Building, Times Square and Central Park. It is also a cultural heartland of the US, hosting a symphony orchestra, the theatres of Broadway, two opera companies, a ballet company, and numerous museums and art galleries. New York is also the home of US TV, radio, and book publishing.

North Carolina

Admission to Statehood: November 21 1789 – 12th state

State Capital: Raleigh

Nickname: Old North State/Tar Heel State

Motto: To be and not to seem

Area: 53,821 square miles

Population: 8,049,313

Sports Teams: Carolina Cobras (AFL); Carolina Hurricanes (NHL); Carolina Panthers (NFL); Charlotte Hornets (NBA); Charlotte Sting (WNBA)

Famous North Carolinians:
Roberta Flack, singer; Ava Gardner, actress; Richard Gatling, inventor; Andrew Johnson, US president; Thelonious Monk, pianist; James K. Polk, US president; Soupy Sales, comedian

Agriculture:
Poultry and eggs, tobacco, hogs, milk, nursery stock, cattle, soybeans

Industry:
Tobacco products, textile goods, chemical products, electric equipment, machinery, tourism

Physical Geography:
North Carolina lies oastal plains and tidewater in two-fifths of state; southern Appalachian Mountains contain Blue Ridge and Great Smokey Mountains.

General Information:
one of the original thirteen colonies, North Carolina's history is closely allied to that of its southern neighbour, South Carolina. North Carolina is the industrial centre of the south, and the nation's leading tobacco producer

North Dakota

Admission to Statehood: November 2 1889 – 39th state

State Capital: Bismarck

Nickname: Peace Garden State/Flickertail State/Roughrider State

Motto: Liberty and union, now and forever, one and inseperable.

Area: 70,704 square miles

Population: 642,200

Sports Teams: North Dakota has no major league sports teams

Famous North Dakotans:
Angie Dickinson, actress; Louis L'Amour, Western author; Peggy Lee, singer

Agriculture:
Wheat, cattle, barley, sunflowers, milk, sugar beets

Industry:
Food processing, machinery, mining, tourism

Physical Geography:
North Dakota lies in the north central USA. It consists of the central lowlands in the east, leading into the flat Red River Valley and the rolling drift prairie, and the Missouri plateau of the Great Plains in the west.

General Information:
settled early on by Scottish and Irish immigrants, North Dakota became more populous after the arrival of the railway in the 1870s. It is still, however, one of the most sparsely populated states in the USA. The name is a Sioux word meaning 'friend'.

Ohio

Admission to Statehood: March 1 1803 – 17th state

State Capital: Columbus

Nickname: Buckeye State

Motto: With God, all things are possible

Area: 44,828 square miles

Population: 11,353,140

Sports Teams: Cincinnati Bengals (NFL); Cincinnati Reds (MLB); Cleveland Browns (NFL); Cleveland Cavaliers (NBA); Cleveland Indians (MLB); Cleveland Rockers (WNBA); Columbus Blue Jackets (NHL); Columbus Crew (MLS)

Famous Ohioans:
Neil Armstrong, astronaut; Nancy Cartwright, voice of Bart Simpson; Doris Day, singer; Thomas Edison, inventor; Clark Gable, actor; James Abram Garfield, US president; John Glenn, astronaut; Ulysses S. Grant, US president and Civil War general; Paul Newman, actor; Jack Nicklaus, golfer; William Sherman, army general; Steven Spielberg, film director; Gloria Steinem, feminist theorist; James Thurber, author and humourist; Orville Wright, pioneer aviator

Agriculture:
Soybeans, dairy products, corn, tomatoes, hogs, cattle, poultry and eggs

Industry:
Transportation equipment, fabricated metal products, machinery, food processing, electric equipment

Physical Geography:
Ohio lies in the midwest of the US, to the south of Lake Erie. It is generally rolling plain, with the Allegheny plateau located in the east. The Lake Erie plains extend southward into the central plains in the west.

General Information:
after disputes between France and Britain, Ohio eventually came under British control in 1763, acquired by the USA twenty years later. Ohio is second only to Virginia in the number of US presidents it has supplied (seven).

Oklahoma

Admission to Statehood: November 16 1907 – 46th state

State Capital: Oklahoma City

Nickname: Sooner State

Motto: Labour conquers all things

Area: 69,903 square miles

Population: 3,450,654

Sports Teams: Oklahoma Wranglers (AFL)

Famous Oklahomans:
Gordon Cooper, astronaut; Garth Brooks, singer; Woody Guthrie, singer and composer; Ron Howard, actor and director; Shannon Miller, Olympic gymnast; Brad Pitt, actor

Agriculture:
Cattle, wheat, milk, poultry, cotton

Industry:
Transportation equipment, machinery, electric products, rubber and plastic products, food processing

Physical Geography:
Oklahoma lies in south central USA, on the northern Texas border. High plains predominate in the west, hills and small mountains in the east; the east central region is dominated by the Arkansas River Basin, and the Red River Plains are in the south.

General Information:
Oklahoma formed part of the Louisiana Purchase (q.v) of 1803, and was originally kept as an Indian reservation. Whites began to settle Oklahoma after the US Civil War, when they began to exploit the rich oil deposits found in the state.

Oregon

Admission to Statehood: February 14 1859 – 33rd state

State Capital: Salem

Nickname: Beaver State

Motto: She flies with her own wings

Area: 98,386 square miles

Population: 3,421,399

Sports Teams: Portland Fire (WNBA); Portland Forest Dragons (AFL); Portland Trail Blazers (NBA)

Famous Oregonians:
Raymond Carver, writer and poet; Douglas Engelbart, inventor; Matt Groening, cartoonist; Sally Struthers, actress

Agriculture:
Cattle, vegetables, nursery stock, fruits and nuts, dairy products, wheat

Industry:
Lumber and wood products, tourism, food processing, paper products, machinery, scientific instruments

Physical Geography:
Rugged coast range; fertile Willamette River Valley to east and south; Cascade Mountain range of volcanic peaks east of the valley; plateau east of Cascades, in remaining two-thirds of the state.

General Information:
originally the home of several different Indian tribes, Oregon was settled in the mid-nineteenth century, by way of the Oregon Trail, a 2000-mile route across the central United States, along the Missouri River.

Pennsylvania

Admission to Statehood: December 12 1787 – 2nd state

State Capital: Harrisburg

Nickname: Keystone State

Motto: Virtue, Liberty and Independence

Area: 46,058 square miles

Population: 12,281,054

Sports Teams: Philadelphia Eagles (NFL); Philadelphia 76ers (NBA); Philadelphia Flyers (NHL); Philadelphia Phillies (MLB); Pittsburgh Penguins (NHL); Pittsburgh Pirates (MLB); Pittsburgh Steelers (NFL)

Famous Pennsylvanians:
Louisa May Alcott, author; Daniel Boone, frontiersman; James Buchanan, US president; Bill Cosby, actor; W.C Fields, comedian; Robert Fulton, inventor; Tom Mix, actor; Robert Peary, explorer; Gertrude Stein, author; James Stewart, actor; John Updike, author

Agriculture:
Dairy products, poultry, cattle, nursery stock, mushrooms, hogs, hay

Industry:
Food processing, chemical products, machinery, electric equipment, tourism

Physical Geography:
Allegheny Mountains run southwest to northeast, with piedmont and coastal plain in southeast triangle; Allegheny Front a diagonal spine across the states center; northwest rugged plateau falls to Lake Erie lowlands.

General Information:
first colonised by the Swedes, then the Dutch, whose influence can still be seen throughout the state, the land was granted to the Quaker William Penn in 1682 by King Charles II of England. Penn used the land to found the colony of Pennsylvania, intended as a sanctuary for Quakers and other Nonconformists. Pennsylvania is also home to the Amish people, and is the site of the infamous Battle of Gettysburg.

Rhode Island

Admission to Statehood: May 29 1790 - 13th state

State Capital: Providence

Nickname: The Ocean State

Motto: Hope

Area: 1545 square miles

Population: 1,048,319

Sports Teams: Rhode Island has no major league sports teams

Famous Rhode Islanders:
Harry Anderson, actor; Nelson Eddy, baritone and actor; Robert Gray, sea captain; H.P Lovecraft, horror writer

Agriculture:
Nursery stock, vegetables, dairy products, eggs

Industry:
Fashion jewelry, fabricated metal products, electric equipment, machinery, shipbuilding and boatbuilding, tourism

Physical Geography:
Rhode Island lies on the northeast coast of the USA, the smallest state of the US. It comprises lowlands of Narragansett Basin, inset by Narrangansett Bay and western uplands of flat rolling hills.

General Information:
one of the original thirteen colonies, Rhode Island was settled as early as 1636, and was the first state to declare independence from Britain. It belongs to the group of states collectively known as New England.

South Carolina

Admission to Statehood: May 23 1788 – 8th state

State Capital: Columbia

Nickname: Palmetto State

Mottoes: Prepared in mind and resources / While I breathe, I hope

Area: 32,007 square miles

Population: 4,012,012

Sports Teams: South Carolina has no major league sports teams

Famous South Carolinians:
James Brown, Godfather of Soul; Joe Frazier, prizefighter; Dizzy Gillespie, jazz trumpeter; Andrew Jackson, US president; Jesse Jackson, civil rights leader; Eartha Kitt, singer; Ronald McNair, astronaut

Agriculture:
Tobacco, poultry, cattle, dairy products, soybeans, hogs

Industry:
Textile goods, chemical products, paper products, machinery, tourism

Physical Geography:
South Carolina lies on the south-east coast of the USA. The southern coastal plain covers two-thirds of the state, rising to the northwestern uplands of the Blue Ridge province.

General Information:
South Carolina was one of the original thirteen colonies of the United States. Originally settled by the Spanish in the 16th century, it quickly passed into English control. It is named after King Charles I of England. South Carolina was the first state to secede from the Union in 1860, and was a major force in the Confederacy during the US Civil War. The state is the site of the Fort Sumter National Monument.

South Dakota

Admission to Statehood: November 2 1889 – 40th state

State Capital: Pierre

Nickname: Mount Rushmore State

Motto: Under God the people rule

Area: 77,121 square miles

Population: 754,844

Sports Teams: South Dakota has no major league sports teams

Famous South Dakotans:
Crazy Horse, Oglala Sioux chief; Hubert H. Humphrey, senator and vice president;
Cheryl Ladd, actress; Red Cloud, Oglala Sioux chief; Sitting Bull, Hunkpappa Sioux
chief; Jess Thomas, opera singer

Agriculture:
Cattle, hogs, wheat, soybeans, milk, corn

Industry:
Food processing, machinery, lumber and wood products, tourism

Physical Geography:
South Dakota is one of the Plains states of North Central USA. It consists of prairie
plains in the east, rolling hills of the Great Plains in the west and the Black Hills in
the southwest corner.

General Information:
South Dakota was part of the 1803 Louisiana Purchase (q.v), expanding rapidly as a
result of the gold rush and land boom in the 1880s. South Dakota is the site of the
Mount Rushmore National Monument, a 1700-metre high granite carving of the
heads of Presidents Washington, Jefferson, Lincoln and Theodore Roosevelt, carved
between 1927 and 1941 by Gutzon Borglum.

Tennessee

Admission to Statehood: June 1 1796 – 16th state

State Capital: Nashville

Nickname: Volunteer State

Motto: Agriculture and commerce

Area: 42,146 square miles

Population: 5,689,283

Sports Teams: Nashville Predators (NHL); Nashville Kats (AFL); Tennessee Titans (NFL)

Famous Tennesseans:
Chet Atkins, guitarist; Davy Crockett, frontiersman; Tennessee Ernie Ford, singer; Morgan Freeman, actor; Aretha Franklin, singer; Sondra Locke, actress; Dolly Parton, singer; Cybil Shepherd, actress; Tina Turner, singer

Agriculture:
Soybeans, cotton, tobacco, livestock and livestock products, dairy products, cattle, hogs

Industry:
Chemicals, transportation equipment, rubber, plastics

Physical Geography:
Tennessee lies in the south central United States. Tennessee can be divided into three regions; East, a thickly-wooded upland region; Middle, rolling hills and upland plateau situated in a loop in the Tennessee River; and West, an area of lowland plains and swamps.

General Information:
Tennessee was disputed between the French and British in the seventeenth century, eventually coming under British rule, where it remained until the end of the Revolutionary War. The state was a supporter of the Confederacy in the Civil War. Memphis was the site of the assassination of Martin Luther King in 1968; on a happier note, Memphis was the site of Sun Studio, where the young Elvis Presley made his first recordings. Nashville was, and remains, the spiritual capital city of Country and Western music.

Texas

Admission to Statehood: December 29 1845 – 28th state

State Capital: Austin

Nickname: Lone Star State

Motto: Friendship

Area: 268,601 square miles

Population: 20,851,820

Sports Teams: Dallas Burn (MLS); Dallas Cowboys (NFL); Dallas Mavericks (NBA); Dallas Stars (NHL); Houston Astros (MLB); Houston Rockets (NBA); Houston Texans (NFL); Houston ThunderBears (AFL); San Antonio Spurs (NBA); Texas Rangers (MLB)

Famous Texans:
Red Adair, oil well firefighter; Clyde Barrow, outlaw; Dwight D. Eisenhower, US president and World War Two general; Larry Hagman, actor; Buddy Holly, musician; Lyndon B. Johnson, US president; Michael Johnson, Olympic champion; Janis Joplin, blues singer; Tommy Lee Jones, actor; Audie Murphy, actor and war hero; Roy Orbison, singer; Bonnie Parker, outlaw; Gene Roddenberry, screenwriter

Agriculture:
Cattle, cotton, dairy products, nursery stock, poultry, sorghum, corn, wheat

Industry:
Chemical products, petroleum and natural gas, food processing, electric equipment, machinery, mining, tourism

Physical Geography:
Texas lies in the south-west of the US. The four main regions are the Gulf Coast Plain in the south and southeast; the North Central Plains; the Great Plains, extending over the Panhandle, broken by low mountains; and Trans-Pecos, southern extention of the Rocky Mountains.

General Information:
After colonisation by the Spanish in 1682, Texas rose up in revolt against the Mexican dictatorship of Santa Anna in 1836. After the renowned Battle of the Alamo, the Texans finally defeated the Mexican army, and Texas became a republic for almost a decade, until its incorporation into the United States. Texas is the second largest and third most populous state of the US. It is the leading producer of oil and gas, and also has the largest area of farmed land in the country. After

Utah

Admission to Statehood: January 4 1896 – 45th state

State Capital: Salt Lake City

Nickname: The Beehive State

Motto: Industry

Area: 84,904 square miles

Population: 2,233,169

Sports Teams: Utah Jazz (NBA); Utah Starzz (WNBA)

Famous Utahns:
Butch Cassidy, outlaw; Donny Osmond, singer; Roseanne Barr, actress; Joseph Smith, religious leader; Brigham Young, religious leader

Agriculture:
Cattle, dairy products, hay, turkeys

Industry:
Machinery, aerospace, mining, food processing, electric equipment, tourism

Physical Geography:
Utah is a mountainous state in the southwestern USA, Utah consists of two arid regions, the Great Basin and the Great Salt Lake Desert, divided by the Rocky Mountains.

General Information:
first settled by Mormons fleeing persecution in New York, Utah remains a state strongly dominated by the Mormon faith; it is the only 'dry' state in the USA, for example. Utah recently hosted the 2002 Winter Olympics.

Vermont

Admission to Statehood: March 4 1791 – 14th state

State Capital: Montpelier

Nickname: Green Mountain State

Motto: Freedom and unity

Area: 9615 square miles

Population: 608,827

Sports Teams: Vermont has no major league sports teams

Famous Vermonters:
Chester Alan Arthur, US president; Calvin Coolidge, US president; John Deere, inventor; John Dewey, philosopher and educator;

Agriculture:
Dairy products, cattle, hay, apples, maple products.

Industry:
Electronic equipment, fabricated metal products, printing and publishing, paper products, tourism.

Physical Geography:
Vermont lies in the north-east of the USA, in New England. It consists mainly of a Green Mountains backbone 20-36 miles wide, running north to south, with an average altitude of 1,000 feet.

General Information:
Vermont was settled by the British in 1724, becoming a state in 1791. Its chief products are granite and marble, although the maple syrup produced in the state is also well known. The main industry is tourism, appealing to the outdoors tourist, with the emphasis on skiing, hunting and fishing.

Virginia

Admission to Statehood: June 25 1788 – 10th state

State Capital: Richmond

Nickname: Old Dominion State

Motto: Thus Always to Tyrants

Area: 42,769 square miles

Population: 7,078,515

Sports Teams: Virginia has no major league sports teams

Famous Virginians:
Arthur Ashe, tennis player; Warren Beatty, actor; Richard E. Byrd, polar explorer; Ella Fitzgerald, singer; William H. Harrison, US president; Patrick Henry, statesman; Thomas Jefferson, US president; Shirley Maclaine, actress; James Madison, US president; James Monroe, US president; Zachary Taylor, US president; John Tyler, US president; George Washington, first US president; Woodrow Wilson, US president; Tom Wolfe, journalist and author.

Agriculture:
Cattle, poultry, dairy products, tobacco, hogs, soybeans.

Industry:
Transportation equipment, textiles, food processing, printing, electric equipment, chemicals.

Physical Geography:
Virginia lies along the mid-Atlantic coast of the US. It consists of mountains in the west, including the Blue Ridge Mountains, and coastal plain to the eastern shore.

General Information:
Virginia was one of the original thirteen states, and the site of the first settlement in the New World at Jamestown, by the Virginia Company. The settlement was also the site of the first representative legislation. The state itself was named after Elizabeth I, the Virgin Queen, of England. Virginia provided four of the first five US presidents, but perhaps paradoxically, was an important stronghold of the Confederacy during the US Civil War. It was and remains a major tobacco producer.

Washington

Admission to Statehood: November 11 1889 – 42nd state

State Capital: Olympia

Nickname: The Evergreen State

Motto: By and By

Area: 71,303 square miles

Population: 5,894,120

Sports Teams: Seattle Mariners (MLB); Seattle Seahawks (NFL); Seattle Sonics (NBA); Seattle Storm (WNBA)

Famous Washingtonians:
Kurt Cobain, musician; Bing Crosby, singer and actor; Frances Farmer, actress; Jimi Hendrix, musician; Adam West, actor

Agriculture:
Seafood, dairy products, apples, cattle, wheat, potatoes, nursery stock

Industry:
Aerospace, software development, food processing, paper products, lumber and wood products, chemical products, tourism

Physical Geography:
Washington lies on the Pacific coast of the northwest USA. The state is mostly surrounded by mountains, including Mount St Helens, and the Olympic mountains along the northwest peninsula, blending into the flat terrain of Puget Sound.

General Information:
Named after George Washington, the area was first exploited by the British Hudson Bay Company until the 1840s. The boundary between Washington and Canada was finally fixed in 1846, and it became a state in 1889, when it took the name.

West Virginia

Admission to Statehood: June 20 1863 – 35th state

State Capital: Charleston

Nickname: Mountain State

Motto: Mountaineers are always free

Area: 24,231 square miles

Population: 1,808,344

Sports Teams: West Virginia has no major league sports teams

Famous West Virginians:
Pearl S. Buck, author; Thomas Stonewall Jackson, Confederate general; Mary Lou Retton, gymnast; Chuck Yeager, test pilot

Agriculture:
Cattle, dairy products, poultry, apples

Industry:
Chemical products, mining, primary metals, stone, clay, and glass products, tourism

Physical Geography:
Virginia lies in the east central USA. The terrain ranges from hilly to mountainous, with the Allegheny plateau, in the west, covering two-thirds of the state. There are many mountains over 4,000 feet.

General Information:
although originally part of Virginia, West Virginia refused to secede during the US Civil War, becoming a separate state of the union in 1863. Among the main landmarks of the state are the New River Gorge and Harpers Ferry.

Wisconsin

Admission to Statehood: May 29 1848 - 30th state

State Capital: Madison

Nickname: Badger State

Motto: Forward

Area: 65,500 square miles

Population: 5,363,675

Sports Teams: Green Bay Packers (NFL); Milwaukee Brewers (MLB); Milwaukee Bucks (NBA); Milwaukee Mustangs (AFL)

Famous Wisconsinites:
Don Ameche, actor; Tyne Daly, actress; August Derleth, author; Harry Houdini, escapologist; Liberace, pianist; Jackie Mason, comedian; Spencer Tracy, actor; Frank Lloyd Wright, architect

Agriculture:
cheese, dairy products, cattle, hogs, vegetables, corn, cranberries

Industry:
Machinery, food processing, paper products, electric equipment, fabricated metal products, tourism

Physical Geography:
Wisconsin lies in the north central USA. It is bounded to the west by the Mississippi River, to the east by Lake Michigan, and to the north by Lake Superior. The central lowlands in the south of the state give rise to the higher ground of the Superior Uplands in the north, which contain abundant forest and minor lakes.

General Information:
Wisconsin was originally settled by the French, who handed it over to the British in 1763. Acquired by the USA in 1783, Wisconsin became the 30th state of the union in 1848. Wisconsin is probably best known for its beer-brewing industries, although it is also the site of the St Croix National Scenic Riverway, and a perennially popular destination for the outdoors type of tourist. It is also the site of Pendarvis, a restored Cornish mining village.

Wyoming

Admission to Statehood: July 10 1890 – 44th state

State Capital: Cheyenne

Nickname: Equality state

Motto: Equal rights

Area: 97,818 square miles

Population: 493,782

Sports Teams: Wyoming has no major league sports teams

Famous Wyomingites:
June Etta Downey, educator; Jackson Pollock, painter

Agriculture:
Cattle, sugar beets, sheep, hay, wheat

Industry:
Mining, chemical products, lumber and wood products, printing and publishing, machinery, tourism

Physical Geography:
Wyoming lies in the north-west of the USA. The terrain is mountains – the foothills of the Rockies – and plains.

General Information:
Part of the Louisiana Purchase (q.v) of 1803, Wyoming was opened up to settlement with the arrival of the Union Pacific Railway in the mid-nineteenth century. Its most famous visitor attraction is Yellowstone National Park, the largest National Park in the USA, covering an area of approximately 3400 square miles, and home of the renowned geyser, 'Old Faithful'.

European Institutions

How much do you know about European Institutions? (1)

QUESTIONS.

1. What does EBRD mean?
2. What does EBU mean?
3. What does CoE mean?
4. What does CDI mean?
5. What does CEA mean?
6. What does EFAH mean?
7. What does EPO mean?
8. What does ESA mean?
9. What does ETUC mean?
10. What does IEEP mean?
11. What does FEE mean?
12. What does EIPA mean?
13. What does CEPS mean?
14. What does CEN mean?
15. What does AER mean?

ANSWERS.
1. European Bank for Reconstruction and Development. 2. European Broadcasting Union. 3. Council of Europe. 4. Centre for the Development of Industry.
5. Confederation of European Agriculture. 6. European Federation of Animal Health.
7. European Patent Office. 8. European Space Agency. 9. European Trade Union Confederation. 10. Institute for European Environmental Policy. 11. Federation of European Employers. 12. European Institute of Public Administration. 13. Centre for European Policy Studies. 14. Comite Europeen de Normalisation. 15. Assembly of European Regions.

How much do you know about European Institutions? (2)

QUESTIONS.

1. What does CENELEC mean?
2. What does AMUE mean?
3. What does BFEU mean?
4. What does AECA mean?
5. What does BEUC mean?
6. What does OECD mean?
7. What does SEAP mean?
8. What does TCARC mean?
9. What does WEU mean?
10. What does UIECE mean?
11. What does OSCE mean?
12. What does EFTA mean?
13. What does EUDUG mean?
14. What does EUROCONTROL mean?
15. What does Eurochambres mean?

ANSWERS.
1. European Committee for Electrotechnical Standardisation. 2. Association for the Monetary Union in Europe. 3. Banking Federation of the European Union. 4. America-European Community Association. 5. Bureau Europeen des Unions de Consommateurs. 6. Organisation for Economic Co-operation and Development. 7. Society of European Affairs Practitioners. 8. Technical Centre for Agricultural and Rural Co-operation. 9. Western European Union. 10. Union of Industrial and Employers' Confederations of Europe. 11. Organisation for Security and Co-operation in Europe. 12. European Free Trade Association. 13. E.U. Databases User Group. 14. European Organisation for the Safety of Air Navigation. 15. Association of European Chambers of Commerce and Industry.

How much do you know about European Institutions? (3)

QUESTIONS.

1. What does ACE mean?

2. What does CEE mean?

3. What does ECMT mean?

4. What does ECF mean?

5. What does EIA Mean?

6. What does FCA mean?

7. What does EYP mean?

8. What does IPT mean?

9. What does IEA mean?

10. What does LDEG mean?

11. What does EUW mean?

12. What does EPF mean?

13. What does ELEC mean?

14. What does EM mean?

15. What does EIM mean?

ANSWERS.
1. Action Centre for Europe. 2. Conservative Enterprise Europe. 3. European Conference for Ministers of Transport. 4. European Cultural Foundation. 5. European Information Association. 6. Federation of Commodity Associations. 7. European Youth Parliament. 8. Industry and Parliament Trust. 9. Institute of European Affairs. 10. Liberal Democrat European Group. 11. European Union of Women. 12. European Policy Forum. 13. European League for Economic Co-operation.14. European Movement. 15. European Institute for the Media.

Capital Cities

What is the capital city of the following countries?

QUESTIONS.

1. United Arab Emirates?

2. Republic of Malawi?

3. Republic of Estonia?

4. Republic of Georgia?

5. Republic of Iraq?

6. Jamaica?

7. Republic of Liberia?

8. Republic of Tajikstan?

9. Kingdom of Lesotho?

10. Socialist Republic of Vietnam?

11. Federal Democratic Republic of Ethiopia?

12. Commonwealth of Dominica?

13. Dominican Republic?

14. Republic of the Fiji Islands?

15. Republic of Kyrgyzstan?

ANSWERS
1. Abu Dhabi. 2. Lilongwe. 3. Tallinn. 4. Tbilisi. 5. Baghdad. 6. Kingston. 7. Monrovia. 8. Dushanbe. 9. Maseru. 10. Hanoi. 11. Addis Ababa. 12. Roseau. 13. Santo Domingo. 14. Suva. 15. Bishkek.

What is the capital city of the following countries?

1. Republic of Latvia?

2. Hashemite Kingdom of Jordan?

3. Republic of Honduras?

4. Republic of Iceland?

5. Republic of Uzbekistan?

6. Federal Republic of Yugoslavia?

7. Czech Republic?

8. Republic of Croatia?

9. Republic of Cote d'Ivoire?

10. Republic of Botswana?

11. State of Brunei?

12. State of Cambodia?

13. Republic of Kazakhstan?

14. Democratic Republic of Madagascar?

15. Federal Republic of Nigeria?

ANSWERS
1. Riga. 2. Amman. 3. Tegucigalpa. 4. Reykjavik. 5. Tashkent. 6. Belgrade. 7. Prague. 8. Zagreb. 9. Yamoussoukro. 10. Gaborone. 11. Bandar Seri Begawan. 12. Phnom Penh. 13. Astana. 14. Antananarivo. 15. Abuja.

What is the capital city of the following countries?

1. Dominion of New Zealand?

2. Former Yugoslav Republic of Macedonia?

3. Grenada?

4. Republic of Guinea?

5. Republic of The Niger?

6. State of Qatar?

7. Republic of Yemen?

8. Republic of Zambia?

9. Commonwealth of the Bahamas?

10. State of Bahrain?

11. Republic of Belarus?

12. Republic of Costa Rica?

13. Democratic Republic of Congo?

14. State of Eritrea?

15. Republic of Gabon?

ANSWERS
1. Wellington. 2. Skopje. 3. St George's. 4. Conakry. 5. Niamey. 6. Doha. 7. San'a. 8. Lusaka. 9. Nassau. 10. Al Manamah. 11. Minsk. 12. San Jose. 13. Kinshasa. 14. Asmara. 15. Libreville.

What is the capital city of the following countries?

1. Kingdom of Morocco?
2. Republic of Nicaragua?
3. Sultanate of Oman?
4. Federation of St. Kitts and Nevis?
5. Republic of Rwanda?
6. Independent State of Samoa?
7. Republic of Seychelles?
8. Republic of Sierra Leone?
9. Slovak Republic?
10. Republic of Suriname?
11. Kingdom of Swaziland?
12. Republic of Togo?
13. United Republic of Tanzania?
14. Republic of Vanuatu?
15. Republic of Turkmenistan?

ANSWERS
1. Rabat. 2. Managua. 3. Muscat. 4. Basseterre. 5. Kigali. 6. Apia. 7. Victoria. 8. Freetown. 9. Bratislava. 10. Paramaribo. 11. Mbabane. 12. Lome. 13. Dodoma. 14. Port-Vila. 15. Ashgabat.

Great Railway Journeys

If you were sitting on the following trains, you would be heading from where – to where?

1. The Canadian?

2. The Coast Starlight?

3. The Copper Canyon Railway?

4. The Puno – Cuzco Line?

5. The Royal Scotsman?

6. The Settle and Carlisle?

7. The Flam Railway?

8. The Viverais Line?

9. The InterCity Express?

10. The Glacier Express?

11. El Transcantabrico?

12. El Andalus?

13. The Venice – Simplon –– Orient Express?

14. The Trans-Mongolian Express?

15. The Trans-Siberian Express?

ANSWERS
1. From Toronto to Vancouver, Canada. 2. From Los Angeles to Seattle, U.S.A. 3. From El Fuerte to Chihuahua, Mexico. 4. From Puno to Cuzco, Peru. 5. From Edinburgh to the Highlands, Scotland. 6. From Leeds to Carlisle, England. 7. From Myrdal to Flam, Norway. 8. From Tournon to Lamastre, France. 9.   From Berlin to Munich, Germany. 10. From Zermatt to St. Moritz, Switzerland. 11. From Santiago de Compostela to San Sebastian, Spain. 12. From Seville – back to Seville on the Andalucia circuit. 13. From Venice, Italy to London, England. 14. From Beijing, China to Moscow, Russia. 15. From Moscow to Vladivostock, Russia.

If you were sitting on the following trains, you would be heading from where – to where?

1. The Khyber Pass Line?

2. The Darjeeling – Himalayan?

3. The Royal Orient Express?

4. The Eastern and Oriental Express?

5. The China to Vietnam?

6. The Ghan?

7. The Indian Pacific Railroad?

8. The Tranzalpine?

9. The Blue Train?

10. The Pride of Africa?

11. The Union Limited?

12. The China Orient Express?

13. The Great South Pacific Express?

14. The Cumbres and Toltec Scenic Railroad?

15. The Durango to Silverton Narrow Gauge?

ANSWERS

1. From Lahore to the Khyber Pass, Pakistan. 2. From New Jalpaiguri to Darjeeling, India. 3. From Delhi to Jaipur, through Rajasthan and Gujarat, India. 4. From Singapore to Bangkok, Thailand. 5. From Beijing, China to Hanoi, Vietnam. 6. From Adelaide to Alice Springs, Australia. 7. From Sydney to Perth, Australia. 8. From Christchurch to Greymouth, New Zealand. 9. From Pretoria to Cape Town, South Africa. 10. From Cape Town, South Africa to Dar Es Salaam, Tanzania. 11. The 'Garden Route' from Cape Town to Oudtshoorn, South Africa. 12. The 'Silk Route' from Urumchi to Beijing, China. 13. From Sydney to Cairns, Australia. 14. From Chama to Antonito, New Mexico, U.S.A. 15. From Durango to Silverton, New Mexico, U.S.A.

If you were sitting on the following trains, you would be heading from where – to where?

1. The CoastaL Pacific?

2. The Capitol Limited?

3. The South-West Chief?

4. The California Zephyr?

5. The Arctic Circle Express?

6. The Bergen Railway?

7. The Golden Panoramic Express?

8. The Glacier Express?

9. The William Tell Express?

10. The Cisalpino?

11. The Donauwalzer?

12. The Arabona?

13. The Hungaria?

14. The Alois Negrelli?

15. The Royal Hungarian Express?

ANSWERS
1. From Vancouver, Canada to San Diego, U.S.A. 2. From Washington to Chicago,
U.S.A.3. From Chicago to Flagstaff, Arizona, U.S.A. 4. From San Francisco to
Chicago, U.S.A. 5. From Stockholm, Sweden to Trondheim, Norway, via Kiruna and
Narvik. 6. From Oslo to Voss, Norway. 7. From Montreux to Interlaken, Switzerland.
8. From Brig to Chur, Switzerland. 9. From Lucerne to Locarno, Switzerland.
10. From Lausanne, Switzerland to Venice, Italy. 11. From Brussels, Belgium to
Vienna, Austria. 12. From Vienna, Austria to Budapest, Hungary 13. From Budapest,
Hungary to Prague, Czech Republic. 14. From Prague, Czech Republic to Berlin,
Germany. 15. From Budapest to Egen; Lake Balatan; Szeged, Hungary.

International Airports

What is the name of the international airport serving the following cities?

1. Chicago, U.S.A.?

2. Amsterdam, The Netherlands?

3. London, U.K (5)?

4. Rome, Italy (2)?

5. Paris, France (2)?

6. Rio de Janeiro, Brazil?

7. Montreal, Canada?

8. Washington, U.S.A.?

9. Venice, Italy?

10. Mexico City, Mexico (2)?

11. Bombay, India?

12. Saint John's, Antigua and Barbuda?

13. Stockholm, Sweden (2)?

14. Bangkok, Thailand?

15. Boston, U.S.A.?

ANSWERS
1. O'Hare. 2. Schipol. 3. Heathrow, Gatwick, Stansted, London City and Luton. 4. Leonardo da Vinci and Ciampino. 5. Charles de Gaulle and Orly. 6. Santos Dumont. 7. Mirabel. 8. Dulles. 9. Marco Polo. 10. Benito Juarez and Morelos. 11. Sahar. 12. V.C Bird. 13. Arlanda and Bromma. 14. Don Muang. 15. Logan.

What is the name of the international airport serving the following cities?

1. Milan, Italy?

2. New York, U.S.A.?

3. Toronto, Canada?

4. Port of Spain, Trinidad?

5. Seoul, South Korea?

6. Budapest, Hungary?

7.   Oslo, Norway?

8. Tokyo, Japan?

9. Warsaw, Poland?

10. Copenhagen, Denmark?

11. Barcelona, Spain?

12. Bucharest, Romania?

13. Florence, Italy?

14. Calcutta, India?

15. Montevideo, Uruguay?

ANSWERS
1. Linate. 2. (A) John F. Kennedy; (B) La Guardia. 3. Lester B. Pearson. 4. Piarco. 5. Kimp'o. 6. Ferihegy. 7. Fornebu. 8. (A) Narita and (B) Hanedi. 9. Okecie. 10. Kastrup. 11. Prat de Llobregat. 12. Otopeni. 13. Peretola. 14. Dum Dum. 15. Carrasco.

What is the name of the international airport serving the following cities?

1. Santiago, Chile?

2. Conakry, Guinea?

3. Tijuana, Mexico?

4. Antananarivo, Madagascar?

5. Toulouse, France?

6. Antwerp, Belgium?

7. Addis Ababa, Ethiopia?

8. Al Khobar, Saudi Arabia?

9. Tangiers, Morocco?

10. Salvador, Brazil?

11. St. Denis, Reunion Island?

12. Alajuela, Costa Rica?

13. Lilongwe, Malawi?

14. Ljubljana, Slovenia?

15. Reykjavik, Iceland?

ANSWERS
1. Arturo Marino Benitez. 2. G'Bessia. 3. General Abelard L. Rodriguez. 4. Ivato. 5. Blagnac. 6. Deurne. 7. Bole. 8. Dhahran. 9. Boukhalef. 10. Dois de Julho. 11. Gillot. 12. Juan Santa Maria. 13. Kamazu. 14. Brnik. 15. Keflavik.

International Currencies

Can you name both the major and the minor currencies used in the following countries?

1. Algeria?

2. Portugal?

3. South Africa?

4. Bulgaria?

5. China?

6. Greece?

7. Laos?

8. Iran?

9. Norway?

10. Saudi Arabia?

11. Tajikstan

12. Uruguay?

13. Zambia?

14. Mongolia?

15. Nigeria?

ANSWERS
1. 1 Dinar = 100 centimes. 2. 1 escudo = 100 centavos. 3. 1 Rand = 100 cents. 4. 1 Lev = 100 stotinki. 5. 1 Renmenbi Yuan = 10 jiao = 100 fen. 6. 1 Drachma = 100 leptae. 7. 1 Kip = 100 at. 8. 1 Rial = 100 dinars. 9. 1 Krone = 100 ore. 10. 1 Riyal = 20 qursh = 100 halala. 11. 1 Rouble = 100 tanga. 12. 1 New Peso = 100 centesimos. 13. 1 Kwacha = 100 ngwee. 14. 1 Tugrik = 100 mongo. 15. 1 Naira = 100 kobo.

What is the main, official language of the following countries – NOT including the language of a colonising nation, if that applies?

1. Bangladesh?

2. Cambodia?

3. Congo?

4. Ethiopia?

5. Iran?

6. Kenya?

7. Luxembourg?

8. Netherlands Antilles?

9. Pakistan?

10. Peru?

11. Sierra Leone?

12. Sri Lanka?

13. Vanuatu?

14. Papua New Guinea?

15. Central African Republic?

ANSWERS
1. Bengali. 2. Khmer. 3. Kikongo; Lingala. 4. Amharic. 5. Farsi. 6. Swahili. 7. Letzebuergesch. 8. Papiamento. 9. Urdu. 10. Quechua. 11. Mende; Temnel. 12. Sinhala; Tamil. 13. Bislama. 14. Tok Pisin; Hiri Motu. 15. Sango.

Natural World

Active volcanoes

Volcano Name	Country	Continuous Eruptions
Etna	Italy	3500 years
Stromboli	Italy	2000 years
Yasur	Vanuatu	800 years
Erta Ale	Ethiopia	1967- present
Manam	Papua New Guinea	1974- present
Langila	Papua New Guinea	1960- present
Bagana	Papua New Guinea	1972- present
Semeru	Indonesia	1967- present
Dukono	Indonesia	1933- present
Sakura-jima	Japan	1955- present
Suwanose-jima	Japan	1949- present
Santa Maria	Guatemala	1922- present
Pacaya	Guatemala	1965- present
Arenal	Costa Rica	1968 - present
Sangay	Ecuador	1934- present
Erebus	Antarctica	1972- present

Highest mountains

The Highest Peaks in the World[1]

Peak	Location	Feet	Metres
1. Mount Everest	Nepal	29,035 ft.	8,850 m.
2. K2	Pakistan/China	28,250 ft.	8,611 m.
3. Kangchenjunga	Nepal/India	28,169 ft.	8,586 m.
4. Lhotse	Nepal	27,920 ft.	8,501 m.
5. Makalu	Nepal	27,765 ft.	8,462 m.
6. Cho Oyu	Nepal	26,906 ft.	8,201 m.
7. Dhaulagiri	Nepal	26,794 ft.	8,167 m.
8. Manaslu	Nepal	26,758 ft.	8,156 m.
9. Nanga Parbat	Pakistan	26,658 ft.	8,125 m.
10. Annapurna	Nepal	26,545 ft.	8,091 m.
11. Gasherbrum I	Pakistan/China	26,470 ft.	8,068 m.
12. Broad Peak	Pakistan/China	26,400 ft.	8,047 m.
13. Gasherbrum II	Pakistan/China	26,360 ft.	8,035 m.
14. Shisha Pangma	Nepal/Tibet	26,289 ft.	8,013 m.

[1] *Mauna Loi on Hawaii 33,132 ft from base to summit; 13,448 ft above sea level*

The Highest Peaks of the Seven Continents

Peak	Continent	Feet	Metres
1. Mount Everest	Asia	29,035 ft.	8,850 m.
2. Aconcagua	South America	22,841 ft.	6,962 m.
3. Mount McKinley	North America	20,320 ft.	6,194 m.
4. Mount Kilimanjaro	Africa	19,563 ft.	5,963 m.
5. Mount Elbrus	Europe	18,481 ft.	5,633 m.
6. Puncak Jaya	Australia/Oceania	16,502 ft.	5,030 m.
7. Vinson Massif	Antarctica	16,066 ft.	4,897 m.

Largest islands

	Island	Location	Square miles	Square kilometres
1	Greenland[1]	North Atlantic (Danish)	839,999	2,175,597
2	New Guinea (divided into Irian Jaya, Indonesia, and Papua New Guinea)	Southwest Pacific	316,615	820,033
3	Borneo (shared by Indonesia and Malaysia)	West mid-Pacific	286,914	743,107
4	Madagascar (Malagasy Republic)	Indian Ocean	226,657	587,042
5	Baffin	North Atlantic (Canadian)	183,810	476,068
6	Sumatra[2] (Indonesian)	Northeast Indian Ocean	182,859	473,605
7	Honshu (Japanese)	Sea of Japan–Pacific	88,925	230,316
8	Great Britain (England,Scotland, Wales)	Off coast of NW Europe	88,758	229,883
9	Ellesmere	Arctic Ocean (Canadian)	82,119	212,688
10	Victoria	Arctic Ocean (Canadian)	81,930	212,199
11	Sulawesi (Celebes)	West mid-Pacific (Ind.)	72,986	189,034
12	South Island	South Pacific (New Zealand)	58,093	150,461
13	Java	Indian Ocean (Indonesian)	48,990	126,884
14	North Island	South Pacific (New Zealand)	44,281	114,688
15	Cuba	Caribbean Sea (Republic)	44,218	114,525

Notes
1) Greenland, is almost three times as big as the third largest, Borneo.
2) Sumatra is more than twice as big as the next largest island, Honshu.
  All the islands below are less than 100, 000 square miles in size.

Longest Rivers

River name	Location	Length
Nile	Africa	4,145 miles
Amazon-Ucayali	South America	4,000 miles
Yangtze	Asia	3,900 miles
Mississippi-Missouri	North America	3,740 miles
Huang	Asia	3,395miles
Ob-Irtysh	Asia	3,362 miles
Rio de la Plata-Parana	South America	3,030 miles
Congo	Africa	2,900 miles
Parana	South America	2,800 miles
Amur-Ergun	Asia	2,761 miles

Ocean Depths

Name	Depth	Place of greatest known depth
Pacific Ocean	(35,837 ft) (10,924 meters)	Challenger Deep, Marianas Trench
Atlantic Ocean	(30,246 ft) (9,219 meters)	Puerto Rico
Indian Ocean	(24,460 ft) (7,455 meters)	Sunda Trench
Caribbean Sea	(22,788 ft) (6,946 meters)	Off the Cayman Islands
Arctic Ocean	(18,456 ft) (5,625 meters)	77°45'N; 175°W
South China Sea	(16,456 ft) (5,016 meters)	West of Luzon
Bering Sea	(15,659 ft) (4,773 meters)	Off Buldir Island
Mediterranean Sea	(15,197 ft) (4,632 meters)	Off Cape Matapan, Greece
Gulf of Mexico	(12,425 ft) (3,787 meters)	Sigsbee Deep
Japan Sea	(12,276 ft) (3,742 meters)	Central Basin

Ocean Areas

Pacific (155,557,000 sq km)   Southern (20,327,000 sq km)
Atlantic (76,762,000 sq km)   Arctic (14,056,000 sq km)
Indian (68,556,000 sq km)

2

HISTORY

Year by year 1900-1909

How much do you know about 1900?

QUESTIONS.

1. The noble gas Radon is discovered. By whom?

2. The Chicago ship canal opens, connecting the Mississippi River with what?

3. In May 1900 an uprising against foreigners begins in China. It was afterwards given what name?

4. Puccini premieres which of his operas in Rome?

5. The Box Brownie camera is launched by which company?

6. Which organisation publishes its first restaurant guide?

7. Manufacture begins of which famous handgun?

8. Frank L. Baum publishes a children's book destined for great fame. What is it called?

9. Who is released from exile in Siberia?

10. In which American city is there is an outbreak of bubonic plague?

11. The trial flight of which aircraft takes place in Germany in July of this year?

12. In which European capital does the Great Exhibition open?

13. In which city does the 2nd modern Olympic games takes place?

14. The U.S.A. win the first of which international tennis tournament?

15. Which physicist reveals the Quantum Theory?

ANSWERS
1. The German chemist Friedrich Dorn. 2. The Great Lakes. 3. The Boxer Rebellion. 4. Tosca. 5. Eastman Kodak. 6. Michelin. 7. The Luger Pistol. 8. The Wizard of Oz. 9. Lenin. 10. San Francisco. 11. Zeppelin airship. 12. Paris. 13. Paris. 14. The Davis Cup. 15. Professor Max Planck.

How much do you know about 1901?

QUESTIONS.

1. The worlds first billion dollar corporation, U.S Steel, is founded by whom?

2. The first ever transatlantic telegraphic transmission is sent. Who demonstrated its possibilities?

3. Which set of awards for intellectual achievement are handed out for the first time?

4. Which Academic Institute is responsible for choosing the winners?

5. Which Italian opera composer dies at the age of 88?

6. Which country is unified as a commonwealth and a British dominion?

7. The first major oil 'gusher' is brought in at Bearmont, Texas. What is it called?

8. An American zoologist proposes that sex in mammals and animals is determined by an extra chromosome. His name?

9. What uprising is formally ended in China by the Peace of Peking?

10. William McKinley becomes the third U.S. President to be assassinated in office. His assassin is a Polish born anarchist. What is his name?

11. Who is McKinley's Vice-President, sworn in to the Presidency after McKinley's shooting?

12. Which reigning British monarch dies on the 22nd of January this year?

13. What does Russia demand from China?

14. For the first time a music hall performer is invited to perform before King Edward VII. Who is he?

15. Which novel, telling the story of an Indian-born orphan who joins the British Secret Service, is published this year?

ANSWERS
1. J.P.Morgan. 2. Guglielmo Marconi. 3. The Nobel Prizes. 4. The Karolinska Institute.
5. Giuseppe Verdi. 6. Australia. 7. Spindletop. 8. Clarence E. McClung. 9. The Boxer
Rebellion. 10. Leon Czolgosz. 11. Theodore Roosevelt. 12. Nova Persei. 13. The
province of Manchuria. 14. Dan Leno. 15. Kim.

How much do you know about 1902?

QUESTIONS.

1. In Britain, secondary level schooling for all children is ensured by the passing of which Act of Parliament?

2. Which country is the first to introduce universal suffrage?

3. Two British physiologists. Sir William Bayliss and Ernest Starling discover secretin and propose a term for secretions which act upon other organs through the bloodstream. What is the term?

4. Which Russian revolutionary activist escapes from Siberia?

5. Which volcano in Martinique erupts, killing 50,000 people?

6. Which country officially abolishes the death penalty?

7. Which Russian-born, naturalised British author writes the novel Heart of Darkness, published this year?

8. Name the King of Spain crowned this year.

9. The Boer War ends with the signing of which treaty?

10. A new Sherlock Holmes mystery is published. What is it called?

11. Which great French man of letters dies in Paris at the age of 62?

12. Which British monarch is crowned this year?

13. A man whose name has become synonymous with British imperialism dies. Who is he?

14. Which English physicist asserts the existence of an ionised, gaseous layer capable of reflecting radio waves?

15. The famous author and satirist, writer of 'Erewhon' and 'The Way of all Flesh' dies this year. What is his name?

ANSWERS
1. The Education Act. 2. Australia. 3. Hormones. 4. Leon Trotsky. 5. Mount Pelee. 6. Russia. 7. Joseph Conrad. 8. Alfonso XIII. 9. The Peace of Vereeniging. 10. The Hound of the Baskervilles. 11. Emile Zola. 12. King Edward VII. 13. Cecil Rhodes. 14. Oliver Heaviside. 15. Samuel Butler.

How much do you know about 1903?

QUESTIONS.

1. Emmeline Pankhurst establishes an organisation to campaign for female suffrage. What is it called?

2. A Scottish born chemist is awarded the Nobel prize for the discovery of krypton and xenon gases. Who is he?

3. The first narrative feature film is made. What is its title?

4. Which famous French literary award is made for the first time?

5. The first professional baseball World series is won by which team?

6. In the U.S. the first of a famous make of motorcycles takes to the road. What is it called?

7. The first crossing of the continental U.S. by car is made. How many days does it take?

8. Which great French impressionist dies at the age of 73?

9. June 10th – King Alexander and Queen Draga of which country are murdered?

10. Foundation of which motor manufacturing company takes place?

11. Which American artist and portrait painter dies at the age of 70?

12. The first heavier-than-air flight is made by whom?

13. Who was the first woman to win a Nobel prize, sharing the 1903 prize for Physics with her husband and another colleague?

14. The first motor driven taxi cabs take to the streets of which capital?

15. At its London congress, the Russian Social Democratic Party splits into two factions; the Mensheviks, and which other?

ANSWERS
1. Women's Social & Political Union. 2. Sir William Ramsay. 3. The Great Train Robbery. 4. Prix Goncourt. 5. Boston Red Sox. 6. Harley Davidson. 7. 52 days. 8. Camille Pissarro. 9. Serbia. 10. Ford Motor Company. 11. James McNeill Whister. 12. Orville and Wilbur Wright. 13. Marie Curie. 14. London. 15. Bolsheviks.

How much do you know about 1904?

QUESTIONS.

1. Russia goes to war with which other country?

2. Premiere of which Puccini opera takes place?

3. First performance of Peter Pan, by which playwright?

4. Anglo-French problems solved in an agreement which becomes known as what?

5. Which famous theatre opens in Dublin?

6. Which famous motor car manufacturing company is founded?

7. The general theory of radioactivity is put forward by whom?

8. War breaks out in the Far East, between which two countries?

9. Death of which British explorer, at the age of 63?

10. In the U.S.A. the first power boat race is held on the River Hudson. What is it called?

11. U.S presidential election won by which candidate?

12. Underground railway opens in which city?

13. What drinks-related object is invented by Thomas Sullivan in the U.S.A?

14. Britain sends military expedition to which country?

15. Violent general strike takes place in which country?

ANSWERS
1. Japan. 2. Madame Butterfly. 3. J.M. Barrie. 4. Entente Cordiale. 5. Abbey Theatre. 6. Rolls-Royce. 7. Ernest Rutherford and Frederick Soddy. 8. Russia and Japan. 9. Henry Morton Stanley. 10. The Gold Cup. 11. Theodore Roosevelt. 12. New York. 13. The teabag. 14. Tibet. 15. Italy

How much do you know about 1905?

QUESTIONS.

1. On Sunday January 22nd, Russian imperial troops fire on a peaceful crowd of protesters in St. Petersburg, killing 105 and wounding several hundreds more. This becomes known as .....?

2. The sailors mutiny in which battleship in Odessa?

3. The first actor to receive a knighthood dies. What is his name?

4. How are the group of French artists led by Henri Matisse known?

5. Franz Lehar produces his most famous operetta. What is it called?

6. The plays Man and Superman and Major Barbara premiere. Which Irish playwright wrote them?

7. Which distinguished American statesman and Ambassador to Great Britain dies at 67?

8. What is the name of the battle in which the Japanese navy annihilates the Russian fleet?

9. Which Spanish born American philosopher, poet and writer publishes Life of Reason?

10. Name the two new provinces officially formed in Canada.

11. War between Japan and Russia ends with which U.S.-mediated peace treaty?

12. Death of which Irish-born doctor and philanthropist?

13. What is the name of Albert Einstein earth shaking paper, published this year?

14. Work begins on the Singer Tower in New York designed by which architect?

15. Revolution breaks out in which country?

ANSWERS
1. Bloody Sunday. 2. The Potemkin. 3. Sir Henry Irving. 4. Les Fauves (Wild Beasts). 5. The Merry Widow. 6. George Bernard Shaw. 7. John Hay. 8. Battle of Tsushima Straits. 9. George Santayana. 10. Saskatchewan and Alberta. 11. Treaty of Portsmouth. 12. Thomas J. Barnardo. 13. Special Theory of Relativity. 14. Ernest Flagg. 15. Persia.

How much do you know about 1906?

QUESTIONS.

1. Which aristocratic Prussian Field-Marshal is appointed Chief of the German general staff?

2. The British general election provides a landslide victory for which party?

3. And who becomes Prime Minister?

4. The Simplon rail tunnel opens between which two European countries?

5. Which state elects a delegate to the U.S Congress for the first time?

6. The first Grand Prix motor race is held at which course?

7. What is the name of the volcano that erupts in Italy, killing hundreds?

8. In the U.S the first National Monument is named. What is its name?

9. Which Norwegian playwright dies at the age of 78?

10. Which powerful novel by Upton Sinclair about the unhealthy practices of American meat industry drives the U.S Congress to pass the Pure Food and Drug Act?

11. France, Britain and Italy officially guarantee the independence of which East African country?

12. The use of opium is banned in which country?

13. Cunard launches which new transatlantic liner?

14. The crisis between France and Germany over control of Morocco is resolved at a conference in which Spanish town?

15. Which French scientist and Nobel Prize winner dies at the age of 46?

ANSWERS
1. Helmuth von Moltke. 2. Liberals. 3. Henry Campbell-Bannerman. 4. Switzerland and Italy. 5. Alaska. 6. Le Mans. 7. Vesuvius. 8. Devil's Tower, Wyoming. 9. Henrik Ibsen. 10. The Jungle. 11. Ethiopia. 12. China. 13. The Mauretania. 14. Algeciras. 15. Pierre Curie.

How much do you know about 1907?

QUESTIONS.

1. The first of a long line of domestic labour-saving devices appears in the U.S. What is it?

2. By whom is the International New Service press agency is founded?

3. Pablo Picasso paints one of his best known works. Which one?

4. Women receive the vote in which Scandinavian countries?

5. At the opening night of a new play by J.M.Synge, there are riots at Dublin's Abbey Theatre. What is the name of the play?

6. The Boy Scout movement is formed in England. By whom?

7. A major earthquake kills over 700 on which island?

8. Mohamed Ali Mirza takes on what high responsibility?

9. The 'Triple Alliance' is renewed between which three European countries?

10. The French fleet bombards which Moroccan city after anti-foreign disturbances.

11. Which U.S state is admitted as the 46th state of the union?

12. What is the name of the French brothers who invent colour photography?

13. Which Scottish born mathematician and physicist who gave his name to a scale of temperature in which zero is absolute zero, dies at the age of 84?

14. What political organisation is formed from a merger of political clubs in Ireland?

15. Which leading revolutionary figure leaves Russia?

ANSWERS
1. The electric washing machine. 2. William Randolph Hearst. 3. Les Demoiselles d'Avignon. 4. Sweden and Finland. 5. The Playboy of the Western World. 6. Sir Robert Baden-Powell. 7. Jamaica. 8. Shah of Persia. 9. Germany, Italy and Austria. 10. Casablanca. 11. Oklahoma. 12. Lumiere. 13. Lord Kelvin. 14. The Sinn Fein League. 15. Lenin.

How much do you know about 1908?

QUESTIONS.

1. Which major law enforcement agency is established in the United States?

2. The first model of which famous motor car goes on sale?

3. Which British explorer leads his team to within 100 miles of the South Pole?

4. Which German physicist, working under Ernest Rutherford at Manchester, invents a machine to measure beta-ray radioactivity?

5. What is the name of the British businessman who discovers enormous oil reserves in Persia?

6. The King and Crown Prince of which nation are murdered?

7. In Turkey, widespread reforms are forced upon the rulers of the Ottoman Empire by which pressure group?

8. The fourth modern Olympic games takes place in which capital?

9. In the U.S, which association begins placing bibles in hotel rooms?

10. Crete declares political union with which European state?

11. Austria annexes which other state?

12. Which major motor manufacturing company is formed in the U.S.?

13. Also in the U.S, which Republican candidate wins the Presidential elections?

14. Which Democrat candidate does he defeat?

15. Kenneth Grahame publishes a children's book which becomes loved by millions. Its name please?

ANSWERS
1. The Federal Bureau of Investigation. 2. Model T Ford. 3. Sir Ernest Shackleton. 4. Hans Geiger. 5. William D'Arcy. 6. Portugal. 7. The Young Turks. 8. London. 9. Gideon International. 10. Greece. 11. Bosnia – Herzegovina. 12. General Motors. 13. William Howard Taft. 14. William Jennings Bryan. 15. The Wind in the Willows.

How much do you know about 1909?

QUESTIONS.

1. Who launches the Indian Nationalist Movement?

2. Britain creates two secret services. What are they called?

3. Which French/Italian writer/editor publishes a manifesto urging the creation of a Futurist Movement in Art and Music?

4. Paul Ehrlich, a German bacteriologist discovers salvarsan, a cure for what?

5. Which American businessman opens a major store on Oxford Street, London?

6. A telegraphic link is established between Britain and which other country?

7. Which American naval officer leads an expedition to the North Pole, or at least to within 30 miles of it?

8. Which Eastern European country obtains independence from Turkey?

9. Which organisation for young girls is founded in England this year?

10. Which French warrior is beatified by Pope Pius X?

11. Which English writer, playwright, poet and critic dies at the age of 72?

12. What does Louis Bleriot achieve in 37 minutes this year?

13. Formation of which important race relations association in the U.S?

14. Importation of Opium is banned in which country?

15. First performance of the opera Electra by which Austrian composer?

ANSWERS.
1. Mahatma Gandhi. 2. MI5 and MI6. 3. Fillipo Marinetti. 4. Syphilis. 5. Harry Selfridge. 6. India. 7. Commander Robert Peary. 8. Bulgaria. 9. The Girl Guides. 10. Joan of Arc. 11. Algernon Swinburne. 12. Crosses the Channel by monoplane. 13. National Association for the Advancement of Coloured People. 14. U.S.A. 15. Richard Strauss.

Year by year 1910-1919

How much do you know about 1910?

QUESTIONS.

1. Which European capital is brought to a standstill by massive flooding?

2. The Postal Savings Bank is established in which country?

3. What is the name of the Premier of Egypt, assassinated by a nationalist fanatic?

4. Japan annexes which other country?

5. Revolution leads to civil war in which Central American state?

6. Which British protectorate is granted dominion status?

7. Which European country declares itself a republic?

8. The Principia Mathematica is published by which British philosopher?

9. The British monarch Edward VII dies. Who is his successor?

10. Which motor pioneer becomes the first British pilot to die in a flying accident?

11. What is celebrated for the first time in the U.S on the 19th of June?

12. Which much beloved American writer dies at 74?

13. Which famous bridge in New York is opened?

14. Death of Mary Baker Eddy, founder of which religious association?

15. What was Mark Twain's real name?

ANSWERS
1. Paris. 2. U.S.A. 3. Boutros Ghali. 4. Korea. 5. Mexico. 6. Union of South Africa. 7. Portugal. 8. Bertrand Russell. 9. His son, George V. 10. Charles Stewart Rolls. 11. Father's Day. 12. Mark Twain. 13. Manhattan Bridge. 14. Christian Scientists. 15. Samuel Langhorne Clemens.

How much do you know about 1911?

QUESTIONS.

1. Which country first uses aeroplanes in combat, in its war with Turkey in Libya?

2. Which Norwegian explorer reaches the South Pole, days ahead of Captain Scott and his party?

3. Russia invades and occupies which other country?

4. Britain passes an Act of Parliament relating to the confidentiality of state information. What is it called?

5. Revolution erupts in Mexico led by two charismatic figures. Who are they?

6. Which famous painting is stolen from the Louvre in Paris in August this year?

7. Which point on the global map becomes the international standard for calculating time?

8. Which American author and educator writes the poem America The Beautiful?

9. The theory of the nuclear atom is propounded. By whom?

10. The first in a series of international Rugby contests is held. By what name is this contest known?

11. Frank Lloyd Wright builds a home/architectural school near Spring Green, Wisconsin, which he names after a Welsh bard. What is the name?

12. Which great Czech-Austrian composer dies at the age of 51?

13. On his way to the South Pole, Amundsen names a chain of mountains after which member of the Norwegian Royal Family?

14. Which Scots-born American industrialist endows a peace foundation?

15. George V, the first British monarch to visit India, holds a ceremonial meeting in public. By what name does this event become known?

ANSWERS.
1. Italy. 2. Roald Amundsen. 3. Iran (Persia). 4. Official Secrets Act. 5. Pancho Villa and Emiliano Zapata. 6. Mona Lisa. 7. Greenwich. 8. Katherine Lee Bates. 9. Sir Ernest Rutherford. 10. Five Nations. 11. Taliesen. 12. Gustav Mahler. 13. Queen Maud Mountains. 14. Andrew Carnegie. 15. The Delhi Durbar.

How much do you know about 1912?

QUESTIONS.

1. Which U.S. state becomes the 47th state in the union?

2. In Britain a new military service is formed. What is it called?

3. Polish born American biochemist Casimir Funk introduces a new word into the medical lexicon. What is it?

4. Which collection of letters is adopted as the universal symbol of distress?

5. What dubious archaelogical artefact is discovered by Charles Dawson in S.E England?

6. The liner SS Titanic hits an iceberg in the North Atlantic and sinks on her maiden voyage. By which shipping line was she owned?

7. And what is the name of the liner, the first on the scene, which picks up survivors?

8. Which British explorer reaches the South Pole but loses his life during the return journey?

9. Morocco becomes a protectorate of which major power?

10. Fifth Olympic Games opens in which city?

11. Which Swedish playwright dies, at the age of 63?

12. What is the name of the new ballet by Igor Stravinsky, performed this year?

13. Which French born actress plays the title role in the film Queen Elizabeth?

14. What is the name of the pioneer of antiseptic surgery, who dies this year?

15. Which Democrat candidate wins the U.S. presidential elections?

ANSWERS.
1. New Mexico. 2. The Royal Flying Corps. 3. Vitamins. 4. SOS. 5. 'Piltdown Man'. 6. White Star. 7. S.S Carpathia. 8. Robert Falcon Scott. 9. France. 10. Stockholm. 11. August Strindberg. 12. Petruschka. 13. Sarah Bernhardt. 14. Joseph Lister. 15. Woodrow Wilson.

How much do you know about 1913?

QUESTIONS.

1. In the U.S the banking system is strengthened by the establishment of what?

2. Which Danish physicist uses the quantum theory to extend the model of the atom?

3. Which country does Serbia invade at the beginning of the second Balkan War?

4. Civil War breaks out again in which Central American country?

5. Which army officer seizes control of Mexico City, deposing the President, who is afterwards murdered?

6. In Turkey, the Young Turks stage a coup and establish a military junta. Who is their leader?

7. In the U.S. what type of tax is levied for the first time?

8. Which classical guitarist makes his public debut?

9. Recovery of which great work of art, stolen from the Louvre in 1911?

10. Publication of Death in Venice by which German author?

11. Who becomes the new British Poet Laureate?

12. Which French statesman is elected President?

13. Suffragettes demonstrate in Britain, and which other country?

14. In the U.S., President Woodrow Wilson establishes the precedent for a political tradition. What does he do?

15. Construction of which feat of engineering is completed?

ANSWERS.
1. The Federal Reserve. 2. Niels Bohr. 3. Albania. 4. Mexico. 5. Victoriana Huerta. 6. Enver Pasha. 7. Federal Income Tax. 8. Andres Segovia. 9. Da Vinci's Mona Lisa. 10. Thomas Mann. 11. Robert Bridges. 12. Raymond Poincarè. 13. The U.S.A. 14. Gives the first State of the Union address to Congress. 15. The Panama Canal.

How much do you know about 1914?

QUESTIONS.

1. Edgar Rice Burroughs publishes a novel destined for fame. What is it called?

2. Mme Caillaux, wife of the French Minister of Finance, shoots dead Gaston Calmette. Who is Calmette?

3. Which contentious piece of legislation throws the British Parliament into disarray?

4. The U.S.A finds itself in a state of armed confrontation with which neighbouring country?

5. Archduke Francis Ferdinand and his wife are assassinated in which city?

6. Which French socialist deputy is murdered in Paris?

7. Henri Matisse paints one of his most famous works. What is it called?

8. The death is announced of which British statesman and radical politician?

9. July 28th. Austria-Hungary declare war on which state?

10. August 1st. Germany declares war on which country?

11. August 3rd. Germany declares war on…?

12. August 4th. Britain declares war on…?

13. September, German and Allied armies try to outflank each other, in what becomes known as…?

14. October 30th. First battle of…?

15. December 8th. Royal Navy defeats German squadron in a battle off which South Atlantic islands?

ANSWERS
1. Tarzan of the Apes. 2. Editor of *Figaro*. 3. The Irish Home Rule Bill. 4. Mexico. 5. Sarajevo. 6. Jean Jaures. 7. The Red Studio. 8. Joseph Chamberlain. 9. Serbia. 10. Russia. 11. France. 12. Germany. 13. The Race to the Sea. 14. Ypres. 15. The Falkland Islands.

How much do you know about 1915?

QUESTIONS.

1. What does Britain suffer for the first time on January 19th?

2. January 30th. Another first in warfare takes place. What is it?

3. February 19th. British and French fleets bombard Turkish positions where?

4. German airships bomb which Allied capital in March of this year?

5. April 22nd. Germans introduce yet another first on the Western Front. What is it this time

6. April 25th. Anglo-French forces meet heavy resistance in landings in Turkey. Where, exactly?

7. May 7th. What is the name of the famous liner, sunk by German U-Boats?

8. June 16th. Who is appointed Minister of Munitions in Britain?

9. July 18th. A second battle begins between Italian and Austrian troops, for a place called ......?

10. August 5th. German troops take which Eastern European capital?

11. September 18th. German troops take another Eastern European capital. Which one?

12. October 29th. After the resignation of French Premier Vivian, who forms a new Ministry?

13. November 13th. Which member of the British cabinet resigns over Gallipoli?

14. December 16th. Who succeeds John French as C-in-C of British forces in France and Belgium?

15. Who publishes the General Theory of Relativity?

ANSWERS
1. Air raids. 2. First German submarine attack. 3. In the Dardanelles. 4. Paris. 5. Poison gas. 6. Gallipoli. 7. The Lusitania. 8. David Lloyd-George. 9. Isonzo. 10. Warsaw. 11. Vilnius, Lithuania. 12. Aristide Briand. 13. Winston Churchill. 14. Douglas Haig. 15. Albert Einstein.

How much do you know about 1916?

QUESTIONS.

1. January. Austria-Hungary attacks which Central European state?

2. February 9th. In Britain the Military Service Act comes into force, introducing what for the first time?

3. February 21st. A battle begins in France which will not end until mid-December. What is it called?

4. March 9th. Germany declares war on which other country?

5. April 24th. Sinn Fein organise what in Dublin?

6. May 31st. Indecisive battle between British and German Fleets, with heavy casualties. What is it called?

7. June 21st. In the Americas there is a battle between U.S and Mexican troops, at which place?

8. July 1st. British and French forces begin an offensive which continues with massive casualties until November. Where?

9. August. Which General becomes Chief of the German General Staff?

10. September 15th. First use by the British of which offensive weapon?

11. October 16th. The Allies occupy which central European capital?

12. November. In the U.S. elections the first female Member of Congress is returned by Montana. Her name please?

13. The 6th Olympic Games are cancelled this year. Where were they scheduled to be held?

14. December 11th. After resignation of British premier Asquith, who becomes the leader of a coalition government?

15. Which self-styled Russian holy man who exercises a strong influence over the Tzarina, is murdered in St. Petersburg?

ANSWERS
1. Montenegro. 2. Conscription. 3. Battle of Verdun. 4. Portugal. 5. Easter Rising. 6. Battle of Jutland. 7. Carrizal, Mexico. 8. The Somme. 9. Paul von Hindenburg. 10. Tanks. 11. Athens. 12. Miss Jeanette Rankin. 13. Berlin. 14. David Lloyd-George. 15. Gregory Rasputin.

How much do you know about 1917?

QUESTIONS.

1. January 31st. Germany warns neutrals about what change in its naval policy?

2. February 2nd. What form of austerity begins in Britain?

3. February 3rd. Which two countries break off diplomatic relations?

4. March 16th. Which Emperor is forced to abdicate?

5. March 31st. The U.S.A takes over which group of islands from Denmark?

6. April 6th. The U.S.A declares war on which country?

7. May 15th. Who is instated as Commander in Chief of French forces?

8. June 24th. Where does the mutiny of the Russian Black Sea fleet take place?

9. July 9th. In the U.S the government takes direct control of which essential commodities?

10. August 13th. In Spain, a revolt demands home rule for which province?

11. November 20th. Where does the first notable tank battle take place?

12. October 7th. Who storms the Winter Palace in Russia, and proclaims the Soviet of People's Commissars as the new government?

13. Which two newspapers are founded following the October Revolution?

14. Death of which famous French artists?

15. In the U.S. prizes are awarded for the first time for literature, drama, music and journalism, endowed by which Hungarian-born American newspaperman?

ANSWERS
1. Unrestricted submarine warfare. 2. Bread rationing. 3. U.S.A and Germany. 4. Tsar Nicholas II. 5. The Virgin Islands. 6. Germany. 7. Marshal Petain. 8. Sevastopol. 9. Fuel and food. 10. Catalonia. 11. Riga, Latvia. 12. Cambrai. 13. Lenin and the Bolsheviks. 14. Degas and Rodin. 15. Joseph Pulitzer.

How much do you know about 1918?

QUESTIONS.

1. January 8th. Which world leader proposes his Fourteen Point Peace Plan?

2. January 14th. Which former premier of France is arrested for treason?

3. February 6th. Death of which popular Viennese artist?

4. March 3rd. Which powers sign the Peace Treaty of Brest-Litovsk?

5. To what does the Bolshevik Party change its name?

6. April 14th. German troops occupy which Scandinavian capital?

7. Roughly how many people are killed worldwide, by an epidemic of Spanish Influenza?

8. July 17th. Where are Nicholas II and his family murdered, on the orders of the Ural Regional Council?

9. August 8th – 11th. British and Commonwealth troops win which great victory?

10. September 12th. American troops win a decisive victory in their first major battle. Where did it take place?

11. Allied advances on all fronts becomes known as what?

12. November 11th. Where is the Armistice signed by Allies and Germany?

13. December 4th. A new kingdom, made up of three previously independent states is proclaimed. What is its name?

14. Whose Collected Poems are published posthumously?

15. And Edward Elgar presents a composition destined for enormous popularity. What is it?

ANSWERS
1. President Woodrow Wilson. 2. Joseph Caillaux. 3. Gustav Klimt. 4. Russia and Germany. 5. Russian Communist Party. 6. Helsinki. 7. 20 million. 8. Ekaterinburg. 9. Battle of Amiens. 10. St. Mihiel. 11. The 'Final Push'. 12. Compiegne. 13. Yugoslavia. 14. Rupert Brooke and Gerald Manley Hopkins. 15. His Cello Concerto.

How much do you know about 1919?

QUESTIONS.

1. Civil War grows, in which country?

2. An uprising takes place in Berlin, led by Rosa Luxembourg and Karl Liebknecht, leaders of which extreme left wing organisation?

3. In the U.S. the 18th amendment to the Constitution is ratified. What legal measure does it provide for?

4. As part of the Paris Peace Conference, President Woodrow Wilson presents the articles of a new world organisation, designed to avoid conflict. What is it called?

5. Which American Senator begins an ultimately successful Lodge campaign to distance the U.S.A from this new organisation?

6. In Italy, who is the founder of the organisation 'Fasci di Combattimento'?

7. Alcock and Brown are the first aviators to fly the Atlantic non-stop. From where to where?

8. The Bauhaus School of Design, Building and Crafts is founded in Weimar. By whom?

9. The ballet The Three Cornered Hat is performed to great acclaim. Which Spanish composer is the writer?

10. For a few months a renowned pianist and composer becomes Premier of Poland. Who is it?

11. A 'soviet' republic is set up in a German city, but it is suppressed within two months. Which province?

12. Where does the German fleet scuttle itself?

13. Who is the American born woman who becomes the first female Member of Parliament in the U.K?

14. Which famous French impressionist painter dies?

15. And which former American President dies, at 61?

ANSWERS
1. Russia. 2. Spartacists. 3. Prohibition. 4. League of Nations. 5. Henry Cabot. 6. Benito Mussolini. 7. Newfoundland to Ireland. 8. Walter Gropius. 9. Manuel de Falla. 10. Ignace Paderewski. 11. Munich. 12. Scapa Flow. 13. Nancy Astor. 14. Pierre-August Renoir. 15. Theodore Roosevelt

Year by year 1920–1929

How much do you know about 1920?

QUESTIONS.

1. Which new political party is founded in Germany?

2. In the U.S, the 19th amendment to the Constitution comes into force. What does it do?

3. Which country signs a peace treaty with the U.S.S.R whilst insisting upon its independence?

4. Death of which Italian painter and sculptor, whose last exhibition in Paris in 1918 had been closed for indecency?

5. Which two stars of the silver screen marry?

6. What political entity is dismantled by the Allies?

7. 7th modern Olympic Games are held in which city?

8. Which American tennis player wins the Wimbledon Lawn Tennis Championships?

9. Which President of a Central American country is assassinated?

10. Which city is chosen as the venue for the permanent International Court of Justice?

11. Who is the newly elected President of Turkey?

12. Which contest is held for the first time in Atlantic City, New Jersey, and won by Miss Margaret Gorman?

13. In the U.S, who is the newly elected Republican President?

14. Which ex-enemy country is admitted to the League of Nations?

15. What new form of information and entertainment begins?

ANSWERS
1. National Socialist German Workers Party (Nazi Party). 2. It gives women the right to vote. 3. Estonia. 4. Amedo Modigliani. 5. Mary Pickford and Douglas Fairbanks. 6. Ottoman Empire. 7. Antwerp. 8. Bill Tilden. 9. President of Mexico. 10. The Hague. 11. Mustafa Kemal. 12. Miss America. 13. Warren G. Harding. 14. Austria. 15. Broadcasting in the U.K and the U.S.A.

How much do you know about 1921?

QUESTIONS.

1. What is set by the Allies at the Paris Conference?

2. First Parliament takes place in which country?

3. Which house is presented to the nation to become the country residence of the British Prime Minister?

4. Ernest Rutherford and James Chadwick disintegrate the majority of the known elements, as a preliminary to doing what?

5. French troops occupy which part of Germany?

6. In which European country do Fascists win heavily in elections?

7. Nationalists riot in which Egyptian city?

8. First Parliament sits in which part of the U.K.?

9. Death occurs of which great Opera star?

10. Which three Eastern European countries are admitted to the League of Nations?

11. What is the name of the Japanese premier, assassinated this year?

12. Which new state is created by treaty with Britain?

13. Which Liberal leader becomes Premier of Canada?

14. Which world-renowned perfume is launched in May this year?

15. Death of which German composer?

ANSWERS
1. German reparations. 2. India. 3. Chequers. 4. Splitting the atom. 5. The Ruhr. 6. Italy. 7. Alexandria. 8. Northern Ireland. 9. Enrico Caruso. 10. Estonia, Latvia, and Lithuania. 11. Takashi Hara. 12. Irish Free State. 13. Mackenzie King. 14. Chanel No. 5. 15. Engelbert Humperdinck

How much do you know about 1922?

QUESTIONS.

1. Who is chosen as the Premier of the first Irish government?

2. Which famous British explorer dies in the Antarctic this year?

3. The sovereign independence of China is guaranteed by a nine power conference, ending in which treaty?

4. In India, who is jailed for six years for sedition?

5. Which poem by T.S Eliot, published this year, opens with the declaration 'April is the cruellest month'?

6. Canadian physiologist Frederick Banting leads a team which isolates the hormone which controls the level of sugar in the blood. What is the name of the hormone?

7. A Hollywood scandal destroys the career of which star?

8. Who is appointed General Secretary of the Communist Party of Russia?

9. The German foreign minister is murdered by Nationalists. What is his name?

10. Which Eastern European state is admitted to the League of Nations?

11. Death of the famous Scots-American inventor of the telephone. What is his name?

12. The book Ulysses is published and makes its already well-known author a world figure. What is his name?

13. Howard Carter discovers the tomb of which Pharaoh?

14. First radio broadcast by which future giant of the airwaves?

15. Who is the Danish physicist who wins the Nobel Prize for his work on the structure of the atom?

ANSWERS
1. Michael Collins. 2. Sir Ernest Shackleton. 3. Treaty of Washington. 4. Mahatma Gandhi. 5. The Waste Land. 6. Insulin 7. Roscoe 'Fatty' Arbuckle. 8. Joseph Stalin. 9. Walter Rathenau. 10. Hungary. 11. Alexander Graham Bell. 12. James Joyce. 13. Tutankhamen. 14. B.B.C. 15. Niels Bohr.

How much do you know about 1923?

QUESTIONS.

1. Fascist militia formed in which European country?

2. What causes tension to rise between France and Germany?

3. First NAZI rally held in Germany, in which town?

4. In the U.S, what is introduced for the first time, in the states Nevada and Montana?

5. Death of which great French-born actress?

6. In the U.K the Duke of York gets married. To whom?

7. Which famous Mexican bandit is shot to death?

8. After the death of President Warren Harding, the U.S. Vice-President is sworn in. What is his name?

9. Russia formally changes its name to what?

10. Which Turkish statesman is elected President?

11. A massive earthquake brings death to 150,000 people and devastates which capital?

12. Which German physicist who discovered X-Rays dies this year?

13. Death of which French engineer, renowned for his bridges and viaducts, and for one tower in particular?

14. An abortive coup in Munich brings to the world's attention, for the first time …..?

15. First F.A. Cup Final to be played at Wembley Stadium results in a win for which club?

ANSWERS
1. Italy. 2. War reparations. 3. Munich. 4. Old-age pensions. 5. Sarah Bernhardt. 6. Lady Elizabeth Bowes-Lyon. 7. Pancho Villa. 8. Calvin Coolidge. 9. Union of Soviet Socialist Republics. 10. Mustafa Kemal. 11. Tokyo. 12. Wilhelm von Rontgen. 13. Gustav Eiffel. 14. Adolf Hitler. 15. Bolton Wanderers.

How much do you know about 1924?

QUESTIONS.

1. Death of which "architect of the Russian revolution"?

2. France signs an alliance agreement with which other state?

3. In the U.S. George Gershwin gives the first performance of which masterpiece?

4. And who becomes the long-serving head of the F.B.I.?

5. American troops are sent to which central American country?

6. Which European country declares itself a republic?

7. Britain is the first major power to recognise which state?

8. In the U.S a notorious murder case happens. The perpetrators?

9. Which great Italian composer dies this year?

10. … leaving his last opera unfinished. Its name?

11. The German author Thomas Mann publishes which great novel?

12. In the U.S a bill is passed to limit ….. what?

13. In elections in South Africa, Smut's South African Party is defeated by which other Party?

14. A mysterious affair undermines the first Labour government in Britain. What is at the heart of the matter?

15. The 8th modern Olympic Games takes place in which city?

ANSWERS
1. Lenin. 2. Czechoslovakia. 3. Rhapsody in Blue. 4. J. Edgar Hoover. 5. Honduras. 6. Greece. 7. U.S.S.R. 8. Leopold and Loeb. 9. Giacomo Puccini. 10. Turandot. 11. The Magic Mountain. 12. Immigration. 13. The Nationalist Party. 14. The Zinoviev Letter. 15. Paris.

How much do you know about 1925?

QUESTIONS.

1. In the U.S, for the first time, a woman becomes a State Governor. Of which state?

2. Who is elected President of Germany?

3. The 'Father of modern China' dies. What is his name?

4. The U.S state of Tennessee bans teaching about … what?

5. A young American teacher is taken to court in Tennessee for teaching 'Darwinism'. What is his name?

6. In the ensuing 'Monkeyville' trial, two great lawyers come face to face. Their names please?

7. Which military leader is elected President of Germany?

8. Which island is added to the British Empire as a colony?

9. A huge Klu Klux Klan parade takes place in which city?

10. Italian troops invade which African country?

11. Which Irish playwright wins the Nobel prize for literature?

12. The "Dawes Plan" for the reconstruction of Germany wins the Nobel Prize for Peace for its two architects. One was obviously the U.S. Vice President Charles Gates Dawes. Who was the other?

13. A new Noel Coward comedy opens in the West End. What is its title?

14. Which work by Franz Kafka is published posthumously?

15. Death of which British military leader who took the title 1st Earl of Ypres when ennobled?

ANSWERS
1. Wyoming. 2. Paul von Hindenburg. 3. Dr Sun Yat-Sen. 4. Evolution. 5. John T. Scopes. 6. Clarence Darrow and William Jennings Bryan. 7. Paul von Hindenburg. 8. Cyprus. 9. Washington D.C. 10. Somaliland. 11. G.B. Shaw. 12. British Foreign Secretary, Sir Austen Chamberlain. 13. Hay Fever. 14. The Trial. 15. John French.

How much do you know about 1926?

QUESTIONS.

1. Which country returns to the Gold Standard?

2. Who succeeds Sun Yat-sen as leader of China's Nationalist Party?

3. Scottish engineer John Logie Baird gives a demonstration of his new invention. What is it?

4. Ibn Saud replaces Hussein as King of Hejaz and immediately changes the name of the country to ..... what?

5. In Ireland the head of Sinn Fein resigns and sets up a new party called Fianna Fail. Who is he?

6. In Britain the general strike of nine days, which grew from the miner's strike, which lasted seven months, ends in defeat for whom?

7. A military coup in Poland installs which army officer and statesman as virtual dictator?

8. Which classic children's book, concerning the doings of the inhabitants of the Hundred Acre Wood, is published this year?

9. General Gomes da Costa leads a military coup in which European country?

10. Germany is admitted to the League of Nations, in consequence which other European country quits?

11. Theodore Dreiser publishes his latest novel, called ....?

12. Spanish architect Antonio Gaudi dies in the same year as his greatest work (begun in 1883) is completed. What is it?

13. Expulsion from the Politburo of which leading Soviets?

14. Death of which great French impressionist painter?

15. Death of which Czech-born Austrian lyric poet at 51?

ANSWERS
1. France. 2. Chiang Kai-Shek. 3. Television. 4. Saudi Arabia. 5. Eamon de Valera. 6. The Trades Union Council. 7. Josef Pilsudski. 8. Winnie the Pooh. 9. Portugal. 10. Spain. 11. An American Tragedy. 12. The Church of the Sagrada Family, Barcelona. 13. Trotsky and Zinoviev. 14. Claude Monet. 15. Rainer Maria Rilke.

How much do you know about 1927?

QUESTIONS.

1. Capital punishment reintroduced and trial by jury abolished in which European country?

2. Allied military control of which European country ends?

3. Revolt against military dictatorship in which European country?

4. Which 10-year-old violin prodigy brings his Paris audience to its feet?

5. Which British sportsman sets a new world land speed record?

6. Which other British sportsman then raises the world land speed record yet again?

7. In Australia, the new Parliament house is opened, in which city?

8. Collapse of Germany's economy is called … ?

9. Which American aviator is the first to fly the Atlantic solo?

10. Which two Italian-born anarchists are executed in the U.S.A. for robbery and murder after a dubious trial?

11. What revolution occurred in the field of entertainment?

12. Death of which American-born Irish politician, renowned for the violence of his language in speeches?

13. In China, the tomb of which Mongol war lord is discovered?

14. British author Henry Williamson publishes which novel about wildlife, destined to become famous?

15. Which German physicist publishes a theory of uncertainty in the field of quantum physics?

ANSWERS
1. Italy. 2. Germany. 3. Portugal. 4. Yehudi Menuhin. 5. Malcolm Campbell. 6. Henry Segrave. 7. Canberra. 8. Black Friday. 9. Charles Lindbergh. 10. Sacco and Vanzetti. 11. Talking pictures ('talkies'). 12. John Dillon. 13. Genghis Khan. 14. Tarka the Otter. 15. Werner Heisenberg.

How much do you know about 1928?

QUESTIONS.

1. The first commercial transatlantic airship flight is made this year. What is the name of the airship?

2. And which British literary giant dies this year?

3. In the U.S the first performance of George Gershwin's new masterpiece. What is it called?

4. And in Germany, which musical by Kurt Weil and Bertolt Brecht has its premiere?

5. Women's suffrage reduced from 30 to what age in Britain?

6. Assassination of the president of which Central American country?

7. Coup d'etat in Egypt leads to the dissolution of Parliament for 3 years and suppression of free press. Who leads the coup?

8. With which country does Italy sign a twenty-year treaty of friendship?

9. In Paris, 23 nations sign the Kellogg-Briand pact which sets out to do... what?

10. First performance of an exciting piece of music by Spanish composer Maurice Ravel . What is it called?

11. Albania declares itself a kingdom, under which king?

12. Death of Britain's first lady of the Shakespearean stage and one-time partner of Henry Irving. What is her name?

13. Sir Alexander Fleming makes, by accident, a medical discovery of immense significance. What name does he give to it?

14. Ninth modern Olympic Games staged, in which city?

15. First state pensions handed out in which country?

ANSWERS
1. The Graf Zeppelin. 2. Thomas Hardy. 3. An American In Paris. 4. The Threepenny Opera (Dreigroschenoper). 5. 21. 6. Mexico. 7. King Fuad. 8. Ethiopia. 9. To outlaw war. 10. Bolero. 11. Zog. 12. Ellen Terry. 13. Penicillin. 14. Amsterdam. 15. United Kingdom.

How much do you know about 1929?

QUESTIONS.

1. Which American astronomer propounds the theory which states that the apparent velocities of receding universes are proportional to their distance from us?

2. In Britain a woman becomes a Member of the Cabinet as Minister of Labour, for the first time. What is her name?

3. In Germany, author Erich Maria Remarque publishes which classic anti-war novel?

4. The Lateran Treaty establishes the independence of which part of Rome?

5. An R.A.F. plane makes the first non-stop flight from Britain to...?

6. Hollywood institutes a tradition with the first Academy Awards ceremony. How do the awards later come to be known?

7. Which American boot-legger and gangster lost seven members of his gang to Al Capone's killers, in the Saint Valentine's Day Massacre?

8. Violent clashes in Palestine between Arabs and Jews about the right of Jewish access to which sacred site?

9. Which French 'Generalissimo' of allied forces, who drove back the Germans on the Western Front in 1918, dies this year?

10. Death which Austrian poet and librettist for Richard Strauss and co-founder of the Salzburg Festival?

11. Death of Russian born impresario and founder of the Ballets Russes. What is his name?

12. What happens on what is called 'Black Thursday'?

13. This event leads to an era, known internationally as?

14. Which province of China is invaded by Japan?

15. Death of which French statesman, known as 'The Tiger', whose intransigence towards Germany in 1919 may have contributed towards the outbreak of the 2nd World War.

ANSWERS
1. Edwin Hubble. 2. Margaret Bondfield. 3. All Quiet On The Western Front (Im Westen Nichts Neues). 4. Vatican City. 5. India. 6. The Oscars. 7. George 'Bugs' Moran. 8. The Wailing Wall. 9. Ferdinand Foch. 10. Hugo von Hofmannsthal. 11. Sergei Diaghilev. 12. The Wall Street Crash. 13. The Depression. 14. Manchuria. 15. Georges Clemenceau.

Year by year 1930–1939

How much do you know about 1930?

QUESTIONS.

1. As part of the drive to collectivise farms in the USSR, Stalin displaces 10,000,000 peasant farmers. By what name are these peasants known?

2. Approximately how many die as a result?

3. In India, Ghandi organises what protest against the Salt Tax?

4. Which British airship crashes in Northern France in October, killing 44 people?

5. Death of which British lyric poet, particularly well known for his last work The Testament of Beauty?

6. The German Admiral responsible for rebuilding the German Navy to compete with the Royal Navy dies this year. What is his name?

7. Which American author wins the Nobel Prize?

8. Amy Johnson makes an epic solo flight from London to…?

9. Which ethnic minority rebels in Persia and Turkey?

10. What invention changes photography?

11. Which nation wins football's inaugural World Cup competition?

12. Which new Noel Coward comedy opens in the West End?

13. France begins building a major defence system, called ….?

14. Ras Tafari becomes the new Emperor of Ethiopia. What name does he take?

15. Which German boxer becomes World Heavyweight Champion?

ANSWERS
1. Kulaks. 2. 6,000,000. 3. March to the Sea. 4. R101. 5. Robert Bridges. 6. Admiral Alfred von Tirpitz. 7. Sinclair Lewis. 8. Australia. 9. The Kurds. 10. The flash bulb. 11. Uruguay. 12. Private Lives. 13. Maginot Line. 14. Haille Selassie. 15. Max Schmeling.

How much do you know about 1931?

QUESTIONS.

1. Who becomes Prime Minister of France?

2. Unemployment reaches 5,000,000 in which country?

3. In the U.K. which former Conservative, Independent and now Labour MP quits to form the 'New Party' which, he claims, "will save Britain"?

4. Which American physicist develops the world's first cyclotron (atom smasher)?

5. In the U.S.A, Al Capone is convicted and sentenced to 11 years in prison. On what charges?

6. Abdication and flight of the King of Spain. His name ....?

7. Which statesman becomes President of France?

8. Which Swiss born Belgian physicist is the first, with his colleague Paul Kipfer, to ascend to the stratosphere in a balloon?

9. Abortive Fascist coup in which European country?

10. In New York the longest suspension bridge yet built in the world, is opened. Its name?

11. In the U.S, publication of a dramatic novel about China, The Good Earth which earns for its author the Nobel Prize in 1938. By which author is the novel?

12. Spain adopts a republican constitution under which President?

13. NAZI party formed in which European country?

14. First performance of a major Charles Chaplin movie, called?

15. The first film version of Mary Shelley's Frankenstein appears, starring which actor as the monster?

ANSWERS
1. Pierre Laval. 2. Germany. 3. Oswald Mosley. 4. Ernest Lawrence. 5. Tax evasion. 6. Alfonso XIII. 7. Paul Doumer. 8. Professor Auguste Piccard. 9. Austria. 10. George Washington Bridge. 11. Pearl Buck. 12. Alcala Zamora. 13. The Netherlands. 14. City Lights. 15. Boris Karloff.

How much do you know about 1932?

QUESTIONS.

1. The first super star of the horse racing world is accidentally poisoned during a visit to the U.S.A. The horse's name?

2. Whose baby dies in a botched kidnapping?

3. Reports of famine in which country?

4. Which two scientists transmute one material (lithium atoms) into another (helium atoms) with a particle accelerator?

5. Japanese forces occupy which Chinese city?

6. What is the title of the rather startling book, published by Aldous Huxley this year?

7. In which Eastern European state is there a fascist coup?

8. Fist solo transatlantic flight by which American aviatrix?

9. In which city are the tenth modern Olympic games staged?

10. What is the name of the party founded this year by Oswald Mosley?

11. By what name are its members more commonly known?

12. Ernest Hemingway publishes a book about bullfighting which becomes a best-seller. What does he call it?

13. Spain grants autonomy to which province, allowing it to have its own flag, language and parliament?

14. Death of which prolific British thriller writer?

15. Which very young Hollywood star makes her debut?

ANSWERS
1. Phar Lap. 2. Charles and Anne Lindbergh. 3. U.S.S.R. 4. John Cockcroft and Ernest Walton. 5. Shanghai. 6. Brave New World. 7. Lithuania. 8. Amelia Earhart. 9. Los Angeles. 10. British Union of Fascists. 11. Blackshirts. 12. Death In The Afternoon. 13. Catalonia. 14. Edgar Wallace. 15. Shirley Temple.

How much do you know about 1933?

QUESTIONS.

1. Who becomes Chancellor of Germany and assumes dictatorial powers?

2. Who becomes the new French Prime Minister?

3. Which English bowler earns a disagreeable reputation for his 'bodyline bowling' during the tour of Australia?

4. Which country quits the League of Nations after world condemnation of its behaviour in China?

5. Which government building in Berlin is burnt down, apparently by a Communist?

6. After a military coup, who becomes President of Cuba?

7. All opposition parties are banned in which country?

8. France gives political asylum to which Russian émigré?

9. Roosevelt persuades Congress to adopt his National Industry Recovery Act, as part of what he calls his… ?

10. Which British tennis player wins the U.S. Open?

11. The 21st Amendment to the U.S. Constitution is passed by Congress. What does it do?

12. Who is the star of the Reuben Mamoulian film Queen Christina?

13. Death of the German poet whose work contained neither punctuation nor capitals. His name please ?

14. The first concentration camp in Germany opens where?

15. Which American aviator flies around the world in less than eight days?

ANSWERS

1. Adolf Hitler. 2. Edouard Daladier. 3. Harold Larwood. 4. Japan. 5. The Reichstag. 6. Fulgencio Batista. 7. Germany. 8. Leon Trotsky. 9. New Deal. 10. Fred Perry. 11. Repeals prohibition. 12. Greta Garbo. 13. Stefan George. 14. Dachau, near Munich. 15. Wiley Post.

How much do you know about 1934?

QUESTIONS.

1. In France, a large scale perpetrator of bonds frauds, dies in bizarre circumstances, leading to a political crisis and the resignation of the Prime Minister. What is his name?

2. Confidentiality of banking services, facilities and activities is guaranteed by Act of Parliament. In which country?

3. The King of Belgium dies and is succeeded by his son, who takes what title?

4. The Japanese appoint the last Emperor of China (before it becomes a republic) Emperor of Manchuria. His name is ....?

5. What are introduced in Britain for the first time?

6. Italian born nuclear physicist splits the nuclei of uranium atoms by bombarding them with neutrons. His name please?

7. What name is given to the Hitler purge of the Nazi party of his opponents?

8. Mount Everest claims the life of British climber...?

9. The Austrian Chancellor is assassinated in an abortive fascist coup. His name, please?

10. In the U.S. Public Enemy No. 1 is caught and shot dead by the agents of the F.B.I. What is his name?

11. Which visiting European monarch is assassinated in France?

12. In Germany, after the death of President von Hindenburg, Adolf Hitler combines the Presidency with the Chancellorship and takes a new title. What is it?

13. Which country is admitted to the League of Nations?

14. In China, the Communist retreat becomes known as...?

15. Three gifted British composers die. Name any of them.

ANSWERS
1. Alex Stavinsky. 2. Switzerland. 3. King Leopold III. 4. Pu Yi. 5. Driving tests. 6. Enrico Fermi. 7. The Night of the Long Knives. 8. Maurice Wilson. 9. Engelbert Dolfuss. 10. John Dillinger. 11. King Alexander of Yugoslavia. 12. Der Führer. 13. U.S.S.R. 14. The Long March. 15. Elgar, Holst, Delius.

How much do you know about 1935?

QUESTIONS.

1.   Which airline is the first to inaugurate regular trans-Pacific flights?

2.   Which country is the first to legalise abortion?

3.   The first broadcast quiz programme ever is aired in which country?

4.   First performance of which T.S. Eliot drama …?

5.   Death of T.E. Lawrence, British scholar and soldier who played a leading role in the Arab revolt against the Turks. By what name is he better known?

6.   Premiere in the U.S of which George Gershwin opera?

7.   What is the name of the scale formulated to measure the intensity of earthquakes?

8.   What is the name of the British inventor of RADAR?

9.   In Utah, Malcolm Campbell sets a new world land speed of 301.337 m.p.h. What is the name of his racing car?

10. Italy renames its North African colonies Cyrenaica, Tripoli and Fezzan. What does it call them?

11. In China the 'Long March' ends, during which one man establishes himself as undisputed Communist leader. Who?

12. In Germany, the Luftwaffe is formed, under whose command?

13. As what is Persia renamed?

14. Abyssinia invaded by troops from which European power?

15. In Britain, who is chosen as new leader by the Labour party?

ANSWERS
1. Pan Am. 2. Iceland. 3. Canada. 4. Murder in the Cathedral. 5. Lawrence of Arabia. 6. Porgy and Bess. 7. Richter Scale. 8. Robert Watson-Wyatt. 9. Bluebird. 10. Libya. 11. Mao Tse-Tung. 12. Herman Goering. 13. Iran. 14. Italy. 15. Clement Attlee.

How much do you know about 1936?

QUESTIONS.

1. Death of British monarch George V. He is succeeded by his son, who takes what title?

2. Death of British writer whose stories about India delight millions. Who is he?

3. In India who emerges as the new leader of the Indian Congress Party?

4, In defiance of the Treaty of Versailles, Germany reoccupies which officially demilitarised province?

5. Which well known British economist publishes his Theory of Employment, Interest and Money?

6. Death of King Fuad of Egypt, who is succeeded by his son, named…?

7. Spanish Civil War begins with a mutiny in the army. What is the name of the leader who quickly emerges?

8. The Irish State governments outlaws which organisation?

9. Eleventh modern Olympic games staged in which city?

10. Which black U.S. athlete wins four gold medals, prompting Hitler to walk out in disgust?

11. In the U.S, the presidential elections lead to an extended mandate for which President?

12. King Edward VIII abdicates in order to marry which American divorcee?

13. In the U.S, Margaret Mitchell publishes which best selling novel?

14. In Paris, which Sergei Prokofiev opus is first performed?

15. In Hollywood, Charles Chaplin produces his satire on…?

ANSWERS
1. King Edward VIII. 2. Rudyard Kipling. 3. Jawaharlal Nehru. 4. The Rhineland. 5. John Maynard Keynes. 6. Farouk. 7. Francisco Franco. 8. The I.R.A. 9. Berlin. 10. Jesse Owens. 11. F.D. Roosevelt. 12. Mrs Wallis Simpson. 13. Gone With The Wind. 14. Peter and the Wolf. 15. Modern Times.

How much do you know about 1937?

QUESTIONS.

1. In the U.S., which great bridge opens for business?

2. Which painting by Pablo Picasso depicts the bombing of a Spanish city by German aeroplanes?

3. In the elections in India, which party takes the most seats?

4. Ernest Hemingway publishes a novel destined to become famous. What is its title?

5. Which British monarch is crowned in Westminster Abbey?

6. Who replaces S. Baldwin as Prime Minister of the U.K.?

7. Tragic death of which beautiful American film star?

8. In the U.S, Roosevelt signs an act designed to keep America out of Europe's problems. What is it called?

9. A steam engine breaks speed record for the Edinburgh–London run. It becomes so famous that a piece of music is written for it. What is it?

10. The Irish Free State takes a new name. What is it?

11. Death of which famous U.S. composer who had done so much to get American music respected around the world?

12. At the Nuremberg Rally, Hitler demands more what for Germany?

13. Which German airship expodes attempting to moor at Lakehurst Naval Station, New Jersey?

14. A world fair is held in which European capital?

15. Death of an American statesman, ex-secretary of war and of state; winner of the Nobel peace prize in 1912. What is his name?

ANSWERS
1. The Golden Gate Bridge. 2. Guernica. 3. Congress Party. 4. To Have and Have Not. 5. King George VI. 6. Neville Chamberlain. 7. Jean Harlow. 8. U.S Neutrality Act. 9. Coronation Scot. 10. Eire. 11. George Gershwin. 12. Lebensraum (living-space). 13. The Hindenburg. 14. Paris. 15. Elihu Root.

How much do you know about 1938?

QUESTIONS.

1. The name please of the German physical chemist who bombards uranium with neutrons and discovers nuclear fission?

2. The third football World Cup is won by Italy after Mussolini sends the players a telegram saying what?

3. Adolf Hitler takes which other office for himself?

4. German troops invade Austria, incorporating it into Germany. How is this action known?

5. In which country are American and British oil properties nationalised?

6. Which socialist forms a coalition government in Belgium?

7. Which invention is patented by Hungarians J Ladisla and Georg Biro?

8. Publication of which Graham Greene novel, featuring the gangster Pinkie?

9. Which eccentric American millionaire flies around the world in less than four days?

10. What was he publicising?

11. In Munich, Chamberlain and Daladier agree to Hitler annexing Sudetenland. They return promising what?

12. Germany signs a pact of 'inviolability of existing frontiers' with which neighbouring country?

13. The U.S.S.R. signs a pact of friendship and non-aggression with which neighbouring country?

14. In Germany, a night of orchestrated violence against Jews becomes known as what ?

15. Death of the Czech author who first gave us the word 'robot' in the title of one of his works of science fiction Rossum's Universal Robots. What is his name?

ANSWERS
1. Otto Hahn. 2. 'Win or Die'. 3. War Minister. 4. Anschluss. 5. Mexico. 6. Paul Spaak. 7. The ballpoint pen. 8. Brighton Rock. 9. Howard Hughes. 10. New York World Fair. 11. 'Peace in our time'. 12. France. 13. Poland. 14. Kristallnacht (Night of Broken Glass). 15. Karel Capek.

How much do you know about 1939?

QUESTIONS.

1. In Spain, Franco's troops capture which major city?

2. Death of Pope Pius XI. Who is his successor?

3. What is the name of the Swiss chemist who invents the insecticide D.D.T.?

4. Germany invades which neighbouring country?

5. Italy invades which neighbouring country?

6. Spanish Civil War comes to an end as Nationalists take which city?

7. Hitler and Mussolini sign which pact?

8. Germany signs a non-aggression pact with which country?

9. Germany invades Poland and annexes which city?

10. Which two countries declare war on Germany?

11. Poland is also invaded by which other country?

12. U.S.S.R invades which other neighbouring country?

13. In the U.S a sentimental Jerome Kern song becomes very popular. Its title is?

14. Death of which famous Austrian psychologist?

15. What is the name of the screaming dive bomber used so effectively by the Germans in the conquest of Poland?

ANSWERS
1. Barcelona. 2. Pius XII. 3. Paul Müller. 4. Czechoslovakia. 5. Albania. 6. Madrid. 7. Pact of Steel. 8. USSR. 9. Danzig. 10. Britain and France. 11. USSR. 12. Finland. 13. The Last Time I Saw Paris. 14. Sigmund Freud. 15. The Stuka.

Year by year 1940–1949

How much do you know about 1940?

QUESTIONS.

1. What austerity measure is introduced in Britain?

2. In France, Daladier resigns and is replaced by whom?

3. Germany invades which two neighbouring countries in April?

4. In Britain, Prime Minister Neville Chamberlain resigns and is replaced by whom?

5. Germany invades which three neighbouring countries in May?

6. More than 4,000 Polish army officers massacred by the Soviet Army. Where did this take place?

7. Britain breaks which German communications code?

8   Evacuation of 200,000 British and 140,000 Allied forces from which French port and beach?

9. War is declared on France and Britain, by which country?

10. Soviet forces occupy which three neighbouring states?

11. Which French military hero comes out of retirement to negotiate the armistice with Germany?

12. From where is the unoccupied part of France governed?

13. Who becomes the leader of the Free French, in Britain?

14. To prevent German use of French warships, the French fleet is sunk by the Royal Navy, in which North African port?

15. German troops occupy which British territory?

ANSWERS
1. Food rationing. 2. Paul Reynaud. 3. Denmark and Norway. 4. Winston Churchill. 5. Holland, Luxembourg and Belgium. 6. Katyn, Poland. 7. Enigma. 8. Dunkirk. 9. Italy. 10. Lithuania, Latvia, and Estonia. 11. Marshal Petain. 12. Vichy. 13. General de Gaulle. 14. Oran. 15. Channel Islands.

How much do you know about 1940? (continued)

QUESTIONS.

1. What famous air battle begins?

2. The Luftwaffe begins all-night bombing raids on London and other cities. By what name are these raids more commonly known?

3. German bombing of British cities causes what level of casualties?

4. What does Hitler call his planned invasion of Britain?

5. The United States enacts a law which allows Britain to borrow war supplies against a promise to pay after the war. How is this agreement commonly known?

6. Italy invades which British protectorate?

7. What treaty is signed by Germany, Italy and Japan?

8. Which passenger liner carrying children, refugees from Britain is sunk by a German U-Boat off the coast of Ireland?

9. Italy invades which neighbouring country?

10. British warships cripple the Italian fleet. Where?

11. In the Dordogne, in France, four young 'cavers' stumble on incredible examples of pre-historic art. Where?

12. In the U.S, who is re-elected for a third term?

13. Who is appointed British Foreign Secretary?

14. Charlie Chaplin's new satire opens. It is called?

15. Death of the American author of The Great Gatsby and Tender is the Night. His name please?

ANSWERS
1. Battle of Britain. 2. The 'Blitz'. 3. 300-600 per day. 4. Operation Sealion. 5. Lend-Lease. 6. Egypt. 7. The Tripartite Pact. 8. Empress of Britain. 9. Greece. 10. At Taranto. 11. In the Lascaux Grotto. 12. F. D. Roosevelt. 13. Anthony Eden. 14. The Great Dictator. 15. F. Scott Fitzgerald.

How much do you know about 1941?

QUESTIONS.

1. The U.S atomic research project commences. By what name is the project known?

2. Which national memorial is completed in the U.S.A?

3. In North Africa, British troops occupy which major port?

4. After signing a pact with Hitler, which central European monarch is deposed in a coup d'etat?

5. Which industrial town in the midlands of England is virtually destroyed in the 'Blitz'?

6. Which German general sweeps all before him in North Africa?

7. Which two Balkan states are invaded by the Axis powers?

8. What is the name of the Nazi party deputy leader who flies to Scotland to attempt peace negotiations?

9. Which German battleship sinks the British cruiser H.M.S. Hood, and is then sunk in turn by other ships of the Royal Navy?

10. Germany invades the U.S.S.R. What codename is given to this operation?

11. The unofficial alliance between Great Britain and the U.S.A becomes more solid when Churchill and Roosevelt meet in Newfoundland and sign which document?

12. President Roosevelt describes the events of 7th December, 1941 as a 'day of infamy'. To what events is he referring?

13. Japanese troops invade which three key Eastern areas?

14. A new Noel Coward comedy opens in the West End. It is called?

15. While over in the U.S, Orson Welles' new film also impresses. What is it called?

ANSWERS
1. The Manhattan Project. 2. Mount Rushmore. 3. Benghazi. 4. Prince Paul of Yugoslavia. 5. Coventry. 6. Erwin Rommel. 7. Greece and Yugoslavia. 8. Rudolf Hess. 9. The Bismarck. 10. Operation Barbarossa. 11. The Atlantic Charter. 12. Japanese attack on Pearl Harbour. 13. Malaya, the Philippines and Hong Kong. 14. Blithe Spirit. 15. Citizen Kane.

How much do you know about 1942?

QUESTIONS.

1. What is the name of the infamous conference during which senior Nazi officers plot the 'final solution' for Jews?

2. Japanese troops occupy the capital of Malaysia. Its name

3. Which new premier, whose name later becomes synonymous with 'traitor' is appointed in Norway by the Germans?

4. Japanese troops occupy the largest port in south-east Asia, part of a highly strategic island. Its name please?

5. In the US mass-produced 'Liberty Ships' are designed by?

6. American scientists build the first electronic brain. What do they call it?

7. British and Canadian commandos raid a French port in German hands, with great losses. What is its name?

8. First US air raids on which Japanese city?

9. Which high-ranking SS officer is assassinated by the Czech underground, leading to savage German reprisals in the towns of Lidice and Lezàky?

10. First thousand-bomber air raid made by RAF on which German town?

11. US Navy defeats Japanese fleet in the South Pacific in which battle?

12. Allied landings begin where in the Mediterranean?

13. Soviet counter offensive encircles German armies in which Russian city?

14. The people of Malta receive which commendation for their courage under continual attack?

15. In Hollywood, Humphrey Bogart and Ingrid Bergman star in which film destined to become a classic?

ANSWERS
1. The Wannsee Conference. 2. Kuala Lumpur. 3. Vidkun Quisling. 4. Singapore. 5. William Gibbs. 6. ENIAC. 7. Dieppe. 8. Tokyo. 9. Reinhard Heydrich. 10. Cologne. 11. Battle of Midway. 12. French North Africa. 13. Stalingrad. 14. George Cross. 15. Casablanca.

How much do you know about 1943?

QUESTIONS.

1. What is the name of the German Field Marshal who surrenders to the Russians at Stalingrad?

2. First heavy RAF raid on which German city?

3   Allied special forces begin operations behind the Japanese lines in Burma. These forces are called?

4. And the name of their charismatic leader is…?

5. In North Africa, Rommels forces are pushed back by the British Eighth Army. What is the name of the officer commanding?

6. Germans massacre the Jewish occupants of the ghetto in which Eastern European capital?

7. U.S forces go on the offensive in the Pacific, starting by taking back which group of islands?

8. Which of the Axis powers surrenders unconditionally to the Allies?

9. Benito Mussolini rescued from an Italian jail by German special forces. Who is their commander?

10. November 28th. Roosevelt, Churchill and Stalin meet where to plan the overthrow of Germany?

11. The Royal Navy sinks which German battleship?

12. In the U.S. the 'bobby-soxers' have a new idol. His name?

13. Premiere of a new kind of musical show with words and music by Rodgers and Hammerstein. What is its title?

14. Death of which Russian composer?

15. Ukraine born American biologist Selman Waksman develops a very important antibiotic, named…?

ANSWERS
1. Von Paulus. 2. Berlin. 3. The Chindits. 4. Orde Wingate. 5. Bernard Montgomery. 6. Warsaw. 7. Solomon Islands. 8. Italy. 9. Otto Skorzeny. 10. Tehran. 11. The Scharnhorst. 12. Frank Sinatra. 13. Oklahoma! 14. Sergei Rachmaninov. 15. Streptomycin.

How much do you know about 1944?

QUESTIONS.

1. In the Soviet Union, which besieged city is relieved?

2. In Italy, Allied troops attack German positions, in which battle?

3. U.S. bombers begin daylight raids on which German city?

4. June 6th. Allied landings in Normandy. What is the codename for this operation?

5. British and Indian troops fight overwhelming Japanese force to a standstill in which famous confrontation?

6. U.S. Air Force inflicts heavy losses on Japanese Air Force in which battle?

7. Germany launches a new weapon against Britain. What is it?

8. Where do the Allies open a new front in Europe?

9. August 25th. The Allies liberate which European capital?

10. September 4th and 5th. Allies liberate which Belgian towns?

11. Germany launches yet another weapon of terror against Britain. It is called...?

12. What is the codename given to the operation which drops Allied troops into Holland to secure routes into the Ruhr?

13. U.S. troops retake what islands in the Pacific?

14. American bacteriologist proves that DNA is indeed the carrier of genetic information. What is his name?

15. In the U.S., a monetary conference held where, leads to the founding of the World Bank and International Monetary Fund?

ANSWERS
1. Leningrad. 2. Monte Cassino. 3. Berlin. 4. Operation Overlord. 5. Battle of Kohima. 6. Battle of the Philippine Sea. 7. The V.1 flying bomb. 8. Southern France. 9. Paris. 10. Antwerp and Brussels. 11. The V.2. rocket. 12. Operation Market Garden. 13. The Philippines. 14. Oswald T. Avery. 15. Bretton Woods.

How much do you know about 1945?

QUESTIONS.

1. The westward-moving Soviet armies cross which German river?

2. The 'Big Three', Roosevelt, Churchill and Stalin meet where?

3. General MacArthurs troops enter which Pacific capital?

4. Soviet puppet governments set up in which Eastern European countries?

5. Eastward-moving U.S. armies cross which German river?

6. Death of U.S. President Roosevelt. He is succeeded by?

7. April 20th. Which allied army enters Berlin?

8. Which new International Institution is set up?

9. Who is executed in Italy by the partisans?

10. Who commits suicide in the ruins of Berlin?

11. Which German general surrenders to Eisenhower near Reims?

12. General von Keitel surrenders in Berlin to which Soviet marshal?

13. The 'Big Three', Truman, Attlee and Stalin meet to settle the problems of the occupation of Germany. Where?

14. August 6th and 9th. U.S drops atom bombs on which two Japanese cities?

15. Japan signs surrender on board which U.S. ship?

ANSWERS
1. The Oder. 2. Yalta. 3. Manila. 4. Poland and Romania. 5. The Rhine. 6. Harry S. Truman. 7. USSR. 8. United Nations. 9. Mussolini. 10. Adolf Hitler. 11. General Jodl. 12. Zhukov. 13. Potsdam. 14. Hiroshima and Nagasaki. 15. U.S.S Missouri.

How much do you know about 1946?

QUESTIONS.

1. First assembly of the United Nations in which capital?

2. In Britain, William Joyce is hanged for treason. By what name is he better known?

3. Albania is proclaimed a 'Peoples Republic' under which leader?

4. Who is elected first Secretary General of the U.N?

5. An important British financial institution is nationalised. Which one?

6. Who is elected President of Argentina?

7. "An iron curtain has descended across Europe". Who said this in a speech in Fulton, U.S.A. on March 5th?

8. A partly communist government is installed in Czechoslovakia. What is the name of its Premier?

9. Civil war between monarchists and communists in which central European country?

10. Which Japanese emperor is forced to admit that he is not divine?

11. Which European country votes overwhelmingly to become a Republic?

12. What important social service is established in the U.K.?

13. In the U.S, which boxer successfully defends his world heavyweight title for the 23rd time?

14. War Crimes Tribunal held in which German town?

15. In the U.S, Chester Carlson invents what aid to office efficiency?

Answers
1. London. 2. Lord Haw-Haw. 3. Enver Hoxha. 4. Trygve Lie. 5. Bank of England. 6. Juan Peron. 7. Winston Churchill. 8. Klement Gottwald. 9. Greece. 10. Hirohito. 11. Italy. 12. National Health Service. 13. Joe Louis. 14. Nuremberg. 15. Xerography

How much do you know about 1947?

QUESTIONS.

1. Labour government in Britain nationalises which industry?

2. Who is elected President of France?

3. The U.S is obliged to break off attempts at conciliation between warring factions, Communist and Nationalist, in which far eastern country?

4. In the U.S, the President outlines a plan to aid Greece and Turkey and any other country menaced by Communism in what comes to be known as ....?

5. Lord Wavell resigns as Viceroy of India. Who is appointed to succeed him?

6. Norwegian anthropologist Thor Heyerdahl journeys from Peru to Tuamotu Island in the Pacific in a balsa raft named ....?

7. The theory that all massive rotating bodies are magnetic is propounded by which British physicist?

8. In the U.S the first supersonic airflight by a Bell X-1 rocket plane takes place, piloted by which USAF Captain?

9. In a speech at Harvard, the U.S. Secretary of State proposes a European Recovery Programme. What is his name?

10. Warsaw Communist conference establishes a body to co-ordinate activities of European parties. Its name?

11. Belgium, Netherlands and Luxembourg ratify a customs union. What is the name given to the union?

12. In London, who does Princess Elizabeth marry?

13. The United Nations announces plan to partition which Middle Eastern state?

14. What is the title of the new play by Tennessee Williams, which receives its first performance this year?

15. Death of which Italian motor manufacturer famed for his high performance racing cars?

ANSWERS
1. Coal. 2. Vincent Auriol. 3. China. 4. The Truman Doctrine. 5. Lord Mountbatten. 6. Kon-Tiki. 7. P.M.S Blackett. 8. Chuck Yeager. 9. George Marshall. 10. Cominform. 11. Benelux. 12. Philip Mountbatten. 13. Palestine. 14. A Streetcar Named Desire. 15. Ettore Bugatti.

How much do you know about 1948?

QUESTIONS.

1. A young Hindu fanatic named Nathuram Godse kills a world leader, idolised by millions. Who?

2. The United Nations General Assembly adopts which central principle?

3. Which new institution is formed which is destined to play a significant international role ?

4. In the U.S., scientists at Bell Telephone invent a type of semi-conductor. What is it called?

5. Which Hungarian-born American inventor produces the first Long Playing record?

6. A communist coup d'etat occurs in Czechoslovakia after the mysterious death of which Czech statesman?

7. Britain, France and the Benelux countries sign which agreement of mutual support?

8. Which new state is proclaimed in the Middle East?

9. The armies of which neighbouring countries invade the new state?

10. U.S.S.R blocks road and rail traffic between Berlin and the West. The Western powers organise what?

11. The new government in South Africa under Daniel Malan introduces which infamous policy?

12. Fourteenth Olympic Games opens in which city?

13. Queen Wilhelmina of the Netherlands abdicates and is succeeded by whom?

14. The United Nations mediator in Palestine is murdered by Jewish terrorists. His name is?

15. Death of the 'Father of Pakistan'. His name?

ANSWERS
1. Mahatma Gandhi. 2. Universal Declaration of Human Rights. 3. World Health Organisation. 4. Solid state transistor. 5. Peter Goldmark. 6. Jan Masaryk. 7. The Brussels Treaty. 8. Israel. 9. Egypt, Jordan, Iraq and Syria. 10. The Berlin Airlift. 11. Apartheid. 12. London. 13. Queen Juliana. 14. Count Folke Bernadotte. 15. Mohammed Ali Jinnah

How much do you know about 1949?

QUESTIONS.

1. Which American scientist publishes theories on Quantum Electrodynamics?

2. Which landmass joins Canada as its tenth province?

3. Which major pact of mutual assistance is signed by eleven countries in Washington?

4. George Orwell publishes a very disturbing book. Its title?

5. In New York, a new musical by Rodgers and Hammerstein opens. Its name?

6. Ten European countries meet in London to found a new European institution. What is it called?

7. The De Havilland 'Comet' makes its first flight. What is so remarkable about it?

8. The U.S.S.R surprises the West by demonstrating what?

9. Which country declares itself to be a Communist Republic?

10. Chinese nationalists under Chiang Kai-shek retreat to where?

11. Which country takes the name Thailand?

12. The Irish Free State declares itself a republic, leaves the Commonwealth, and changes its name to what?

13. The German Federal Republic comes into being and takes which town for its capital?

14. Death of which British comedian, famous for his show ITMA during the war?

15. Which film set in post-war Vienna, co-written by Graham Greene, directed by Carol Reed and starring Orson Welles and Trevor Howard, has its premiere this year?

ANSWERS
1. Richard Feynman. 2. Newfoundland. 3. North Atlantic Treaty. 4. 1984. 5. South Pacific. 6. The Council of Europe. 7. First jet passenger plane. 8. Nuclear capability. 9. China. 10. Formosa. 11. Siam. 12. Eire. 13. Bonn. 14. Tommy Handley. 15. The Third Man.

Year by year 1950–1959

How much do you know about 1950?

QUESTIONS.

1. What does U.S. President Truman instruct the U.S. Atomic Energy Commission to develop?

2. In the U.S which well known State Department official is jailed for perjury?

3. The U.S and Britain formally recognise whom as ruler of South Vietnam?

4. Which party wins the general elections in Britain?

5. Which German-born British atomic scientist is convicted of passing atomic secrets to the U.S.S.R?

6. American nuclear chemist Glenn T. Seaborg, professor at Berkeley University, California, discovers which two elements?

7. Death of which charismatic Russian ballet dancer?

8. For what was Kurt Weill, who dies this year, well-known?

9. What line is fixed as the border between Poland and East Germany?

10. Which European country joins the Council of Europe?

11. War breaks out when South Korea is invaded by forces from which country?

12. Which famous U.S General is appointed commander of U.N forces in Korea?

13. Which U.S Senator causes chaos when he claims that the State Department has been infiltrated by communists?

14. Brazil are beaten by which other South American country in the final of the fourth football World Cup?

15. Chinese troops invade which two countries?

ANSWERS
1. The hydrogen bomb. 2. Alger Hiss. 3. Emperor Bao Dai. 4. The Labour Party. 5. Klaus Fuchs. 6. Berkelium (97) and Californium (98). 7. Vaslav Nijinsky. 8. As a composer. 9. The Oder–Neisse Line. 10. West Germany. 11. North Korea. 12. Douglas MacArthur. 13. Joseph McCarthy. 14. Uruguay. 15. Tibet and South Korea.

How much do you know about 1951?

QUESTIONS.

1. In Korea, North Korean and Chinese troops break through the U.N lines and take the capital of South Korea. Its name?

2. In the U.S, death of Nobel prize winning author Sinclair Lewis. The title of one of his books is still the synonym for middle class vulgarity and the commonplace. What is it?

3. In Germany, death of the designer of Hitler's 'Peoples Car', and of an impressive sports car. His name?

4. The U.S Constitution is amended to limit Presidents to a maximum of two terms. The number of the amendment?

5. The U.N creates a commission to deal with a large andgrowing human problem. What is it named?

6. Which Act of Parliament first passed in 1735, is repealed in Britain?

7. In Europe, the Schuman plan of 1950 leads to the creation of what institution?

8. General MacArthur is relieved of Command in the Far East and replaced by whom?

9. In U.S, a Senate Committee begins hearings on organised crime, under which Senator?

10. In which Middle Eastern country is the oil industry nationalised?

11. Two British diplomats flee in anticipation of exposure as Soviet spies. What are their names?

12. What is the name of the science and technology fair which opens in London, attracting 8 million visitors?

13. In the U.S, which newspaper tycoon dies?

14. Which North African country achieves independence?

15. Nicholas Monsarrat's great novel of the war at sea is published. What is its title?

ANSWERS
1. Seoul. 2. Babbitt. 3. Ferdinand Porsche. 4. 22nd. 5. Commission for Refugees. 6. Witchcraft Act. 7. European Coal and Steel Community. 8. General Matthew Ridgway. 9. Senator Estes Kefauver. 10. Iran. 11. Guy Burgess and Donald Maclean. 12. Festival of Britain. 13. William Randolph Hearst. 14. Libya. 15. The Cruel Sea

How much do you know about 1952?

QUESTIONS.

1. In Britain who succeeds to the throne following the death of King George VII?

2. Who steps down from his post as Supreme Allied Commander in Europe in order to run for Presidency of the U.S?

3. Which Indian statesman becomes Prime Minister?

4. Who is elected first African Prime Minister of Ghana?

5. Fifteenth modern Olympic Games is staged in which city?

6. Which Czech athlete dominates these games?

7. In the U.S, a flying innovation is introduced by T.W.A. What is it?

8. Death of an Italian educationalist who gave her name to a method of teaching children. What is her name?

9. In the U.S, which new form of music is catching on with young people?

10. Death of which charismatic Argentinian figure?

11. A coup d'etat in Egypt forces the abdication of Farouk. Which military leader forms a government?

12. In Jordan, King Talal's reign is terminated by parliamentary decree. He is succeeded by whom?

13. In the U.S, which Vice-Presidential candidate denies charges of corruption in an emotional televised speech?

14. Which heavyweight defeats Jersey Joe Walcott to become World Champion?

15. A State of Emergency is declared in which East African country due to the actions of the Mau-Mau Nationalists?

ANSWERS
1. Queen Elizabeth II. 2. Dwight D. Eisenhower. 3. Pandit Nehru. 4. Kwame Nkrumah. 5. Helsinki. 6. Emil Zatopek. 7. Tourist class. 8. Maria Montessori. 9. Rock 'n' roll. 10. Eva Peron. 11. General Neguib. 12. King Hussein. 13. Richard Nixon. 14. Rocky Marciano. 15. Kenya.

How much do you know about 1953?

QUESTIONS.

1. Which Army officer is elected first President of the Republic of Yugoslavia?

2. Discovery of double helix structure of DNA announced by whom?

3. Death of the most powerful dictator in history. But what is Joseph Stalin's real name?

4. Swedish statesman Dag Hammarskjold is appointed to a very important international position. What is it?

5. In the U.S, which feather-ruffling male-oriented magazine is published for the first time?

6. Massive flooding kills over 1,000 people in which low-lying European country?

7. Which middle eastern country is declared a Republic?

8. Mount Everest is finally conquered by a New Zealander and a Nepalese sherpa. Their names please?

9. Soviet forces brutally suppress a workers' uprising in which city?

10. Which 'apparatchik' is appointed first secretary of the Soviet communist party?

11. In Kenya, who is convicted of leading the Mau Mau uprising?

12. In Germany which statesman forms a new government is formed?

13. Death of Americas leading dramatist, winner of both the Pulitzer prize and the Nobel prize. His name?

14. Which 1912 archaelogical discovery is now shown to have been a fraud?

15. The ex-Minister of the Soviet Interior is executed. His name please?

ANSWERS
1. Marshal Josip Tito. 2. Francis Crick and J D Watson. 3. Iosif Dzhugashvili. 4. U.N Secretary-General. 5. Playboy. 6. The Netherlands. 7. Egypt. 8. Edmund Hillary and Tenzing Norgay. 9. East Berlin. 10. Nikita Kruschev. 11. Jomo Kenyatta. 12. Konrad Adenauer. 13. Eugene O'Neill. 14. Piltdown Man. 15. Lavrenty Beria.

How much do you know about 1954?

QUESTIONS.

1. The fifth football World Cup is won by which country?

2. The U.S launches its first nuclear powered submarine, named...?

3. A Greek terrorist organisation is formed to fight for the union of Cyprus with Greece. What is it called?

4. In the U.S, Dr Jonas Salk develops a vaccine for the treatment of which disease?

5. And who does baseball hero Joe DiMaggio marry?

6. Power in Egypt is taken over – briefly – by whom?

7. Which European wide television network is formed?

8. During rebuilding in the City of London, an historically interesting structure is uncovered. What is it?

9. In Indochina, French troops surrender to the VietMinh, after the siege of which village?

10. In the U.S racial segregation in schools is outlawed by which legal authority?

11. Meeting of President Eisenhower and Prime Minister Churchill in Washington. Which six point declaration of Western Policy is issued?

12. Plans for a European Defence Community are wrecked by the rejection of which National parliament?

13. Death of which French artist, renowned for his use of colour?

14. Anti-French uprising in which North African colony?

15. First part of the trilogy The Lord of the Rings published, by which English philologist?

ANSWERS
1. West Germany. 2. U.S.S Nautilus. 3. EOKA. 4. Dr Jonas Salk. 5. Marilyn Monroe. 6. Colonel Nasser. 7. Eurovision. 8. A temple to the ancient Persian god Mithras. 9. Dien Bien Phu. 10. Supreme Court. 11. The Potomac Charter. 12. The French. 13. Henri Matisse. 14. Algeria. 15. J.R.R Tolkien.

How much do you know about 1955?

QUESTIONS.

1. Britain in dispute with Argentina and Chile about what?

2. What is the name of the science fiction writer who creates the Church of Scientology?

3. Premier Malenkov of the U.S.S.R. resigns. He is succeeded by whom?

4. Iraq and Turkey sign an agreement of mutual defence. What is the agreement called?

5. Death of American jazz saxophonist with an enormous international following. What is his name?

6. The worlds most celebrated scientist dies at his home in Princeton, New Jersey. His name?

7. At a meeting in Prague, Soviet Prime Minister Bulganin and the leaders of the other Eastern bloc nations, sign a Treaty of Friendship, Co-operation and Mutual Assistance, known ever afterwards as .... ?

8. West Germany is admitted to membership of which international organisation?

9. A new organisation for the co-ordination of European defence comes into being. What is it called?

10. The Pope excommunicates which South American dictator?

11. Death of a young American film star with 'cult' status. His name please?

12. Publication of the diary of a young Dutch Jewish girl who died in a concentration camp. Who was she?

13. First performance in London of which Samuel Beckett play?

14. The film The Blackboard Jungle launches a rock song destined to become a classic. What is it called?

15. In Alabama, U.S.A, a woman is arrested for violating the segregated seating laws on a bus. What is her name?

ANSWERS
1. The Falkland Islands. 2. L. Ron Hubbard. 3. N.A Bulganin. 4. Baghdad Pact. 5. Charlie 'Bird' Parker. 6. Albert Einstein. 7. The Warsaw Pact. 8. NATO. 9. The Western European Union. 10. Peron of Argentina. 11. James Dean. 12. Anne Frank. 13. Waiting For Godot. 14. Rock Around The Clock. 15. Rosa Parks.

How much do you know about 1956?

QUESTIONS.

1. Which French North African colonies gain independence?

2. Death of which Hungarian born British film-maker?

3. Which British soldier loses command of the Arab Legion?

4. Which film does British MP Robert Boothby call for the banning of, following disturbances around the country?

5. Which country of the Commonwealth declares itself an Islamic Republic?

6. President Nasser nationalises the Suez Canal, leading to the invasion of Egypt by forces of which three countries?

7. Brutal suppression by Soviet forces of uprising in which Eastern bloc country, calling for more democracy?

8. Which Far Eastern country is admitted to the United Nations?

9. In the U.S who does leading American dramatist Arthur Miller marry?

10. And American film star Grace Kelly marries whom?

11. Scientists working at the Los Alamos Laboratory, U.S.A detect the existence of particles without electrical charges. What do they call them?

12. Britain starts up its largest nuclear power station to date. Where is it situated?

13. Which famous Russian ballet company visits London?

14. Sixteenth modern Olympic games staged in which city?

15. Death of British chemist, close colleague of Sir Ernest Rutherford, and inventor of the term 'isotope'. His name ?

ANSWERS
1. Morocco and Tunisia. 2. Sir Alexander Korda. 3. Glubb Pasha. 4. Rock Around The Clock. 5. Pakistan. 6. Britain, France and Israel. 7. Hungary. 8. Japan. 9. Marilyn Monroe. 10. Prince Rainier of Morocco. 11. Neutrinos. 12. Calder Hall. 13. The Bolshoi. 14. Melbourne. 15. Frederick Soddy.

How much do you know about 1957?

QUESTIONS.

1. In Britain, Prime Minister Anthony Eden resigns. Who is his successor?

2. In the U.S.S.R., who is appointed Foreign Secretary?

3. Which West African country becomes an independent State within the Commonwealth and joins the U.N?

4. In the U.S., the Senate approves the use of U.S. forces to protect political independence of Middle East States. How is this proposition known?

5. Belgium, France, West Germany, Italy, Luxembourg and The Netherlands sign what document to create a Common Market?

6. Martial law is declared in which Middle Eastern state?

7. Which Far Eastern island and former British possession becomes a self-governing state?

8. Death of which German born film actor and director?

9. In Canada, the Progressive Conservatives win the elections. Who becomes Prime Minister?

10. A new organisation is formed to try to control the spread of use of Atomic Energy. What is it called?

11. Death of which Finnish composer and patriot?

12. Queen Elizabeth II visits Canada and the U.S. and addresses which assembly?

13. A regular air service opens between London and which other capital city?

14. In U.S, Leonard Bernstein's new musical based on Romeo and Juliet opens in New York. What is it called?

15. One of Hollywoods favourite 'tough guys' loses the battle against cancer. What is his name?

ANSWERS
1. Harold Macmillan. 2. Andrei Gromyko. 3. Ghana. 4. The Eisenhower Doctrine. 5. The Treaty of Rome. 6. Jordan. 7. Singapore. 8. Erich von Stroheim. 9. John Diefenbacker. 10. International Atomic Energy Agency. 11. Jean Sibelius. 12. United Nations. 13. Moscow. 14. West Side Story. 15. Humphrey Bogart.

How much do you know about 1958?

QUESTIONS.

1. In China, Mao Tse-tung launches a modernisation programme. What is it called?
   2. A dispute over fishing rights between Britain and Iceland rumbles on into the 70s and becomes known as ?

3. In the U.S, what do scientists begin measuring?

4. And what giant space exploration agency is created?

5. U.S nuclear powered submarine Nautilus goes where?

6. Russian poet and author Boris Pasternak publishes his romance of the Russian revolution, entitled what?

7. An air crash in Germany kills eight members of the Manchester United football team. By what name were the team affectionately known?

8. What anti-nuclear arms organisation is founded in Britain?

9. In Haiti, an abortive coup gives the President the chance to take dictatorial powers. What is his name?

10. Which nation wins the football World Cup final?

11. Leslie Caron and Maurice Chevallier co-star in which film?

12. A giant exhibition in Belgium attracts 40,000,000 visitors. What is it called?

13. British author Lawrence Durrell publishes the first part of his Alexandrian Quartet. What is it called?

14. A world conference on the law of the sea is held where?

15. 1958 was also designated as what?

ANSWERS
1. The Great Leap Forward. 2. The Cod War. 3. The ozone layer. 4. NASA. 5. Under the North Pole. 6. Dr Zhivago. 7. Busby's Babes. 8. Campaign for Nuclear Disarmament. 9. Francois 'Papa Doc' Duvalier. 10. Brazil. 11. Gigi. 12. Brussels World Fair. 13. Justine. 14. Geneva. 15. International Geophysical Year.

How much do you know about 1959?

QUESTIONS.

1. Which charismatic rebel leader defeated the dictator of Cuba, turning it into a communist state?

2. In France, which wartime hero returns as President of the Fifth Republic?

3. The Republics of Senegal and French Sudan unite to form which Federal State?

4. What is rejected by a referendum in Switzerland on Federal elections?

5. A Soviet spacecraft is the first to escape Earth's gravity. What is it called?

6. In the U.S, which 'epic' film maker dies this year?

7.   And which creator of the 'hard-boiled private eye'?

8. In Tibet, an uprising against Chinese occupation fails. Which Buddhist leader is forced to flee to India?

9. In Japan, Crown Prince Akihito breaks with thousands of years of tradition. How?

10. First meeting at Strasbourg of which supra-national legal body?

11. And which 'special' year begins on June 1st, designed to draw attention to a human rights problem?

12. First crossing of the channel by a Hovercraft, invented by whom?

13. Which two new states join the Union, to become the 49th and 50th respectively?

14. Seven European and Scandinavian countries sign a trading agreement to become what?

15. Bernard Miles opens a theatre in the City of London, the first for 300 years. What is its name?

ANSWERS
1. Fidel Castro. 2. Charles de Gaulle. 3. Mali. 4. Female suffrage. 5. Lunik I. 6. Cecil B. De Mille. 7. Raymond Chandler. 8. The Dalai Lama. 9. By marrying a commoner. 10. European Court of Human Rights. 11. World Refugee Year. 12. Christopher Cockerill. 13. Alaska and Hawaii. 14. European Free Trade Association. 15. The Mermaid Theatre.

Year by year 1960–1969

How much do you know about 1960?

QUESTIONS.

1. By what name does the new military force, formed this year by North Vietnam, become widely known?

2. Israeli agents abduct from Argentina the Nazi officer responsible for the Jewish 'Final Solution' His name?

3. The novel Lady Chatterley's Lover is the subject of an obscenity trial in Britain. What is its author's name ?

4. Which underwater pioneer descends to a depth of more than 10 km, to the bottom of the worlds deepest abyss, the Mariana Trench, in a bathyscape?

5. South African police shoot down unarmed protesters in which town?

6. Which Ceylonese leader becomes the first female Prime Minister in the Commonwealth?

7. British Prime Minister addresses the South African Parliament in Cape Town; warns about what?

8. Which city is named the new capital of Brazil?

9. Seventeenth modern Olympic games staged in which city?

10. And which American boxer wins a gold medal at the games?

11. What is the name of the American pilot of the U2 Spy plane shot down in the Soviet Union?

12. Who becomes head of the Soviet state?

13. In the U.S the Presidential elections are won by the Democrat Senator from Massachusetts. His name?

14. In Paris, The U.S, Canada and 18 European Community member states sign a convention to create which Atlantic economic community?

15. First performance of Robert Bolt's play about Sir Thomas More. What is it called?

ANSWERS
1. The Vietcong. 2. Adolf Eichmann. 3. D. H. Lawrence. 4. Jacques Piccard. 5. Sharpeville. 6. Sirimavo Bandarainake. 7. The 'Wind of Change in Africa'. 8. Brasilia. 9. Rome. 10. Cassius Clay (Muhammad Ali). 11. Gary Powers. 12. Leonid Brezhnev. 13. John F. Kennedy. 14. Organisation for Economic Co-operation and Development. 15. A Man For All Seasons.

How much do you know about 1961?

QUESTIONS.

1. In the U.S, a voluntary body to provide practical help anywhere in the world is formed. Its name?

2. An international organisation designed to protect wild animals the world over is founded. Its name please?

3. Assassination of former leader of the Congo. His name?

4. A Soviet cosmonaut becomes the first man in space. What is his name?

5. A U.S-backed invasion of Cuba goes sadly awry, with most of the Cuban exile invaders being killed or captured. Where did they land?

6. A KGB spy in Britain is sentenced to 42 years in prison. His name please?

7. Which country declares its independence of Britain, becomes a Republic and leaves the Commonwealth?

8. Which former German Nazi is found guilty in Israel of crimes against the Jewish people during the Holocaust?

9. Death of which influential Swiss psychologist?

10. East Germany closes border with West in Berlin. Construction begins on what monument to communism?

11. The President of Iraq declares that which neighbouring state is an integral part of his country?

12. Who becomes acting Secretary General of the U.N following the death of Dag Hammarskjold in an air crash?

13. Tanganyika gains independence under which Prime Minister?

14. John Osborne's new play opens in London, entitled?

15. Which U.S astronaut pioneers re-entry through the atmosphere in a capsule?

ANSWERS
1. The Peace Corps. 2. World Wildlife Fund. 3. Patrice Lumumba. 4. Yuri Gagarin. 5. Bay of Pigs. 6. George Blake. 7. South Africa. 8. Adolf Eichmann. 9. Carl Jung. 10. The Berlin Wall. 11. Kuwait. 12. U Thant. 13. Julius Nyerere. 14. Luther. 15. Alan Shepherd.

How much do you know about 1962?

QUESTIONS.

1. The member nations of the European Economic Community reach agreement on their first major policy. Which one?

2. Who is the first U.S astronaut to orbit the earth?

3. Which North African colony achieves independence from France?

4. Prime Minister Debre of France resigns and is succeeded by whom?

5. The European Space Research Organisation is founded in which European capital?

6. Death of which American writer and Nobel prize winner?

7. Publication of Capitalism and Freedom by which U.S economist?

8. Death of which Hollywood screen icon?

9. China launches attacks on the border of which neighbouring country?

10. In Britain, an Admiralty clerk is sentenced for spying for the KGB. His name please?

11. U.S blockades which Caribbean island?

12. Riots in which state of the U.S over desegregation of education?

13. Death of the widow of one president, the niece of another, and a great lady in her own right. Her name?

14. In Britain, a fiercely satirical newspaper makes its first appearance. Its name please?

15. Alfred Hitchcock's new film opens, based on a story by Daphne du Maurier about attacks on humans from an unexpected quarter. What is it called?

ANSWERS
1. Common Agricultural Policy. 2. John Glenn. 3. Algeria. 4. Georges Pompidou. 5. Paris. 6. William Faulkner. 7. Milton Friedman. 8. Marilyn Monroe. 9. India. 10. William Vassall. 11. Cuba. 12. Mississippi. 13. Eleanor Roosevelt. 14. Private Eye. 15. The Birds.

How much do you know about 1963?

QUESTIONS.

1. What is the name of the leader of the British Labour Party who dies aged 56?

2. And the name of the former MI6 agent who turned out to be a Soviet spy and had to seek asylum in the Soviet Union?

3. In the U.S which infamous prison on a small, rocky island off San Francisco is closed for good?

4. What is the name of the Premier of Nyasaland who leads his country to independence?

5. In Canada, who forms a government after the resignation of John Diefenbaker?

6. What is the name of the KGB officer sentenced to death in the Soviet Union, for spying for the West?

7. Which British government minister resigns after lying to the Commons about an extra-marital relationship?

8. An earthquake in Yugoslavia destroys which ancient city?

9. What first did Valentina Tereshkova achieve?

10. In the U.S, which charismatic Black leader heads a civil rights march to Washington?

11. Malaya, North Borneo, Sarawak and Singapore form a new national grouping. What is it called?

12. Death of which much admired French singer?

13. One day which remains fixed in the memory of all who were alive at the time, is 22/11/63. Why?

14. The book Silent Spring about the dangers of chemical pest control is published. By whom?

15. And whose disc She Loves You makes the 'Liverpool sound' famous?

ANSWERS
1. Hugh Gaitskell. 2. Kim Philby. 3. Alcatraz. 4. Hastings Banda. 5. Lester Pearson. 6. Oleg Penkovsky. 7. John Profumo. 8. Skopje. 9. First woman into space. 10. Martin Luther King. 11. Federation of Malaysia. 12. Edith Piaf. 13. The assassination of President Kennedy. 14. Rachel Carson. 15. The Beatles.

How much do you know about 1964?

QUESTIONS.

1. Who becomes the first premier of an independent Northern Rhodesia, renamed Zambia?

2. Who takes control of South Vietnam after a military coup?

3. In the U.S, Cassius Clay defeats who in the World Heavyweight Boxing Championship?

4. In the U.S, President Johnson presents a $344 million project to Congress. For what purpose?

5. U.N peace-keeping force arrives in which Eastern Mediterranean island?

6. A "Pirate Radio" ship begins broadcasting off the east coast of England. What is its name?

7. In Southern Rhodesia, who forms a government?

8. Zanzibar and Tanganyika unite to become…?

9. Which leader of the A.N.C is sentenced by a South African court to life imprisonment for treason?

10. Which great piece of civil engineering is opened in Egypt?

11. Spy swop. Soviet spy Gordon Lonsdale is exchanged for which British spy?

12. In the Gulf of Tonkin, North Vietnamese torpedo boats attack a U.S destroyer. What is the name of the destroyer?

13. What is the name of the U.S Supreme Court Chief Justice who issues his report on the Kennedy assassination?

14. Where do the eighteenth modern Olympic Games take place?

15. In Britain a new Labour government is formed under which Prime Minister?

ANSWERS
1. Kenneth Kaunda. 2. Nguven Khanh. 3. Sonny Liston. 4. To combat poverty. 5. Cyprus. 6. Radio Caroline. 7. Ian Smith. 8. Tanzania. 9. Nelson Mandela. 10. Aswan Dam. 11. Greville Wynne. 12. U.S.S Maddox. 13. Earl Warren. 14. Tokyo. 15. Harold Wilson.

How much do you know about 1965?

QUESTIONS.

1. Who died of a stroke at his London home aged 90 and receives the first state funeral for a commoner since the death of the Duke of Wellington in 1852?

2. In the U.S, which Black Muslim leader is shot dead in Manhattan?

3. Death of which American pianist and singer?

4. A Russian cosmonaut is the first man to 'walk in space'. His name please?

5. In Britain two political celebrations take place. What are they, and what do they celebrate?

6. American forces invade which Caribbean island?

7. Which U.S satellite transmits close-ups of Mars?

8. Yale University Press claim that the 'Vinland Map' proves America was discovered in 11th century, by whom?

9. Which Scots motor racing champion wins six Grand Prix titles plus the Indianapolis 500?

10. After the resignation of Sir Alec Douglas-Home, who becomes leader of the Conservatives in his place?

11. Death in Equatorial Africa of the man described as 'the noblest figure of the 20th Century'. What is his name?

12. A 'Unilateral Declaration of Independence' is made by which member of the Commonwealth?

13. Where are new reserves of oil discovered?

14. Death of influential Swiss architect Charles Edouard Jeanneret, better known by which pseudonym?

15. In the U.S, Norman Mailer publishes a new novel. What is it called?

ANSWERS
1. Sir Winston Churchill. 2. Malcolm 'X'. 3. Nat King Cole. 4. Alexei Leonov. 5. Magna Carta, and the 700th anniversary of the founding of Parliament. 6. Dominican Republic. 7. Mariner IV. 8. Leif Ericsson. 9. Jim Clark. 10. Edward Heath. 11. Albert Schweitzer. 12. Rhodesia. 13. In the North Sea. 14. Le Corbusier. 15. An American Dream.

How much do you know about 1966?

QUESTIONS.

1. What is the name of the new ideological police in China?

2. In the U.S, the militant black rights group 'The Black Panthers' is founded by whom?

3. What is the name given to the Vietcong network of supply routes from North to South Vietnam, through Laos?

4. What is the name of the soldier on active duty who sells over a million copies of The Ballad of the Green Berets?

5. Which cult television programme begins its run?

6. In India, who becomes the new Prime Minister?

7. In China, over 400,000 die due to which of Mao Tse-tung's latest brainchilds?

8. In South Africa, the Prime Minister and architect of Apartheid is assassinated. His name please?

9. France withdraws from which international body?

10. Which American comedian dies from a drug overdose?

11. In the final of the football World Cup, England beat Germany. But which country did they beat in the semi-finals?

12. In the final, Geoff Hurst scored a hat-trick. But who scored the other goal for England?

13. And who captained England on that day?

14. Who has a hit with Strangers in the Night?

15. Death of which Hollywood comedy legend?

ANSWERS
1. The Red Guard. 2. Bobby Seale and Huey Newton. 3. Ho Chi Minh Trail. 4. Sergeant Barry Sadler. 5. Star Trek. 6. Indira Gandhi. 7. Cultural Revolution. 8. Dr Hendrik Verwoerd. 9. NATO. 10. Lenny Bruce. 11. Portugal. 12. Martin Peters. 13. Bobby Moore. 14. Frank Sinatra. 15. Buster Keaton.

How much do you know about 1967?

QUESTIONS.

1. Which spacecraft blows up on the launch pad at Cape Kennedy, killing three astronauts?

2. What is the name of the oil tanker which goes aground in Cornwall, causing severe environmental damage?

3. In Britain what new tests are introduced to identify drivers who have had too much to drink?

4. And which new surgical operation holds out new hope for people with heart problems?

5. Cambridge radio astronomers discover a source of rapid, regular pulses of radio waves. What do they christen them?

6. Which British yachtsman completes the first solo round-the-world expedition?

7. In New York, the first 'hippie' musical opens. Its name?

8. Death of which British driver, attempting to break the world water speed record?

9. Who rigs the elections to become President of Nicaragua?

10, Svetlana Alliluyeva defects from the Soviet Union to the West. Her parenthood makes this very newsworthy. Why?

11. Which province tries, unsuccessfully, to break away from the newly independent Nigeria?

12. War flares up again between Israel and her Arab neighbours. What name is given to this outbreak?

13. Death of influential American jazz saxophonist. His name?

14. First heart transplant operation successfully carried out by a South African surgeon. What is his name?

15. Which Columbian writer publishes his most famous work One Hundred Years of Solitude?

ANSWERS
1. Saturn 1. 2. The Torrey Canyon. 3. Breathalysers. 4. Coronary by-pass operation. 5. Pulsars. 6. Francis Chichester. 7. Hair. 8. Donald Campbell. 9. Anastasio Somoza. 10. She is the dughter of the late Joseph Stalin. 11. Biafra. 12. Six Day War. 13. John Coltrane. 14. Christian Barnard. 15. Gabriel Garcia Marquez.

How much do you know about 1968?

QUESTIONS.

1. German terrorist group the 'Red Army Faction' is founded. By what other name was the group known?

2. After the resignation of Antonin Novotny as First Secretary of the Czech Communist Party, who takes over?

3. What is the name of the U.S intelligence-gathering boat captured by the North Koreans?

4. What name is given to the co-ordinated attack launched on over 100 urban areas of South Vietnam by the Vietcong?

5. April 4th 1968, Memphis, Tennessee. Martin Luther King is assassinated. Who is eventually convicted of his murder?

6. Which British politician attacks the concept of a peaceful multiracial Britain, with his rivers of blood speech?

7. Which Democrat candidate for the U.S Presidency is murdered by a Palestinian immigrant?

8. Which Canadian politician becomes Prime Minister?

9. Warsaw pact countries find Czech reforms unacceptable and invade, putting an end to what came to be known as…?

10. Nineteenth modern Olympic games open in which city?

11. In the U.S, who is the Republican candidate who is elected President?

12. Death of which American Nobel Prize-winning author?

13. U.S. astronauts orbit the Moon for the first time. What is the name of their spacecraft?

14. Which company is founded to develop and manufacture microchips?

15. And Dustin Hoffman stars alongside Anne Bancroft as…?

ANSWERS
1. The Baader–Meinhoff Gang. 2. Alexander Dubcek. 3. U.S.S Pueblo. 4. The Tet Offensive. 5. James Earl Ray. 6. Enoch Powell. 7. Robert Kennedy. 8. Pierre Trudeau. 9. Prague Spring. 10. Mexico. 11. Richard Nixon. 12. John Steinbeck. 13. Apollo 8. 14. Intel. 15. The Graduate.

How much do you know about 1969?

QUESTIONS.

1. U.S Forces bomb Vietcong positions, not in Vietnam but in which neighbouring country?

2. In the U.S, a new home-grown group of terrorists begins activities. What is its name?

3. In Britain, the voting age is set at what age?

4. And which form of punishment is abolished by law?

5. The U.S government launches an anti-trust action against which business giant?

6. Who is the Australian newspaper magnate who buys The Sun?

7. A Czech student immolates himself in protest at Soviet occupation of his country. What is his name?

8. Who becomes leader of the P.L.O?

9. What is the mission called which sees American astronauts walk on the Moon?

10. Who succeeds as President of France after the resignation of Charles de Gaulle?

11. In mid-August a 'happening' occurrs at Bethel in up-state New York. What is it called?

12. Death of which American jazz saxophonist?

13. Senator Edward Kennedy has an accident in which his car passenger drowns. Where does this happen?

14. What is the name of the black journalist and author of Soul On Ice who becomes 'Minister of Information' for the Black Panthers?

15. Death of which much-beloved American singer and actress?

ANSWERS
1. Cambodia. 2. Weathermen. 3. 18. 4. Capital punishment. 5. IBM. 6. Rupert Murdoch. 7. Jan Palach. 8. Yasser Arafat. 9. Apollo 11. 10. Alain Poher. 11. Woodstock. 12. Coleman Hawkins. 13. Chappaquiddick. 14. Eldridge Cleaver. 15. Judy Garland.

Year by year 1970–1979

How much do you know about 1970?

QUESTIONS.

1. In the U.S.A., an 'ecologically friendly' organisation is founded. What is its name?

2. The underground train system opens in which Central American city?

3. Which new advanced educational organisation aimed at adults is launched in the U.K?

4. Palestinian terrorists kill 47 people and destroy an airliner belonging to which airline?

5. Death of Britain's greatest logician and philosopher. Who was he?

6. A massive earthquake kills over 70,000 in which South American country?

7. Death of which dictator who has dominated Portuguese politics for over thirty years?

8. Salvador Allende wins the Presidential elections in which South American country?

9. Who succeeds as President of Egypt after the death of Nasser?

10. Death of which American rock guitarist?

11. What is the name of the Japanese writer who commits ritual suicide?

12. Riots in which Polish port over food shortages?

13. Canadian Minister of Labour, Pierre Laporte, is kidnapped and murdered by whom?

14. In the U.S, I.B.M develops a major aid to effective I.T. What is it?

15. Australian feminist Germaine Greer publishes a thought-provoking work entitled…?

ANSWERS
1. Environmental Protection Agency. 2. Mexico. 3. Open University. 4. Swissair. 5. Bertrand Russell. 6. Peru. 7. Antonio Salazar. 8. Chile. 9. Anwar Sadat. 10. Jimi Hendrix. 11. Yukio Mishima. 12. Gdansk. 13. Quebec separatists. 14. The floppy disk. 15. The Female Eunuch.

How much do you know about 1971?

QUESTIONS.

1. Which Soviet space probe is the first to land on Mars?

2. Which environmental pressure group is founded?

3. A new development in medicine allows doctors to see inside the patient's stomach. What is it called?

4. The I.T company INTEL pushes back the frontiers of information processing with the development of… what?

5. In New York, which major musical by Andrew Lloyd-Webber and Tim Rice opens?

6. There is a military coup in Uganda. Milton Obote is deposed. Who takes control of the country?

7. In Britain, life is simplified in one stroke. How?

8. In the U.S, which heavyweight boxing champion defeats Muhammad Ali to retain his world title?

9. Which East German 'apparatchik' succeeds Party Leader Walter Ulbricht after his resignation?

10. The New York Times begins publication of what report showing how the U.S. military had misrepresented its involvement in Vietnam?

11. In the U.S, the 26th amendment to the Constitution is ratified by Congress. What does it do?

12. Death of internationally loved American trumpet player, one of the fathers of Jazz. Who is it?

13. Mysterious death of American rock legend, lead singer of The Doors. What was his name?

14. Bangladesh declares its independence. What was its name previously?

15. Which populous nation is finally allowed to become a member of the United Nations?

ANSWERS
1. Mars 3. 2. Greenpeace. 3. Endoscopy. 4. The micro-processor. 5. Jesus Christ Superstar. 6. Idi Amin. 7. The pound goes decimal. 8. Joe Frazier. 9. Erich Honecker. 10. The 'Pentagon Papers'. 11. Lowers voting age to 18. 12. Louis Armstrong. 13. Jim Morrison. 14. East Pakistan. 15. Communist China.

How much do you know about 1972?

QUESTIONS.

1. Who declares martial law and assumes dictatorial powers in the Philippines?

2. Which anti-terrorist measure is rescinded in Northern Ireland by William Whitelaw?

3. Who becomes world chess champion by defeating Boris Spassky?

4. Nineteenth modern Olympic games are staged in which city?

5. Which brutal event marks these games out from all others?

6. Which American swimmer wins 7 gold medals?

7. Death of which legendary French actor and singer?

8. President Nixon becomes the first U.S President to visit which Communist country?

9. NASA launches Pioneer 10, an unmanned mission. To which planet?

10. Death of a former British monarch, now called…?

11. In the U.S, death of which former head of the FBI?

12. In June, Washington police arrest five intruders in the Democratic Party headquarters, leading to which major political scandal?

13. The Governor of Alabama is paralysed after an assassination attempt. What is his name?

14. Death of which American poet who had sided with the Italian fascists in the war and spent many years in an asylum for the insane?

15. A new system for instant photographs is marketed. What is it called?

ANSWERS
1. Ferdinand Marcos. 2. Internment without trial. 3. Bobby Fischer. 4. Munich. 5. Murder of Israeli athletes by PLO terrorists. 6. Mark Spitz. 7. Maurice Chevalier. 8. China. 9. Jupiter. 10. Duke of Windsor. 11. J. Edgar Hoover. 12. Watergate. 13. George Wallace. 14. Ezra Pound. 15. Polaroid.

How much do you know about 1973?

QUESTIONS.

1. Britain, Ireland and which other country join the E.E.C.?

2. The musical A Little Night Music opens in New York. Who is it by?

3. In the U.S, who knocks out Joe Frazier to become world heavyweight champion?

4. Death of perhaps the most influential artist of the 20th century. Born in Spain, he dies in Provence, aged 91. Who is he?

5. British Honduras changes its name to…what?

6. Which country abolishes the monarchy, and proclaims itself a republic?

7. Which CIA-backed army general and evil git stages a coup in Chile, and murders the elected President?

8. Death of which U.S film director, renowned for his Westerns?

9. Egypt and Syria attack Israel on which Jewish holy day?

10. Meanwhile, Britain is embroiled in a 'war' of its own, over fishing rights. With which other country?

11. Mass kidnapping of schoolchildren by terrorists in which East African country?

12. Which mainly Arab agency holds the world to ransom and quadruples the price of crude oil?

13. Which Bernardo Bertolucci film, starring Marlon Brando, upsets the censors with its idiosyncratic use of dairy produce?

14. In which country is a state of emergency declared, and a three-day working week and petrol rationing introduced?

15. What does France resume on Mururoa Atoll, despite protests from virtually every country in the region?

ANSWERS
1. Denmark. 2. Stephen Sondheim. 3. George Foreman. 4. Pablo Picasso. 5. Belize. 6. Greece. 7. General Augusto Pinochet. 8. John Ford. 9. Yom Kippur. 10. Iceland. 11. Rhodesia. 12. Organisation of Petroleum Exporting Countries. 13. Last Tango in Paris. 14. Great Britain. 15. Nuclear testing.

How much do you know about 1974?

QUESTIONS.

1. Death of U.S film producer, famous for his malapropisms. His name?

2. Patty Hearst, daughter of the chairman of the Hearst media empire is kidnapped by which would-be revolutionaries?

3. Which British Prime Minister goes to the polls under the slogan 'Who runs the country?', and loses?

4. Which dissident and author of The Gulag Archipelago is deported from the Soviet Union?

5. Which Labour leader forms a minority government in Britain?

6. An IRA attempt to kidnap which member of the British Royal family is foiled?

7. Which Israeli Prime Minister resigns?

8. In France, after the death of Georges Pompidou, who is elected President?

9. Which band wins the Eurovision Song Contest, launching them on a career of international stardom and outlandish stage costumes?

10. Death of which legendary U.S composer and pianist?

11. What is the name of the East German spy who had become a close aide to West Germany's Chancellor Willy Brandt, obliging Brandt to resign?

12. Troops from which country invade Cyprus?

13. U.S. President Nixon resigns; is replaced by whom?

14. In Britain which peer disappears after the murder of his children's nanny?

15. In the U.S, the mysterious death of a female worker in a nuclear plant occurs before she can reveal safety flaws. Her name?

ANSWERS
1. Sam Goldwyn. 2. Symbionese Liberation Army. 3. Alexander Solzhenitsyn. 4. Harold Wilson. 5. Princess Anne. 6. Golda Meir. 7. Valery Giscard d'Estaing. 8. Abba (the song is Waterloo). 9. Duke Ellington. 10. Gunter Guillaume. 11. Turkey. 12. Gerald Ford. 13. Edward Heath. 14. Lord Lucan. 15. Karen Silkwood.

How much do you know about 1975?

QUESTIONS.

1. Who is the British doctor imprisoned and tortured in Chile?

2. The 'colonels' junta' of former leaders of which country are convicted of treason and imprisoned?

3. In the U.S, what are marketed for the first time?

4. And which computer software company, destined to have a major impact in the future, is founded?

5. Europe shows its willingness to get into the space industry by the creation of what organisation?

6. The British Conservative Party chooses whom as its first female leader?

7. Death of the Greek shipping magnate who married the widow of a late U.S. President. His name?

8. Death of long-term President of Nationalist China. What was his name?

9. In which European country is there a military coup, followed by several months of Communist inspired unrest, followed by a seizure of power by the moderate left?

10. Which African countries gain their independence from Portugal?

11. In a rare example of space friendliness, the U.S spacecraft Apollo 18 docks with which Soviet spacecraft?

12. Which Soviet scientist and dissident wins the Nobel Prize for Peace?

13. A group of people are sentenced to life imprisonment in the U.K, after being convicted of an IRA bombing campaign. How do they come to be known?

14. Which British journalist is murdered by the IRA?

15. Who ascends the throne of Spain, after the death of Franco?

ANSWERS
1. Sheila Cassidy. 2. Greece. 3. Personal computers. 4. Microsoft. 5. European Space Agency. 6. Margaret Thatcher. 7. Aristotle Onassis. 8. Chiang Kai-Shek. 9. Portugal. 10. Mozambique and Angola. 11. Soyuz 19. 12. Andrei Sakharov. 13. The Guildford Four. 14. Ross McWhirter. 15. King Juan Carlos.

How much do you know about 1976?

QUESTIONS.

1. What is the name of the U.S aircraft manufacturer around which a bribery and corruption scandal breaks?

2. What is founded in Northern Ireland by Mairead Corrigan and Betty Williams?

3. Which Anglo-French supersonic airliner begins commercial flights?

4. In the U.S, Steve Jobs and Stephen Wozniak begin manufacture of which new desktop computer?

5. And Australian born media mogul Rupert Murdoch buys which leading U.S newspaper?

6. The oil industry in which South American country is nationalised?

7. After a fiery anti-Communist speech by Margaret Thatcher, what nickname is given to her by the Soviet newspaper Red Star?

8. Death of the British doyenne of mystery writers. Who is she?

9. At the 21st Olympic Games in Montreal, for the first time ever, a gymnast achieves 7 perfect scores of 10. Who?

10. In Britain, who succeeds as Prime Minister after the resignation of Harold Wilson?

11. In the U.S death of one of the worlds richest men, who became a total recluse. His name?

12. In what turns out to be a bad year for the rich, the world's richest man also dies this year. What is his name?

13. The Israeli Army rescues hostages held where?

14. In U.S the 200th Anniversary of what event is celebrated?

15. And which Democrat candidate is elected President?

ANSWERS
1. Lockheed. 2. The Peace Movement. 3. Concorde. 4. Apple. 5. New York Post. 6. Venezuela. 7. The 'Iron Lady'. 8. Agatha Christie. 9. Nadia Comaneci of Romania. 10. James Callaghan. 11. Howard Hughes. 12. Jean Paul Getty. 13. Entebbe, Uganda. 14. Declaration of Independence. 15. Jimmy Carter.

How much do you know about 1977?

QUESTIONS.

1. At great risk to themselves Czech dissidents publish a human rights manifesto called…what?

2. In the U.K, what event is celebrated by Queen and country?

3. Punk band the Sex Pistols offer their own musical tribute to the Queen. What is the record called?

4. The world of rock 'n' roll is further shaken by the death of one its favourite sons in the U.S. Who is it?

5. New York is terrorized by a series of murders carried out by a killer calling himself…what?

6. Who is the new Israeli Prime Minister?

7. First elections held for 41 years in which country?

8. Who has the dubious honour of becoming the first person executed in the U.S for over ten years?

9. Who takes over as leader in China?

10. NASA launches two probes to explore the outer planetary system. What are they called?

11. A 30-year-old black activist is found dead in his police cell in South Africa. What is his name?

12. The first film of what becomes the highest-grossing trilogy in the history of cinema is released. What is its name?

13. And the death of which beautiful, fiery, Greek opera diva?

14. In Britain, which horse wins the Grand National for an unprecedented third time?

15. Which English-born comic genius, writer, director and star of many silent film comedies also dies this year?

ANSWERS
1. Charter 77. 2. The Queen's Silver Jubilee. 3. God Save The Queen. 4. Elvis Presley. 5. Son of Sam. 6. Menachem Begin. 7. Spain. 8. Gary Gilmore. 9. Deng Xiaoping. 10. Voyagers 1 and 2. 11. Steve Bilko. 12. Star Wars. 13. Maria Callas. 14. Red Rum. 15. Charlie Chaplin.

How much do you know about 1978?

QUESTIONS.

1. Economic refugees start fleeing from Vietnam in their hundreds. What do they come to be known as?

2. A previously unknown moon is found orbiting Pluto. What name is given to it?

3. Soviet probes Venera 11 and 12 land on which planet?

4. What is the name of the supertanker which goes aground on rocks off the Brittany coast, causing an ecological disaster?

5. The Italian terrorists Brigate Rosso abduct and murder the five-times Prime Minister of Italy. What is his name?

6. What is the name of the Bulgarian defector who was murdered in London by the Bulgarian secret police?

7. And how was he killed?

8. Which cartoon strip featuring a particularly obnoxious cat goes into syndication?

9. Which South American country wins the football World Cup?

10. Muhammad Ali loses world heavyweight title (but regains it five months later). To whom does he lose?

11. World's first 'test tube baby' is born in Manchester, England. What is her name?

12. Who succeeds as President of Kenya after the death of Jomo Kenyatta?

13. Death of German aircraft manufacturer with a very evocative name. What is it?

14. Death of much loved U.S. artist whose illustrations were the very symbol of the American way of life. Who is he?

15. Which Pope dies after only 33 days in office?

ANSWERS
1. Boat People. 2. Charon. 3. Venus. 4. Amoco Cadiz. 5. Aldo Moro. 6. Georgi Markov. 7. With a poison-tipped umbrella. 8. Garfield. 9. Argentina. 10. Leon Spinks. 11. Louise Brown. 12. Daniel Arap Moi. 13. Willi Messerschmidt. 14. Norman Rockwell. 15. John Paul I.

How much do you know about 1979?

QUESTIONS.

1. In the U.S a right-of-centre political pressure group is founded. What is it called?

2. Which Middle Eastern monarch is forced into exile by radical Islamists?

3. And which religious leader becomes the de facto dictator of Iran?

4. The invasion of Cambodia (then Kampuchea) by forces from Vietnam, allows the world to see the horrors of what?

5. Which Khmer Rouge leader is principally responsible for the deaths of up to 2.5 million Cambodians?

6. In the U.S, an accident occurs at which nuclear power plant?

7. Death of which Hungarian–British physicist, inventor of Holography and Nobel Prizewinner?

8. Which close relative of the Queen, war hero and last Viceroy of India is murdered by the IRA?

9. Who is the British Conservative Politician and war hero murdered by the IRA?

10. Where is there a huge oilwell blow-out, which causes the world's worst environmental pollution incident?

11. What is the nuclear weapon treaty called which Soviet Premier Brezhnev and U.S. President Carter sign in Vienna?

12. Who becomes President of Iraq?

13. First direct elections are held to which Parliament?

14. Afghanistan is invaded by which one of its neighbours?

15. What is the name of the art historian identified in the House of Commons as a member of the 'Cambridge' Soviet spy ring?

ANSWERS
1. Moral Majority. 2. Shah of Iran. 3. Ayatollah Khomeini. 4. The Killing Fields. 5. Pol Pot. 6. Three Mile Island. 7. Dennis Gabor. 8. Lord Mountbatten. 9. Airey Neave. 10. The Gulf of Mexico. 11. SALT 2. 12. Saddam Hussein. 13. European Parliament. 14. Soviet Union. 15. Anthony Blunt.

Year by year 1980–1989

How much do you know about 1980?

QUESTIONS.

1. The Japanese company Sony launches the personal cassette player. What is it called?

2. In the U.S, a political corruption scandal opens up. What name does the F.B.I give to it?

3. What is the name of the Austrian born naturalist made famous by her book Born Free who is killed in January?

4. Which British television film causes a diplomatic row with Saudi Arabia?

5. Who becomes the first Prime Minister of Zimbabwe?

6. Who becomes the first President of Zimbabwe?

7. What is the name of the oil platform belonging to Phillips Petroleum which capsizes in the North Sea?

8. Who succeeds to the throne of the Netherlands after the abdication of Queen Juliana?

9. Death of which famous French existentialist author?

10. Death in Hollywood of British-born master of film suspense. His name please?

11. Eruption of which volcano in Washington State, U.S.A?

12. The Iranian Embassy in London is seized by terrorists. Which branch of the British army takes it back?

13. The 22nd modern Olympic Games are staged in which city?

14. In Poland, the first independent trade union to exist in the Eastern bloc is formed. What is it called?

15. Which Republican candidate is elected 40th President of the U.S.A?

ANSWERS
1. The Walkman. 2. 'Abscam'. 3. Joy Adamson. 4. Death of a Princess. 5. Robert Mugabe. 6. Canaan Banana. 7. The Alexander Keilland. 8. Her daughter, Princess Beatrix. 9. Jean-Paul Sartre. 10. Alfred Hitchcock. 11. Mount St Helens. 12. S.A.S. 13. Moscow. 14. Solidarity. 15. Ronald Reagan

How much do you know about 1981?

QUESTIONS.

1. What new world-wide disease is officially recognised?

2. I.B.M produces its first...what?

3. End of the Iranian hostage crisis. For how long had the American embassy staff been held prisoner?

4. Four senior members of the British Labour Party resign to form a new political party. What do they call it?

5. In the U.S, what is the name of the 'drifter' who attempts to assassinate President Reagan?

6. Who becomes the first woman Prime Minister of Norway?

7. What is the name of the first space shuttle, launched in April of this year?

8. In Rome, a 23-year-old Turkish criminal makes an attempt on the life of Pope John Paul II. His name?

9. The Israeli Air Force destroys a nuclear reactor in which nearby country?

10. Who becomes President of France?

11. The Panamanian leader Herrera is killed in an air crash. Who succeeds him?

12. To whom does the Prince of Wales get married?

13. Who succeeds to the Presidency of Egypt after the assassination of Anwar Sadat?

14. Which musical by Andrew Lloyd-Webber, based upon poems by T. S. Eliot, opens in London?

15. In the U.S, release of Steven Spielberg's first film featuring Indiana Jones. What is it called?

ANSWERS
1. AIDS. 2. Personal Computer. 3. 444 days. 4. Social Democratic Party. 5. John Hinckley. 6. Gro Brundtland. 7. Columbia. 8. Mehmet Ali Agca. 9. Iraq. 10. François Mitterand. 11. Colonel Manuel Noriega. 12. Lady Diana Spencer. 13. Hosni Mubarak. 14. Cats. 15. Raiders of the Lost Ark.

How much do you know about 1982?

QUESTIONS.

1. The Vietnam Veterans Memorial in Washington D.C is designed by which U.S architect?

2. The novel The House of the Spirits is published by which Chilean writer?

3. Which 'wonder' car plant in Northern Ireland fails?

4. Death of which very influential U.S jazz pianist?

5. What is the name of the German composer, particularly well known for his Carmina Burana who dies in March?

6. British dependency in the South Atlantic, the Falkland Islands, invaded by troops from which country?

7. The Argentine cruiser General Belgrano is sunk off the Falklands, by which British nuclear submarine?

8. Israel drives the P.L.O out of which neighbouring country?

9. Which Mexican politician is elected President?

10. Crops fail for the fourth year in succession in which country?

11. In the entertainment field, what new audio system is launched?

12. What highly successful T.V programme set in a bar debuts in the U.S.?

13. Which country wins the football World Cup?

14. What position did Yuri Andropov hold before he became General Secretary of the Communist Party, on the death of Leonid Brezhnev?

15. Which Polish-born American piano virtuoso dies this year?

ANSWERS
1. Maya Lin. 2. Isabel Allende. 3. De Lorean. 4. Thelonius Monk. 5. Carl Orff. 6. Argentina. 7. HMS Conqueror. 8. The Lebanon. 9. Miguel Hurtado. 10. U.S.S.R. 11. Compact Discs. 12. Cheers. 13. Italy. 14. Head of the KGB. 15. Artur Rubinstein.

How much do you know about 1983?

QUESTIONS.

1. Which U.S Government Agency is rocked by corruption scandals?

2. In Britain, the wearing of what safety device is made compulsory by law?

3. Death by suicide of Hungarian born British journalist and writer, author of Darkness at Noon. His name please?

4. Death of one of Americas favourite playwrights, author of A Streetcar Named Desire and many others. Who is it?

5. Which party wins the general election in West Germany?

6. President Reagan launches what defence initiative?

7. In West Germany a major fraud is foiled when a book awaiting publication proves to be a fake. What book?

8. Who is the 'Solidarity' leader who is awarded the Nobel Peace prize?

9. The U.S Embassy and the U.S Marine Headquarters are both the subject of devastating terrorist bomb attacks. These attacks occur in which Middle Eastern city?

10. Who is the Philippine opposition leader assassinated upon his return to Manila?

11. A Boeing 747 'Jumbo' airliner of which eastern airline is shot down by Soviet fighters after straying into Soviet air space?

12. Who succeeds Menachem Begin as Prime Minister of Israel?

13. In Britain, who is elected leader of the Labour Party?

14. First cruise missiles arrive in Britain. Where are anti-nuclear demonstrators arrested?

15. American designer, inventor and philosopher, best known for his 'Geodesic Dome' dies. His name please?

ANSWERS
1. Environment Protection Agency. 2. Car safety belts. 3. Arthur Koestler. 4. Tennessee Williams. 5. Christian Democrats. 6. Strategic Defence Initiative. 7. Hitler's Diaries. 8. Lech Walesa. 9. Beirut. 10. Benigno Aquino. 11. Korean Airlines. 12. Yitzhak Shamir. 13. Neil Kinnock. 14. Greenham Common. 15. Buckminster Fuller.

How much do you know about 1984?

QUESTIONS.

1. Riots in the streets of which North African capital over increases in the price of bread?

2. Which British protectorate since 1888 in North Borneo gains its independence?

3. British scientist Alec Jeffreys develops a technique which will have huge significance in the solving of crimes. What is it?

4. Who succeeds as Soviet Premier on the death of Yuri Andropov?

5. Death of which American jazz pianist and band leader?

6. Sikh extremists seize which holy monument at Amritsar?

7. What is the name of the Civil Servant charged with breaking the Official Secrets Act over the 'Belgrano affair'?

8. What is the name of the hotel in Brighton devastated by an IRA bomb, in an attempt to kill the Prime Minister?

9. Death of which British actor, veteran star of many 1940's dramas, like The Seventh Veil and The Wicked Lady?

10. The 23rd modern Olympic Games are staged in which city?

11. Who becomes Prime Minister of Canada?

12. What is the name of the pro-Solidarity priest murdered by the Polish secret police?

13. Who is the leader of the Sandinista Front who wins the elections in Nicaragua?

14. And who is elected Prime Minister of India following the assassination of Indira Gandhi.

15. What is the name of the South African bishop awarded the Nobel Peace Prize?

ANSWERS
1. Tunis. 2. Brunei. 3. Genetic fingerprinting. 4. Konstantin Chernenko. 5. Count Basie. 6. The Golden Temple. 7. Clive Ponting. 8. Grand Hotel. 9. James Mason. 10. Los Angeles. 11. Brian Mulrooney. 12. Jerzy Popiluszko. 13. Daniel Ortega. 14. Rajiv Gandhi. 15. Desmond Tutu.

How much do you know about 1985?

QUESTIONS.

1. Who becomes the new leader of the Soviet Union, after the death of Konstantin Chernenko?

2. Death of Enver Hoxha, communist dictator of which central European state since 1946?

3. Parallel pop concerts in Philadelphia, U.S.A and Wembley, England, raise £50 million for famine relief. What are they called?

4. French secret service agents sink which Greenpeace ship in Auckland Harbour, New Zealand?

5. Around 10,000 people are killed and 100,000 rendered homeless in an earthquake in which central American city?

6. Death of which U.S film actor and maker, and one-time 'wunderkind'?

7. Who is the 57-year-old Georgian who replaces Gromyko, long-time U.S.S.R Foreign Secretary?

8. 39 Juventus fans are killed and 400 injured in a disaster involving Liverpool F.C, at which stadium in Brussels, Belgium?

9. Death of which British fashion designer known for her romantic style and use of natural fabrics?

10. Which Hollywood star is the first major celebrity to die from AIDS?

11. What is the name of the Italian cruise liner, sailing from Alexandria, Egypt, seized by P.L.O terrorists?

12. Death of the Hollywood star who proved that 'bald' could mean 'sexy'. His name please?

13. In the Irish Republic, the Dail legalises the sale of what goods in shops for the first time?

14. Death of Russian born Paris based artist, for whom the term 'surrealist' was said to have been coined. His name?

15. In which European city do U.S President Reagan and U.S.S.R Premier Gorbachev hold their first meeting?

ANSWERS
1. Mikhail Gorbachev. 2. Albania. 3. Live Aid. 4. Rainbow Warrior. 5. Mexico City. 6. Orson Welles. 7. Eduard Shevardnadze. 8. Heysel Stadium. 9. Laura Ashley. 10. Rock Hudson. 11. The Achille Lauro. 12. Yul Brynner. 13. Contraception. 14. Marc Chagall. 15. Geneva.

How much do you know about 1986?

QUESTIONS.

1. What is the name of the NASA space shuttle which blew up over Cape Canaveral, 70 seconds into its flight?

2. Which video game craze sweeps the U.S.?

3. Which dictator, son of a dictator, is forced to flee from his Caribbean island?

4. Which presidential aide resigns in the wake of the Iran-Contra arms scandal in the U.S?

5. Which two countries join the E.E.C.?

6. U.S. space probe Voyager II reaches which planet?

7. Who becomes President of the Philippines after Marcos flees into exile?

8. What is the name of the Prime Minister of Sweden who is assassinated in February?

9. Who is the leader of the Afrikaner Resistance Movement, the AWB, opposed to any reform in South Africa?

10. In the U.S, what is the name of the Wall Street trader who confesses to have made a fortune from 'insider trading'?

11. Disaster at a Soviet nuclear plant, near which city?

12. In the U.S a Soviet diplomat is arrested and charge with spying. What is his name?

13. Death of which U.S maestro clarinettist?

14. Death of which British-born American actor, renowned for his charm?

15. The last volume of the Oxford English Dictionary is published. When did the first volume come out?

ANSWERS
1. Challenger. 2. Nintendo. 3. Jean-Claude 'Baby Doc' Duvalier. 4. Lt. Colonel Oliver North. 5. Spain and Portugal. 6. Uranus. 7. Corazon Aquino. 8. Olof Palme. 9. Eugene Terre' Blanche. 10. Ivan Boesky. 11. Chernobyl. 12. Gennady Zakharov. 13. Benny Goodman. 14. Cary Grant. 15. In 1884.

How much do you know about 1987?

QUESTIONS.

1. Soviet General Secretary Mikhail Gorbachev announces his policy of perestroika and glasnost, meaning what ?

2. Death of one the founding fathers of 'Pop Art'. His name?

3. What is the name of the Townsend Thoreson ferry which capsizes off Zeebrugge, with a loss of 200 lives?

4. The leader of a major Columbian drug cartel is arrested, then extradited to the U.S.A. His name ?

5. In the U.S., who replaces Donald Regan as White House Chief of Staff?

6. Resignation of Italian socialist Prime Minister. His name?

7. An affair with a model puts leading contender for the Democrat candidature Senator Gary Hart out of the running. Name the boat on which they holidayed together?

8. What is the name of the U.S. frigate attacked by Iraqi fighter planes in the Persian Gulf?

9. A 19 year old German student lands a light plane in Red Square, Moscow. What is his name?

10. Death of Spanish classical guitar virtuoso. His name?

11. In France, who is the ex-NAZI officer condemned for crimes against humanity during the war?

12. In which small Northern Ireland town is a poppy-day parade blown to pieces by an I.R.A. bomb?

13. Death of which British cellist after a serious illness?

14. Which participant in the 'Iran-Contra Affair' emerges from the hearings as something of a patriot to the American people?

15. The U.S. and U.S.S.R. sign a treaty for reducing nuclear weapons. What is the treaty called?

ANSWERS
1. Freedom and openness. 2. Andy Warhol. 3. Herald of Free Enterprise. 4. Carlos Rivas. 5. Howard Baker. 6. Bettino Craxi. 7. Monkey Business. 8. U.S.S. Stark. 9. Mathias Rust. 10. Andres Segovia. 11. Klaus Barbie. 12. Enniskillen. 13. Jacqueline Du Pre. 14. Lt.-Col. Oliver North. 15. Intermediate Nuclear Forces Treaty. (INF)

How much do you know about 1988?

QUESTIONS.

1. Death of Irish statesman and founder of Amnesty International. His name please?

2. In the U.S, which 'tele-evangelist' went on the air to admit visiting a prostitute?

3. Death of U.S. physicist, winner of the Nobel Prize for his work in the field of quantum electrodynamics. His name?

4. Where are three IRA terrorists shot dead by the SAS in March?

5. Following a coup in Pakistan, who takes control, dissolving the national assembly?

6. Where do police kill 3,000 demonstrating students?

7. What is the name of the North Sea oil rig which suffers an explosion and fire, with the loss of 160 lives?

8. Who succeeds as Premier of Pakistan after the death of Zia ul-Haq?

9. Death of which Italian designer of high performance and racing cars?

10. The 24th modern Olympic games are staged in which city?

11. Which U.S. female track athlete wins 3 gold medals?

12. Which Middle Eastern war ends in stalemate and over a million deaths?

13. Which country does the Red Army pull out of, following a nine-year occupation?

14. In the U.S, which Republican candidate wins the Presidential Election?

15. And in Chile, which U.S-backed fascist dictator is forced to step down?

ANSWERS
1. Sean McBride. 2. Jimmy Swaggart. 3. Richard Feynman. 4. On Gibraltar. 5. Mohammed Zia ul-Haq. 6. Rangoon, Burma. 7. Piper Alpha. 8. Benazir Bhutto. 9. Enzo Ferrari. 10. Seoul. 11. Florence Griffith Joyner. 12. Iran – Iraq War. 13. Afghanistan. 14. George Bush. 15. General Augusto Pinochet

How much do you know about 1989?

QUESTIONS.

1. Who succeeds to the throne of Japan on the death of Emperor Hirohito?

2. Cuban troops begin withdrawal from which South West African country?

3. Death of which famous Spanish surrealist artist?

4. What is the name of the newly elected President of Argentina?

5. In Britain, 95 football fans are crushed to death at which English football ground?

6. Death of which leading British actor?

7. Where is the focal point of student unrest in China, and its subsequent brutal suppression?

8. In the U.S, which charismatic hotel proprietor is convicted of tax evasion?

9. What is the name of the new President of South Africa?

10 The East German government is forced to allow free access to the West, leading to the destruction of which major symbol of communist rule?

11. The long standing communist President of Czechoslovakia steps down. His place is taken by which man of letters?

12. In Czechoslovakia the fall of communism is achieved with so little fighting, that it becomes known as what?

13. U.S troops invade which Central American country?

14. Anti-government demonstrations break out and are brutally put down in which Transylvanian city?

15. This action leads to revolution in Romania and the summary execution of which dictator?

ANSWERS
1. Akihito. 2. Angola. 3. Salvador Dali. 4. Carlos Menem. 5. Hillsborough . 6. Sir Laurence Olivier. 7. Tiananmen Square. 8. Leona Helmsley. 9. F.W. de Klerk. 10. The Berlin Wall. 11. Vaclav Havel. 12. The 'Velvet Revolution'. 13. Panama. 14. Timisoara. 15. Nicolae Ceausescu.

Year by year 1990–1999

How much do you know about 1990?

QUESTIONS.

1. Which South West African country gains its independence from South Africa?

2. Fighting breaks out between Serbs and Albanians in which autonomous region of Yugoslavia?

3. In Britain, widespread disturbances against the most unpopular measure of Margaret Thatcher's premiership. What is it?

4. Azerbaijan declares war on what neighbouring country?

5. The designer of a 'super-gun' made for Iraq, is found dead in Brussels. His name please?

6. Which northern European state secedes from the Soviet Union, and elects its own President, Vitautas Landsbergis?

7. Death of retired Swedish film actress, famous for her desire to be alone. Her name?

8. What is the name of Ireland's first ever female President?

9. What is the name of the U.S. space probe which goes into orbit around Venus?

10. Iraq sends a 100,000 invasion force into which neighbouring state?

11. After 45 years of partition, which European country is finally re-unified?

12. Death of which U.S composer and conductor?

13. Who succeeds Margaret Thatcher as Prime Minister of the U.K. ?

14. Who wins the Presidential elections in Serbia?

15. Who does Lech Walesa replace as President of Poland?

ANSWERS
1. Namibia. 2. Kosovo. 3. The Poll Tax (Community Charge). 4. Armenia. 5. Dr Gerald Bull. 6. Lithuania. 7. Greta Garbo. 8. Mary Robinson. 9. Magellan. 10. Kuwait. 11. Germany. 12. Leonard Bernstein. 13. John Major. 14. Slobodan Milosevic. 15. General Jaruzelski.

How much do you know about 1991?

QUESTIONS.

1. What is stated by UN Resolution 678?

2. What is the name of the American General who is made Commander of the Allied Forces?

3. What is the name of the U.N Secretary General who flies to Baghdad in a last effort to stop hostilities?

4. In Russia, what pre-Revolution name does Leningrad revert to?

5. Which major bank crashes amid allegations (later proven) of theft, fraud and money laundering?

6. Which international political and military organisation is dissolved?

7. What is the name of the young black motorist filmed being beaten by four Los Angeles police officers?

8. Death of which British prima ballerina?

9. A failed coup in the Soviet Union, sees Gorbachev sidelined and a new Russian leader emerging. His name?

10. Which two 'autonomous regions' secede from Yugoslavia and declare their independence?

11. Mysterious death of Czech-born British newspaper tycoon. His name please?

12. In the U.S, which Supreme Court nominee is accused of sexual harassment?

13. The release of the album Nevermind by Nirvana heralds the arrival of which musical style?

14. Rock star and lead singer of the group 'Queen' dies of AIDS. What is his name?

15. In the U.S, one of the most successful and popular basketball players announces that he is HIV positive. What is his name?

ANSWERS.
1. Final warning to Iraq to quit Kuwait. 2. General 'Stormin' Norman' Schwarzkopf. 3. Javier Perez de Cueller. 4. St Petersburg. 5. Bank of Credit and Commerce International. 6. The Warsaw Pact. 7. Rodney King. 8. Dame Margot Fonteyn. 9. Boris Yeltsin. 10. Croatia and Slovenia. 11. Robert Maxwell. 12. Clarence Thomas. 13. Grunge. 14. Freddie Mercury. 15. Earvin 'Magic' Johnson.

How much do you know about 1992?

QUESTIONS.

1. Who is the newly appointed Secretary-General of the UN?

2. Who is the Irish Prime Minister forced to resign due to scandal this year?

3. Which computer game character, created by Sony, begins to rival Nintendo's Mario Bros in popularity?

4. In the U.S, the world heavyweight boxing champion is convicted of rape. What is his name?

5. In Britain, after his second successive electoral defeat, Neil Kinnock resigns as Labour party leader. Who succeeds him?

6. In the U.S, which Mafia chieftain is convicted on racketeering charges?

7. Death of Russian-born American biochemist, the best-known writer on science and science fiction. His name?

8. The twenty-fifth modern Olympic Games are staged in which city?

9. And who runs the race of his life to take gold in the Men's 100m?

10. In the U.S, the presidential elections are won by the Democrat governor of Arkansas. His name please?

11. A well-intentioned U.S. military intervention ordered by the new President turns sour in which East African country?

12. Which other autonomous region of Yugoslavia declares its independence?

13. In England, football's First Division is won for the final time before becoming the Premier League by which side?

14. What is the name of the hurricane which causes devastation in Florida and the Caribbean?

15. In which great city does the United Nations organise a conference on the environment?

ANSWERS
1. Boutros-Boutros Ghali. 2. Charles Haughey. 3. Sonic the Hedgehog. 4. Mike Tyson. 5. John Smith. 6. John Gotti. 7. Isaac Asimov. 8. Barcelona. 9. Linford Christie. 10. Bill Clinton. 11. Somalia. 12. Bosnia-Herzegovina. 13. Leeds United. 14. Hurricane Andrew. 15. Rio de Janeiro.

How much do you know about 1993?

QUESTIONS.

1. Czechoslovakia decides to divide itself into two separate republics. What do they call this action?

2. Canada, the U.S.A and Mexico sign an agreement to set up what?

3. Italy reforms its electoral system, abandoning which system of voting?

4. In the U.S, what is the name of the Act of Congress which is passed, ensuring a certain level of gun control?

5. In Europe, what is brought to the point of collapse by money market speculators?

6. In the U.S, who is the first woman to be appointed to the post of Attorney-General?

7. Which British adventurer completes the first crossing of Antarctica on foot?

8. What mathematical riddle, unsolved since the 17th century, is finally deciphered by British mathematician Andrew Wiles?

9. In Britain, what historic decision is made by Queen Elizabeth and the Prince of Wales?

10. Death of which U.S Jazz trumpeter and pioneer of be-bop?

11. Which country gains independence from Ethiopia?

12. The siege of which sect in Waco, Texas, turns into an inferno which takes many lives?

13. Who becomes Canada's first woman Prime Minister?

14. Who becomes Turkey's first woman Prime Minister?

15. Who becomes world heavyweight boxing champion?

ANSWERS
1. The 'Velvet Divorce'. 2. North American Free Trade Area. 3. Proportional Representation. 4. The Brady Act. 5. The Exchange Rate Mechanism. 6. Janet Reno. 7. Ranulph Fiennes. 8. Fermant's Last Theorem. 9. They agree to pay income tax, for the first time ever. 10. Dizzy Gillespie. 11. Eritrea. 12. Branch Davidians. 13. Kim Campbell. 14. Tansu Ciller. 15. Evander Holyfield.

How much do you know about 1994?

QUESTIONS.

1. In the U.S, allegations of impropriety are made about President Clinton's involvement in which Arkansas Development Corporation?

2. And a woman is acquitted of charges of assault on her husband. What is her name?

3. Which former C.I.A official is arrested for espionage?

4. Who is the media baron who wins the Italian presidential elections?

5. In Britain, which political leader dies suddenly?

6. Suicide of lead singer of the grunge band 'Nirvana'. What is his name?

7. Massacre in which Central African State?

8. In the U.S, sexual harassment charges are filed against President Clinton, by whom?

9. Completion of which major piece of civil engineering designed to bring Britain and Europe closer together?

10. Who is the internationally infamous terrorist arrested in the Sudan?

11. What is lowered to the age of 18 for the first time in the U.K?

12. Which Scandinavian country rejects membership of the European Union in a referendum?

13. What is launched to turn Britain into a nation of gamblers?

14. Which 'autonomous region' of the Russian Federation declares itself independent, leading to war with Russia?

15. Who becomes the first black President of South Africa?

ANSWERS
1. Whitewater. 2. Lorena Bobbitt. 3. Aldrich Ames. 4. Silvio Berlusconi. 5. John Smith.
6. Kurt Cobain. 7. Rwanda. 8. Paula Jones. 9. Channel Tunnel. 10. Carlos the Jackal. 11.
Age of homosexual consent. 12. Norway. 13. National Lottery. 14. Chechnya. 15.
Nelson Mandela.

How much do you know about 1995?

QUESTIONS.

1. Which three countries join the European Union?

2. Kobe, Japan is struck by what disaster?

3. In the U.S, who is appointed Speaker of the House of Representatives?

4. In Chechnya, Russian troops take which city?

5. Barings Bank is bankrupted by which 'rogue trader'?

6. Death of U.S thriller writer, author of Strangers On A Train. The name please?

7. Terrorists of which Japanese cult release nerve gas in the Tokyo underground during rush hour?

8. Who is responsible for the bombing of the federal building in Oklahoma City?

9. What is the name of the Burmese opposition leader released from long house arrest?

10. In the U.S, the separatist 'Nation of Islam' organises a protest march in Washington to hear their leader. What is his name?

11. Which former Italian Prime Minister goes on trial, accused of connections with the Mafia?

12. In which European country is the ban on divorce lifted?

13. Assassination of which Israeli Prime Minister?

14. In the U.S, Microsoft releases which operating system?

15. In which town in Ohio, U.S.A, do warring Balkan leaders meet to forge a peace agreement, later signed in Paris?

ANSWERS
1. Sweden, Finland and Austria. 2. Earthquake. 3. Newt Gingrich. 4. Grozny. 5. Nick Leeson. 6. Patricia Highsmith. 7. "Supreme Truth". 8. Timothy McVeigh 9. Aung San Suu Kyi. 10. Louis Farrakhan. 11. Giulio Andreotti. 12. Ireland. 13. Yitzhak Rabin. 14. Windows '95. 15. Dayton.

How much do you know about 1996?

QUESTIONS.

1. Why doe the European Commission impose a world wide ban on exports of British beef?

2. Opening in London of a reproduction Shakespearean theatre. What is it called ?

3. NASA launches a space probe to explore Mars. What is it called?

4. Who is elected President of Palestine?

5. Death of U.S actor and dancer, he who liked to go Singin' in the Rain?

6. Thomas Kaczynski, America's most wanted terrorist is arrested. By what name is he better known?

7. What is the name of the anti-government militia, forced to surrender after a siege of 81 days in Montana?

8. Death of America's first lady of jazz. The one and only...?

9. The twenty-sixth modern Olympic Games are staged in which city?

10. Which U.S athlete wins both the men's 200 and 400 metres?

11. In Afghanistan, an Islamic fundamentalist force captures the capital, Kabul. What is the name of the force?

12. In the U.S presidential elections who is the Republican candidate defeated by the Democrat incumbent?

13. In Britain, two penniless ecological campaigners are defeated by McDonalds in a law suit that comes to be known as what?

14. Who is the new Secretary General of the UN?

15. Death of which U.S comedian renowned for his longevity?

ANSWERS
1. Fear of 'mad cow disease'. 2. The Globe. 3. Pathfinder. 4. Yasser Arafat. 5. Gene Kelly 6. The 'Unabomber'. 7. The 'Freemen'. 8. Ella Fitzgerald. 9. Atlanta, Georgia. 10. Michael Johnson. 11. Taliban. 12. Bob Dole. 13. The 'McLibel Case'. 14. Kofi Annan. 15. George Burns.

How much do you know about 1997?

QUESTIONS.

1. In the U.S, the government ends federal funding of what kind of scientific research?

2. Which NASA space probe gets the closest yet to Jupiter?

3. After 43 years, Ford Motors calls a halt to the production of what type of car?

4. What is the name of the comet which passes in view of Earth?

5. And which internet-oriented religious cult in the U.S takes the comet as a sign to mass suicide?

6. Who becomes the first female U.S Secretary of State?

7. Construction begins on which building in London, designed by Richard Rogers?

8. In France, who becomes Prime Minister?

9. In Britain, who is chosen as the new leader of the defeated Conservative Party?

10. Death of which famous French undersea explorer?

11. What does Britain return to China?

12. What is the name of the Italian fashion designer shot dead outside his home in Miami?

13. Amazing outpouring of public grief follows the death of probably the most prominent woman in the world. Who?

14. In the U.S, what is the name of the young British nanny charged with the murder of the child in her care?

15. Death of two Hollywood greats. Who are they?

ANSWERS.
1. Cloning. 2. Galileo. 3. Thunderbird. 4. Hale-Bopp. 5. Heaven's Gate. 6. Madeleine Allbright. 7. The Millenium Dome. 8. Lionel Jospin. 9. William Hague. 10. Jacques Cousteau. 11. Hong Kong. 12. Gianni Versace. 13. Princess Diana. 14. Louise Woodward. 15. James Stewart and Robert Mitchum.

How much do you know about 1998?

QUESTIONS.

1. In the U.S, scandal erupts as the nation learns of the President's relationship with whom?

2. Pro-democracy anti-government riots in which South-East Asian republic?

3. Which two Asian countries demonstrate their nuclear capabilities?

4. Which European country wins the football World Cup?

5. State of Emergency declared in which republic in the Indian Ocean?

6. Which long-term Chancellor is defeated in the German elections?

7. An astronaut returns to space, at age 77. His name?

8. Which former Chilean dictator is arrested in London?

9. Who is thrown out of Iraq by Saddam Hussein?

10. U.S Congress votes to impeach President Clinton after the publication of the Starr Report into what?

11. The European Union announces the arrival of what?

12. An IRA bomb kills 28 and injures more than 200 in which Northern Ireland town?

13. Which British pop star admits his homosexuality?

14. Stephen Spielberg's anti-war film opens to acclaim. What is it called?

15. War breaks out again between which two East African countries?

ANSWERS.
1. Monica Lewinsky. 2. Indonesia. 3. India and Pakistan. 4. France. 5. Sri Lanka. 6. Helmut Kohl. 7. John Glenn. 8. General Augusto Pinochet. 9. United Nations arms inspectors. 10. 'Zippergate'. 11. The 'Euro' Currency. 12. Omagh. 13. George Michael. 14. Saving Private Ryan. 15. Ethiopia and Eritrea.

How much do you know about 1999?

1. In Britain, which former Cabinet Minister admits to committing perjury?

2. Who is the ex-M.I.6 agent who defies extradition?

3. In Canada, Innuit Indians are given their own self-governing territory. What name do they give to it?

4. Researchers at the Houses of Parliament are accused of downloading what from the Internet onto the government computers?

5. Who succeeds as King of Jordan, after the death of King Hussein?

6. U.S astronomers use the Hubble telescope to identify the oldest galaxy in the universe. How old is it?

7. A 'life-time achievement' award at the Oscar ceremonies causes controversy. To whom is it given?

8. Which Anglo-Swiss balloon team completes the first round-the-world flight and wins the $1 million prize?

9. In the U.S, which High School in Colorado is the scene of a massacre, carried out by two students?

10. One of the most popular television presenters in Britain is murdered in front of her home. Who is it?

11. Who is the 22-year-old charged with having committed a series of nail-bombings in Soho, London?

12. NATO planes accidentally bomb the Chinese Embassy in which Eastern European city?

13. Which long-term British resident sees his application for British citizenship rejected again?

14. Queen Elizabeth's youngest son Prince Edward marries whom in St. George's Chapel, Windsor?

15. In South Africa, who replaces Nelson Mandela as President of South Africa?

ANSWERS.
1. Jonathan Aitken. 2. David Shayler. 3. Nunavut. 4. Pornography. 5. Prince Abdullah. 6. 14.25 billion years. 7. Elia Kazan. 8. The 'Breitling' team. 9. Columbine High. 10. Jill Dando. 11. David Copeland. 12. Belgrade. 13. Mohammed al-Fayed. 14. Sophie Rhys-Jones. 15. Thabo Mbeki.

Great British Royalty

Monarchs since 802

House of Wessex
802- 839 Egbert
839- 855 Aethelwulf
855- 860 Aethelbald
860- 866 Aethelbert
866- 871 Aethelred I
871- 899 Alfred the Great
899- 924 Edward the Elder
924- 939 Athelstan First monarch of
all England
939- 946 Edmund I
946- 955 Eadred
955- 959 Eadwig
959- 975 Edgar
975- 979 Edward the Martyr
979- 1016 Aethelred the Unready
1016 Edmund II (Ironside)
1016- 1035 Cnut I
1037- 1040 Harold I
1040- 1042 Cnut II (Harthcanute)
1042- 1066 Edward the Confessor
1066 Harold II

House of Normandy
1066-1087 William I (the Conqueror)
1087-1100 William II
1100-1135 Henry I (Beauclerc)
1135-1154 Stephen

House of Plantagenet
1154-1189 Henry II (Curtmante)
1189-1199 Richard I (Lionheart)
1199-1216 John (Lackland)
1216-1272 Henry III
1272-1307 Edward I (Longshanks)
1307-1327 Edward II
1327-1377 Edward III
1377-1399 Richard II

House of Lancaster
1399-1413 Henry IV
1413-1422 Henry V
1422-1461 Henry VI

House of York
1461-1483 Edward IV
1483 Edward V
1483-1485 Richard III

House of Tudor
1485-1509 Henry VII
1509-1547 Henry VIII
1547-1553 Edward VI
1553-1558 Mary I
1558-1603 Elizabeth I

House of Stuart
1603-1625 James I
1625-1649 Charles I
1649-1653 Commonwealth
1653-1658 Protectorate of
Oliver Cromwell
1658-1659 Protectorate of
 Richard Cromwell
1660-1685 Charles II
1685-1688 James II
1689-1694 William and Mary (jointly)
1694-1702 William III (sole ruler)
1702-1714 Anne

House of Hanover
1714-1727 George I
1727-1760 George II
1760-1820 George III
1820-1830 George IV
1830-1837 William IV
1837-1901 Victoria

House of Saxe-Coburg
1901-1910 Edward VII

House of Windsor
1910-1936 George V
1936   Edward VIII
1936-1952 George VI
1952-   Elizabeth II

Monarchs since the conquest

House of Normandy
1066-1087 William I (the Conqueror)
1087-1100 William II
1100-1135 Henry I (Beauclerc)
1135-1154 Stephen

House of Plantagenet
1154-1189 Henry II (Curtmante)
1189-1199 Richard I (Lionheart)
1199-1216 John (Lackland)
1216-1272 Henry III
1272-1307 Edward I (Longshanks)
1307-1327 Edward II
1327-1377 Edward III
1377-1399 Richard II

House of Lancaster
1399-1413 Henry IV
1413-1422 Henry V
1422-1461 Henry VI

House of York
1461-1483 Edward IV
1483 Edward V
1483-1485 Richard III

House of Tudor
1485-1509 Henry VII
1509-1547 Henry VIII
1547-1553 Edward VI
1553-1558 Mary I
1558-1603 Elizabeth I

House of Stuart
1603-1625 James I
1625-1649 Charles I
1649-1653 Commonwealth
1653-1658 Protectorate of
Oliver Cromwell
1658-1659 Protectorate of
 Richard Cromwell
1660-1685 Charles II
1685-1688 James II
1689-1694 William and Mary (jointly)
1694-1702 William III (sole ruler)
1702-1714 Anne

House of Hanover
1714-1727 George I
1727-1760 George II
1760-1820 George III
1820-1830 George IV
1830-1837 William IV
1837-1901 Victoria

House of Saxe-Coburg
1901-1910 Edward VII

House of Windsor
1910-1936 George V
1936   Edward VIII
1936-1952 George VI
1952-   Elizabeth II

U.S Presidents

		President	Vice-President
1	1789-1797	George Washington	John Adams
2	1797-1801	John Adams	Thomas Jefferson *
3	1801-1809	Thomas Jefferson	Aaron Burr, George Clinton
4	1809-1817	James Madison	George Clinton, Elbridge Gerry
5	1817-1825	James Monroe	Daniel D Tompkins
6	1825-1829	John Quincy Adams	John C Calhoun
7	1829-1837	Andrew Jackson	John C Calhoun +, Martin Van Buren
8	1837-1841	Martin Van Buren	Richard M Johnson #
9	1841	William Henry Harrison	John Tyler
10	1841-1845	John Tyler	None
11	1845-1849	James Polk	George M Dallas
12	1849-1850	Zachary Taylor	Millard Fillmore
13	1850-1853	Millard Fillmore	None
14	1853-1857	Franklin Pierce	William R King
15	1857-1861	James Buchanan	John C Breckinridge
16	1861-1865	Abraham Lincoln	Hannibal Hamlin, Andrew Johnson *
17	1865-1869	Andrew Johnson	None
18	1869-1877	Ulysses Simpson Grant	** Schuyler Colfax, Henry Wilson
19	1877-1881	Rutherford Birchard Hayes	William A Wheeler
20	1881	James Abram Garfield	Chester A Arthur
21	1881-1885	Chester Alan Arthur	None
22	1885-1889	Stephen Grover Cleveland	Thomas Hendricks
23	1889-1893	Benjamin Harrison	Levi P Morton
24	1893-1897	Grover Cleveland	Adlai E Stevenson
25	1897-1901	William McKinley	Garret A Hobart, Theodore Roosevelt
26	1901-1909	Theodore (Teddy) Roosevelt	Charles W Fairbanks
27	1909-1913	William Howard Taft	James S Sherman
28	1913-1921	Thomas Woodrow Wilson	Thomas R Marshall
29	1921-1923	Warren Gamaliel Harding	Calvin Coolidge

U.S Presidents (continued)

		President	Vice-President
30	1923-1929	John Calvin Coolidge	Charles G Dawes
31	1929-1933	Herbert Clark Hoover	Charles Curtis
32	1933-1945	Franklin Delano Roosevelt	John N Garner, Henry A Wallace, Harry S Truman
33	1945-1953	Harry S Truman ##	Alben W Barkley
34	1953-1961	Dwight David Eisenhower	Richard M Nixon
35	1961-1963	John (Jack) Kennedy	Lyndon B Johnson
36	1963-1969	Lyndon Baines Johnson	Hubert Humphrey
37	1969-1974	Richard Milhous Nixon +	Spiro T Agnew +, Gerald Ford %
38	1974-1977	Gerald Rudolph Ford	Nelson Rockefeller %
39	1977-1981	James (Jimmy) Earl Carter	Walter Mondale
40	1981-1989	Ronald Wilson Reagan	George Bush
41	1989-1993	George Herbert Walker Bush	Dan Quayle
42	1993-2001	William (Bill) Jefferson Clinton	Al Gore
43	2001-	George Walker Bush	Dick Cheney

**   He was baptised Hiram Ulysses Grant
The S stood for nothing
      Vice Presidents whose names are in italics later became President
*   the only times the President and Vice President have been of different parties. In the Adams/Jefferson case this was as a result of the pre-1804 electoral system.
      In the Lincoln/Johnson case it was by agreement during the Civil War.
\#   elected by the Senate
%   appointed under the XXVth Amendment
+   resigned

Historical personalites

How much do you know about notable Americans? (1)

QUESTIONS.

1. The Declaration of Independence' was officially the work of a committee. It is acknowledged however that one man contributed more than any other. Who was he?

2. Who was the motive force behind the Federal Party, and its leader until his death in 1804?

3. What function did Hamilton have in the first two U.S. governments, resigning in 1795?

4. Hamilton died from wounds received in a duel with his political enemy …who?

5. Who was considered to have been the 'colossus of the debate' on the subject of independence at the first Continental Congress in 1774? He went on to become the first Vice-President of the U.S. and its second President.

6. The 'manifesto' of the Federal party, 'The Federalist', was written by Hamilton, with many contributions from two other notables. One was James Madison. Who was the other?

7. Which U.S. President established the principal in 1823 that the American continent was henceforth out of bounds to European powers with colonisation in mind?

8. Which ex-President, whose brilliant political career began at fourteen years of age, died in the Speakers room of the lower house of congress, February 23 1848?

9. Which US President won a second term on the stand he took against renewing the charter of the Bank of the United States in 1832?

10. Who was the American soldier, veteran of the War of 1812, veteran of the Indian Wars and hero of the Mexican War 1846-48, who became President in 1849?

11. During whose presidency did the repeal of the Missouri Compromise and the passing of the Kansas-Nebraska Act kindle a flame which ultimately led to the civil war?

12. 'Government of the people, by the people, for the people'. These words, and many others just as inspiring, were part of the Gettysburg Address, made in 1863 by whom?

13. Who was the first U.S. President to be impeached?

14. Which war hero President served his two terms and then became a sleeping partner in a bank, only to be robbed of everything he possessed by his crooked partners?

15. Who was the first Democrat to win election as President after the civil war, and become the President to serve two non-consecutive terms?

ANSWERS.

1. Thomas Jefferson. 2. Alexander Hamilton. 3. Secretary of the Treasury. 4. Aaron Burr 5. John Adams. 6, John Jay. 7. James Monroe. 8. John Quincy Adams. 9. Andrew Jackson. 10. Zachary Taylor. 11. Franklin Pierce. 12. Abraham Lincoln. 13. Andrew Johnson. 14. Ulysses S. Grant. 15. Grover Cleveland.

How much do you know about notable Americans? (2)

QUESTIONS.

1. The election of which Republican candidate as President in 1888 was seen as a triumph of protectionism over free trade?
2. Whose presidential election campaigns in 1896 and 1900 were enlivened by exciting contests with democratic contender William Jennings Bryan?
3. Who was the assistant secretary of the navy who quit to lead his famous 'roughriders' during the war with Cuba in 1898?
4. Whose two periods of presidency from 1912 to 1920 were marked by the amendments to the constitution allowing women's suffrage and the establishment of prohibition; American participation in the first World War and his championship of the League of Nations?
5. Who was the only U.S. President to be elected four times?
6. Whose eventful presidencies caused him to have a sign made for his desk which said 'The Buck Stops Here'?
7. Whose presidencies were mainly concerned with the policy of 'containment' of communism, and whose political inexperience was counter-balanced by his integrity and sincerity?
8. Who became in 1960, the first Catholic and youngest man ever to be elected President?
9. The ever increasing escalation of the war in Vietnam led to unpopularity for ……who?
10. Who resigned in August 1974 under threat of impeachment after the Watergate scandal broke?
11. Who was appointed Vice-President after the resignation of Spiro Agnew in 1973 and then took over as President after the resignation of Nixon?
12. The milestones of whose presidency were the handing over of the Panama Canal Zone to Panama; the Camp David peace agreements and the seizure of the American Embassy in Tehran by the Iranians?
13. Which U.S. President was called 'The Great Communicator'?
14. Who was U.S. President at the time of the Iraqi invasion of Kuwait and the consequent Gulf War?
15. Despite many positive aspects of his presidency, who was the 42nd President who is more likely to be remembered because he was only the second president to be impeached?

ANSWERS.
1. Benjamin Harrison. 2. William McKinley. 3. Theodore Roosevelt. 4. Woodrow Wilson. 5. Franklin Delano Roosevelt. 6. Harry S. Truman. 7. Dwight D. Eisenhower. 8. John F. Kennedy. 9. Lyndon Baines Johnson. 10. Richard Nixon. 11. Gerald Ford. 12. James Carter. 13. Ronald Reagan. 14. George Bush. 15. Bill Clinton.

How much do you know about notable Americans? (3)

QUESTIONS.

1. Who is the German-born U.S. diplomat, Secretary of State to two Presidents, negotiated the U.S. withdrawal from Vietnam and set up Nixon's visits to Beijing and Moscow?

2. Who is the U.S. lawyer and former First Lady who, in 2000, became the Senator for New York?

3. Who is the Vietnam veteran and former chair of the U.S. Joint Chiefs of Staff, who in 2000 became the first black Secretary of State?

4. Who was the Commander of the Allied Forces in the Gulf war?

5. Who was the U.S. diplomat who was charged with brokering the peace in Kosovo and in the ensuing NATO/Serbia conflict in 1999?

6. Who is the Canadian-born U.S. economist who has had enormous influence on contemp orary economic thinking? Best-known publication 'The Affluent Society' 1958.

7. Who is the astronaut who went back into space in October '98 at the age of 77?

8. Who became, in 1997, the first woman to be appointed to the post of Secretary of State?

9. Who was the U.S. architect, engineer and social philosopher who invented the geodesic dome, and warned that 'no instruction book came with the Spaceship Earth'?

10. Who was the U.S. civil-rights leader who said 'Injustice anywhere is a threat to justice everywhere'? He was assassinated in Memphis, Tennessee in April 1968.

11. Who became the U.S.'s first female Attorney General in 1993?

12. Who was the U.S. Secretary of State during the George Bush administration?

13. Who was the Secretary of the Treasury and then Chief of Staff for two years in the Ronald Reagan administration, who was forced to resign over the Irangate affair?

14. Who was the democratic U.S. senator who through an act of Congress named after him, made it possible for thousands of Americans to study abroad and for thousands of overseas students to study in America?

15. Who was the school teacher who lost her life in the 1986 'Challenger' space disaster?

ANSWERS.
1. Henry Kissinger. 2. Hillary Rodham Clinton. 3. General Colin Powell. 4. General Norman Schwarzkopf. 5. Richard Holbrook. 6. John Kenneth Galbraith. 7. John Glenn. 8. Madeleine Allbright. 9. Buckminster Fuller. 10. Martin Luther King. 11. Janet Reno. 12. James Baker. 13. Donald Regan. 14. William Fulbright. 15. Christa McAuliffe.

How much do you know about notable Americans? (4)

QUESTIONS.

1. Who was the Director of the National Security Council and presidential assistant – National Security Affairs in the Carter administration?

2. Who was Jimmy Carter's Vice President?

3. Who was the pilot of the Bell X-1 rocket plane which was the first to pass the sound barrier on 14th October 1947?

4. Who is the co-founder and driving force behind the company Microsoft?

5. Who was the billionaire businessman, aviator and film producer who died a tormented recluse in 1976?

6. Who was the German-born American physicist who, in 1907, became the first American scientist to win a Nobel prize, and whose work on ether drift set Einstein on the way to his theory of relativity?

7. Who were the two surgeons, brothers, who founded the Mayo Clinic and the Mayo Foundation for Medical Education and Research?

8. Who was the 19th century American inventor from Barnesville, Ohio, who took out more than sixty patents, including several for the telephone and telegraph?

9. What was the name of the woman who spied for the South in the American Civil War?

10. Who was the U.S. army Chief of Staff in World War II, secretary of state 1947-49 and secretary of defence September 1950-September 1951? He was responsible for drawing up a generous financial plan to assist European powers to recover from the war.

11. Who was the U.S. politician who was closely associated with George Marshall in drawing up the Marshall Plan and succeeded him as secretary of state?

12. Who was the U.S. social reformer and feminist, who founded Hull House community welfare centre, Chicago; was V.P. of the American Women's Suffrage Alliance and leader of the Women's Peace Party and organised the first Women's Peace Congress?

13. Who was the U.S. military leader who formed the 'Green Mountain Boys' in 1770?

14. Who were the two U.S. social reformers who together founded the National Woman Suffrage Association in 1869?

15. Who was the commander in chief of the U.S. occupation forces in Germany 1947-49 who defeated the Soviet blockade by organising an 'air-lift'?

ANSWERS.
1. Zbigniew Brzezinski. 2. Walter Mondale. 3. Chuck Yeager. 4. Bill Gates. 5. Howard Hughes. 6. Albert Michelson. 7. Charles and William Mayo. 8. Elisha Gray. 9. Rose O'Neal Greenhow. 10. George Marshall 11. Dean Acheson. 12. Jane Addams. 13. Ethan Allen. 14. Elizabeth Cady Stanton and Susan B. Anthony. 15. Lucius Clay.

How much do you know about notable Americans? (5)

QUESTIONS.

1. Who was the 18th/19th century pioneer who campaigned vigorously for U.S. control of Texas and after the war of 1836 became secretary of state of the independent Republic?

2. Who was the 17th century Virginia plantation owner whose rebellion brought attention to the brutality of the governor, William Berkeley, who was removed from his post?

3. Who was the 19th century health worker who founded the American Red Cross in 1881?

4. Who was the leader of the Sauk tribe who violently resisted the resettlement of his people off their original homelands, ending in a battle named after him in 1832?

5. Who was the U.S. general who led the U.S. troops in the 1944 invasion of France?

6. Who was the 2nd World War U.S. general known to his troops as 'Blood and Guts'?

7. Who was the leading Democrat and Speaker of the House whose tenure, 1912-1961, was the longest on record?

8. Who was the director of the F.B.I. from 1924 until his death in 1972?

9. Who was the Democrat politician, FDR's secretary of state 1933-44, often called the 'father' of the United Nations?

10. What was the name of the leader of the Chiricahua Apaches who fought relentlessly against white encroachment on his territory, until captured by General Crook in 1871?

11. Who was the Scottish-born American naval officer who led a small French squadron into action off the English coast in 1779, capturing HMS Serapis (although his own vessel the 'Bonhomme Richard' sank two days later?

12. Who was the U.S. swimmer who won 7 gold medals at the Munich Olympics in 1977?

13. He was born in 1900 in New Orleans and brought up in extreme poverty; his skill as a jazz trumpeter in the '20's conquered one world; his fabulous personality helped him conquer many others. He became an Ambassador for the United Nations. Who was he?

14. Who was the civil-rights lawyer to be appointed the first black judge in the U.S. Supreme Court in 1967?

ANSWERS.
1. Stephen Austin. 2. Nathaniel Bacon. 3. Clara Barton. 4. 'Black Hawk.' 5. Omar Bradley. 6. George S. Patton. 7. Samuel Rayburn. 8. J. Edgar Hoover. 9. Cordell Hull. 10. Cochise. 11. John Paul Jones. 12. Mark Spitz. 13. Louis Armstrong. 14. Thurgood Marshall.

Kings and Queens of Britain

How much do you know about British monarchs? (1)

QUESTIONS.

1. What was the name of the Chieftain of the British tribe the Catuvellauni who led the resistance to the Romans under Caesar in 54 BC ?

2. Who was the grandson of the above, also hereditary Chieftain of the Catuvellauni who was still fighting the Romans a hundred years later AD 5-40?

3. Who was the widow of King Prasutagas of the Iceni, whose territory was violently annexed by the Romans AD 60, who led a revolt burning the Roman towns of London, Colchester and St.Albans, and who poisoned herself rather than be taken alive?

4. What was the name of the King of Kent 560-616 who received the Christian missionary Augustine in 597, and was the first ruler of Anglo-Saxon England to become a Christian?

5. Who was the 7th century King of the East Angles whose burial chamber at Sutton Hoo, Suffolk, contained a huge wooden row-boat and many items of treasure?

6. Who was the great 8th century King of the Mercians who corresponded with Charlemagne, introduced silver coinage and dug a great dyke to separate his kingdom from Wales?

7. Who was the 9th century King of the West Saxons whose reputation rests on his defence of Wessex against the Danes, and his embodiment of the ideals of Christian kingship?

8. Who was the famous King of the Scots and the Picts who ruled from AD 841-858?

9. Who was the 9th century King who succeeded in uniting the three largest kingdoms in Wales, Gwynedd, Powys and Deheubarth?

10. Who was the King of the West Saxons AD 899-924, son of Alfred, who reconquered most of England from the Danes, and united Mercia and Wessex ?

11. Who was the son who succeeded Edward, even though illegitimate, and became the first to claim kingship 'of the English' AD 924-939?

12. Who was the King of England 968-1016 who spent most of his reign at war with Sweyn I of Denmark, and with Sweyn's successor?

13. Who was the King of the English, Danes and Norwegians, AD 1016-35?

ANSWERS.
1. Cassivelaunus. 2. Cymbeline. 3. Boudicca. (Boadicea). 4. Aethelberht. 5.Raedwald. 6. Offa.7.Alfred the Great. 8. Kenneth mac Alpin.9. Rhodri Mawr. 10. Edward the Elder. 11.Athelstan. 12. Ethelred the Unready. 13. Cnut.

How much do you know about British monarchs? (2)

QUESTIONS.

1. He was the illegitimate son of Robert I 'the Magnificent', duke of Normandy and Herleve, the daughter of a tanner. Who was he?

2. What was the name of his wife, the daughter of the count of Flanders?

3. What was the name of his son who became the second Norman king of England?

4. In 1058 Scotland acquired a new king, Malcolm III, son of Duncan I. Who was the ruling king at the time, whom he had to kill to take the crown?

5. What was the name of the king who died in 1135 of food poisoning or over-eating, in any case of 'a surfeit of lampreys'?

6. His daughter Matilda being married to Geoffrey of Anjou was unacceptable to the English and Norman barons, who chose as their king ....who?

7. Who, from 1137 to 1170 ruled over Gwynedd and was acknowledged as the principal ruler in Wales?

8. Who, from 1124 until 1153, was the king of the Scots?

9. Whose reign as King of England 1153-89, was overshadowed by the murder of Thomas a Becket, and by the ambitions of his remaining – and quarrelsome – sons?

10. Who was the vivacious, talented lady who became his wife and mother of his nine children?

11. Who was the king who spent only six months of a ten year kingship in England, the rest of the time on crusade, imprisoned by the Germans, and warring on the French?

12. Who was the king of Deheubarth 1155-97, who, after the death of Owain in 1170 was acknowledged as the leading ruler in Wales?

13. Which king of the Scots from 1165 until 1214 was called 'the Lion'?

14. Which English king 1199-1216 was nicknamed 'Softsword' for losing Normandy and Anjou?

15. In 1244, David the younger but legitimate son of Llywelyn ab Iorwerth, prince of Gwynedd was the first person to be given what title in partiicular?

ANSWERS.
1. William the Conqueror (reigned 1066-1087). 2. Matilda. 3. William II (Rufus).(r. 1087-1100). 4. Macbeth. 5. Henry I (r. 1100-35). 6. Stephen of Blois. 7. Owain. 8. David I. 9. Henry II. 10. Eleanor of Aquitaine. 11. Richard I. (Lionheart).(r. 1189-99) 12. Rhys ap Gruffydd. 13. William I. 14. John. 15. 'Prince of Wales'.

How much do you know about British monarchs? (3)

QUESTIONS.

1. Who was the king of the Scots 1214-49, who was known as 'the little red fox'?

2. Who inherited the English throne at the age of nine, rebuilt and enlarged Westminster Abbey, and ruled so incompetently that he nearly lost his crown to Simon de Montfort?

3. What was the name of the French Princess who became his wife in 1236?

4. What was the name of the Queen of England who never set foot in England?

5. Who was the king of Scotland 1249-86, knighted by Henry III of England in 1251 when hemarried Henry's daughter Margaret?

6. The tragedies of Alexander's life were the death of his wife (1275) and two sons. His daughter Margaret married Eric , king of Norway also died (1283) but not before giving birth to a daughter who became the heir to the Scottish throne. How was she known?

7. Which English king was nicknamed 'The Hammer of the Scots'?

8   What was the name of his Spanish wife, after whose death he built a cross at every place where her body rested on it's final journey from Nottingham to Westminster in 1290?

9. For political reasons he entered into a second marriage. Who was his second wife?

10. Who was king of England 1307-27?

11. Which European princess did he make his Queen?

12. But which handsome young Gascon knight enjoyed his favours to the point of indiscretion?

13. On midsummer day 1314 Edward II and his military advisers made a complete hash of abattle against a Scottish force one third of their size at Bannockburn. Who led the Scots?

14. Who inherited the Scottish throne in 1329 after the death of Robert Bruce?

15. Who inherited the English throne after the murder of Edward II in 1327?

ANSWERS.
1.Alexander II. 2. Henry III (r. 1216-72). 3. Eleanor of Provence. 4. Berengaria, wife of Richard I 5. Alexander III. 6. Margaret, Maid of Norway. 7. Edward I (r.1272-1307). 8. Eleanor of Castile. 9. Margaret of France. 10. Edward II. 11. Isabella of France. 12. Piers Gaveston. 13. Robert Bruce. 14. David II (r. 1329-71) 15. Edward III.

How much do you know about British monarchs? (4)

QUESTIONS.

1. The son and heir of Edward III, was also called Edward and was the first English Prince of Wales. But his valour on the field of battle earned him another title. What was it?

2. Regretfully he died a year before his father and the crown passed in 1377 to his son who was crowned as ......?

3. Who was Richard's famous and charismatic uncle, and for a while, guide?

4. In 1381 when Richard was only 14, he rode out to meet the armies of peasants who were staging 'the Peasant's Revolt'. Who was the leader of the revolt?

5. By whom was Richard II deposed, and apparently murdered in 1399?

6. Richard II was the last of which dynasty which had ruled England since 1154?

7. What title did Bolingbroke take for his reign 1399-1413?

8. And was the first of which royal dynasty?

9. Who was the first Stuart king of the Scots, 1371-1390?

10. Who was the 2nd Stuart king of the Scots, 1390-1406, disadvantaged by his illegitimacy?

11. He was the eldest son of Henry IV, renewed the 100 years war, occupied half of France and became heir to the dual monarchy France/England. What was his name?

12. As a result of the Battle of Agincourt 1415, Henry V also won for himself a French Princess the daughter of King Charles VI, as a bride. What was her name?

13. Who was the son and heir of Robert III who ruled the Scots 1406-1437? From 1406 until 1424 he was held in honourable captivity in England at the request of certain Scots nobles, during which time he married a kinswoman of Henry V.

14. Who was the only English sovereign to be crowned in both France and England, and was crowned a second time in England in 1470 after having spent nine years in the Tower?

15. Who was the king of the Scots 1437-1460, who married Mary of Gueldres andstabbed to death the intractable earl of Douglas?

ANSWERS.
1. 'The Black Prince'. 2. Richard II. 3. John of Gaunt. 4. Wat Tyler. 5. Henry Bolingbroke, son of John of Gaunt. 6. The Plantagenets. 7. Henry IV. 8. The House of Lancaster. 9. Robert II 10. Robert III, 11. Henry V. 12. Catherine de Valois. 13. James I. 14. Henry VI. 15. James II.

How much do you know about British monarchs? (5)

QUESTIONS.

1. Who was King of the Scots 1460-88, whose reign was troubled by poor relations with England and by ambitious and quarrelsome relatives? He was murdered at Sauchieburn.

2. Who was the first English King of the house of York, whose reign (1461-70; 1471-83) was interrupted when the Earl of Warwick ('Kingmaker') reinstated the bemused Henry VI?

3. Who was the 2nd English King of the house of York 1483-85, the last King to die in hand to hand fighting in battle (at Bosworth), and apparently, the murderer of his nephews?

4. Who was the first King of the house of Tudor, 1485-1509, whose detailed control of the administration of the country became legendary?

5. Who was King of the Scots 1488-1513? He married Margaret, daughter of Henry VII but still invaded England in 1513 where he was defeated and killed at Flodden.

6. Who was the first English King to be given the title 'Defender of the faith' and later. to be excommunicated?

7. Who was King of the Scots 1513-42, son of James IV and nephew of Henry VIII of England? Much influenced by his catholic wife Mary of Guise, he sent an invasion force into England where it was destroyed at Solway Moss in 1542. Within a month he was dead.

8. Who was King of England 1547-53, son of Henry VIII and Jane Seymour? His mother died at his birth, his father when he was nine and he himself only survived until he was fifteen.

9. Who was Queen of England 1553-58, and wife of Philip of Spain?

10. Who was Queen of England 1558-1603 remaining unmarried all her life?

11. Who was the much-married Queen of the Scots 1542-1567 when she was beheaded for plotting against the life of Elizabeth?

12. Who was King of England and Scotland 1603-25, son of Mary Queen of Scots and Darnley?

13. Who was the second son of James I of England and Anne of Denmark who reigned 1625-49, becoming the only English King to be beheaded following a revolution? 14. Who, in 1657, refused the throne of England, preferring to remain the country's 'Lord Protector'?

15. Who was the third King of the House of Stuart, restored to the throne in 1660 he reigned until 1685?

ANSWERS.
1. James III. 2. Edward IV. 3. Richard III. 4. Henry VII. 5. James IV. 6. Henry VIII.
7. James V. 8. Edward VI. 9. Mary I. 10. Elizabeth I. 11. Mary, queen of Scots. 12. James (I of England; VI of Scotland) 13. Charles I. 14. Oliver Cromwell. 15. Charles II.

How much do you know about British monarchs? (6)

QUESTIONS.

1. Who was the King of England 1685-1688? He was brother of Charles II, a convert to Catholicism, and was chased from the throne by William of Orange, the husband of his own daughter Mary.

2. Who were the joint rulers 1689-94?

3. After Mary's death in 1694 at the age of thirty two, William ruled alone until his death in1702. Who then inherited the crown?

4. Queen Anne was the last of the Stuarts. She died in 1714, predeceased by both her husband George of Denmark in 1708 and their son William Duke of Gloucester in 1700. The crown therefore passed to yet another dynasty. Which one?

5. Who was the first King of the Hanoverian dynasty, 1714-27?

6. Within a year of George I's accession, a rather pathetic attempt was made to mount a rebellion was made. It fizzled out rapidly, but who was behind it?

7. Who was the second King of the Hanoverian dynasty, 1727-60?

8. In 1745 a second and somewhat more successful attempt was made to foster rebellion in Scotland. It ended at the Battle of Culloden in April 1746. Who was the prime mover?

9. Who was the third King of the Hanoverian dynasty, 1760-1820? His reign was marked by the loss of the American colonies, for which he must share the blame with his Prime Minister, Lord North, as well as by his own mental illness, probably porphyria.

10. And what was the name of his Queen who bore him fifteen children?

11. Who was the fourth King of the Hanoverian dynasty, 1820-30?

12. And who was his Queen, with whom he claimed, he only spent one night?.

13. Who was the fifth and final King of the House of Hanover, 1830-37?

14. William leaving no direct descendants, the crown passed to his niece. Her name?

15. How old was Victoria when she was crowned Queen?

ANSWERS.
1. James II. 2. William III and Mary II. 3. Anne. 4. The House of Hanover. 5. George I. 6. James Francis Edward Stuart , known as 'The Old Pretender' and son of James II by his second wife. 7. George II. 8. Charles Edward Stuart, known as 'The Young Pretender' or 'Bonnie Prince Charlie'. 9. George III. 10. Charlotte. 11. George IV. 12. Caroline of Brunswick. 13. William IV. 14. Victoria. 15. Eighteen.

How much do you know about British monarchs? (7)

QUESTIONS.

1. How long did Queen Victoria reign?

2. Her first Prime Minister became her mentor, unofficial tutor and close friend. Who was he?

3. And who was the man whom she chose to be her Prince Consort?

4. How old was Prince Albert when he died of typhoid?

5. With the death of Victoria, the crown passed to yet another dynasty. The name please?

6. Who was the first King of this dynasty, who reigned from 1901 to 1910?

7. And what was the name of his Queen?

8. Who was the second Windsor King who reigned from 1910 to 1936?

9. And what was the name of his Queen?

10. Who was the third King of the Windsor dynasty, who came to the throne in 1936?

11. What was the name of the American divorcee for whom Edward VIII gave up the throne?

12. His place was taken by his younger brother. By what name did he reign?

13. George was King of England from 1936 to 1952. What was the name of his Queen before their marriage?

14. Who succeeded him after his death in 1952?

15. And who became the Queen's consort in November 1947?

ANSWERS.
1. 64 years (1837-1901). 2. Lord Melbourne. 3. Albert of Saxe-Coburg-Gotha. 4. 42
5. Windsor. 6. Edward VII. 7. Alexandra 8. George V. 9. Mary. 10. Edward VIII.
11. Mrs Wallis Simpson. 12. George VI. 13. Lady Elizabeth Bowes-Lyon. 14. Queen Elizabeth II. 15. Prince Philip of Greece, Duke of Edinburgh.

3

LITERATURE

Classical Literature

How much do you know about classical literature? (1)

QUESTIONS.

1. The first 'sequel' novel to be written in English was published in 1820 by Sir Walter Scott. What was its title?

2. And it was a sequel to ....?

3. Who wrote A Comic History of England in 1847/48?

4. Which book by Robert Burton published in 1621, appears at first to be a medical treatise, but in fact is an amusing satire on some of mankind's weaknesses?

5.   In which Henry Fielding novel does Squire Allworthy appear?

6. According to Coleridge in Kublai Khan what was the name of the sacred river of Xanadu?

7. In which George Eliot novel is the central figure an unhappy young woman named Hetty Sorrel?

8. What was the name of The American Senator in Anthony Trollope's novel of that title?

9. In which novel by Henry James does Chadwick Newsome appear?

10. In The Amazing Marriage by George Meredith, the heroine is abandoned on her wedding night. What is her name?

11. In The Mourning Bride by William Congreve, the heroine Is abandoned on her wedding night. What is her name?

12. Who, according to Ariosto's 1532 poem Orlando Furioso, journeys to the moon on a hippogriff to bring back Orlando's lost wits?

13. In which of Sheridan's plays does Sir Anthony Absolute play a part?

14. In which comedy by Ben Jonson is the central character a rogue called 'Face'?

15. In the ballad La Belle Dame sans Merci by Keats, a knight makes the fatal mistake of falling in love with a woman who is no ordinary woman, but what?

ANSWERS
1. The Abbot. 2. The Monastery. 3. Gilbert a Beckett. 4. The Anatomy of Melancholy. 5. Tom Jones. 6. The Alph. 7. Adam Bede. 8. Elias Gotobed. 9. The Ambassadors. 10. Carinthia. 11. Almeria. 12. Astolfo. 13. The Rivals. 14. The Alchemist. 15. An elf.

How much do you know about classical literature? (2)

QUESTIONS.

1. Who was the 1st century North African Roman poet and philosopher whose best-known work is The Golden Ass?

2. The Arabian classic The Thousand and One Nights was translated into English in the definitive version by whom?

3. What was the name of the Great enchanter, symbolising hypocrisy, in Spenser's Faerie Queene?

4. What was the masterpiece of the French novelist Pierre Choderlos de Laclos?

5. In which of Dicken's novels did Miss La Creevy appear?

6. Who was the English writer whose works, such as The Lady's Not For Burning in 1949 were heralded as the return of the classic poetic drama?

7. Who published The Lays of Ancient Rome in 1842?

8. Who was the author of best-sellers like Uncle Silas and In a Glass Darkly in the 1860's/1880's, who is now considered a master of the sinister and the supernatural?

9. Squire Hardcastle, his wife and daughter are characters in which successful comedy by Oliver Goldsmith?

10. What is the name of Thomas Hardy's first published novel, which appeared in 1871?

11. Hardy himself classified his novels and short stories in three different groups. The first was 'Novels of Character and Environment'; the second was 'Romances and Fantasies'. What was the third group?

12. In which work by Aristophanes do the women of Athens deny their husbands their conjugal rights until they will end the war with Sparta?

13. Who was the poet author of Sohrab and Rustum and Tristram and Yseult, acknowledged to be the leading critic of the Classics of his day?

14. Who was the author of Tom Brown's Schooldays?

15. Who was Michael Henchard?

ANSWERS
1. Apuleius. 2. Sir Richard Burton. 3. Archimage. 4. Les Liaisons Dangereuses. 5. Nicholas Nickleby. 6. Christopher Fry. 7. Thomas Babington Macaulay. 8. Joseph Sheridan Le Fanu. 9. She Stoops to Conquer. 10. Desperate Remedies. 11. Novels of Ingenuity. 12. Lysistrata. 13. Matthew Arnold. 14. Thomas Hughes. 15. The Mayor of Casterbridge.

How much do you know about classical literature? (3)

QUESTIONS

1. Whose first novel Love and Friendship was written (but not published) when she was only fourteen?

2. Who delivered a course of six lectures in 1840 which were published in 1841, on 'Heroes, Hero-Worship and the Heroic in History'?

3. Which 16th/17th century dramatist is best known for such works as A Woman Killed with Kindness?

4. Who wrote the humorous collection of Bab Ballads?

5. Who was the 19th century professor of anatomy and physiology at Harvard University who was also a prolific writer, starting with The Autocrat at the Breakfast Table?

6. Who was the highly successful 19th century author of over 80 novels, written mainly for boys, including The Coral Island and The Young Fur Traders?

7. Who was the prolific 19th century French author who wrote 91 separate complete novels, all part of a series of co-ordinated and connected works called collectively the Comedie Humaine?

8. What was the name of the principal character in Marlowe's The Jew of Malta?

9. What was the name of the author of the Barsetshire series?

10. What was the name of Mr Pickwick's landlady in Pickwick Papers, who sued him for breach of promise?

11. Who was the prolific 19th century French poet, novelist and dramatist who was the central figure of the Romantic movement in France and author of Les Miserables?

12. In which play by Philip Massinger does Sir Giles Overreach appear?

13. What is the name of the heroine of Hardy's Far From The Madding Crowd?

14. Who was the French dramatist and author of The Barber of Seville and The Marriage of Figaro?

15. What name does Don Quixote give to his beloved?

ANSWERS
1. Jane Austen. 2. Thomas Carlyle. 3. Thomas Heywood. 4. W.S Gilbert. 5. Oliver Wendell Holmes. 6. R. M Ballantyne. 7. Honore de Balzac. 8. Barabas. 9. Anthony Trollope. 10. Mrs Bardell. 11. Victor Hugo. 12. A New Way to Pay Old Debts. 13. Bathsheba Evans. 14. Beaumarchais. 15. Dulcinea del Toboso.

Contemporary American Literature

How much do you know about contemporary American literature? (1)

QUESTIONS.

1. Which American author was inspired by the 'Oresteia' of Aeschylus to write 'Mourning Becomes Electra'?

2. The first volume of whose autobiography is called I Know Why The Caged Bird Sings?

3. What is the name of the private detective hired to solve the mystery of The Lady in the Lake?

4. Who is the American author of science fiction, whose works include the Earthsea Trilogy and are admired as much for the quality of their prose as for their imagination?

5. The American authoress Susan Sontag wrote a fictionalized account of the life of Sir William and Lady Emma Hamilton in Naples, and of their meeting with Nelson. What is it called?

6. Who was the American author of the novel The Magnificent Ambersons better remembered as an Orson Welles' film?

7. Who is the American poet, first of the 'New York School' and author of Self-Portrait in a Convex Mirror?

8. Who is the hero of Ernest Hemingway's The Sun Also Rises published in 1926?

9. William Sydney Porter, in prison for embezzlement, began to write short stories which became very popular and he became very successful. What pen-name did he take?

10. According to the Science Fiction novel A Canticle for Leibowitz by Walter Miller, for what crime was Leibowitz executed?

11. Who was the English/Scots/German-born, American-educated writer whose crime novels have a distinctively black humour, especially the series about the criminally-minded Mr Tom Ripley?

12. Who was the black American author who made such an impact on America's consciousness with his first book Go Tell It On The Mountain in 1953?

13. What is the name of the author of the 'Godfather' series about the Corleone family?

14. Who is the American novelist and short-story writer, best known, perhaps, for his Slaughterhouse Five?

15. Harry Angstrom is the hero of which John Updike series of four books?

ANSWERS
1. Eugene O' Neill. 2. Maya Angelou. 3. Philip Marlowe. 4. Ursula Le Guin. 5. The Volcano. 6. Booth Tarkington. 7. John Ashbery. 8. Hake Barnes. 9. O. Henry. 10. For booklegging (smuggling books). 11. Patricia Highsmith. 12. James Baldwin. 13. Mario Puzo. 14. Kurt Vonnegut Jr. 15. The 'Rabbit' series.

How much do you know about contemporary American Literature? (2)

QUESTIONS.

1. Who was the Leningrad-born American writer who expounded her political philosophy 'Objectivism' through novels such as Atlas Shrugged, The Fountainhead and We, The Living?

2. Who is the playwright and author of Death of a Salesman, The Crucible and other powerful dramas?

3. Who was the novelist who was perhaps more famous for his way of life than for his books, although Junkie (1953) and Naked Lunch (1959) caused quite a stir when they came out?

4. For what best-selling novel did Saul Bellow win the National Book Award for fiction in 1965?

5. Who won the 1984 Pulitzer Prize for fiction in 1984 for Glengarry Glen Ross?

6. What was Walt Whitman's major work?

7. Whose best-known work was Ship of Fools?

8. Who wrote Tender is the Night?

9. Who was the author of the trilogy of novels known collectively as U.S.A?

10. Who wrote the political satire Washington DC which was so successful in the 1960's?

11. William Saroyan was a prolific writer of short stories and plays, for one of which he was awarded the Pulitzer Prize, which he refused to accept. What was it called?

12. Who wrote the partly autobiographical novel The Bell Jar?

13. What was the name of the play with which Thornton Wilder won the Pulitzer Prize?

14. Who wrote the social drama The Children's Hour?

15. Who is the author of Giles Goat-Boy and The Sot-Weed Factor?

ANSWERS
1. Ayn Rand. 2. Arthur Miller. 3. William Burroughs. 4. Herzog. 5. David Mamet. 6. Leaves of Grass. 7. Katherine Anne Porter. 8. F. Scott Fitzgerald. 9. John Dos Passos. 10. Gore Vidal. 11. The Time of Your Life. 12. Sylvia Plath. 13. Our Town. 14. Lillian Helman. 15. John Barth.

How much do you know about contemporary American Literature? (3)

QUESTIONS.

1, Who was the American exile in Paris who founded the bookshop 'Shakespeare and Company, which became a meeting-place for other American literary exiles?

2. Whose reputation was established in 1961 by his anti-war novel Catch 22?

3. Whose work includes The Heart is a Lonely Hunter and Reflections in a Golden Eye?

4. Who won the National Book award for his novel of narcotic addiction The Man With the Golden Arm?

5. In 1997, Charles Frazier reworked the Odyssey into a tale set during the American Civil War. What is it called?

6. And which author rewrote much of the Arthurian legend told this time from the point of view of the women involved, in The Mists of Avalon?

7. In 1979 Norman Mailer was awarded the Pulitzer Prize. For which book?

8. One of America's foremost Jewish writers won both the National Book Award and the Pulitzer Prize for The Fixer. What was his name?

9. Who was the writer who could make the transition from Breakfast at Tiffany's to In Cold Blood with no problem?

10. Who wrote The Martian Chronicles and many other highly imaginative works?

11. Who is the main character in Upton Sinclair's 'roman fleuve' entitled World's End?

12. What was the title of the John Steinbeck story, published in 1939, about a family fleeing the dust bowl of Oklahoma to a better life in California?

13. In which play by Tennessee Williams does Blanche Du Bois play a central role?

14. Who is the author of The Day After Tomorrow and Day of Confession?

15. Whose legal dramas are set in fictitious Kindle County?

ANSWERS
1. Sylvia Beach. 2. Joseph Heller. 3. Carson McCullers. 4. Nelson Algren. 5. Cold Mountain. 6. Marion Zimmer Bradley. 7. The Executioner's Song. 8. Bernard Malamud. 9. Truman Capote. 10. Ray Bradbury. 11. Lanny Budd. 12. The Grapes of Wrath. 13. A Streetcar Named Desire. 14. Allan Folsom. 15. Scott Turow

Contemporary European literature

How much do you know about contemporary European literature? (1)

QUESTIONS.

1. Who wrote the James Bond novel Colonel Sun under the pseudonym Robert Markham?

2. One part of whose autobiography is entitled Bury My Heart at W.H. Smiths?

3. What is the term coined by Terence Blacker in Publishing News in 1992 to depict novels which dwell on English middle class country life and values?

4. Waiting for Godot by Samuel Becket is the ultimate example of what kind of theatre?

5. Which famous book in seven sections (each published separately) ends with the narrator discovering his artistic vocation, leading him to write the book that the reader has just finished reading?

6. Who was the author whose biographies of D.H. Lawrence and T.E. Lawrence, in the '50's, caused great controversy?

7. Who was the popular and prolific writer, many of whose novels celebrate life in the North East of England?

8. Who was the popular French dramatist whose works include Antigone and Becket?

9. Lady Chatterley's lover was of course the gamekeeper. But what was his name?

10. Whose first volume of autobiography described 'a village girl who baptized him with cidrous kisses behind a haycock'?

11. Radclyffe Hall's book about lesbian relationships, published in 1928, caused a scandal and led to a trial for obscenity. What was it called?

12. Who was the Scots dramatist and novelist whose major creation was the 'boy who never grew up – Peter Pan'?

13. Who is the Italian Nobel Laureate satirist and author of 'Can'tPay? Won't Pay!'?

14. Who is the Czech dramatist, author of The Garden Party and The Memorandum, perhaps best known for his political successes?

15. For which play is the Spanish poet and dramatist Federico Garcia Lorca best remembered?

ANSWERS

1. Sir Kingsley Amis. 2. Brian Aldiss. 3. The 'Aga Saga'. 4. The Theatre of the Absurd. 5. A la Recherche du Temps Perdu. 6. Richard Aldington. 7. Catherine Cookson. 8. Jean Anouilh. 9. Oliver Mellors. 10. Laurie Lee, in Cider With Rosie. 11. The Well of Loneliness. 12. J. M. Barrie. 13. Dario Fo. 14. Vaclav Havel. 15. The House of Bernarda Alba.

How much do you know about contemporary European literature? (2)

QUESTIONS.

1. Who was the author who wrote tellingly about love crossing social barriers, in The Go-Between, The Hireling, etc.?

2. For which work is Czech writer Jaroslav Hasek best remembered?

3. M.P. for Oxford University; author, satirist and humorist, his best known works included The Water Gipsies.

4. Who was the German-Swiss Nobel Laureate and author of several novels with a mystical slant, including The Glass Bead Game?

5. Who was the phonetician in G. B. Shaw's Pygmalion?

6. Who is the contemporary dramatist whose first London success Relatively Speaking in 1967 has been followed by many others, including the series Talking Heads written specially for television?

7. In 1993 Susan Hill published a sequel to Daphne du Maurier's Rebecca. What is it called?

8. Who was the author of Lost Horizon and Good-bye Mr Chips?

9. By which name was the French satirist and actor Jean-Baptiste Poquelin better known?

10. Who was the 1934 Italian Nobel Laureate and author, amongst many other works, of Six Characters in Search of an Author?

11. Who was the hero of Jules Vernes' Around the World in Eighty Days?

12. George Bernard Shaw is reported as having said : " Reading his plays makes me want to tear up my own". Of whom was he speaking?

13. Who was the author of A Clockwork Orange?

14. Whose 1999 Booker Prize 'Disgrace' is set in post-apartheid South Africa?

15. In Cold Comfort Farm by Stella Gibbons, the heroine Flora Poste visits relatives in the Sussex countryside. What is the family name?

ANSWERS
1. L.P. Hartley. 2. The Good Soldier Schweik. 3. A. P. Herbert. 4. Herman Hesse. 5. Henry Higgins. 6. Sir Alan Ayckbourn. 7. Mrs de Winter. 8. James Hilton. 9. Moliere. 10. Luigi Pirandello. 11. Phineas Fogg. 12. Anton Chekov. 13. Anthony Burgess. 14. J.M. Coetzee. 15. Starkadder.

How much do you know about contemporary European literature? (3)

QUESTIONS.

1. What is the name of the fantasy trilogy written by C. S. Lewis?

2. Who was the author of Hobson's Choice the most successful and most often performed play of the 'Manchester' school?

3. What was George Orwell's account of his participation in the Spanish Civil War entitled?

4. What is the name of the hero of C.S. Forester's series of novels set in the time of the Napoleonic Wars?

5. Who was the author of The Chalk Garden and National Velvet upon which the 1944 Elizabeth Taylor film was based?

6. Who is the Scottish novelist whose first publication The Wasp Factory caused something of a sensation?

7. What is the title of Patricia Barker's book, published in 1991, about the First World War which did so much to establish her reputation?

8. Who wrote, amongst many other works, The Shropshire Lad?

9. And who was the author of the novel Howard's End?

10. What is the title of the book by Richard Hughes about a family of children captured by pirates in the Caribbean?

11. Who was the U.K. Poet Laureate from 1984 until his death in 1998?

12. Whose Playboy of the Western World caused a minor scandal when it was performed for the first time in Dublin?

13. Whose work has never ceased to attract attention, from Rosencratz and Guildenstern are dead in 1966 to the screenplay for Shakespeare in Love in 1998?

14. Who wrote An Intelligent Woman's Guide to Socialism, Capitalism, Sovietism and Fascism?

15. Who came to prominence in 1989 with The Remains of the Day?

ANSWERS
1. Out of the Silent Planet. 2. Harold Brighouse. 3. Homage to Catalonia. 4. Horatio Hornblower. 5. Enid Bagnold. 6. Iain M. Banks. 7. Regeneration. 8. A. E. Housman. 9. E. M. Forster. 10. A High Wind in Jamaica. 11. Ted Hughes. 12. J. M. Synge. 13. Tom Stoppard. 14. George Bernard Shaw. 15. Kazuo Ishiguro.

Cops and Robbers

How much do you know about non-police investigators, e.g. pathologists; doctors; monks; etc.?

QUESTIONS.

1. Way back in 1907 R. Austin Freeman wrote The Red Thumb Mark, a thriller in which the detective was a doctor. His name?

2. 'The Paddington Mystery' by John Rhode featured which doctor?

2. Who did John Dickson Carr introduce us to in Hag's Nook?

4. And Josephine Bell, in 'Murder in Hospital' gave us …?

5. And V.C. Clinton-Baddeley wrote about a doctor named …?

6. When The Bough Breaks by Jonathon Kellerman introduced us to a psychologist working often with the police called …?

7. In The Alienist by Caleb Carr we met which psychiatrist ?

8. Post Mortem in 1990 was the first of a whole series by Patricia Cornwell, featuring Virginia's chief medical examiner …?

9. And Deja Dead by Kathy Reichs introduced us to which forensic anthropologist?

10. The 'Silent Witness' series by Nigel McRery centres around the work of Britain's favourite pathologist …?

11. Aaron Elkins also writes about a forensic anthropologist, named?

12. And Sharyn McCrumb's medical examiner heroine is …?

13. In 1977, Edith Pargeter writing under her pseudonym Ellis Peters introduced us, in A Morbid Taste For Bones to her medieval monk investigator …?

14. Have you met Chris Roger's creation, a Houston based bounty hunter ? She first appeared in Bitch Factor and her name is …?

15. Like Ellis Peters, Susanna Gregory takes us back a few years, to around 1350 in fact, to follow the efforts of her physician detective …what was that name again?

ANSWERS
1. Dr Thorndyke. 2. Dr Lancelot Priestley. 3. Dr Gideon Fell. 4. Dr David Wintringham. 5. Dr R.V. Davie. 6. Dr Alex Delaware. 7. Dr Laszlo Kreizler. 8. Dr Kay Scarpetta. 9. Dr Temperance Brennan. 10. Professor Samantha Ryan. 11. Dr Gideon Oliver. 12. Dr Elizabeth MacPherson. 13. Brother Cadfael. 14. Dixie Flanagan. 15. Matthew Bartholomew.

How much do you know about fictitious policemen? (1)

QUESTIONS.

1. Who was the policeman hero of A.E.W. Mason's novel At The Villa Rosa?

2. In 1967, Edith Pargeter writing as Ellis Peters published Black is the Colour of My True Love's Heart, introducing …?

3. D.I. Thomas Lynley and D.S. Barbara Havers are creations of?

4. Naked in Death by J.D. Robb (Nora Roberts) introduced us to which New York Police Department Lieutenant?

5. In 1929 Arthur W. Upfield published The Barakee Mystery, introducing which unconventional policeman?

6. And in the same year Josephine Tey wrote The Man in the Queue as a challenge for her detective of what name?

7. It was in 1931 that the world famous Inspector Jules Maigret appeared first in The Death of Monsieur Gallet. His creator?

8. In 1934, Chief Inspector Roderick Alleyn put in an appearance in A Man Lay Dead by which famous mystery writer?

9. And in 1935 Georgette Heyer published Death in the Stocks to introduce her formidable duo Superintendant Hannasyde and …?

10. Michael Innes wrote Death at the President's Lodging in 1936 which allowed us to meet …who?

11. What is the name of the Detective Sergeant about whom Faye Kellerman writes with such authority?

12. District Attorney Lily Forrester appeared in Mitigating Circumstances by …?

13. In The Chinese Bell Murders in 1951, the investigating officer was not a policeman but a Judge – Judge Dee. Who was the author?

14. Cop Hater in 1956 introduced us to the men and women of the 87th Precinct, created by …?

15. And For Love Of Imabelle in 1957 introduced two unforgettable Harlem-based cops, Gravedigger Jones and Coffin Ed Johnson. What was the name of their creator?

ANSWERS
1. Inspector Hanand. 2. D.I George Felse. 3. Elizabeth George. 4. Eve Dallas. 5. Inspector Napoleon Bonaparte. 6. Inspector Alan Grant. 7. Georges Simenon. 8. Ngaio Marsh. 9. Inspector Hemingway. 10. Inspector John Appleby. 11. Peter Decker. 12. Nancy Taylor. 13. Robert H. Van Gulik. 14. Ed McBain. 15. Chester Himes.

How much do you know about fictitious policemen? (2)

QUESTIONS.

1. In 1958 Colin Watson introduced us to Inspector Purbright, in?

2. In 1962, in Love in Amsterdam we had the pleasure of meeting Inspector Piet Van Der Valk, whose creator was …?

3. And in Cover Her Face, P.D James introduced us to her great fictitious policeman …?

4. In 1964, in The Perfect Murder by H.R.F Keating we met, for the first time, which wily Indian policeman ?

5. Also in '64, we met Chief Inspector Reginald Wexford in From Doom With Death. Who is his famous creator?

6. Skin Deep in 1968 by Peter Dickinson introduced us to which high-ranking policeman?

7. In the curiously entitled Wobble to Death the author Peter Lovesey handed the investigation over to his creation …?

8. And in A Clubbable Woman by Reginald Hill in 1970, we encountered which sometimes uncomfortable pairing?

9. In The Steam Pig, James McClure introduced which detective?

10. Whom did Colin Dexter introduce in 1975 in Last Bus to Woodstock?

11. In 1979 James Melville published The Wages of Zen which featured a Japanese policeman. His name?

12. And who did Campbell Armstrong's Jig introduce us to?

13. In 1981 Martin Cruz Smith transported us to Moscow in Gorky Park, the first outing for his inimitable detective …?

14. Whereas Donna Leon sets the scene of her murder mysteries in Venice, home of which senior policeman?

15. Open Season by Archer Mayor introduced us to …?

ANSWERS
1. Coffin, Barely Used. 2. Nicholas Freeling. 3. Chief Inspector Adam Dalgliesh. 4. Inspector Ghote. 5. Ruth Rendell. 6. Superintendent James Pibble. 7. Sgt. Richard Cribb. 8. Superintendent Andy Dalziel and Inspector Peter Pascoe. 9. Lieutenant 'Tromp' Kramer. 10. Chief Inspector Morse. 11. Superintendent Tetsuo Otami. 12. Frank Pagan. 13. Senior Investigator Arkady Renko. 14. Commisario Guido Brunetti. 15. Lieutenant Joe Gunther.

How much do you know about fictitious policemen? (3)

QUESTIONS.

1. In his series of police investigation novels all of which contain the word 'Prey' in their titles, John Sandford presents which hero?

2. Ian Rankin has put Edinburgh on the map with his series featuring which Detective Inspector?

3. And J. Wallis Martin did the same thing for Manchester in her Bird Yard, leaving the investigation to whom?

4, In 1997 Lisa See introduced us to crime in China with The Flower Net featuring which policewoman?

5. Michael Connelly began a series about a Los Angeles Police Dept. detective in The Black Echo. What is the detective's name?

6. And James Patterson has a series, including Cat and Mouse all about the same detective. What is his name?

7. John Connolly began a series about Detective Charlie 'Bird' Parker in 1999 with which murder mystery?

8. In 2000 Mo Hayder's first thriller was called Birdman and it introduced us to whom?

9. In Prayer For The Dead, Close To The Bone and The Edge of Sleep, David Wiltse has created an unusual investigator. His name?

10. A classic series with a Scotland Yard background was created by John Creasey under the pseudonym J.J.Marric, about which detective?

11. What is the name of Greg Iles' Louisiana-based cop?

11. In Hornet's Nest and Southern Cross Patricia Cornwell presents two new female cops, a Police Chief and her Deputy. Can you name either of them?

12. Linda Fairstein's heroine is not a policewoman but an Assistant D.A in New York. The subject of three books, her name is …?

13. James Patterson's new thriller 1st To Die is about a female homicide inspector in San Francisco. Her name please?

15. What is the name of Martina Cole's policewoman heroine?

ANSWERS
1. Deputy Chief Lucas Davenport. 2. D.I John Rebus. 3. D.S Parker. 4. Detective Lin Hulan. 5. Harry Bosch. 6. Alex Cross. 7. Every Dead Thing. 8. D.I Jack Caffery. 9. John Becker. 10. Gideon of the Yard. 11. Dave Robicheaux. 12. Judy Hammer and Virginia West. 13. Alexandra Cooper. 14. Lindsay Boxer. 15. D.I Kate Burrows.

How much do you know about fictitious private detectives? (1)

QUESTIONS.

1. Who introduced the detective C. Auguste Dupin in The Murders in the Rue Morgue, in 1841?

2. In which book did Sir Arthur Conan-Doyle introduce his detective Sherlock Holmes in 1887?

3. In 1907 Maurice Leblanc, in his mystery The Seven of Hearts introduced us to whom?

4. G.K. Chesterton's famous priest-detective appeared in 1910 in The Secret Garden. His name, please?

5. Melville Davisson Post created a homespun character detective called Uncle Abner in 1911, in which mystery?

6. More sophisticated readers appreciated E .C. Bentley's smooth detective Philip Trent who appeared in 1913 in which novel?

7. In 1914 Ernest Bramah used the name of his detective for the title of his book. What was it?

8. And in 1920, H. C. Bailey used a similar formula to present his detective Reggie Fortune, in which book?

9. In the same year Agatha Christie published The Mysterious Affair at Styles, introducing her famous Belgian detective, named…?

10. But for her Secret Adversary in 1922 she preferred a very English young married couple as detectives. Who were they?

11. In 1923 Dorothy L. Sayers in Whose Body? introduced which aristocratic detective?

12. The Rasp published in 1924 introduced us to an ex-Army officer turned investigator, Col. Anthony Gethryn. His author?

13. In The Layton Court Mystery in 1925, Anthony Berkeley introduced us to his detective hero named…?

14. Also in 1925 the American author Earl Derr Biggs set the scene for his famous Chinese-American detective in The House Without A Key. The detective's name please?

15. In The Benson Murder Case in 1926, S.S. Van Dine introduced us to … who, exactly?

ANSWERS

1. Edgar Allan Poe. 2. A Study In Scarlet. 3. Arsene Lupin. 4. Father Brown. 5. The Doomdorf Mystery. 6. Trent's Last Case. 7. Max Carrados. 8. Call Mr Fortune. 9. Hercule Poirot. 10. Tommy and Tuppence Beresford. 11. Lord Peter Wimsey. 12. Philip MacDonald. 13. Roger Sheringham. 14. Charlie Chan. 15. Philo Vance.

How much do you know about fictitious private detectives? (2)

QUESTIONS.

1. 1929 was a good year for private investigators. In The Crime at Black Dudley Margery Allingham introduced us to …whom?

2. And Frederic Dannay and Manfred B. Lee published their Roman Hat Mystery in which who made a first appearance?

3. Tough P.I. Sam Spade arrived on the scene in The Maltese Falcon by which author?

4. And Gladys Mitchell's charismatic detective Dame Beatrice Lestrange Bradley impressed in which novel?

5. In 1930 Agatha Christie introduced Miss Jane Marple in which novel with an ecclesiastical flavour?

6. And Miles Burton solved The Secret of High Eldersham through the efforts of his creation named …?

7. In 1932 Dashiel Hammett returned with a vintage detective story The Thin Man featuring which husband and wife team?

8. In 1933 the famous lawyer Perry Mason appeared for the first time in The Case of the Velvet Claws. His creator?

9. In 1934 Mignon Eberhart introduced us to her well-named female detective, Susan Dare in what?

10. In the same year another aristocratic detective, Sir Henry Merrivale appeared in The White Priory Murders by which author?

11. And Rex Stout introduced a detective who solved complex cases whilst growing orchids in Fer-de-Lance. His name?

12. Nicholas Blake's 1935 novel A Question of Proof brought his detective to our attention. What was his name?

13. In the same year we met detective Kent Murdock in Murder With Pictures. Who was the author?

14. And Murder in the Madhouse by Jonathon Latimer featured …?

15. In Dance of Death in 1938, Helen McCloy introduced which investigator?

ANSWERS
1. Albert Campion. 2. Ellery Queen. 3. Dashiell Hammett. 4. Speedy Death. 5. Murder At The Vicarage. 6. Desmond Merron. 7. Nick and Nora Charles. 8. Erle Stanley Gardner. 9. The Cases of Susan Dare. 10. Carter Dickson. 11. Nero Wolfe. 12. Nigel Strangeways. 13. George Harmon Coxe. 14. Bill Crane. 15. Basil Willing.

How much do you know about fictitious private detectives? (3)

QUESTIONS.

1. Also in 1938, British P.I. Slim Callaghan made his first appearance in The Urgent Hangman. Who was his creator?

2. In 1939 Erle Stanley Gardner, under the pseudonym A.A.Fair, published The Bigger They Come featuring which detective team?

3. The same year one of the greatest names in this genre appeared in The Big Sleep by Raymond Chandler. His name ?

4. Contemporary writer Frank Lean uses Manchester as the background for the work of his private investigator named …?

5. What is the name of the series which features Stephen R. Donaldson's Ginny Fistoulari and Mick 'Brew' Axbrewder?

6. 1947 saw the arrival of the toughest private eye of all, Mike Hammer in I, The Jury by which great U.S writer?

7. A truly great American private eye appeared on the scene in 1949 in The Moving Target by F. Ross Macdonald. His name?

8. Who is the creator of the laconic private eye 'Spenser'?

9. Everyone knows Sara Paretsky's famous feisty female sleuth …?

10. In 1964, in The Deep Blue Goodbye by John D. MacDonald, we met a different kind of detective hero, named ?

11. In 1965 Swedish writers Maj Sjowall and Per Wahloo created who, in their book Roseanna?

12. Who is Sue Grafton's female P.I. in the alphabet series?

13. In 1972, P.D. James departed from her police based novels to introduce gutsy female private detective Cordelia Gray in which book?

14. In 1977 Antonia Fraser abandoned her historical biographies to write Quiet As A Nun, a thriller which introduced us to which female investigator?

15. And Val McDermid has two series going about Private Eyes. Can you name either of them?

ANSWERS
1. Peter Cheyney. 2. Bertha Cool and Donald Lam. 3. Philip Marlowe. 4. Dave Cunane. 5. 'The Man Who' series. 6. Mickey Spillane. 7. Lew Archer. 8. Robert Parker. 9. V.I. Warshanski. 10. Travis McGee. 11. Martin Beck. 12. Kinsey Millhone. 13. An Unsuitable Job For A Woman. 14. Jemima Shore. 15. Kate Brannigan and Lindsay Gordon.

Lord of the Rings

How much do you know about the Fellowship of the Ring? (1)

QUESTIONS.

1.   When the book opens, it is with news that someone in the Shire is planning a birthday party. Who?

2.   Which birthday is he celebrating?

3.   What is the name of Bilbo's home?

4.   He shares his home with his nephew and heir, whose name is…?

5.   Bilbo leaves The Shire for one last journey. What does he leave behind for his nephew?

6.   Many years later Frodo learns from Gandalf the Wizard that the ring is a thing of great power belonging to…?

7.   To avoid bringing danger to The Shire, Frodo sets out to seek the counsel of ….whom?

8.   Who does he take with him as his companion?

9.   Four other young hobbits help him, although only two decide to go on the whole journey. Their names are…?

10. Walking through The Shire they realise that they are being pursued by what?

11. Leaving The Shire behind they ride through The Old Forest, where they are nearly trapped by Old Man Willow, a very evil-hearted tree. Who comes to their rescue?

12. What is the name of Tom Bombadil's lady?

13. Tom comes their aid yet again, to save them from whom?

14. They arrive safely at the village of Bree. What is the name of the Inn at which they take a room?

15. What is the name of the innkeeper?

ANSWERS
1. Bilbo Baggins. 2. His eleventy-first (111). 3. Bag End. 4. Frodo. 5. A gold ring. 6. Sauron the Great, the Dark Lord. 7. Elrond Halfelven. 8. His gardner, Sam Gamgee. 9. Merry Brandybuck and Pippin Took. 10. The Black Riders. 11. Tom Bombadil. 12. Goldberry. 13. The Barrow Wights. 14. The Prancing Pony. 15. Barliman Butterbur.

How much do you know about the Fellowship of the Ring? (2)

QUESTIONS.

1. For the night at the inn, who does Frodo pass himself off as?

2. During the evening they meet a Ranger, named…?

3. Frodo is wounded by a dagger from one of the Black Riders in a fight on which hill?

4. What is the house of Elrond Halfelven called?

5. Frodo sees the daughter of Elrond, what is her name?

6. At the Council of Elrond Frodo meets many people who will play a part – or who have already played a part in the trials of the ring-bearer. Who are the two dwarves?

7. Who is the Elf from Northern Mirkwood?

8. Who is the warrior who has come from Gondor?

9. And Strider is revealed as …who?

10. And it is revealed that the Black Riders are …what?

11. What is forged anew by the Elven smiths?

12. What two gifts does Bilbo give to Frodo before the Company of the Ring set out on the Quest of Mount Doom?

13. What is the name of the mountain upon which they are trapped by a snowfall?

14. Having failed to cross over the mountains, the Company is obliged to cross under them. Where does the path lead to?

15. What is the password to enter the Doors of Durin?

ANSWERS
1. Mr Underhill. 2. Strider. 3. Weathertop. 4. Rivendell. 5. Arwen Evenstar. 6. Gloin, one of Bilbo's original twelve companions, and his son, Gimli. 7. Legolas. 8. Boromir. 9. Aragorn, son of Arathorn, heir of Elendil. 10. Nazgul (Ringwraiths). 11. The Sword of Elendil. 12. His sword Sting, and his coat of mithril (dwarf chainmail). 13. Mount Caradhras. 14. Moria. 15. 'Friend'

How much do you know about the Fellowship of the Ring? (3)

QUESTIONS.

1. Whose tomb do they find in the mines of Moria?

2. With what creature does Gandalf fight on the Bridge of Khazad-Dum?

3. What is the Elvish name for the Golden Wood?

4. Who are the people who live in Lothlorien?

5. And who are their leaders?

6. Into what device were Frodo and Sam allowed to look?

7. What special food for travellers do the Galadhrim give the Company to help their journey?

8. What gift does Galadriel give to Sam Gamgee before the Company leaves?

9. What gift does Gimli request of Galadriel?

10. And what is in the crystal phial which Galadrial gives to Frodo?

11. What is the name of the tributary of the Great River on which they take up their journey once more?

12. They pass the Argonath, the Pillars of Kings, which are statues hewn from rock. Of which kings?

13. What is the name of the sheer rocky island of which they then come to?

14. And, frightened by Boromir, Frodo sits upon Amon Hen, which means ....?

15. After seeing war and desolation everywhere, Frodo and Sam set off without the others, over the grey hills of Emyn Muil; and down into where?

ANSWERS
1. Balin the dwarf. 2. A Balrog. 3. Lothlorien. 4. The Galadhrim. 5. Lord Celeborn and Lady Galadriel. 6. The Mirror of Galadriel. 7. Lembas or waybread. 8. A box of earth from her orchard and a Mallorn nut. 9. A lock of her hair. 10. The light of Earindil's star. 11. The Silverlode. 12. Isildur and Anarion. 13. Tol Brandir. 14. The Hill of Seeing. 15. The Land of Mordor.

How much do you know about the Two Towers? (1)

QUESTIONS.

1. At the beginning of Part 2, Gandalf was apparently killed in the Mines of Moria; Frodo and Sam have left their other companions to go to Mordor; what happens to Boromir?

2. Pursuing the Orcs and their prisoners, what is the first thing that Aragorn, Gimli and Legolas find to confirm that the hobbits are still alive?

3. On the fourth day of their pursuit who do they meet?

4. Who is the leader of the Riders?

5. Merry and Pippin are captives of the Orcs. Some belong to Sauron, but others belong to Saruman the White, a great Wizard. What are Saruman's orcs called?

6. Who is the leader of the Orcs from Mordor?

7. And who leads the Uruk-Hai ?

8. After escaping from the Orcs, Merry and Pippin enter a forest. What is the forest called?

9. And who do they meet there?

10. What is Treebeard?

11. Concerned by Saruman's treachery, what does he organise?

12. And at the Entmoot, the Ents decide to march on Saruman's stronghold, which is called …what?

13. To the joy of Aragorn, Gimli and Legolas, who do they find again in Fangorn?

14. What is the name of the great horse given to Gandalf by the Lord of the Mark of Rohan?

15. What is the name of the Golden Hall where the King of Rohan resides?

ANSWERS
1. He is killed by Orcs whilst trying to protect Frodo and Sam. 2. Pippin's elven brooch. 3. A troop of the Riders of Rohan. 4. Eomer, Third Marshal of the Riddermark. 5. The Uruk-Hai. 6. Grishnakh. 7. Ugluk. 8. Fangorn. 9. Treebeard. 10. An Ent. 11. An Entmoot. 12. Isengard. 13. Gandalf. 14. Shadowfax. 15. Meduseld.

How much do you know about the Two Towers? (2)

QUESTIONS.

1. What is the name of the King of Rohan?

2. By what epithet is Grima, Theoden's counsellor known?

3. And how is Theoden's niece, sister of Eomer, called?

4. What is the emblem, white upon green, of the House of Eorl?

5. What is the name of the mountain fortress in which the Orcs of Saruman besiege the Riders of Rohan?

6. How many orcs do Legolas and Gimli each kill in the battle?

7. When Theoden and Aragorn lead the warriors out of Helm's Deep, driving Saruman's host before them, they find that the countryside has changed. How?

8. What happens to any Orc which enters the forest?

9. What is the name of Theoden's war-horse?

10. What are Huorns?

11. Saruman's citadel in the centre of Isengard is a great tower made of rock. What is it called?

12. When the Companions ride through the gate of Isengard they find Merry and Pippin, doing what?

13. What does Grima hurl at Gandalf from the tower?

14. What does Sauron send to Saruman to collect the hobbit that he has seen in the Palantir?

15. On their way into the Land of Shadow, who do Frodo and Sam take on as their guide?

ANSWERS
1. Theoden. 2. 'Wormtongue'. 3. Eowyn, Lady of Rohan. 4. A running horse. 5. Helm's Deep. 6. 41 and 42. 7. A great forest has appeared on the plain before the deep. 8. It is never seen again. 9. Snowmane. 10. Ents that have become very like trees. 11. Orcthanc. 12. Pippin is sleeping, Merry is smoking. 13. A Palantir. 14. A flying Nazgul. 15. Gollum (Smeagol).

How much do you know about the Two Towers? (3)

QUESTIONS.

1. As Frodo and Sam leave Emyn Muil behind them a sheer cliff causes a problem. Which gift of the Galadhrim helps them through?

2. Gollum leads them through a swamp, the site of a terrible battle many years before. What is it called?

3. What does Gollum call The Ring?

4. To which entrance into Mordor does Gollum lead them?

5. The entrance to the pass is closed by a rampart of stone in which is set …what?

6. When it becomes evident that this way is impassable, Gollum tells them about a second possibility. What is it?

7. And tells them of a secret way near to the tower, a secret way through a high mountain path called …?

8. Chance brings them a cooked meal, of what?

9. They are caught by men of Gondor, led by whom?

10. A fight between the men of Gondor and the Southrons (on their way to join Sauron) gives Sam the chance to see which exotic beast?

11. How is the ring known to the people of Gondor?

12. They come to Cirith Ungol and after climbing many stairs reach the entrance to a tunnel. What is it called?

13. What does Frodo use to drive Shelob away, the first time?

14. Thinking Frodo dead, killed by Shelob, what does Sam decide to do?

15. What does he realise after overhearing some Orcs talking?

ANSWERS
1. A length of rope. 2. The Dead Marshes. 3. His 'precious'. 4. To Cirith Gorgor (The Haunted Pass). 5. The Black Gate. 6. The tower of Minas Morgul. 7. Cirith Ungol. 8. Stewed rabbit. 9. Prince Faramir. 10. An Oliphaunt. 11. As Isildur's Bane. 12. Torech Ungol. 13. Galadriel's starglass. 14. Take the Ring to Mount Doom himself. 15. That Frodo is alive, but has been captured by Sauron's forces.

How much do you know about the Return of the King? (1)

QUESTIONS.

1. What is the name of the great city of Gondor?

2. Who is the Lord of Minas Tirith, Steward of Gondor?

3. What is the name of the Guard of the Tower of Gondor who befriends Pippin?

4. And his son, who also takes Pippin under his wing?

5. Who is the Prince of Dol Amroth?

6. As Aragorn, Gimli, Legolas and Merry accompany King Theoden back to Meduseld, they are joined by a troop of riders. Thirty of them are Rangers, Dunedain and kindred of Aragorn, led by whom?

7. And two of them are the sons of Elrond. What are their names?

8. What is the name of Aragorn's horse?

9. By which way is Aragorn and the company that rides with him appointed to go to war?

10. Who are summoned by Aragorn to the Stone of Erech?

11. Where does the Muster of Rohan take place?

12. Hirgon, errand-rider of Denethor brings Theoden a token of war. What is it?

13. What is the name of the young rider who offers to take Merry into battle with him on his horse?

14. Faramir returns to Minas Tirith but leaves again almost immediately to take charge of the garrison at … where?

15. Sorcerer, Ringwraith, Lord of the Nazgul, who leads the first army of Sauron against Gondor: who?

ANSWERS
1. Minas Tirith. 2. Denethor, father of Boromir and Faramir. 3. Beregond. 4. Bergil. 5. Imrahil. 6. Halbarad. 7. Elrohir and Elladan. 8. Roheryn. 9. By 'the Paths of the Dead'. 10. The dead who had broken their oath in Isildur's time. 11. In the Hold of Dunharrow. 12. A red arrow. 13. Dernhelm. 14. Osgiliath. 15. The long-dead King of Angmar.

How much do you know about the Return of the King? (2)

QUESTIONS.

1. How is Faramir wounded during the retreat from Osgiliath?

2. In the siege of Gondor the army of Sauron make use of a great battering ram. What is it called?

3. Unexpected help comes to the Rohirrim. Who is it from?

4. What is the name of their head-man?

5. What does he offer to do?

6. Which of Sauron's chieftains does King Theoden kill in mortal combat?

7. Which knight defies the Lord of the Nazgul to protect the fallen king?

8. Who turns out to be none other than ....?

9. The ships of the Corsairs of Umbar arrive, but who is sailing in them?

10. What is the name of the battle which takes place before the walls of Minas Tirith?

11. Who fights and destroys the Lord of the Nazgul?

12. What does Denethor order to be prepared for himself and for the unconscious Faramir?

13. After the death of Denethor, Faramir is transported to .....?

14. What do the Healers call the malady which comes from the Nazgul?

15. Who was the wise woman of Gondor who said 'The hands of the King are the hands of a healer'?

ANSWERS

1. He is pierced by a dart from a flying Nazgul. 2. Grond. 3. The Woses; Wild Men of Druadan Forest. 4. Ghan-buri-Ghan. 5. To lead the Riders through the forest by a forgotten path. 6. The King of the Southrons. 7. Dernhelm. 8. Eowyn. 9. Aragorn and his Company. 10. The Battle of the Pelennor Fields. 11. Eowyn and Merry. 12. A funeral pyre. 13. The Houses of Healing. 14. The Black Shadow. 15. Ioreth.

How much do you know about the Return of the King? (3)

QUESTIONS.

1. What is the name of the herb which Aragorn sends for to help him heal Faramir, Eowyn and Merry?

2. What counsel does Gandalf now give?

3. How many are there in the army which Aragorn leads to Mordor?

4. Before the Black Gates they are met by the Lieutenant of the Tower of Barad-dur, who is called …what?

5. What does he show to the Company?

6. What enemy does Pippin destroy, saving the life of Beregond?

7. And what cry does he hear as he loses consciousness?

8. What is the name of the Orc Captain of the Tower of Cirith Ungol?

9. After rescuing Frodo from the Tower, Sam leads him into Mordor. Their first test is to get past …what?

10. As they go further and further into Mordor, the Ring gets heavier and heavier. In Frodo's mind it becomes …?

11, And how do they manage the last few miles up to 'The Cracks of Doom'?

12. When, finally, he is standing above the fires of Mount Doom, what does Frodo do?

13. Sauron becomes aware of him and sends what, flying 'faster than the winds'?

14. What does Gollum do?

15. And with one last cry of 'Precious!' he …what?

ANSWERS
1. Athelas or Kingsfoil. 2. To march on Mordor. 3. About 7000. 4. 'The Mouth of Sauron'. 5. Frodo's mithril coat and elven cloak. 6. A chief of the hill trolls. 7. 'the Eagles are coming!'. 8. Shagrat. 9. The Silent Watchers. 10. 'A great wheel of fire'. 11. Sam carries Frodo on his back. 12. He claims the Ring for his own and puts it on. 13. The eight remaining Nazgul. 14. Bites off Frodo's finger with the Ring on it. 15. Falls into the fires of Mount Doom.

How much do you know about the Return of the King? (4)

QUESTIONS.

1. What is the name of the great eagle who bears Gandalf into Mordor?

2. And when Frodo and Sam wake up, where are they?

3. What is the song which the minstrel of Gondor sings when the Company of The Ring is reunited?

4. In a ceremony before the gates of Minas Tirith, Aragorn is crowned King, and takes what name?

5. Gandalf takes Aragorn to the foot of Mount Mindolliun where he finds ...what?

6. And in great joy, who does Aragorn, the King Elessar marry?

7. And to whom does Eowyn of Rohan plight her troth?

8   Treebeard charges Pippin and Merry to keep their eyes open for ...who?

9. The Company of The Ring return to Rivendell in time for Bilbo's birthday. How old is he?

10. The Company breaks up, leaving the Hobbits to return to the Shire alone. They find that is has been taken over by which mysterious person?

11. After a run-in with some of the villain's ruffianly men, what do the four decide to do?

12. To their surprise and shock, the villain is revealed to be who?

13. After putting the Shire to rights, who does Sam decide to marry?

14. On Bilbo's 131st birthday he comes through the shire with Elrond and Galadriel and many other elves on their way to The Havens to take ship and, with Gandalf ...do what?

15. And, using Arwen Evenstar's gift, who goes with them?

ANSWERS
1. Gwaihir the Windlord. 2. In the land of Ithilien (Gondor). 3. Of Frodo of the Nine Fingers and the Ring of Doom. 4. Elessar, the Elfstone. 5. A sapling of the White Tree, the symbol of his realm and reign. 6. Arwen Evenstar. 7. To Faramir of Ithilien. 8. Entwives. 9. 129. 10. The Chief, or 'Sharkey'. 11. Raise the Shire! 12. Saruman. 13. Rosie Cotton. 14. Sail away into the West. 15. Frodo, the Ringbearer.

Literature facts

Guardian Fiction Award (since 1999 First Book Award)

Year	Winner
1965	Clive Barry, Crumb Borne
1966	Archie Hind, The Dear Green Place
1967	Eva Figes, Winter Journey
1968	P. J. Kavanagh, A Song and a Dance
1969	Maurice Leitch, Poor Lazarus
1970	Margaret Blount, Where Did You Last See your Father?
1971	Thomas Kilroy, The Big Chapel
1972	John Berger, G
1973	Peter Redgrover, In the Country of the Skin
1974	Beryl Bainbridge, The Bottle Factory Outing
1975	Sylvia Clayton, Friends and Romans
1976	Robert Nye Hamish, Falstaff
1977	Michael Moorcock, The Condition of Muzak
1978	Neil Jordan, Night in Tunisia
1979	Dambudzo Merechera, The House of Hunger
1980	J. L. Carr, A Month in the Country
1981	John Banville, Kepler
1982	Glyn Hughes, Where I Used to Play on the Green

Year	Winner
1983	Graham Swift, Waterland
1984	J. G. Ballard, Empire of the Sun
1985	Peter Ackroyd, Hawksmoor
1986	Jim Crace, Continent
1987	Peter Benson, The Levels
1988	Lucy Ellman, Sweet Desserts
1989	Carol Lake, Rosehill: Portrait from a Midlands City
1990	Pauline Melville, Shape-Shifter
1991	Alan Judd, The Devil's Own Work
1992	Alasdair Gray, Poor Things
1993	Pat Barker, The Eye in the Door
1994	Candia McWilliam, Debatable Land
1995	James Buchan, Heart's Journey in Winter
1996	Seamus Deane, Reading in the Dark
1997	Anne Michaels, Fugitive Pieces
1998	Jackie Kay, Trumpet
1999	Philip Gourevitch, We Wish to Inform You That Tomorrow We Will be Killed with Our Families
2000	Zadie Smith, White Teeth

Hugo Awards for Science Fiction

The Mule by Isaac Asimov, 1946

The Demolished Man by Alfred Bester, 1953

They'd Rather Be Right by Mark Clifton and Frank Riley, 1955

Double Star by Robert A. Heinlein, 1956

A Case of Conscience by James Blish, 1959

Starship Troopers by Robert A. Heinlein, 1960

A Canticle for Leibowitz by Walter M. Miller, Jr., 1961

Stranger in a Strange Land by Robert A. Heinlein, 1962

The Man in the High Castle by Philip K. Dick, 1963

Way Station by Clifford D. Simak, 1964

The Wanderer by Fritz Leiber, 1965

Dune by Frank Herbert, 1966 (tie)

...And Call Me Conrad by Roger Zelazny, 1966 (tie)

The Moon Is a Harsh Mistress by Robert A. Heinlein, 1967

Lord of Light by Roger Zelazny, 1968

Stand on Zanzibar by John Brunner, 1969

The Left Hand of Darkness by Ursula K. Le Guin, 1970

Ringworld by Larry Niven, 1971

To Your Scattered Bodies Go by Philip José Farmer, 1972

The Gods Themselves by Isaac Asimov, 1973

Rendezvous with Rama by Arthur C. Clarke, 1974

The Dispossessed by Ursula K. Le Guin, 1975

The Forever War by Joe Haldeman, 1976

Where Late the Sweet Birds Sang by Kate Wilhelm, 1977

Gateway by Frederik Pohl,m 1978

Dreamsnake by Vonda McIntyre, 1979

The Fountains of Paradise by Arthur C. Clarke, 1980

The Snow Queen by Joan D. Vinge, 1981

Downbelow Station by C. J. Cherryh, 1982

Foundation's Edge by Isaac Asimov, 1983

Startide Rising by David Brin, 1984

Neuromancer by William Gibson, 1985

Ender's Game by Orson Scott Card, 1986

Speaker for the Dead by Orson Scott Card, 1987

The Uplift War by David Brin, 1988

Cyteen by C. J. Cherryh, 1989

Hyperion by Dan Simmons, 1990

The Vor Game by Lois McMaster Bujold, 1991

Barrayar by Lois McMaster Bujold, 1992

A Fire Upon the Deep by Vernor Vinge, 1993 (tie)

Doomsday Book by Connie Willis, 1993 (tie)

Green Mars by Kim Stanley Robinson, 1994

Mirror Dance by Lois McMaster Bujold, 1995

The Diamond Age by Neal Stephenson, 1996

Blue Mars by Kim Stanley Robinson, 1997

Forever Peace by Joe Haldeman, 1998

To Say Nothing of the Dog by Connie Willis, 1999

A Deepness in the Sky by Vernor Vinge, 2000

James Tait Black Memorial Prizes for Fiction

1920 Hugh Walpole The Secret City

1921 D. H. Lawrence The Lost Girl

1922 Walter de la Mare Memoirs of a Midget

1923 David Garnett Lady Into Fox

1924 Arnold Bennett Riceyman Steps

1925 E. M. Forster A Passage to India

1926 Liam O'Flaherty The Informer

1927 Radcliffe Hall Adam's Breed

1928 Francis Brett Young The Portrait of Clare

1929 Siegried Sassoon Memoirs of a Foxhunting Man

1930 J. B. Priestley The Good Companions

1931 E. H. Young Miss Mole

1932 Kate O'Brien Without My Cloak

1933 Helen Simpson Boomerang

1934 A. G. Macdonnell England, Their England

1935 Robert Graves I, Claudius and Claudius the God

1936 L. H. Myers The Root and the Flower

1937 Winifred Holtby South Riding

1938 Neil M. Gunn Highland River

1939 C. S. Forester A Ship of the Line and Flying Colours

1940 Aldous Huxley After Many a Summer Dies the Swan

1941 Charles Morgan The Voyage

1942 Joyce Cary A House of Children

1943 Arthur Waley Translation of Monkey by Wu Ch'êng-ên

1944 Mary Lavin Tales from Bective Bridge

1945 Forrest Reid Young Tom

1946 L. A. G. Strong Travellers

1947 Oliver Onions Poor Man's Tapestry

1948 L. P. Hartley Eustace and Hilda

1949 Graham Greene The Heart of the Matter

1950 Emma Smith The Far Cry

1951 Robert Henriquez Through the Valley

1952 W. C. Chapman-Mortimer Father Goose

1953 Evelyn Waugh Men at Arms

1954 Margaret Kennedy Troy Chimneys

1955 C. P. Snow The Men and the Masters

1956 Ivy Compton-Burnett Mother and Son

1957 Rose Macauley The Towers of Trebizond

1958 Anthony Powell At Lady Molly's

1959 Angus Wilson The Middle Age of Mrs. Eliot

1960 Rex Warner Imperial Caesar

1961 Jennifer Dawson The Ha-Ha

1962 Ronald Hardy Act of Destruction

1963 Gerda Charles A Slanting Light

1964 Frank Tuohy The Ice Saints

1965 Muriel Spark The Mandelbaum Gate

1966 Christine Brooke-Rose Such, and Aidan Higgins Langrishe, Go Down

1967 Margaret Drabble Jerusalem The Golden

1968 Maggie Ross The Gasteropod

1969 Elizabeth Bowen Eva Trout

1970 Lily Powell The Bird of Paradise

1971 Nadine Gordimer A Guest of Honour

1972 John Berger G

1983 Iris Murdoch The Black Prince

1974 Lawrence Durrell Monsieur, or the Prince of Darkness

1975 Brian Moore The Great Victorian Collection

1976 John Banville Doctor Copernicus

1977 John Le Carré The Honourable Schoolboy

1978 Maurice Gee Plumb

1979 William Golding Darkness Visible

1980 J. M. Coetzee Waiting for the Barbarians

1981 Salman Rushdie Midnight's Children, and Paul Theroux The Mosquito Coast

1982 Bruce Chatwin On the Black Hill

1983 Jonathan Keates Allegro Postillions

1984 J. G. Ballard Empire of the Sun, and Angela Carter Nights at the Circus

1985 Robert Edric Winter Garden

1986 Jenny Joseph Persephone

1987 George Mackay Brown The Golden Bird: Two Orkney Stories

1988 Piers Paul Read A Season in the West

1989 James Kelman A Disaffection

1990 William Boyd Brazzaville Beach

1991 Iain Sinclair Downriver

1992 Rose Tremain Sacred Country

1993 Caryl Phillips Crossing the River

1994 Alan Hollinghurst The Folding Star

1995 Christopher Priest The Prestige

1996 Graham Swift Last Orders, and Alice Thompson Justine

1997 Andrew Miller Ingenious Pain

1998 Beryl Bainbridge, Master Georgie

1999 Timothy Mo, Renegade, or Halo2

2000 Zadie Smith, White Teeth

Nobel Prize in Literature Winners 2001-1901

2001 V. S. NAIPAUL
2000 GAO XINGJIAN
1999 GUNTER GRASS
1998 JOSE SARAMAGO
1997 DARIO FO
1996 WISLAWA SZYMBORSKA
1995 SEAMUS HEANEY
1994 KENZABURO OE
1993 TONI MORRISON
1992 DEREK WALCOTT
1991 NADINE GORDIMER
1990 OCTAVIO PAZ
1989 CAMILO JOSÉ CELA
1988 NAGUIB MAHFOUZ
1987 JOSEPH BRODSKY
1986 WOLE SOYINKA
1985 CLAUDE SIMON
1984 JAROSLAV SEIFERT
1983 SIR WILLIAM GOLDING
1982 GABRIEL GARCÍA
  MÁRQUEZ
1981 ELIAS CANETTI
1980 CZESLAW MILOSZ
1979 ODYSSEUS ELYTIS (pen-
  name of ODYSSEUS
  ALEPOUDHELIS)
1978 ISAAC BASHEVIS SINGER
1977 VICENTE ALEIXANDRE
1976 SAUL BELLOW
1975 EUGENIO MONTALE
1974 The prize was divided
  equally between: EYVIND
  JOHNSON & HARRY
  MARTINSON
1973 PATRICK WHITE
1972 HEINRICH BÖLL
1971 PABLO NERUDA
1970 ALEKSANDR ISAEVICH
  SOLZHENITSYN
1969 SAMUEL BECKETT
1968 YASUNARI KAWABATA
1967 MIGUEL ANGEL ASTURIAS
1966 The prize was divided
  equally between: SHMUEL
  YOSEF AGNON & NELLY
1965 MICHAIL ALEKSAN-
  DROVICH SHOLOKHOV
1964 JEAN-PAUL SARTRE
1963 GIORGOS SEFERIS (pen-
  name of GIORGOS
  SEFERIADIS)
1962 JOHN STEINBECK
1961 IVO ANDRI´C
1960 SAINT-JOHN PERSE (pen-

name of ALEXIS LÉGER)
1959 SALVATORE
1958 BORIS LEONIDOVICH
1957 ALBERT CAMUS
1956 JUAN RAMÓN JIMÉNEZ
1955 HALLDÓR KILJAN
  LAXNESS
1954 ERNEST MILLER
  HEMINGWAY
1953 SIR WINSTON LEONARD
  SPENCER CHURCHILL
1952 FRANÇOIS MAURIAC
1951 PÄR FABIAN LAGERKVIST
1950 EARL BERTRAND ARTHUR
  WILLIAM RUSSELL
1949 WILLIAM FAULKNER
1948 THOMAS STEARNS ELIOT
1947 ANDRÉ PAUL GUILLAUME
1946 HERMANN HESSE
1945 GABRIELA MISTRAL (pen-
  name of LUCILA GODOY Y
  ALCA-YAGA)
1944 JOHANNES VILHELM
  JENSEN
1943-1940 The prize money was
  allocated to the Main Fund
  (1/3) and to the Special Fund
  (2/3) of this prize section.
1939 FRANS EEMIL SILLANPÄÄ
1938 PEARL BUCK (pen-name
  of PEARL WALSH née
  SYDENSTRICKER)
1937 ROGER MARTIN DU
  GARD
1936 EUGENE GLADSTONE
  O'NEILL
1935 The prize money was
  allocated to the Main Fund
  (1/3) and to the Special Fund
  (2/3) of this prize section.
1934 LUIGI PIRANDELLO
1933 IVAN ALEKSEYEVICH
  BUNIN for the strict artistry
  with which he has carried on
  the classical Russian traditions
  in prose writing.
1932 JOHN GALSWORTHY
1931 ERIK AXEL KARLFELDT
1930 SINCLAIR LEWIS
1929 THOMAS MANN
1928 SIGRID UNDSET
1927 HENRI BERGSON
1926 GRAZIA DELEDDA (pen-
  name of GRAZIA MADESANI

née DELEDDA)
1925 GEORGE BERNARD SHAW
1924 WLADYSLAW STANISLAW
  REYMONT (pen-name of
  REYMENT)
1923 WILLIAM BUTLER YEATS
1922 JACINTO BENAVENTE
1921 ANATOLE FRANCE (pen-
  name of JACQUES ANATOLE
  THIBAULT)
1920 KNUT PEDERSEN
  HAMSUN
1919 CARL FRIEDRICH GEORG
  SPITTELER
1918 The prize money for 1918
  was allocated to the Special
  Fund of this prize section.
1917 The prize was divided
  equally between: KARL
  ADOLPH GJELLERUP &
  HENRIK PONTOPPIDAN
1916 CARL GUSTAF VERNER
  VON HEIDENSTAM
1915 ROMAIN ROLLAND
1914 The prize money for 1914
  was allocated to the Special
  Fund of this prize section.
1913 RABINDRANATH TAGORE
1912 GERHART JOHANN
  ROBERT HAUPTMANN
1911 COUNT MAURICE
  (MOORIS) POLIDORE MARIE
  BERNHARD MAETERLINCK
1910 PAUL JOHANN LUDWIG
  HEYSE
1909 SELMA OTTILIA LOVISA
  LAGERLÖF
1908 RUDOLF CHRISTOPH
  EUCKEN
1907 RUDYARD KIPLING
1906 GIOSUÈ CARDUCCI
1905 HENRYK SIENKIEWICZ
1904 The prize was divided
  equally between: FRÉDÉRIC
  MISTRAL & JOSÉ ECHEGARAY
  Y EIZAGUIRRE
1903 BJØRNSTJERNE
  MARTINUS BJØRNSON
1902 CHRISTIAN MATTHIAS
  THEODOR MOMMSEN
1901 SULLY PRUDHOMME
  (pen-name of RENÉ FRANÇOIS
  ARMAND)

The Pulitzer Prize (fiction)

1918 His Family by Ernest Poole (Macmillan)

1919 The Magnificent Ambersons by Booth Tarkington (Doubleday)

1920 (No Award)

1921 he Age of Innocence by Edith Wharton (Appleton)

1922 Alice Adams by Booth Tarkington (Doubleday)

1923 One of Ours by Willa Cather (Knopf)

1924 The Able McLaughlins by Margaret Wilson (Harper)

1925 So Big by Edna Ferber (Doubleday)

1926 Arrowsmith by Sinclair Lewis (Harcourt)

1927 Early Autumn by Louis Bromfield (Stokes)

1928 The Bridge of San Luis Rey by Thornton Wilder (Boni)

1929 Scarlet Sister Mary by Julia Peterkin (Bobbs)

1930 Laughing Boy by Oliver Lafarge (Houghton)

1931 Years of Grace by Margaret Ayer Barnes (Houghton)

1932 The Good Earth by Pearl S. Buck (John Day)

1933 The Store by T. S. Stribling (Doubleday)

1934 Lamb in His Bosom by Caroline Miller (Harper)

1935 Now in November by Josephine Winslow Johnson (Simon & Schuster)

1936 Honey in the Horn by Harold L. Davis (Harper)

1937 Gone With the Wind by Margaret Mitchell (Macmillan)

1938 The Late George Apley by John Phillips Marquand (Little)

1939 The Yearling by Marjorie Kinnan Rawlings (Scribner)

1940 The Grapes of Wrath by John Steinbeck (Viking)

1941 (No Award)

1942 In This Our Life by Ellen Glasgow (Harcourt)

1943 Dragon's Teeth by Upton Sinclair (Viking)

1944 Journey in the Dark by Martin Flavin (Harper)

1945 A Bell for Adano by John Hersey (Knopf)

1946 (No Award)

1947 All the King's Men by Robert Penn Warren (Harcourt)

1948 Tales of the South Pacific by James A. Michener (Macmillan)

1949 Guard of Honor by James Gould Cozzens (Harcourt)

1950 The Way West by A. B. Guthrie, Jr. (Sloane)

1951 The Town by Conrad Richter (Knopf)

1952 The Caine Mutiny by Herman Wouk (Doubleday)

1953 The Old Man and the Sea by Ernest Hemingway (Scribner)

1954 (No Award)

1955 A Fable by William Faulkner (Random)

1956 Andersonville by MacKinlay Kantor (World)

1957 (No Award)

1958 A Death In The Family by the late James Agee (a posthumous publication) (McDowell, Obolensky)

1959 The Travels of Jaimie McPheeters by Robert Lewis Taylor (Doubleday)

1960 Advise and Consent by Allen Drury (Doubleday)

1961 To Kill A Mockingbird by Harper Lee (Lippincott)

1962 The Edge of Sadness by Edwin O'Connor (Little)

1963 The Reivers by William Faulkner (Random)

1964 (No Award)

1965 The Keepers Of The House by Shirley Ann Grau (Random)

1966 Collected Stories by Katherine Anne Porter (Harcourt)

1967 The Fixer by Bernard Malamud (Farrar)

1968 The Confessions of Nat Turner by William Styron (Random)

1969 House Made of Dawn by N. Scott Momaday (Harper)

1970 Collected Stories by Jean Stafford (Farrar)

1971 (No Award)

1972 Angle of Repose by Wallace Stegner (Doubleday)

1973 The Optimists Daughter by Eudora Welty (Random)

1974 (No Award)

1975 The Killer Angels by Michael Shaara (McKay)

1976 Humboldt's Gift by Saul Bellow (Viking)

1977 (No Award)

1978 Elbow Room by James Alan McPherson (Atlantic Monthly Press)

1979 The Stories of John Cheever by John Cheever (Knopf)

1980 The Executioner's Song by Norman Mailer (Little, Brown)

1981 A Confederacy of Dunces by the late John Kennedy Toole (a posthumous publication) (Louisiana State U. Press)

1982 Rabbit Is Rich by John Updike (Knopf), the latest novel in a memorable sequence

1983 The Color Purple by Alice Walker (Harcourt Brace)

1984 Ironweed by William Kennedy (Viking)

1985 Foreign Affairs by Alison Lurie (Random House)

1986 Lonesome Dove by Larry McMurtry (Simon & Schuster)

1987 A Summons to Memphis by Peter Taylor (Alfred A. Knopf)

1988 Beloved by Toni Morrison (Alfred A. Knopf)

1989 Breathing Lessons by Anne Tyler (Alfred A. Knopf)

1990 The Mambo Kings Play Songs of Love by Oscar Hijuelos (Farrar, Straus & Giroux)

1991 Rabbit At Rest by John Updike (Alfred A. Knopf)

1992 A Thousand Acres by Jane Smiley (Alfred A. Knopf)

1993 A Good Scent from a Strange Mountain by Robert Olen Butler (Henry Holt)

1994 The Shipping News by E. Annie Proulx (Charles Scribner's Sons)

1995 The Stone Diaries by Carol Shields (Viking)

1996 Independence Day by Richard Ford (Alfred A. Knopf)

1997 Martin Dressler: The Tale of an American Dreamer by Steven Millhauser (Crown)

1998 American Pastoral by Philip Roth (Houghton Mifflin)

1999 The Hours by Michael Cunningham (Farrar, Straus and Giroux)

2000 Interpreter of Maladies by Jhumpa Lahiri (Mariner Books/Houghton Mifflin)

2001 The Amazing Adventures of Kavalier & Clay by Michael Chabon (Random House)

2002 Empire Falls by Richard Russo (Alfred A. Knopf)

The Booker prize

Financed by Booker McConnell, a multinational conglomerate company, and awarded annually for the best full length novel in the British Commonwealth of Nations.

1969: P. H. Newby Something to Answer For

1970: Bernice Rubens The Elected Member

1971: V. S. Nailpul In a Free State

1972: John Berger G

1973: J. G. Farrell Siege of Krishnapur

1974: Stanley Middleton Holiday

1975: Nadine Gordimer The Conversationalist and Ruth Prower Jhabvala Heat and Dust

1976: David Storey Saville

1977: Paul Scott Staying On

1978: Iris Murdoch The Sea, The Sea

1979: Penelope Fitzgerald Offshore

1980: William Golding Rites of Passage

1981: Salman Rushdie Midnight's Children

1982: Thomas Keneally Schindler's Ark

1983: J. M. Coetzee Life and Times of Michael K.

1984: Anita Brookner Hotel Du Lac

1985: Keri Hulme Bone People

1986: Kingsley Amis The Old Devils

1987: Penelope Lively Moon Tiger

1988: Peter Carey Oscar and Lucinda

1989: Kazuo Ishiguro The Remains of the Day

1990: A. S. Byatt Possession

1991: Ben Okri The Famished Road

1992: Michael Ondaatje The English Patient and Barry Unsworth Sacred Hunger

1993: Roddy Doyle Paddy Clarke Ha Ha Ha

1994: James Kelman How Little It Was, How Late

1995: Pat Barker The Ghost Road

1996: Graham Swift Last Orders

1997: Arundhati Roy The God of Small Things

1998: Ian McEwan Amsterdam

1999: J.M. Coetzee Disgrace

2000: Margaret Atwood The Blind Assassin

2001: Peter Carey True History of the Kelly Gang

Whitbread winners

2001
* Book of the Year and Children's Book of the Year: The Amber Spyglass Philip Pullman
* Novel: Twelve Bar Blues Patrick Neate
* First Novel: Something Like A House Sid Smith

2000
* Book of the Year: English Passengers Matthew Kneale
* First novel: White Teeth Zadie Smith
* Novel: English Passengers Matthew Kneale

1999
* Book of the Year: Beowulf Seamus Heaney
* First Novel: White City Blue Tim Lott
* Novel: Music and Silence Rose Tremain

1998
* Book of the Year: Birthday Letters Ted Hughes
* First Novel The Last King of Scotland Giles Foden
* Novel: Leading the cheers Justin Cartwright

1997
* Book of the Year and First Novel: The Ventriloquist's Tale Pauline Melville
* Novel: Quarantine Jim Crace

1996
* Book of the Year and First Novel: A Debt to Pleasure John Lanchester
* Novel: Every Man for Himself Beryl Bainbridge

1995
* Book of the Year and First Novel: Behind the Scenes at the Museum Kate Atkinson
* Novel: The Moor's Last Sigh Salman Rushdie

1994
* Novel and Book of the Year: Felicia's Journey William Trevor

* First Novel: The Longest Memory Fred D'Aguiar

1993
* Novel and Grand Prize: Theory of War Joan Brady
* First Novel: Saving Agnes Rachel Cusk

1992
* Novel: Poor Things Alasdair Gray
* First Novel: Swing Hammer Swing! Jeff Torrington

1991
* Novel: The Queen of the Tambourine Jane Gardam
* First Novel: Alma Cogan Gordon Burn

1990
* Novel: Hopeful Monsters Nicholas Mosley
* First Novel: The Buddha of Suburbia Hanif Kureishi

1989
* Novel: The Chymical Wedding Lindsay Clarke
* First Novel: Gerontius James Hamilton-Paterson

1988
* Novel: Satanic Verses Salman Rushdie
* First Novel and Grand Prize: The Comforts of Madness Paul Sayer

1987
* Novel: The Child in Time Ian McEwan
* First Novel: The Other garden Francis Wyndham

1986
* Novel and Grand Prize: An Artist of the Floating World Kazuo Ishiguro
* First Novel: Continent Jim Crace

1985
* Novel: Hawksmoor Peter Ackroyd
* First Novel: Oranges are not the only fruit Jeanette Winterson

1984
* Novel: Kruger's Alp Christopher Hope
* First Novel: A Parish of rich women James Buchan

1983
* Novel: Fools of Fortune William Trevor
* First Novel: Flying to Nowhere John Fuller

1982
* Novel: Young Shoulders John Wain
* First Novel: On the Black Hill Bruce Chatwin

1981
* Novel: Silver's City Maurice Leitch
* First Novel: A Good Man in Africa William Boyd

1980
* Novel and Book of the Year: How Far Can You Go? David Lodge

1979
* Novel: The Old Jest Jennifer Johnston

1978
* Novel: Picture Palace Paul Theroux

1977
* Novel: Injury Time Beryl Bainbridge

1976
* Novel: The Children of Dynmouth William Trevor

1975
* Novel: Docherty William McIlvanney

1974
* Novel: The Sacred and Profane Love Machine Iris Murdoch

1973
* Novel: The Chip-chip gatherers Shiva Naipaul

W.H. Smith Award

W.H. Smith Award

1959	Patrick White, Voss
1960	Laurie Lee, Cider With Rosie
1961	Nadine Gordimer, Friday's Footprint
1962	J. R. Ackerley, We Think the World of You
1963	Gabriel Fielding, The Birthday King
1964	Ernst H. Gombrich, Meditations on a Hobby-Horse
1965	Leonard Woolf, Beginning Again
1966	R. Ch Hutrchinson, A Child Possessed
1967	Jean Rhys, Wide Sargasso Sea
1968	V. S. Naipaul, The Mimic Men
1969	Robert Gittings, John Keats
1970	John Fowles, The French Lieutenant's Woman
1971	Nan Fairbrother, New Lives, New Landscapes
1972	Kathleen Raine, The Lost Country
1973	Brian Moore, Catholics
1974	Anthony Powell, Temporary Kings
1975	Jon Stallworthy, Wilfred Owen
1976	Seamus Heaney, North
1977	Ronald Lewin, Slim: The Standardbearer
1978	Patrick Leigh Fermor, A Time of Gifts
1979	Mark Girouard, Life in the English Country House
1980	Thom Gunn, Selected Poems 1959-1975
1981	Isabel Colegate, The Shooting Party
1982	George Clare, Last Waltz in Vienna
1983	A. N. Wilson, Wise Virgin
1984	Philip Larkin, Required Writing
1985	David Hughes, The Pork Butcher
1986	Doris Lessing, The Good Terrorist
1987	Elizabeth Jennings, Collected Poems 1953-1985
1988	Robert Hughes, The Fatal Shore
1989	Christopher Hill, A Turbulent, Seditious and Factious People: John Bunyan and His Church
1990	V. S. Pritchett, A Careless Widow and Other Stories
1991	Derek Walcott, Omeros
1992	Thomas Pakenham, The Scramble for Africa
1993	Michèle Roberts, Daughters of the House
1994	Vikram Seth, A Suitable Boy
1995	Alice Munro, Open Secrets
1996	Simon Schama, Landscape and Memory
1997	Orlando Figes, A People's Tragedy–The Russian Revolution
1998	Ted Hughes, Tales From Ovid
1999	Beryl Bainbridge, Master Georgie
2000	Melvyn Bragg, The Soldier's Return
2001	Philip Roth, The Human Stain
2002	Ian McEwan, Atonement

4

MYTHOLOGY

Greek Mythology

How much do you know about the Greek Gods? (1)

QUESTIONS.

1. Who was the goddess of the earth, who sprang from Chaos?

2. Who was the sky god, son and husband of Gaia?

3. Who was the ancient fertility god, son of Gaia and Uranus and father of Zeus?

4. Who were the race of giants, with Cronos the offspring of Gaia and Uranus?

5. Who was the fertility goddess, a Titan, wife of Cronos, mother of Zeus?

6. Who was the chief of the gods, dispenser of good and evil?

7. Who was the god of the underworld, the brother of Zeus?

8. Who was the chief god of the sea, also the brother of Zeus?

9. Who was the goddess of women, consort to Zeus?

10. Who was the goddess of war, wisdom, arts and crafts, who sprang fully grown from the head of Zeus?

11. Who was the god of war, son of Zeus and Hera?

12. Who was the god of fire and metalcraft, son of Zeus and Hera?

13. Who was the goddess of youth, daughter of Zeus and Hera?

14. Who was the goddess of agriculture, daughter of Cronos and Rhea?

15. Who was the primordial god of darkness, who – like Gaia – sprang from Chaos?

ANSWERS

1. Gaia. 2. Uranus. 3. Cronos. 4. The Titans. 5. Rhea. 6. Zeus. 7. Hades. 8. Poseidon. 9. Hera. 10. Athena. 11. Ares. 12. Hephaestus. 13. Hebe. 14. Demeter. 15. Erebos.

How much do you know about the Greek Gods? (2)

QUESTIONS.

1. Who was the god of the sun, music, poetry, prophecy, agriculture and pastoral life; the son of Zeus and Leto?

2. Who was the goddess of the moon, the hunt, chastity, and the young of all creatures, twin sister of Apollo?

3. Who was the goddess of justice and retribution?

4. Who was the sea goddess, daughter of Uranus and Gaia?

5. Who was the god of merchants, thieves and travellers, also the messenger of the gods; son of Zeus and Maia?

6. Who was the god whose spirit embodied the ocean, believed to be a great river encircling the earth?

7. Who was the goddess queen of the underworld, daughter of Zeus and Demeter?

8. Who was the mother goddess of Phrygia, always shown flanked by two lions, to show her control over wild nature?

9. Who was the goddess of love, wife of Hephaestus and mother of Eros?

10. Who was the merman sea-god, son of Poseidon and the sea goddess Amphitrite?

11. Who was the god of wine, ecstasy and orgiastic excess, son ofZeus and Semele?

12. Who was the goddess of the underworld and magic?

13. Who was the god of medicine, son of Apollo?

14. Who was the goddess of health, daughter of Asclepius?

15. Who was the god of flocks and herds, and a very famous player of pipes?

ANSWERS
1. Apollo. 2. Artemis. 3. Nemesis. 4. Tethys. 5. Hermes. 6. Oceanus. 7. Persephone. 8. Cybele. 9. Aphrodite. 10. Triton. 11. Dionysius. 12. Hecate. 13. Asclepius. 14. Hygieia. 15. Pan.

How much do you know about the Greek Gods? (3)

QUESTIONS.

1. Who was the goddess of memory, a Titan, and mother by Zeus of the nine muses?

2. Who were the Nine Muses?

    2.1. The muse of epic poetry?

    2.2. The muse of love poetry?

    2.3. The muse of lyric poetry?

    2.4. The muse of history?

    2.5. The muse of sacred song?

    2.6. The muse of comedy?

    2.7. The muse of tragedy?

    2.8. The muse of astronomy?

    2.9. The muse of dance?

3. Who was the god of the winds, who held them prisoner on the Island of Lipari?

4. Who was the goddess of victory, sometimes represented as winged?

5. Who was the god of sleep, father of Morpheus?

6. Who was the sun god, who traversed the heavens each day in his fiery chariot?

7. Who was the son of Helios, who abused the privilege of driving his fathers' chariot?

ANSWERS
1. Mnemosyne. 2.1 Calliope. 2.2 Erato. 2.3 Euterpe. 2.4 Clio. 2.5 Polyhymnia. 2.6 Thalia. 2.7 Melpomene. 2.8 Urania. 2.9 Terpsichore. 3. Aeolus. 4. Nike. 5. Hypnos. 6. Helios. 7. Phaeton.

How much do you know about the Greek Gods? (4)

QUESTIONS.

1. Who was the god of the north wind?

2. Who was the child-god of love, son of Aphrodite?

3. Who was the goddess of the hearth?

4. Who were the three goddesses who controlled human life?

   4.1. Who was 'the spinner' who spun the thread of life?

   4.2. Who was the 'caster of lots' who measured the thread?

   4.3. Who was 'death's inevitability' who cut the thread?

5. Who was the goddess of wisdom, who helped Zeus overcome his father Cronos; daughter of Oceanus and Tethys?

6. Who was the goddess of peace and wealth?

7. Who were the goddesses with terrible faces who brought retribution on criminals and oath-breakers?

   7.1. Who was the 'relentless' goddess?

   7.2. Who was the 'resentful' goddess?

   7.3. Who was the 'avenger of murder'?

8. Who was the god of wealth?

9. Who was the goddess of the moon, sister of Helios?

ANSWERS
1. Boreas. 2. Eros. 3. Hestia. 4. The Fates. 4.1 Klotho. 4.2 Lachesis. 4.3 Atropus. 5. Metis. 6. Irene. 7. The Furies. 7.1 Alecto. 7.2 Megara. 7.3 Tisiphone. 8. Pluto. 9. Selene.

How much do you know about the Greek Gods? (5)

QUESTIONS.

1. Who was the Titan who was the father of Helios (the Sun), Selene (the Moon), and Eon (the Dawn)?

2. Who was the rainbow goddess, messenger of the Gods?

3. Who are the goddesses who personified beauty, grace and good nature?

   3.1. Who was the goddess whose name meant 'splendour'?

   3.2. Who was the goddess whose name meant 'rejoicing of the heart'?

   3.3. Who was the goddess whose name meant 'blossom'?

4. Who was the god of water, of the sea in particular; older than Poseidon and father of 50 daughters by the sea nymph Doris who were called the 'Nereids'?

5. Who was the god of fertility, son of Dionysius and Aphrodite?

6. Who was the sea god with oracular and shape-changing powers?

7. Who was the god of the west wind and husband of Iris?

8. Who was the goddess of the dawn, daughter of Hyperion and Thea?

9. Who was the half-god half-human, renowned for his physical strength, who became a full god after his death?

10. Who was the great river god, son of Oceanus and Tethys, defeated in battle by Heracles for the hand of Deianeira?

11. Who was the god of weddings?

12. Who was the goddess of quarrels and strife?

ANSWERS
1. Hyperion. 2. Iris. 3. The Graces (The Charities). 3.1 Aglaia. 3.2 Euphrosyne. 3.3 Thalia. 4. Nereus. 5. Priapus. 6. Proteus. 7. Zephyrus. 8. Eos. 9. Heracles. 10. Achelous. 11. Hymen. 12. Eris.

How much do you know about Heracles ?

QUESTIONS.

1. By what name is Heracles known in Roman mythology?

2. Zeus was the father of Heracles. Who was his mother?

3. Heracles was sent by the oracle of Apollo at Delphi to serve his cousin for twelve years. What was his cousin's name?

4. Eurystheus set him twelve tasks, or labours. What were they?

   4.1. To kill and take back the skin of what animal?

   4.2. To kill which monster with the body of a dog and nine serpent heads?

   4.3. To catch which creature with brazen feet and golden antlers?

   4.4. To catch a giant wild boar, called ...?

   4.5. To clean out the filthy stables of which King of Elis?

   4.6. To drive away the giant, man-eating birds from which marshy area in northern Arcadia?

   4.7. To capture which magnificent white animal sent by Poseidon to Minos?

   4.8. To catch the man-eating pets of a king of the Bistones in Thrace, which were known as ...what?

   4.9. To fetch which item of clothing from the Queen of the Amazons?

   4.10. To steal the cattle belonging to which three-bodied monster living on the island of Erythia?

   4.11. To bring back the fruit belonging to the 'daughters of evening' living at the western end of the world, called ...?

   4.12. To capture the savage dog which guarded Hades, named ...?

ANSWERS
1. Hercules. 2. Alcmene. 3. Eurystheus. 4.1 The Nemean Lion. 4.2 The Hydra of Lerna.
4.3 The Ceryneian Hind. 4.4 The Erymanthian Boar. 4.5 Augeus. 4.6 Lake Stymphal.
4.7 The Cretan Bull. 4.8 The horses of Diomedes. 4.9 The golden girdle of Hippolyte.
4.10 Geryon. 4.11 The golden apples of Hesperus. 4.12 Cerberus.

How much do you know about the Hindu Gods? (1)

QUESTIONS.

1. Who was the principle god of creation, for members of the sect of Vaishnavism?

2. Who was the principle god of creation, for members of the sect of Shaivism?

3. Who was the goddess of wealth and good fortune, wife of Vishnu?

4. Who was the goddess of destruction, the evil wife of Shiva?

5. Who was the goddess, the good wife of Shiva, the opposite of Kali?

6. Who, for followers of both sects, was the minor god of creation?

7. Who was the goddess, third wife of Shiva?

8. Who was the goddess, consort to Shiva?

9. Who was the goddess, consort to Shiva?

10. Who was the incarnation of Vishnu who corresponded to the perfect deification of life?

11. Who was the goddess of romantic love, the consort of Krishna?

12. Who was the mother goddess of art, music and learning, the female counterpart of Brahma?

13. Who was the god of desire and sexual lust?

14. Who was the storm god, who brings rain?

15. Who was the astral god, who brings ill fortune?

ANSWERS
1. Vishnu. 2. Shiva. 3. Lakshmi. 4. Kali. 5. Parvati. 6. Brahma. 7. Durga. 8. Mahishasuramardini. 9. Pidari. 10. Krishna. 11. Radha. 12. Sarasvati. 13. Kama. 14. Indra. 15. Shani.

How much do you know about the Hindu Gods? (2)

QUESTIONS.

1. Who was the elephant headed son of Shiva?

2. Who was the incarnation of Shiva as lord of the dance and rhythm?

3. Who was the goddess, the female incarnation of energy?

4. Who was the goddess, the foster mother of Krishna?

5. Who was the god-incarnation of Vishnu?

6. Who was the god half-brother of Rama?

7. Who was the six-headed, twelve-armed god who rode on a peacock?

8. Who was the goddess, the gracious and ascetic?

9. Who was the sun god, the illuminator?

10. Who was the god of fire, a three headed god who rode on a ram?

11. Who was the bird-god on which Shiva rode?

12. Who was the incarnation of Vishnu as a man-lion?

13. Who was the god who was the terrifying, violent aspect of Shiva?

14. Who was the god creator of truth and justice?

15. Who was the mother goddess and teacher, often depicted playing the cymbals?

ANSWERS
1. Ganesh. 2. Nataraja. 3. Shakti. 4. Yashoda. 5. Rama. 6. Lakshmana. 7. Karrttikeya. 8. Uma. 9. Surya. 10. Agni. 11. Garuda. 12. Narasimha. 13. Rudra. 14. Savitri. 15. Karaikkal-Ammaiyar.

How much do you know about the Hindu Gods? (3)

QUESTIONS.

1. Who was the monkey god?

2. Who was the god who corresponded to nature and the human soul. (Collectively represented by Brahma, Vishnu and Shiva as 'Trimurti')?

3. Who was the incarnation of Vishnu as a giant with the head of a horse?

4. Who was the goddess, wife of Rama?

5. Who was the incarnation of Vishnu as a tortoise?

6. Who was the god known as he who enlightens, he who enhances, he who makes prosper?

7. Who was the supreme goddess, corresponding to the Absolute (Brahman) and facilitates its manifestation?

8. Who was the incarnation of Vishnu as a dwarf?

9. Who was the incarnation of Vishnu as a fish?

10. Who was the incarnation of Vishnu as a boar?

11. Who was the god-bull vehicle of Shiva?

12. Who was the god who was yet another incarnation of Shiva?

13. Who was the god who was yet another incarnation of Vishnu?

14. Who was the god brother of Krishna?

15. Who was the god half-brother of Rama?

ANSWERS
1. Hanuman. 2. Iswara. 3. Kalkin. 4. Sita. 5. Kurma. 6. Pushan. 7. Mahadevi-Shakti. 8. Vamana. 9. Matsya. 10. Varaha. 11. Nandin. 12. Bhairava; Virabhadra. 13. Narada; Parashurama. 14. Balarama. 15. Shatrughna.

How much do you know about the Celtic Gods? (1)

QUESTIONS.

1. Who was the ancestor deity, worshipped by the Druids as a god of wisdom and power?

2. Who was the supreme, divine 'mother' goddess?

3. Who was the god of the sea, and of patience and wisdom?

4. Who was the 'horned one', ruler and protector of the animal kingdom, and Lord of the Underworld?

5. Who was the god associated with solar symbolism and light, whose worship was replaced in the Christian church by the worship of the Archangel Michael?

6. Who was the god of healing?

7. Which goddess was patroness of war, battles and valour; also associated with festivals and games?

8. Who was the goddess of beauty and peace?

9. Who was the god of eloquence and strength?

10. Who was the goddess of plenty?

11. Who were the goddesses and divine consorts who usually appeared in groups of three, symbolising the Earth mother, fecundity and childbirth?

12. Who was the Irish goddess who ruled the wild animals of the forest?

13. Who was the goddess of the Otherworld, maiden of joy and sorrow?

14. Who was the god of cultivated fields?

15. Who was the female warrior and goddess of sexuality and physical love?

ANSWERS
1. Daghdha. 2. Modron. 3. Manawydan. 4. Cernunnos. 5. Belinus. 6. Grannos. 7. Macha. 8. Cliodna. 9. Ogmia. 10. Anna. 11. The Matronae. 12. Flidhais. 13. Edain. 14. Ialonus. 15. Medhbh of Connacht.

How much do you know about the Celtic Gods? (2)

QUESTIONS.

1. Who was the god of war and leadership, equivalent of Jupiter?

2. Who was the god associated with the sovereignty of the land and the protection of kingship?

3. Who was the horse goddess, patroness of cavalry?

4. Who was the god of commerce, arts and crafts?

5. Who was the goddess of livestock and growing things; of the crafts, of therapy and poetic inspiration who was later worshipped by Christians as St. Brigit or St. Bride?

6. Who was the god of healing and thermal waters?

7. Who was the goddess who, like many others, concerned herself with wild animals, in her case in particular, the wild boar?

8. Who was the Welsh goddess of Nature and Inspiration, endowed with dark prophetic powers?

9. Who was the 'god of the rock'?

10. Who was the god of crafts and of strength, the Celtic equivalent of the Greek god Hephaestus?

11. Who was the god of fortified places?

12. Who was the god associated partly with the Underworld and partly with the fertility of the earth?

13. Who was the goddess of water, consort to Sucellus?

14. Who was the 'Phantom Queen' one of the three goddesses associated with war and destruction?

15. Who was the god of confluence?

ANSWERS
1. Taranis. 2. Nodons. 3. Epona. 4. Lleu. 5. Brighid. 6. Borvo. 7. Dea Arduinna. 8. Cerridwen. 9. Alisanos. 10. Gofannon. 11. Dunatis. 12. Sucellus. 13. Nantosvelta. 14. Morrighan. 15. Condatis.

How much do you know about the Celtic Gods? (3)

QUESTIONS.

1. Who was the 'flower maiden', the goddess of loving and giving?

2. Who was the goddess concerned with the wild bear?

3. Who was one of the three goddesses of war whose presence on the battlefield incited frenzy?

4. Who was the Welsh goddess called the 'Great Queen'?

5. Who was the guardian god of the land, one of the aspects of the 'Son of Light'?

6. Who was the Welsh goddess, mother of the gods Llew and Dylan?

7. Who was the Welsh god associated with sacred kingship and 'Threefold Death'?

8. Who was the Welsh god of the sea?

9. Who was the god of music, healing and youth, sometimes seen as a hunter?

10. Who was the great river goddess, mother of the god Oenghus?

11. What were the names of the three goddesses who together form the goddess of Irish sovereignty?

12. What was the name of the third of the war goddesses?

13. By what name was the god Mabon known in Ireland?

14. Into what deity did early Christianity transform the god Cernunnos?

15. By what name was the god Sucellus known in Gaul?

ANSWERS
1. Blodeuwedd 2. Dea Artio 3. Nemhain 4. Rhiannon 5. Merlin 6. Arianrhod 7. Llew 8. Dylan 9. Mabon 10. Boann 11. Banbha; Fodla and Eriu 12. Badhbh 13. Oenghus 14. The Devil 15. Sylvanus

How much do you know about the Egyptian Gods? (1)

QUESTIONS.

1. Who was the god of the air?

2. Who was the goddess of water, consort of Shu?

3. Who was the god of earth, son of Shu and Tefnet?

4. Who was the creator goddess, the fundamental female principle, consort to Geb

5. Who was the principal goddess of ancient Egypt, daughter of Geb and Nut, sister-wife of Osiris?

6. Who was the embodiment of goodness, who ruled the Underworld after being murdered by the god of night

7. Who was the hawk-headed sun god, son of Isis and Osiris, of whom the pharaohs were thought to be the incarnation?

8. Who was the divine potter, the personification of the creative force, who brought male and female genders into being?

9. Who was the goddess of war, the 'powerful she' portrayed as a lioness, consort to Ptah.

10. Who was the god who represented the divine lotus, son of Ptah and Sekhmet?

11. Who was the sun god and creator of the universe?

12. Who was the sun god, often portrayed with a falcon's head, who became god of Heliopolis after Atum?

13. Who was the god of wisdom and learning, often represented as a scribe with the head of an ibis?

14. Who was the god of night, the desert and all evils, the murderer of Osiris?

15. Who was the goddess of the dead, sister-wife of Set?

ANSWERS
1. Shu. 2. Tefnet. 3. Geb. 4. Nut. 5. Isis. 6. Osiris. 7. Horus. 8. Ptah. 9. Sekhmet. 10. Neferten. 11. Atum. 12. Ra. 13. Thoth. 14. Set. 15. Nephthys.

How much do you know about the Egyptian Gods? (2)

QUESTIONS.

1. Who was the 'king of the gods', a sun god often portrayed with the head of a ram?

2. Who was the god who personified the chaos which existed before form?

3. Who was the god of the rising sun, often portrayed as a scarab?

4. Who was the cat-headed goddess of sexual pleasure?

5. Who was the sun god, the supreme deity, worshipped as the one true god in the monotheistic religion introduced by the Pharaoh Akhenaten?

6. Who was the sky goddess, wife of Horus, goddess of dance, music and love?

7. Who was the god of war in Upper Egypt, often portrayed as a man with the head of a bull or a hawk?

8. Who was the moon god, sometimes portrayed with the head of a falcon?

9. Who was the goddess of order, justice and truth who carried an ostrich feather against which the hearts of the dead were weighed to judge their purity?

10. Who was the jackal-headed god, son of Osiris, who oversaw the weighing of hearts?

11. Who was the god of music and dance?

12. Who was the goddess who was the counterpart of Sekhmet in Upper Egypt, whose sacred bird was the vulture?

13. Who was the crocodile god?

14. Who was the bull god, believed to be the personification of Ptah?

15. Who was the god of the Nile, shown as an overweight man with the breasts of a woman, symbolising nourishment in abundance?

ANSWERS
1. Ammon (Amun-Re). 2. Nu. 3. Khepre. 4. Batet. 5. Aton. 6. Hathor. 7. Montu. 8. Khonsu. 9. Maat. 10. Anubis. 11. Bes. 12. Mut. 13. Sebek. 14. Apis. 15. Hapi.

How much do you know about the Roman Gods? (1)

QUESTIONS.

1. Who was the chief Roman god, god of the sky, arbiter of victory in battle?

2. Who was the principal goddess, consort to Jupiter?

3. Who was the god of the sea?

4. Who was the god of the underworld?

5. Who was the earth goddess, mother of Mercury?

6. Who was the god of past, present and future; the god who gave law to mankind; the god of doorways and passageways?

7. Who was the goddess of the dawn?

8. Who was the god of agriculture?

9. Who was the goddess of the moon?

10. Who was the god of light, truth and the plighted word (adopted by the Romans from the Persians)?

11. Who was the goddess of love and beauty, the patroness of spring?

12. Who was the god of medicine?

13. Who was the goddess of flocks and shepherds?

14. Who was the messenger of the gods and protector of commerce?

15. Who was the goddess of the hearth and home?

ANSWERS
1. Jupiter (Jove). 2. Juno. 3. Neptune. 4. Pluto. 5. Maia. 6. Janus. 7. Aurora. 8. Saturn. 9. Luna. 10. Mithras. 11. Venus. 12. Aesculapius. 13. Pales. 14. Mercury. 15. Vesta.

How much do you know about
the Roman Gods? (2)

QUESTIONS.

1. Who was the goddess of the underworld?

2. Who was the god of love?

3. Who was the goddess of intelligence and of the arts?

4. Who was the god of wine and of fertility?

5. Who was the goddess of flowers, youth and spring?

6. Who was the god of the sun, music, poetry, prophecy, agriculture and the pastoral life?

7. Who was the goddess of chastity, hunting and the Moon; twin sister of Apollo?

8. Who was the god of fire and destruction?

9. Who was the goddess of agriculture?

10. Who was the god of fertility and prophecy; with goat's ears, horns, tail and hind legs?

11. Who was the goddess of the harvest and the growth of seed; consort to Saturn?

12. Who was the goddess of peace?

13. Who was the god of war?

14. Who was the goddess of war?

15. Who was the goddess of fruit trees, often depicted in art holding a cornucopia, from which pours forth the fruits of the earth?

ANSWERS
1. Prosperine. 2. Cupid. 3. Minerva. 4. Bacchus. 5. Flora. 6. Apollo. 7. Diana. 8. Vulcan. 9. Ceres. 10. Faunus. 11. Ops. 12. Pax. 13. Mars. 14. Bellona. 15. Pomona.

How much do you know about the Roman Gods? (3)

QUESTIONS.

1. Who was the goddess of horses?

2. Who was the god of honesty?

3. Who was the god of trees and forests?

4. Who was the goddess of victory?

5. Who was the goddess of nursing mothers?

6. Who was the god of fertility?

7. Who was the god of seed-sowing?

8. Who was the god of death?

9. Who was the god who protected individuals and groups?

10. Who was the god of husbands?

11. Who was the goddess of childbirth and of fountains?

12. Who was the goddess of chance?

13. Who was the goddess of funerals?

14. Who was the god of human fertility?

15. Who was the goddess of spring flowers?

ANSWERS
1. Epona. 2. Fides. 3. Silvanus. 4. Victoria. 5. Rumina. 6. Vertumnus. 7. Consus. 8. Orcus.
9. Genius. 10. Portunus. 11. Egreria. 12. Fortuna. 13. Libitina. 14. Liber Pater. 15.
Feronia.

How much do you know about the Roman Gods? (4)

QUESTIONS.

1. What was the name of the Trojan hero regarded by the Romans as their ancestor?

2. What was the name of the Latin city which was in fact as well as in legend, the mother city of Rome?

3. Everyone knows that Romulus was the first King of Rome, but who was the second?

4. What was the name of the college of priestesses devoted to the cult of Vesta, goddess of the hearth and home?

5. What was the name of the precipice on the south-west corner of the Capitol, from which traitors were thrown to their deaths?

6. What are the books of prophecy, first destroyed in 83 BC, replaced, and finally destroyed in the 4th century AD.?

7. Who was the third King of Rome?

8. The Temple of Saturn in Rome, which was consecrated in 497 BC had a secondary function. What was it?

9. What 'event' did Romulus organise in order to populate Rome?

10. Apart from the major deities, Romans also had many domestic gods who protected their homes and belongings. What were they called?

11. What was the name of the wife of Tarquinius Collatinus whose rape by Sextus son of the seventh King of Rome, Tarquinius Superbus led her to kill herself in shame?

12. Can you name any of the three original tribes into which Rome was divided, believed to date back to the time of Romulus?

13. Who was the Etruscan chief who besieged Rome in 6th century BC?

14. Who was the legendary one-eyed Roman warrior who held the Etruscans at bay, until the bridge behind him was destroyed?

15. What was the Roman name for the spirits of the dead?

ANSWERS

1. Aeneas. 2. Alba Longa. 3. Numa. 4. The Vestal Virgins. 5. The Tarpeian Rock. 6. The Sibylline Books. 7. Tullus Hostilius. 8. The State Treasury. 9. The Rape of the Sabine Women. 10. Penates. 11. Lucretia. 12. The Luceres, the Ramnes and the Tities. 13. Lars Porsena. 14. Horatius. 15. The Manes.

How much do you know about the Nordic Gods? (1)

QUESTIONS.

1. Who was the chief god, the sky god who lived in Asgard (Valhalla) at the top of the world tree?

2. Who was the creator god, who helped Odin make the first humans, endowing them with the senses?

3. Who was the third creator god, who helped Odin make the humans, endowing them with life and energy?

4. Who was the goddess of married love and the hearth, wife of Odin and mother of Thor?

5. Who was the god of thunder, son of Odin and Freya?

6. Who was the best, wisest and most beloved of all the Gods, son of Odin and Freya, killed at the instigation of Loki?

7. Who was the goddess, wife of Baldur, who died of a broken heart after his murder?

8. Who was the god of light who was present at the birth of the world, and who watches over the other gods?

9. Who was the corn goddess, wife of Thor?

10. Who was the god of mischief, a principal god, but sly, cunning and the cause of dissension amongst the gods?

11. Who was the goddess wife of Loki?

12. Who was the god of fertility, brother of Freya?

13. Who was the goddess of virginity and fertility?

14. Who was the god of battles?

15. Who was the god of sailors and fishermen?

ANSWERS
1. Odin. 2. Hoenir. 3. Lodur. 4. Freya. 5. Thor. 6. Baldur. 7. Nanna. 8. Heimdall. 9. Sif. 10. Loki. 11. Sigyn. 12. Frey. 13. Gefion. 14. Tyr (Anglo-Saxon Tiw). 15. Njord.

How much do you know about the Nordic Gods? (2)

QUESTIONS.

1. What was the name of the race of warlike sky gods to which most of the familiar deities belonged?

2. Who was the chief goddess, sometimes mistaken for Freya?

3. Who was the god of justice and fertility, son of Sif?

4. Who was the god brother of Odin?

5. Who was the blind god who was tricked into killing Balder by Loki?

6. Who was the brother of Balder who avenged his death by killing Hoder?

7. Who was the god of the sea, whose daughters were the waves?

8. Who was the goddess of storms, wife of Aegir?

9. Who was the guardian of the well of knowledge?

10. Who was the goddess of the underworld?

11. Who was the goddess, keeper of the golden apples of eternal youth?

12. Who was the mountain goddess, wife of Njord, mother of Frey and Freya?

13. Who was the sun goddess who drove her chariot across the sky

14. Who was the son of Odin who avenged his father's death by slaying the wolf responsible?

15. Who were the female warrior spirits who helped Odin by training and watching over his warriors in battle?

ANSWERS
1. The Aesir. 2. Frigg. 3. Ull. 4. Ve. 5. Hoder. 6. Vali. 7. Aegir. 8. Ran. 9. Mimir. 10. Hel. 11. Idun. 12. Skadi. 13. Sol. 14. Vidar. 15. The Valkyries.

How much do you know about the Nordic Gods? (3)

QUESTIONS.

1. Who was the father of the great god Odin?

2. Who was the god who watched over craftsmen?

3. Who was the god of fire?

4. Who was the son of Odin and half-brother to Thor?

5. Who was the god of poetry?

6. Who was the god of wise statements?

7. Who was the otter god?

8. Who was the goddess of plenty?

9. What was the name of Thor's hammer?

10. Who was the dragon god?

11. Who was the goddess of earth?

12. According to Nordic mythology, the three goddesses of fate are known collectively as ...what?

13. Of these three, which is the goddess of the past?

14. Which the goddess of the present?

15. And which the goddess of the future?

ANSWERS
1. Bor. 2. Weyland the Smith. 3. Loki. 4. Hermod. 5. Bragi. 6. Kvasir. 7. Otr. 8. Nehallenia. 9. Mjollnir. 10. Fafnir. 11. Nerthus. 12. The 'Norn'. 13. Urd. 14. Verdande. 15. Skuld.

5

MUSIC

Classical Music

How much do you know about ballet? (1)

QUESTIONS.

1. Who composed the ballet 'Appalachian Spring' for which he received the 1945 Pulitzer Prize?

2. Who composed the music for the ballets 'The Sleeping Princess' and 'Swan Lake'?

3. Who composed the music for the ballets 'Coppelia' and 'Sylvia'?

4. Who composed the music for the ballet 'Cinderella'?

5. Who composed the music for the ballets 'The Rite of Spring' , 'The Fire Bird' and 'Petrouchka'?

6. Who composed the music for the ballet 'Prelude a L'Apres-Midi d'un Faune'?

7. Who composed the music for the ballet 'The Three Cornered Hat'?

8. Who composed the music for the ballet 'Les Sylphides'?

9. Who composed the music for the ballet 'The Swan'?

10. Who composed the music for the ballet 'Le Spectre de la Rose'?

11. Who composed the music for the ballet 'The Skaters'?

12. Who composed the music for the ballet 'The Good-Humoured Ladies'?

13. Who composed the music for the ballet 'The Gods Go a-Begging'?

14. Who composed the music for the ballet 'Façade'?

15. Who composed the music for the ballet 'Giselle'?

ANSWERS
1. Aaron Copland 2. Peter Tchaikovsky 3. Leo Delibes 4. Sergei Prokofiev 5. Igor Stravinsky 6. Claude Debussy 7. Manuel de Falla 8. Frederic Chopin 9. Camille Saint-Saens 10. Anton Weber 11. Giacomo Meyerbeer 12. Domenico Scarlatti 13. George Frederic Handel 14. William Walton 15. Adolphe Charles Adam

How much do you know about ballet? (2)

QUESTIONS.

1. Who composed the ballets 'Checkmate' and 'Miracle in the Gorbals'?

2. Who composed the music for the ballet 'La Boutique Fantasque'?

3. And who arranged the music for this ballet?

4. Who composed the music for the ballet 'Daphnis and Chloe'?

5. What is the name of the spirits of dead girls who dance at night and lure men to their destruction in 'Giselle'?

6. Who composed the ballet (or 'masque for dancing' as the composer preferred to call it), entitled 'Job'?

7. Which ballet by Aram Khatchaturian includes the famous 'Sabre Dance'?

8. From which of Tchaikovsky's ballets does 'The Dance of the Sugar-Plum Fairy' come?

9. In which ballet by Stravinsky are the central characters three puppets?

10. In which of Tchaikovsky's ballets do we meet the villainous magician Von Rothbart?

11. What is the name of the ballet choreographed by Fokine to a number of piano compositions by Chopin?

12. Stravinsky's most famous ballet scores (Fire Bird, Petrouchka and Rite of Spring) were commissioned by which great leader of the Russian ballet ?

13. Who composed the ballet which became a vehicle for the superb talents of Fonteyn and Nuryev : 'Romeo and Juliet'?

14. Who was the Russian dancer considered to be the greatest of all prima ballerinas?

15. Who was called 'the god of the dance'?

ANSWERS
1. Sir Arthur Bliss 2. Gioacchino Rossini 3. Ottorino Respighi 4. Maurice Ravel 5. The Wilis 6. Vaughan Williams 7. 'Gayaneh' 8. 'The Nutcracker' 9. 'Petrouchka' 10. 'Swan Lake' 11. 'Les Sylphides' 12. Diaghilev 13. Prokofiev 14. Anna Pavlova 15. Nijinsky

How much do you know about musical terms?

QUESTIONS.

1 What is a 'couplet'?

2. What is a 'fanfare'?

3. What is a 'nefer'?

4. What is a 'chorist'?

5. What does 'francamente' mean?

6. What does 'calando' mean?

7. What does 'calcando' mean?

8. What does 'andante' mean?

9 What does 'appassionato' mean?

10. What is a 'ballonchio'?

11. What does the instruction 'alla moderna' mean?

12. What is a 'pentachium'?

13. What does 'rococo' mean?

14. What is a 'seguidilla'?

15. What does 'sordamente' mean?

ANSWERS
1. Two notes occupying the same time as a triplet. 2. Musical flourish with trumpets 3. An Egyptian guitar 4. Choral singer; member of choir 5. Play frankly, boldly 6. Diminishing and slowing 7. Hurrying 8. Moderately slowly; restfully 9. With passion 10. A country dance 11. In the modern style 12. A composition in five parts 13. Old-fashioned or eccentric 14. Spanish dance in 3/4 time, usually slow and in a minor key 15. Softly

How much do you know about classical music in general? (1)

QUESTIONS.

1. Who was the American-born harmonica player who raised the harmonica to the level of a classical instrument?

2. Who was the composer of the 'Warsaw Concerto', written for the 1942 film 'Dangerous Moonlight'?

3. The 2nd movement of J.S. Bach's orchestral suite No 3 in D, Is better known as …what?

4. What was the name of the Italian family who made Cremona famous as a centre of violin making in 16th – 18th centuries?

5. The Spanish 'Ritual Fire Dance' comes from which ballet with songs by Manuel De Falla?

6. The 2nd movement of the string quartet No 1 in D by Tchaikovsky is better known as …what?

7. 'Anitra's Dance' is part of the incidental music written by Grieg for the poetic play by Ibsen, called …?

8. Who was the English conductor, son of an Italian father and a French mother; composer of an oboe concerto, long-term chief conductor of the New York Philharmonic and Halle Orchestras?

9. Which town in Bavaria is host to the Wagner festival?

10. Which great composer left three letters hidden in his writing-table after his death, addressed to his 'Immortal Beloved', the identity of whom is still in question?

11. Which of the Strauss's was called 'The Waltz King'?

12. Whose symphonies bore such a resemblance to those of Haydn, although so much milder and less virile, that he was given the nickname "Mrs Haydn"?

13. What did Maurice Ravel say that he considered his composition 'Bolero' to be?

14. What is the name of the Belgian national anthem?

15. Johannes Brahms composed a double concerto in A minor, Opus 102. For which two instruments?

ANSWERS
1. Larry Adler 2. Richard Addinsell 3. 'Air on the G String' 4. Amati 5. 'El Amor Brujo' (Love the Magician) 6. The 'Andante Cantabile' 7. 'Peer Gynt' 8. Sir John Barbirolli 9. Bayreuth 10. Ludwig van Beethoven 11. Johann Strauss the Younger 12. Luigi Boccherini 13. A lewd dance 14. 'La Brabanconne' 15. Violin and Cello

How much do you know about classical music in general? (2)

QUESTIONS.

1. Of whom was Albert Einstein speaking when he said 'His symphonies breathe a cosmic spirit'?

2. Who composed the 'Capriccio Espagnol'?

3. Who composed the 'Capriccio Italien'?

4. Who composed the 'Caprice Viennois'?

5. Which of his compositions did Saint-Saens consider to be a 'musical joke'?

6. Mascagni's 'Cavalleria Rusticana' is an opera in two acts masquerading as an opera in one act. How does the curtain remains open and the composer get away with the deception?

7. Who is the patron saint of music?

8. Which great Russian bass singer's career was put in jeopardy by terrible stage fright as a young man?

9. About which other composer did Schumann write a newspaper article which concluded with the words 'Hats off, gentlemen – a genius!'?

10. Which of his compositions did Richard Strauss describe as 'Fantastic variations on a knightly theme'?

11. Who was the composer of the symphonic poem 'The Sorcerer's Apprentice'?

12. By what name is Mozart's Serenade for string orchestra K. 525 better known?

13. What is an 'elegy'?

14. On the flyleaf of the published score of the Violin Concerto in B minor, Opus 61 are the words 'Here is enshrined the soul of ... '. Who was the composer?

15. What is the name of the Oratorio for solo voices, choir and orchestra, Opus 70 composed by Felix Mendelssohn?

ANSWERS
1. Anton Bruckner 2. Rimsky-Korsakov 3. Tchaikovsky 4. Fritz Kreisler 5. 'The Carnival of the Animals' 6. During the interval the curtain remains open and the 'Intermezzo' is played 7. Saint Cecilia 8. Feodor Chaliapine 9. Chopin 10. 'Don Quixote' 11. Paul Dukas 12. 'Eine Kleine Nachtmusik' 13. A song of lamentation 14. Sir Edward Elgar 15. 'Elijah'

How much do you know about classical music in general? (3)

QUESTIONS.

1. Sir Edward Elgar's 'Enigma Variations' are 14 variations on an original theme. Each variation represents ...what?

2. The 'Enigma' in the title is not however the mystery of the identities of the friends, but rather ...what?

3. Who composed the orchestral rhapsody 'Espana'?

4. Who composed the 'Music for the Royal Fireworks'?

5. Ottorino Respighi composed three orchestral suites inspired by his favourite city – Rome. One was ' The Fountains of Rome'; another was 'The Pines of Rome'. What was the third?

6. Which Belgian-born composer and organist was awarded a 'Grand Prix d'Honneur' by the Paris Conservatoire at a piano competition, the only time such an award has been made?

7. The 'Fugue' is the most exacting of all musical forms, the voices or parts appearing to flee from each other. What does the word mean exactly?

8. The Leipzig Gewandhaus is one of the world's most famous concert halls, dating back to the mid-18th century. The name gives away the original use of the building. What does 'Gewandhaus' mean?

9. Gounod's 'meditation' on Bach's Prelude in C major – 'The Well-Tempered Clavier', is famous as ...what?

10. The ashes of which composer who died in 1907 are buried in a cave dug into a mountain near his old country home?

11. The famous maker of violins Nicolo Amati had two pupils who became equally famous in this field. What were their names?

12. What was the name of the Coronation Anthem composed by George Frederick Handel?

13. What infirmity affected the last years of Handel's life?

14. Which Russian-American violinist gave his first public performance in 1908 at 7 years of age?

15. What is the name of the orchestral suite by Zoltan Kodaly in which a soldier returned home from the Napoleonic Wars tells a series of tall stories about his imagined exploits?

ANSWERS

1. A characteristic of a friend of the composer 2. Another well-known tune interwoven with the variations but unheard and – as yet - unidentified! 3. Emmanuel Chabriere 4. George Frederick Handel 5. 'Roman Festivals' 6. Cesar Franck 7. 'Flight' 8. Warehouse 9. 'Ave Maria' 10. Edvard Grieg 11. Andrea Guarneri and Antonio Stradivari 12. 'Zadok the Priest' 13. Blindness 14. Jascha Heifetz 15. Hary Janos

How much do you know about classical music in general? (4)

QUESTIONS.

1. Who was popularly considered to have been the greatest guitar virtuoso of all time?

2. Who was the American composer known as 'The March King'?

3. Who was the London-born, American conductor, one of the 20th century 'greats' who always conducted without book or baton? He appeared in several films including Disney's 'Fantasia'?

4. Which of the three Strauss brothers composed the famous waltz 'Village Swallows'?

5. Which of the three Strauss brothers composed the famous waltz 'The Blue Danube'?

6. What was the name of the third Strauss brother who also composed many waltzes?

7. A famous orchestral piece by Richard Straus gained even greater fame when it was used by Stanley Kubrick in the opening sequence to his 1963 film '2001: A Space Odyssey'. What is it called?

8. Who composed the oratorio 'A Child of Our Time' in 1945, inspired by the Nazi persecution of the Jews?

9. Who composed the 'Poeme Symphonique' in 1962 in which 100 wind-up metronomes tick away at different speeds, gradually winding down until there is only one, and then silence?

10. In which work by Jacques Ibert do you hear a policeman's whistle?

11. Who is the American composer of operas with a political theme, such as 'Nixon in China' or based on current events, like 'Achille Lauro'?

12. Who, with Pavarotti and Domingo, is the third of the Three Tenors?

13. Claudio Abbado has been principal conductor of the Berlin Philharmonic since 1990. Who will succeed him in 2002?

14. Whose famous Symphony No. 3 is known also as the 'Symphony of Sorrowful Songs'?

15. Who is the American composer who has made operas out of a number of Doris Lessing's novels?

ANSWERS

1. Andres Segovia 2. John Phillip Sousa 3. Leopold Stokowski 4. Joseph Strauss 5. Johann the Younger 6. Edward Strauss 7. 'Thus Spake Zarathustra' 8. Michael Tippett 9. Gyorgy Ligeti 10. 'Divertissement' 11. John Adams 12. Carreras 13. Sir Simon Rattle 14. Henryk Gorecki 15. Philip Glass

How much do you know about marches? (1)

QUESTIONS.

1. Who composed the march 'Hands Across the Sea'?

2. Who composed the march 'Entry of the Gladiators'?

3. Who composed the march 'Pomp and Circumstance'?

4. Who composed the 'Marche Slave'?

5. Who composed the 'Persian' and 'Egyptian' marches?

6. Who composed the 'Polovtsian March'?

7. Who composed the 'Wedding March'?

8. Beethoven composed a 'Turkish March'. But so also did ...?

9. Who composed the 'Rakoczy (or Hungarian) March'?

10. Who composed the 'March of the Smugglers'?

11. Who composed the 'Emperor March'?

12. Who composed the 'Funeral March of a Marionette'?

13. Who composed the march 'Colonel Bogey'?

14. Who composed the 'Coronation March'?

15. Who composed the march 'Pack Up Your Troubles'?

ANSWERS
1. John Philip Sousa 2. Julius Fucik 3. Sir Edward Elgar 4. Tchaikovsky 5. J. Strauss the Younger 6. Borodin 7. Mendelssohn 8. Mozart 9. Berlioz 10. Bizet (in Carmen) 11. Wagner 12. Gounod 13. Kenneth Alford 14. Meyerbeer 15. Felix Powell

How much do you know about marches? (2)

QUESTIONS.

1. In which of Verdi's operas does a 'Grand March' feature?

2. Who composed the 'Funeral March'?

3. Who composed the march 'Garde Republicaine'?

4. Who composed the 'Homage March'?

5. Who composed the march 'Alla Marcia'?

6. Who composed the march 'Knightsbridge'?

7. Who composed the march 'Liberty Bell'?

8. Who composed the 'Marche Lorraine'?

9. Who composed the 'Marche Militaire'?

10. Who composed the 'March of the Little Lead Soldiers'?

11. Who composed the march 'On The Mall'?

12. Who composed the Royal Air Force March Past?

13. Who composed the march 'Strike Up The Band'?

14. Who composed the march 'Stars and Stripes Forever'?

15. Who wrote the words and who arranged the music of an old Scottish tune, to come up with 'Waltzing Matilda'?

ANSWERS
1. 'Aida' 2. Chopin 3. Emmerson 4. Grieg 5. Sibelius (from 'Karelia Suite') 6. Eric Coates 7. Sousa 8. Ganne 9. Schubert 10. Pierne 11. Goldman 12. Walford Davies 13. Gershwin 14. Sousa 15. A.B Paterson and Marie Cowan

How much do you know about opera? (1)

QUESTIONS.

1. Who composed the opera 'Aida'?

2. Who composed the opera 'If I Were King'?

3. Who composed the opera 'L'Africaine' (The African Girl)?

4. Who composed the humorous opera 'Albert Herring'?

5. Who composed the opera 'The Barber of Seville'?

6. Who composed the opera 'The Bartered Bride'?

7. Beethoven only composed one opera. What is its name?

8. Which is the best known opera by Vincenzo Bellini?

9. Who composed the opera 'The Damnation of Faust'?

10. Georges Bizet composed three operas : 'Carmen'; 'The Fair Maid of Perth' and which other?

11. Who composed the opera 'La Boheme'?

12. 'They call me Mimi …' sings the heroine of 'La Boheme'. But what is her real name?

13. Who was the composer of the musical folk drama 'Boris Godunov'?

14. Which friend of Mussorgsky carried out a 'technical revision' of the opera after his death, and some say saved it from oblivion?

15. Alexander Borodin wrote only one opera. Its name …?

ANSWERS
1. Giuseppe Verdi 2. Adolphe Charles Adam 3. Giacomo Meyerbeer 4. Benjamin Britten 5. Gioacchino Rossini 6. Bedrich Smetana 7. 'Fidelio' 8. 'Norma' 9. Hector Berlioz 10. 'The Pearl Fishers' 11. Giacomo Puccini 12. 'Lucia' 13. Modest Mussorgsky 14. Nicolai Rimsky-Korsakov 15. Prince Igor

How much do you know about opera? (2)

QUESTIONS.

1. Who composed the music for the opera 'Cavalleria Rusticana'?

2. Who composed the music for the opera 'Lakme'?

3. What is the most famous aria from this opera?

4. Who composed the music for the opera 'Dido and Aeneas'?

5. What is the name of Don Giovanni's manservant in Mozart's opera?

6. And who or what is the unwelcome guest at the banquet who carries Don Giovanni off to hell?

7. Who composed the music for the operas 'Lucia di Lammermoor' and 'Don Pasquale'?

8. Who composed the opera 'The Flying Dutchman'?

9. Who composed the opera 'Der Freischutz'?

10. Who composed the first genuinely American opera, 'Porgy and Bess'?

11. Which great tenor became ill with internal bleeding during a performance of ''The Elixir of Love' in Brooklyn in 1920 and died a few months later, without having sung again?

12. Which other great Italian tenor was often referred to, to his annoyance, as the second Caruso?

13. Who composed the opera 'Russlan and Ludmilla'?

14. Two of whose operas were about the same character, Iphigenia, daughter of Agammemnon, King of Mycenae?

15. Where can you hear world-class performances of opera in the auditorium of a private house?

ANSWERS
1. Pietro Mascagni 2. Leo Delibes 3. 'The Bell Song' 4. Henry Purcell 5. Leporello 6. The stone statue of the dead Commandant of Seville 7. Gaetano Donizetti 8. Richard Wagner 9. Carl Maria von Weber 10. George Gershwin 11. Enrico Caruso 12. Beniamino Gigli 13. Michael Ivanovitch 14. Christoph Gluck 15. At Glyndebourne, Sussex

How much do you know about opera? (3)

QUESTIONS.

1. Who was the 19th century French composer of several operas' the best-known being 'Faust' and 'Romeo and Juliet' ?

2. The very beautiful largo 'Ombra mai fu' comes from which of Handel's operas?

3. Who composed the opera 'Hansel and Gretel'?

4. The very first jazz opera ever was German! Composed by Ernst Krenek and performed in Leipzig in 1927, what was its name?

5. The fame of which Italian opera composer rests on just one work 'I Pagliacci' ?

6. What was Beethoven's only opera 'Fidelio' originally entitled?

7. And how many overtures to 'Leonora' did Beethoven write?

8. Benjamin Britten composed a 'musical play for children' in which the audience also participates. What is it called?

9. Giuseppe Verdi composed two operas based upon characters from Shakespearean plays. Who were they?

10. Who, in Puccini's opera, is Madame Butterfly?

11. On September 30th, 1791, in a suburban theatre of Vienna, Mozart conducted the first night of which opera, only two months before his death?

12. In which of Mozart's operas is the role of the page-boy Cherubino, played by a girl?

13. Who was the composer of the operas 'Manon' and 'Le Cid'?

14. Richard Wagner only composed one comic opera. What is its name?

15. What is the name of the beautiful and famous intermezzo from Act II of the opera 'Thais' by Massenet?

ANSWERS
1. Charles Gounod 2. 'Serse' 3. Englebert Humperdinck 4. Johnny Spielt Auf (Johnny Strikes Up) 5. Ruggiero Leoncavallo 6. 'Leonora' or 'Conjugal Bliss' 7. Five (four still exist) 8. 'Let's Make An Opera' 9. 'Falstaff' and 'Macbeth' 10. Cho-Cho-San 11. 'The Magic Flute' 12. 'The Marriage of Figaro' 13. Jules Massenet 14. 'The Mastersingers' 15. 'Meditation'

How much do you know about operetta? (1)

QUESTIONS.

1. If 'Opera' is a drama set to music, in which the dialogue is sung, what is the definition of 'Operetta'?

2. Who composed the operetta 'The Beautiful Galatea' based on the Greek Myth of Pygmalion and Galatea?

3. Who composed the operettas 'Die Fledermaus' (The Bat) and 'The Gypsy Baron'?

4. Who composed the operettas 'Frederica', 'The Merry Widow', 'The Land of Smiles' and many more?

5. Who composed the operettas 'The Firefly', 'The Vagabond King' and 'Rose Marie'?

6. Who composed the operettas 'Merrie England', 'Tom Jones' and 'The Princess of Kensington'?

7. Which of Gilbert and Sullivan's famous comic operas has the secondary title 'The King of Barataria'?

8. Sir W. S Gilbert died in 1911 at the age of 74. How did he die?

9. Who was the American composer of many musical comedies including the well-remembered 'Naughty Marietta'?

10. Who was the Hungarian composer of a number of popular operettas, including 'Countess Maritza'?

11. Who was the American composer of many delightful operettas, such as 'Showboat' and 'Roberta'?

12. Which other American composer gave us so many enjoyable operettas (and films) such as 'Kiss Me Kate'?

13. 'Girls were made to love and kiss' comes from which Lehar operetta?

14. Which 'musical play' is based upon a fictitious event in the life of the composer Schubert?

15. Who composed 'Desert Song' and 'The Student Prince'?

ANSWERS
1. A small, light opera 2. Franz von Suppe 3. Johann Strauss the Younger 4. Franz Lehar 5. Rudolf Frimi 6. Sir Edward German 7. 'The Gondoliers' 8. He was drowned attempting to save a young woman 9. Victor Herbert 10. Emmerich Kalman 11. Jerome Kern 12. Cole Porter 13. 'Paganini' 14. 'Lilac Time' 15. Sigmund Romberg

How much do you know about operetta? (2)

QUESTIONS.

1. From which Gilbert and Sullivan operetta does the song 'Three Little Maids' come?

2. Who was the Welsh-born composer of such 'musical plays' as 'Glamorous Nights', 'Careless Rapture', 'The Dancing Years' and 'King's Rhapsody'?

3. What is the most famous song from Victor Herbert's operetta 'Naughty Marietta'?

4. Who composed the music for the modern operetta 'Oklahoma!'?

5. And who wrote the libretto?

6. From which musical romance does the song 'The Indian Love Call' come?

7. Who was the composer of the operettas 'The Chocolate Soldier' and 'The Last Waltz'?

8. The first major professional work for which Franz Schubert was paid was the operetta ....what was its name?

9. Who composed the operettas 'La Belle Helene' and 'La Vie Parisienne'?

10. With which of his operettas did Offenbach shock the audience with the 'Can-Can' in the last act?

11. Who was the American composer of the musicals 'Funny Face' and 'Lady be Good'?

12. And who composed 'Annie Get Your Gun' and 'Call Me Madame'?

13. Who composed the music for the hugely successful 'West Side Story'?

14. Who composed the music to Alphonse Daudet's play 'L'Arlesienne'?

15. Who wrote the operetta 'Bitter Sweet'?

ANSWERS
1. 'The Mikado' 2. Ivor Novello 3. 'Ah! Sweet Mystery of Life' 4. Richard Rogers 5. Oscar Hammerstein II 6. 'Rose Marie' 7. Oscar Strauss 8. 'The Twin Brothers' 9. Jacques Offenbach 10. 'Orphee aux enfers' (Orpheus in the Underworld) 11. George Gershwin 12. Irving Berlin 13. Leonard Bernstein 14. Bizet 15. Noel Coward

How much do you know about overtures?

QUESTIONS.

1. Who composed 'The Academic Festival overture'?

2. Who composed the overture 'Roman Carnival'?

3. Who composed the overture 'Calm Sea and Prosperous Voyage'?

4. The overture is the best known piece from the light opera 'Donna Diana'. Who composed it?

5. The 'Egmont' overture is the prelude to the incidental music to Goethe's tragedy of the same name. Who was the composer?

6. Who was the composer of the Festival Overture 1812?

7. Sir Edward Elgar composed an overture about London. What is its name?

8. Where exactly is 'Fingal's Cave' which inspired Mendelssohn to compose an overture named for it?

9. Who was the composer of 'The London Overture'?

10. Who composed the fantasy overtures 'Romeo and Juliet' and 'Hamlet'?

11. Who composed the operas 'The Thieving Magpie' and 'William Tell' with their famous overtures?

12. Who composed the incidental music to Byron's play 'Manfred' of which the overture is most often performed?

13. Who composed the overture 'Portsmouth Point'?

14. Who composed the operas 'Susanna's Secret' and 'The Jewels of the Madonna' of which only the overtures are played today?

15. Who composed the concert overture 'Carnival' Opus 92?

ANSWERS
1. Johannes Brahms 2. Hector Berlioz 3. Felix Mendelsohn 4. Emil Nikolaus von Reznicek 5. Beethoven 6. Tchaikovsky 7. 'Cockaigne' 8. On the island of Staffa in the Hebrides 9. John Ireland 10. Tchaikovsky 11. Rossini 12. Schumann 13. Sir William Walton 14. Ermanno Wolf-Ferrari 15. Dvorak

How much do you know about piano music? (1)

QUESTIONS.

1. Who composed the 48 preludes and fugues which are collectively known as 'The Well-Tempered Clavier'?

2. Who composed the 80 pieces of piano music collectively entitled 'For Children'?

3. Beethoven wrote five piano concertos, only one of which the 5th in E flat major was given a name. What is it?

4. By what name is Beethoven's piano sonata in C minor, Opus 13 better known?

5. By what name is Chopin's Etude No 12 in C minor, Opus 10, better known?

6. The 3rd movement of the 'Suite Bergamasque' for piano by Debussy is better known as ...what?

7. Who is called 'the father of modern piano playing'?

8. Dvorak composed a set of eight light pieces for the piano, Opus 101. What did he call them?

9. Who composed 'Ludus Tonalis' (Tonal Game) which he referred to as a 'play on keys'?

10. Who composed the 'Hungarian Dances' for piano?

11. Who composed the ' Hungarian Rhapsodies' for piano?

12. Who composed a suite of 12 pieces for piano which he called 'Iberia'?

13. Who composed a set of thirty piano pieces which he called 'Inventions'?

14. Who was the composer of the concert waltz 'Invitation to the Dance'?

15. Which outstanding concert pianist was born in a tent in a mining camp in Tasmania and didn't learn to read or write until she was twelve? The people of Kalgoorlie collected £1,000 to send her to the Leipzig Conservatoire.

ANSWERS
1. Johann Sebastian Bach 2. Bela Bartok 3. 'The Emperor' 4. The 'Pathetique' 5. The 'Revolutionary' 6. 'Clair de Lune' 7. Muzio Clementi 8. 'Humoresques' 9. Paul Hindemith 10. Brahms 11. Liszt 12. Albeniz 13. J.S Bach 14. Weber 15. Eileen Joyce

How much do you know about piano music? (2)

QUESTIONS.

1. Of whom was Beethoven speaking when he said 'We shall hear more from him' after a concert in Vienna on December 1st, 1823?

2. Who was the French court musician and composer who created the French National Opera?

3. How did Grieg refer to his 47 immensely popular 'Lyric Pieces'?

4. Who was the composer of the 'Songs Without Words'?

5. Tchaikovsky composed a suite of twelve pieces for piano, Opus 37a, on a particular theme. What is it called?

6. Beethoven's piano sonata in C sharp minor, Opus 27, No. 2, is better known as what?

7. Who was the British pianist who achieved world fame as the greatest accompanist to singers of lieder? His autobiography was entitled 'The Unashamed Accompanist'.

8. Who composed the piano suite for four hands 'Mother Goose'?

9. Who composed the piano suite 'Pictures at an Exhibition'?

10. Who composed three nocturnes for piano and orchestra called 'Nights in the Gardens of Spain'?

11. Who composed the eight piano pieces called 'Novelettes'?

12. Schumann also composed 12 short, light fluttery pieces for the piano, his Opus 2. What did he call these pieces?

13. What was Rachmaninov's last major work for piano and orchestra?

14. Chopin composed a suite of 24 piano pieces, Opus 28 which called …what?

15. What is unusual about Maurice Ravel's Piano Concerto in D?

ANSWERS
1. Franz Liszt 2. Jean-Baptiste Lully 3. His 'hot cakes' 4. Mendelssohn 5. 'The Months' 6. 'Moonlight Sonata' 7. Gerald Moore 8. Ravel 9. Mussorgsky 10. De Falla 11. Robert Schumann 12. 'Papillons' (Butterflies) 13. 'Rhapsody on a Theme of Paganini' 14. 'Preludes' 15. It is for the left-hand only

How much do you know about symphonies? (1)

QUESTIONS.

1. Who composed, in 1915, the 'Alpine Symphony'?

2. By what name is Beethoven's 5th Symphony, in C minor, known?

3. Whose Symphony No 2 is known as 'The Age of Anxiety'?

4. By what name is Dvorak's Symphony No 9 in E, better known?

5. By what name is Beethoven's 3rd Symphony in E flat major Opus 55 better known?

6. It was originally dedicated to Napoleon Bonaparte, but Beethoven changed that when he heard ....what?

7. Which Symphony by Hector Berlioz was sub-titled 'Episode in the Life of an Artist'?

8. By what name is Haydn's Symphony No 45 in F sharp minor better known?

9. What is unusual about the way it ends?

10. Tchaikovsky was inspired to compose a symphonic fantasy by a character from Dante's 'Inferno'. Which character?

11. By what collective name are Haydn's symphonies numbers 93 – 104 known?

12. What did Haydn do which affected the way symphonies were written ever afterwards?

13. Mendelssohn's 4th Symphony in A, Opus 90, is better known as ...what?

14. Mozart's last symphony, in C major, (K. 551) was given what name, many years after his death?

15. Who, other than Haydn, composed a 'London Symphony'?

ANSWERS
1. Richard Strauss 2. The 'Fate' Symphony 3. Leonard Bernstein 4. 'From the New World' 5. The 'Eroica' 6. That Bonaparte had declared himself Emperor 7. 'Symphonie Fantastique' 8. The 'Farewell' Symphony 9. Each musician leaves as he finishes his part 10. 'Francesca da Rimini' 11. The 'London Symphonies' 12. He introduced the four-movement symphony 13. 'The Italian Symphony' 14. 'Jupiter' 15. Vaughan Williams

How much do you know about symphonies? (2)

QUESTIONS.

1. Gustav Mahler did not number his 9th Symphony. What did he call it instead?

2. Why was he so reluctant to give it a number?

3. Did Mahler successfully avoid the same fate?

4. By what name is Mozart's Symphony No 38 in D major, (K. 504) known?

5. Haydn's symphony No.94 in G major Opus 80, is also known as …?

6. By what name is Beethoven's 6th Symphony in F, Opus 68, known?

7. By what name is Tchaikovsky's 6th Symphony in B minor, Opus 74, known?

8. Who composed a choral symphony called 'The Bells'?

9. Who composed the symphonic poems 'En Saga' and 'Finlandia',

10. What is the unusual element in Saint-Saens Symphony number 3 in C minor, Opus 78?

11. Rimsky-Korsakov composed a symphonic suite based upon tales from the Arabian Nights. What did he call it?

12. Which of Franz Schubert's symphonies is known as 'The Unfinished'?

13. Who composed his Symphony No 7 in C major (Opus 60) whilst enduring the siege of Leningrad by the German army in 1941?

14. Who composed the cycle of 6 symphonic poems entitled 'Ma Vlast' (My Country)?

15. Whose 7th symphony is called the 'Sinfonia Antarctica'?

ANSWERS
1. 'Das Lied von der Erde' (Song of the Earth) 2. Because Beethoven, Bruckner and Schubert had all died after completing their 9th symphonies 3. No. He died before the first performance 4. 'Prague' 5. The 'Surprise' 6. Pastoral Symphony 7. Symphonie Pathetique 8. Sergei Rachmaninov 9. Sibelius 10. It contains a part for an organ 11. 'Scheherazade' 12. The No. 8 in B minor 13. Shostakovich 14. Smetana 15. Ralph Vaughan Williams

Jazz

How much do you know about great makers of Jazz? (1)

QUESTIONS.

1. Who was the 'Father of the Blues'?

2. Who was the 'Prince of Darkness' who gave us 'cool' jazz?

3. Who led what is considered today to have been the first 'real' jazz band?

4. Who was the Kansas city based pianist and leader of big band 'swing' who composed 'One O' Clock Jump'?

5. Which other great jazz 'original' persuaded Louis Armstrong to give up the cornet and concentrate on the trumpet?

6. Freddie Keppard was one of New Orlean's leading jazz trumpet players. What was his nick-name?

7. Which New Orleans-born saxophonist and clarinettist began his career with Freddie Keppard's band at only eight years of age? He died in France in 1959.

8. Who was the trumpeter and band-leader renowned for improvisation, especially with 'Dippermouth Blues'?

9. Who, with his 'Red Hot Peppers' made the best recordings ever of New Orleans music in the 1920's?

10. Who developed a unique trumpet-style of piano playing? He had an influential duet recording of 'Weather Bird' with Louis Armstrong.

11. Who was the brilliant jazz trumpeter with the 'Wolverines' and the Frankie Trumbauer and Paul Whiteman orchestras whose career was cut short when he died at 28?

12. Which chemist's assistant and gramophone company accompanist, led his own band from 1923 to 1939 then became arranger for Benny Goodman?

13. Who was the jazz drummer par excellence who turned the drums into a solo instrument?

14. Which big band leader was called the 'King of Swing'?

15. Which trumpeter was the first major jazz virtuoso, 'scat' singer, film star and U.N. Ambassador?

ANSWERS
1. W.C Handy 2. Miles Davis 3. Buddy 'Kid' Bolden 4. Wm 'Count' Basie 5. Wm 'Bunk' Johnson 6. 'Whalemouth' 7. Sidney Bechet 8. Joseph 'King' Oliver 9. Ferdinand 'Jelly Roll' Morton 10. Earl 'Fatha' Hines 11. Leon 'Bix' Beiderbecke 12. Fletcher Henderson 13. Gene Krupa 14. Benny Goodman 15. Louis Armstrong

How much do you know about great makers of Jazz? (2)

QUESTIONS.

1. Which jazz pianist was the leading pioneer of Boogie-Woogie?

2. Which trombonist and big band leader was called 'The Sentimental Gentleman of Swing'?

3. Who has been called the 'King of Bop' because of his pioneering role in the development of be-bop?

4. Which virtuoso alto-saxophonist was also in at the birth of bebop, collaborating with Dizzy Gillespie on such recordings as 'Ornithology' and 'Now's The Time'?

5. Who composed 'Round Midnight' and 'Straight, No Chaser'? He was often called the 'Prophet' and the 'High Priest' of bebop.

6. Which famous jazz trumpeter was given the nickname 'Little Jazz'?

7. Who is celebrated in the history of jazz as the founder of the so-called 'Piano School of Harlem'?

8. Which pianist and bandleader died in Kansas City at only 39 years of age? An outstanding improvisational soloist, a charismatic singer of his own songs such as 'Honeysuckle Rose', his left hand was so powerful that a rhythm section was almost superfluous.

9. Who was the Toledo, Ohio born jazz pianist who, although near blind since birth, was the most influential of the 'swing' style pianists in his day? His unrivalled technique won him acclaim as one of the all-time greats. Recordings include 'Body and Soul' and 'Tea For Two'.

10. Who was the pianist and bandleader who pioneered 'progressive' jazz in the '40's?

11. Who was the Chicago born and based blind pianist and composer who anticipated the 'Free Jazz' movement of the '60's with such recordings as 'Intuition' and 'Digression'?

12. Who was the London-born blind pianist who went to the U.S. in 1947, created his own jazz quintet; recorded jazz hits like 'September in the Rain' and 'Lullaby of Birdland' and went on to collaborate with great vocalists like Peggy Lee, Nat 'King' Cole and Mel Torme.?

13. Who succeeded Thelonius Monk as pianist with the Dizzy Gillespie band; recorded with Miles Davis and Charlie Parker, and went on to be a founder of the Modern Jazz Quartet.

14. Who was the self-taught pianist who developed an instantly recognisable style which comes through well on recordings of 'Misty', 'Laura' and the award winning 'Concert by the Sea'?

15. Who do you think of when you hear 'Take Five' or 'Unsquare Dance'?

ANSWERS.
1. Jimmy Yancey. 2. Tommy Dorsey. 3. Dizzy Gillespie. 4. Charlie 'Bird' Parker. 5. Thelonius Monk. 6. Roy Eldridge. 7. James P. Johnson. 8. Thomas 'Fats' Waller. 9. Art Tatum. 10. Stan Kenton. 11. Lennie Tristano. 12. George Shearing. 13. John Lewis. 14. Erroll Garner. 15. Dave Brubeck.

How much do you know about great non-American makers of Jazz?

QUESTIONS.

1. Who was the Danish-born trombonist, played with many of the jazz greats, co-founder with J. J. Johnson of their own jazz quintet?

2. Who was the Belgian-born, self-taught guitarist of gypsy background who lost two fingers in a caravan fire, and still became a potent influence on the American jazz scene?

3. Who is the Argentinian-born clarinettist. tenor saxophonist. composer and multi jazz stylist who won the 'Grammy' for the soundtrack to 'Last Tango in Paris'?

4. Who was the Anglo-Indian clarinettist and composer, leader of the Fairweather All-Stars?

5. Who is the English-born alto-saxophonist, band leader and composer of all kinds of jazz, including 'Experiments With Mice', 'African Waltz' and many film scores?

6. Who was the Canadian-born pianist whose collaboration with Miles Davis led to the birth of 'cool jazz'?

7. Which Norwegian-born saxophonist's style is described as 'distilled thought'?

8. Who was the French-born violinist, co-founder of 'Le Club Hot' with Django Rheinhardt and France's first name in jazz?

9. Who was the South African-born pianist who worked with Duke Ellington in the U.S. in the '60's, formed the Jazz Epistles and made South Africa's first black jazz album?

10. Who is the English trumpeter and band-leader whose albums include 'Bad Penny Blues'?

11. Who is the English electric guitarist and bandleader with impressive speed and rhythm technique, whose music developed into a synthesis of Afro-American and Indian music?

12. Who was the Belgian-born guitarist and harmonica player; Quincy Jones's favourite soloist; played with many greats; played the soundtrack to 'Midnight Cowboy'?

13. Who is the Canadian-born piano virtuoso, great accompanist and flamboyant soloist, many recordings to his name including 'Oscar's Blues'?

14. Who is the Algerian-born pianist, composer and bandleader, renowned for his imagination and capacity for improvisation?

15. Who is the English-born saxophonist and clarinettist of Jamaican background who has formed two bands : 'The Jazz Warriors' and ' World's First Saxophone Posse'?

ANSWERS.
1. Kai Winding 2. Django Rheinhardt 3. Gato Barbieri 4. Sandy Brown 5. Johnny Dankworth 6. Gil Evans 7. Jan Garbarek 8. Stephane Grapelli 9. Abdullah Ibrahim 10. Humphrey Lyttleton 11. John McLaughlin 12. 'Toots' Thielemans 13. Oscar Peterson 14. Martial Solal 15. Courtney Pine

How much do you know about great Jazz tunes?

QUESTIONS.

1.   Who composed 'Maple Leaf Rag'?

2:   Who composed 'Tiger Rag'?

3.   Who composed 'Muskrat Ramble'?

4.   Who composed 'Basin Street Blues'?

5.   Who composed 'High Society'?

6.   Who composed 'Body and Soul'?

7.   Who composed 'Twelfth Street Rag'?

8.   Who composed 'St. Louis Blues'?

9.   Who composed 'Bugle Call Rag'?

10. Who composed 'Jazz Me Blues'?

11. Who composed 'Ain't Misbehavin''?

12. Who composed 'Sophisticated Lady'?

13. Who composed 'Stormy Weather'?

14. Who composed 'After You've Gone'?

15. Who composed 'Limehouse Blues'?

ANSWERS
1. Scott Joplin 2. Nick La Rocca 3. Edward 'Kid' Ory 4. Spencer Williams 5. Porter Steele and Walter Melrose 6. Johnny Green 7. Euday L. Bowman 8. W.C Handy 9. Jack Pettis and Elmer Schoebel 10. Tom Delaney 11. Fats Waller and Harry Brooks 12. Duke Ellington 13. Harold Arlen 14. Turner Layton and Henry Creamer 15. Philip Braham and Douglas Furber

How much do you know about great Jazz singers?

QUESTIONS.

1. Who sang the blues before anyone else? And received the homely nickname of 'Ma'?

2. Who was called the 'Empress of the Blues'?

3. Who was called the 'Queen of the Blues'?

4. Who was called the 'Queen of Soul' and 'Lady Soul'?

5. Who was called 'Lady Day'?

6. Who was the highly regarded 1930's blues singer who had such hits as 'Stormy Weather'?

7. Who started his career with Tommy Dorsey and went on to film and concert fame. He was known as 'The Voice'?

8. Who was the pianist, composer and bandleader who sang his own songs like 'Aint Misbehavin'' and 'Honeysuckle Rose'?

9. Who sang bebop with Charlie Parker and Dizzy Gillespie, and was known as 'Sassy'?

10. Who was the charismatic guitarist who accompanied himself on recordings like 'Sweet Black Angel' and the 1981 Grammy winner 'There Must Be A Better World Somewhere'?

11. Who is the eclectic leading lady of the British jazz scene, who first came to notice in the 1950's with the Johnny Dankworth Seven?

12. Who was the most talented jazz singer of them all, renowned for her 'scat singing' as well as her mellow treatment of love songs?

13. Who is the blind singer, pianist and composer of songs like 'Georgia' and 'Hit The Road Jack'?

14. Who was the singer, pianist and composer who developed the modern concept of a trio with piano, guitar and double bass.? Sang 'Unforgettable', 'Stardust' and 'Too Young'?

15. Which singer and guitarist and a very relaxed style led to recordings such as 'Boogie Chillen' and ' Boogie With The Hook'?

ANSWERS.
1. Gertrude Rainey 2. Bessie Smith 3. Dinah Washington 4. Aretha Franklin 5. Billie Holiday 6. Ethel Waters 7. Frank Sinatra 8. 'Fats' Waller. 9. Sarah Vaughan 10. B. B. King 11. Cleo Laine 12. Ella Fitzgerald 13. Ray Charles 14. Nat 'King' Cole 15. John Lee Hooker.

Pop Music

How much do you know about great hit albums 1950 - 1999? (1)

QUESTIONS.

1. Which American group brought out the album 'Recycler' in 1990?

2. Which British group brought out the album 'World Outside' in 1991?

3. Who had a hit album in 1990 with 'Rhythm of Love'?

4. Which Australian group brought out the album 'Full Moon, Dirty Hearts' in 1993?

5. Which British group brought out the album 'The Great Escape' in 1995?

6. 'Autogeddon' is the name of the album brought out in 1994 by ...?

7. Which group expressed a 'Wish' on album in 1992?

8. And who recorded 'The Songs of Distant Earth' in 1994?

9. Which group brought out the album 'Be Here Now' in 1997?

10. 'OK Computer' was the work of which group in 1997?

11. And which group rang 'The Division Bell' in 1994?

12. And which group led us into 'Hell's Ditch' in 1990?

13. Which much admired lady warned us that she was 'The Force Behind The Power' in 1991?

14. And which Canadian soloist brought out the album 'Mirror Ball' in 1995?

15. The Bee Gees brought out a very reassuring album in 1993. What was its title?

ANSWERS
1. ZZ Top 2. The Psychedelic Furs 3. Kylie Minogue 4. INXS 5. Blur 6. Julian Cope 7. The Cure 8. Mike Oldfield 9. Oasis 10. Radiohead 11. Pink Floyd 12. The Pogues 13. Diana Ross 14. Neil Young 15. 'Size Isn't Everything'

How much do you know about great hit albums 1950 - 1999? (2)

QUESTIONS.

1. Who issued her 'Birthday Concert' album in 1997?

2. Which American group brought out the album 'Good Stuff' in 1992?

3. What was the name of the album brought out in 1995 by Black Sabbath?

4. Who asked us to 'Keep The Faith' in 1992?

5. And who was the 'Earthling' in 1997?

6. Which charismatic lady issued an album in 1991 complaining that 'Love Hurts'?

7. Whose 1994 album showed clearly what he had been doing since he leapt 'From The Cradle'?

8. In 1997 Fleetwood Mac returned to issue an album which was actually an invitation to …what?

9. Which ageing Welsh heart-throb proved he was still capable of 'Carrying a Torch' in 1991?

10. Who sang the soundtrack to 'Even Cowgirls Get The Blues' in 1993?

11. Who issued their 'BBC Sessions' in 1997?

12. Who was 'Back To Front' in his 1992 album?

13. And who could you have met in 1994 in their 'Voodoo Lounge'?

14. Whose 1992 album promoted the idea of 'Love Deluxe'?

15. Which group sang 'Urban Hymns' in 1997?

ANSWERS
1. Shirley Bassey 2. The B52's 3. 'Forbidden' 4. Jon Bon Jovi 5. David Bowie 6. Cher 7. Eric Clapton 8. 'The Dance' 9. Tom Jones 10. K.d lang 11. Led Zeppelin 12. Lionel Richie 13. The Rolling Stones 14. Sade 15. The Verve

How much do you know about great hit albums 1950 - 1999? (3)

QUESTIONS.

1.   In 1984 Madonna had her first really, really big hit ...?

2.   And Prince also made a splash with his album ...?

3.   Which group issued 'Alive in America' in 1995?

4.   And which group sent 'Good News From the Next World'?

5.   In 1994 '30 Years of Maximum R&B' came out for ...?

6.   During the same year George Michael released his album ...?

7.   In 1983 Michael Jackson produced the album which set the standard by which all albums since have been judged. It was called ...?

8.   1993 produced 'Promises and Lies' by ...?

9.   In 1998 Madonna shone again, with ...?

10. 'Down Under' did rather well for ...?

11. As did 'Let's Dance' for ...?

12. Which group released the albums 'Dirty Deeds Done Dirt Cheap' and 'For Those About To Rock' in 1981?

13. In 1984 which group released the album 'Parade'?

14. Who had a hit album called 'She Works Hard For The Money' in 1983?

15. And who were 'So Excited!' in 1982?

ANSWERS
1. 'Like A Virgin' 2. 'Purple Rain' 3. Steely Dan 4. Simple Minds 5. The Who 6. 'Faith' 7. 'Thriller' 8. UB40 9. 'Ray of Light' 10. Men at Work 11. David Bowie 12. AC/DC 13. Spandau Ballet 14. Donna Summer 15. The Pointer Sisters

How much do you know about great hit albums 1950 - 1999? (4)

QUESTIONS.

1. Who came on a 'Ship Arriving Too Late To Save A Drowning Witch' in 1982?

2. Which group asked 'Who's Better, Who's Best' in '88?

3. Whose 1980 album was entitled 'Women and Children First'?

4. Which group sang 'Live Under A Blood Red Sky' in 1983?

5. Which group issued an album in 1987 entitled 'Strangeways, Here We Come'?

6. And which group, also in 1987, went 'Through The Looking-glass'?

7. Which group issued an album in 1988 advising you to 'Blow Up Your Video'?

8. Who is the British soloist whose album, also issued in 1988, was 'The Shouting Stage'?

9. In 1987, Joe Cocker had a big hit with …?

10. Who made 'False Accusations' in 1985?

11. Which American group had a hit in 1983 with 'Allies'?

12. Which British group had a massive hit in 1982 with 'Sweet Dreams Are Made Of This'?

13. Which group had a hit in 1988 with the album 'Seventh Son of a Seventh Son'?

14. Which group issued 'The Roaring Silence' in 1986?

15. And who had 'New Sensations' in 1984?

ANSWERS
1. Frank Zappa 2. The Who 3. Van Halen 4. U2 5. The Smiths 6. Siouxsie and the Banshees 7. AC/DC 8. Joan Armatrading 9. 'Unchain My Heart' 10. Robert Cray 11. Crosby, Stills, Nash and Young 12. Eurythmics 13. Iron Maiden 14. Manfred Mann 15. Lou Reed

How much do you know about great hit albums 1950 - 1999? (5)

QUESTIONS.

1. In 1978 Blondie released the album …?

2. The Police released an album in 1979 called ……?

3. In 1970 Eric Clapton had a major success on his hands with the album named …?

4. Who started all the 'Rumours' in 1977 which became the biggest-selling album ever up to that date?

5. In 1976 'Songs in the Key of Life' was whose album?

6. Which group released the album 'Toys in the Attic' in 1975?

7. And which group released, in the same year, the album 'That's The Way Of The World'?

8. Whose was the album 'The Stranger' released in 1977?

9. 1974 heard an album 'Tubular Bells' being played everywhere. By whom?

10. Who was responsible for the 1979 album 'The Wall'?

11. And whose was the 1973 album 'Goats Head Soup'?

12. Which group produced the 1971 album 'Coal Miner's Daughter'?

13. Which group was going in 'All Directions' in their 1972 album?

14. Which Irish heavy rock group claimed, in their 1978 album to be 'Live and Dangerous'?

15. And which British group claimed, in their 1972 album, to be 'Fragile'?

ANSWERS
1. 'Parallel Lines' 2. 'Regatta de Blanc' 3. Eric Clapton 4. Fleetwood Mac 5. Stevie Wonder 6. Aerosmith 7. Earth, Wind & Fire 8. Billy Joel 9. Mike Oldfield 10. Pink Floyd 11. The Rolling Stones 12. The Lovin' Spoonful 13. The Temptations 14. Thin Lizzy 15. Yes

How much do you know about great hit albums 1950 - 1999? (6)

QUESTIONS.

1. Whose album 'Unicorn' came out in 1970?

2. The Beatles had an enormous hit with an album which they put out in 1970. What was the name of the album, taken from the lead number?

3. Who wrote 'Plastic Letters' in 1977?

4. In 1972 David Bowie issued an album which caught the imagination of a generation. What was it called?

5. Who had an absolutely massive hit in 1970 with 'Close To You'?

6. Who put out the album 'Can't Get Enough' in 1974 as a launch-pad for the number 'Can't Get Enough of Your Love Babe'?

7. Who had a hit with 'Fear of Music' in 1979?

8. In the same year, which group put out 'Cool For Cats'?

9. Who was 'Born to Run' in 1975?

10. Which group were 'Flogging A Dead Horse' in '79?

11. Who sang of the 'Moonflower' in 1977?

12. Which British group, who were obviously fans of the Marx brothers, had an album 'A Night at the Opera' in 1975, followed by 'A Day at the Races' in 1976?

13. Who had a fair-sized hit with 'Lust for Life' in 1977?

14. Which group had an album entitled 'Heartbeat City' in '84?

15. Which group was 'Dressed to Kill' in 1975?

ANSWERS
1. Marc Bolan and T Rex 2. 'Let It Be' 3. Blondie 4. 'The Rise and Fall of Ziggy Stardust and the Spiders From Mars' 5. The Carpenters 6. Barry White 7. Talking Heads 8. Squeeze 9. Bruce Springsteen 10. The Sex Pistols 11. Carlos Santana 12. Queen 13. Iggy Pop 14. The Cars 15. Kiss

How much do you know about great hit albums 1950 - 1999? (7)

QUESTIONS.

1. Which group had a hit in 1965 with 'Rubber Soul'?

2. Which group cut an album in 1962 called 'Green Onions'?

3. The American group The Byrds had two hit albums in 1966. One was 'Turn, Turn, Turn'. What was the other?

4. Who was the British soloist who had a hit with 'The Universal Soldier' in 1966?

5. In 1967 The Doors put out two major albums. One was called 'The Doors'. What was the other?

6. Which pop icon issued an album in 1968 in honour of 'John Wesley Hardin'?

7. Who admitted on the cover of her album issued in 1967, 'I Never Loved A Man The Way I Love You'?

8. And who, also in 1967, asked 'Are You Experienced'?

9. Also 1967, which group had a big hit with 'Surrealistic Pillow', containing 'Nothing's Gonna Stop Us Now'?

10. And who raised the roof in 1969 with 'I Got Dem Oll' Kozmic Blues Again, Mama!'?

11. Who was 'Confessin' the Blues' in 1966?

12. And which British group set up the ' Village Green Preservation Society' in 1968?

13. Which other British group sang, in 1967, of 'Days of Future Passed'?

14. Who, in 1968, issued an album which he called his own 'Story'?

15. Which young singer from Northern Ireland issued an album in 1967 called 'Blowin' Your Mind'?

ANSWERS 1. The Beatles 2. Booker T And the MGs 3. 'Fifth Dimension' 4. Donovan 5. 'Strange Days' 6. Bob Dylan 7. Aretha Franklin 8. Jimi Hendrix 9. Jefferson Airplane 10. Janis Joplin 11. B.B King 12. The Kinks 13. The Moody Blues 14. Otis Redding 15. Van Morrison

How much do you know about great hit albums 1950 - 1999? (8)

QUESTIONS.

1. Which group put out an album in 1968 with the title 'White Light, White Heat'?

2. In the same year, who had a hit with her album 'Any Day Now'?

3. In 1967 The Beatles issued an album that is still thought of as an absolute masterpiece. What is it called?

4. Who wove an album called 'Tapestry' in 1971?

5. 1980 was a great year for albums. Witness one called 'Off The Wall' by ......?

6. Another called 'Double Fantasy' put out by...?

7. Yet another was the groundbreaking 'London Calling' by ...?

8. And yet another was entitled 'Zenyatta Mondatta' by ...?

9. Who sang 'Like a Prayer' in 1989?

10. Which British group issued the album 'Wheels of Fire' in 1968?

11. Who is the American soloist who had a number of hit albums in the '90's. including 'Daydream' and 'Butterfly'?

12. Which group had a hit in 1983 with 'Pyromania'?

13. In 1993 'Songs of Faith and Devotion' brought which group back into the charts?

14. And which group said 'Thankyou' in 1995?

15. And who kept the 'Best Kept Secret' in 1983?

ANSWERS 1. Velvet Underground 2. Joan Baez 3. 'Sergeant Pepper's Lonely Hearts Club Band' 4. Carol King 5. Michael Jackson 6. John Lennon 7. The Clash 8. The Police 9. Madonna 10. Cream 11. Mariah Carey 12. Def Leppard 13. Depeche Mode 14. Duran Duran 15. Sheena Easton

How much do you know about great hit albums 1950 - 1999? (9)

QUESTIONS.

1. Whose was the 1994 album 'Mamouna'?

2. Which group had a hit in 1984 with 'Welcome to the Pleasure Dome'?

3. It was back in 1972 that Aretha Franklin brought out an album named for it's lead song and established a classic. What is it called?

4. Which group had a hit in 1995 with 'Octopus'?

5. Who put out an album called 'Imagine' in 1971 which quickly became a classic?

6. Who got a 'Wake Up Call' in 1993?

7. And who had a hit with 'Sail Away' in 1972?

8. Which group had a successful album in 1987 with 'Men And Women' and another in 1995 with 'Life'?

9. Whose 'Dream Of Life' came out in 1988?

10. Which 1969 album brought together all those great Dusty Springfield love songs?

11. And what was the title of Bruce Springsteen's 1995 album?

12. Whose hit album 'Piledriver' released in 1973 really launched their career?

13. And who had such a big hit in 1986 when he released 'Every Beat Of My Heart'?

14. 'Rattus Norvegicus' was the first album, issued in 1977 of which British group?

15. Who were sure they were going to 'Make It Big!' in 1984?

ANSWERS
1. Bryan Ferry 2. Frankie Goes To Hollywood 3. 'Amazing Grace' 4. The Human League 5. John Lennon 6. John Mayall 7. Randy Newman 8. Simply Red 9. Patti Smith 10. 'Dusty in Memphis' 11. 'The Ghost of Tom Joad' 12. Status Quo 13. Rod Stewart 14. The Stranglers 15. Wham!

How much do you know about great hit singles 1950 - 1999? (1)

QUESTIONS.

1. Who had a big hit in 1990 with 'Nothing Compares 2 U'?

2. In 1994 which group claimed that 'Love Is All Around'?

3. Who had a hit with 'All I Wanna Do' in the same year?

4. And which group suggested that 'Things Can Only Get Better'?

5. 'Firestarter' was something of a winner in 1996 for …?

6. 'Killing Me Softly' came around again, this time as a hit for…?

7. And the third big one of the year '96 was the Spice Girls' …?

8. In 1991 'Everything I Do' (I do it for you) was a huge hit for…?

9. Which group rode on 'Wonderwall' in 1995?

10. And which group sang about 'Common People'?

11. And which group claimed to be 'Back For Good'?

12. The massive hit single of 1992 was 'I Will Always Love You' from the film 'The Bodyguard' sung by …?

13. Also popular in '92 was 'Achy Breaky Heart' by …?

14. In 1997 'Don't Speak' was a hit for…?

15. But the biggest hit of all in 1997, and for all the wrong reasons, was 'Candle In The Wind' reworked and sung by …?

ANSWERS
1. Sinead O'Connor 2. Wet Wet Wet 3. Sheryl Crow 4. D:Ream 5. Prodigy 6. The Fugees 7. 'Wannabe' 8. Bryan Adams 9. Oasis 10. Pulp 11. Take That 12. Whitney Houston 13. Billy Ray Cyrus 14. No Doubt 15. Elton John

How much do you know about great hit singles 1950 - 1999? (2)

QUESTIONS.

1. In 1992 Take That returned with the hit …?

2. And Jazzy Jeff and the Fresh Prince stirred things up with …?

3. Who sang 'hello Mary Lou' in 1972?

4. In the same year 'Never Ever' was a hit for …?

5. 'Mmm Bop' was a '97 hit for …?

6. In '95 'A Girl Like You' made it for …?

7. And 'Country House' was a hit for …?

8. What was the first solo single by ex-Spice Girl Geri Halliwell, which was a hit in 1999?

9. In the same year, 'My Vida Loca' was a hit for …?

10. And soap opera star Martine McCutcheon sang …?

11. Who had a hit with 'Just My Imagination (Running Away With Me)'?

12. 'Never Too Much' was a hit in the late eighties for American soul singer …?

13. Long before it became the title of an album in 1993, 'What's Love Got To Do With It' was a hit single for …?

14. For whom was 'Morning Has Broken' such a big, big hit?

15. Who, in 1976, complained that 'Breaking Up Is So Hard To Do'?

ANSWERS
1. 'Could It Be Magic?' 2. 'Boom! Shake the Room' 3. Ricky Nelson 4. All Saints 5. Hanson 6. Edwyn Collins 7. Blur 8. 'Look At Me' 9. Ricky Martin 10. 'This Is My Moment' 11. The Temptations 12. Luther Vandross 13. Tina Turner 14. Cat Stevens 15. Neil Sedaka

How much do you know about great hit singles 1950 - 1999? (3)

QUESTIONS.

1. In 1986 'The Lady in Red' was an outstanding succes for ...?

2. 'West End Girls' was a minor hit for ...?

3. And 'Walk Like An Egyptian' did alright for ...?

4. In 1988 'Sweet Child O' Mine' made it for ...?

5. Who released 'Call Me' in 1976?

6. Or 'The Winner Takes It All' in 1980?

7. Or 'Brass in Pocket' in 1979?

8. In 1982 Simple Minds had a hit single with ...?

9. And which group released 'Everybody Wants To Rule The World' in 1983?

10. Who had a winner with 'Teardrops' in 1988?

11. And which group brought out 'Hangin' Tough' in 1989?

12. In 1982 Paul McCartney and Stevie Wonder collaborated on ...?

13. 'A Town Called Malice' was a hit for which group?

14. 'Golden Brown' was released in 1977 by ...?

15. And in 1979 'Our House' was relatively successful for ..?

ANSWERS
1. Chris De Burgh 2. Pet Shop Boys 3. The Bangles 4. Guns 'n Roses 5. Blondie 6. Abba 7. The Pretenders 8. 'Don't You Forget About Me' 9. Tears For Fears 10. Womack and Womack 11. New Kids On The Block 12. 'Ebony and Ivory' 13. The Jam 14. The Stranglers 15. Madness

How much do you know about great hit singles 1950 - 1999? (4)

QUESTIONS.

1. In 1987 'Livin' On A Prayer' was a hit single for …?

2. In the same year, U2 had a big hit called … ?

3. Who declared to the world 'I Want Your Sex' in 1987?

4. And which group released 'Don't Dream It's Over'?

5. In 1981 'Stand and Deliver' was a hit for …?

6. 'Bette Davis Eyes' did quite well for …?

7. 'Ghost Town' was a British number one for …?

8. 'Tainted Love' did well for which Leeds-based duo?

9. And 'Don't You Want Me' was a hit for whom?

10. 1983 saw a massive hit with 'Every Breath You Take' for whom?

11. 'Relax' was released in 1984 by which Liverpool group?

12. George Michael had two big winners in 1984. One was 'Wake Me Up Before You Go Go'. What was his solo hit?

13. The Christmas time hit was 'Do They Know It's Christmas' by which collaboration of artists?

14. Which group sang 'Do You Really Want To Hurt Me' in 1983?

15. In 1986 Prince had another hit, with …?

ANSWERS
1. Bon Jovi 2. 'With or Without You' 3. George Michael 4. Crowded House 5. Adam and the Ants 6. Kim Carnes 7. The Specials 8. Soft Cell 9. The Human League 10. The Police 11. Frankie Goes To Hollywood 12. 'Careless Whisper' 13. Band Aid 14. Culture Club 15. 'Kiss'

How much do you know about great hit singles 1950 - 1999? (5)

QUESTIONS.

1. What was the title of Paul McCartney's hit of 1978?

2. What did Gloria Gaynor promise in her hit single of the same year?

3. 'My Sharona' did quite well for …?

4. And 'Le Freak' was quite a hit for …?

5. From the album of the same name, 1970 was the year that Simon and Garfunkel released a single destined to become a classic …?

6. In 1973, who asked us to 'Help Me Make It Through The Night'?

7. 'Let it Be' was a massive single hit for …?

8. And 'Tears of a Clown' did rather well for …?

9. 'Tears of a Clown' was re-recorded in 1979 by which English ska outfit, featuring Dave Wakeling and Rankin' Roger?

10. Who sang 'Rhinestone Cowboy'?

11. And who sang 'The Hustle'?

12. In 1973 'Killing Me Softly' was a great success for the first time. It was sung by …..?

13. And who sang 'You're So Vain' with great results?

14. 'Wuthering Heights' was a 1978 hit for solo female artist?

15. In 1977 the Bee Gees released the hit single …?

ANSWERS
1. Mull of Kintyre 2. 'I Will Survive' 3. The Knack 4. Chic 5. 'Bridge Over Troubled Water' 6. Gladys Knight 7. The Beatles 8. Smokey Robinson and the Miracles 9. The Beat 10. Glen Campbell 11. Van McCoy 12. Roberta Flack 13. Carly Simon 14. Kate Bush 15. 'How Deep Is Your Love?'

How much do you know about great hit singles 1950 - 1999? (6)

QUESTIONS.

1. In 1972 the most unlikely 'Long Haired Lover from Liverpool' was a hit single for …?

2. And 'Let's Stay Together' did quite well for …?

3. 1976 punk music arrives with 'Anarchy in the U.K' by …?

4. And 'New Rose' by …?

5. In the same year 'Bohemian Rhapsody' was a hit for …?

6. And 'Love to Love You, Baby' by …?

7. And 'Dancing Queen' by …?

8. In 1978 'Night Fever' did well for …?

9. Who in the same year thought you were not once, not twice, but 'Three Times A Lady'?

10. 1974 saw the release of possibly Abba's greatest hit single …?

11. And who, in 1972, confessed 'I Shot The Sheriff'?

12. In 1971 'My Sweet Lord' was a great hit single for …?

13. 'What's Going On' was a hit for …?

14. As was 'Maggie May' for …?

15. Whose opinion was it in 1971 that it 'Might As Well Rain Until September'?

ANSWERS
1. Little Jimmy Osmond 2. Al Green 3. The Sex Pistols 4. The Damned 5. Queen 6. Donna Summer 7. Abba 8. The Bee Gees 9. The Commodores 10. 'Waterloo' 11. Bob Marley 12. George Harrison 13. Marvin Gaye 14. Rod Stewart 15. Carol King

How much do you know about great hit singles 1950 - 1999? (7)

QUESTIONS.

1. Who released his hit single 'Are You Lonesome Tonight' in 1960?

2. Who had a hit single in 1961 with 'Let's Twist Again'?

3. Who released 'Surfin' Safari' in 1962?

4. The Beatles had two major hit singles in 1963. One was 'Twist and Shout'. What was the other?

5. They also had two hit singles in 1964. One was 'I Want To Hold Your Hand'. What was the other?

6. The Beach Boys also had a hit single in '64. It was …?

7. And 'I Only Want To Be With You' made an international star of …….?

8. Who, in 1965, complained that 'You've Lost That Lovin' Feelin'?

9. In the same year, who thought that 'It's Not Unusual'?

10. Who was 'King of the Road'?

11. Who sang 'I Got You Babe'?

12. Who couldn't get no 'Satisfaction'?

13. The Beatles had their usual two top hit singles. One was 'Help'. What was the other?

14. In 1966, who heard 'The Sound of Silence' (and sang a song about it)?

15. And the Beach Boys were back up there again, with …?

ANSWERS
1. Elvis Presley 2. Chubby Checker 3. The Beach Boys 4. 'She Loves You' 5. 'Can't Buy Me Love' 6. 'Fun, Fun, Fun' 7. Dusty Springfield 8. The Righteous Brothers 9. Tom Jones 10. Roger Miller 11. Sonny and Cher 12. The Rolling Stones 13. 'Yesterday' 14. Simon and Garfunkel 15. 'Good Vibrations'

How much do you know about great hit singles 1950 - 1999? (8)

QUESTIONS.

1. In 1967 who won the Eurovision Song contest for the UK with 'Puppet On A String'?

2. Which group recorded the hit single 'I'm A Believer'?

3. And which group had a hit single with 'Light My Fire'?

4. And which father/daughter pairing had a hit with 'Something Stupid'?

5. Who wooed the girls with hits like 'Maybelline' and 'Nadine' and 'Sweet Little Sixteen'?

6. 1968 produced a wonderful hit single 'Those Were The Days' for …?

7. As well as which hit single for the Beatles?

8. And the trumpet-led 'This Guy's In Love With You' from …?

9. Marvin Gaye had another top single with …?

10. Who insisted that 'It's a Man's Man's Man's World'?

11. Who was 'Leaving On A Jet Plane' in 1962?

12. In 1969 'Wichita Lineman' was a runaway hit for …?

13. And who told us that 'The Times They Are A' Changing' in 1963?

14. In 1964 'The House of the Rising Sun' and 'We've Gotta Get Out Of This Place' were individual hits extracted from an album put out by …?

15. And who took us on a trip down the 'Tunnel of Love' in 1980?

ANSWERS
1. Sandie Shaw 2. The Monkees 3. The Doors 4. Frank & Nancy Sinatra 5. Chuck Berry 6. Mary Hopkins 7. 'Hey Jude' 8. Herb Alpert 9. 'I Heard It Through The Grapevine' 10. James Brown 11. Peter, Paul & Mary 12. Glen Campbell 13. Bob Dylan 14. The Animals 15. Dire Straits

How much do you know about great hit singles 1950 - 1999? (9)

QUESTIONS.

1. Who is the American soloist with a whole list of hits to his name, like 'Georgia', Hit the Road Jack', and many more?

2. Whose hits included 'Annie's Song' and 'Take Me Home Country Road'?

3. Who shared the big, big hit 'You Don't Bring Me Flowers' with Barbra Streisand?

4. Which pianist and soloist had any number of hits including 'Blueberry Hill' and 'Ain't That A Shame'?

5. 'Bye Bye Love' was an early hit for …?

6. Which British group had a big hit with 'You Can't Hurry Love'?

7. 'See You Later Alligator' was one of whose big hits?

8. What was the name of the group, one of the earliest, who had many hits, including 'Mrs Brown You've Got A Lovely Daughter'?

9. Which group had an early smash hit with 'Stop! In The Name of Love'?

10. Who had a hit with 'This Old Heart Of Mine'?

11. And whose 1986 big hit single was 'When I Think Of You'?

12. 'Love Will Tear Us Apart' was whose message on the 1979 hit single?

13. And who sang 'Stand By Me'?

14. Who was the 'Dedicated Follower of Fashion'?

15. And who claimed that 'Girls Just Want to Have Fun'?

ANSWERS
1. Ray Charles 2. John Denver 3. Neil Diamond 4. Fats Domino 5. The Everly Brothers 6. Genesis 7. Bill Haley and the Comets 8. Herman's Hermits 9. The Hollies 10. The Isley Brothers 11. Janet Jackson 12. Joy Division 13. Ben E. King 14. Gilbert O' Sullivan 15. Cyndi Lauper

How much do you know about great hit singles 1950 - 1999? (10)

QUESTIONS.

1. Who was the top pop artist who had hits like 'Peggy Sue' and 'That'll Be The Day'?

2. What was the name of the group which specialised in hit singles like 'California Dreamin' and 'Dedicated to the One I Love'?

3. Who sang 'And I Love You So'?

4. With what hit single did Kylie Minogue break upon the scene in 1987?

5. Who was the American singer with many hits to his name, like 'Dream Baby' and 'Pretty Woman'?

6. 'The Man Who Shot Liberty Valance' was a hit for …?

7. 'One Night' was a big hit for …?

8. Who sang 'This Is Not A Love Song' in 1981, but it sold anyway?

9. Who invaded the charts with 'A Crazy Little Thing Called Love'?

10. Who had a big, big hit with a single called 'Cry'?

11. Who took 'A Walk On The Wild Side'?

12. Some time in the mid-sixties, who suggested 'Let's Spend The Night Together'?

13. And who sang 'I'm Ready For Love'?

14. 'My Only Love' was a big hit for …?

15. Who claimed to be a 'Smooth Operator'?

ANSWERS
1. Buddy Holly 2. The Mamas and the Papas 3. Don McLean 4. 'I Should Be So Lucky'
5. Roy Orbison 6. Gene Pitney 7. Elvis Presley 8. Public Image Ltd 9. Queen 10.
Johnnie Ray 11. Lou Reed 12. The Rolling Stones 13. Martha Reeves and the
Vandellas 14. Roxy Music 15. Sade

How much do you know about great hit singles 1950 - 1999? (11)

QUESTIONS.

1. Who sang about 'The Leader of the Pack'?

2. Which British vocalist had hits with 'Puppet On A String' and 'Always Something There To Remind Me'?

3. And who sang the background song to the James Bond film 'The Spy Who Loved Me' – 'Nobody Does It Better'?

4. Who had a major hit single in 1959 with 'Living Doll'?

5. And who turned 'Mack the Knife' from The Threepenny Opera into a hit single in the same year?

6. And who had a big hit with the single 'C'mon Everybody'?

7. Who had a big hit single in 1958 with 'Great Balls of Fire'?

8. And who, in that same year, told us to 'Dream'?

9. Elvis Presley has two big hit singles in 1956. One of them was 'Heartbreak Hotel'. What was the other?

10. And which female vocalist and film star had a very successful single release 'Che Sera Sera'?

11. In 1955 Bill Haley and the Comets released a rock single which quickly became a classic. What was it called?

12. Who offered a 'Small Blue Thing'?

13. Which day of the week did U2 make peculiarly their own?

14. Who made her own arrangement of 'House of the Rising Sun' and scored a major hit?

15. Which group had a non-vocal hit with 'Apache'?

ANSWERS
1. The Shangri-Las 2. Sandie Shaw 3. Carly Simon 4. Cliff Richard 5. Bobby Darin 6. Eddie Cochran 7. Jerry Lee Lewis 8. The Everly Brothers 9. 'Hound Dog' 10. Doris Day 11. 'Rock Around The Clock' 12. Suzanne Vega 13. 'Sunday, Bloody Sunday' 14. Nina Simone 15. The Shadows

How much do you know about who is who in the pop business?

QUESTIONS.

1. By what name is REGINALD KENNETH DWIGHT better known?

2. And DAVID ROBERT JONES?

3. And DECLAN PATRICK McMANUS?

4. And ROBERT ALLEN ZIMMERMAN?

5. And YVETTE MARIE STEVENS?

6. And MARIE McDONALD McLAUGHLAN LAWRIE?

7. And YORGOS KYRIATOU PANAYIOTOU?

8. And ROBERTA JOAN ANDERSON?

9. And JAMES NEWELL OSTERBURG?

10. And FREDERICK BULSARA?

11. And HARRY RODGER WEBB?

12. And EUNICE WAYMAN?

13. And ANNIE MAE BULLOCK?

14. And MARY O'BRIEN?

15. And STEVEN DEMITRI GEORGIOU?

ANSWERS
1. Elton John 2. David Bowie 3. Elvis Costello 4. Bob Dylan 5. Chaka Khan 6. Lulu 7. George Michael 8. Joni Mitchell 9. Iggy Pop 10. Freddie Mercury 11. Cliff Richard 12. Nina Simone 13. Tina Turner 14. Dusty Springfield 15 Cat Stevens

6

SCIENCE
&
TECHNOLOGY

Astronomy

How much do you know about Astronomy? (1)

QUESTIONS.

1. What is the term for the study of the properties, processes and evolution of the universe?

2. What is the term for the study of how the universe was formed?

3. What is the word that describes the apparent path of the Sun, the planets and the Moon as seen from the earth?

4. What is the name given to a concentration of gas and dust in the galaxy?

5. What is the term for matter in the form of electrically charged particles?

6. What do you call a spherical, self-luminating, celestial body, consisting of a large mass of hot gas held together by its own gravity?

7. What is the movement of an object around a central body called?

8. What is the path of an object around a central body called?

9. What is the condition called when three celestial objects find themselves arranged in a straight line, e.g. during a solar or lunar eclipse?

10. How do you refer to the number of degrees above the horizon of an object on the celestial sphere?

11. What is the term for the average distance from Earth to the Sun, about 93 million miles?

12. How do we refer to the passage of Mercury or Venus between the Earth and the Sun?

13. What term is applied to the measure of a celestial object's brightness?

14. What term defines the line separating sunlight and darkness on a planet or moon?

15. What do we call the movement of a celestial body as it turns on its axis?

ANSWERS.
1. Cosmology 2. Cosmogony 3. Ecliptic 4. Nebula 5. Plasma 6. Star 7. Revolution 8. Orbit 9. Syzygy 10. Altitude 11. An 'astronomical unit' 12. An 'inferior conjunction' 13. Magnitude 14. 'Terminator' 15. Rotation.

How much do you know about Astronomy? (2)

QUESTIONS.

1. What are thought to be the most distant objects in the universe?

2. What is the term given to the Sun's apparent figure eight path during the course of a year?

3. What do we call particularly bright meteor, one with an apparent magnitude ranging from –5 to –20 (the Sun having an apparent magnitude of -26,7)?

4. What name is given to the apparent uniform and mutual recession of celestial objects because of the expansion of the universe?

5. What description do we give to a planet or natural satellite that is not completely spherical but bulges in the centre and is flattened at the poles?

6. What name do we give to the stream of particles, primarily protons and electrons, that constantly flow outwards from the Sun?

7. What term is applied to the area in shadow, from which light is completely cut off, e.g. the whole of the Moon during a total lunar eclipse?

8. What term is applied to the entirety of all that is know to exist?

9. What do we call matter that is thought to exist in the universe but which has not yet been observed?

10. How do we refer to stars that are gravitationally attracted to each other, becoming part of a double star system?

11. What do we call the measurement of the positions and apparent motions of celestial objects and the study of the factors influencing such movements?

12. What name is given to a nearly spherical, dense cluster of hundreds of thousands to millions of stars?

13. What term is applied to the phenomenon in which, as a source of waves (either sound or light) and an observer move relative to each other, the emitted wavelength appears to change?

14. What is the co-ordinate on a celestial sphere that is analogous to latitude on Earth?

15. What is the crossing of one body in front of another, relative to an observer?

ANSWERS.
1. Quasi-stellar radio sources (QUASARS) 2. Analemma 3. Fireball 4. The Hubble Flow 5. Oblate 6 Solar wind 7. Umbra 8. The Universe 9. Dark matter 10. Binary star 11. Astrometry 12. 'Globular cluster' 13. The Doppler effect 14. Declination 15. Occultation

Biology

How much do you know about biological terms? (1)

QUESTIONS.

1. What is the name of the branch of archaeology that includes the study of how ancient civilisations used plants in their everyday life?

2. What is the name of the process by which plants use light to convert water and carbon dioxide into sugar?

3. What do you call a plant whose parents are from two different genera?

4. In the life cycle of an animal or a plant, what is the term used for the young, immature form that undergoes major change in structure as it becomes adult?

5. What is a chemical that kills certain plants, usually used for weed control?

6. What is the name of the male part of a flower, the pollen bearing anther is at its tip?

7. What is the name of the female part of a flower, part of the pistil, it is where the pollen from the male stamen is deposited?

8. What is the major structural part of the flower called? It transports water and minerals from the roots to the leaves, and the food made in the leaves to other parts of the plant.

9. What is the biological term for any individual living entity?

10. What is any spontaneous change in an organism's inherited characteristics called?

11. What is the term applied to the transfer of pollen from the male anther to a female stigma, being the first step in flower reproduction?

12. What is the dark, thick material that is produced when organic matter decays?

13. What is the stalk of a flower's stamen which bears the anther?

14. What are the complex protein substances that accelerate chemical activities in a living organism, often referred to as organic catalysts?

15. What term describes a group of flowers on a plant?

ANSWERS.
1. Ethnology. 2. Photosynthesis. 3. Bigeneric. 4. Larva. 5. Herbicide.6. Stamen. 7. Stigma. 8. Stem. 9. Organism. 10. Mutation. 11. Pollination.12. Humus. 13. Filament. 14. Enzymes. 15. Inflorescence.

How much do you know about biological terms? (2)

QUESTIONS.

1. What do you call a plant that is not native to the area in which it is growing?

2. What term is applied to the change from one stage in an organism's life cycle to another?

3. What is the name for a unit of a chromosome that codes for specific hereditary traits?

4. What is the term for the single-celled organisms, either plant or animal, that float on or near the surface of the oceans, including small crustaceans, algae and protozoa?

5. What is the main root of a plant called, the one which reaches deep underground?

6. What name is given to any invertebrate animal that resembles a plant, e.g. coral?

7. What are the basic chemical units called, from which proteins are synthesised by the body?

8. What name is given to the fully developed ovule containing a dormant embryo plant?

9. What is the fertilised egg cell of a plant or animal called?

10. What is the material found within the nucleus of a call called?

11. What is the first stage in the development of a plant seed called?

12. What name is given to the outer covering of a plant or animal that is essentially waterproof and protective?

13. What term is given to the successive stages, usually functional and morpho-logical, through which organisms pass?

14. What is the name give to the relationship between two organisms in which one organism benefits but the other does not, or is harmed?

15. What is the relationship between two organisms in which both partners benefit?

ANSWERS.
1. Exotic. 2. Metamorphosis. 3. Gene. 4. Plankton. 5. Taproot. 6. Zoophyte. 7. Amino acids.   8. Seed. 9. Zygote. 10. Nucleoplasm. 11. Germination. 12. Epidermis. 13. Life cycle. 14. Parasitism. 15. Mutualism.

Chemistry

How much do you know about chemical terms? (1)

QUESTIONS.

1. What is the term for a compound having basic (as opposed to acidic) properties?

2. What is the emission of heat and light through rapid oxidation called?

3. What is the name given to organic compounds, including fats, waxes and steroids?

4. What is the term for anything that occupies space and has mass when at rest?

5. What are high-frequency electromagnetic waves, similar to X-rays but of higher frequency?

6. What is energy produced by molecular motion?

7. What number is given to protons in the nucleus of an atom?

8. What is a substance that changes the speed of a chemical reaction without itself being permanently changed?

9. What is the conversion of a gas or vapor into a liquid, by cooling?

10. What is an atom (or group of atoms) that is electrically charged as a result of a gain or a loss of electrons?

11. What is a substance that slows down the rate of a chemical reaction?

12. What is the change of state from a liquid to a gas?

13. What is a compound composed solely of carbon and hydrogen (e.g. methane)?

14. What is the process in which an atom, ion or molecule loses electrons?

15. What is the name given to the smallest particle of an element or compound that contains the chemical properties of that material?

ANSWERS.
1. Alkali. 2. Combustion. 3. Lipids. 4. Matter. 5. Gamma-rays. 6. Heat. 7. Atomic number. 8. Catalyst. 9. Condensation. 10. Ion. 11. Inhibitor. 12. Evaporation. 13. Hydrocarbon. 14. Oxidation. 15 Molecule.

How much do you know about chemical terms? (2)

QUESTIONS.

1. What is the term used to express the breakdown of atomic nuclei accompanied by the release of radiation, in alpha-, beta- or gamma-rays?

2. What is the term for a specific amount of energy released or absorbed in a process?

3. What are atoms that have the same atomic number but different atomic mass, due to the different number of neutrons in their nuclei?

4. What is the term for the property of matter, either positive or negative, that gives rise to electrical forces?

5. What term denotes a chemical reaction in which heat is released, (e.g. combustion)?

6. What is the term for the bonding or the chemical reaction that produces a polymerfrom two or more monomers?

7. What do you call a substance, chemical or solution used in the laboratory to detect or measure other substances, chemicals or solutions?

8. What is a system in which particles of a solid or liquid are dispersed in a liquid or a gas?

9. What is the process of removing suspended particles from a fluid, by passing or forcing the fluid through a porous material, called?

10. What term refers to matter that does not enter chemical reactions?

11. That part of an atom in which electrons are most likely to be found is ...?

12. What is the change in a substance from a liquid to a solid known as?

13. What term refers to the conversion of one element into another by means of nuclear change?

14. What is the sum of the atomic masses in a compound's formula called?

15. What is the decomposition of a substance by passing an electric current through a liquid?

ANSWERS.
1. Radioactivity. 2. Quantum. 3. Isotopes. 4. Electric charge. 5. Exothermic.
6. Polymerisation. 7. Reagent. 8. Suspension. 9. Filtration.   10. Inert. 11. Orbital.
12. Solidify. 13.Transmutation. 14. Formula mass. 15. Electrolysis.

The Environment

How much do you know about Environmental Science? (1)

QUESTIONS.

1. What term is applied to the entire zone of the Earth that is capable of sustaining life, e.g. the atmosphere; the hydrosphere and parts of the lithosphere?

2. What do we call the characteristic surroundings of an area, mainly determined by the vegetation?

3. What is the term used for an animal which eats both flesh and plants?

4. What describes a substance that has a poisonous effect on humans and/or other organisms through physical contact; ingestion and/or inhalation?

5. What do we call coal, oil and natural gas, which were formed from the remains of decaying plants and animals, and which are non-renewable?

6. What are particles so small that they tend to remain in suspension in the air for years?

7. What term do we use for the continual contest between living organisms for the available space, food resources and light?

8. What is the term used to describe water that is fit for human consumption?

9. What term is used to indicate the existence of different species in a community?

10. What is the term for the more or less permanent structural breakdown of a molecule into its components (atoms or molecules)? It is also used for the decay of organic material.

11. What do we call any feature of an organism that increases its chance of survival?

12. What term describes any organism that can only survive in the presence of oxygen?

13. And what describes any organism that does not need oxygen to survive?

14. What term is applied to a substance that is shown to cause cancer?

15. What do we call precipitation that contains a high level of dissolved chemical pollutants, e.g. sulphur, nitrogen oxide?

ANSWERS.
1. Biosphere. 2. Habitat. 3. Omnivore. 4. Toxic. 5. Fossil fuels. 6. Aerosols. 7. Competition. 8. Potable. 9. Diversity 10. Decomposition. 11. Adaptation. 12. Aerobic. 13. Anaerobic. 14. Carcinogen. 15. Acid rain.

How much do you know about Environmental Science? (2)

QUESTIONS.

1. What is the name of the hypothesis put forward that proposes that the Earth should be regarded as a living organism?

2. Who was the environmentalist who proposed this hypothesis?

3. What is the name of the principle of competitive exclusion which states that two similar species cannot occupy the same ecological niche for any length of time?

4. This principle came out of the collaboration of a Russian ecologist and an American naturalist. What are their names?

5. What is the name given to an animal whose diet is mainly of insects, e.g. the bat?

6. What is the theory and practice of establishing and managing stands of trees?

7. What are those metals called, that are found in chemical products and in nature, that often find their way into water and soil?

8. What is the name given to the colourless gas which is produced by a photochemical reaction involving oxygen and ultraviolet radiation from the sun?

9. What is the naturally occurring, invisible, odourless gas that is produced as a result of radioactive decay of uranium in rock and soil?

10. What name is given to the combustible gas, mostly methane, that is produced from the decay of vegetation in stagnant water?

11. What is the destruction or impairment of the purity of a natural environment by contaminants of any sort?

12. What is the growing of marine and freshwater organisms, e.g. fish, in a controlled environment called?

13. What is the name for that property of a material that ensures that it will degrade into components that are easily accepted into the local environment?

14. Which gas is, in general, released by animal respiration and taken in by plants during photosynthesis?

15. What name is given to the border between two major ecosystems, e.g the region between the tundra and the northern forests?

ANSWERS.
1. The Gaia Hypothesis 2. James Lovelock. 3. Gause's Principle. 4. G. F. Gause and J. Grinnell. 5. Insectivore. 6. Silviculture. 7. Trace metals. 8. Ozone. 9. Radon. 10. Marsh gas. 11. Pollution. 12. Aquaculture. 13. Biodegradable. 14. Carbon dioxide. 15. Ecotone.

Geology

How much do you know about Geology? (1)

QUESTIONS.

1.   What name is given to the hot molten rock found under the earth's surface?

2.   What does this material become when it reaches the earth's surface?

3.   What forms on the surface of the earth when this material erupts violently upwards?

4.   What is the Japanese word used everywhere for a seismic sea wave caused by underwater earthquake or volcanic activity?

5.   What term is applied to the alternate rising and falling of water surfaces caused mainly by the pull of the Moon?

6.   What is the name of the instrument which measures the intensity and direction of seismic waves caused by earthquakes, aftershocks or tremors?

7.   What term is given to a mineral's resistance to scratching by another mineral or object?

8.   What name is given to any animal which resembles human beings?

9.   What do we call those flowing bodies of land ice that develop in colder regions and higher latitudes of the planet, originating on land by the accumulation and compression of snow?

10. What do we call a flat-topped plateau with steep sides, in which the top surface rock is more resistant to erosion than the underlying rock?

11. Into which other rock formation does a mesa eventually erode?

12. What is a large, natural elevation of the earth's surface rising abruptly from the surrounding level?

13. What word is used to refer to the action of water e.g erosion, along water courses?

14. What is the finest rock material ejected from a volcanic eruption called?

15. What is the name given to the measurement of of the ocean depths to establish sea floor topography?

ANSWERS.
1. Magma 2. Lava 3. A Volcano 4. Tsunami 5. Tides 6. Seismograph 7. Hardness 8. Hominoid 9. Glaciers 10. A Mesa 11. A Butte 12. A Mountain 13. Fluvial 14. Ash 15. Bathymetry.

How much do you know about Geology? (2)

QUESTIONS.

1. What is the term applied to a crack or fracture in the Earth, usually created by the movement of the Earth's crust?

2. What is the name give to the wide, tidal part of a coastal river, close to its mouth, where freshwater mixes with seawater?

3. What are remains of a plant or animal buried in sediment called?

4. What is the term used for that property of a mineral that allows it to break along a smooth plane surface?

5. What is the name of the solid, black or brownish-black combustible material that was formed through the partial decomposition of vegetation?

6. What term do we give to the solid rock that makes up the Earth's crust, and also to the exposed solid mass of rock after soil has been removed?

7. What is the deep, roughly round depression at the mouth of a volcano called?

8. What name is given to a natural – or artificial – body of inland water?

9. What is the 'wobbling' effect of the Earth as it turns on its axis called?

10. What is the name given to permanently frozen ground?

11. What name is given to a circular, steep-sided basin associated with a volcano or meteorite impact?

12. What is a long, steep-sided valley formed in dry regions by running water?

13. What term is applied to a rock layer that can store a large amount of groundwater?

14. What do we call Geologic time measured in years from information gathered by direct means, e,g, radioactive dating?

15. What term relates to materials such as rocks, meteorites, etc., that contain carbon?

ANSWERS.
1. Fault. 2. Estuary. 3. Fossils. 4. Cleavage. 5. Coal. 6. Bedrock. 7. Caldera. 8. Lake.
9. 'Nutation'. 10. Permafrost. 11. Crater. 12. Canyon. 13. Aquifer. 14. 'Absolute time'.
15. Carbonaceous

The Industrial Revolution

How much do you know about the Industrial Revolution? (1)

QUESTIONS.

1. Who was the English clock maker who, in 1733, revolutionised the cloth industry by inventing the flying shuttle?

2. Who was the French scientist who, in 1743, invented a process for galvanising steel?

3. In 1759 the first marine chronometer was invented. By whom?

4. Who invented the 'spinning jenny' in 1764, only to see it destroyed by his fellow spinners?

5. Who was the English inventor who, in 1769, invented the hydraulic spinning frame?

6. In 1782, the double-action steam engine is invented in Britain. By whom?

7. Who was the inventor who, in 1787, produced the steam-powered loom?

8. Who was the American inventor who, in 1787, built the first workable steam boat?

9. Who was the American inventor who, in 1790 obtained the first U.S. Patent ever issued for a cotton spinning and weaving machine?

10. Who was the American inventor who, in 1793, invented the cotton gin?

11. Who invented ball-bearings in 1794?

12. Who was the English engineer who made the first operational steam locomotive in 1796?

13. Who was the Czech-born, Bavarian inventor who, in 1798, invented lithography?

14. In 1803 Soho became the first part of London to be lit by coal gas lighting. Who was the Scottish engineer who invented the process?

15. In 1813, who invented the miner's safety-lamp?

ANSWERS.
1. John Kay 2. Paul Malouin 3. John Harrison 4. James Hargreaves 5. Richard Arkwright 6. James Watt 7. Edmond Cartwright 8. John Fitch 9. William Pollard 10. Eli Whitney 11. Philip Vaughan 12. Richard Trevithick 13. Aloys Senefelder 14. William Murdock 15. Humphrey Davy

How much do you know about the Industrial Revolution? (2)

QUESTIONS.

1. Who was the Scottish businessman who, in 1815, introduced a method of road construction which still bears his name today?

2. 1825. The Stockton – Darlington railway opens, with a locomotive designed by ......?

3. Which American gunsmith patented the six-shooter revolver in 1835?

4. In 1838 an English ex – M.P. succeeded in making photographic prints on silver chloride paper. What was his name?

5. Who was the Scottish engineer who, in 1839, patented the giant steam hammer?

6. Who was the American inventor who, in 1844, patented the vulcanisation of rubber?

7. Who was the French physicist who, in 1852, invented the gyroscope?

8. Who was the American who, in 1852, installed the very first passenger elevator?

9. Who sank the first successful oil well in Pennsylvania in 1859?

10. What was the name of the Swedish physicist who invented dynamite in 1867?

11. Who was the American engineer who, in 1868, invented the air brake?

12. Who was the Scottish-American inventor who, in 1876, gave us the telephone?

13. The first phonograph was invented in 1877, in the U.S.A. By whom?

14. Who was the German engineer who invented the electric railway in 1878?

15. Who was the German engineer who, in 1886, produced his first four-wheeled, petrol powered automobile?

ANSWERS.
1. John Loudon McAdam 2. George Stephenson. 3. Samuel Colt. 4. William Fox Talbot. 5. James Nasmyth. 6. Charles Goodyear. 7. J.B.L. Foucault. 8. Elisha Otis. 9. Edwin Drake. 10. Alfred Nobel. 11. George Westinghouse. 12. Alexander Graham Bell. 13. Thomas Edison. 14. Werner von Siemens. 15. Gottlieb Daimler.

How much do you know about the Industrial Revolution? (3)

QUESTION.

1. Who was the German inventor who gave us the first contact lens in 1887?

2. Who was the American inventor who, in 1888, two years after successfully inventing the 'roll-film' produced the first 'roll-film' camera – the 'Kodak'?

3. In 1890 the first electric-powered underground rail system went into operation. Where?

4. What did Thomas Edison patent in 1891?

5. In 1893, Crompton and Company, England, brought out the first ....what?

6. Who was the inventor of the first moving escalator to appear in 1893?

7. Who invented the first electric hand-drill in 1895?

8. In 1900, a Dutchman Johann Vaaler introduced to the world the most important aid to office efficiency ever invented. What was – and still is – it?

9. Who invented the electric typewriter in 1901?

10. Who invented air conditioning in 1902?

11. Disc brakes came on the market in 1903. Who invented them?

12. In 1904 the diode vacuum tube was invented. By whom?

13. In 1907 two French brothers, pioneers in the field of cinematography, invented colour photography. What was their name?

14. In 1908 a patent was issued relating to the invention of cellophane. By whom?

15. In 1908, mass production began in the U.S. of which motor car?

ANSWERS.
1. Eugene Frick. 2. George Eastman. 3. London. 4. The Movie Camera. 5. Electric toaster. 6. Jesse W. Reno. 7. Wilhelm Fein. 8. The Paper Clip. 9. Thaddeus Cahill. 10. Willis H. Carrier. 11. Frederick Lanchester. 12. John Fleming. 13. Lumiere. 14. J. E. Brandenberger. 15. Model T Ford.

How much do you know about post-Industrial Revolution inventions? (1)

QUESTIONS.

1. Which Belgian – American founder of the plastics industry invented 'Bakelite' in 1909?

2. Who was the French scientist who, in 1910, invented neon lighting?

3. Which German engineer invented stainless steel, in 1913?

4. What domestic product did the Universal Company, in U.S., put onto the market in 1918?

5. Who were the British pioneers of light who were the first to fly across the Atlantic, Newfoundland to Ireland, on June 14th, 1919.

6. Who invented the lie detector in 1921?

7. In 1924, the Savage Arms Corp., in U.S. put a domestic product on the market for the first time, which was in no way a reflection of their name. What was it?

8. What did the German company I. G. Farben produce for the first time in 1926?

9. First public broadcast in Britain in 1927 of ....what?

10. A German airship flies around the world in 1928. Who invented it?

11. Three major industrial corporations in the U.S., Dupont; Carbon Chemical and Carbide Corp., share in the launch of a new plastic product with enormous potential in 1928. What is it called?

12. In 1929 Bell Telephone Laboratories rack up two important 'firsts'. One is the invention of coaxial cable. What is the other?

13. In 1930, I. G. Farben of Germany also bring out a new form of plastic with widespread potential applications. What is it called?

14. In 1931, the very first electric razor goes on sale. Who is its inventor?

15. 1932. The technology of aerodynamics impacts on the Ford Motor Co. What do they build?

ANSWERS.
1. Leo Hendrik Baekeland. 2. Georges Claude. 3. Harry Brearley. 4. Electric food mixer. 5. Alcock and Brown. 6. John Larsen. 7. Washing/Spin Drying Machine. 8. Synthetic rubber. 9. Television. 10. Graf von Zeppelin. 11. PVC. (Polyvinylchloride). 12. First colour television image transmission. 13. Polystyrene. 14. Jacob Schick. 15. Their first wind tunnel.

How much do you know about post-Industrial Revolution inventions? (2)

QUESTIONS.

1. Who was the American scientist who, in 1934, invented nylon?

2. Who was the Scottish-born physicist who, in 1935, invented radar?

3. Who was the American engineer who, in 1938, invented the photo-copying machine?

4. Who was the Russian-born American inventor who, in 1939, produced the first truly operational helicopter?

5. In 1940, General Motors produced an innovation in automobile engineering. What was it?

6. 1940. Who was the British engineer whose work led to the first flight of a jet-engined plane?

7. Who was the French naval officer who, in 1943, invented the aqualung?

8. Who, in 1944, made Tupperware available for the first time?

9. Who invented holography in 1947?

10. Who, in 1948, invented the long playing gramophone record?

11. What did the Sony Corp. of Japan invent in 1952, which spread throughout the world?

12. Who was the English engineer who, in 1955, invented the hovercraft?

13. Who was the inventor of the heart pacemaker in 1957?

14. Who invented the ion engine in 1959?

15. In 1960, Frank Taylor and his team of engineers at Short Bros. and Harland, Belfast, developed an aeroplane with a very distinctive capability. What was it exactly?

ANSWERS.
1. Wallace Carothers. 2. Robert Watson-Watt. 3. Chester F. Carlson. 4. Igor Sikorsky. 5. Automatic transmission. 6. Frank Whittle. 7. Jacques-Yves Cousteau. 8. Earl W. Tupper. 9. Dennis Gabor. 10. Peter Goldmark. 11. Transistor Radio. 12. Christopher Cockerill. 13. Clarence Lillehie. 14. Alvin T. Forrester. 15. Vertical take off.

How much do you know about post-Industrial Revolution inventions? (3)

QUESTIONS.

1. Who was the American scientist who, in 1960, invented the laser?

2. In 1962, the Rand Corporation and I.B.M. opened up a whole new techno-logical realm. What was it called?

3. In 1963, the Philips Company in the Netherlands, introduced a new vehicle for sound distribution. What was it?

4. In 1964 the Japanese introduced a new concept of high-speed trains, called ....what?

5. Who was the inventor in 1966 of a noise reduction system for audio tapes which rapidly became the industry standard?

6. In 1969 the Anglo-French supersonic passenger took to the air. Its name please?

7. In 1970, Monarch Marketing, U.S.. and Plessey Telecommunications, U.K. jointly launched a new aid to speed up mass shopping. What was it?

8. In 1971 George Theiss and Willy Crabtree developed an entirely new type of personal timepiece. What was it?

9. In 1972, no sooner had Philips in the Netherlands invented the video disk, than someone came along and invented the video game. Who was it?

10. In 1974, technology had sufficiently advanced to allow Honeywell, U.S., to make a major innovation to the world of printing. What did they invent?

11. Although Sony had been the first to attack the home entertainment market in 1964, by 1975 the market was sufficiently large to encourage other Japanese companies to market …….. what kind of appliances?

12. What 'first' was launched in Chicago, U.S. in 1984?

13. In 1984, Hitachi introduced what seemed to be the ultimate sound distribution system?

14. Who was the English geneticist responsible for providing law enforcement agencies every-where with a key new weapon in the fight against crime in 1986 --DNA fingerprinting?

15. What innovation pointing to a brave new world was launched in 1994?

ANSWERS.
1. Theodore Maiman. 2. Robotics. 3. Cassette tapes. 4. Shinkansen. 5. Ray M. Dolby. 6. Concorde. 7. Bar code system. 8. Quartz digital watch. 9. Noland Bushnel. 10. Non-impact printing. 11. Home video systems. 12. First Cellphone network.. 13. Compact Disk player. 14. Alex Jeffreys. 15. Worldwide Web.

How much do you know about early inventions and discoveries? (1)

QUESTIONS.

1. In roughly what period did man first start using sharp-edged stones as tools and weapons?

2. In roughly what period did man first start shaping stones for more precise use?

3. In roughly what period did man first start building semi-permanent shelters?

4. In what period did man start building seaworthy boats, allowing the colonisation of land masses like Australia?

5. In what period did man start sewing his clothing and building more permanent shelters from mammoth bones?

6. When did the bow and arrow appear, revolutionising hunting?

7. When did man learn how to make fire?

8. Skill in pottery developed in Japan around what date?

9. When did wild dogs allow themselves to be domesticated in different parts of the world?

10. When was the boomerang developed in Australia and copper smelting, kiln-fired pottery and irrigation began to appear in western Asia?

11. When did woven cloth make its first appearance in Mesopotamia, and pottery began to be made in the Amazon basin?

12. When was copper smelted in what is now the Balkans and the plough and sailing boats appeared in Mesopotamia?

13. When did flint and copper mining begin in Europe?

14. When did wheeled vehicles and the potters wheel appear in Mesopotamia?

15. When did the Egyptians construct the Great Pyramid of Cheops

ANSWERS.
1. Around 2.5 million years BC. 2. Around 1.5 million years BC. 3. Around 400,000 BC. 4. Around 60,000 BC. 5. Around 30,000 BC. 6. Around 18,000 BC. 7. Around 12,000 BC. 8. Around 11,000 BC. 9. Around 10,000 BC. 10. Around 8,000 BC. 11. Around 5,000 BC. 12. Around 4,500 BC. 13. Around 4,000 BC. 14. Around 3,800 BC. 15. Around 2,700 BC

How much do you know about early inventions and discoveries? (2)

QUESTIONS.

1. When did the first four-wheeled war chariot and reflex composite bow appear in Mesopotamia; the first ox-drawn plough and simple objects in glass appear in Egypt ; the first bronze working in Southeast Asia and the first crude skis in Scandinavia?

2. When was bronze casting developed in China?

3. When was gold being worked in the Andes, and bronze in Korea?

4. When did iron start coming into widespread use in West Asia, India, China and Europe?

5. When did the Chavin culture in Peru begin producing fine goldwork and underground irrigation canals were constructed in Iran and Central Asia?

6. From around 700 BC to around 680 BC major irrigation works were carried out for Hezekiah, King of Judah and Sennacherib, King of Assyria, including the first known aquaducts. Sennacherib went on to build his 'Palace without rival'. In which city?

7. In which period did coinage start being used in India?

8. When did ironworking begin in China and in the Sudan, and copper mining begin in China?

9. About when did the Persian King Darius complete the canal connecting the Red Sea and the River Nile?

10. When did the Chinese invent the crossbow?

11. In what year was the completion of the Pharos lighthouse in Alexandria?

12. When was Archimedes screw used to pump water for irrigation?

13. About 193 BC concrete was invented. By whom?

14. When were techniques of glass blowing invented in the Levant?

15. In a major feat of engineering for the period (36 – 30 BC), a three storey palace is built at Masada on the orders of …whom?

ANSWERS.
1. 2,500 BC. 2. 1,900 BC. 3. 1,500 BC. 4. 1,000 BC. 5. 800 BC. 6. Nineveh. 7. 700 BC 8. 600 BC. 9. 500 BC. 10. 450 BC. 11. 279 BC. 12. 200 BC 13. The Romans. 14. 50 BC. 15. Herod.

How much do you know about early inventions and discoveries?

QUESTIONS.

1. What domestic device was invented in China around the year 110?

2. What useful tool for explorers was invented, also in China, in the year 271?

3. From 531 to 537 builders in Constantinople laboured on a religious edifice of major significance, today a huge tourist attraction. What is it?

4. What important constructional 'first' is also attributed to China, around 580?

5. In Iran, windmills were used for the first time to grind flour. When?

6. Around 650, Chinese scholars develop a technique using engraved wooden blocks in order to create the first what?

7. Around 850, Chinese scholars with different specialities invent …what?

8. Around 980, the Chinese inventor Ch'iao Wei-yo makes a very significant contribution to inland transportation. What did he invent?

9. Around 1250 the magnifying glass is invented by which English Franciscan philosopher?

10. Around 1340, marshes are drained for the first time in Holland, with the aid of …what?

11. Around 1445 the first printing press is set up in Germany. By whom?

12. Around 1505 a German clockmaker invented the first pocket watch. What was his name?

13. In 1589 the stocking-frame knitting machine is invented by the English cleric …?

14. In 1701 the machine seed drill is invented by which English farmer?

15. In 1712 a steam-powered water pump is invented by the English inventor …?

ANSWERS.
1. The wheelbarrow. 2. Magnetic compass. 3. Church of Hagia Sophia. 4. Iron-chain suspension bridge. 5. Around 600, 6. Printing. 7. Gunpowder. 8. The canal lock. 9. Francis Bacon. 10. Wind pumps. 11. Johann Gutenberg. 12. Peter Henlein. 13. Rev. William Lee. 14. Jethro Tull. 15. Thomas Newcomen.

Information Technology

How much do you know about terms used in Information Technology? (1)

QUESTIONS.

1. What term is used for any object on which data can be stored, e.g. floppy disk?

2. What do we call the small pictures used to represent commands or files?

3. What term is applied to a location in the memory where a specific unit of data is stored?

4. What is a symbol or a letter that requires a byte of storage called?

5. What name is given to a type of virus that affects the computer's memory but cannot attach itself to other programs?

6. What do we call the process or removing errors or defects in hardware or software?

7. What term is used for the preparation of a storage medium for use?

8. What is a code used to communicate with a computer called?

9. What do we call the programmed steps that manipulate data and produce the required result?

10. What name is given to the area in random-access memory in which data is stored temporarily?

11. What is a computer program that translates from assembly to machine language called?

12. What term is used for the continuous repetition of a command?

13. What term is given to the capacity of a computer to perform more than one task at a time?

14. What term do we use for the transfer of information from one computer to another?

15. What term do we use for copying information from one computer to another?

ANSWERS.
1. Medium. 2. Icons. 3. Address. 4. Character. 5. Worm. 6. Debug. 7. Format. 8. Language. 9. Algorithms. 10. Buffer. 11. Assembler. 12. Do loop. 13. Multitasking 14. Upload. 15. Download.

How much do you know about terms used in Information Technology? (2)

QUESTIONS.

1. What term is applied to a group of two or more computers linked together?

2. What do we call a picture element, that is a single point in a graphic image?

3. What term do we use for a small square of semiconducting material that holds an integrated circuit?

4. What is a collection of data that is stored either on the computer's hard drive or on a floppy disk called?

5. What term is applied to a key, character or symbol that substitutes for a combination of keystrokes?

6. What do we call an internal or external device that allows us to send and receive data over the telephone lines?

7. What name is given to the main directory in a file system?

8. What term refers to copyrighted software programs that are distributed on the basis of an honour system

9. What term defines starting the system up again from the beginning without switching off the computer?

10. What term is given to moving among consecutive lines of data on a computer screen?

11. What is the circle on a disk where the data is written called?

12. What do we call a program that transforms a high level programming language from source code to object code?

13. What is a list of commands in a program from which we choose to initiate an action?

14. What term is applied to the degree of clarity of an image on the screen or on paper?

15. What do we call those special programs that manage numerous 'housekeeping' tasks?

ANSWERS.
1. Network. 2. Pixel. 3. Chip. 4. File. 5. Macro. 6. Modem. 7. Root directory. 8. Shareware. 9. Reboot. 10. Scrolling. 11. Track. 12. Compiler. 13. Menu. 14. Resolution. 15. Utilities.

How much do you know about terms used in Information Technology? (3)

QUESTIONS.

1. What term describes a computer that processes data represented by a continuous physical variable, e.g. an electric current?

2. What term describes a computer that processes data represented as a series of binary digits or other similar discrete form?

3. What do we call a computer program that performs a specific task, e.g word-processing?

4. What term is used for copies of files on disk or tape, for archival purposes?

5. What term is given to paper printout from a computer?

6. What term is applied to the physical or electronic means of connecting two separate parts of the computer system?

7. What do we call a malfunction of the disk drive?

8. Information fed into a computer is called ......what?

9. What term is applied to a device that protects hardware and software from a sudden marked increase in voltage of an electric current?

10. What do we call a hostile coded instruction that enters a computer and causes damage?

11. What is the device that draws mostly line images, working usually in a continuous line?

12. What is the interface called that connects an external device to a printer and allows more than one bit of data to be sent at the same time?

13. What term is applied to a program that allows the computer to check its systems in order to find a bug or problem in either the hardware or the software?

14. What is the name given to the conductor by which data is transferred from one place to another in a computer?

15. What term is applied to the chip (or integrated circuit) that contains a central processor?

ANSWERS.
1. Analog. 2. Digital. 3. Application. 4. Back-up. 5. Hard copy. 6. Interface. 7. Head crash. 8. Input. 9. Surge protector. 10. Virus. 11. Plotter. 12. Parallel port. 13. Diagnostic routine. 14. Bus. 15. Microprocessor.

How much do you know about computer languages?

QUESTIONS.

1. Which is the most commonly used language for business data processing?

2. Which is the language designed for internet applications?

3. Which language is aimed at educational and games applications for beginners?

4. Which language was created for complex, on-line, real-time monitoring and control applications e.g. military applications?

5. What name was given to a highly specific object orientated language?

6 Which was the first translation language, designed for mathematical, scientific and engineering applications?

7. Which is a popular language for educational and mathematical problems, particularly those concerned with multi-dimensional arrays?

8. Which language was designed specifically for Web Page construction?

9. Which language is used for simulation programmes?

10. Which language was created to meet the needs of Artificial Intelligence applications?

11. Which language is specific to computer-aided design applications?

12. Which language is for applications that operate machine tools using numeric codes?

13. Which language was designed for applications in the fields of Linguistics, Artificial Intelligence and manipulation of mathematical logic?

14. Which language is used in applications designed to query databases?

15. Which language was designed for military applications?

ANSWERS.
1. COBOL. (Common Business Oriented Language). 2. JAVA. 3. BASIC. (Beginners All-purpose Symbolic Instruction Code). 4. Ada. 5. Smalltalk. 6. FORTRAN (Formula Translation). 7. APL. (A Programming Language). 8. HTML (Hypertet Markup Language). 9. GPSS (General Purpose Systems Simulation). 10. OCCAM. 11. AED (Algol Extended for Design). 12. APT (Automatically Programmed Tools). 13. LISP (List Processing). 14. SQL (Structured Query Language). 15. CORAL (Computer On-line Real-time Application Language).

How much do you know about the milestones on the way to an information society? (1)

QUESTIONS.

1. Which instrument, the first invention on the long road to electronic computing, appeared in Mesopotamia around 3000 BC?
2. Who was the Scottish mathematician who in 1614 invented logarithms?
3. Who was the English mathematician who in 1615 invented the slide rule?
4. Who was the German scientist who, in 1623 invented the first mechanical calculating machine?
5. Who was the French philosopher who, in 1642 invented the second mechanical calculating machine, an adding machine?
6. Who was the German mathematician who in 1673 invented a calculator which could not only count, but also multiply, divide and calculate square roots?
7. Who was the French silk weaver who, in 1804 invented a loom controlled by punched cards?
8. Who was the French scientist who in 1820 produced the first commercially available calculator, the Arithmometer?
9. Who was the English inventor who in 1822 built a prototype of his Difference Engine?
10. In the 1830's, Babbage conceived the idea for an automatic digital computer, which however, he never completed. What did he call it?
11. Who was the English logician who in 1847 published his Mathematical Analysis of Logic. His theory, with its logic operators on binary numbers became the basis for the logic operations performed by modern computers. What is it called?
12. Who was the American inventor who, in 1886 invented the first mechanical desk adding- machine?
13. Who was the American inventor who in 1890 developed the electromechanical machine controlled by punched cards to process the results of the U.S. 1890 census?
14. What was the name of the company founded by Hollerith in 1896?
15. To what did this company change its name shortly afterwards?

ANSWERS.
1. The Abacus. 2. John Napier. 3. William Oughtred. 4. Wilhelm Schickard.
5. Blaise Pascal. 6. Gottfried Leibnitz. 7. Joseph-Marie Jacquard. 8. Charles de Colmar.
9. Charles Babbage. 10. The Analytical Engine. 11. Boolean algebra. 12. William Burroughs 13. Herman Hollerith. 14. Tabulating Machine Coy. 15. I.B.M..

How much do you know about the milestones on the way to an information society? (2)

QUESTIONS.

1. Who was the English mathematician who in 1936, published his theory of computing and supervised the construction of the ACE computer at the National Physical Laboratory?

2. Who was the American mathematician who in 1939 put into operation the Complex Number Calculator, a computer in which binary numbers were represented by relays?

3. Who was the German engineer who in 1941 constructed the first fully operational program-controlled electromechanical binary calculator, or digital computer, using Boolean algebra?

4. Who was the American physicist and mathematician who was responsible in 1942 for building the first electronic digital computer, the ABC?

5. What was the name given to the enormous vacuum-tube computer built at Bletchley Park, England in 1943 to decode German military signals?

6. Who was the American engineer who led the IBM team in the construction in 1944 of the 'Harvard Mark 1' automatic sequence-controlled calculator?

7. In 1946 J. Presper Eckert and John W. Mauchly of Pennsylvania University, constructed the first general purpose fully electronic digital computer. What was it called?

8. In 1948 stored-program computers arrived, with the Ferranti Mark 1, built at Manchester University, England by ....whom?

9. Quickly followed by the EDSAC (Electronic Delay Storage Automatic Calculator) built at Cambridge University, England by ......whom?

10. Also in 1948, William Shockley, John Bardeen and Walter Brattain of Bell Labs made their mark on the future by inventing ....what?

11. In 1951, eight examples of the Ferranti Mark 1 were sold commercially; production of ORDVAC, Whirlwind 1 and the IBM 701 went ahead in the U.S. and the compiler computer   program was invented by which American mathematician and computer pioneer?

12. In 1952 John von Neumann at the Institute for Advanced Study, Princeton, built .....what?

13. What form of memory system was developed in 1953?

14. What name was given to the formula translation programming language developed in '56?

15. Which U.S. company built the first 'mini' computer in 1963?

ANSWERS.

1. Alan Turing. 2. George R. Stibitz. 3. Konrad Zuse. 4. John V. Altasanoff. 5. 'Colossus'. 6. Howard Aiken. 7. ENIAC. (Electronic numerical integrator and computer). 8. T. M. Kilburn and F. C. Williams. 9. Maurice Wilkes. 10. The Transistor. 11. Grace Hopper. 12. EDVAC. (Electronic Discrete Variable Computer). 13. Magnetic Core. 14. FORTRAN. 15. Digital Equipment.

How much do you know about the milestones on the way to an information society? (1)

QUESTIONS.

1. A major milestone was reached in 1959 when Jack Kilby at Texas Instruments invented ......?

2. In 1964 IBM launched their first compatible family of business computers, called ......?

3. In 1965 the first supercomputer, the CD 6600, is constructed by ......which U.S. company?

4. The first microprocessor was introduced in 1971. What was it called?

5. In 1974 the company MITS, launched the first personal computer in kit form. Its name ......?

6. 1977 saw the arrival of a major new player in the P. C. business. Who was it?

7. In 1981 the first 32-bit silicon chip was announced by ......which U.S. manufacturer?

8. In 1982/83/84 which of the major players launched a) laser printers; b) 512 K dynamic access memory chips and c) megabit computer chips?

9. Which company announced the arrival in 1984 of the CD-ROM?

10. In 1983 Apple produced the Apple Lisa, with the first graphical user interface. Better known as ....?

11. In 1984 Apple went all Scottish with the launch of which series of P.C.'s?

12. In 1985 it became possible to buy a transputer off the shelf in order to build your ownparallel computer. What was it called?

13. What is the name of the popular windowing environment released by Microsoft in 1990?

14. What is the name of the microprocessor launched by Intel in 1995?

15. In an effort to bypass congestion on the Internet, what was announced for the U.S. in 1995?

ANSWERS.

1. The Integrated Circuit. 2. The System 360. 3. Control Data Corp. 4. The Intel 4004 5. The Altair 8800. 6. Apple. 7. Hewlett-Packard. 8. IBM 9. Hitachi. 10. A Mouse. 11. The Macintosh. 12. The Inmos T414, 13. Windows 3. 14. Pentium Pro. 15. Internet 2.

Measurement and Mathematics

How much do you know about the terms used in measurement and mathematics?

QUESTIONS.

1. What term do we use for a symbol, such as a letter or a number, used to represent an indeterminate quantity that can change or be changed?

2. What do we call a quantity that has been chosen as a standard in terms of which other quantities may be expressed?

3. What is the term applied to a measured unit that is recognised as having a permanent value?

4. What term do we give to any whole number: positive and negative numbers, and zero?

5. What term do we apply to a measured amount of material?

6. What term do we use when we determine the quantity of a measurement?

7. What do we call the relationship between two measurements of different units, e.g the change in distance with respect to time (m.p.h.)?

8. What is the quantitative relation between two similar units determined by the number of times one can contain the other, either fractionally or integrally?

9. What is the change from one measurement system to another by use of a common value?

10. What do we call the assumption(s) upon which a mathematical theory is based?

11. What is the measurement of a two-dimensional surface?

12. What do we call an instrument for measuring the mass of an object?

13. What do we call the state of balance between opposing forces or effects?

14. What do we call the result of a multiplication problem?

15. What do we call the result of a division problem?

ANSWERS.
1. Variable. 2. Unit. 3. Standard. 4. Integer. 5. Mass. 6. Quantify. 7. Rate. 8. Ratio. 9. Conversion. 10. Axiom. 11. Area. 12. Balance. 13. Equilibrium. 14. Product. 15. Quotient.

How much do you know about the terms used in measurement and mathematics?

QUESTIONS.

1. What do we call something which has no boundaries, limits or end?

2. What do we call the outer boundary of an enclosed area?

3. What do we call the line or boundary that forms the perimeter of a circle?

4. What is a unit of angular measurement?

5. What is the longest side of a right angled triangle called?

6. What is a quantity that has magnitude e.g. mass, density, but no direction?

7. What do we call an object that has three dimensions: length, width and height?

8. What term is applied to an equality of ratios between two pairs of quantities?

9. What do we call the x and y co-ordinates that define a point on a graph?

10. What is the bottom line in a fraction called?

11. What term is given to a straight line that passes from side to side through the centre of body or figure, usually a sphere or a circle,

12. What do we call a number or letter placed before a variable in an algebraic expression, which is used as a multiplier?

13. What term is used of a fraction whose numerator is the same or higher than the denominator?

14. What is the system of weights called that is used to weigh precious metals?

15. What term describes a body or line at right angles to a line or plane?

ANSWERS.
1. Infinite. 2. Perimeter. 3. Circumference. 4. Degree. 5. Hypotenuse. 6. Scalar. 7. Solid. 8. Proportion. 9. Ordered pair. 10. Denominator 11. Diameter. 12. Coefficient. 13. Improper fraction. 14. Troy weight. 15. Perpendicular.

Medicine and Health

How much do you know aboout medical terminology? (1)

QUESTIONS.

1. What is a substance that kills or inhibits the growth of microorganisms?

2. What is the study of the structure of the body and its component parts called?

3. What is the study of bodily functions called?

4. What is the name of the medical speciality which concerns itself with the care of children?

5. What is the study of the properties of drugs and their effects on the human body called?

6. What is the name given to any measure taken to prevent disease?

7. What is the name given to any illness specific to hot climates?

8. Any word used in a medical sense with the prefix 'opthalm(o)' would be used in connection with what part of the body?

9. And with the prefix 'phleb(o)' ?

10. And with the prefix 'osteo'?

11. And with the prefix 'nephr(o)'?

12. And with the prefix 'vesico'?

13. What is the name given to a physical symptom or disease thought to emanate from emotional or mental factors?

14. What is the name given to any of a family of viruses containing the genetic material RNA rather than the more usual DNA?

15. What are any events occurring immediately after childbirth called?

ANSWERS.
1. Antiseptic. 2. Anatomy. 3. Physiology. 4. Paediatrics. 5. Pharmacology. 6. Prophylaxis. 7. A 'Tropical Disease'. 8. The Eye. 9. The Veins. 10. The Bones. 11. The Kidneys. 12. The Bladder. 13. Psychosomatic. 14. A 'Retrovirus.' 15. Postpartum.

How much do you know aboout medical terminology? (2)

QUESTIONS.

1. What is the name of the treatment of injury or disease by physical means, exercise; heat; massage, manipulation, etc?

2. What is the name given to any microorganism that causes disease?

3. What is the medical speciality concerned with the study and treatment of disorders of the brain, spinal cord and peripheral nerves?

4. What is the use of radioactive isotopes in the diagnosis and treatment of disease called?

5. What is the name of the medical speciality concerned with the diagnosis and treatment of neoplasms, particularly cancer?

6. What is the name of the medical speciality concerned with the study of disease processes and the structural and functional changes to the body provoked by these processes?

7. What is the removal of a living tissue sample from the body for diagnostic examination?

8. Any word used in a medical sense with the prefix 'cardi(o)' would be used in connection with what part of the body?

9. And with the prefix 'cerebr(o)'?

10. And with the prefix 'enter(o)'?

11. And with the prefix 'my(o)'?

12. And with the prefix 'hepat(o)'?

13. What is the technique of using X-rays or ultrasound waves to obtain images of structures deep within the body for diagnostic purposes?

14. What is the laboratory study of cells and tissues called?

15. What is the name of the medical speciality concerned with the diagnosis and treatment of hormone disorders?

ANSWERS.
1. Physiotherapy. 2. A 'Pathogen'. 3. Neurology. 4. 'Nuclear medicine'. 5. Oncology. 6. Pathology. 7. 'Biopsy'. 8. The Heart. 9. The Brain. 10. The Intestine. 11. Muscle. 12. The Liver. 13. 'Tomography'. 14. Histology. 15. Endocrinology.

Meteorology

How much do you know about meteorology? (2)

QUESTIONS.

1. What do we call the long-term weather conditions, i.e. temperature, rainfall and other atmospheric factors, prevalent in a given region over a given length of time?

2. What is an electrical discharge in the atmosphere?

3. What is a measurement of average kinetic energy?

4. What do we call local, short-term changes in temperature, humidity, rainfall and barometric pressure in the atmosphere?

5. What are lines connecting areas of equal pressure on a weather map?

6. What term is applied to a narrow, elongated area of low atmospheric pressure, usually running north to south?

7. What term is applied to the movement of air with respect to the Earth's surface, caused locally by the Sun heating the ground and globally by the Sun's radiation and the rotation of the Earth?

8. What kind of fog forms when warmer, humid air flows over cooler ground or water?

9. What is the force per unit area, that the air exerts on any surface, resulting from the collision of air molecules?

10. What is the process called in which a liquid is transformed into a gas?

11. What is the process called in which water vapour is transformed into liquid water?

12. What do we call a collection of water droplets or ice crystals suspended in the air which forms when the air is cooled to dew point and condensation occurs?

13. What do we call the temperature at which air becomes saturated, unable to hold more water vapour?

14. What is the general term for the gases that make up the atmosphere?

15. What do we call the droplets that form when water vapour condenses?

ANSWERS.
1. Climate. 2. Lightning. 3. Temperature. 4. Weather. 5. Isobars. 6. Trough. 7. Wind. 8. Advection fog. 9. Air pressure. 10. Evaporation. 11. Condensation. 12. Cloud. 13. Dew Point. 14. The air. 15. Dew.

How much do you know about terms used in meteorology? (2)

QUESTIONS.

1. What is a high-pressure area with closed circulation, which rotates clockwise in the Northern Hemisphere and anti-clockwise in the Southern Hemisphere?

2. What is the name of the instrument used to measure atmospheric pressure?

3. What is the term applied to the boundary between two air masses of varying temperature and humidity, usually warm and cold air masses?

4. What do we call the condition when the air on the ground is cooler that the air at a higher latitude?

5. What name do we give to those small balls of ice with space between them, which form when small drops of water freeze on contact with an object?

6. What name do we give to a snow storm that is accompanied by high winds?

7. What is the branch of meteorology that studies the atmosphere by comparing statistical variations in both space and time, as seen in weather conditions over many years?

8. What is the name of the force which causes winds to deviate in a clockwise direction in the Northern Hemisphere and in an anti-clockwise direction in the Southern hemisphere, as a result of the Earth's rotation?

9. What is water vapour that condenses from the atmosphere? It can fall as rain, snow, ice, frost, dew or other forms of atmospheric water.

10. What is the name of the technique using substances such as silver iodide and dry ice in order to increase precipitation?

11. What is the amount of water vapour in the air, as a percentage of the amount of water vapour which the air could hold at that temperature?

12. What name do we give to a wind with a velocity that ranges from 32 to 63 miles per hour?

13. What do we call those tiny, airborne crystals of ice that reflect sunlight?

14. What do we call intermittent precipitation, that can be heavy or light, rain or snow?

15. What are particles of water that fall from clouds but evaporate before touching ground?

ANSWERS.
1. Anticyclone. 2. Barometer. 3. Front. 4. Inversion. 5. Rime. 6. Blizzard. 7. Climatology.
8. Coriolis Effect. 9. Precipitation. 10. Cloud seeding. 11. Relative humidity. 12. Gale.
13. 'Diamond dust'. 14. Shower. 15. Virga.

Natural History

How much do you know about terms used in natural history? (1)

QUESTIONS.

1. What is the name of the type of bony fish thought to be long extinct until a living example was discovered in 1938?

2. What do we call the system of high pitched pulses of sound that bounce off surrounding objects used by certain nocturnal animals e.g. bats, and aquatic animals e.g. dolphins?

3. What is the name for the study of past climates through the study of tree growth rings?

4. What is the term used to describe a plant with little or no woody stem, in which all the green parts die back at the end of each season?

5. What is the order of the class Insecta to which butterflies and moths belong?

6. The presence of a pouch on the lower abdomen of the female is a distinctive feature of which sub-class of mammals?

7. What is the term applied to the seasonal mass movement of some animals?

8. What is the term used to describe any organisms living in the sea between the surface and the middle depths?

9. What do we call the uppermost, surface layer of a lake or a sea into which sufficient light penetrates to allow photosynthesis to take place?

10. What is the name of the order of mammals to which mice, rats, and squirrels belong?

11. What is the term applied to one of the major divisions of the animal or vegetable kingdoms containing one or more classes?

12. What is the collective term for a group of individuals that belong to the same species?

13. What is the shallow water environment of a lake or of a sea lying close to the shore?

14. What is the name of the order of placental mammals to which elephants belong, characterised by having a trunk and tusks?

15. What is the vertebrate class to which salamanders, frogs and toads belong?

ANSWERS.
1. Coelacanth. 2. Echo-location. 3. Dendrochronology. 4. Herbaceous. 5. Lepidoptera. 6. Marsupials. 7. Migration. 8. Pelagic. 9. Photic zone. 10. Rodentia. 11. Phylum. 12. Population. 13. Littoral. 14. Proboscidea. 15. Amphibia.

How much do you know about terms used in natural history? (2)

QUESTIONS.

1. What do we call the mammalian order to which monkeys, lemurs, apes and humans belong?

2. What term is applied to a group of individuals that is different in one or more ways from other members of the same species?

3. What term is used to define a specific area that animals, whether singly or in groups, will defend to exclude other members of their species?

4. What is the name given to the study of changes in population numbers, whether plant or animal, and the factors that have an influence on these changes?

5. What term is used for the shallow water marine zone near the shore that extends from low tide to a depth of approximately 200 metres?

6. What term is applied to all the environmental factors that affect an organism within its community, e.g living space; available food, and all the conditions necessary for the survival and reproduction of the species?

7. What term refers to the ability of animals, especially birds, to find their way home?

8. What term is applied to that sleep-like state in which certain animals pass the winter?

9. What term is used for all the biological life and non-biological components e.g. minerals in the soil, within an given area, and the inter-relationships which exist between them all?

10. What term is given to a plant that grows on another plant and is not rooted to the ground?

11. What do we call water that is to be found in estuaries, a mixture of salt and fresh water?

12. What term describes all the organisms that live at the bottom of a sea, lake or river?

13. What is the name of the order of marine mammals to which dolphins and whales belong?

14. What is the collective term applied to a group of individual organisms of the same species that are living together and are, to some extent or other dependent on each other?

15. What do we call a group of animals or plants that bear a close resemblance to each other, bearing similar progeny, and capable of sharing genes and interbreeding?

ANSWERS.
1. Primates. 2. Race. 3. Territory. 4. Population dynamics. 5. Neritic zone. 6. Niche. 7. Homing. 8. Hibernation. 9. Ecosystem. 10. Epiphyte. 11. Brackish. 12. Benthic. 13. Cetacea. 14. Colony. 15. Species.

Physics

How much do you know about the development of physics? (1)

QUESTIONS.

1. Around 450 BC the first 'atomic' theory was suggested, by which Greek thinker?

2. Who was the Greek physicist who, around 350 BC, suggested that heavier bodies fall faster than lighter ones?

3. Around 250 BC the 'principle of buoyancy' was established by which Greek scientist?

4. By the year 1010 the Arabian physicist Abu Ali Al-hasan ibn Al-haytham had worked out how lenses function, and also made a significant invention. What was it?

5. Who was the Genoa-born explorer who observed in 1492, that the needle on a magnetic compass varied it's position according to the longitude it was in?

6. Who was the Dutch mathematician who established, in 1586 AD, that objects in a vacuum fall at an equal rate, whatever their individual weights?

7. Who was the English physician who established the magnetic nature of the earth in 1600 and was the first person to use the word 'electricity'?

8. 1602. The constancy of a swinging pendulum is established by which Italian scientist?

9. Who was the Dutch scientist who, in 1608, invents the refracting telescope?

10. Who was the Dutch mathematician who discovered the law of refraction known as Snell's Law in 1617?

11. Who was the French physicist whose experiments with mercury in glass tubes in 1642, paved the way for the invention of the barometer, the hydraulic press and the syringe ?

12. Who was the Italian scientist who invented the first mercury barometer in 1643?

13. Who was the Dutch physicist who, in 1656 invented the first pendulum clock?

14. Who was the Irish physicist who, in 1662, established his law relating to the expansion of gases?

15. Who was the English scientist who, around 1665, proposed his law of gravity?

ANSWERS.
1. Leucippus of Miletus. 2. Strato. 3. Archimedes. 4. The Parabolic Mirror. 5. Christopher Columbus. 6. Simon Stevin. 7. William Gilbert. 8. Galileo Galilei. 9. Hans Lippershey. 10. Willebrod van Roijen (Known as 'Snellius'). 11. Blaise Pascal. 12. Evangelista Torricelli. 13. Christian Huygens. 14. Robert Boyle. 15. Isaac Newton.

How much do you know about the development of physics? (2)

QUESTIONS.

1. Who was the English physicist and chemist who, in 1665, compared light to waves in water?

2. Who was the first known person to calculate the speed of light, in 1675?

3. Who was the English astronomer and mathematician who, in 1684, persuaded Isaac Newton to extend his thinking about the problems of gravitation?

4. In 1687 Isaac Newton establishes his three laws of motion and publishes his theory of gravity in ......what?

5. Who was the English physicist whose experiments in 1705 proved that sound needs a medium through which to travel?

6, Who was the German physicist who, in 1714, invented the first mercury thermometer?

7. Who was the Swedish astronomer who in 1742 invented the centigrade thermometer?

8. Who was the German scientist who in 1745 invented the 'Leyden Jar' a condenser designed to accumulate and preserve electricity?

9. Who was the American scientist and statesman whose experiments in 1747 showed that a conductor can draw an electric charge from a charged body?

10. Which French mathematician and physicist established the laws of electrodynamics in 1822 and left his name to the unit of electrical current?

11. Who was the French scientist who was the founder of thermodynamics in 1824?

12. Who was the German physicist who established the law of electrical resistance which is named after him, in 1827?

13. Who was the Scottish physicist who, in 1829, established the 'law of gaseous diffusion'?

14. Who was the English chemist whose work on electricity and other subjects over more than 40 years was totally influential? In 1831 – 34 he established the laws of electromagnetic induction and self-induction.

15. Who was the German physicist who, in 1842, promulgated the 'law of conservation of energy'?

ANSWERS.
1. Robert Hooke. 2. Olaus Romer. 3. Edmund Halley. 4. His 'Philosophiae Naturalis Principia Mathematica'. 5. Francis Hawksbee. 6. Gabriel Daniel Fahrenheit. 7. Anders Celsius. 8. E. G. von Kleist. 9. BenjaminFranklin. 10. Andre Ampere. 11. Sadi Carnot. 12. Georg Ohm. 13. Thomas Graham. 14. Michael Faraday. 15. Julius von Mayer.

How much do you know about the development of physics? (3)

QUESTIONS.

1. Who was the English physicist whose experiments in the 1840's established the mechanical equivalent of heat, and who left his name as a SI unit of work, energy and heat?

2. Who was the French physicist who was the first, in 1849, to measure the speed of light?

3. Who was the French physicist who suspended a pendulum from the ceiling of the Pantheonin Paris in the 1850's, in order to prove the rotation of the earth?

4. In 1858, the mirror galvanometer, an instrument for measuring limited electric currents was invented by a Scottish-born mathematician and physicist. What was his name?

5. Who were the two German physicists who together discovered spectrum analysis in 1859?

6. Who was the Scottish physicist who, in 1873, proposed his theory of electro-magnetic radiation?

7. Who was the English physicist who did valuable work on the theory of sound, the wave theory of light and vibratory motion? He discovered the rare gas argon and was a Nobel laureate.

8. Who was the French physicist who, in 1880, discovered piezoelectricity?

9. In 1887 a German physicist confirmed the predictions of James Clerk-Maxwell by his discovery that electromagnetic waves behave, with the exception of wavelength, like light waves. He also predicted the existence of radio waves. Who was he?

10, In 1895 a German physicist discovers X-rays. What was his name?

11. Who was the French physicist who, in 1896, whilst working with the Curies, discovered 'rays' emitted by uranium salts, leading to the isolation of radium and the foundations of modern nuclear physics?

12. Who was the outstanding English mathematical physicist who, in 1897, discovered the electron?

13. Who was the New Zealand-born British physicist, a pioneer of atomic science, who in 1899, discovered the three types of uranium radiations : alpha, beta and gamma rays?

14. Who was the German physicist who, in 1900, propounded his 'Quantum Theory'?

15. Who was the English physicist who discovered the ionosphere in 1902?

ANSWERS.

1. James Joule. 2. Armand Fizeau. 3. Jean Foucault. 4. William Thomson (later Lord Kelvin). 5. Robert Bunsen and Gustav Kirchhoff. 6. James Clerk-Maxwell 7. John William Strutt, Baron Rayleigh. 8. Pierre Curie. 9. Heinrich Hertz. 10. Wilhelm Rontgen. 11. Antoine Becquerel. 12. Joseph Thomson. 13. Ernest Rutherford. 14. Max Planck. 15. Oliver Heaviside.

How much do you know about the development of physics? (4)

QUESTIONS.

1. In 1904 the general theory of radioactivity is published, by which British scientists?

2. Who was the German scientist who rocked the scientific world with his 'special theory of relativity', published in 1905?

3. In 1911 the discovery of the atomic nucleus is made public, by ....Whom?

4. Who was the German physicist who, whilst working under Rutherford at Manchester, devised an apparatus for measuring beta-ray radioactivity ?

5. Who was the Danish physicist who, whilst working under Rutherford at Manchester, published the orbiting electron atomic theory in 1913?

6. Also in 1913, what was the term coined by Frederick Soddy to describe forms of the same element with identical chemical qualities but different atomic weights?

7. Who were the father and son English scientists who discovered X-ray crystallography?

8. What did Einstein publish in 1916 which took his work to new heights?

9. Also in 1916, who was the English scientist who invented the mass spectograph?

10. On May 29th 1919 study of a particular phenomenon allowed scientists to confirm Einstein's theory of relativity. What was the phenomenon?

11. Also in 1919 came news of Rutherfords experiments in which alpha-ray bombardments induced transmutation of .....what?

12. 1921 Rutherford succeeded in disintegrating all known elements but four, as a preliminary to splitting the atom. In this work he was assisted by another brilliant physicist, named ......?

13. Which English physicist begins in 1924 a series of investigations of the ionosphere which will lead to his Nobel prize in 1947?

14. Who was the German theoretical physicist who in 1927 propounded the 'uncertainty principle' in quantum physics?

15. In 1929, Einstein goes a step further and publishes his ...what?

ANSWERS,
1. Ernest Rutherford and Frederick Soddy. 2. Albert Einstein. 3. Ernest Rutherford. 4. Hans Geiger. 5. Niels Bohr. 6. 'Isotopes'. 7. William and Lawrence Bragg. 8. His 'general theory of relativity'. 9. William Aston. 10. A total eclipse of the sun. 11. Complex atoms into simpler ones. 12. James Chadwick. 13. Edward Appleton. 14. Werner Heisenberg. 15. Unitary Field Theory.

How much do you know about the development of physics? (5)

QUESTIONS.

1. Who was the Dutch-American physicist who, in 1930, began investigating the structure of molecules with the assistance of X-rays?

2. Who was the American physicist who, in 1931, constructed the world's first cyclotron?

3. Who was the English nuclear physicist who, in 1931, succeeded in disintegrating lithium (one of the four which eluded Rutherford in 1921), going on to build a British cyclotron?

4. Who was the astronomer, considered by many to have been the greatest of modern English astronomers who, in 1931, published one of his keys works 'The World of Physics'?

5. Who was the English physicist and former student and colleague of Rutherford, who, in 1932 discovered the neutron?

6. Who was the Russian-American physicist who in 1932 invented the electron microscope?

7. Who are the two American physicists who in 1933 whilst analysing cosmic rays, discover positive electrons (positrons)?

8. Who were the French couple, both nuclear physicists who, in 1934 succeeded in inducing artificial radioactivity?

9. Who was the Italian physicist who, also in 1934, split the nuclei of uranium atoms by bombarding them with neutrons, producing artificial radioactive substances?

10. Who was the German physical chemist who, in 1939, used the techniques developed by the Joliot-Curies and Fermi to obtain the first chemical evidence of nuclear fission?

11. What was the name given to the atomic research programme launched in Chicago and Los Angeles in 1941?

12. December 2nd 1942. Enrico Fermi creates the first controlled nuclear chain-reaction. Where was this carried out?

13. Who was the English physicist who, independent of Anderson also discovered the positron and went on in 1947 to propose that all massive rotating bodies are magnetic?

14. What was satisfactorily produced from atomic energy at Arcon, Idaho December 1951?

ANSWERS.
1. Peter Debye. 2. Ernest O. Lawrence. 3. John Cockcroft. 4. Arthur Eddington.
5. James Chadwick. 6. Vladimir Zworykin. 7. Carl Anderson and Robert Millikin.
8. Frederic and Irene Joliot-Curie. 9. Enrico Fermi. 10. Otto Hahn. 11. The Manhattan Project. 12. Chicago University. 13. Patrick Blackett. 14. Electricity.

How much do you know about terms used in physics? (1)

QUESTIONS.

1. How is the science of the production, transmission and effect of sound waves known?

2. How is a force that opposes a change in motion or shape better known?

3. What is a quantity or measurement that never changes in magnitude?

4. What term would you use for the resulting vertical force on an object, by a static fluid in which the object is floating or submerged?

5. What would you call the reflection of sound from a surface?

6. What would you call the density of a material divided by the density of water?

7. What is the distance travelled divided by the time it takes to travel that distance?

8. How would you describe matter which does not allow light to pass through?

9. What is the term for the tendency for matter to cling to other types of matter, due to intermolecular forces?

10. What is the term describing the transfer of heat by molecular motion from a region of high temperature to a region of lower temperature, tending towards equalisation of temperatures?

11. What is the term given to a four-dimensional space that specifies the location and time co-ordinates of a specific event?

12. What is the resistance to motion between two surfaces moving over each other which is usually measured in terms of force and velocity?

13. What is the term for anything small and discrete, such as a proton, a neutron, an atom, or a molecule?

14. What do you call a description of certain behaviour in nature, e.g. the fact that an object does not change its position until acted upon by an outside force?

15. What is the term for tension forces exerted on a body that tend to produce a deformation of that body?

ANSWERS.
1. Acoustics. 2. Resistance. 3. A constant. 4. Buoyancy. 5. An echo. 6. Relative density. (Also known as specific gravity). 7. Speed. 8. Opaque. 9. Adhesion. 10. Conduction. 11. Space-time. 12. Friction. 13. Particle. 14. A physical law. 15. Stress.

How much do you know about terms used in physics? (2)

QUESTIONS.

1. What is the term given to that property of a liquid that makes it resist flow or any change in the arrangement of its molecules?

2. What name is given to a particle having mass, lifetime and spin identical to a particle of matter, but opposite to it in charge and magnetic moment?

3. What is matter composed of antiparticles?

4. What is the increase in velocity per unit time?

5. What is the mass per unit volume of a material?

6. What is the term given to the change in a shape or size of a body caused by pressure and movement?

7. What is a physical quantity that is the measurement of the amount of disorder in a system?

8. What is a hot, ionized (that is electrically charged) gas?

9. What is the force acting upon a per unit area of a surface?

10. What is the term for the emission and propagation of radiant energy – either atomic, by radioactive substances, or spectral, as in light?

11, What is the term given to the absence of matter, or, as in space the total – or almost total – exhaustion of air or other gases?

12. What is the term relating to a solid or liquid medium through which light will pass but no clear image is formed, e.g. frosted glass?

13. What is the term for the speed and direction that an object travels over a specified distance during a measured period of time?

14. What is the term given to the capacity or ability to do work?

15. What is the matter through which a wave travels?

ANSWERS.
1. Viscosity. 2. Antiparticle. 3. Antimatter. 4. Acceleration. 5. Density. 6. Strain. 7. Entropy. 8. Plasma. 9. Pressure. 10. Radiation. 11. Vacuum. 12. Translucent. 13. Velocity. 14. Energy. 15. Medium.

How much do you know about terms used in physics? (3)

QUESTIONS.

1. What term is used for the regular oscillation, backwards and forwards, of a material?

2. What is the study of motion that ignores the forces creating the motion?

3. What is the name given to the study of the movement of heat from one body to another, and the relations between heat and other forms of energy?

4. What is the effect opposite of an action?

5. What is an instrument that precisely measures light, sound and radio waves through interference patterns?

6. What is the name given to the band of varying colour observed when a beam of white light is passed through a prism or diffraction grating that separates each component of the light into its respective wavelengths?

7. What is a quantity that has both magnitude and direction called?

8. What name is given to the collapse of a body that has become so massive that the forces of attraction are more powerful than the forces of repulsion?

9. What is the term applied to the ability of an object to generate a voltage when mechanical force is applied (e.g. as in crystal oscillators and microphones)?

10. What do you call the cooling of a liquid at a given pressure to a temperature below its freezing point at that pressure, without any change to its phase state being generated?

11. What do you call the raising of a liquid's temperature above its boiling point, by increasing the pressure, without causing any change to its phase state?

12. What is the term used for the ratio of the radiant flux reflected from a given surface, to the total light that falls upon that surface?

13. What is the name of an instrument with a rapidly spinning, heavy mass that maintains a ixed reference direction by conserving angular momentum?

14. What term is used to indicate the state of matter of a material: solid, liquid, gas or plasma?

15. What term is applied to the effect produced by a force?

ANSWERS.
1. Vibration. 2. Kinematics. 3. Thermodynamics. 4. Reaction. 5. Interferometer. 6. Spectrum. 7. Vector. 8. Gravitational collapse. 9. Piezoelectric effect. 10. Supercooling. 11. Superheating. 12. Reflectance. 13. Gyroscope. 14. Phase. 15. Action.

How much do you know about terms used in physics? (4)

QUESTIONS.

1. What term is used for the mechanical transfer of heated molecules of a gas or liquid from a source to another area, as when a room is warmed by the mass movement of air molecules heated by a radiator?

2. What is the force that causes the movement of electrons through an electrical circuit?

3. What is the name of the instrument used to determine the spectrum or wavelength of a ray of light emanating from an object?

4. What term is used to describe the property of a liquid in which the surface molecules show a strong inward attraction, forming an apparent membrane across the surface of the liquid?

5. What is a device that converts power into a very narrow, intense monochromatic beam of visible or infrared light? The light is amplified by the stimulated emission of radiation.

6. What term applies to the limitation of electromagnetic waves' oscillation to a specific plane.

7. What is the term relating to a solid or liquid medium through which light will travel and form a clear image?

8. What do you call the spreading out of any type of wave (e.g. sound; light) when it passes through an opening smaller than – or equal to – the wavelength?

9. What name is given to all fundamental particles, that is, those particles that are constituents of all matter?

10. What do you call an ideal object that absorbs all incident radiation and radiates according to Planck's law?

11. What is the name given to that branch of mechanics that deals with objects at rest, and with the interaction of forces in equilibrium?

12. Whose law relates temperature to wavelength, stating that hotter objects radiate most at shorter wavelengths?

13. What is the point called at which the constants of a circuit change, and cause reflection of any wave being propagated along the circuit?

14. What is the name used for a tank in which elementary atomic particles are detected?

15. What name is given to space-time in the absence of a gravitational field?

ANSWERS.
1. Convection. 2. Electromotive force. 3. Spectroscope. 4. Surface tension. 5. Laser. 6. Polarisation. 7. Transparent. 8. Diffraction. 9. Elementary particles. 10. Black body. 11. Statics. 12. Planck's Law. 13. Transition point. 14. Bubble chamber. 15. Minkowski space.

Psychology

How much do you know about phobias? (1)

QUESTIONS.

1. 'Aerophobia' is the fear of ....what?

2. 'Bibliophobia' is the fear of ......what?

3. 'Ailurophobia' or 'Gatophobia' is the fear of ......what?

4. 'Traumatophobia' is the fear of ....what?

5. 'Agoraphobia' is the fear of ....what?

6. 'Olfactophobia' is the fear of ......what?

7. 'Hedonophobia' is the fear of .....what?

8. 'Batrachophobia' is the fear of .....what?

9. 'Peccatophobia' is the fear of .....what?

10. 'Akousticophobia' is the fear of ....what?

11. 'Mysophobia' is the fear of .....what?

12. 'Maniaphobia' or 'Lyssophobia' is the fear of ....what?

13. 'Gynophobia' is the fear of ......what?

14. 'Demonophobia' is the fear of .....what?

15. 'Haematophobia' or 'Hemophobia' is the fear of ......what?

ANSWERS.
1. Flying, or the air. 2. Books. 3. Cats. 4. Being wounded or injured. 5. Open spaces. 6. Smells. 7. Pleasure. 8. Reptiles. 9. Sinning. 10. Sound. 11. Infection. 12. Insanity. 13. Women. 14. Demons. 15. Blood.

How much do you know about phobias? (2)

QUESTIONS.

1. 'Frigophobia' or 'Cheimatophobia' is the fear of ....what?

2. 'Cardiophobia' is the fear of ......what?

3. 'Phasmophobia' is the fear of .....what?

4. 'Hippophobia' is the fear of .....what?

5. 'Astraphobia' is the fear of ....what?

6. 'Gamophobia' is the fear of .....what?

7. 'Androphobia' is the fear of .....what?

8. 'Musophobia' is the fear of .....what?

9. 'Anginophobia' is the fear of .....what?

10. 'Hodophobia' is the fear of ......what?

11. 'Siderodromophobia' is the fear of ......what?

12. 'Hypegiaphobia' is the fear of .....what?

13. 'Erotophobioa' is the fear of ..... what?

14. 'Triskaidekaphobia' or 'Terdekaphobia' is the fear of .....what?

15. 'Gymnotophobia' is the fear of .....what?

ANSWERS.
1. Cold. 2. Heart disease. 3. Ghosts. 4. Horses. 5. Lightning. 6. Marriage. 7. Men. 8. Mice. 9. Suffocating. 10. Travelling. 11. Travelling by train. 12. Responsibility. 13. Physical love. 14. The number '13'. 15. Nudity.

Transport

How much do you know about the development of the motor car? (1)

QUESTIONS.

1.   Who was the French engineer who in 1769, built a three-wheeled steam driven carriage or tractor, now acknowledged to be the forerunner of the motor car?

2.   Who was the English engineer who invented a steam carriage which ran from Camborne to Tuckingmill and back, at between 4 and 9 mph, in 1801?

3.   In 1865 the British Government passed the 'Red Flag Act' requiring any 'horseless carriage' to be preceded on the road by ......what?

4.   Who was the German engineer who in 1876 invented the four-stroke combustion engine?

5.   Who was the German engineer who in 1885 fitted a lightweight petrol engine to a three-wheeled carriage, thus inventing the first motor car?

6.   Who was the German engineer who in 1886 fitted his combustion engine to a four-wheeled carriage, thus inventing the first four-wheeled motor car?

7.   In the first motor race ever, Paris in 1888, whose steam quadricycle defeated a steam tricycle made by Leon Serpollet who was supported by Armand Peugeot?

8.   Who were the French engineers who in 1891improved on the German design by mounting the engine on the front of the motor car, and attaching it to the chassis?

9.   Who was the British engineer who in 1896 patented epicyclic gearing, paving the way for automatic transmission?

10. The first London to Brighton motor rally took place in which year?

11. Who was the German engineer who in 1897 successfully demonstrated the compression-ignition engine that today still bears his name?

12. In 1901 Emil Jellinek, the German Consul-General at Nice ordered 36 models of a new Daimler-Benz car, on the condition that they were marketed not as Daimlers, but taking the name of his daughter, that is to say ....?

13. In 1901 there were 8,000 cars on the roads of the U.S., of which 4,000 were which make?

14. Who was the American engineer whose Oldsmobile Curved Dash replaced the Locomobile as the 'popular' car of the first five years of the century?

15. And who, in 1908, introduced the Model T, which was to sweep the world?

ANSWERS.
1. Nicolas Joseph Cugnot. 2. Richard Trevithick. 3. A walking person carrying a red flag. 4. Nikolaus August Otto. 5. Karl Benz. 6. Gottllieb Daimler. 7. Albert de Dion and Georges Bouton. 8. Rene Panhard and Emile Levassor. 9. Frederick Lanchester. 10. 1896. 11. Rudolph Diesel. 12. Mercedes. 13. Locomobiles. 14. Ransom Olds. 15. Henry Ford.

How much do you know about the development of the motor car? (2)

QUESTIONS.

1. Who was the French driver who exceeded 100 mph, in a Gobron-Brille at Nice in 1904?

2. In 1906 Rolls-Royce produced the car that set the standard for quality automobiles from then on. What was it called?

3. In 1908 the race from New York to Paris – via China and Siberia – was won by ......what car?

4. The electric starter was introduced in 1911 by which great US manufacturer?

5. Which French maker proudly announced that for 1913 its output exceeded 10,000 cars?

6. Who was the American entrepreneur who in 1918 launched the General Motors Corporation, by combining the General Motors Company with Chevrolet Company?

7. Who was the American manager who quit GMC (where he had been head of Buick) in 1923 to start his own company, which within a few years was one of the 'big three'?

8. Which Italian maker introduced unitary (all-in-one) construction and independent front suspension on its 'Lambda' model in 1923?

9. Who was the British driver who exceeded 200 mph in a Sunbeam in 1927?

10. What technological innovation facilitating gear changing did Cadillac announce in 1928?

11. What did Citroen pioneer in their 7CV model in 1934?

12. Which Italian manufacturer introduced its 'baby car, the Topolino' 500 cc in 1936?

13. In 1938 Germany brought out the 'peoples car'. What was it called?

14. In 1948 which British manufacturer introduced the XK 120 sports car?

15. In the same year Goodrich introduced the tubeless tyre; and ...... who brought our the radial-ply tyre?

ANSWERS
1. Louis Rigolly. 2. Silver Ghost. 3. A Thomas Flyer. 4. Cadillac. 5. Renault. 6. William Durant. 7. Walter Chrysler. 8. Lancia. 9. Henry Segrave. 10. The synchromesh gearbox. 11. Front-wheel drive. 12. Fiat. 13. Volkswagen Beetle. 14. Jaguar. 15. Michelin.

How much do you know about the development of the motor car? (3)

QUESTIONS.

1. Which manufacturer of motor car parts announced the disc brake in 1950?

2. In 1951 two major U.S. car makers launched power steering. Who were they?

3. What was the name of the British car manufacturer whose experimental gas-turbine car set a speed record of 152 mph in 1952?

4. Which German component manufacturer introduced fuel injection in 1954?

5. In 1955 appeared the first family saloon to have disc-brakes and hydrop-neumatic suspension to be fitted as standard. Which car was it?

6. Who was the Italian born engineer responsible for the design of the revolutionary BMC Mini- Minor in 1959?

7. What was so special about the German NSU Special, when it arrived in 1964?

8. What was the name of the first mass-produced car with four wheel drive, which arrived in 1980?

9. Which manufacturer was the first to introduce an on-board computer to monitor engine performance in 1981?

10. Which two European manufacturers launched electric passenger cars in 1990?

11. Which two Japanese manufacturers launched an image-processing system for cars in 1992, designed to view the road ahead for obstacles, road signs etc.?

12. What is the name of the Japanese electric car that reached speeds of 109 mph in 1993?

13. What innovation did Daimler-Benz unveil in 1996?

14. What was the name of the RAF fighter pilot who broke the sound barrier in Thrust SCC in 1997 with a ground speed of 714.1 mph?

15. What new model of an earlier, very successful British car, went on sale in 2001?

ANSWERS.
1. Dunlop. 2. Buick and Chrysler. 3. Rover. 4. Robert Bosch. 5. Citroen DS-19.
6. Alec Issigonis. 7. It was the first car to be fitted with the Wankel rotary engine.
8. Audi Quattro. 9. BMW. 10. Fiat and Peugeot. 11. Mazda and NEC. 12. The IZA, 13.
The first fuel-cell-powered car. 14. Andy Green. 15. The new Mini.

How much do you know about the development of the Railways? (1)

QUESTIONS.

1. The first rails, wooden tracks along which trolleys were pushed by men (or women and children), later pulled by horses, were installed in European mines. In which century?

2. Who was the English engineer who in 1785, developed cast-iron rails along which flanged wheels could run, for improved efficiency and safety?

3. In which county in England were the first tracks laid in 1797 for horse drawn trams?

4. In 1804 English engineer Richard Trevithick adapted a steam engine which had been used for many years for pumping water, to drive a wheeled locomotive to haul wagons. Where?

5. Who was the English inventor who in 1820, began building on the work of Henry Cort to use wrought iron for the manufacture of rails?

6. Who was the English engineer who in 1825 built the first public railway to carry freight, from Stockton to Darlington, using his locomotive 'Locomotion'?

7. What was the name of Stephenson's much improved locomotive, which he made in 1829?

8. What was the name of the railway Stephenson built in 1830, the first to carry passengers?

9. In 1830 also, the first US built steam locomotive, the 'Best Friend of Charleston' went into service for which railroad company?

10, Within months a second US railroad started operations. What was its name?

11. Who was the German designer who in 1832 built the first proper passenger carriages?

12. In 1835 a steam locomotive built by Stephenson was the first to go into service in Germany. What name did its new owners give to it?

13. Who was the Scottish engineer who in 1863 patented a locomotive with pivoting driving bogies allowing curved in the track to be much sharper?

14. Also in 1863, London opened the world's first underground steam-powered railway. What was the line called?

15. In 1869 the first U.S. transcontinental railroad was completed when the Union Pacific and the Central Pacific met ....where?

ANSWERS.
1. 16th century. 2. William Jessop. 3. Shropshire. 4. South Wales, the Pen-y-Darren ironworks. 5. John Birkenshaw. 6. George Stephenson. 7. 'Rocket'. 8. Liverpool and Manchester. 9. South Carolina. 10. Baltimore – Ohio. 11. Franz Anton von Gerstner. 12. Der Adler (The Eagle). 13. Robert Fairlie. 14. The Metropolitan. 15. Promontory, Utah.

How much do you know about the development of the Railways? (2)

QUESTIONS.

1. In 1863 he introduced sleeping-cars to the railways; then dining-cars. Then in 1867 he founded his 'Palace Car Company'. What was his name?

2. Under the pressure of the Governor-General Lord Dalhousie, the first coast-to-coast railroad was constructed in India in 1870. From where to where?

3. Where was the first transalpine train tunnel built in 1871 to connect France to Italy?

4. Who was the Belgian entrepreneur who founded the European 'International Sleeping Car Company' in 1876?

5. Who was the German inventor who demonstrated an electric train at an exhibition in Berlin in 1879?

6. Who was the British imperialist who in 1880, established the planning and the finance for a railroad from Capetown, South Africa to link up with the Cairo-Suez railroad in Egypt?

7. A milestone for the industry occurred in 1881 when Siemens launched the world's first public service in Berlin of ......what?

8. What is the name of the mountain in Central Switzerland through which a railway pass was dug in 1881?

9. In 1883 an electric railway began offering a public service along the seafront of which English town?

10. More important, also in 1883, which steam train, synonymous with luxury and mystery, began its regular run from Paris to Constantinople?

11. Who was the French inventor who built an experimental monorail in Ireland, also in 1883?

12. Which US railroad was launched in 1883?

13. Which Australian railroad was launched in 1883?

14. November 7th 1886 saw the completion of which major North American railroad?

15. In what year did the first refrigerated railroad goods van roll in the US and the first railway was constructed in China?

ANSWERS.
1. George Pullman. 2. Bombay to Calcutta. 3. Mont Cenis (Frejus). 4. Georges Nagelmakers. 5. Werner von Siemens. 6. Cecil Rhodes. 7. Electrically powered trams. 8. St. Gotthard. 9. Brighton. 10. The Orient Express. 11. Charles Lartique. 12. Northern Pacific. 13. Sydney – Melbourne. 14. Canadian Pacific. 15. 1888.

How much do you know about the development of the Railways? (3)

QUESTIONS.

1. 1890 saw the arrival of the first trains with corridors and also the first electrically powered 'tube' train in London, which passed under the Thames. What was its name?

2. In 1891 construction began on what was to become the longest railway line in the world. Its name please?

3. The world's first automatic railway signals went into operation in 1893. Where?

4. In 1901 the world's longest operating monorail, the Schweberbahn, went into service in which German town?

5. In 1904 the New York subway system opened, with electric trains on which line?

6. 1912 and 1913. The first diesel electric locomotives entered service in which two European countries?

7. The largest railway station in Europe opened in 1915. In which German town?

8. Which British locomotive set a steam-rail speed record of 126 mph in 1938?

9. In October 1964 Japan National Railways inaugurated their 'New Trunk Line' between Tokyo and Osaka. Others have been built since. What speeds are regularly achieved on these lines?

10. In 1981 France's TGV trains began operations between Paris and Lyon (later extended to Marseilles). What does 'TGV' stand for?

11, In 1987 British Rail set a new diesel-traction speed record of ....what?

12 In 1988 the West German Intercity Experimental train reached what speed on a test run between Wurzburg and Fulda?

13. In 1989 a second Trans-Siberian line opened, the Baikal-Amur Magistral. How long is it?

14. What is the name of the private consortium franchised to introduce high-speed trains to the Dallas – Austin network?

15. What year did the first direct rail service from London to Paris begin operations through the Channel tunnel?

ANSWERS.
1. City and South London. 2. Trans-Siberian Railway. 3. Liverpool, England. 4. Wuppertal. 5. Broadway. 6. Germany and Sweden. 7. Leipzig. 8. 'Mallard'. 9. 150 mph. 10. 'Trains a Grande Vitesse'. 11. 148.5 mph. 12. 252 mph. 13. 1,954 miles. 14. Texas TGV. 15, 1994.

How much do you know about the development of ships? (1)

QUESTIONS.

1. Around what period were reed boats being developed in Mesopotamia and Egypt, and dug-out canoes used in north west Europe?

2. Around what period did the Egyptians begin using single-masted square-rigged ships on the Nile?

3. Who was the Egyptian Pharaoh who sent small fleets to explore the Mediterranean, the Red Sea, the Indian Ocean and the east coast of Africa, around 2,500 BC?

4. Around what period did the Phoenicians start building keeled boats with hulls of wooden planks?

5. Also around 1,200 BC, what nation of sea-faring islanders were defeated by Ramses III, with the aid of a new and very warlike innovation – ships fitted with rams?

6. Which sea-faring nation is credited with the invention of the bireme, the classical warship with a double row of oarsmen on each side?

7. Around what period did the Greeks begin building three-masted ships?

8. In the 1st century BC whilst the Chinese were inventing the rudder, the Romans were defeating which other nation for control of the Mediterranean?

9. In the 2nd century AD, who, other than the Romans, were developing fore and aft rigging that allows boats to sail across the direction of the wind?

10. What was the name of the famous Viking 'drakkar' from which the Norwegian King Olaf Tryggvesson leapt to his death after being defeated at the Battle of Svolde in AD 1000?

11. What aid to navigation was invented by the Chinese in AD 1090?

12. What type of vessel was developed in the Eastern Mediterranean from about 600 BC onwards and became the warships used by the Saracens to battle the Crusaders 500 – 600 years later?

13. What was the name of the Chinese admiral whose flagship, in 1410, was 130 meters (427 feet) long, had five masts and twelve decks?

14. What type of ships were the Pinta, the Nina and the Santa Maria in which Columbus set out in 1492?

15. What was the name of the most famous ship built on the orders of Henry VIII in 1514?

ANSWERS.
1. Around 7,500 BC. 2. Around 3,500 BC. 3. Sahure. 4. Around 1,200 BC. 5. The Cretans. 6. The Phoenicians. 7. Around 220 BC. 8. The Carthaginians. 9. The Arabs. 10. 'The Long Serpent'. 11. The Magnetic Compass. 12. The Dromon. 13. Zheng He. 14. They were Caravels. 15. 'Henry Grace a Dieu' (or 'Great Harry').

How much do you know about the development of ships? (2)

QUESTIONS.

1. In 1571 the last battle between oared galleys was fought. By what name is it known?

2. In 1577 – 1580 Francis Drake sailed around the world. What was the name of his ship?

3. What was the name of the Swedish man-of-war which sank on her maiden voyage in 1628, but was recovered some 450 years later in a remarkable state of preservation?

4. What name was given to the galleon launched in 1637, and built to be – on the orders of Charles I, 'the largest man of war afloat'?

5. What was the name of the ship in which Captain James Cook sailed in 1668 in the first of his three voyages to the Pacific?

6. Who was the English clockmaker who in 1759 invented the first marine chronometer?

7. What was the name of Nelson's flagship at the Battle of Trafalgar in 1805?

8. What was the name of the Scottish engineer who in 1802 launched the first stern paddle-wheel steamer, the 'Charlotte Dundas'?

9. What was the name of the American engineer who built the first successful steamboat, the 'Clermont' which sailed between New York and Albany in 1807?

10. Who was the English engineer who patented the screw propeller in 1836 and also launched the first screw steamship, the 'Rattler' in 1843?

11. What was the name of Isambard Kingdom Brunel's steamship, the first to be built specifically for the transatlantic passenger trade, launched in 1838?

12. What was the name of the first clipper ship, launched in the US in 1845?

13. What was the name of the French built submarine powered by an air-driven engine which took to the seas in 1863?

14. In 1866 two British clippers completed the tea race from China to London in 99 days. One was the 'Taeping'. What was the other one called?

15. Who was the German engineer who built the first boat powered by an internal combustion engine in 1886?

ANSWERS.
1. The Battle of Lepanto. 2. The Golden Hind. 3. The Vasa. 4. The 'Royal Sovereign'.
5. The Endeavour. 6. John Harrison, 7. The Victory. 8. William Symington. 9. Robert
Fulton. 10. Francis Pettit Smith. 11. The 'Great Western'. 12. The 'Rainbow'.
13. The 'Plongeur'. 14. The 'Ariel'. 15. Gottlieb Daimler.

How much do you know about the development of ships? (3)

QUESTIONS.

1. What was the name of the first propeller-driven iron ship to cross the Atlantic in 1845?

2. Who was the English engineer who fitted a steam-turbine to the 'Turbinia' in 1897, making it the fastest boat of its time?

3. Who was the American inventor who in 1900 designed the first modern submarine?

4. What was the name of the French ship which in 1902 was the first to be powered by a diesel engine?

5. Who was the American inventor who in 1905 patented the outboard motor?

6. Who was the American inventor who in 1911, after previously patenting gyrostabilisation, patented the gyro compass?

7. What was the first nuclear-powered submarine which was launched by the US in 1955 called?

8. Also in 1955, what did innovative British engineer Christopher Cockerill present?

9. In 1959 the world's first nuclear-powered ice-breaker was commissioned, as was the first nuclear-powered merchant ship. The first was the 'Lenin', the second was named …what?

10. What appeared on the world's oceans for the first time in 1968?

11. The Japanese tanker Shin-Aitoku-Maru was launched in 1980. What was unusual about it?

12. 1986 saw the launch of another technologically advanced ship, in which control of the sails is computerised. What name was given to this ship?

13. What was the name of the wave-piercing catamaran which in 1990 crossed the Atlantic in a world record time for passenger vessels of 3 days, 7 hours and 52 minutes?

14. In 1992 the propeller-less Japanese ship Yamato was launched. How is it powered?

15. In 1997 the largest cruise ship ever built was launched. Its name please?

ANSWERS.
1. The 'Great Britain'. 2. Charles Parsons. 3. John Philip Holland. 4. The 'Petit Pierre'. 5. Cameron Waterman. 6. Elmer Sperry. 7. The 'Nautilus'. 8. The Hovercraft. 9. The 'Savannah'. 10. Supertankers. 11. It was the first wind-assisted ship for over 50 years. 12. The 'Windstar'. 13. The 'Hoverspeed Great Britain'. 14. By magnetohydrodynamics. (It uses water in the same way as a jet plane uses air). 15. The 'Carnival Destiny'

How much do you know about the development of flight? (1)

QUESTIONS.

1. The first known human flight occurred in Paris in 1783 in a hot air balloon made by the Montgolfier brothers. Do you know the names of the balloonists?

2. Later in the same year the first ascent of a hydrogen-filled balloon, also took place in Paris. Can you name the two balloonists in this adventure?

3. In 1785 a hydrogen-filled balloon made the first air crossing of the Channel. Who were the balloonists in this case?

4. For what other flying-connected invention are we indebted to Blanchard?

5. Who was the French balloonist who flew an airship with a 3 h.p. engine over Paris in 1852?

6. Which English pioneer made a successful flight in a glider in 1853?

7. Who was the German aeronautical inventor who made many short flights in gliders, before dying in a crash in 1896?

8. Who was the Paris based Brazilian inventor who won a prize of 100,000 francs in 1901 for flying an airship across Paris and round the Eiffel Tower?

9. Who was the American pioneer who made the first powered and controlled flight of a heavier-than-air craft at Kitty Hawk, North Carolina in 1903?

10. Who were the French brothers who made the first significant controlled flight of 62 km in an airship in November 1903?

11. Who was the first person to fly a heavier-than-air craft in the U.K. in 1908?

12. Who was the French aviator who was the first to cross the Channel in an aircraft on July 25, 1909?

13. Which completely new military service came into existence in Britain on 13th April 1912?

14. In 1919 Ross and Keith Smith made the first flight from Britain to Australia in 135 hours, and Alcock and Brown caught the public imagination with the first non-stop Atlantic flight from Newfoundland to Ireland. What sort of plane did they use for their exploit?

15. Who, in 1923, was the first person to fly an autogiro with a rotating wing?

ANSWERS.

1. Jean Pilatre de Rozier and the Marquis d'Arlandes. 2. Jacques Charles and M. N. Robert. 3. Jean-Pierre Blanchard and John J. Jeffries. 4. The parachute. 5. Henri Giffard. 6. George Cayley. 7. Otto Lilienthal. 8. Alberto Santos-Dumont . 9. Orville Wright. 10. Paul and Pierre Lebaudy. 11. Samuel Cody. 12. Louis Bleriot. 13. Royal Flying Corps. 14. A Vickers Vimy. 15. Juan de la Cieva

How much do you know about the development of flight? (2)

QUESTIONS.

1. Who was the American aviator who in 1927, made the first solo non-stop Atlantic crossing?

2. Who were the two pilots who in 1928, made the first transpacific flight from San Francisco to Brisbane, Australia?

3. Who was the English engineer who patented the jet engine in 1930?

4. Who was the English aviator who made a solo flight from Britain to Australia in 9.5 days, also in 1930?

5. In 1932 this same aviator made a record sole flight from Britain to ....where?

6. The first fully pressurised aircraft came into service in 1937. What make was it?

7. Who was the German aviator who flew the first German jet, a Heinkel, in 1939?

8. Although the first attempts to design a Helicopter dated back to 1907, it was 1939 before a fully functional model was made by ....whom?

9. Two British fighter planes made an enormous contribution to the winning of the Battle of Britain in 1940. What were they called?

10. In May 1941 Frank Whittles' jet engine flew successfully, in what type of plane?

11. What was the rocket powered USAF plane to fly faster than the speed of sound in 1947?

12. What was the first jet airliner to come into commercial service in 1949?

13. Also in 1949, a Boeing Stratocruiser, the commercial passenger version of the bomber Superfortress, made another significant first. What was it?

14. What was the name given to the Rolls-Royce vertical take-off test model in 1953?

15. In 1968 the world's first supersonic airliner flew for the first time. What was it?

ANSWERS.
1. Charles Lindbergh. 2. Charles Kinsford Smith and C.T.P.Ulm 3. Frank Whittle. 4. Amy Johnson. 5. Capetown, South Africa. 6. A Lockheed XC-35. 7. Erich Warsitz. 8. Igor Sikorsky. 9. Supermarine Spitfire and Hawker Hurricane. 10. Gloster E 28/39. 11. Bell X-1. 12. De Havilland Comet. 13. First non-stop round-the-world flight. 14. Flying Bedstead. 15. The Russian TU-144.

How much do you know about the development of flight? (3)

QUESTIONS.

1. In 1969 the first vertical-take-off fighter entered service with the R.A.F. What was it called?

2. Which was the first of the wide-bodied passenger carriers which entered commercial service in 1970?

3. Who was the British engineer who, in 1971, designed the 'swing wing' which was incorporated into the design of the American F1-11 and the French Dassault Mirage G.8?

4. What was the fourth of the wide-bodied passenger airliners called? The only European manufactured model,, it entered commercial service in 1974.

5. What was the Anglo-French supersonic airliner which entered commercial service in 1976, reducing the transatlantic crossing to three hours?

6. Also in 1976, a new world air-speed record of almost 2,200 mph, was set in California, by .....what type of plane?

7. What was the helium-filled balloon called that made the first transatlantic crossing in 1978?

8. Who piloted his human-powered aircraft, Gossamer Albatross, across the English Channel in 1979?

9. In 1981 there was the first crossing of the English Channel by a solar-powered aircraft. What was it called?

10. The 'Virgin Atlantic Challenger' made the first hot-air balloon crossing of the Atlantic in 1987. Who were the balloonists?

11. In 1988 Kanellos Kanellopoulos piloted his human-powered aircraft 74 miles across the Aegean Sea. What name did he give to the craft?

12. In 1992 U.S. engineers successfully demonstrated a radio-controlled model of an aircraft that was propelled and manoeuvred by flapping its wings. What did they call it?

13. In 1994 U.S. engineers successfully demonstrated a model of a supersonic combustion ramjet at speeds up to 5,590 mph (Mach 8.2). What did they call it?

14. In 1998 Swiss balloonist set a record for the longest non-stop, non-refuelled flight : 9days, 17 hours and 55 minutes. What is the name of his balloon?

15. Also in 1998, a 14 kg robot aircraft designed by Australian and U.S. researchers carried out a successful crossing of the Atlantic. How long did it take?

ANSWERS.
1. British Aerospace Harrier. 2. Boeing 747. 3. Barnes Wallis 4. Airbus A300B. 5. Concorde. 6. Lockheed SR-17A. 7. Double Eagle II. 8. Bryan Allen. 9. Solar Challenger. 10. Richard Branson and Per Lindstrand. 11. Daedelus. 12. An 'Ornithopter'. 13. A 'Scramjet'. 14. Breitling Orbiter. 15. 26 hours.

Communications

How much do you know about the Internet? (1)

QUESTIONS.

1. What name is given to a hypertext system for publishing information on the Internet?

2. What do we call any company that sells dial-up access to the Internet?

3. What term is given for the behaviour guidelines for the Internet users?

4. What is the opening page on any particular site on the World Wide Web called?

5. What term is applied to a centre for the electronic storage of messages?

6. What is the name of the world's largest bulletin board system?

7. What is the system administrator for a server on the World Wide Web called?

8. What term applies to the imaginary, inter-active 'worlds' created by networked computers?

9. What is the facility to eliminate messages from irritating users called?

10. What term is used for the protocol used for communications between server and client?

11. What do we call an image or item of text in a WWW document that acts as an indicator to another Web page or document?

12. What term is applied to exploring the internet?

13. What term is used for the service that allows users to chat with each other?

14. What name is given to a user who reads a USENET newsgroup without making a contribution?

15. What term is applied to a security system that blocks access to a particular computer or network, while allowing some types of data to flow to and from the Internet?

ANSWERS.
1. World Wide Web. 2. Internet Service Provider. 3. Netiquette. 4. Home Page. 5. Bulletin board. 6. USENET. 7. Webmaster. 8. Cyberspace. 9. Bozo filter. 10. HTTP (Hypertext Transfer Protocol). 11. Link. 12. Surfing. 13. Internet Relay Chat. 14. Lurker. 15. Firewall

How much do you know about the Internet? (2)

QUESTIONS.

1. What term is applied to programs that are used to deny access to categories of information considered dangerous or offensive?

2. What do we call the set of rules applied by the service provider or backbone network, limiting the use to which their services may be put?

3. What term is used to describe advertising on the Internet by sending messages to any or all newsgroups regardless of relevance?

4. What term is applied to posting a deliberately misleading message to a newsgroup in order to solicit an intemperate reply?

5. What is the name of the relatively powerful encryption program that runs on personal computers and is distributed free of charge on the Internet?

6. What term is used for a request for information sent to a WWW site?

7. What is the term for a program that allows access to USENET newsgroups, interpreting standard commands in simple, user-friendly language?

8. What is the term, a contraction of electronic magazine, for a periodical sent by e-mail?

9. What term is applied to the list of routing that appears in the heading of a message sent across the Internet, showing how it arrived at its destination?

10. What do they call the campaign established to protest against moves towards censorship on the Internet?

11. What is the practice of sending a message to more than one newsgroup on USENET called?

12. What term is given to on-line sexual fantasy, spun by two or more participants in live chat?

13. What is any program that allows a user to search for and view data called?

14. What is a program that downloads Web pages onto a computer so that they can be viewed without being connected to the Internet?

15. What is the term for any automated, indexing program that trawls the Web for new or updated sites?

ANSWERS.
1. Blocking software. 2. Acceptable use. 3. Spamming. 4. Trolling. 5. PGP (Pretty Good Privacy). 6. Hit. 7. Newsreader. 8. E-zine. 9. Bang path. 10. Blue-ribbon campaign. 11. Crossposting. 12. Cybersex. 13. Browser. 14. Off-line browser. 15. Crawler.

How much do you know about the Internet? (3)

QUESTIONS.

1. What is the term used to describe a discussion group on the Internet's USENET?

2. What name is given to an inter-active multi-player game?

3. What term is applied to a popular MUD site in which the players take on the imaginary shapes and characters of furry, anthropomorphic animals?

4. What is the term applied to any angry electronic mail message?

5. What do we call an automated program that performs specific tasks on the Internet?

6. What is the name given to a magazine published on the WWW instead of on paper?

7. What is the term applied to a series of numbers and/or letters which give the location of a document on the WWW.?

8. What do we call a file that filters out types of information that the user does not wish to see when accessing a newsgroup?

9. What is the term used for that area in cyberspace, either text-based or graphical, that uses the model of a city to facilitate the retrieval of specific types of information?

10. What name is given the system that uses links to lead visitors to related graphics, in the same way that hypertext systems link related pieces of text?

11, What is the term, a contraction of system operator, for the operator of a bulletin board system?

12. What is the name given to any passionate believer in the right of free access to an encryption service on the Internet (in the interests of free speech and privacy)?

13. What is term used for a service that allows Internet users to post to USENET and send e-mail without revealing their true identity or e-mail address?

14. What is software used for creating Web pages, e.g. HTML, called?

15. What name is given to a new user of a USENET newsgroup?

ANSWERS.
1. Newsgroup. 2. MUD (Multi-User Dungeon) 3. FurryMUCK. 4. Flame 5. 'bot (Abbreviation of Robot). 6. Webzine. 7. URL (Uniform Resource Locator). 8. Killfile. 9. Digital city. 10. Hypermedia. 11. Sysop. 12. Cypherpunk. 13. Anonymous remailer. 14. Web authoring tool. 15. A newbie.

How much do you know about expressions used on the Internet? (1)

QUESTIONS.

What do the following commonly used abbreviations and acronyms mean?

1. FOCL?

2. TYVM?

3. IOW?

4. FWIW?

5. NIMBY?

6. BTDT?

7. TIC?

8. AIUI?

9. ROTFL?

10. OTOH?

11. BTW?

12. CUL?

13. IKWYM?

14. TPTB?

15. IYSWIM?

ANSWERS.
1. Falls off chair laughing. 2. Thank you very much. 3. In other words. 4. For what it's worth. 5. Not in my back yard. 6. Been there, done that. 7. Tongue in cheek. 8, As I understand it. 9. Rolling on the floor laughing. 10. On the other hand. 11. By the way. 12. See you later. 13. I know what you mean. 14. The powers that be. 15. If you see what I mean.

How much do you know about expressions used on the Internet? (2)

QUESTIONS.

What do the following commonly used abbreviations and acronyms mean?

1. OIC?

2. SO?

3. TIA?

4. LCW?

5. IRL?

6. NALOPKT?

7. DQM?

8. FOAF?

9. FUD?

10. FYI?

11. ISTM?

12. TTBOMK?

13. LOL?

14. LOL?

15. PMFJ

ANSWERS.
1. Oh! I see. 2. Significant other. 3. Thanks, in anticipation. 4. Loud, confident and wrong. 5. In real life. 6. Not a lot of people know that. 7. Don't quote me. 8. Friend of a friend. 9. Fear, uncertainty and doubt. 10. For your information. 11. It seems to me. 12. To the best of my knowledge. 13. Lots of luck. 14. Laughing out loud. 15. Pardon me for jumping in.

How much do you know about expressions used on the Internet? (3)

QUESTIONS.

What do the following commonly used abbreviations and acronyms mean?

1. IIRC?

2. TTFN?

3. AFAICR?

4. OTT?

5. SOTA?

6. PIM?

7. TTYL?

8. YKWIM?

9. WYSIWYG?

10. FAQ?

11. IMO?

12. NAFAIK?

13. FOC?

14. POV?

15. ATM?

ANSWERS.
1. If I remember correctly. 2. Tata (goodbye) for now. 3. As far as I can recall. 4. Over the top. 5. State of the art. 6. Personal Information Manager 7. Talk to you later. 8. You know what I mean. 9. What you see is what you get 10. Frequently asked question. 11. In my opinion. 12. Not as far as I know. 13. Free of charge. 14. Point of view. 15. At the moment.

How much do you know about the history and development of communications? (1)

QUESTIONS.

1. When did the Sumerians make their first attempts at a system of writing?

2. By what date did the Egyptians have their hieroglyphic script developed?

3. By what date did the Mesopotamians have their cuneiform script developed?

4. By what date was the Minoan Linear A script developed?

5. By what date was the Mycenaean Linear B script developed?

6. When did writing start to be put to widespread use in China?

7. When was the 22 letter alphabet invented by the Phoenicians?

8. When did the first musical notations appear, in Syria?

9. When was the alphabet adopted in Greece?

10. When did the Etruscans adopt the alphabet?

11. When did calendric writing begin to be used in Central America?

12. By what date had Brahmi syllabic script appeared in India?

13. By what date had paved roads improved physical communications in Rome?

14. By what date had parchment (vellum) been invented in Pergamum, Asia Minor?

15. What year was 'The Periplus of Erythraean Sea', a Greek pamphlet detailing sea trade routes between the Roman world, Africa and South Asia written?

ANSWERS.
1. Around 3,500 BC. 2. Around 2,900 BC. 3. Around 2,600 BC. 4. Around 1,700 BC. 5. Around 1,450 BC. 6. Around 1,400 BC 7. Around 1,350 BC. 8. Around 1,300 BC. 9. Around 800 BC. 10. Around 700 BC. 11. Around 550 BC. 12. Around 500 BC. 13. Around 170 BC. 14. Around 165 BC. 15. Around 60 BC.

How much do you know about the history and development of communications? (2)

QUESTIONS.

1. When did the first Arab paper factory open in Baghdad? 2. When did the Abbasid Caliph al-Mamun open his 'House of Wisdom', a library and translation academy in Baghdad?

3. When did Johannes Gutenberg set up a printing press in Mainz, Germany?

4. What year did Konrad Gesner invent the graphite pencil?

5. What year did French educationalist Louis Braille invent his reading system for the blind?

6. When did American artist and inventor Samuel Morse demonstrate his magnetic telegraph to the U.S. Congress?

7. In what year did Samuel Morse invent the Morse Code?

8. In what year did British physicists Charles Wheatstone and William Cooke take out the patents for the electric telegraph?

9. In what year was the first telegraph line established in the U.S., between Washington and Baltimore, after Morse received a grant of $30,000 from congress?

10. The first known typewriter was patented in England by Henry Mills in 1714. However the first fully functional typewriter was made by Christopher Sholes in the U.S. In what year?

11. In what year did William Thompson (later Lord Kelvin) supervise the laying of the first transatlantic telegraph cable?

12. In what year did Guglielmo Marconi launch wireless telegraphy?

13. In what year was the American telecommunications satellite TELSTAR launched?

14. In what year was the first cellphone network launched in Chicago, U.S.A. ?

15. In what year was the Worldwide web created, heralding the explosion of Internet?

ANSWERS.
1. Around 784. 2. Around 825. 3. Around 1445. 4. 1565. 5. 1837. 6. 1837. 7. 1838. 8. 1840. 9. 1843. 10. 1867. 11. 1886. 12. 1895. 13. 1962. 14. 1984. 15. 1994.

7

ENTERTAINMENT

The Cinema

How much do you know about action films?

QUESTIONS.

1. Everybody knows that in the 1938 release 'The Adventures of Robin Hood' the part of Robin Hood was played by Errol Flynn, but who played the villainous Sir Guy of Gisbourne?

2. What was the title of the Mel Gibson 1990 release about C.I.A. pilots playing fast and loose over and in Laos?

3. Who starred in the 1997 blockbuster 'Air Force One'?

4. Who starred in the 1998 release about an asteroid threatening the earth 'Armageddon'?

5. Who starred in the 2000 release 'The Art of War'?

6. What was the title of the 1979 release based upon a spy novel by Colin Forbes, centred upon a cross-Europe train journey?

7. What sad events marked the making of this film?

8. Who played the two male leads in the 1995 release 'Bad Boys'?

9. Who played the name part in the 1996 release 'Barb Wire'?

10. Who played the lead role in the 1996 release 'Daylight;?

11. Who played the lead role in the 1995 release 'Sudden Death'?

12. Who played the lead in the 1998 release 'Black Dog'?

13. Who were the male and female stars of the 1994 release 'True Lies'?

14. Who was the director of the 2000 release 'Crouching Tiger, Hidden Dragon'?

15. What was the title of the 2000 release in which Tom Hanks is marooned on a desert island?

ANSWERS.
1. Basil Rathbone 2. 'Air America' 3. Harrison Ford 4. Bruce Willis 5. Wesley Snipes.
6. 'Avalanche Express' 7. The death of the star (Robert Shaw) and of the director (Mark Robson) in mid-production 8. Will Smith and Martin Lawrence 9. Pamela Anderson 10. Sylvester Stallone 11. Jean-Claude van Damme 12. Patrick Swayze 13. Arnold Schwarzenegger and Jamie Lee Curtis 14. Ang Lee 15. 'Castaway'

Comedies

How much do you know about film comedies? (1)

QUESTIONS.

1. Who were the stars of the 1979 French film comedy 'A Nous Deux' released as 'The Two of Us' in English speaking markets?

2. Who played the male and female leads in the 1942 release 'To Be or Not To Be'? (Not to be confused with the very inferior remake from 1983.)

3. Who wrote, directed and starred in the 1975 release 'The Adventures of Sherlock Holmes' Smarter Brother'?

4. Who directed the black comedy released in 1985 'After Hours'?

5. What was the title of Satyajit Ray's last film, released in 1991 about a phony uncle who comes to stay?

6. Who played the hero and heroine of the 1980 release 'Airplane'?

7. Who played the name part in the highly successful 1966 release 'Alfie'?

8. Who played the male and female leads in the 1999 release 'American Beauty'?

9. Who played the lead male role in the 1973 release 'American Graffiti'?

10. Who played the two male lead parts in the 1999 release 'Analyse This'?

11. Who directed the 1983 release 'And the Ship Sails On'?

12. Who wrote, directed and starred in the 1977 release 'Annie Hall'?

13. And who played his leading lady?

14. What was so unusual about the 1992 release 'Another Girl, Another Planet'?

15. Who were the two male leads in the 1987 release 'Stakeout'?

ANSWERS
1. Catherine Deneuve and Jacques Dutronc 2. Jack Benny and Carole Lombard. 3. Gene Wilder 4. Martin Scorsese 5. 'Agantuk' (The Stranger) 6. Robert Hays and Julie Hagerty 7. Michael Caine 8. Kevin Spacey and Annette Bening 9. Richard Dreyfuss 10. Robert de Niro and Billy Crystal 11. Federico Fellini 12. Woody Allen 13. Diane Keaton 14. It was filmed with a Fisher-Price PXL 2000 child's camcorder 15. Richard Dreyfuss and Emilio Estevez

How much do you know about film comedies? (2)

QUESTIONS.

1. Who were the male and female leads in the classic comedy thriller released in 1934 'The Thin Man'?

2. Who were the male and female leads in the 1960 release 'The Apartment'?

3. What was the title of the Italian film which won the Oscar in the category best foreign film in 1997?

4. And who wrote, directed and starred in this film?

5. What was the name of the 1944 release starring Cary Grant about two sweet old ladies who poison lonely old men and bury them in the cellar?

6. Who won the Oscar in the supporting actor category in 1981 for his performance as Dudley Moore's butler in 'Arthur'?

7. Who played the male and female leads in the 1997 release 'As Good as it Gets'?

8. Who played the leading role in the 1996 release 'The Associate'?

9. Who played the part of Austin Powers in 1997 and again in 1999?

10. Who was the female star of the 1987 release 'Baby Boom'?

11. Who was the male star of the 1999 release 'The Bachelor'?

12. Who were the two male stars who appeared in all three 'Back to the Future' films?

13. What was the name of the 1988 release which was an unexpected success and gave rise to a television series, in which a middle-aged Bavarian woman left stranded in the Mojave desert, transforms a seedy motel she happens across?

14. What was the title of the 1971 Woody Allen release about an angst-ridden New Yorker who accidentally becomes a South American revolutionary hero?

15. What was the title of the film which took an unprecedented three prizes at the 1991 Cannes Film Festival, best actor, best film, best director?

ANSWERS
1. William Powell and Myrna Loy 2. Jack Lemmon and Shirley MacLaine. 3. 'Life is Beautiful' 4. Roberto Benigni 5. 'Arsenic and Old Lace' 6. John Gielgud 7. Jack Nicholson and Helen Hunt 8. Whoopi Goldberg 9. Mike Myers 10. Diane Keaton 11. Chris O'Donnell 12. Michael J. Fox and Christopher Lloyd. 13. 'Bagdad Café'. 14. 'Bananas'. 15. 'Barton Fink'.

How much do you know about film comedies? (3)

QUESTIONS.

1. What was the title of the 'ultimate disaster movie' released in 1997, starring Rowan Atkinson?

2. Who played the two female leads in the 2000 release 'Beautiful Creatures'?

3. What was the title of the 1999 release in which Serbian and Croatian refugees try to carry on their dispute in 1993 London?

4. Who played the part of the Devil in the 2000 release 'Bedazzled'?

5. What was the title of the 1951 release in which a chimpanzee is brought up as a human baby? It starred a future President of the U.S.

6. And who was the future President?

7. Who played the lead in the 1999 release 'Being John Malkovich'?

8. What was the title of the 2000 release set in a dog show in Philadelphia?

9. Who played the male and female leads in the 1993 release 'Dave' in which a Baltimore businessman is invited to the White House to impersonate the President?

10. Who wrote and directed the 1973 French comedy 'La Nuit Americaine'?

11. What was the title of the 1996 release in which a wronged wife and her family drive from Long Island to confront her husband in Manhattan?

12. Who played the lead in the 1982 release 'Dead Men Don't Wear Plaid'?

13. Who played the two female leads in the 1992 release 'Death Becomes Her'?

14. What was the title of Woody Allen's 1997 release about a writer who goes to a ceremony in his honour at his old school?

15. Who played the male and female leads in the 1999 release 'Galaxy Quest'?

ANSWERS
1. 'Bean' 2. Rachel Weisz and Susan Lynch 3. 'Beautiful People' 4. Elizabeth Hurley 5. 'Bedtime for Bonzo' 6. Ronald Reagan 7. John Cusack 8. 'Best in Show'.9. Kevin Kline and Sigourney Weaver 10. Francois Truffaut 11. 'The Daytrippers'. 12. Steve Martin 13. Meryl Streep and Goldie Hawn 14. 'Deconstructing Harry' 15. Tim Allen and Sigourney Weaver.

How much do you know about film comedies? (4)

QUESTIONS.

1. Who wrote, directed and starred in the 1996 release 'Big Night' ?

2. Who played the part of the Scottish hairdresser in Los Angeles in the 1999 release 'The Big Tease'?

3. What was the name of the 1963 release starring Tom Courteney as an undertaker's clerk living in a world of fantasy?

4. Who played the male and female leads in the 1987 Italian release 'Dark Eyes' (U.S. - Black Eyes)?

5. Who played the lead role in the 1980 release 'Private Benjamin'?

6. Who took the male and female leads in the 1985 release 'Prizzi's Honour'?

7. Who played the two lead male roles in the 1983 release 'Trading Places'?

8. Who was the male star of the 1994 release 'Trapped in Paradise'?

9. Who played the male and female leads in the 1990 release 'Tune in Tomorrow'?

10. Who played the part of Turner in the 1989 release 'Turner and Hooch'?

11. What is the title of the 1997 release in which five friends on the way to a wedding decide to commit a bank robbery, which goes wrong?

12. Who played the lead male role in the 1990 release 'Betsy's Wedding'?

13. Who played the part of Axel Foley in the series of films between 1984 and 1994 about a 'Beverley Hills Cop'?

14. Who played the male and female leads in the 1959 release 'A Touch of Larceny', one of those very rare films which contained moments when audiences applauded?

15. Who starred in the 1999 release 'Big Daddy'?

ANSWERS
1. Stanley Tucci 2. Craig Ferguson 3. 'Billy Liar' 4. Marcello Mastroianni and Silvana Mangano 5. Goldie Hawn 6. Jack Nicholson and Kathleen Turner 7. Dan Aykroyd and Eddie Murphy 8. Nicholas Cage 9. Keanu Reeves and Barbara Hershey 10. Tom Hanks 11. 'Best Men' 12. Alan Alda 13. Eddie Murphy 14. James Mason and Vera Miles 15. Adam Sandler.

How much do you know about film comedies? (5)

QUESTIONS.

1. Who part-wrote and directed the 1974 release 'Blazing Saddles'?

2. Who starred in the 1999 release 'Man On The Moon'?

3. Who starred in the 1997 release 'The Man Who Knew Too Little'?

4. In London, three young men pursue three women at a salsa club. That is the storyline of which 2000 release?

5. Three young incompetents decide to embark on a life of crime. That is the storyline of a 1996 US release. What was its title?

6. Who played the male and female leads in the 2000 release 'Bounce'?

7. Who played the two male leads in the 1998 release 'Bowfinger'?

8. What was the title of the 1996 release in which Michael Keaton stars as a workaholic who clones himself so as to be able to spend more time with his family?

9. What was the title of the 1961 release which starred Audrey Hepburn as Holly Golightly?

10. Who played the starring part in the 1999 release 'Breakfast of Champions'?

11. Who played the part of the central character in the 2001 release 'Bridget Jones's Diary'?

12. Who wrote, directed and starred in the 1984 release 'Broadway Danny Rose'?

13. What was the title of the 1998 release about an ambulance service team in Los Angeles?

14. Who part-wrote, directed and starred in the 1998 release 'Bulworth' about a politician who tells the truth during an election campaign, having arranged for his own assassination?

15. Who played the male lead in the black comedy 1997 release 'Butcher Boy'?

ANSWERS
1. Mel Brooks 2. Jim Carrey 3. Bill Murray 4. 'Born Romantic' 5. 'Bottle Rocket'.
6. Ben Affleck and Gwyneth Paltrow 7. Steve Martin and Eddie Murphy 8.
'Multiplicity'.   9. 'Breakfast at Tiffany's' 10. Bruce Willis 11. Renee Zellweger
12. Woody Allen 13. 'Broken Vessels' 14. Warren Beatty 15. Stephen Rea.

Costume drama

How much do you know about costume drama? (1)

QUESTIONS.

1. Who played the lead role in the 1964 release 'Angelique, Marquise des Anges'?

2. Who played the lead role in the 1945 release 'The Wicked Lady'?

3. And who played the same part in the 1983 remake?

4. Who played the male and female leads in the 1995 release 'Angels & Insects'?

5. Who wrote and directed the 1982 release 'The Draughtsman's Contract'?

6. The 1999 release 'Anna and the King' is a remake of a film that has been made several times before, notably as a musical. However, who played the role of Anna in this version?

7. Who played the male and female lead roles in the 1997 remake of Leo Tolstoy's 'Anna Karenina'?

8. Who played Henry VIII and Anne Boleyn in the 1969 release 'Anne of a Thousand Days'?

9. Who played the parts of 'Robin and Marian' in the 1976 release of that name?

10. What was the title of the 1997 French/German/Italian release about the scandals surrounding a 17th century female artist?

11. Who played the parts of Henry II and Eleanor of Aquitaine in the 1968 release 'The Lion in Winter'?

12. What was the title of the 1993 Peter Greenaway film about a miraculous infant in the mid-17th century?

13. Who wrote and directed the 1975 release about an 18th century Irish gentleman-of-fortune 'Barry Lyndon'?

14. Who played the two leading roles of Thomas a Becket and Henry II in the 1964 film version of Jean Anouilh's play 'Becket'?

15. Who won the 1998 Oscar in the category Best Supporting Actress for her role as Queen Elizabeth I in "Shakespeare in Love'?

ANSWERS.
1. Michele Mercier. 2. Margaret Lockwood. 3. Faye Dunaway. 4. Mark Rylance and Kristin Scott-Thomas. 5. Peter Greenaway. 6. Jodie Foster. 7. Sean Bean and Sophie Marceau. 8. Richard Burton and Genevieve Bujold. 9. Sean Connery and Audrey Hepburn. 10. 'Artemisia'. 11. Peter O'Toole and Katherine Hepburn. 12. 'The Baby of Macon'. 13. Stanley Kubrick. 14. Richard Burton and Peter O'Toole. 15. Judi Dench.

How much do you know about costume drama? (2)

QUESTIONS.

1. In 16th century Venice, a woman becomes a celebrated courtesan when the man she loves marries for money. This is the story-line of which 1998 release?

2. Who played the male and female leads in the 1988 release 'Dangerous Liaisons'?

3. Who played the lead role in the French 1994 release 'D'Artagnan's Daughter'?

4. Who played the name part in the 1995 release 'Rob Roy'?

5. Who played the name part in the 1995 release 'Braveheart'?

6. Who played the male and female leads in the 1950 release 'The Black Rose' about a 13th century English scholar in the land of the Mongols?

7. And who played the leader of the Mongols in this film?

8. Power and Welles had already shared the lead in a previous costume drama in 1949, about an adventurer at the court of the Borgias in medieval Italy. What was it called?

9. Who played the brothers: actor Edwin Booth and assassin of Abraham Lincoln John Wilkes Booth in the 1955 release 'Prince of Players'?

10, Who played a cameo role as Henry VIII in the 1977 release 'The Prince and the Pauper'?

11. Who played the male and female leads in the 1952 remake of 'The Prisoner of Zenda'?

12. Who played the role of the austere music teacher in the 1992 French production 'Tous les matins du monde'?

13. Who played the lead in the 1998 remake 'The Man in the Iron Mask'?

14, Which two actors played the parts of Sir Thomas More and Henry VIII in the 1966 release 'A Man for All Seasons'?

15. Who played the two male leads in the 1975 release, John Huston's 'The Man Who Would Be King'?

ANSWERS.
1. 'Dangerous Beauty'. (In the U.K. – 'The Honest Courtesan') 2. John Malkovich and Glenn Close 3. Sophie Marceau 4. Liam Neeson 5. Mel Gibson 6. Tyrone Power and Cecile Aubry 7. Orson Welles 8. 'Prince of Foxes' 9. Richard Burton and John Derek, respectively 10. Charlton Heston 11. Stewart Granger and Deborah Kerr 12. Jean-Pierre Marielle 13. Leonardo DiCaprio 14. Paul Scofield and Robert Shaw 15. Sean Connery and Michael Caine.

Drama

How much do you know about drama films? (1)

QUESTIONS.

1. Who played the two leading roles in the 1981 drama 'Absence of Malice'?

2. Who played the male and female lead roles in the 1999 drama 'Titus'?

3. Who played the male and female leads in the 1997 drama ''Titanic'?

4. Who was the director of 'Titanic'?

5. What was the title of the 1962 film for which Gregory Peck received an Oscar? In it he played a lawyer in a small Southern town who defends a black man against the charge of raping a white woman.

6. Who played the male and female leads in the French, New Wave 1960 release 'A Bout de Souffle' (Breathless) about a young car thief who kills a policeman and goes on the run with his girl-friend?

7. Who was the actress who starred opposite Jodie Foster in the 1988 release 'The Accused' for which Jodie won an Oscar?

8. Who directed the brilliant 1951 release 'Ace in the Hole' starring Kirk Douglas?

9. Who were the male and female leads in the 1997 release 'Affliction'?

10. Who were the male and female leads of the 1992 release 'Afraid of the Dark'?

11. What was the English title of the 1998 Japanese release in which people who die are allowed to take one memory with them?

12. Who played the male and female leads in the 1997 release 'Afterglow'?

13. Who played the male and female leads in Martin Scorsese's 1993 film 'Age of Innocence'?

14. Who played the name part in the 1999 Irish release 'Agnes Brown'?

15. Who starred in Werner Herzog's spellbinding 1972 release 'Aguirre, Wrath of God'?

ANSWERS
1. Paul Newman and Sally Field 2. Anthony Hopkins and Jessica Lange 3. Leonardo DiCaprio and Kate Winslet 4. James Cameron 5. 'To Kill a Mockingbird' 6. Jean-Paul Belmondo and Jean Seberg 7. Kelly McGillis 8. Billy Wilder 9. Nick Nolte and Sissy Spacek 10. James Fox and Fanny Ardant 11. 'After Life' 12. Nick Nolte and Julie Christie. 13. Daniel Day-Lewis and Michelle Pfeiffer 14. Anjelica Huston 15. Klaus Kinski.

How much do you know about drama films? (2)

QUESTIONS.

1. Who were the two male leads in Carol Reed's 'The Agony and the Ecstasy' (1965)?
2. Who played the chief pilot and the air hostess in the 1970 release 'Airport'?
3. And who played the air hostess who had to take over the controls of the Jumbo Jet in the 1975 sequel?
4. Who were the two actresses who played the two leading roles in the 1950 release 'All About Eve'?
5. Who were the two actors who played the two leading roles in the 1976 release 'All the Presidents Men' about the breaking of the Watergate affair?
6. Who played the part of Salieri, the composer rival to Mozart who claims to have been the cause of Mozart's death in the 1984 film version of Peter Schaffer" play "Amadeus"
7. What was the title of the Anglo/French 1992 release about a 15 year old French girl in Vietnam who begins an obsessive affair with a Chinese businessman?
8. Who played the female lead in the 1991 release 'Les Amants du Pont Neuf'?
9. Who played the part of 'the highest paid lover in Beverley Hills' in the 1980 release 'American Gigolo'?
10. What was the name of the 1997 Steven Spielberg film, based on the true story of a group of African slaves who killed the crew of the slave ship on the way to America?
11. Who played the male and female leads in the 1956 release 'Anastasia'?
12. What was the name of the 1993 release, full of stars, based on the book by Randy Shilts, about the development of AIDS in America
13. What was the name of the 1999 release based upon a very successful book describing a writer's poverty-stricken upbringing in Ireland before his emigration to the U.S?
14. What was the title of the 2001 release which, topically deals with the ethics of the head of a leading software company, and his ambition to control the market?
15. Who were the male and female leads in the 1999 release about American football, 'Any Given Sunday'?

ANSWERS

1. Charlton Heston and Rex Harrison 2. Dean Martin and Jacqueline Bisset 3. Karen Black 4. Bette Davis and Anne Baxter 5. Robert Redford and Dustin Hoffman 6. F. Murray Abraham 7. 'L'Amant' 8. Juliette Binoche 9. Richard Gere 10. 'Amistad' 11. Yul Brynner and Ingrid Bergman 12. 'And the Band Played On' 13. 'Angela's Ashes' 14. 'Antitrust' 15. Al Pacino and Cameron Diaz.

How much do you know about drama films? (3)

QUESTIONS.

1. Who took the roles of mother and daughter in the 1999 release 'Anywhere But Here'?
2. Who played the lead in the 1995 release 'Apollo 13' which recounted the story of that fated space flight?
3. What was the title of the 1997 release, written, directed by and starring Robert Duvall as a preacher?
4. Who played the lead role in the 1992 release 'Article 99' set in a US vet's hospital?
5. Who played the male and female leads in the 1981 release of Louis Malle's elegant drama 'Atlantic City'?
6. Louis Malle returned to France to direct a very moving story of childhood and inadvertent betrayal which was released in 1988. What was it called?
7. What was the title of the 1995 release directed by and starring Anthony Hopkins, which transposed a play by Chekov from Russia to Wales?
8. What was the romantic drama starring Richard Gere and Winona Ryder released in 2000?
9. Who were the two male stars of the 1990 release dealing with suspended animation and called 'Awakenings'?
10. In 1952 Kirk Douglas and Lana Turner headed a strong cast in a film about Hollywood and what makes it tick. What was it called?
11. What was the title of the 1973 release which became a bit of a cult movie, following the movements of a couple of low lifers played by Martin Sheen and Sissy Spacek as they wander across America leaving a trail of murder behind them?
12. Who wrote and directed the 2000 release 'Bamboozled'?
13. The 1994 GB/India release 'Bandit Queen' was about a low-caste, illiterate, much-abused woman who revenged herself on her tormentors before becoming a member of the Indian Parliament, and being assassinated. What was her name?
14. A rebellious teenager at a Catholic school becomes a heroin addict, prostitute and thief. Which 1995 release starring Leonardo Di Caprio does this describe?
15. What is the title of the 2000 release in which Leonardo Di Caprio plays a hippy in Thailand?

ANSWERS.
1. Susan Sarandon and Natalie Portman 2. Tom Hanks 3. 'The Apostle' 4. Ray Liotta 5. Burt Lancaster and Susan Sarandon 6. 'Au Revoir Les Enfants' 7. 'August' 8. 'Autumn in New York' 9. Robert De Niro and Robin Williams 10. 'The Bad and the Beautiful' 11. 'Badlands' 12. Spike Lee 13. Phoolan Devi 14. 'The Basketball Diaries' 15. 'The Beach'.

How much do you know about drama films? (4)

QUESTIONS.

1. What was the title of the 1994 GB/France/Macedonia joint production about an expatriate Macedonian photographer who returns to witness the conflict in Yugoslavia?

2. Who played the lead in the 1967 French release 'Belle de Jour' in which a surgeon's wife spends afternoons working in a brothel?

3. And who directed it?

4. Who played the male and female leads in the 1998 release 'Beseiged'?

5. What was the title of the 1992 Swedish film which won the Cannes Film Festival awards for best film and best actress? It recounted the history of the marriage of a cleric and a nurse.

6. What was the title of the 1992 release starring Jeremy Irons and Juliette Binoche which told of the destruction of an M.P. by his obsessive love for his son's girlfriend?

7. Who is the pop-star who appeared in her first film in 2000 – 'Dancer in the Dark'?

8. Who was the star of the 1995 release 'Dangerous Minds' about an ex-marine who becomes a teacher at a tough inner-city school?

9. Who played the male and female leads in the 1997 release 'Dante's Peak'?

10. Who played the name role in the 1965 release 'Darling'?

11. Who played the male and female leads in the 1990 release 'Days of Thunder'?

12. Who played the male and female leads in the 1995 release 'Dead Man Walking'?

13. Who played the lead role in the 1989 release 'The Dead Poets Society'?

14. Who played the part of the identical twins in the 1988 release 'Dead Ringers'?

15. Who played the two male leads in the 1997 release 'The Edge'?

ANSWERS.
1. 'Before the Rain' 2. Catherine Deneuve 3. Luis Bunuel 4. David Thewlis and Thandie Newton 5. 'The Best Intentions' 6. 'Damage' 7. Bjork 8. Michelle Pfeiffer 9. Pierce Brosnan and Linda Hamilton 10. Julie Christie 11. Tom Cruise and Nicole Kidman 12. Sean Penn and Susan Sarandon 13. Robin Williams 14. Jeremy Irons 15. Anthony Hopkins and Alec Baldwin.

How much do you know about drama films? (5)

QUESTIONS.

1. What was the title of the 1995 film version of the play by Ariel Dorfman, starring Sigourney Weaver and Ben Kingsley?

2. Who starred in the 1971 release 'Death in Venice'?

3. Who played the lead role in the 1951 film version of the classic play by Arthur Miller 'Death of a Salesman'?

4. Who played the lead in the 1999 release 'The Debt Collector'?

5. What was the title of the 1999 release starring Samuel L. Jackson about sharks with enhanced intelligence turning on the personnel at the underwater research facility?

6. Who play the husband and wife devastated by the disappearance of their three -year-old son in the 1999 release 'The Deep End of the Ocean'?

7. Who played the name part in the 1982 release 'Gandhi'?

8. And who directed it?

9. Who directed the 1970 Italy/Germany release 'The Garden of the Finzi-Continis'?

10. What was the name of the 1993 France/Italy production based upon an Emile Zola novel of the same name about the terrible working and living conditions of miners?

11. What was the title of the 1996 release starring Alec Baldwin and James Woods about the third trial of the racist who murdered a black civil rights activist 20 years previously?

12. Who played the three lead roles in the 1956 release 'Giant'?

13. Who played the three lead roles in the 1959 release 'Suddenly, Last Summer'?

14. Who directed the 1992 release 'A River Runs Through It'?

15. Who played the name part in the 1995 version of 'Richard III, in which Shakespeare's play was transposed to the '30's in a fascist state?

ANSWERS.
1. 'Death and the Maiden' 2. Dirk Bogarde 3. Fredric March 4. Billy Connolly 5. 'Deep Blue Sea' 6. Treat Williams and Michelle Pfeiffer 7. Ben Kingsley 8. Richard Attenborough 9. Vittorio de Sica 10. 'Germinal' 11. 'Ghosts of Mississippi' 12. Rock Hudson, Elizabeth Taylor and James Dean 13. Montgomery Clift, Elizabeth Taylor and Katherine Hepburn 14. Robert Redford 15. Ian McKellen

How much do you know about drama films? (6)

QUESTIONS.

1. What was the title of the 2000 release about the eleven year-old miner's son who defies his father and learns ballet instead of boxing?

2. Who played the female and male leads in the 1991 release 'Prince of Tides'?

3. Who starred in the 1969 release 'The Prime of Miss Jean Brodie'?

4. Who played the title role in the 1994 release 'Priest'?

5. Who played the male and female leads in the 1998 release 'Primary Colours'?

6. This was the film version of a book about which American politician's first presidential campaign?

7. Who played the male and female roles in the 1995 release 'Desperado'?

8. What was the title of the 2000 release about the drugs problem which starred the recently married Michael Douglas and Catherine Zeta-Jones?

9. What was the title of the 1996 release about four friends in Scotland enjoying the highs and lows of drug addiction, sex, booze and violence?

10. Who played the two male leads in the 1948 release 'The Treasure of Sierra Madre'?

11. Who were the stars of the 1990 release 'Truly, Madly, Deeply'?

12. Who played the lead in the 1957 release 'Twelve Angry Men'?

13. What was the title of the 1946 Award winning film about three men returning home from the war and the difficulties they encounter?

14. Who starred as the young, American doctor in the 1995 release 'Beyond Rangoon'?

15. Who played the lead in the 1999 release 'Bicentennial Man' about an android becoming more human?

ANSWERS
1. 'Billy Elliot' 2. Barbra Streisand and Nick Nolte 3. Maggie Smith 4. Linus Roache 5. John Travolta and Emma Thompson 6. Bill Clinton 7. Antonio Banderas and Salma Hayek 8. 'Traffic' 9. 'Trainspotting 10. Humphrey Bogart and Walter Huston 11. Juliet Stevenson and Alan Rickman 12. Henry Fonda 13. 'The Best Years of Our Lives' 14. Patricia Arquette 15. Robin Williams

How much do you know about drama films? (7)

QUESTIONS.

1. Who was the director of the 1948 Italian release 'Bicycle Thieves' which was considered to be the epitome of Italian neo-realism, brilliantly acted, winning many awards?

2. Who was the star of the 1997 release 'The Blackout', in which Claudia Schiffer appeared?

3. Who played the two female lead parts in the 2000 release 'The Man Who Cried'?

4. Who played the lead role in the 1999 release 'Boys Don't Cry'?

5. The storyline for a 1991 US release goes: 'young blacks try to survive in the hostile urban world of Los Angeles gangs'. What was the name of the film?

6. What is the name of the young actress who received an Oscar nomination in 1996 for her first film performance, in 'Breaking the Waves'?

7. What was the title of the 1999 release in which Nicholas Cage plays a New York ambulance driver heading for a breakdown? (Him – not the ambulance).

8. And the film was directed by which iconoclastic director?

9. Who were the two young actresses who starred in the 1999 release 'Brokedown Palace'?

10. What was the title of the 1996 release starring Robert Carlyle about a Glaswegian bus driver in Nicaragua?

11. Who played the female lead in the 1995 release 'Carrington'?

12. Everybody knows that Bogart and Bergman were the stars of the 1942 release 'Casablanca', but can you remember who played the part of Victor Laszlo?

13. Who was the female star of the 2000 release 'The Cell'?

14. What was the title of the 1993 Anglo/French/German release which deals with the matter of incest?

15. Who played the title role in the 1992 biopic 'Chaplin'?

ANSWERS
1. Vittorio de Sica 2. Matthew Modine 3. Christina Ricci and Cate Blanchett 4. Hilary Swank 5. 'Boyz N The Hood' 6. Emily Watson 7. 'Bringing Out The Dead' 8. Martin Scorsese 9. Claire Danes and Kate Beckinsale 10. 'Carla's Song' 11. Emma Thompson 12. Paul Henreid 13. Jennifer Lopez 14. 'The Cement Garden' 15. Robert Downey Jnr.

Epics

How much do you know about epics? ·

QUESTIONS.

1. Who played the name part in the 1956 epic 'Alexander the Great'?

2. Who was the famous director of the great Russian epic of 1938 'Alexander Nevsky'?

3. Who played the starring role of Phileas Fogg in the 1956 Mike Todd release 'Around the World in Eighty Days'?

4. And who played the part of his faithful manservant, Passepartout?

5. Who played the name part in the 1962 release 'Barabbas'?

6. Who played the name part in the 1959 version of 'Ben-Hur'?

7. Who played the name parts in the 1951 release 'David and Bathsheba'?

8. Who played the name parts in the 1949 release 'Samson and Delilah'?

9. Who played the two male leads in the 1974 release 'The Towering Inferno'?

10. Who directed the 1966 release 'The Bible'?

11. What was the title of the screen's very first epic, written and directed by D.W. Griffith and released in 1915?

12. Who played the male and female leads in the 1953 release 'The Robe'?

13. Who played the part of the wizard Gandalf in the 2002 release 'The Fellowship of the Ring', the first part of the trilogy 'The Lord of the Rings'?

14. Who directed the 1956 release 'The Ten Commandments'?

15. Who directed the 1960 release 'Spartacus'?

ANSWERS
1. Richard Burton 2. Sergei Eisenstein 3. David Niven 4.Cantinflas 5.Anthony Quinn 6. Charlton Heston 7. Gregory Peck and Susan Hayward 8. Victor Mature and Hedy Lamarr 9. Paul Newman and Steve McQueen 10. John Huston 11. 'Birth of a Nation' 12. Richard Burton and Jean Simmons 13. Ian McKellan 14. Cecil B. de Mille 15. Stanley Kubrick.

Family Films

How much do you know about family films? (1)

QUESTIONS.

1. Who starred in the 1993 release 'The Adventures of Huck Finn'?

2. Who was the narrator of the 1986 release about the friendship between a puppy and a kitten 'Adventures of Milo and Otis'?

3. What was the name of the film which was released in 1996 starring Martin Landau, which was a remake with real actors of a classic Disney cartoon?

4. What was the name of the 1967 release starring John Mills and Hugh O'Brian about a Kenyan settler who hires two cowboys to help wild game ranching?

5. What was the title of the 1997 Disney release about a golden retriever which plays basketball?

6. In the 1992 Disney release 'Aladdin', which actor supplied the voice of the genie?

7. What was the title of the 1994 release in which a seven year-old girl befriends a baby seal?

8. What was the title of the 1994 Disney release about a boy who enlists the aid of angels to transform a baseball team?

9. What was the title of the 1998 animated cartoon in which a worker falls in love with a princess and foils the plans of her soldier fiance to mount a coup?

10. What was the title of the 2000 cartoon in which a circus rooster helps chickens to escape from their jail-like farm?

11. What was the title of the 1999 release, about France's most loved cartoon character and national symbol?

12. And who played the part of Obelix?

13. What was the title of the film about a pig which thought it was a sheepdog, a 1995 release?

14. What was the title of another 1995 release about a dog, half-wolf/half-dog which led a sled team to save the people of the town of Nome, Alaska from an epidemic of diptheria?

15. What was the title of the 1942 Disney animated release about a forest deer?

ANSWERS
1. Elijah Wood 2. Dudley Moore 3. 'The Adventures of Pinocchio' 4. Africa, Texas Style 5. 'Air Bud' 6. Robin Williams 7. 'Andre'. 8. 'Angels in the Outfield' 9. 'Antz'. 10. 'Chicken Run' 11. 'Asterix and Obelix take on Caesar' 12. Gerard Depardieu 13. 'Babe' 14. 'Balto' 15. 'Bambi'

How much do you know about family films? (2)

QUESTIONS.

1. Who was the Director of the 1989 French release about an orphaned bear cub which falls in with a full-grown male grizzly? The film was called simply 'The Bear'.

2. What was the title of the 1991 Disney animated musical based upon a fairy story about a prince turned into a monstrosity by enchantment, and the girl who saves him?

3. What was the title of the Disney 1992 release about a St Bernard and his family?

4. What was the title of the 1985 Disney cartoon in which a medieval hero combats magic swords, wicked witches and skeletal tyrants?

5. What was the title of the 1995 release, the first totally computer generated animated feature, with characters such as Buzz Lightyear and Randy the Cowboy?

6. Who played the unforgettable Long John Silver in the 1950 Disney remake of 'Treasure Island'?

7. Who played the roles of mother and daughter in the 1999 release 'Tumbleweeds'?

8. What was the title of the 1980 release about a boy and a horse castaway together somewhere in Africa, after a shipwreck?

9. Who played the title part in the 1952 release 'Blackbeard, the Pirate'?

10. And who played the title part in the 1967 Disney release 'Blackbeard's Ghost'?

11. What was the title of the 1999 release in which a family emerges from a nuclear fall-out shelter after 35 years?

12. What was the title of the 1995 release in which a teenage delinquent becomes friendly with a gorilla in a research laboratory?

13. What was the title of the 1997 release about a family of tiny people who live under the floorboards of a house?

14. What was the title of the 1998 Disney animated cartoon in which a young Chinese girl disguises herself as a warrior to rescue the Emperor?

15. What was the title of the 1995 release about a friendly little ghost?

ANSWERS
1. Jean-Jacques Annaud 2. 'Beauty and the Beast' 3. 'Beethoven' 4. 'The Black Cauldron' 5. 'Toy Story' 6. Robert Newton 7. Janet McTeer and Kimberley Brown 8. 'The Black Stallion' 9. Robert Newton 10. Peter Ustinov 11. 'Blast from the Past' 12. 'Born to Be Wild' 13. 'The Borrowers' 14. 'Mulan' 15. 'Casper'.

How much do you know about great lines?

QUESTIONS.

The following lines were said in which movies?

1. 'Frankly, my dear, I don't give a damn'.

2. 'Well, here's another nice mess you've gotten me into'.

3. 'Remember you're fighting for this woman's honour. Which is probably more than she ever did'.

4. 'Of all the gin joints in all the towns in all the world, she had to walk into mine'.

5. 'I'll be back'.

6. 'I read you were shot five times in the tabloids'.

   'It's not true. He didn't come anywhere near my tabloids'.

7. 'It's alive!'

8. 'Mrs Robinson. You're trying to seduce me, aren't you?'

9. 'I'll have what she's having'.

10. 'Gentlemen! You can't fight in here! This is the War Room!'

11. 'You know how to whistle don't you Steve? You just put your lips together – and blow'.

12. 'You're gonna need a bigger boat!'

13. 'I'm not living with you. We occupy the same cage, that's all'.

14. 'They call me Mr Tibbs'.

15. 'I'm as mad as hell, and I'm not going to take this anymore!'

ANSWERS.
1. Gone With The Wind (1939). 2. Sons of the Desert (Laurel and Hardy – 1933).
3. Duck Soup. (The Marx Bros. – 1933). 4. Casablanca. (1942). 5. The Terminator (1984). 6. The Thin Man. (1934). 7. Frankenstein. (1931). 8. The Graduate (1967).
9. When Harry Met Sally. (1989). 10. Dr. Strangelove. (1964). 11. To Have and Have Not. (1944). 12. Jaws. (1975). 13. Cat on a Hot Tin Roof. (1958). 14. In the Heat of the Night. (1967). 15. Network. (1976).

How much do you know about horror films?

QUESTIONS.

1. Who was the well-known American supporting actor who became the top star of horror films, starting with 'House of Wax' in 1953?

2. A young actor, then at the beginning of his career, who went on to be a top star in action roles, played the part of the mad professor's mute assistant in 'House of Wax'. His name?

3. In what 1971 British horror, did Vincent Price play a disfigured musical genius who invoked ten curses of a Pharaoh on the surgeons who failed to save his wife?

4. What was the title of the 1976 release starring Richard Widmark and Christopher Lee which was based upon a famous satanic novel by Dennis Wheatley?

5. Who played the lead male part in the 2000 release 'American Psycho'?

6. American Werewolves show up in Europe from time to time, Can you name the two cities visited in 1981 and 1997?

7. What was the name of the highly successful 1973 release in which Linda Blair played a young girl possessed by the devil

8. What was the name of the 1979 release in which a young couple move into an old house, but are driven out by satanic manifestations?

9. Who played the male and female leads in the 1997 release 'Anaconda'?

10. What was the title of the first British film to receive the H (for Horror) certificate?

11. What was the title of the 1995 Spanish release about a priest hunting for the Anti-Christ which is about to be born in Madrid?

12. What was the title of the 1998 release which presented itself as an amateur movie, and received tremendous international public and critical acclaim?

13. Who played the female lead in the 2000 release 'Bless the Child'?

14. Who played the male and female leads in the 1999 release 'The Mummy' and the sequel, the 2001 release 'The Mummy Returns'?

15. What was the title of the 1992 release in which an anthropology student becomes convinced of the existence of a mythical hook-handed serial killer?

ANSWERS
1. Vincent Price 2. Charles Bronson 3. 'The Abominable Dr. Phibes' 4. 'To The Devil, A Daughter' 5. Christian Bale 6. a) London and b) Paris 7. 'The Exorcist' 8. 'The Amityville Horror' 9. Jon Voight and Jennifer Lopez 10. 'The Dark Eyes of London (1939) 11. 'The Day of the Beast' 12. 'The Blair Witch Project' 13. Kim Basinger 14. Brendan Fraser and Rachel Weisz 15. 'Candyman'

James Bond Films

How much do you know about James Bond films? (1)

QUESTIONS.

1. Who played the part of 'M' in the first eleven Bond films, from 'Dr No' to 'Moonraker'?

2. What was the title of the only Bond film to appear without someone in the role of 'M'?

3. Who played the part of 'M' in four Bond films, from 'Octopussy' to 'Licence To Kill'?

4. And who took over as 'M' in 'GoldenEye'?

5. Who was the Canadian actress who played Moneypenny in the first fourteen Bond films, from 'Dr No' to 'A View To A Kill'?

6. Who played the part of Moneypenny in the two Timothy Dalton Bond films?

7. And who took over as Moneypenny in 'GoldenEye'?

8. Who played the part of 'Q', the gadget master, in every Bond film with the exception of the first one, up until his death in a car accident in 1999.?

9. Amazingly enough, in his last appearance in 'The World Is Not Enough' he introduced Bond to his successor 'R', played by ....?

10. What is the name of the C.I.A. agent who has turned up in a number of Bond films, played by a different actor each time?

11. What is the name of the American actor who played the villainous Brad Whitaker who met his end at Bond's hands in 'The Living Daylight' and then turned up as a C.I.A. agent in each of the following two Bond films?

12. The K.G.B. were never far away in at least three different Bonds, generally in the person of the ubiquitous General ....who?

13. Who was the British character actor who played the part of General Gogol?

14. And General Gogol had an assistant. What was her name?

15. Who was the actress who played this part?

ANSWERS.
1. Bernard Lee. 2. 'For Your Eyes Only' 3. Robert Brown. 4. Judi Dench.
5. Lois Maxwell. 6. Caroline Bliss. 7. Samantha Bond. 8. Desmond Llewellyn.
9. John Cleese. 10. Felix Leiter. 11. Joe Don Baker. 12. General Gogol.
13. Walter Gotell. 14. Rubelvitch. 15. Ex-Miss World Eva Rueber-Staier.

How much do you know about James Bond films? (2 *The Villains*)

QUESTIONS..

1, Who played the part of 'Dr. No' in the first Bond film? (We do not count 'Casino Royale').

2. Who played the part of Rosa Klebb in 'From Russia With Love'?

3. Who played the part of Auric Goldfinger in 'Goldfinger'?

4. Who played the part of Emilio Largo in 'Thunderball'?

5. Who played the part of Ernst Stavro Blofeld in 'You Only Live Twice'?

6. Who played the part of Blofeld in 'On Her Majesty's Secret Service'?

7. Who played the part of Blofeld in 'Diamonds Are Forever'?

8. Who played the part of Dr Kananga in 'Live And Let Die'?

9. Who played the part of Scaramanga in 'The Man With The Golden Gun'?

10. Who played the part of Stromberg in 'The Spy Who Loved Me'?

11. Who played the part of Hugo Drax in 'Moonraker'?

12. Who played the part of Kristatos in 'For Your Eyes Only'?

13. Who played the part of Kamal Khan in 'Octopussy'?

14. Who played the part of Max Zorin in 'A View To A Kill'?

15. Who played the part of General Georgi Koskov in 'The Living Daylights'?

ANSWERS.
1. Joseph Wiseman. 2. Lotte Lenya. 3. Gert Frobe. 4. Adolfo Celi. 5. Donald Pleasence. 6. Telly Savalas. 7. Charles Gray. 8. Yaphet Kotto. 9. Christopher Lee. 10. Curt Jurgens. 11. Michael Lonsdale. 12. Julian Glover. 13. Louis Jourdan. 14. Christopher Walken 15. Jeroen Krabbe.

How much do you know about James Bond films? (3 *The Villains continued*)

QUESTIONS.

1. Who played the part of Franz Sanchez in 'Licence To Kill'?

2. Who played the part of Alexander Trevelyan in 'GoldenEye'?

3. Who played the part of Elliott Carver in 'Tomorrow Never Dies'?

4. Who played the part of Renard in 'The World Is Not Enough'?

   Well, that takes care of the principal villains. Now, some of the hired hands were pretty remarkable too, so what do you know about them?

5. Who played the part of the SPECTRE assassin Red Grant in 'From Russia ....'?

6. What was the name of Goldfinger's Korean manservant, and who was the actor who played the role?

7. What were the names of the two professional killers who camped it up in 'Diamonds Are Forever'?

8. What was the name of the actor who played Jaws in 'The Spy Who ....' and 'Moonraker'?

9. Who was the striking actress who played May Day in 'A View To A Kill'? A baddie from the beginning she died an almost heroic death in the last reel but one.

10 Who played the Tangier based arms dealer Brad Whitaker in 'The Living Daylights'?

11. Who played the SPECTRE assassin Fiona Volpe in 'Thunderball'?

12. Who played the murderous Miss Xenia Onatopp in 'Goldeneye'?

13. Who played the very professional killer Dr. Kaufman in 'Tomorrow Never Dies'?

14. Who was the actor who portrayed Professor Dent in 'Dr No', nearly ending James Bond's career before it got off the ground by putting a large, poisonous spider in his bed?

15. Who played the part of Elektra King with whom Bond falls in love in 'The World is Not Enough', only to find that she is a fully paid-up member of Renard's terrorist group?

ANSWERS.
1. Robert Davi. 2. Sean Bean 3. Jonathan Pryce. 4. Robert Carlyle. 5. Robert Shaw. 6. 'Oddjob'/Harold Sakata. 7. Mr Kidd and Mr Wint. 8. Richard Kiel. 9. Grace Jones. 10. Joe Don Baker. 11. Luciana Paluzzi. 12. Famke Janssen. 13. Vincent Schiavelli. 14. Anthony Dawson. 15. Sophie Marceau.

How much do you know about James Bond films? (4 *The Girls*)

QUESTIONS.

1. Who was the actress who appeared as Sylvia Trench in the prologues to both 'Dr No' and 'From Russia With Love'

2. Who played the part of Honey Rider in 'Dr No'?

3. Who played the part of Tatiana Romanova in 'From Russia With Love'?

4. Who played the part of Pussy Galore in 'Goldfinger'?

5. And who wound up covered from head to foot in gold paint in the same film?

6. Who played the part of Domino in 'Thunderball'?

7. Who played the part of Helga Brandt in 'You Only Live Twice'?

8. Who played the part of Tracy in 'On Her Majesty's Secret Service'?

9. Who played the part of Tiffany Case in 'Diamonds Are Forever'?

10. Who played the part of Solitaire in 'Live And Let Die'?

11. Who played the part of Mary Goodnight in 'The Man With The Golden Gun'?

12. Who played the part of Major Anya Amasova in 'The Spy Who Loved Me'?

13. Who played the part of Holly Goodhead in 'Moonraker'?

14. Who played the part of Melina Havelock in 'For Your Eyes Only'?

15. Who played the part of 'Octopussy'?

ANSWERS.
1. Eunice Gayson. 2. Ursula Andress. 3. Daniela Bianchi. 4. Honor Blackman.
5. Shirley Eaton. 6. Claudine Auger. 7. Karin Dor. 8. Diana Rigg.
9. Jill St. John. 10. Jane Seymour. 11. Britt Ekland. 12. Barbara Bach.
13. Lois Chiles. 14. Roger Moore. 15. Maud Adams.

How much do you know about James Bond films? (5 *The Girls continued*)

QUESTIONS.

1. Who played the part of Stacey Sutton in 'A View To A Kill'?

2. Who played the part of Kara Milovy in 'The Living Daylights'?

3. Who played the part of Pam Bouver in 'Licence to Kill'?

4. Who played the part of Natalya Simonova in 'GoldenEye'?

5. Who played the part of Wai Lin in 'Tomorrow Never Dies'?

6. Who played the part of Christmas Jones in 'The World Is Not Enough'?

    Well, that takes care of, what you might call Bond's first team. But there were others, oh, so many others in the reserves who also deserve a question or two.

7. Who played the knife throwing 'cigar-girl' in 'The World Is ....'?

8. Who played the part of Dr Molly Warmflash in 'The World Is ....'?

9. Who played the part of Paris Carver whose assignation with Bond leads to her death, in 'Tomorrow Never Dies'?

10. Who played the bit part of Irina, Zukovsky's mistress, a very off-key country and western singer in 'GoldenEye'?

11. Who played the role of Lupe Lamora in 'Licence To Kill'?

12. Who played the part of Pola Ivanova in 'A View To A Kill'?

13. Who played the part of Jenny Flex, May Day's right-hand girl in 'A View To A Kill'?

14. Who played the part of Magda in 'Octopussy'?

15. Who played the part of Naomi, Stromberg's in-house killer in 'The Spy Who Loved Me' who attemped to assassinate Bond and Anya Amasova by helicopter?

ANSWERS
1. Tanya Roberts. 2. Maryam d'Abo. 3. Carey Lowell. 4. Izabella Scorupco 5. Michelle Yeoh. 6. Denise Richards. 7. Maria Grazia Cucinotta. 8. Serena Scott-Thomas. 9. Teri Hatcher. 10. Minnie Driver. 11. Talisa Soto. 12. Fiona Fullerton. 13. Alison Doody. 14. Kristina Wayborn. 15. Caroline Munro

How much do you know about musicals?

QUESTIONS.

1. What was the title of the 1949 release about three sailors on shore leave in New York?

2. Who directed the 1979 release 'All That Jazz' starring Roy Scheider and Jessica Lange?

3. Whose music was celebrated in the 1951 release 'An American in Paris'?

4. And who played the lead male and female roles?

5. Who played the male and female leads in the 1950 release 'Annie Get Your Gun'?

6. Who played the male and female leads in the 1953 release 'The Band Wagon'?

7. Who played the name role in the 1958 release 'Gigi'?

8. And who provided the words and the music?

9. Who were the stars of the 1953 remake of 'The Desert Song'?

10. What was the title of the 1999 release about the trials and tribulations behind Gilbert and Sullivan's creation of The Mikado?

11. What was the title of the 1956 release which tells the story of the songwriting team de Sylva, Brown and Henderson?

12. And who played the parts of the three songwriters?

13. What was the title of the 1998 release, a documentary (more or less) about a group of elderly Cuban musicians who are brought back into the limelight?

14. Who played the part of Sally Bowles in the 1972 release 'Cabaret'?

15. Who played the male and female leads in the 1955 release 'Oklahoma!'?

ANSWERS
1. 'On The Town' 2. Bob Fosse 3. George Gershwin 4. Gene Kelly and Leslie Caron
5. Howard Keel and Betty Hutton 6. Fred Astaire and Cyd Charisse 7. Leslie Caron 8.
Alan Jay Lerner and Frederick Loewe 9. Kathryn Grayson and Gordon MacRae 10.
'Topsy-Turvy' 11. 'The Best Things in Life Are Free' 12. Gordon MacRae; Ernest
Borgnine and Dan Dailey 13. 'The Buena Vista Social Club' 14. Liza Minnelli 15.
Gordon MacRae and Shirley Jones.

Romantic comedies

How much do you know about romantic comedies?

QUESTIONS.

1. Who played the two leading roles in the 2000 romantic comedy 'About Adam'?

2. Who played the two leading roles in the 1986 romantic comedy 'About Last Night'?

3. Who played the male and female leads in Hitchcocks' 1955 'To Catch A Thief'?

4. Who played the male and female leads in the 1997 release 'Addicted to Love'?

5. Who played the male and female lead in the 1957 release 'An Affair to Remember'?

6. Who played the male and female leads in the 1951 release 'The African Queen'?

7. Who directed the 1989 release 'Always' in which a dead pilot returns as a ghost to sort out the romantic problems of another flyer?

8. Who played the male and female leads in the 1995 release 'The American President'?

9. Who played the male and female leads in the 1993 release 'Sleepless in Seattle'?

10. Who played the part of 'the woman' in the 1957 release of Roger Vadim's 'And God Created Woman'?

11. Who played the name part in the 1994 release 'Angie'?

12. What was the title of the 1991 release in which Johnny Depp falls for an older woman played by Faye Dunaway?

13. Who played the name part in the 1970 release 'Darling Lili'?

14. Who played the male and female leads in the 1947 release 'The Ghost and Mrs Muir'?

15. Who played the male and female leads in the 1957 release 'The Prince and the Showgirl'?

ANSWERS.
1. Stuart Townsend and Kate Hudson 2. Demi Moore and Rob Lowe 3. Cary Grant and Grace Kelly 4. Matthew Broderick and Meg Ryan 5. Cary Grant and Deborah Kerr 6. Humphrey Bogart and Katherine Hepburn 7. Steven Spielberg 8. Michael Douglas and Annette Bening 9. Tom Hanks and Meg Ryan 10. Brigitte Bardot 11. Geena Davis 12. 'Arizona Dream' 13. Julie Andrews 14. Rex Harrison and Gene Tierney 15. Laurence Olivier and Marilyn Monroe

Science fiction Films

How much do you know about science fiction films? (1)

QUESTIONS.

1. Who wrote and directed the 1970 film 'THX 1138'?

2. Who played the male and female leads in the 1989 Sci-Fi thriller 'The Abyss'?

3. And who wrote and directed it?

4. Who is the actor who played the part of the man who 'gave birth' to the baby monster in the very first 'Alien' in 1979?

5. Who directed 'Alien'?

6. Who directed the first sequel to 'Alien', which was called 'Aliens'?

7. Who was the star of the 1982 release 'Android'?

8. What was the name of the first Michael Crichton story to be filmed in 1970?

9. What was the title of the 1996 release starring Charlie Sheen as an astronomer who realises that aliens are amongst us?

10. Who played the male and female leads in the 1999 release 'The Astronaut's Wife'?

11. What was the title of the 1980 release which was a rip-off of the Seven Samurai?

12. Who starred in the 2000 release 'Battlefield Earth'?

13. Who played the lead role in the 1998 release 'Dark City'?

14. What was the title of the 1982 animated cartoon in which two different species turn out to be two halves of the same specie which had somehow become separated?

15. Who played the part of the Alien in the 1951 release 'The Day the Earth Stood Still'?

ANSWERS.
1. George Lucas. 2. Ed Harris and Mary Elizabeth Mastrantonio. 3. James Cameron. 4. John Hurt. 5. Ridley Scott. 6. James Cameron. 7. Klaus Kinski. 8. 'The Andromeda Strain'. 9. 'The Arrival'. 10. Johnny Depp and Charlize Theron. 11. 'Battle Beyond the Stars'. 12. John Travolta. 13. Rufus Sewell. 14. 'The Dark Crystal' 15. Michael Rennie.

How much do you know about science fiction films? (2)

QUESTIONS.

1. Who starred in the 1994 release, 'Death Machine'?

2. Who played the male and female leads in the 1998 release 'Deep Impact'?

3. What was the title of the 1998 release about a gigantic octopus-like creature which attacks a luxury liner?

4. Who played the male and female leads in the 1997 release 'Gattaca'?

5. Who played the name part in the 1987 release 'Robocop'?

6. Who played the two male lead parts in the 1979 Disney release 'The Black Hole'?

7. Who played the two male leads in the 1995 release 'Twelve Monkeys'?

8. Who played the lead male role in the 1990 release 'Total Recall'?

9. Who played the two male leads in the 1982 release 'Blade Runner'?

10. Who directed it?

ANSWERS.
1. Brad Dourif. 2. Robert Duvall and Tia Leoni. 3. 'Deep Rising'. 4. Ethan Hawke and Uma Thurman. 5. Peter Weller. 6. Maximilian Schell and Anthony Perkins. 7. Bruce Willis and Brad Pitt.. 8. Arnold Schwarzenegger. 9. Harrison Ford and Rutger Hauer. 10. Ridley Scott.

Spy Films

How much do you know about spy films?

QUESTIONS.

1. Who played the male and female leads in the 2001 spy saga 'The Tailor of Panama'?

2. Who played the male and female leads in 'The Spy Who Came In From The Cold' (1965)?

3. Who played the male lead in the 1966 film 'The Quiller Memorandum'?

4. In 1942 Warner Bros. made a spy film which reunited three of the stars of 'The Maltese Falcon' - Bogart, Astor and Greenstreet. What was it called?

5. What was the name of the 1965 film version of a popular Len Deighton book which introduced us to an intelligence agent named Harry Palmer, played by Michael Caine?

6. In 1966 James Mason starred in a film version of John Le Carre's spy novel 'Call for the Dead'. What was it called?

7. Who played the female lead role in the 2001 release 'Enigma'?

8. Who played the male and female leads in the Alfred Hitchcock 1935 release 'The 39 Steps', still the best version despite being remade several times since?

9. Who played the two lead male roles in the 1959 release 'Our Man in Havana'?

10. Who played the starring role in the 1960's/1970's series about 'Our Man Flint'?

11. And who played the starring role in the even sillier 1960's/1970's series about a secret agent named Matt Helm?

12. Who starred in the 1996 release Mission: Impossible and its sequel in 2000?

13. Who played the male and female leads in the 1990 release 'The Russia House'?

14. Who played the male lead role in the 1985 release 'The Man with One Red Shoe'?

15. Who played the male and female leads in the 1938 Hitchcock release 'The Lady Vanishes'?

ANSWERS.
1. Pierce Brosnan and Jamie Lee Curtis. 2. Richard Burton and Claire Bloom. 3. George Segal. 4. 'Across the Pacific'. 5. 'The IPCRESS File'. 6. 'The Deadly Affair'. 7. Kate Winslet. 8. Robert Donat and Madeleine Carroll. 9. Alec Guinness and Noel Coward. 10. James Coburn. 11. Dean Martin. 12. Tom Cruise. 13. Sean Connery and Michelle Pfeiffer. 14. Tom Hanks. 15. Michael Redgrave and Margaret Lockwood.

Thrillers

How much do you know about thrillers? (1)

QUESTIONS.

1. Who played the male and female leads in the 1947 thriller 'Odd Man Out'?

2. Who played the male and female leads in the 1949 thriller 'The Third Man'?

3. And who played the part of the 'third man' (Harry Lime)?

4. Who played the male and female leads in the 1953 thriller 'The Man Between'?

5. What did these three films have in common, apart from the use of the 'Man' in the titles?

6. Who played the male and female leads in the 1946 thriller 'The Killers'?

7. And who played the parts of the killers?

8. And who played the part of the ex-boxer waiting to be killed?

9. Who played the male and female leads in the 1950 thriller 'The Asphalt Jungle'?

10. Who played the male and female leads in the 1941 thriller 'The Maltese Falcon'?

11. And who played the two chief villains?

12. Who played the male and female leads in the 1948 thriller 'Key Largo'?

13. Who was the director of the films mentioned in questions 9, 10 and 12?

14. Who played the part of the chief villain in 'Key Largo'?

15. Who played the male and female leads in the 1949 thriller 'White Heat'?

ANSWERS.
1. James Mason and Kathleen Ryan. 2. Joseph Cotton and Alida Valli. 3. Orson Welles. 4. James Mason and Claire Bloom. 5. They were all directed by Carol Reed. 6. Ava Gardner and Edmond O'Brien. 7. Charles McGraw and William Conrad. 8. Burt Lancaster. 9. Sterling Hayden and Jean Hagen. 10. Humphtey Bogart and Mary Astor. 11. Sydney Greenstreet and Peter Lorre. 12. Humphrey Bogart and Lauren Bacall. 13. John Huston. 14. Edward G. Robinson. 15. James Cagney and Virginia Mayo.

How much do you know about thrillers? (2)

QUESTIONS.

1. Who played the male and female leads in the 1999 thriller 'The Talented Mr Ripley'?

2. A previous version of this film had already been made in France in 1960 with the rising young star Alain Delon in the principal role. Do you know what that version was called?

3. What is the name of another French thriller, released in 1955, in which the central thirty minutes of the film pass in total silence as a robbery is carried out?

4. Who starred in the 1985 thriller 'Target', playing Matt Damon's father?

5. What was the title of the 1990 thriller in which Richard Gere played (unusually for him) the villain, a crooked and extremely vicious cop?

6. What was the title of the 1997 thriller about an ageing burglar who sees the US President become an accessory in the murder of a woman?

7. Who played the burglar and who played the President?

8. Who played the lead in a tough, clever thriller released in 1972 called 'Across 110th Street'?

9. Who played the male and female leads in the 1984 release 'Against All Odds'?

10. Who played detective Alex Cross in 'Kiss the Girls' (1997) and 'Along Came a Spider' (2001)?

11. Who played the male lead in the 1990 release 'The Ambulance'?

12. What was the name of the 1955 release directed by and starring Mark Stevens as an insurance investigator assigned to a robbery he committed himself?

13. Who played the male and female leads in the 1942 classic thriller 'This Gun for Hire'?

14. What was Ladd and Lake's second film together, also released in 1942?

15. Who wrote and directed the 1956 release 'The Killing' starring Sterling Hayden?

ANSWERS.
1. Matt Damon and Gwyneth Paltrow. 2. 'Plein Soleil'. 3. 'Rififi'. 4. Gene Hackman. 5. 'Internal Affairs'. 6. 'Absolute Power'. 7. Clint Eastwood and Gene Hackman. 8. Anthony Quinn. 9. Jeff Bridges and Rachel Ward. 10. Morgan Freeman. 11. Eric Roberts. 12. 'Timetable'. 13. Alan Ladd and Veronica Lake. 14. 'The Glass Key'. 15. Stanley Kubrick.

How much do you know about thrillers? (3)

QUESTIONS.

1. What is the title of the 1999 release in which Jeff Bridges suspects Tim Robbins of being a terrorist?

2. Who was the director who began his career with a number of tough, tight little thrillers like 'Armoured Car Robbery' (1950) and 'The Narrow Margin' (1952)?

3. And who was the gravel-voiced, hard-faced actor who played the lead in both of those films?

4. Who played the starring role in the 1999 release 'The Limey'?

5. Who played the principal antagonists in the seminal thriller from 1955 'Bad Day at Black Rock'?

6. What was the title of the 1991 release starring Michael Douglas and Sharon Stone?

7. What was the title of the 1999 release starring Alessandro Nivola and Reese Witherspoon about a thief for whom robberies always go wrong?

8. What was the title of the semi-classic thriller released in 1950 in which the victim (played by Edmond O'Brien) of a slow poison tracks down his own killer?

9. Who was the star of the 1995 release 'Danger Zone'?

10. Who played the name part in the 1944 release 'Laura' which brought a new approach to the thriller genre?

11. And who played three men in her life: her mentor; her fiance and the detective who investigated her murder?

12. And who directed them all?

13. Who played the male and female lead in the 1946 release 'The Dark Corner'?

14. What was the title of the Bogart-Bacall vehicle of 1947 in which Bogie played a convicted murderer who escaped from jail to prove his innocence?

15. Who starred in the 1991 release 'Dark Wind', playing a Navajo cop?

ANSWERS.
1. 'Arlington Road'. 2. Richard Fleischer. 3. Charles McGraw. 4. Terence Stamp. 5. Spencer Tracy and Robert Ryan. 6. 'Basic Instinct'. 7. 'Best Laid Plans'. 8. 'D.O.A.' (Dead On Arrival). 9. Billy Zane. 10. Gene Tierney. 11. Clifton Webb; Vincent Price and Dana Andrews. 12. Otto Preminger. 13. Mark Stevens and Lucille Ball. 14. 'Dark Passage'. 15. Lou Diamond Phillips.

How much do you know about thrillers? (4)

QUESTIONS.

1. The 1971 release 'The Day of the Jackal' shows how a professional killer goes about carrying out the attempted assassination of which French President?

2. Who played the male and female leads in the 1991 release 'Dead Again'?

3. Who played the lead role in the 1996 Canadian release 'Dead Innocent'?

4. Who played the lead role in the 1992 release 'Deep Cover'?

5. Who played the lead role in the 1997 release 'The Game'?

6. Who directed the 1998 release about an IRA gangster 'The General'?

7. Who played the male and female leads in the 1999 release 'The General's Daughter'?

8. Who played the two lead male roles in the 1995 release 'Get Shorty'?

9. Who played the male and female leads in the 1994 release 'The Getaway'?

10. This was a remake of a 1972 release which starred ......who and who?

11. What was the title of the curiously successful 1990 release starring Patrick Swayze, Demi Moore and Whoopi Goldberg

12. Who played the lead in the strangely named 1999 release 'Ghost Dog: The Way of the Samurai'?

13. What was the title of the 1954 release which had Frank Sinatra cast as a professional assassin lying in wait for the US President?

14. Who played the two male lead parts in the 1993 release 'Rising Sun'?

15. Who played the lead in the 1991 release 'Ricochet'?

ANSWERS.
1. Charles de Gaulle. 2. Kenneth Branagh and Emma Thompson. 3. Genevieve Bujold. 4. Laurence Fishburne. 5. Michael Douglas. 6. John Boorman. 7. John Travolta and Madeleine Stowe. 8. John Travolta and Gene Hackman. 9. Alec Baldwin and Kim Basinger. 10. Steve McQueen and Ali MacGraw. 11. 'Ghost'. 12. Forest Whitaker. 13. 'Suddenly'. 14. Sean Connery and Wesley Snipes. 15. Denzel Washington.

How much do you know about thrillers? (5)

QUESTIONS.

1. Who played the male and female leads in the 1949 release, which has become something of a cult film, 'Gun Crazy'?

2. Who played the lead role in the 2000 release 'The Gift'?

3. Who played the male and female leads in the famous 1946 release 'Gilda'?

4. Who played the lead in the 1997 release 'The Gingerbread Man'?

5. And who directed it?

6. Who played the cop and who the killer in the 1953 release 'The Big Heat' directed by Fritz Lang?

7. Who played the lead in the 1953 French production 'The Wages of Fear', which was considered by some to be the greatest suspense thriller ever?

8. Who played the male and female leads in the 1967 release 'Point Blank'?

9. What was the title of the 1990 French release about a young, female drug addict who is turned into a professional assassin by an intelligence service?

10. Who starred as the girl in the 1993 American copy 'Point of No Return' (The Assassin in the U.K.) ?

11. And who took the Lee Marvin role in the 1999 remake of Point Blank – 'Payback'?

12. Who played the lead role in the 1998 release 'The Big Lebowski'?

13. By now everyone knows that Bogart and Bacall starred in the 1946 release ;The Big Sleep', but how many know which ex-cowboy film star played the part of the gunman Canino?

14. Who directed the 1963 release 'The Birds'?

15. What was the title of the 1989 release starring Michael Douglas and Andy Garcia as American cops in Tokyo?

ANSWERS.
1. John Dall and Peggy Cummins. 2. Cate Blanchett. 3. Glenn Ford and Rita Hayworth. 4. Kenneth Branagh. 5. Robert Altman. 6. Glenn Ford and Lee Marvin. 7. Yves Montand. 8. Lee Marvin and Angie Dickenson. 9. 'Nikita'. 10. Bridget Fonda. 11. Mel Gibson. 12. Jeff Bridges. 13. Bob Steele. 14. Alfred Hitchcock. 15. 'Black Rain'.

How much do you know about thrillers? (6)

QUESTIONS.

1. Who played the part of the lawyer who defends a shy choirboy accused of murdering an archbishop in the 1996 release 'Primal Fear'?

2. Who played the male and female leads in the 1968 release 'Bullitt'?

3. What was the title of the extremely scary 1954 French release starring Simone Signoret, Paul Meurisse and Vera Clouzot?

4. Who played the leads in the 1967 release 'Bonnie and Clyde'?

5. Who played the part of the female Sheriff in the 1996 release 'Fargo'?

6. What was the title of the 1975 remake of the film based on a Raymond Chandler novel with Robert Mitchum as Philip Marlowe and Charlotte Rampling as the femme fatale?

7. Who played the two male leads in the 1958 release 'Touch of Evil'?

8. Who was the star of the 1993 release 'Trespass' in which two firemen go in search of a gold cross?

9. Who played the role of the chief villain in the 1993 release 'True Romance'?

10. Who played the male and female leads in the 1991 release 'Billy Bathgate'?

11. Who played the two female lead roles in the 1987 release 'Black Widow'?

12. What was the title of Alfred Hitchcock's first film, released in 1929?

13. Who starred as the psychopath in the 1993 release 'Blind Side'?

14. Who were the two male leads in the 1996 release 'Blood and Wine'?

15. Who played the male and female leads in the 1999 release 'The Bone Collector'?

ANSWERS.
1. Richard Gere. 2. Steve McQueen and Jacqueline Bisset. 3. 'Les Diaboliques' (The Fiends). 4. Warren Beatty and Faye Dunaway. 5. Frances McDormand. 6. 'Farewell, My Lovely'. 7. Charlton Heston and Orson Welles. 8. Bill Paxton. 9. Dennis Hopper. 10. Dustin Hoffman and Nicole Kidman, 11. Debra Winger and Theresa Russell. 12. 'Blackmail'. 13. Rutger Hauer. 14. Jack Nicholson and Michael Caine. 15. Denzel Washington and Angelina Jolie.

How much do you know about vampire films?

QUESTIONS.

1. What was the title of the 1995 release starring Christopher Walken and Lili Taylor about a philosophy student who turns into a vampire after reading Nietsche?

2. Who played the starring role in the 1970 release 'Daughters of Darkness', a lesbiavampire, the re-incarnation of Elizabeth of Bathory, a medieval Hungarian countess?

3. What was the alternative title to the 1967 release 'The Fearless Vampire Killers'?

4. And who played the two male lead roles?

5. What was the title of the 1972 spoof in which a 150 year old African Prince, one of Dracula's victims, is taken to Los Angeles and revivified?

6. Who was the star of the 1998 release 'Blade' in which he plays a half-human, half-vampire?

7. Who played the starring role in the 1992 release 'Bram Stoker's Dracula'?

8. And who played the female lead?

9. What was the title of the 1992 release starring Kristy Swanson which gave birth to a much more successful TV series starring Sarah Michelle Gellar?

10. Who starred in the 1995 release 'A Vampire in Brooklyn'?

11. Who were the male and female stars of the 1979 French/German release 'Nosferatu, the Vampyre'?

12. Who was the star of the original, 1931 release 'Dracula'?

13. And who played the part of Dracula in the 1958 remake, the first of many remakes?

14. Who was the star of the 1994 release 'Interview with the Vampire: The Vampire Chronicle'?

15. Who plays the part of Van Helsing in the 2000 release 'Dracula 2000'?

ANSWERS.
1, 'The Addiction'. 2. Delphine Seyrig. 3. 'Pardon Me, Your Teeth Are in My Neck'. 4. Jack MacGowran and Roman Polanski. 5. 'Blacula'. 6. Wesley Snipes. 7. Gary Oldman8. Winona Ryder. 9, 'Buffy the Vampire Slayer'. 10. Eddie Murphy. 11. Klaus Kinski and Isabelle Adjani. 12. Bela Lugosi. 13. Christopher Lee. 14. Tom Cruise 15. Christopher Plummer.

How much do you know about war films?

QUESTIONS.

1. What was the title of the 1955 release which starred Audie Murphy in the film version of his own book about his own World War 2 experiences?

2. What was the title of the prisoner-of-war film released in 1953 about the Royal Navy P.O.W.'s who construct a lifelike dummy to cover the absence of an escapee?

3. Some say it was the greatest anti-war film ever made. Based, in 1930, on the greatest anti-war novel ever written, by Erich Maria Remarque. What was it called?

4. Who played the leading role in Francis Ford Coppola's 1979 release 'Apocalypse Now'?

5. Who played the two lead male roles in the 1988 Vietnam war release 'Bat 21'?

6. What was the title of the 1988 release about a Russian tank crew in Afghanistan?

7. Who played the two leading male roles in the 1965 release 'The Bedford Incident'?

8. What was the title of the 1956 release in which a British Colonel and an American Captain on the way to invade France in 1944, reminisce about the woman they both love?

9. And which two actors played the two roles?

10. Who played the part of Barnes Wallis in the 1954 release 'The Dam Busters'?

11. Who played the name part in the 1997 release 'G. I. Jane'?

12. What was the title of the 1993 release about the decisive batltle of the American Civil War, starring Tom Berenger and Martin Sheen?

13. Who played Rommel in the 1951 release 'The Desert Fox' and then again in the 1953 'Desert Rats'?

14. What was the title of the 1999 release about a platoon of British soldiers at the start of the Somme offensive in 1916?

15. Who starred in the 1949 release 'Twelve O' Clock High' about the commander of a US bomber unit in Britain who begins to crack under the strain?

ANSWERS.
1. 'To Hell and Back'. 2. Albert, R.N. 3. 'All Quiet on the Western Front'. 4. Martin Sheen5. Gene Hackman and Danny Gover. 6. ' The Beast of War'. 7. Richard Widmark and Sidney Poitier. 8. 'D-Day 6th of June'. 9. Richard Todd and Robert Taylor. 10. Michael Redgrave.11. Demi Moore. 12. 'Gettysburg'. 13. James Mason. 14. 'The Trench'. 15. Gregory Peck.

How much do you know about westerns? (1)

QUESTIONS..

Who played the two main antagonists in the following films?

1. Duel in the Sun?

2. Jubal ?

3. The Man from Laramie?

4. Unforgiven?

5. Johnny Guitar?

6. The Comancheros?

7. The Big Country?

8. The Professionals?

9. Last Train from Gun Hill?

10. Across the Wide Missouri?

11. 3.10 to Yuma?

12. Vera Cruz?

13. The Naked Spur?

14. True Grit?

15. Gunfight at the O.K. Corral?

ANSWERS.
1. Gregory Peck and Jennifer Jones. 2. Glenn Ford and Rod Steiger. 3. James Stewart and Arthur Kennedy. 4. Clint Eastwood and Gene Hackman. 5. Joan Crawford and Mercedes McCambridge. 6. John Wayne and Nehemiah Persoff. 7. Burl Ives and Charles Bickford. 8. Lee Marvin and Jack Palance. 9. Kirk Douglas and Anthony Quinn 10. Clark Gable and Ricardo Montalban. 11. Van Heflin and Glenn Ford. 12. Gary Cooper and Burt Lancaster. 13. James Stewart and Robert Ryan. 14. John Wayne and Robert Duvall. 15. Burt Lancaster and Lyle Betger.

How much do you know about westerns? (2)

QUESTIONS.

1. Which unknown actress gained stardom in the notorious western 'The Outlaw'?

2. Who played the part of Marshal Will Kane in 'High Noon'?

3. And which young actress at the beginning of her career played his wife?

4. And who sang the song in the background?

5. Who played the part of 'The Searchers'?

6. And who played the part of the young girl for whom they were searching?

7. Who played the part of the Indian chief Cochise in 'Broken Arrow'?

8. Who played the part of the eponymous hero 'Shane'?

9. Who played the female lead in 'Rio Bravo' opposite John Wayne?

10. Who played the name part in Joan Crawford's western 'Johnny Guitar'?

11. Who played the lead in the film version of Stephen Crane's best-seller 'The Red Badge of Courage'?

12. Who played the female lead opposite Burt Lancaster in the 1960 film 'The Unforgiven'?

13. Marlene Dietrich made two westerns in her career. The first was 'Destry Rides Again'. What was the other?

14. Who played the female lead opposite Gregory Peck in the 1968 film 'The Stalking Moon'?

15. What was the first film in which John Wayne played the part of Rooster Cogburn?

ANSWERS.
1. Jane Russell. 2. Gary Cooper. 3. Grace Kelly. 4. Gene Autry. 5. John Wayne and Jeffery Hunter. 6. Natalie Wood. 7. Jeff Chandler. 8. Alan Ladd. 9. Angie Dickenson. 10. Sterling Hayden. 11. Audie Murphy. 12. Audrey Hepburn. 13. 'Rancho Notorious'. 14. Eve Marie Saint. 15. 'True Grit'.

How much do you know about westerns? (3)

QUESTIONS.

1. Who were the four male leads in the 1985 western 'Silverado'?

2. Who directed 'Silverado'?

3. Which British comedian/comic actor had a cameo role in 'Silverado' as Sheriff of a small western town?

4. Which two Western legends starred together in the 1962 film 'Ride the High Country'?

5. And which legendary director of artistic violence directed it?

6. What was the title of the 1969 Western also directed by Peckinpah which starred William Holden, Robert Ryan and Ernest Borgnine?

7. Who was the actor, better known for his roles in sophisticated comedies who starred as the patriarch in the 1954 western 'Broken Lance'?

8. What was the title of the great song written for the film 'The Alamo' released in 1960?

9. Who played the lead role in the 2000 release 'All the Pretty Horses'?

10. What was the title of the 1954 release in which Burt Lancaster and Jean Peters played Indians at war with the whites?

11. Who was the star of the 1966 release 'The Appaloosa'?

12. Who played the male and female leads in the 1956 release 'Backlash'?

13. What was the title of the curiously compelling Sam Peckinpah western starring Jason Robards which was released in 1970?

14. Who played the two male lead roles of bank-robbing brothers in the 1963 Andrew McLaglen release 'Bandolero!'?

15. Who played the male lead in the 1952 release 'Where the River Bends'?

ANSWERS.
1. Scott Glenn; Kevin Costner; Kevin Kline and Danny Glover. 2. Lawrence Kasdan. 3. John Cleese. 4. Joel McCrea and Randolph Scott. 5. Sam Peckinpah. 6. 'The Wild Bunch'. 7. Spencer Tracy. 8. 'The Green Leaves of Summer'. 9. Matt Damon. 10. 'Apache'. 11. Marlon Brando. 12. Richard Widmark and Donna Reed, 13. 'The Ballad of Cable Hogue'. 14. James Stewart and Dean Martin. 15. James Stewart.

How much do you know about westerns? (4)

QUESTIONS.

1. Who directed and starred in the 1990 release 'Dances with Wolves'?

2. Who starred in the 1950 release 'Dallas'?

3. Who played the name part in the 1955 release 'Davy Crockett'?

4. Who played the lead role in the 1996 release 'Dead Man'?

5. Who played the three principal roles in the 1954 release 'Garden of Evil'?

6. Who starred in the 1958 release 'Buchanan Rides Alone'?

7. Who played the young soldier in the 1999 release 'Ride With The Devil'?

8. Who played the lead role in the 1964 release 'Rio Conchos'?

9. Who played the male and female leads in the 1954 release 'River of No Return'?

10. What was the name of the actor who appeared in a series of spaghetti Westerns in the 1970''s as the character 'Trinity'?

11. Who starred in the 1952 release 'The Big Sky'?

12. Who played the name part in the 1970 release 'A Man Called Horse'?

13. Who played the main antagonists in the 1958 release 'Man of the West'?

14. Who played the part of the baddie Liberty Valance in the 1962 release 'The Man Who Shot Liberty Valance'?

15. Who played the two male leads in the 1969 release 'Butch Cassidy and the Sundance Kid'?

ANSWERS.
1. Kevin Costner. 2. Gary Cooper. 3. Fess Parker. 4. Johnny Depp. 5. Gary Cooper; Susan Hayward and Richard Widmark. 6. Randolph Scott. 7. Skeet Ulrich. 8. Richard Boone. 9. Robert Mitchum and Marilyn Monroe. 10. Terence Hill. 11. Kirk Douglas. 12. Richard Harris. 13. Gary Cooper and Lee J. Cobb. 14. Lee Marvin. 15. Paul Newman and Robert Redford

The Oscars

1927-28

Best Picture: Wings

Best Actor: Emil Jannings,
   "The Last Command," and "The Way
   of All Flesh"

Best Actress: Janet Gaynor, "Seventh
   Heaven," "Street Angel" and "Sunrise"

Best Director: Frank Borzage, "Seventh
   Heaven"

1928-29

Best Picture: Broadway Melody

Best Actor: Warner Baxter, "In Old
   Arizona"

Best Actress: Mary Pickford, "Coquette"

Best Director: Frank Lloyd, "The Divine
   Lady"

1929-30

Best Picture: All Quiet On the Western
   Front

Best Actor: George Arliss, "Disraeli"

Best Actress: Norma Shearer, "The
   Divorcee"

Best Director: Lewis Milestone, "All
   Quiet On the Western Front"

1930-31

Best Picture: Cimarron

Best Actor: Lionel Barrymore, "A Free
   Soul"

Best Actress: Marie Dressler, "Min and
   Bill"

Best Director: Norman Taurog, "Skippy"

1931-32

Best Picture: Grand Hotel

Best Actor: Wallace Beery, "The Champ"
   and Frederic March, "Dr. Jekyll and Mr.
   Hyde" (tie)

Best Actress: Helen Hayes, "The Sin of
   Madelon Claudet"

Best Director: Frank Borzage, "Bad Girl"

1932-33

Best Picture: Cavalcade

Best Actor: Charles Laughton, "The
   Private Life of Henry VIII"

Best Actress: Katharine Hepburn,
   "Morning Glory"

Best Director: Frank Lloyd, "Cavalcade"

1934

Best Picture: It Happened One Night

Best Actor: Clark Gable, "It Happened
   One Night"

Best Actress: Claudette Colbert, "It
   Happened One Night"

Best Director: Frank Capra, "It Happened
   One Night"

1935

Best Picture: Mutiny on the Bounty

Best Actor: Victor McLaglen, "The
   Informer"

Best Actress: Bette Davis, "Dangerous"

Best Director: John Ford, "The Informer"
   1936

Best Picture: The Great Ziegfeld

Best Actor: Paul Muni, "The Story of

Louis Pasteur"

Best Actress: Luise Rainer, "The Great Ziegfeld"

Best Director: Frank Capra, "Mr. Deeds Goes to Town"

1937

Best Picture: The Life of Emile Zola

Best Actor: Spencer Tracy, "Captains Courageous"

Best Actress: Luise Rainer, "The Good Earth"

Best Director: Leo McCarey, "The Awful Truth"

1938

Best Picture: You Can't Take It With You

Best Actor: Spencer Tracy, "Boys Town"

Best Actress: Bette Davis, "Jezebel"

Best Director: Frank Capra, "You Can't Take It With You"

1939

Best Picture: Gone With The Wind

Best Actor: Robert Donat, "Goodbye, Mr. Chips"

Best Actress: Vivien Leigh, "Gone With The Wind"

Best Director: Victor Fleming, "Gone With The Wind"

1940

Best Picture: Rebecca

Best Actor: James Stewart, "The Philadelphia Story"

Best Actress: Ginger Rogers, "Kitty Foyle"

Best Director: John Ford, "The Grapes of Wrath"

1941

Best Picture: How Green Was My Valley

Best Actor: Gary Cooper, "Sergeant York"

Best Actress: Joan Fontaine, "Suspicion"

Best Director: John Ford, "How Green Was My Valley"

1942

Best Picture: Mrs. Miniver

Best Actor: James Cagney, "Yankee Doodle Dandy"

Best Actress: Greer Garson, "Mrs. Miniver"

Best Director: William Wyler, "Mrs. Miniver"

1943

Best Picture: Casablanca

Best Actor: Paul Lukas, "Watch on the Rhine"

Best Actress: Jennifer Jones, "The Song of Bernadette"

Best Director: Michael Curtis, "Casablanca"

1944

Best Picture: Going My Way

Best Actor: Bing Crosby, "Going My Way"

Best Actress: Ingrid Bergman, "Gaslight"

Best Director: Leo McCarey, "Going My Way"

1945

Best Picture: The Lost Weekend

Best Actor: Ray Milland, "The Lost Weekend"

Best Actress: Joan Crawford, "Mildred Pierce"

Best Director: Billy Wilder, "The Lost Weekend"

1946

Best Picture: The Best Years of Our Lives

Best Actor: Frederic March, "The Best Years of Our Lives"

Best Actress: Olivia de Havilland, "To Each His Own"

Best Director: William Wyler, "The Best Years of Our Lives"

1947

Best Picture: Gentleman's Agreement

Best Actor: Ronald Coleman, "A Double Life"

Best Actress: Loretta Young, "The Farmer's Daughter"

Best Director: Elia Kazan, "Gentleman's Agreement"

1948

Best Picture: Hamlet

Best Actor: Laurence Olivier, "Hamlet"

Best Actress: Jane Wyman, "Johnny Belinda"

Best Director: John Huston, "Treasure of The Sierra Madre"

1949

Best Picture: All The King's Men

Best Actor: Broderick Crawford, "All The King's Men"

Best Actress: Olivia de Havilland, "The Heiress"

Best Director: Joseph L. Mankiewicz, "A Letter to Three Wives"

1950

Best Picture: All About Eve

Best Actor: Jose Ferrer, "Cyrano de Bergerac"

Best Actress: Judy Holliday, "Born Yesterday"

Best Director: Joseph L. Mankiewicz, "All About Eve"

1951

Best Picture: An American In Paris

Best Actor: Humphrey Bogart, "The African Queen"

Best Actress: Vivien Leigh, "A Streetcar Named Desire"

Best Director: George Stevens, "A Place In the Sun"

1952

Best Picture: The Greatest Show On Earth

Best Actor: Gary Cooper, "High Noon"

Best Actress: Shirley Booth, "Come Back, Little Sheba"

Best Director: John Ford, "The Quiet Man"

1953

Best Picture: From Here To Eternity

Best Actor: William Holden, "Stalag 17"

Best Actress: Audrey Hepburn, "Roman Holiday"

Best Director: Fred Zinnemann, "From Here To Eternity"

1954

Best Picture: On The Waterfront

Best Actor: Marlon Brando, "On The Waterfront"

Best Actress: Grace Kelly, "The Country Girl"

Best Director: Elia Kazan, "On The Waterfront"

1955

Best Picture: Marty

Best Actor: Ernest Borgnine, "Marty"

Best Actress: Anna Magnani, "The Rose Tattoo"

Best Director: Delbert Mann, "Marty"

1956

Best Picture: Around the World In 80 Days

Best Actor: Yul Brynner, "The King and I"

Best Actress: Ingrid Bergman, "Anastasia"

Best Director: George Stevens, "Giant"

1957

Best Picture: The Bridge on the River Kwai

Best Actor: Alec Guinness, "The Bridge on the River Kwai"

Best Actress: Joanne Woodward, "The Three Faces of Eve"

Best Director: David Lean, "The Bridge on the River Kwai"

1958

Best Picture: Gigi

Best Actor: David Niven, "Separate Tables"

Best Actress: Susan Hayward, "I Want To Live!"

Best Director: Vincente Minelli, "Gigi"

1959

Best Picture: Ben-Hur

Best Actor: Charlton Heston, "Ben-Hur"

Best Actress: Simone Signoret, "Room at the Top"

Best Director: William Wyler, "Ben-Hur"

1960

Best Picture: The Apartment

Best Actor: Burt Lancaster, "Elmer Gantry"

Best Actress: Elizabeth Taylor, "Butterfield 8"

Best Director: Billy Wilder, "The Apartment"

1961

Best Picture: West Side Story

Best Actor: Maximillian Schell, "Judgment at Nuremberg"

Best Actress: Sophia Loren, "Two Women"

Best Director: Robert Wise and Jerome Robbins, "West Side Story"

1962

Best Picture: Lawrence of Arabia

Best Actor: Gregory Peck, "To Kill A Mockingbird"

Best Actress: Anne Bancroft, "The Miracle Worker"

Best Director: David Lean, "Lawrence of Arabia"

1963

Best Picture: Tom Jones

Best Actor: Sidney Poitier, "Lilies of the Field"

Best Actress: Patricia Neal, "Hud"

Best Director: Tony Richardson, "Tom Jones"

1964

Best Picture: My Fair Lady

Best Actor: Rex Harrison, "My Fair Lady"

Best Actress: Julie Andrews, "Mary Poppins"

Best Director: George Cukor, "My Fair Lady"

1965

Best Picture: The Sound of Music

Best Actor: Lee Marvin, "Cat Ballou"

Best Actress: Julie Christie, "Darling"

Best Director: Robert Wise, "The Sound of Music"

1966

Best Picture: A Man For All Seasons

Best Actor: Paul Scofield, "A Man For All Seasons"

Best Actress: Elizabeth Taylor, "Who's Afraid of Virginia Woolf?"

Best Director: Fred Zinnemann, "A Man For All Seasons"

1967

Best Picture: In the Heat of the Night

Best Actor: Rod Steiger, "In the Heat of the Night"

Best Actress: Katharine Hepburn, "Guess Who's Coming to Dinner"

Best Director: Mike Nichols, "The Graduate"

1968

Best Picture: Oliver!

Best Actor: Cliff Robertson, "Charly"

Best Actress: Katharine Hepburn, "The Lion in Winter" and Barbra Streisand, "Funny Girl" (tie)

Best Director: Carol Reed, "Oliver!"

1969

Best Picture: Midnight Cowboy

Best Actor: John Wayne, "True Grit"

Best Actress: Maggie Smith, "The Prime of Miss Jean Brodie"

Best Director: John Schlesinger, "Midnight Cowboy"

1970

est Picture: Patton

Best Actor: George C. Scott, "Patton"

Best Actress: Glenda Jackson, "Women in Love"

Best Director: Franklin J. Schaffner, "Patton"

1971

Best Picture: The French Connection

Best Actor: Gene Hackman, "The French Connection"

Best Actress: Jane Fonda, "Klute"

Best Director: William Friedkin, "The French Connection"

1972

Best Picture: The Godfather

Best Actor: Marlon Brando, "The Godfather"

Best Actress: Liza Minelli, "Cabaret"

Best Director: Bob Fosse, "Cabaret"

1973

Best Picture: The Sting

Best Actor: Jack Lemmon, "Save the Tiger"

Best Actress: Glenda Jackson, "A Touch of Class"

Best Director: George Roy Hill, "The Sting"

1974

Best Picture: The Godfather, Part II

Best Actor: Art Carney, "Harry and Tonto"

Best Actress: Ellen Burstyn, "Alice Doesn't Live Here Anymore"

Best Director: Francis Ford Coppola, "The Godfather, Part II"

1975

Best Picture: One Flew Over the Cuckoo's Nest

Best Actor: Jack Nicholson, "One Flew Over the Cuckoo's Nest"

Best Actress: Louise Fletcher, "One Flew Over the Cuckoo's Nest"

Best Director: Milos Forman, "One Flew Over the Cuckoo's Nest"

1976

Best Picture: Rocky

Best Actor: Peter Finch, "Network"

Best Actress: Faye Dunaway, "Network"

Best Director: John G. Avildsen, "Rocky"

1977

Best Picture: Annie Hall

Best Actor: Richard Dreyfuss, "The Goodbye Girl"

Best Actress: Diane Keaton, "Annie Hall"

Best Director: Woody Allen, "Annie Hall"

1978

Best Picture: The Deer Hunter

Best Actor: Jon Voight, "Coming Home"

Best Actress: Jane Fonda, "Coming Home"

Best Director: Michael Cimino, "The Deer Hunter"

1979

Best Picture: Kramer vs. Kramer

Best Actor: Dustin Hoffman, "Kramer vs. Kramer"

Best Actress: Sally Field, "Norma Rae"

Best Director: Robert Benton, "Kramer vs. Kramer"

1980

Best Picture: Ordinary People

Best Actor: Robert De Niro, "Raging Bull"

Best Actress: Sissy Spacek, "Coal Miner's Daughter"

Best Director: Robert Redford, "Ordinary People"

1981

Best Picture: Chariots of Fire

Best Actor: Henry Fonda, "On Golden Pond"

Best Actress: Katharine Hepburn, "On Golden Pond"

Best Director: Warren Beatty, "Reds"

1982

Best Picture: Gandhi

Best Actor: Ben Kingsley, "Gandhi"

Best Actress: Meryl Streep, "Sophie's Choice"

Best Director: Richard Attenborough, "Gandhi"

1983

Best Picture: Terms of Endearment

Best Actor: Robert Duvall, "Tender Mercies"

Best Actress: Shirley MacLaine, "Terms of Endearment"

Best Director: James L. Brooks, "Terms of Endearment"

1984

Best Picture: Amadeus

Best Actor: F. Murray Abraham, "Amadeus"

Best Actress: Sally Field, "Places in the Heart"

Best Director: Milos Forman, "Amadeus"

1985

Best Picture: Out of Africa

Best Actor: William Hurt, "Kiss of the Spider Woman"

Best Actress: Geraldine Page, "The Trip to Bountiful"

Best Director: Sydney Pollack, "Out of Africa"

1986

Best Picture: Platoon

Best Actor: Paul Newman, "The Color of Money"

Best Actress: Marlee Matlin, "Children of a Lesser God"

Best Director: Oliver Stone, "Platoon"

1987

Best Picture: The Last Emperor

Best Actor: Michael Douglas, "Wall Street"

Best Actress: Cher, "Moonstruck"

Best Director: Bernardo Bertolucci, "The Last Emperor"

1988

Best Picture: Rain Man

Best Actor: Dustin Hoffman, "Rain Man"

Best Actress: Jodie Foster, "The Accused"

Best Director: Barry Levinson, "Rain Man"

1989

Best Picture: Driving Miss Daisy

Best Actor: Daniel Day-Lewis, "My Left Foot"

Best Actress: Jessica Tandy, "Driving Miss Daisy"

Best Director: Oliver Stone, "Born on the Fourth of July"

1990

Best Picture: Dances With Wolves

Best Actor: Jeremy Irons, "Reversal of Fortune"

Best Actress: Kathy Bates, "Misery"

Best Director: Kevin Costner, "Dances With Wolves"

1991

Best Picture: The Silence of the Lambs

Best Actor: Anthony Hopkins, "The Silence of the Lambs"

Best Actress: Jodie Foster, "The Silence of the Lambs"

Best Director: Jonathan Demme, "The Silence of the Lambs"

1992

Best Picture: Unforgiven

Best Actor: Al Pacino, "Scent of a Woman"

Best Actress: Emma Thompson, "Howard's End"

Best Director: Clint Eastwood, "Unforgiven"

1993

Best Picture: Schindler's List

Best Actor: Tom Hanks, "Philadelphia"

Best Actress: Holly Hunter, "The Piano"

Best Director: Steven Spielberg, "Schindler's List"

1994

Best Picture: Forrest Gump

Best Actor: Tom Hanks, "Forrest Gump"

Best Actress: Jessica Lange, "Blue Sky"

Best Director: Robert Zemeckis, "Forrest Gump"

1995

Best Picture: Braveheart

Best Actor: Nicolas Cage, "Leaving Las Vegas"

Best Actress: Susan Sarandon, "Dead Man Walking"

Best Director: Mel Gibson, "Braveheart"

1996

Best Picture: The English Patient

Best Actor: Geoffrey Rush, "Shine"

Best Actress: Frances McDormand, "Fargo"

Best Director: Anthony Minghella, "The English Patient"

1997

Best Picture: Titanic

Best Actor: Jack Nicholson, "As Good As it Gets"

Best Actress: Helen Hunt, "As Good As it Gets"

Best Director: James Cameron, "Titanic"

1998

Best Picture: Shakespeare in Love

Best Actor: Roberto Benigni, "Life is Beautiful"

Best Actress: Gwyneth Paltrow, "Shakespeare in Love"

Best Director: Steven Spielberg, "Saving Private Ryan"

1999

Best Picture: American Beauty

Best Actor: Kevin Spacey, "American Beauty"

Best Actress: Hilary Swank, "Boys Don't Cry"

Best Director: Sam Mendes, "American Beauty"

2000

Best Picture: Gladiator

Best Actor: Russell Crowe, "Gladiator"

Best Actress: Julia Roberts, "Erin Brockovich"

Best Director: Steven Soderbergh, "Traffic"

Television

How much do you know about TV comedy? (1)

QUESTIONS.

1. Everybody knows who the stars of 'Absolutely Fabulous' were, but who played the part of Jennifer Saunder's mother?

2. And who played her daughter, Saffron?

3. And who played her dizzy secretary, Bubble?

4. Whose impressions of Angela Rippon and Janet-Street-Porter were high spots of the 1979-82 series 'Not the Nine O' Clock News?

5. Which two members of the 'Not the Nine O' Clock News' team went on to host their own show from 1982 to 1987 and from 1990 to 1995

6. And the name of their show?

7. Whole generations of youngsters had to stay on at school to unlearn everything they had learned about British history from the ''Blackadder' series. OK, we all know who played Blackadder, but who played his companion, the repugnant Baldrick?

8. Who played Queen Elizabeth I in 'Blackadder II'?

9. And who were the other three stalwarts of the series, appearing and reappearing in different roles?

10. Who plays the title role in the series 'Frasier'?

11. Who plays the part of his father Marty, an ex-policeman?

12. Who plays the part of his brother Niles, another psychiatrist?

13. Who plays the part of his studio producer, Roz?

14. Who plays the part of Daphne, a Mancunian physiotherapist, and love of Niles' life?

15. Who plays the part of Lilith, Frasier's ex-wife who pops up from time to time?

ANSWERS.
1. June Whitfield. 2. Julie Sawalha. 3. Jane Horrocks. 4. Pamela Stephenson. 5. Mel Smith and Griff Rhys Jones. 6. Alas Smith and Jones. 7. Tony Robinson. 8. Miranda Richardson. 9. Tim McInnerny, Stephen Fry and Hugh Laurie. 10. Kelsey Grammar. 11. John Mahoney. 12. David Hyde Pierce. 13. Peri Gilpin. 14. Jane Leeves. 15. Bebe Neuwirth.

How much do you know about TV comedy? (2)

QUESTIONS.

1. What was the name of the 1990-98 series set in the newsroom of Globelink TV?

2. Who played the part of the slightly batty office manager, Gus Hedges?

3. Who played the parts of the continuously feuding newsreaders, Henry Davenport and Sally Smedley? 4. Who was the actress who brought a dark, somewhat anarchic quality to the role of the personal assistant, Joy?

5. 'Happy Days' 1974-84, was one of the most popular series in the US. What was the nickname of the minor character who literally hi-jacked the programme?

6. Who was the actor who played the role?

7. The show gave birth to two spin-offs. 'One was 'Laverne and Shirley'. What was the other?

8. Mork was an extra-terrestrial. From which planet?

9. It gave which actor his first major exposure on the way to stardom?

10. Who played the starring role in the 1988-98 series 'Murphy Brown'?

11. The programme was set in which city?

12. Who was the star of the series about life inside, 'Porridge'?

13. What was the name of his character?

14. Who played the part of his naïve cell-mate, Godber?

15. And who played the part of the slightly sadistic Chief Officer Mackay?

ANSWERS.
1. 'Drop the Dead Donkey'. 2. Robert Duncan. 3. David Swift and Victoria Wicks.
4. Susannah Doyle. 5. 'The Fonz'. 6. Henry Winkler. 7. 'Mork and Mindy'. 8. Ork. 9. Robin Williams. 10. Candice Bergen. 11. Washington DC. 12. Ronnie Barker.
13. Norman Stanley Fletcher. 14. Richard Beckinsale. 15. Fulton MacKay.

How much do you know about TV comedy? (3)

QUESTIONS.

1. What was the name of the cult Sci-Fi/Comedy sitcom which first came to the screen in 1988, about the last human being alive?

2. He was a 23rd century Liverpudlian of somewhat dubious hygienic habits. His name?

3. And he was played by ....Which actor?

4. Of course he wasn't alone. There was a hologram of his ex-boss, whose name was .....?

5. Played by ......?

6. And over the centuries in stasis the ship's cat had evolved into a very cool, vain humanoid. Unfortunately for 'Cat' he had a very un-cool alter-ego by the name of ......what?

7. Who was the actor who played the part of 'Cat'?

8. And finally there was an android for the domestic duties. What was he called?

9. What was the name of the actor who played 'Kryten'?

10. 'Holly' the ship's computer was originally played by .....who?

11. But changed sex somewhere along the line and was later played by a female, stand-up comedian. What was her name?

12. A recurring character in the series was Kochanski, Lister's unrequited, holographic love interest. What was the name of the singer who played this role?

13. Who was the young actress who took over this role?

14. What was the title of the first episode?

15. Who made a guest appearance in the episode entitled 'Timeslides' (season 3)?

ANSWERS.
1. 'Red Dwarf'. 2. 'Dave Lister'. 3. Craig Charles. 4. Arnold Rimmer. 5. Chris Barrie. 6. Duane Dibley. 7. Danny John-Jules. 8. 'Kryten'. 9. Robert Llewellyn. 10. Norman Lovett. 11. Hattie Hayridge. 12. Claire Grogan. 13. Chloe Annett. 14. 'The End'. 14. Koo Stark.

How much do you know about TV comedy? (4)

QUESTIONS.

1. Classic sixties sitcom about a character called Rob Petrie, head TV comedy writer for the fictional Alan Brady Show, set in New York, created by Carl Reiner,....which show are we talking about?

2. What was the name of Rob Petrie's wife in the series?

3. And which young actress on her way to stardom played the part?

4. And which actress played the part of Rob Petrie's man-hungry colleague?

5. And who played the part of his other colleague, Buddy Sorrell?

6. Which series, which ran from 1970 to 1977, was set in the newsroom of fictitious TV station WJM-TV in Minneapolis?

7. Who played the part of MTM's irascible boss, Lou Grant?

8. There were five shows which came about as spin-offs, based on characters from the MTM Show. Can you name any of them?

9. Which actors took the roles immortalised by Jack Lemmon and Walter Matthau in the screen version of the Neil Simon play 'The Odd Couple' when it was transferred to TV?

10. A female version of 'The Odd Couple' ran from 1984-88. What was it called?

11. And who were the stars?

12. Jane Curtin went on to have a romance with an alien disguised as a college professor, when she could get him away from his three alien colleagues, In what show?

13. Who played the alien professor?

14. Who starred in the '60's series 'I Dream Of Jeannie' about an astronaut and a genie?

15. And who played the part of Jeannie?

ANSWERS.
1. The Dick Van Dyke Show. 2. Laura. 3. Mary Tyler Moore. 4. Rose Marie. 5. Morey Amsterdam. 6. The Mary Tyler Moore Show. 7. Edward Asner. 8. Lou Grant; Rhoda; Phyllis; The Love Boat and The Betty White Show. 9. Tony Randall and Jack Klugman. 10. 'Kate and Allie' 11. Susan Saint James and Jane Curtin 12. 'Third Rock From The Sun'. 13. John Lithgow. 14. Larry Hagman. 15. Barbara Eden.

How much do you know about TV comedy? (5)

QUESTIONS.

1. What was the name of the comedy series which ran from 1951 to 1961, being virtually the prototype sitcom, and established Lucille Ball as TV's favourite comedienne?

2. Her co-star in the series was her real-life Cuban-born husband. What was his name?

3. What was the name of their production company which filmed the series?

4. From 1961 to 1972 Lucille, now divorced from Desi,, continued with a second series. What was it called?

5. In the second series (which included a title change) she played a Connecticut widow and mother of two. What was her character's name?

6. What was the title of the series which ran originally 1968-77, about the adventures of a Home Guard platoon in the second world war?

7. In which fictitious English south coast town was the series set?

8. Who was the officer in charge of the platoon?

9. And who was the actor who played that role?

10. Who took the part of the diffident lady-killer, Sergeant Wilson?

11. Who played the part of the butcher, Jones, who was the platoon's corporal and the only member of the platoon with real military experience?

12. Who came up with the idea for the show, and were the motive forces behind it?

13. What was the title of the series which ran from 1985 until 1989 set in 'The Blue Moon' Los Angeles private detective agency?

14. Who were the two stars?

15. What were the names of the characters they played?

ANSWERS.
1. 'I Love Lucy'. 2. Desi Arnaz. 3. Desilu. 4. 'The Lucy Show/Here's Lucy' 5. 'Lucy Carmichael'. 6. 'Dad's Army'. 7. Walmington-on-Sea. 8. Captain Mainwaring. 9. Arthur Lowe. 10. John Le Mesurier. 11. Clive Dunn. 12. Jimmy Perry and David Croft. 13. 'Moonlighting'. 14. Cybill Shepherd and Bruce Willis. 15. Maddie Hayes and David Addison.

How much do you know about TV comedy? (6)

QUESTIONS.

1. What was the title of the series which started in 1996 and was set in the offices of the Mayor of New York?

2. What was the name of the central character, the deputy Mayor?

3. And who was the actor who played the part?

4. Who played the part of Mayor Randall Winston?

5. What was the name of the character who was the Public Relations officer?

6. And what was the name of the character who represented black and gay rights in the office?

7. A show exploded onto the little screen in 1977 and ran until 1982. It broke all the rules of family sitcom at the time, outrageously sending up all competitive series and provoking storms of protest. It was hilarious. What was it called?

8. It was a launch platform for a young actor who went on to movie stardom. His name?

9. What was the name of the series that ran from 1972 to 1983, set in a mobile military hospital during the Korean War, developed from the 1970 Robert Altman film?

10. Who were the two main characters, doctors with an irreverent attitude to authority?

11. Who were the actors who played the parts?

12. What was the name – and nickname - of the senior nurse?

13. Who was the actress who played the part?

14. Who was Commanding Officer of the camp? And his replacement?

15. What was the name of the transvestite theatre assistant?

ANSWERS.
1. 'Spin City'. 2. Michael Flaherty. 3. Michael J. Fox.. 4. Barry Bostwick. 5. Paul Lassiter. 6. Carter Heywood. 7. 'Soap'. 8. Billy Crystal. 9. M.A.S.H. 10. 'Hawkeye Pierce' and 'Trapper John McIntyre'. 11. Alan Alda and Wayne Rogers. 12. Major Margaret 'Hotlips' Houlihan 13. Loretta Swit. 14. Lt. Col. Henry Blake/Col. Potter. 15. Cpl. Klinger.

How much do you know about TV comedy? (7)

QUESTIONS.

1. What were the names of the double series set at the heart of the British Government in the '80's?

2. What was the name of the central character?

3. In the first episode he was called into the Cabinet, in what function?

4. Who was the actor who played the part?

5. Within minutes of taking office he met his nemesis, the Head of the Civil Service in the department, by name ....?

6. Played by which distinguished actor?

7. What was the name of his Private Secretary?

8. Played by ....?

9. What was the name of the 1987-90 US show in which an ex-dancer for Les Dawson made good as a variety of characters?

10. This show became the launch-pad for which animated series, which was shown in segments between live-action sketches?

11. What was the name of the off-beat series that ran from 1990 until 1998, about a New York stand-up comedian and his immediate friends for whom everything ultimately goes wrong?

12. Who was the lead player?

13. Who played his ex-girlfriend Elaine?

14. Who played his side-kick, the luckless George?

15. Who played his neighbour with the hair, Cosmo Kramer?

ANSWERS.
1. 'Yes, Minister' and 'Yes, Prime Minister'. 2. Right Honourable James Hacker MP.
3. Minister for Administrative Affairs. 4. Paul Eddington. 5. Sir Humphrey Appleby.
6. Nigel Hawthorne. 7. Bernard Wooley. 8. Derek Fowlds. 9. The Tracey Ullman Show.
10. 'The Simpsons'. 11. 'Seinfeld'. 12. Jerry Seinfeld. 13. Julia Louis-Dreyfus.
14. Jason Alexander. 15. Michael Richards.

How much do you know about TV comedy? (8)

QUESTIONS.

1. What was the name of the series which gave birth to the 'Blues Brothers' and 'Wayne's World' routines, which independently, became movie successes?

2. Who created the roles of the Blues Brothers, in both SNL and the film?

3. And who created the 'Wayne's World routine and starred in the film?

4. Who was the luminary of the first season, who went on to film stardom?

5. Who were the hosts of the great 'Laugh-In' which dominated comedy 1967-73?

6. Who was the giggly blonde who went on to film fame and fortune?

7. Which other 'Laugh-In' regular has had a successful movie career since?

8. Who played the central character in the series 'Roseanne'?

9. Who played the role of Dan Connor, her husband?

10. And who played the part of her sister Jackie?

11. And of her mother, Bev?

12. And of her grandmother Mary?

13. With which other actress did Roseanne share a much-publicised lesbian kiss?

14. What was the name of the diner which Roseanne and Jackie ran in later episodes?

15. What were the names of the three Connor children in the series?

ANSWERS.
1. 'Saturday Night Live'. 2. John Belushi and Dan Aykroyd. 3. Mike Myers and Dana Carvey. 4. Chevy Chase. 5. Dan Rowan and Dick Martin. 6. Goldie Hawn. 7. Lily Tomlin. 8. Roseanne Barr. 9. John Goodman. 10. Laurie Metcalf. 11. Estelle Parsons. 12. Shelley Winters. 13. Mariel Hemingway. 14. The Lunch Box. 15. Becky, Darlene and D.J.

How much do you know about TV comedy? (9)

QUESTIONS.

1. What was the name of the lead character in the 1982 series 'Police Squad'?

2. Who was the actor who played the part, taking it onto movie success in the 'Naked Gun' series?

3. What was the name of the trailblazer of comedy series, set in an army post and featuring a fast-talking sergeant with the heart of a master confidence trickster?

4. What was the name of the lead character, played by Phil Silvers?

5. What was the name of his long-suffering camp commander?

6. Who was the actor who played this role?

7. What was the name of the unfortunate character billed as 'the biggest slob in the world'?

8. What show leaps to mind when you hear the catch-phrase 'And now for something completely different'?

9. Who was the star of 'It's a Square World'?

10. Who was the star of 'The Honeymooners'?

11. Who was the star of 'Home Improvements', playing a character called Tim Taylor?

12. What was the name of Taylor's next-door neighbour, hidden behind a fence?

13. What was the name of the series which ran from 1986 to 1993 about four middle-aged to elderly women sharing a house in Miami?

14. Who played the tall one, with acid tongue and venomous wit?

15. And who played the southern, man-hungry belle?

ANSWERS.
1. Detective Frank Drebin. 2. Leslie Nielsen. 3. 'The Phil Silvers Show'. 4. Sgt Ernie Bilko. 5. Col. John Hall. 6. Paul Ford. 7. Private Doberman. 8. 'Monty Python's Flying Circus'. 9. Michael Bentine. 10. Jackie Gleason. 11. Tim Allen. 12, Wilson. 13. 'Golden Girls'. 14. Bea Arthur. 15. Rue McClanahan.

How much do you know about TV comedy? (10)

1. What was the title of the long running series, 1982-93, set in a Boston bar?

2. Who played the lead part of Sam Malone?

3. What was his nickname, a leftover from his baseball days?

4. In the very first episode he persuaded a young woman to work in the bar. What was her name?

5. Who was the actress playing this part?

6. The first seasons were dominated by Sam and Diane's love/hate relationship, but eventually   she leaves him and goes off to marry a bar regular, a psychiatrist named ....?

7. Who was the other waitress, acid-tongued and sex-mad?

8. Who was the actress who played that role?

9. What was the name of the intellectually challenged, but very sweet, barman?

10. Who was the actor who played that role?

11. One of the true regulars in the bar was an unemployed, overweight accountant named Norm. Who was the actor playing that role?

12. After the death of the actor who played Coach, a new barman was hired. Who was the young actor who played this role?

13. After Diane's definitive departure, a new female lead entered. What was her name?

14. Who was the actress who played that role?

15. Who was the anally retentive mailman, a fount of dubious trivia, who seemed to spend as much time in the bar as Norm?

ANSWERS.

1. 'Cheers'. 2. Ted Danton. 3. 'Mayday'. 4. Diane Chambers. 5. Shelley Long.
6. Frasier Crane. 7. Carla Tortelli. 8. Rhea Perlman. 9. 'Coach' Pantuso. 10. Nicholas Colasanto. 11. George Wendt. 12. Woody Harrelson. 13. Rebecca Howe. 14. Kirstie Alley. 15. Cliff Clavin played by John Ratzenberger.

How much do you know about TV coppers? (1)

QUESTIONS.

1. Who played the part of P.C. 'Fancy' Smith in the original series of 'Z Cars'?

2. Who played the part of FBI Assistant Director Skinner in 'The X Files'?

3. Who played the name part in the series about Detective Superintendent 'Wycliffe'?

4. Who played the part of FBI Agent Dale Cooper in 'Twin Peaks'?

5. Who played the name part in the series about Detective Chief Inspector Jim 'Taggart'?

6. Who were the two male leads in the series 'The Sweeney'?

7. Who were the two male leads in the series ;The Streets of San Francisco'?

8. Who were the two male leads in the series 'Starsky and Hutch'?

9. Who played the role of Sergeant Suzanne 'Pepper' Anderson in the series 'Police Woman'?

10. Who played the part of the policeman who was also a masterchef, Henry Crabbe in 'Pie In The Sky'?

11. Who played the part of Det. Andy Sipowicz in the series 'NYPD Blue'?

12. Who were the two male leads in the series 'Miami Vice'?

13. Who played the leading roles in the police series 'McMillan and Wife'?

14. Who played the title role in the series 'A Man Called Ironside'?

15. Who played the title role in the series 'Kojak'?

ANSWERS.
1. Brian Blessed. 2. Mitch Pileggi. 3. Jack Shepherd. 4. Kyle MacLachlan.
5. Mark McManus. 6. John Thaw and Dennis Waterman. 7. Karl Malden and Michael Douglas. 8. Paul Michael Glaser and David Soul. 9. Angie Dickinson. 10. Richard Griffiths. 11. Dennis Franz. 12. Don Johnson and Philip Michael Thomas. 13. Rock Hudson and Susan St. James. 14. Raymond Burr. 15. Telly Savalas.

How much do you know about TV coppers? (2)

QUESTIONS.

1. Who played the male and female leads in the series 'CSI: Crime Scene Investigation'?

2. Who played the part of Detective Inspector Frank Burnside in the early days of 'The Bill'?

3. Who played the name part in the series about Det. Sgt. Jim 'Bergerac'?

4. Who played the name parts in the series 'Cagney and Lacey'?

5. What was the name of the series which featured Robbie Coltrane as criminal psychologist Eddie 'Fitz' Fitzgerald?

6. Who played the role of Det. Supt. Andrew Dalziell in the series 'Dalziell and Pascoe'?

7. Who were the male and female leads in the series 'Dempsey and Makepeace'?

8. What was the name of the series starring Jack Webb as 'Sgt. Joe Friday'?

9. The series called 'The FBI' featured a character named Inspector Lewis Erskine. Who played this role?

10. Who played the part of Lt. Philip Gerard who spent a whole series in pursuit of 'The Fugitive'?

11. Who was the star of the series 'Hawaii Five-0'?

12. Who played the part of PC Nick Rowan in the series 'Heartbeat'?

13. Who played the part of Captain Frank Furillo in 'Hill Street Blues'?

14. Who played the title role in the TV series based upon the books of Ngaio Marsh, 'The Inspector Alleyn Mysteries'?

15. Everyone knows that the part of Inspector Morse was played by John Thaw, but who played his assistant Det. Sgt. Lewis?

ANSWERS.
1. William Petersen and Marg Helgenberger. 2. Christopher Ellison. 3. John Nettles. 4. Tyne Daly and Sharon Gless. 5. 'Cracker'. 6. Warren Clarke. 7. Michael Brandon and Glynis Barber. 8. 'Dragnet'. 9. Efrem Zimbalist Jnr. 10. Barry Morse. 11. Jack Lord. 12. Nick Berry. 13. Daniel Travanti. 14. Patrick Malahide. 15. Kevin Whately.

How much do you know about TV Private Eyes?

QUESTIONS.

1. Who was the star of the series about a private detective named 'Mannix'?

2. What was the name of the series about a detective agency called 'The Blue Moon'?

3. And who were the two stars?

4. Who played the part of that aristocratic private eye, Lord Peter Wimsey?

5. And who lived the role of 'Magnum PI'?

6. Who was the star of the series 'The Rockford Files'?

7. Everybody knows that the part of 'Remington Steele' was played by Pierce Brosnan, but who was his leading lady?

8. Who played the lead in the series 'Spenser, For Hire'?

9. Who played the part of the classic detective with the classic white Rolls Royce, 'Sexton Blake'?

10. Another member of the Zimbalist family found honest employment in the series '77 Sunset Strip'. That was Efrem who played the part of Stuart Bailey. But who played his partner Jeff Spencer?

11. What was the British private eye series, in which one of the partners is a ghost?

12. What was the name of the private detective frequently called in by 'Perry Mason'?

13. Who starred in the series based upon the books by Lady Antonia Fraser 'Jemima Shore Investigates'?

14. Who was the well-known actor who gave his voice to the unseen Charlie Townshend in the series 'Charlie's Angels'?

15. Who was the star of the series 'Banacek'?

ANSWERS.
1. Mike Connors. 2. 'Moonlighting'. 3. Cybill Hayes and Bruce Willis. 4. Ian Carmichael. 5. Tom Selleck. 6. James Garner. 7. Stephanie Zimbalist. (as Laura Holt). 8. Robert Urich. 9. Laurence Payne. 10. Roger Smith. 11. 'Randall and Hopkirk (Deceased). 12. Paul Drake (played by William Hopper). 13. Patricia Hodge. 14. John Forsythe. 15. George Peppard.

How much do you know about TV science fiction?

QUESTIONS.

1. Who played the leading male part in the series 'V'?

2. And what were the aliens really like, beneath their fake human skins?

3. Who played the part of Professor Maximilian Arturo in 'Sliders'?

4. Who starred in the series 'The Time Tunnel'?

5. Everyone knows that William Shatner played the part of Captain James T. Kirk in the original series of 'Star Trek', but who knows what the 'T' stood for?

6. Who played the starring role as Captain Jean-Luc Picard in the series 'Star Trek – The Next Generation'?

7. And what was the name of the Captain in the third series 'Star Trek - Voyager'?

8. Who played the starring role of Commander Cisco of the Space Station in Star Trek – Deep Space Nine?

9. Who was the star of the series 'Quantum Leap'?

10. Who was the star of the series 'The Invaders'?

11. Who plays the part of the delightful and very brainy scientist Major Carter in 'Stargate SG1'?

12. Who were the married couple who played the leads in the series 'Space: 1999'?

13. Who was the star of the series 'Battleship Galactica'?

14. Who played the part of Blake in the series 'Blake's 7'?

15. Who was the famous British character actor who set his dignity aside to appear as Dr Goodfellow in the series 'Buck Rogers in the 25th Century'?

ANSWERS.
1. Marc Singer. 2. Lizards. 3. John Rhys-Davies. 4. James Darren. 5. Tiberius. 6. Patrick Stewart. 7. Capt. Catherine Janeway. 8. Avery Brooks. 9. Scott Bakula. 10. Roy Thinnes. 11. Amanda Tapping. 12. Martin Landau and Barbara Bain. 13. Lorne Greene. 14. Gareth Thomas. 15. Wilfred Hyde-White.

How much do you know about TV soap operas?

QUESTIONS.

1. Who played the starring role of 'Jock Ewing' in the original series of 'Dallas'?

2. And who was the original 'Miss Ellie', his wife?

3. Who played the part of 'Kathy Mitchell' in 'Eastenders'?

4. Who played the part of 'Elsie Tanner' in the early days of 'Coronation Street'?

5. Who played the part of 'Dominique Deveraux' in 'Dynasty'?

6. Which town was the setting for 'Dynasty'?

7. Who played the part of 'Charlie Fairhead' in 'Casualty'?

8. Who played the part of 'Meg Richardson' in the original 'Crossroads'?

9. Who played the part of 'Beth Jordache' in 'Brookside'?

10. Which fictitious London district is the setting for 'Eastenders'?

11. Who played the part of 'Charlene Mitchell' in 'Neighbours'?

12. Who played the part of 'Joshua Rush' in 'Knots Landing'?

13. Who played the part of 'Frank Tate' in 'Emmerdale'?

14. Who played the part of 'Emma Jackson' in 'Home and Away'?

15. Who played the part of 'Constance Colby' in 'The Colbys'?

ANSWERS.
1. Jim Davis. 2. Barbara Bel Geddes. 3. Gillian Taylforth. 4. Pat Phoenix. 5. Diahann Carroll. 6. Denver, Colorado. 7. Derek Thompson. 8. Noele Gordon. 9. Anna Friel. 10. 'Walford'. 11. Kylie Minogue. 12. Alec Baldwin. 13. Norman Bowler. 14. Dannii Minogue. 15. Barbara Stanwyck

How much do you know about TV westerns?

QUESTIONS.

1. Who was the star of the series 'Wanted, Dead or Alive'?

2. Who was the star of the series 'Wild Bill Hickock'?

3. Who was the star of the series 'The Restless Gun'?

4. Who played the part of Little Joe in the series 'Bonanza'?

5. Who played the part of 'Shotgun Slade'?

6. Who was the star of the series 'Wagon Train' and 'A Man Called Shenandoah'?

7. Who was the star of the series 'The Life and Legend of Wyatt Earp'?

8. Who played the part of 'The Virginian'?

9. What was the title of the western series that gave Clint Eastwood his big chance?

10. But who was the main star of the series?

11. And what was the name of the character of the cook, played by Paul Brinegar?

12. Who played the two male lead parts in the series 'Laramie'?

13. Who played Marshal Matt Dillon in the series 'Gunsmoke'?

14. Who played the starring role as Paladin the Gunfighter, in 'Have Gun, Will Travel'?

15. Who played the part of Cheyenne Bodie in the series 'Cheyenne'?

ANSWERS.
1. Steve McQueen. 2. Guy Madison. 3. John Payne. 4. Michael Landon. 5. Scott Brady. 6. Robert Horton. 7. Hugh O'Brian. 8. James Drury. 9. 'Rawhide'. 10. Eric Fleming 11.'Wishbone'. 12. John Smith and Robert Fuller. 13.James Arness. 14. Richard Boone. 15. Clint Walker.

8

FAMOUS

PERSONALITIES

Autobiographies

Whose autobiographies are these? (1)

QUESTIONS.

1. An American Comedy.

2. Blessings in Disguise.

3. I Owe Russia $2,000.

4. A Postillion Struck by Lightning.

5. What's It All About?

6. The Movies, Mr Griffith and Me.

7. One Man Tango.

8. Stand By Your Man.

9. My Wicked, Wicked Ways.

10. The Moon's A Balloon.

11. To Hell and Back.

12. Nostalgia Isn't What It Used To Be.

13. The Ragman's Son.

14. The Naked Civil Servant.

15. Life Is Too Short.

ANSWERS.
1. Harold Lloyd. 2. Alec Guinness. 3. Bob Hope 4. Dirk Bogarde. 5. Michael Caine.
6. Lilian Gish. 7. Anthony Quinn. 8. Tammy Wynette. 9. Errol Flynn. 10. David Niven.
11. Audie Murphy. 12. Simone Signoret. 13. Kirk Douglas. 14. Quentin Crisp.
15. Mickey Rooney.

Whose autobiographies are these? (2)

QUESTIONS.

1. In My Father's Court.
2. My American Journey.
3. Thursday's Child.
4. Tall, Dark and Gruesome.
5. Laughter In The Next Room.
6. Wanderer.
7. Absolutely Mahvelous.
8. Every Other Inch A Lady.
9. Dear Me..
10. Future Indefinite.
11. By Myself.
12. Citizen Jane.
13. Always Playing.
14. As It Happened.
15. Beginning.

ANSWERS.
1. Isaac Bashevis Singer. 2. Colin Powell. 3. Eartha Kitt. 4. Christopher Lee. 5. Osbert Sitwell. 6. Sterling Hayden. 7 Billy Crystal. 8. Beatrice Lilley. 9. Peter Ustinov. 10. Noel Coward. 11. Lauren Bacall. 12. Jane Fonda. 13. Nigel Kennedy. 14. Clement Attlee. 15. Kenneth Branagh.

Whose autobiographies are these? (3)

QUESTIONS.

1. The Eternal Male

2. Fire Over England.

3. Also Known As Shirley.

4. Beneath the Underdog.

5. Chronicles of Wasted Time.

6. Being Myself.

7. Good Vibrations.

8. Before I Forget.

9. The Good, the Bad and the Bubbly.

10. The Greatest Game of All.

11. Hollywood in a Suitcase.

12. Inside the Third Reich.

13. It Doesn't Take A Hero.

14. Leaving a Doll's House.

15. The Man Who Listens to Horses.

ANSWERS.
1. Omar Sharif. 2. Ken Russell. 3. Shelley Winters. 4. Charlie Mingus. 5. Malcolm Muggridge. 6. Martina Navratilova. 7. Evelyn Glennie. 8. James Mason. 9. George Best. 10. Jack Nicklaus. 11. Sammy Davis Jnr. 12. Albert Speer. 13. Norman Schwarzkopf. 14. Claire Bloom. 15. Monty Roberts.

Whose autobiographies are these? (4)

QUESTIONS.

1. Full Circle.

2. An American Life.

3. Hope Dies Last.

4. Unfinished Journey.

5. As Much As I Dare.

6. Free Agent.

7. Years of Upheaval.

8. The Path to Power/The Downing Street Years

9. This I Remember.

10. Battling For Peace.

11. A Path Of Hope.

12. Disturbing The Peace.

13. The Future Belongs To Freedom.

14. The View From The Kremlin.

15. Strange Places, Questionable People.

ANSWERS.
1. Sir Anthony Eden. 2. Ronald Reagan. 3. Alexander Dubcek. 4. Yehudi Menuhin.
5. Arnold Wesker. 6. Brian Crozier. 7. Henry Kissinger. 8. Margaret Thatcher.
9. Eleanor Roosevelt. 10. Shimon Peres. 11. Lech Walesa. 12. Vaclav Havel.
13. Eduard Shevardnadze. 14. Boris Yeltsin. 15. John Simpson

Whose autobiographies are these? (5)

QUESTIONS.

1.   An Accidental M.P.

2.   Roar of the Crowd.

3.   Peacework.

4.   Me.

5.   Walking Tall.

6.   A Tree is a Tree.

7.   Memoirs of a Professional Cad.

8.   The Life of an American Workman.

9.   Precious Little Sleep.

10. Why Me?

11. With Nails.

12. You See, I Haven't Forgotten.

13. Galina.

14. I Put A Spell On You.

15. On My Way To The Club.

ANSWERS.
1. Martin Bell. 2. 'Gentleman' Jim Corbett. 3. Spike Milligan. 4. Katherine Hepburn.
5. Simon Weston. 6. King Vidor. 7. George Sanders, 8. Walter Chrysler. 9. Wayne Sleep.
10. Sammy Davis Jnr. 11. Richard E. Grant. 12. Yves Montand. 13. Galina
Vishnevskaya. 14. Nina Simone. 15. Ludovic Kennedy.

Historical figures

What do you know about Historical figures? (1)

QUESTIONS.

1. Who was the first woman to qualify as a medical doctor in Britain? She also went on to become the first female mayor.

2. Who was the fanatical Dominican who stabbed to death Henry III of France on August 1st, 1589, bringing to an end the house of Valois?

3. What was the name of the Welsh prince, long believed by his countryman to have been the first to discover America, in the year 1170?

4. Who was the German inventor who patented the metronome?

5. Who was the Dutch physicist who was the first to discover that the electrical resistance of metals, when cooled to near absolute zero, all but disappears?

6. What was the name of the French army officer who composed both the words and the music of the 'Marseillaise'?

7. Who was the 17th century Oxford educated lawyer and polemicist whose criticism of the court life of Charles I led to severe punishment, including the cropping of both ears?

8. What was the name of the Polish countess who became Napoleon Bonaparte's mistress?

9. Who was the only bachelor President of the U.S.?

10. Who was the 17th century soldier who fought for Charles I, then for Oliver Cromwell, and then secured the restoration of Charles II?

11. What was the name of the Queen of Egypt, daughter of Thothmes I; wife of Thothmes II and regent for Thothmes III?

12. Who was the American lawyer who, in 1905, founded the Rotary Club, now Rotary International?

13. What was the name of the Arab geographer who, while residing at the court of Roger II of Sicily, wrote the 'Description of the World' completing it in 1154?

14. What was the name of the wife of Edward I of England? She accompanied him on a Crusade and is reported to have saved his life when he was struck by a poisoned arrow.

15. Who was the Scottish heroine who led Bonnie Prince Charlie to safety in 1746?

ANSWERS.
1. Elizabeth Garrett Anderson. 2. Jacques Clement. 3. Madoc. 4. Johann Maelzel. 5. Heike Onnes. 6. Claude Joseph Rouget de Lisle. 7. William Prynne. 8. Marie Walewska. 9. James Buchanan. 10. George Monk, 1st Duke of Albemarle.. 11. Hatshepsut. 12. Paul Harris. 13. Idrisi. 14. Eleanor of Castile. 15. Flora MacDonald.

What do you know about Historical figures? (2)

QUESTIONS.

1. What was the name of the Chinese poet of the 8th century, considered by many to be the greatest of all, who drowned whilst trying to kiss the reflection of the moon in a river?

2. What was the name of the Shawnee Chief who tried to unite the Indian tribes from Canada to Florida against the encroaching whites, and died in 1813 at the Thames in Canada?

3. Who was the Austrian admiral who defeated the Danish fleet off Heligoland in 1864 in the first sea battle between ironclads?

4. In the 1770's, two chemists working independently, discovered oxygen. One was Swedish, one was English. What were their names?

5. Who was the English public schoolboy who was playing football in 1823 and picked up the ball to run with it, thus inadvertently founding the game of Rugby Football?

6. What was the name of the magistrate who was found murdered on October 17th 1678, only hours after Titus Oates had sworn an oath before him about the so-called 'Popish Plot'

7. Who was the Greek historian who was called the 'father of history' by Cicero?

8. Who was the leader of the plot to assassinate Napoleon Bonaparte, for which he was executed in 1804?

9. What was the name of the French historian and philosopher, author of 'Democracy in America'?

10. Who was the Naples-born Paris-based banker who invented the 'tontine' the life insurance system in which the benefits accrue to the last survivor of a consortium?

11. Who was the very first English poet to be known by name?

12. How old was Benedict IX when he first became Pope in 1032?

13. Who was the Flemish 16th/17th century chemist who invented the word 'gas'?
14. Who was the American philanthropist who presented his strongly held views on slavery in the journal he started in 1831 'The Liberator'?

15. Who was the Greek mathematician who taught in Alexandria around 300 BC whose work 'Elements' is still used as a geometry text book today?

ANSWERS.
1. Li Po. 2. Tecumseh. 3. Baron Wilhelm von Tegethoff. 4. Carl Scheele and Joseph Priestley. 5. William Webb Ellis. 6. Sir Edmund Berry Godfrey. 7. Herodotus. 8. Georges Cadoudal. 9. Alexis de Toqueville. 10. Lorenzo Tonti. 11. Caedmon. 12. 12 years old. 13. Jean Baptiste van Helmont. 14. William Lloyd Garrison. 15. Euclid.

What do you know about Historical figures? (3)

QUESTIONS.

1. She was the youngest daughter of William the Conqueror; she became the wife of Stephen Count of Blois and mother of King Stephen of England, the last of the Norman dynasty. What was her name?

2. Who was the Chief of the German Cherusci who, in the year 9, annihilated a Roman Army in a three day battle in the 'Teutoberg Forest'?

3. What was the name and nationality of the last non-Italian Pope (before John Paul II) ?

4. Who was the 18th century Scottish stonecutter who devoted forty years to repairing and erecting headstones to Covenanting martyrs and who was the inspiration for Sir Walter Scott's 'Old Mortality'?

5. She was the daughter of the King of Epirus, wife of Philip of Macedon and mother of Alexander the Great. What was her name?

6. What was the name of the American landscape architect who co-designed Central Park, New York and other famous parks and planned the layout of Chicago World's Fair 1893?

7. Who was the 15th/16th century French cleric and satirist who published his thoughts through the characters 'Pantagruel' and 'Gargantua'?

8. Who was the 18th/19th century English colonial administrator and natural historian who founded Singapore in 1818?

9. Who was the first Pope to take a double name?

10. Who was the American mariner who made the first known solo cruise around the world 1895 – 1898, and who disappeared on another solo expedition in 1909?

11. What was the name of the first Archbishop of Canterbury?

12. Who, according to the Bible, was the Egyptian official who purchased Joseph as a slave?

13. What was the name of the 18th century French financier whose remedial measures were unacceptable to Louis XVI, but might have saved the country from revolution?

14. Who was the founder of the Society of Jesus (the Jesuits) in 1534?

15. Who was the founder of the Society of Friends (the Quakers) in 1650?

ANSWERS.
1. Adela. 2. Arminius. 3. Adrian VI (1522-23). He was Dutch. 4. Robert Paterson.
5. Olympias. 6. Frederick Law Olmsted. 7. Francois Rabelais. 8. Thomas Stamford Raffles. 9. John Paul I (1978). 10. Joshua Slocum. 11. Augustine (597-604). 12. Potiphar. 13. Jacques Necker. 14. Ignatius Loyola. 15. George Fox..

What do you know about Historical figures? (4)

QUESTIONS.

1. Who was the 19th century Italian statesman who played a leading role in the reunification of Italy and the creation of the Italian nationality?

2. Who was the 15th/16th century Swiss physician, alchemist and scientist who led medicine away from Galen's 'imbalance of four humours' towards physical, external causes?

3. Who was the 13th/14th century Turkish adventurer who laid the foundations of the Ottoman Empire in Bithynia, and conquering the greater part of Anatolia?

4. Who was the best English chronicler of the 13th century and author of the 'Chronica Majora' a history of the world from the date of creation down to 1259, the year of his death?

5. Who was the 4th century Greek priest considered to be the greatest orator of his time, indeed his Saint's name indicates that he was 'golden-mouthed'?

6. Which Queen of Sweden was crowned with the form reserved for King of Sweden in 1650?

7. Who was the French rationalist philosopher and mathematician of the 16th/17th century who has been called 'the father of modern philosophy'?

8. Who was the 16th/17th century Dutch jurist and theologian who, driven from his own country lived in France, eventually becoming Ambassador for Sweden at the French court?

9. Who was the 16th/17th century French scholar, philosopher and jurist, probably the greatest scholar in the world in his day?

10. Who was the 19th century Italian patriot who for around forty years in banishment dreamed, schemed, plotted and conspired towards the unification of Italy?

11. What was the name of the Italian-born courtier who became private secretary to Mary, Queen of Scots, and was murdered by her jealous husband, Charles Darnley?

12. What was the name of the 4th century Athenian courtesan, famous for her wit and beauty, who is supposed to have persuaded Alexander the Great to burn down Persepolis?

13. Who was the 16th century Belgian anatomist whose work greatly advanced the science of biology, although he was sentenced to death by the Inquisition for dissection?

14. Who was the 19th century French meteorologist who separated the strato-sphere from the troposphere in the upper atmosphere?

ANSWERS.

1. Count Camillo Cavour. 2. Paracelsus. 3. Osman I. 4. Matthew Paris. 5. St. John Chrysostom. 6. Christina. 7. Rene Descartes. 8. Hugo Grotius. 9. Claudius Salmasius. 10. Giuseppe Mazzini. 11. David Rizzio. 12. Thais. 13. Andreas Vesalius. 14. Leon Teisserenc de Bort.

What do you know about Historical figures? (5)

QUESTIONS.

1. Who was the daughter of a Ravenna nobleman, who became the mistress of Lord Byron 1819-1823?

2. Who was the French physician and revolutionary who proposed to the Constituent Assembly, the use of an instrument of decapitation which was adopted nationally in 1791?

3. What was the name of the 19th century French sculptor who received the Legion d'honneur in 1887 for making and installing the Statue of Liberty on Bedloe's Island, New York?

4. What was the name of the 16th century Flemish mathematician, geographer and map-maker which is still today synonymous with maps?

5. Who was the 19th century German mathematician mainly known now for his discovery of a one-sided surface formed by giving a rectangular strip a half twist, then joining the ends?

6. Who was the 19th century Polish actress who performed triumphantly in Great Britain and the U.S.A., especially in Shakespearean roles?

7. What was the name of the English inventor of the shorthand system?

8. What was the name of the Spanish discoverer of Brazil in 1499? He had also captained the Nina on the 1492 Columbus expedition.

9. Who was the French revolutionary leader who, for a few months in 1794 was virtually the dictator of France, only to fall victim to the paranoia of the time, partly his own creation?

10. Who succeeded as King of Persia 485-465 BC, after the death of his father, Darius?

11. Who was the English public official in India in the 17th/18th centuries who was a major benefactor to an American University which took his name in gratitude in 1718?

12. Long-term mistress of King George II, Sophia von Walmoden was brought to England after the death of Queen Caroline, and ennobled as ....what?13. Who was the Swiss-French bacteriologist who in 1894 discovered the plague bacillus and developed a serum against it?

14. Who was the 19th century German optician who established his factory at Jena in 1846?

15. Who was the 5th cent. BC Greek philosopher who stated four arguments against motion?

ANSWERS.
1. Teresa Gamba, Countess Guiccioli. 2. Joseph Ignace Guillotin. 3. Auguste Bartholdi. 4. Gerhardus Mercator. 5. August Mobius. 6. Helena Modjeska. 7. Isaac Pitman. 8. Vicente Pinzon. 9. Maximilien Robespierre. 10. Xerxes I. 11. Elihu Yale. 12. Countess of Yarmouth. 13. Alexandre Yersin. 14. Carl Zeiss. 15. Zeno of Elea.

What do you know about Historical figures? (6)

QUESTIONS.

1. Who was the British Tory Prime Minister 1852-1855, who was obliged to resign due to the criticism aroused by his government's mismanagement of the Crimean War?

2. Who, according to the Old Testament, was the founder of the Jewish nation?

3. What was the surname of the first of the three Holy Roman Emperors to share the Christian name Frederick?

4. Who was the 12th century historian and Dean of St Pauls, whose 'Epitome of Chronicles' was a history from the Creation until 1148? His 'Images of History' went from 1148 until 1200.

5. What was the name of the first great Mogul ruler who, in 1526, made Agra, the city in Uttar Pradesh, India, the capital of his empire?

6. Who was the Roman governor of Britain, AD 78-85, who sailed his fleet around the north of Scotland to prove that Britain was an island?

7. Ahab was King of Israel c. 875-854 BC. He married a Princess of Sidon. Who was she?

8. What was the name of the founder and first ruler of Afghanistan?

9. Who was the 15th century Italian reformer, a Dominican monk who criticised the excesses and corruption of Pope Alexander VI (Rodrigo Borgia), who had him put to death?

10. What was the name of the daughter of King Oxyartes of Sogdiana, whom Alexander the Great took to wife during his march east?

11. By what Latin name was the great 17th century Czech-born educational reformer John Komensky better known?

12. Alfonso X was King of Castile from 1252 until his death in 1284. What was his nickname?

13. Who was the 12th/13th century English soldier, courtier and Regent of England for the boy - king Henry III, he rose from obscurity to the highest position in the land?

14. Who was the Spanish conquistador who conquered Peru in 1531 with only 180 soldiers?

15. Who was the Spanish conquistador who conquered Chile in 1536? In 1538 he was assassinated by Pizarro's brother and his supporters assassinated Pizarro in 1541.

ANSWERS.
1. George Gordon, 4th Earl of Aberdeen. 2. Abraham. 3. Barbarossa. 4. Ralph Diceto.
5. Zahir ud-din Muhammad (better known as 'Babur'). 6. Gnaeus Julius Agricola. 7.
Jezebel. 8. Ahmad Shah Durrani (1724-1773). 9. Girolamo Savonarola 10. Roxana. 11.
Comenius. 12. 'El Sabio' (The Wise). 13. William Marshal. 14. Francisco Pizarro. 15.
Diego de Almagro.

What do you know about Historical figures? (7)

QUESTIONS.

1. What was the name of the Berber dynasty which ruled much of Morocco and Spain from 1056 until 1147?

2. What was the name of the Berber dynasty which ruled much of Morocco and Spain from 1140 until 1269? In the name of 'religious purity' they massacred thousands of Jews.

3. Who was the Spanish politician and soldier who was appointed governor of the Netherlands in 1567 and established a reign of terror to suppress Protestantism?

4. Who was the Spanish conquistador who conquered and ruled over Guatemala 1524-41?

5. She was the daughter of Philip III of Spain; Queen of France 1615-1643 and Regent 1643-61. How was she known?

6. What was the name of the 3rd/4th century Egyptian priest whose ideas gave rise to a form of Christianity which denied the complete divinity of Jesus Christ?

7. Who was the 18th/19th century campaigner for Uruguayan independence, despite being made the governor of Montevideo in 1815?

8. Who was the Roman Emperor AD 121 – 180 remembered today more as a philosopher than as a soldier or statesman?

9. What was the name of the third and favourite wife of the prophet Muhammad, who married her when she was nine years of age?

10. Who was the founder of the Order of the Assassins, an off-shoot of the Islamic Isma'ili sect in the 11th century?

11. What was the name of the last emperor of the Incas, murdered by Pizarro in 1533?

12. Who hatched a plot to assassinate Elizabeth I and replace her with Mary, Queen of Scots? The discovery of the plot led to his own death, and that of Mary.

13. What was the title that Mirza Hosein Ali (1817-1892) Persian founder of the Baha'i religion took to himself?

14. Who was the Spanish conquistador who founded a settlement at Darien (Panama) in 1511 and discovered the Pacific Ocean? Intrigued against, he was imprisoned and executed.

15. Who was the 10th century English physician who wrote 'The Leech Book', the earliest surviving medical book in the English language?

ANSWERS.
1. Almoravid. 2. Almohad. 3. Ferdinand Alvarez de Toledo, Duke of Alba. 4. Pedro de Alvaredo. 5. Anne of Austria. 6. Arius (Arianism). 7. Jose Gervasio Artigas. 8. Marcus Aurelius. 9. Ayesha. 10. Hassan Sabah. 11. Atahualpa. 12. Anthony Babington. 13. 'Baha'ullah' (God's Glory). 14. Vasco Nunez de Balboa. 15. Bald.

What do you know about Historical figures? (8)

QUESTIONS.

1. Who was the French revolutionary who helped to overthrow Robespierre in 1794; in 1795 he became a member of the ruling Directory and in 1796 assumed dictatorial powers? He arranged the marriage of his former mistress Josephine de Beauharnais to Napoleon but fell into disgrace after Napoleon's coup d'etat in 1799.

2. Who was elected King of Poland in 1575 and drove the Russians out of his country?

3. Who was the French Liberal aristocrat who served in the American Revolution and was a member of the National Convention of revolutionary France before being guillotined for 'lack of zeal for the revolutionary cause'?

4. What was the name of the venerable 7th/8th century English theologian and historian?

5. Who was the 18th/19th century Argentinian revolutionary, a member of the group which led the 1810 revolt against Spain and commander of the revolutionary army until 1814?

6. Who was the first Governor General of India 1828-35? He suppressed thuggee and suttee.

7. Who was the aggressively expansionist 19th century German chancellor whose wars with Denmark, Austria and France went a long way to unifying Germany?

8. Who were the two stock manipulators who on 24th September 1869 ('Black Friday') tried to corner the market in gold, ultimately making a profit of around $11 million?

9. Who was the British 'general-at-sea' of the Parliamentary forces during the English Civil War who destroyed Prince Rupert's fleet in 1650; won several battles with the Dutch navy in 1652; bombarded the Barbary Corsairs in Tunis in 1654 and took the Spanish treasure fleet in 1657?

10. She was wife of King Louis VIII of France, mother of and regent for Louis IX and in 1229 negotiated the Treaty of Paris, winning Toulouse for the crown. Who was she?

11. Who was the South American nationalist who liberated Columbia from the Spanish in 1819, Venezuela in 1821, Ecuador in 1822 and Peru in 1824?

12. Which 15th century Italian general and illegitimate son of a Pope, was a Cardinal at 17, became the papacy's Captain-General and served as model for Machiavelli's 'The Prince'?

13. Who was the 18th century English admiral known to his men as 'Old Dreadnought'?

ANSWERS.
1. Paul Barras. 2. Stephen Bathory. 3. Alexandre, Vicomte de Beauharnais. 4. Bede. 5. Manuel Belgrano. 6. Lord William Cavendish Bentinck. 7. Otto von Bismarck. 8. Jay Gould and James Fiske. 9. Robert Blake. 10. Blanche of Castile. 11. Simon Bolivar. 12. Cesare Borgia. 13. Edward Boscawen.

What do you know about Historical figures? (9)

QUESTIONS.

1. What was the family name of the royal house of Portugal 1640-1910? Another branch of the family were emperors of Brazil 1822-1889.

2. Who was the Haitian revolutionary leader who was made governor of Haiti by the French revolutionary government, revolted again when Napoleon reintroduced slavery and died in prison in France?=

3. Who was the 19th century English economic lecturer and historian who coined the term 'the Industrial revolution'?

4. Who was the 18th century Russian politician who reformed the army for Catherine II and conquered the Crimea in 1783?

5. Who was the Scottish-born administrator who succeeded Admiral Bligh as governor of New South Wales in 1809 and did much to improve the conditions of the settlement?

6. Who was the first Holy Roman Emperor, 800 – 814 AD?

7. What was the name of the 14th century English religious reformer who attacked abuses in the church and translated the bible into English?

8. Who was the 14th century Bohemian religious reformer who defended Wycliffe's arguments rejected the pope's authority and was burned at the stake in 1415?

9. Who was the first mother-in-law of Henry VIII of England?

10. Who was the Portuguese navigator who in 1497-98 found a sea way to India round the Cape of Good Hope?

11. Who was the 19th century Italian soldier, a member of Mazzini's 'Young Italy' society, he made a major contribution to unifying Italy by capturing Sicily and Naples in 1860?

12. Who was the 11th/12th century Mongol conqueror whose empire stretched from the Yellow Sea to the Black Sea at the time of his death in 1227?

13. By what title was the 11th century Spanish soldier Rodrigo Diaz de Bivar known?

14. Who was the 5th century Merovingian King of the Franks? He defeated the Gallo-Romans and the Alemanni, embraced Christianity and made Paris his capital.

15. Who took command of the British fleet after Nelson's death at Trafalgar?

ANSWERS.
1. Braganza. 2. Pierre Dominique Toussaint L'Ouverture. 3. Arnold Toynbee. 4. Prince Potemkin. 5. Lachlan Macquarie. 6. Charlemagne. 7. John Wycliffe. 8. John Huss.
9. Isabella I of Castile and Aragon. 10. Vasco da Gama. 11. Giuseppe Garibaldi.
12. Genghis Khan. 13. 'El Cid'. 14. Clovis. 15. Admiral Collingwood.

What do you know about Historical figures? (10)

QUESTIONS.

1. She was a French princess, sister of Louis XVI, and like him, was guillotined during the French revolution. What was she called?

2. Who was the illegitimate daughter of Peter the Great and Catherine I ? She was passed over three times, but finally in 1741 became Empress of Russia.

3. With which 19th century English literary genius did the American poet and essayist Ralph Waldo Emerson enjoy a friendship and correspondence which lasted for thirty-eight years?

4. Who was the 19th century American entertainer, originator of the 'Minstrel Show'?

5. He was the grandfather of Charlemagne and in AD 720 became the ruler of all the Franks, driving the Saracens out of Burgundy and Languedoc. What was his name?

6. Which English philosopher was born prematurely, on April 5th 1588, when his mother heard of the arrival of the Spanish Armada?

7. Who was the 19th century Finnish dramatist, now recognised as one of his country's greatest writers, but who died unrecognised, poverty-stricken and insane at thirty-eight?

8. Who was the 19th century leader of the Hungarian revolution who spent his entire adult life trying to free Hungary from Austrian Hapsburg ownership?

9. Who was the 19th century French lexicographer who produced the first 'Grand Dictionnaire Universel' in 15 volumes 1864-76?

10. Who was the brilliant first century Roman poet whose verses so outshone those of the Emperor Nero, that he was ordered to die?

11. Who was the 14th century Tatar chief who conquered Persia, Georgia and the Tatar Empire, and all the states between the Indus and the Ganges? Died on the way to China 1405.

12. Who was the 17th century Dutch explorer who discovered New Zealand in 1642? 13. Who was the 18th century British soldier and administrator who established British rule in India? He defeated French and native forces, and twice became Governor of Bengal.

14. Daughter of a bee-keeper; actress and mistress of the Byzantine Emperor Justinian, she married him to become Empress in AD 525. What was her name?

15. Who was the 16th/17th century French soldier and explorer who founded Quebec in 1608?

ANSWERS.
1. Madame Elizabeth. 2. Elizabeth Petrovna. 3. Thomas Carlyle. 4. Edwin Christy.
5. Charles Martel 'The Hammer'. 6. Thomas Hobbes. 7. Aleksis Kivi. 8. Lajos Kossuth
9. Pierre Larousse. 10. Lucan. 11. Tamerlane. 12. Abel Tasman. 13. Robert Clive 14.
Theodora. 15. Samuel de Champlain.

Last Words

Whose famous last words are these? (1)

QUESTIONS.

1. 'Farewell my friends. I go to glory!'

2. 'Am I dying, or is this my birthday'?

3. 'I have been a most unconscionable time dying, and I beg you to excuse it'.

4. 'It was a great game'. (Of golf)

5. 'Last words are for fools who have not said enough'.

6. 'Dying is easy. Comedy is difficult'.

7. 'Tomorrow I shall no longer be here'.

8. 'Drink to me!'

9. 'Wait a second'.

10. 'Strike man! Strike!'

11. 'Go away. I'm alright'.

12. 'I still live'.

13. 'They couldn't hit an elephant at this dist....'

14. 'Codeine ....Bourbon'.

15. 'What's this?'

ANSWERS.
1. Isadora Duncan, U.S. dancer 1878–1927. 2. Lady Nancy Astor, M.P.,1879–1964.
3. Charles II, King of England, 1630–1685. 4. Bing Crosby, U.S. singer, 1904–1977.
5. Karl Marx, German historian 1818–1883. 6. Edmund Gwenn, U.S. actor, 1875–1959
7. Nostradamus, French astrologer 1503–1566. 8. Pablo Picasso, Spanish painter
1881-1973.9. Marquise de Pompadour, French courtesan, 1721-1764.10. Sir Walter
Raleigh, English adventurer, 1554-1618. (Addressing the executioner).11. H.G. Wells,
English author, 1866-1946. 12. Daniel Webster, U.S. statesman 1782-1852 13. General
John Sedgwick, U.S. Army, 1813-1864 14. Tallulah Bankhead, U.S. actress 1902-1968
15. Leonard Bernstein, U.S. composer, 1918-1990.

Whose famous last words are these? (2)

QUESTIONS.

1. 'It has been a long time since I had champagne'.

2. 'I am mortally wounded. I think'.

3. 'It has all been most interesting'.

4. 'Born in a hotel room – and, God damn it – died in a hotel room!'

5. 'So little done – so much to do'.

6. 'Woe is me. I think I am becoming a God'.

7. 'Everybody has got to die, but I have always believed that an exception would be made in my case. Now what?'

8. 'I wonder why he shot me?'

9. 'I am just going outside. I may be sometime'.

10. 'It is nothing. It is nothing'.

11. 'Now I shall go to sleep. Good-night'.

12. 'Only one man ever understood me. And he didn't really understand me'.

13. 'This is a mortal wound, doctor'.

14. 'This is funny'.

15. 'I' bored. I'm bored'.

ANSWERS
1. Anton Chekhov, Russian author, 1860-1904. 2. Stephen Decatur, U.S. Navy, 1779-1820. 3. Lady Mary Wortley Montagu, 1689-1762. 4. Eugene O'Neill, U.S. playwright 1888-1953. 5. Cecil Rhodes, British statesman 1853-1902. 6. Vespasian, Roman Emperor, AD 9-79. 7. Wm. Saroyan, U.S. writer, 1908-1981. 8. Huey P. Long, U.S. Politician, 1893-1935. 9. Capt. Laurence Oates, English explorer 1880-1912 10. Archduke Francis Ferdinand 1863-1914. 11. Lord Byron, English poet, 1788-1824. 12. G.W.Hegel, German philosopher 1770-1831 13. Alexander Hamilton, U.S. statesman 1757-1804. 14. 'Doc' Holliday, U.S. dentist, 1851-1887. 15. Gabriele D'Annunzio, Italian dramatist, 1863-1938.

Whose famous last words are these? (3)

QUESTIONS.

1. 'All my possessions for a moment of time'.

2. 'Never felt better'.

3. 'Give me 80 men and I'll ride through the whole Sioux nation'.

4. 'Don't let it end like this. Tell them I said something'.

5. 'What! Do they run already? Then I die happy'.

6. 'The show looks good. The show looks good.'

7. 'I have tried so hard to do right'.

8. 'I have lived as a philosopher, and die as a christian'.

9. 'My work is done. Why wait'?

10. 'This the fourth' (of July)?

11. 'My design is to make what haste I can to be gone'.

12. 'How were the receipts at Madison Square Garden?'

13. 'Sergeant, the Spanish bullet hasn't been made that will kill me ……..'

14. 'Well gentlemen, you are about to see a baked apple'.

15. 'How about this for a headline: French Fries?'

ANSWERS.
1. Elizabeth I, Queen of England, 1533-1603. 2. Doug. Fairbanks Snr, U.S. actor, 1883-1939. 3. Capt. Wm. Fetterman, U.S. Army, 1833-66. 4. Pancho Villa, Mexican bandit, 1878-1923. 5. Gen. James Wolfe, British Army, 1727-59. 6. Florenz Ziegfeld, U.S. impresario 1869-1932. 7. Stephen Grover Cleveland, U.S. President, 1837-1908. 8. Giovanni Jacopo Casanova, Italian adventurer, 1725-1798. 9. George Eastman, U.S. inventor, 1854-1932. 10. Thomas Jefferson, U.S. Pres.ident 1743-1826. 11. Oliver Cromwell, 'Protector of England', 1599-1658. 12. Phineas Taylor Barnum, U.S. showman, 1810-1891. 13. William 'Buckeye' O'Neill, U.S. Rough Rider, 1898. 14. Convicted murderer George Appel to warders strapping him into the electric chair 1928. 15. Convicted murderer James French in similar circumstances 1966.

Whose famous last words are these? (4)

QUESTIONS.

1. 'So this is death, well …..'.

2. 'If you will send for the doctor, I will see him now'.

3. 'Doctor, do you think it could have been the sausage?'

4. 'Who's there?'

5. 'Goodnight my darlings. I'll see you tomorrow'.

6. 'I cannot sleep'.

7. 'Dying is a very dull, dreary affair. My advice to you is to have nothing whatever to do with it'.

8. 'Cheer up children! I'm alright'.

9. 'What an artist the world is losing in me!'

10. 'What is the scaffold? A short-cut to Heaven'.

11. 'I am dying, sir, of a hundred good symptoms!'

12. 'I've had 18 straight whiskies. I think that's some sort of a record …..'

13. 'I am dying as I have lived. Beyond my means'. And later: 'either this wallpaper goes or I do'.

14. 'I feel faint'.

15. 'I believe we must adjourn the meeting to some other place'.

AANSWERS.
1. Thomas Carlyle, English historian, 1795-1881. 2. Emily Bronte, Poet and author, 1818-48.. 3. Paul Claudel, French dramatist, 1868-1955. 4. Billy the Kid, U.S. outlaw, 1859-81. 5. Noel Coward, English dramatist, 1899-1973. 6. J.M. Barrie, Scottish author, 1860-1937 7. W.S. Maugham, British writer, 1874-1965, 8. F.J. Haydn, Austrian composer, 1732-1809. 9. Nero, Roman Emperor, 37-68. 10. Charles Peace, murderer, 1832-79. 11. Alexander Pope, English poet, 1688-1744. 12. Dylan Thomas, Welsh poet, 1914-53. 13. Oscar Wilde, Irish dramatist, 1854-1900. 14. Adlai Stevenson, U.S. politician, 1900-65. 15. Adam Smith, Scots economist, 1723-90.

Whose famous last words are these? (5)

QUESTIONS.

1. 'God bless you all. I feel myself again'.

2. 'We are the first victims of American fascism'.

3. 'If this is dying, I don't think much of it'.

4. 'It is well. I die hard, but am not afraid to go'.

5. 'Commend your souls to God. Our bodies are our foe's'.

6. 'I regret that I have but one life to give for my country'.

7. 'We shall this day light such a candle, by God's grace, in England, as I trust shall never be put out'.

8. 'Well, if it must be so'.

9. 'Patriotism is not enough. I must have no hatred or bitterness towards anyone'.

10. 'Die, my dear Doctor? That is the last thing I shall do!'

11. 'Do not hack me, as you did my Lord Russell'.

12. 'I do not suffer, but I feel a sort of difficulty in living longer'.

13. 'That's good. Go on, read some more'.

14. 'Ah! My God! I am dead'.

15. 'I am tired of fighting. I guess this thing is going to get me'.

ANSWERS.
1. Sir Walter Scott, Scots novelist, 1771-1832. 2. Ethel Rosenberg, Russian spy, 1916-53. 3. Lytton Strachey, Eng. biographer, 1880-1932. 4. G. Washington, U.S. President, 1732-99. 5. Simon de Montfort, Earl of Leicester and rebel against King Henry III, 1208-65. 6. Nathan Hale, U.S. soldier/spy, 1755-76. 7. Hugh Latimer, Protestant martyr, 1485-1555. 8. Edvard Greig, Nor, composer, 1843-1907. 9. Edith Cavell, English nurse, 1865-1915. 10. Lord Palmerston, English P.M., 1784-1865. 11. James, Duke of Monmouth, 1649-85. 12. Bernard Fontenelle, French writer,1657-1757. 13. Warren Harding, U.S. Pres.,1865-1923 14. Catharine de Medici, wife of one and mother of three French Kings, 1519-89. 15. Harry Houdini, American escapologist, 1874-1926.

Nicknames

How much do you know about famous people's nicknames? (1)

QUESTIONS.

To whom do these nicknames belong?

1. 'The Bounding Basque'?

2. 'The "It" Girl'?

3. 'The Father of American History'?

4. 'The World's Most Perfectly Developed Man'?

5. 'The Flanders Mare'?

6. 'The Sage of Chelsea'?

7. 'The Father of the Game of Whist'?

8. 'Poor Little Rich Girl'?

9. 'Old Ironsides'?

10. 'Wilt the Stilt'?

11. 'Father of American Democracy'?

12. 'Mother of the Blues'?

13. 'The Sweater Girl'?

14. 'Father of the Railways'?

15. 'The Man in Black'?

ANSWERS. 1. Jean Borotra. 2. Clara Bow. 3. William Bradford. 4. Charles Atlas, 5. Anne of Cleves. 6. Thomas Carlyle. 7. Edmond Hoyle. 8. Barbara Hutton. 9. Oliver Cromwell. 10. Wilton Chamberlain. 11. Thomas Hooker. 12. Ma Rainey. 13. Lana Turner. 14. George Stephenson. 15. A) In the U.S. – Johnny Cash. B) In the U.K. – Valentine Dyall.

How much do you know about famous people's nicknames? (2)

QUESTIONS.

To whom do these nicknames belong?

1. 'Father of Moral Philosophy'?

2. ' The Father of the Pony Express'?

3. 'The Father of English History'?

4. 'Duke'?

5. 'The Iron Duke'?

6. 'The Iron Lady'?

7. 'The Teflon President'?

8. 'America's Sweetheart'?

9. 'The Father of Economics'?

10. 'Red Eminence'?

11. 'The Father of Ragtime'?

12. 'Bluebeard'?

13. 'The Father of the Constitution'?

14. 'Goldenballs'?

15. 'The Father of Comedy'?

ANSWERS.
1. St. Thomas Aquinas. 2. William Hepburn Russell. 3. The Venerable Bede. 4. John Wayne. 5. The Duke of Wellington. 6. Margaret Thatcher. 7. Ronald Reagan. 8. Mary Pickford. 9. Adam Smith. 10. Cardinal Richelieu. 11. Scott Joplin. 12. Henri Landru. 13. James Madison. 14. Sir James Goldsmith. 15. Aristophanes

How much do you know about famous people's nicknames? (3)

QUESTIONS.

To whom do these nicknames belong?

1. 'The Louisville Lip'?

2. 'Doctor Mirabilis'?

3. 'The Father of Scottish Poetry'?

4. 'The Wizard of Dribble'?

5. 'The Maid of Orleans'?

6. 'The Lady with the Lamp'?

7. 'The Father of Modern Chemistry'?

8. 'The Brazilian Bombshell'?

9. 'Bloody Mary'?

10. 'The Sun King'?

11. 'The Velvet Fog'?

12. 'Great White Shark'?

13. 'The Ebony Antelope'?

14. 'Pam'?

15. 'Black Jack'?

ANSWERS.
1. Muhammed Ali. 2. Roger Bacon. 3. John Barbour. 4. Stanley Matthews. 5. Joan of Arc. 6. Florence Nightingale. 7. Antoine Lavoisier. 8. Carmen Miranda. 9. Mary Tudor, Mary I Queen of England. (1516-58) 10. Louis XIV, King of France. (1638-1715) 11. Mel Torme. 12. Greg Norman. 13. Jesse Owens. 14. Lord Henry Palmerston. 15. General John Pershing.

How much do you know about famous people's nicknames? (4)

QUESTIONS.

To whom do these nicknames belong?

1. 'The Father of Chemistry'?

2. 'Father of the American Novel'?

3. 'The Voice'?

4. 'The Ambling Alp'?

5. 'The Father of Medicine'?

6. 'The King of Swing'?

7. 'The Master'?

8. 'Papillon'?

9. 'The Flying Scotsman'?

10. 'The Last of the Red-Hot Mamas'?

11. 'Blackbeard'?

12. 'The Brown Bomber'?

13. 'Superbrat'?

14. 'The Cat'?

15. 'The Handsomest Man in the World'?

ANSWERS.
1. Robert Boyle. 2. William Hill Brown. 3. Richard Burton. 4. Primo Carnera. 5. Hippocrates. 6. Benny Goodman. 7. Noel Coward. 8. Henri Charriere. 9. Eric Liddell. 10. Sophie Tucker. 11. Edward Teach. 12. Joe Louis. 13. John McEnroe. 14. Peter Bonetti. 15. Francis X. Bushman.

How much do you know about famous people's nicknames? (5)

QUESTIONS.

To whom do these nicknames belong?

1. 'The Father of Greek Tragedy'?
2. 'Father of the Royal Navy'?
3. 'Restorer of the Roman Empire'?
4. 'The Father of Inductive Philosophy'?
5. 'Father of Television'?
6. 'The Rockhampton Rocket'?
7. 'Stone Face'?
8. 'Lord Haw Haw'?
9. 'Father of Immunology'?
10. 'Conqueror of the World'?
11. 'The Railway King'?
12. 'Twiggy'?
13. 'The Father of American Poetry'?
14. 'The Vamp'?
15. 'The Black Panther'?

ANSWERS.
1. Aeschylus. 2. George, Baron Anson. 3. Aurelian, Emperor (212-275 AD). 4 Francis Bacon. 5. John Logie Baird. 6. Rod Laver. 7. Buster Keaton. 8. William Joyce. 9. Edward Jenner. 10. Jahangir, son of Akbar the Great. 11. George Hudson. 12. Lesley Hornby. 13. William Cullen Bryant, 14. Theda Bara. 15. Eusebio.

Previous occupations

How much do you know about what the famous did before they became famous? (1)

QUESTIONS.

Prior to becoming famous, how did the following earn their living:

1. Robbie Burns?

2. Jimmy Carter?

3. Karl Marx?

4. Benny Hill?

5. Cary Grant?

6. Giuseppe Garibaldi?

7. Samuel Goldwyn?

8. Franz Liszt?

9. Harold Macmillan?

10. St.Peter?

11. Robert Mitchum?

12. Che Guevara?

13. Modeste Mussorgsky?

14. Albert Einstein?

15. Clint Eastwood?

ANSWERS.
1. Excise officer. 2. Peanut farmer. 3. Newspaper correspondent. 4. Milkman. 5.
Acrobat. 6. Candlemaker. 7. Glove salesman. 8. Priest. 9. Publisher. 10. Fisherman. 11.
Miner. 12. Doctor. 13. Civil Servant. 14. Patent office clerk. 15. Swimming instructor.

How much do you know about what the famous did before they became famous? (2)

QUESTIONS.

Prior to becoming famous, how did the following earn their living:

1. Benjamin Franklin?

2. Clark Gable?

3. Sean O'Casey?

4. David Niven?

5. Bob Hope?

6. Henrik Ibsen?

7. Woody Allen?

8. Sir Arthur Conan Doyle?

9. Errol Flynn?

10. Anthony Trollope?

11. Brigham Young?

12. Rod Stewart?

13. Zane Grey?

14. John Buchan?

15. Alexander Borodin?

ANSWERS.
1. Printer. 2. Lumberjack. 3. Builder's labourer. 4. Army Officer. 5. Boxer. 6. Journalist.
7. Jazz clarinettist. 8. Opthalmologist. 9. Policeman. 10. Post Office employee. 11.
Carpenter. 12. Gravedigger. 13. Dentist. 14. M.P. 15. Professor of Chemistry. .

How much do you know about what the famous did before they became famous? (3)

QUESTIONS.

Prior to becoming famous, how did the following earn their living:

1. Isaac Asimov?

2. Cilla Black?

3. Lewis Carroll?

4. W. Somerset Maugham?

5. Paul Gauguin?

6. Thomas Hardy?

7. W.S. Gilbert?

8. Arthur Rimbaud?

9. Henry Wadsworth Longfellow?

10. William Faulkner?

11. Michael Faraday?

12. Greta Garbo?

13. Herman Melville?

14. Benjamin Disraeli?

15. Giacomo Casanova?

ANSWERS.
1. Biochemist. 2. Coat checker at The Cavern. 3. Mathematics lecturer. 4. Surgeon. 5. Stockbroker. 6. Apprentice architect. 7. Barrister. 8. Gun-runner. 9. Lecturer at Harvard. 10. Postmaster. 11. Apprentice bookbinder. 12. Hat model. 13. Customs officer. 14. Novelist. 15. Abbot.

How much do you know about what the famous did before they became famous? (4)

QUESTIONS.

Prior to becoming famous, how did the following earn their living:

1. John Mills?

2. Nathaniel Hawthorne?

3. Geoffrey Chaucer?

4. Gerald Ford?

5. Thomas Alva Edison?

6. Samuel Morse?

7. Clement Attlee?

8. Juan Fangio?

9. Ian Fleming?

10. Robert Graves?

11. T.S. Eliot?

12. Enoch Powell?

13. Vladimir Lenin?

14. Burt Lancaster?

15. Adolf Hitler?

ANSWERS.
1. Commercial salesman. 2. Customs officer. 3. Customs officer. 4. Male model. 5. Newsboy. 6. Artist. 7. Social worker. 8. Motor mechanic. 9. Journalist. 10. Shop keeper. 11. Bank clerk. 12. Professor of Greek. 13. Lawyer. 14. Acrobat. 15. Postcard painter.

How much do you know about what the famous did before they became famous? (5)

QUESTIONS,

Prior to becoming famous, how did the following earn their living:

1. James Garner?

2. Charles Dickens?

3. John Thaw?

4. Lech Walesa?

5. Leo Tolstoy?

6. Nevil Shute?

7. Laurence Sterne?

8. Christopher Wren?

9. Emile Zola?

10. Freddie Starr?

11. John Prescott?

12. Roger Moore?

13. Daniel Defoe?

14. Bob Newhart?

15. Rene Descartes?

ANSWERS.
1. Swimming trunks model. 2. Factory worker (as a child). 3. Market porter. 4. Electrician. 5. Artillery officer. 6. Aircraft designer. 7. Vicar. 8. Professor of Astronomy. 9. Publisher's clerk. 10. Bricklayer. 11. Merchant seaman. 12. Male model. 13. Government spy. 14. Accountant. 15. Army engineer.

Quotes, ad libs and observations

How much do you know about quotes, ad libs and observations? (1)

QUESTIONS.

Who said:

1. 'It's true that money can't buy you friends. But it gets you a better class of enemy'?

2. 'I always wait for The Times in the morning. I look at the obituary column, and if I'm not in it, I go to work'?

3. 'I don't know what else I could do but pretend to be an actor'?

4. 'I'm no actor, and I've 64 pictures to prove it'?

5. 'I only really exist when I am working on a film'?

6. 'When I was nine I played the Demon King in Cinderella, and it launched me on the long and happy life of being a monster'?

7. 'I can't stand light. I hate weather. My idea of heaven is moving from one smoke-filled room to another'?

8. 'I'm a sausage machine. A perfect sausage machine'?

9. 'It took me fifteen years to discover that I had no talent for writing. But by then I couldn't give it up because I was too famous'?

10. 'On the continent people have good food. In England people have good table manners'?

11. 'It only takes one drink to get me loaded. Trouble is, I can never remember if it's the thirteenth or fourteenth'?

12. 'A man is never drunk if he can lie on the floor without holding on'?

13. 'Doesn't everyone want to lie successfully'?

14. 'Most of the time I don't have much fun. The rest of the time I don't have any fun at all'?

15. 'I have been a film star so long that I don't know what it would feel like not to be one'?

ANSWERS.
1. Spike Milligan. 2. A. E. Matthews. 3. Sir Alec Guinness. 4. Victor Mature. 5. Marcello Mastroianni. 6. Boris Karloff. 7. Peter O'Toole. 8. Agatha Christie. 9. Robert Benchley. 10. George Mikes. 11. George Burns. 12. Joe E. Lewis. 13. Eric Ambler. 14. Woody Allen. 15. Kevin Bacon.

How much do you know about quotes, ad libs and observations? (2)

QUESTIONS.

Who said:

1. 'The only thing I regret about my past is the length of it. If I had it to live over again, I'd make the same mistakes, only sooner'?

2. 'I started out as a lousy actress, and I have remained one'?

3. 'There's one born every minute!'?

4. 'I'm lucky. I grew up being famous, so I don't have any weird things about being famous'?

5. 'I like to be introduced as America's foremost actor. It saves the necessity of further effort'?

6. 'Hollywood is tied hand and foot to the demands for artificiality of the masses all over the world'?

7. 'I'm not the first straight dancer or the last. Anyway it has nothing to do with art'?

8. 'You have to be a little unreal to be in this busiess'?

9. 'I could never become a slave to the movie machine. I must be captain of my own ship. That, to me, is the only imperative'?

10. 'Movies are fun, but they are not a cure for cancer'?

11. 'My claim to literary fame is that I used to deliver meat to a woman who became T.S. Eliot's mother-in-law'?

12. 'It takes a long time to grow up. Longer than they tell you'?

13. The theatre is like a faithful wife. The film is the great adventure – the costly, exacting mistress'?

14. 'I have no regrets. I wouldn't have lived my life the way I did if I was going to worry about what people were going to say'?

15. 'I often think of myself as a beautiful woman walking through a provincial village and being spat on by the locals'?

ANSWERS.
1. Tallulah Bankhead. 2. Brigitte Bardot. 3. Phineas T. Barnum. 4. Drew Barrymore. 5. John Barrymore. 6. Lionel Barrymore. 7. Mikhail Baryshnikov. 8. Kim Basinger. 9. Emmanuelle Beart. 10. Warren Beatty. 11. Alan Bennett. 12. Candice Bergen 13. Ingmar Bergman. 14. Ingrid Bergman. 15. Steven Berkoff.

How much do you know about quotes, ad libs and observations? (3)

QUESTIONS.

Who said:

1. 'I'm fascinated by a man with a twinkle in his eye'?

2. 'It's not my job as an actor to like or dislike the character I'm playing. That way lies sentimentality'?

3. 'I love the camera and it loves me. Well, not very much sometimes. But we're good friends'?

4. 'The trouble with the world is that everybody in it is about three drinks behind'?

5. 'I hate this image of me as a prim Edwardian. I want to shock everyone'?

6. 'I get offered so many bad movies. They're all raging queens or transvestites or Martians'?

7. 'Acting is an empty and useless profession'?

8. 'I know the word 'bumbling' often comes up when people discuss me. I don't mind, but I do prefer 'obsessive"?

9. 'Someday I'd like a part where I can lean my elbow against a mantelpiece and have a cocktail'?

10. 'If you got it, flaunt it'?

11. 'I don't see myself as hunk of the month'?

12. 'I've always found insects exciting'?

13. 'When you are called a character actress it's because you are too ugly to be called a leading lady'?

14. 'Acting is all about honesty. If you can fake that you've got it made'?

15. 'I have done the most awful rubbish in order to have somewhere to go in the morning'?

ANSWERS.
1. Jacqueline Bisset. 2. Cate Blanchett. 3. Dirk Bogarde. 4. Humphrey Bogart. 5. Helena Bonham Carter. 6. David Bowie. 7. Marlon Brando. 8. Richard Briers. 9. Charles Bronson. 10. Mel Brooks. 11. Pierce Brosnan. 12. Luis Bunuel. 13. Kathy Burke. 14. George Burns. 15. Richard Burton.

How much do you know about quotes, ad libs and observations? (4)

QUESTIONS.

Who said:

1. 'I didn't get into acting as much as I got out of the meat business'?

2. 'You get paid the same for a bad film as you do for a good one'?

3. 'So, does this prove once and for all, that size does matter'?

4. 'It doesn't matter what you do in the bedroom, as long as you don't do it in the street and frighten the horses'?

5. 'I'd rather be a friend of mine than an enemy'?

6. 'Real life is scarier than any movie these days'?

7. 'I am terribly shy, but of course no one believes me. Come to think of it, neither would I'?

8. 'Men are luxuries. Not necessities'?

9. 'I'm not a novelist, but a storyteller. I'm not a literary figure at all'?

10. 'Even when you win the rat race, you are still a rat'?

11. 'I've always hated that damn James Bond. I'd like to kill him'?

12. 'I probably have genius. But no talent'?

13. 'I didn't want to peak too early. The worry is that you never know until it is all over whether you peaked at all – and then you're finished and it's too late'?

14. 'I don't think pornography is harmful, but it is terribly, terribly boring'?

15. 'The most important thing a woman can have, next to her talent of course, is her hairdresser'?

ANSWERS.

1. James Caan. 2. Michael Caine. 3. James Cameron (accepting Golden Globe for 'Titanic'). 4. Mrs Patrick Campbell. 5. Truman Capote. 6. John Carpenter. 7. Carol Channing. 8. Cher. 9. James Clavell. 10. Joan Collins. 11. Sean Connery. 12. Francis Ford Coppola. 13. Tom Courtney. 14. Noel Coward. 15. Joan Crawford.

How much do you know about quotes, ad libs and observations? (5)

QUESTIONS.

Who said:

1. 'What keeps a woman young and beautiful is not repeated surgery but constant praise'?

2. 'I don't have a moral plan. I'm a Canadian'?

3. 'Next time I send a dumb sonofabitch to do something, I'll go myself'?

4. 'If I played Hamlet, they'd call it a horror film'?

5. 'When I saw my first film test I ran from the projection room, screaming'?

6. 'You always, in the end, believe you are a fraud'?

7. 'I'm actually a thin, serious person. I only play fat and funny for the movies'?

8. 'I didn't write the Bible and I didn't invent sin'?

9. 'There is a mixture of anarchy and discipline in the way I work'?

10. 'I don't see scary films. I certainly wouldn't go to see my films'?

11. 'She (Catherine Deneuve) is the man I would like to be'?

12. 'My father told me, the best advice I can give you is never to follow my advice'?

13. 'Feet are fascinating, don't you think? They tell you so much about people'?

14. 'The relationship between the make-up man and the film actor is that of accomplices in crime'?

15. 'My kids never had the advantage I had. I was born poor'?

ANSWERS.
1. Quentin Crisp. 2. David Cronenberg. 3. Michael Curtiz. 4. Peter Cushing. 5. Bette Davis. 6. Daniel Day-Lewis. 7. Dom De Luise. 8. Cecil B. De Mille. 9. Robert De Niro. 10. Brian De Palma. 11. Gerard Depardieu. 12. Guillaume Depardieu. 13. Johnny Depp. 14. Marlene Dietrich. 15. Kirk Douglas.

Real names

How much do you know about famous people with assumed names? (1)

QUESTIONS.

What are the real names of the following famous people:

1. Neil Diamond?

2. Margot Fonteyn?

3. Elvis Costello?

4. Tony Curtis?

5. Chubby Checker?

6. Elton John?

7. Whoopi Goldberg?

8. Perry Como?

9. Bobby Davro?

10. Rock Hudson?

11. Karl Malden?

12. Peggy Lee?

13. Anthony Quinn?

14. Yves St. Laurent?

15. Lily Savage?

ANSWERS.
1. Noah Kaminsky. 2. Margaret Hookham. 3. Declan McManus. 4. Bernard Schwartz.
5. Ernest Evans. 6. Reginald Dwight. 7. Caryn Johnson. 8. Nick Perido. 9. Robert
Nankeville. 10. Roy Scherer Jnr. 11. Mladen Sekolovich. 12. Norma Egstrom. 13.
Rudolph Oaxaca. 14. Henri Mathieu. 15. Paul O'Grady.

How much do you know about famous people with assumed names? (2)

What are the real names of the following famous people:

1. Winona Ryder?

2. Del Shannon?

3. Tony Randall?

4. Marty Wilde?

5. Sid Vicious?

6. Tammy Wynette?

7. Sting?

8. Ringo Starr?

9. Pia Zadora?

10. Muddy Waters?

11. Barbara Windsor?

12. Conway Twitty?

13. Shakin' Stevens?

14. Stevie Wonder?

15. Annie Oakley?

ANSWERS.
1. Winona Horowitz. 2. Charles Westover. 3. Leonard Rosenberg. 4. Reginald Smith. 5. John Ritchie. 6. Wynette Pugh. 7. Gordon Sumner. 8. Richard Starkey. 9. Pia Schipani. 10. McKinley Morganfield. 11. Barbara Deeks. 12. Harold Jenkins. 13. Michael Barrett. 14. Steveland Judkins. 15. Phoebe Mozee.

How much do you know about famous people with assumed names? (3)

QUESTIONS.

What are the real names of the following famous people:

1. John Le Carre?

2. Marilyn Monroe?

3. Patsy Kline?

4. Stan Laurel?

5. Pola Negri?

6. Chaka Khan?

7. Tab Hunter?

8. Billie Holiday?

9. Buddy Holly?

10. Samuel Goldwyn?

11. Boy George?

12. Kirk Douglas?

13. John Denver?

14. Alice Cooper?

15. Big Daddy?

ANSWERS.
1. David Cornwell. 2. Norma Jean Baker. 3. Virginia Hensley. 4. Arthur Jefferson. 5. Appolonia Chalupek. 6. Yvette Stephens. 7. Arthur Gellen. 8. Eleanora Fagan. 9. Charles Hardin. 10. Samuel Gelbfisz. 11. George O'Dowd. 12. Issur Demsky. 13. Henry John Deutschendorf Jnr. 14. Vincent Furnier. 15. Shirley Crabtree.

How much do you know about famous people with assumed names? (4)

QUESTIONS.

What are the real names of the following famous people:

1. Michael Caine.

2. Lenny Bruce?

3. Lionel Bart?

4. Anne Bancroft?

5. Bono?

6. Lauren Bacall?

7. Yul Brynner?

8. Bo Derek?

9. Michael Crawford?

10. Nat 'King' Cole?

11. Bobby Darin?

12. Charles Bronson?

13. Jack Higgins?

14. Deborah Kerr?

15. Herbert Lom?

ANSWERS.
1. Maurice Micklewhite. 2. Alfred Schweider. 3. Lionel Begleiter. 4. Anna Maria Italiano. 5. Paul Hewson. 6. Betty Joan Perske. 7. Taidje Khan Jnr. 8. Cathleen Collins. 9. Michael Dumble-Smith. 10. Nathaniel Adams. 11. Robert Cassotto. 12. Charles Buchinski. 13. Henry Patterson. 14. Deborah Trimmler. 15. Herbert Ze Schluderpacheru

How much do you know about famous people with assumed names? (5)

QUESTIONS.

What are the real names of the following famous people:

1. Canaletto?

2. Caravaggio?

3. El Cid?

4. St. Francis of Assisi?

5. Nero?

6. Jacques Offenbach?

7. Ho Chi-Minh?

8. El Greco?

9. Alicia Markova?

10. Dame Nellie Melba?

11. Pele?

12. Joseph Stalin?

13. Tintoretto?

14. Tito?

15. The Sundance Kid?

ANSWERS.
1. Giovanni Antonio Canale. 2. Michelangelo Merisi. 3. Rodrigo Diaz de Vivar. 4. Giovanni de Bernadone. 5. Lucius Domitius Ahenobarbus. 6. Jakob Eberst. 7. Nguyen Van Thann. 8. Domenico Theotocopoulos. 9. Alice Marks. 10. Helen Mitchell. 11. Edson Arantes do Nascimento. 12. Iosif Vissarionovich Dzhugashvili. 13. Jacopo Robusti. 14. Josip Broz. 15. Henry Longabaugh.

Famous Spouses

How much do you know about people with famous spouses? (1)

QUESTIONS.

Who is - or was - married to:

1. Victoria Adams?

2. Albert Finney?

3. Pamela Anderson?

4. Loni Anderson?

5. Blake Edwards?

6. Nicholas Cage?

7. Barbara Bach?

8. Michael Caine?

9. Priscilla Beaulieu?

10. Cary Grant?

11. Phoebe Cates.

12. Vincent Price?

13. Kim Basinger?

14. Sammy Davis Jnr?

15. Ronald Reagan?

ANSWERS.
1. David Beckham. 2. Anouk Aimee. 3. Tommy Lee. 4. Burt Reynolds. 5. Julie Andrews.
6. Patricia Arquette. 7. Ringo Starr. 8. Shakira Baksh. 9. Elvis Presley. 10. Dyan Cannon.
11. Kevin Kline. 12, Coral Browne. 13. Alec Baldwin. 14. May Britt. 15. Nancy Davis.

How much do you know about people with famous spouses? (2)

QUESTIONS.

Who is - or was - married to:

1. Cindy Crawford?

2. Jacqueline Du Pre?

3. Linda Eastman?

4. John Thaw?

5. Audrey Hepburn?

6. Eva Herzigova?

7. Iman?

8. Ffion Jenkins?

9. Vivien Leigh?

10. Sophia Loren?

11. Courtney Love?

12. Maurice Gibb?

13. Noel Gallagher?

14. Patsy Kensit?

15. Iris Murdoch?

ANSWERS.
1. Richard Gere. 2. Daniel Barenboim. 3. Paul McCartney. 4. Sheila Hancock. 5. Mel Ferrer. 6. Tico Torres. 7. David Bowie. 8. William Hague. 9. Laurence Olivier. 10. Carlo Ponti. 11. Kurt Cobain. 12. Lulu. 13. Meg Matthews. 14. Liam Gallagher. 15. John Bayley.

How much do you know about people with famous spouses? (3)

QUESTIONS.

Who is – or was – married to:

1. Sylvia Plath?

2. Brigitte Nielsen?

3. Tatum O'Neal?

4. Lisa Presley?

5. Billy Connolly?

6. Ethan Hawke?

7. Sting?

8. Val Kilmer?

9. Natalie Wood?

10. Joanne Woodward?

11. Barbra Streisand?

12. Andre Agassi?

13. Prunella Scales?

14. Denis Thatcher?

15. Charlotte Rampling?

ANSWERS.
1. Ted Hughes. 2. Sylvester Stallone. 3. John McEnroe. 4. Michael Jackson. 5. Pamela Stephenson. 6. Uma Thurman. 7. Frances Tomelty. 8. Joanne Whalley. 9. Robert Wagner. 10. Paul Newman. 11. James Brolin. 12. Steffi Graf. 13. Timothy West. 14. Margaret Roberts. 15. Jean-Michel Jarre.

How much do you know about people with famous spouses? (4)

QUESTIONS.

Who is - or was - married to:

1. Nicole Kidman?

2. Ursula Andress?

3. Lenny Henry?

4. Ava Gardner?

5. Mike Tyson?

6. Jemima Goldsmith?

7. Betty Grable?

8. Sinead Cusack?

9. Claire Bloom?

10. Steven Spielberg?

11. Brigitte Bardot?

12. Anne Bancroft?

13. Ingrid Bergman.

14. Annette Bening?

15. Christie Brinckley?

ANSWERS.
1. Tom Cruise. 2. John Derek. 3. Dawn French. 4. Frank Sinatra. 5. Robin Givens. 6. Imran Khan. 7. Harry James. 8. Jeremy Irons. 9. Rod Steiger. 10. Amy Irving. 11. Roger Vadim. 12. Mel Brooks. 13. Roberto Rossellini. 14. Warren Beatty. 15. Billy Joel.

How much do you know about people with famous spouses? (5)

QUESTIONS.

Who is - or was - married to:

1. Diahnne Abbott?
2. Hephaestus?
3. Elizabeth Barrett?
4. Catherine of Braganza?
5. Isadora Duncan?
6. Leofric of Mercia?
7. Oona O'Neill?
8. Amy Johnson?
9. Napoleon Bonaparte?
10. Charles Laughton?
11. Johnny Dankworth?
12. Lotte Lenya?
13. Messalina?
14. Hera?
15. Charles Lindbergh?

ANSWERS.
1. Robert De Niro. 2. Aphrodite. 3. Robert Browning. 4. King Charles II of England. 5. Sergei Yessenin. 6. Lady Godiva. 7. Charlie Chaplin. 8. Jim Mollison. 9. Josephine de Beauharnais. 10. Elsa Lanchester. 11. Cleo Laine. 12. Kurt Weill. 13. Nero. 14. Zeus. 15. Anne Morrow.

World figures

How much do you know about figures on the world scene? (1)

QUESTIONS.

1. Who was the English economist whose 'General Theory of Employment, Interest and Money' had an enormous impact on economic thinking when it came out in 1936?

2. Who is the South African statesman who served 27 years in prison and was released to become the first black President of the Republic of South Africa?

3. Who was the King of Jordan from 1952 to 1999 who was a moderating voice in the Middle East conflict of the last half-century?

4. Who is the ex-German Chancellor who was the force behind the reunification of Germany?

5. Who is the ex-President of the Russian Federation (1991-1999) who played a decisive role in defeating the attempted coup against President Gorbachev in 1991?

6. Who is the British politician who was the last Governor of Hong Kong and is now one of the European Commissioners?

7. Who was the former G.P. in England who became the leader of the movement for Nyasaland's independence, becoming Prime Minister and President for 30 years?

8. Who was the most prominent celebrity in the world at the time of her death in 1997?

9. Who is the ex-President whose liberal reforms led to the implosion of the Soviet Union?

10. Who was the Chinese reformer, finally a supporter of market-oriented policies, but who still sanctioned the Army's massacre of over 2,000 pro-democracy demonstrators in 1989.

11. Who is the Egyptian diplomat who was the secretary general of the U.N., 1992-96?

12. Who is the Pakistani politician who is the first woman to have become the leader of a Muslim state, in 1988?

13. Who is the ex-electrician, founding member of Solidarity, and President of Poland 1990-95?

ANSWERS.
1. John Maynard Keynes. 2. Nelson Mandela. 3. King Hussein ibn Talal. 4. Helmut Kohl. 5. Boris Yeltsin. 6. Chris Patten. 7. Hastings Banda. 8. Princess Diana of Wales. 9. Mikhail Gorbachev. 10. Deng Xiaoping. 11. Boutros Boutros-Ghali. 12. Benazir Bhutto. 13. Lech Walesa.

How much do you know about figures on the world scene? (2)

QUESTION.

1. What is the title given to Tenzin Gyatso, a Tibetan Buddhist monk and the political ruler of Tibet, now in exile since the Chinese invasion?

2. What is the name of the Myanmar (Burmese) opposition leader, and winner of the 1991 Nobel Peace Prize

3. Who is the ex-President of Peru whose two mandates from 1990 were mainly concerned with fighting the 'Shining Path' and other urban guerrilla movements?

4. What is the name of the French politician, Mayor of Paris 1977-95, twice Prime Minister and finally (1995) President, who has twice found himself in a 'co-habitation' situation with the opposition parties, once as Prime Minister to socialist Francois Mitterand's President and once as President to Lionel Jospin's socialist government?

5. Who was the Argentinian politician twice elected President in 1989 and 1995?

6. What was the name of the President of Egypt from 1970 to 1981? He visited Israel and signed the Israel-Egypt peace treaty of 1979 for which he was murdered by Islamic fanatics

7. Who was the Indian nationalist leader whose strategy was always one of non-violent noncooperation? He was murdered by a Hindu nationalist in '48 after the partition of India.

8. Who is the ex-Prime Minister of Luxembourg who served as President of the European Commission from 1995 to 1999?

9. In 1993 an American and a British politician worked together to propose a peace plan to end the war in Bosnia. Who were they?

10. Who became Turkey's first female Prime Minister in 1993?

11. Who became Canada's first female Prime Minister, also in 1993?

12. Who is the Australian-born U.S.-naturalised multi-media magnate with worldwide interests?

13. Who is the Czech dramatist and human-rights activist who became President of Czechoslovakia in 1989 and then President of the Czech Republic in 1993?

14. Who is the English physicist whose 1988 book 'A Brief History of Time' became an international best-seller?

15. Who was the Algerian President assassinated by Islamic extremists in 1992?

ANSWERS.
1. Dalai Lama. 2. Aung San Suu Kyi. 3. Alberto Fujimori. 4. Jacques Chirac. 5. Carlos Menem. 6. Anwar Sadat. 7. ' Mahatma' Gandhi. 8. Jacques Santer. 9. Cyrus Vance and Lord Owen. 10. Tansu Ciller. 11. Kim Campbell. 12. Rupert Murdoch. 13. Vaclav Havel. 14. Stephen Hawking. 15. Mohammed Boudiaf.

How much do you know about figures on the world scene? (3)

QUESTIONS.

1. Who is the French socialist politician who became the first female Prime Minister of France in May 1991?

2. Who were the two Prime Ministers, of the U.K. and of Ireland, who issued the joint peace initiative for Northern Ireland in December 1993?

3. What is the name of the Lithuanian politician who became President in 1990, declaring Lithuania's independence from the Soviet Union?

4. Who was the first Prime Minister of independent Northern Rhodesia , then the first President of Zambia from 1964 to 1991?

5. What is the name of the Italian Christian Democrat politician who headed seven post-war governments, was Defence Minister 8 times and Foreign Minister 5 times? Accused of having Mafia connections he was tried and acquitted in October 1999.

6. Who is the Portuguese socialist politician, Prime Minister 1976-78, President 1986-96?

7. Who were the mother and son Prime Ministers of India who both died by assassination?

8. Who is the Peruvian diplomat who was the 5th Secretary General of the United Nations 1982-91, and who became President of Peru in 2000?

9. Who was the Prime Minister of Singapore for 31 years?

10. Who is the four-times Prime Minister of Norway who became head of the W.H.O. in '98?

11. Who became the first female President of the Irish Republic in 1990?

12. Who was the U.K.'s first female Prime Minister from 1979 to 1990?

13. Who was the South African National Party politician and President 1989-94 who effectively brought an end to apartheid, ended the ban on the ANC and liberated Nelson Mandela

14. Who succeeded Emperor Hirohito after his death in 1989?

15. Who is the Malawi politician who defeated Hastings Banda in the presidential election in 1992 and went on to be re-elected in 1999?

ANSWERS.
1. Edith Cresson. 2. John Major and Albert Reynolds. 3. Vytautas Landsbergis. 4. Kenneth Kaunda. 5. Giulio Andreotti. 6. Mario Soares. 7. Indira and Rajiv Gandhi. 8. Javier Perez de Cuellar. 9. Lee Kuan Yew. 10. Gro Harlem Brundtland. 11. Mary Robinson. 12. Margaret Thatcher. 13. F.W. de Klerk. 14. Akihito. 15. Bakili Muluzi

How much do you know about figures on the world scene? (4)

QUESTIONS.

1. Who was the Chinese communist politician, a loyal ally of Mao Tse-tung for 40 years and Prime Minister of China from 1949 until his death in 1976?

2. Who was the Pakistani general,, Army Chief of Staff who led a coup-d'etat in 1977, appointed himself President in 1978, instituting a fundamentalist Islamic regime?

3. Who was the French politician whose career went from a role in Petain's Vichy administration to winning two terms as socialist President (1981-95)?

4. Who was the Hungarian communist leader, in power after suppressing the national uprising in 1956, until deposed in 1988?

5. Who was the Irish statesman who founded 'Amnesty International'?

6. Who was the Chinese nationalist leader, twice President of China (1928-31 and 1943-49) and then President of Taiwan from 1949 until his death in 1975.

7. Who has been President of Egypt since the assassination of Anwar Sadat?

8. Who is the Filipino centrist politician, brought to the fore by the assassination of her husband, who overthrew Marcos and became President 1986-92?

9. Who was the British Conservative politician, Prime Minister 1957-1963, who was given the nickname 'Supermac' by the satirical cartoonist Vicky?

10. Who is the Anglican Archbishop of South Africa who was one of the fiercest critics of Apartheid?

11. Who was the Liberal politician twice Prime Minister of Canada, 1968-79 and 80-84?

12. Who was the French Defence Minister who approved the attack on the 'Rainbow Warrior'?

13. Who was the USSR's Foreign Minister 1957-85 and President 1985-88?

14. Who was the Stalinist communist who controlled Albania from 1944 until 1985?

15. Who is the British Conservative politician, Chancellor of the Exchequer, Foreign Secretary, Deputy Prime Minister and Leader of the House of Commons, under Margaret Thatcher?

ANSWERS.
1. Chou En-lai. 2. Muhammad Zia ul-Haq. 3. Francois Mitterand. 4. Janos Kadar. 5. Sean McBride. 6. Jiang Jie Shi (or Chiang Kai-shek). 7. Hosni Moubarak. 8. Cory Aquino. 9. Harold McMillan. 10. Desmond Tutu. 11. Pierre Trudeau. 12. Charles Hernu. 13. Andre Gromyko. 14. Enver Hoxha. 15. Geoffrey Howe.

How much do you know about figures on the world scene? (5)

QUESTIONS.

1. What was the name of the priest murdered by Polish secret police in an anti-Solidarity action?

2. What was the name of the Soviet leader, general secretary of the CPSU 1964-82 and president 1977-82, the latter a period of external imperialism and internal stagnation?

3. Who succeeded Brezhnev as President of the USSR 1983-84, formerly head of KGB?

4. What is the name of the Panamanian soldier, effective ruler of Panama from 1983, a CIA informer, captured in 1989 and charged with drug smuggling and money laundering?

5. Who was the President, virtual dictator of the Philippines 1965-1986?

6. Who was elected President of Argentina in 1983 ending the military dictatorship?

7. Who is the former British Labour party leader (1983-92) who is now Vice President of the European Commission with responsibility for internal reform?

8. Who was the German socialist politician, formerly Mayor of West Berlin 1957-66; German foreign minister 1966-69; federal chancellor 69-74 and instigator of 'Ostpolitik'?

9. What is the name of the Cardinal elected Pope in 1978, first non-Italian Pope since 1522?

10. And what is his family name?

11. Who was the Sri Lankan Prime Minister in 1977, serving as the 1st President, 1978-88?

12. Who was the Italian Christian Democrat politician and twice Prime Minister due to become President, when he was kidnapped and murdered by the Red Brigade?

13. Who was the nationalist dictator of Spain from 1939 to his death in 1975?

14. Who was the American-born wife of the ruler of Monaco who died in a car accident in' 82?

15. Who is the Lebanese politician largely responsible for ending Lebanon's civil war in 1989?

ANSWERS.
1. Jerzy Popieluszko. 2. Leonid Brezhnev. 3. Yuri Andropov. 4. Manuel Noriega. 5. Ferdinand Marcos. 6. Raoul Alfonsin. 7. Neil Kinnock. 8. Willy Brandt. 9. John Paul II. 10. Karol Wojtyla. 11. Junius Jayawardene. 12. Aldo Moro. 13. Francisco Franco. 14. Princess Grace. 15. Amin Gemayel.

How much do you know about figures on the world scene? (6)

QUESTIONS.

1. Who is the former communist leader who became President of Serbia and initiated a policy of ethnic cleansing in the province of Kosovo in the late '90's?

2. Who is the revolutionary who overthrew King Idris of Libya in 1969 and became the country's president? He has been associated with many international acts of terrorism.

3. Who was the Cambodian communist and leader of the Khmer Rouge? After overthrowing the government in 1975 he slaughtered approximately two million Cambodians.

4. Who was the Iranian Shiite leader who returned from exile to Iran in 1979 and established a fundamentalist Islamic republic, executing thousands of opponents?

5. Who is the President of Iraq, renowned for the savagery of his repression of ethnic minorities and the invasion of Kuwait in 1990? His fanatical hatred of Israel may yet lead to the destruction of all life on earth.

6. Who was the Czech communist leader, who ruthlessly restored control after the Prague Spring of 1968, until he was deposed in the popular uprising of 1989?

7. Who was the much despised East German communist leader from 1973 to 1989?

8. Who is the Chilean military dictator who took over the presidency following the coup which ousted President Allende in 1973 and ruled ruthlessly until 1989?

9. Who is the Ugandan who led the coup which deposed Milton Obote in 1971 and made himself President? His reign of terror ended in 1979. He now lives in Saudi Arabia.

10. Who was the leader of the Chinese Communist Party from 1935 until his death in 1976, during which time his political theories led to the deaths of an estimated 60 million people?

11. Who is the Ethiopian soldier who seized power in a coup in 1977, murdering the Emperor, Haile Selassie and instituting a regime of terror until being overthrown in 1991? He now resides in Zimbabwe.

12. Who is the President of the Palestinian National Authority? A doctor in medicine, co-founder of al-Fatah, leader of the P.L.O. who devised the tactic of blowing up school buses.

13. What is the real name of 'Carlos, the Jackal'?

ANSWERS.
1. Slobodan Milosevic. 2. Moamer al Khaddhafi. 3. Pol Pot. 4. Ayatollah Ruhollah Khomeini. 5. Saddam Hussein. 6. Gustav Husak. 7. Erich Honeker. 8. General Augusto Pinochet. 9. Idi Amin. 10. Mao Tse-tung. 11. Haile Mengistu. 12. Yassir Arafat. 13. Ilich Ramirez Sanchez.

How much do you know about figures on the world scene? (7)

QUESTIONS.

1. Who Is the Zimbabwean guerrilla leader who became Prime Minister in 1980 and President in 1987? His one-party rule has led to economic disaster and unrest.

2. Who was the president, virtual dictator of Haiti from 1957 to 1971, protected by his private security force the 'Tonton Macoutes'?

3. Who was the Irish Prime Minister who signed the Anglo-Irish agreement 1985?

4. What was the name of the Turkish-born assassin whose attempt on the life of the Pope John Paul II in 1981 was very nearly successful?

5. What was the name of the disturbed young man who made an attempt on the life of President Reagan in March 1981?

6. What was the name of the disturbed young man who murdered John Lennon in 1980?

7. Who is the British labour politician who was Chancellor of the Exchequer 1964-67; Home Secretary 1967-70, and Prime Minister 1976 – 79?

8. Who is the German Social Democrat politician who was chancellor 1974 – 83? He continued Brandt's 'Ostpolitik' whilst championing NATO and Europe.

9. Who is the French centre-right politician, Minister of Finance 1962-66 and 1969-74, President 1974-81, founder and leader of the UDF party until 1996?

10. Who was the Prime Minister of Spain in the period immediately following Franco's death?

11. What was the name of the family who held Nicaragua like a family fiefdom until their regime was overthrown by the Sandinistas in 1979?

12. By what name was the Croatian communist soldier/politician Josip Broz, virtual dictator of Yugoslavia from 1943 until his death in 1980, better known?

13. What was the name of the Queen of the Netherlands who abdicated in 1980 in favour of her daughter Beatrix?

14. Which former Irish Minister of Justice was tried on the charge of illegally importing arms. acquitted and went on to become Prime Minister (1979) ?

15. Who was the art historian and Surveyor of the Queen's pictures who turned out to have been a Russian spy as well?

ANSWERS.
1. Robert Mugabe. 2. 'Papa Doc' Duvalier. 3. Garret FitzGerald. 4. Mehmet Ali Agcar. 5. John Hinckley. 6. Mark Chapman. 7. James Callaghan. 8. Helmut Schmidt. 9. Valery Giscard d'Estaing. 10. Adolfo Suarez. 11. Somoza. 12. Tito. 13. Juliana. 14. Charles Haughey. 15. Anthony Blunt.

How much do you know about figures on the world scene? (8)

QUESTIONS.

1. Who was the 2nd World War hero, statesman and cousin of the Queen who was murdered by the IRA in August 1979?

2. Who was the President of the Central African Republic 1966-79 and self-proclaimed Emperor 1977-79, whose grandiose inauguration ceremony nearly bankrupted the state?

3. Who was the Progressive Conservative politician, Prime Minister of Canada 1957-63, who refused to accept atomic warheads for U.S. supplied missiles, and lost his job?

4. Who was the 2nd World War hero who escaped from Colditz Castle, became a Conservative M.P. and was murdered by the IRA in 1979?

5. What was the name of the late Shah of Iran, deposed by an Islamic revolution in 1979?

6. Who was the first woman to be Prime Minister of Israel, 1969-74?

7. Who was the first Prime Minister (1962-63) and then first President (1963-65) of an independent Algeria?

8. Who was the infamous leader of the sect 'The People's Temple' who persuaded 914 members of the cult to commit suicide with him in Guyane in 1978?

9. Who was the Prime Minister of South Africa 1966-78, resigning after the 'information scandal'?

10. Who was the first Prime Minister and then first President of independent Kenya?

11. Who succeeded Jomo Kenyatta as President of Kenya after his death in 1978?

12. What was the name of the Israeli premier who signed the Camp David agreement with President Sadat of Egypt?

13. What is the name of the world's first 'test-tube baby', born in 1978?

14. Who was the Soviet physicist and 'father' of the Soviet hydrogen bomb who became an outspoken human-rights campaigner. elected to the Russian Parliament in 1989?

15. Who was the last white Prime Minister of Zimbabwe (Rhodesia) who made the unilateral declaration of independence in 1965?

ANSWERS.
1. Earl Mountbatten of Burma. 2. Jean-Bedel Bokassa. 3. J. G. Diefenbaker. 4. Airey Neave. 5. Mohammed Reze Pahlavi. 6. Golda Meir. 7. Muhammad Ben Bella. 8. James Jones. 9. B.J. Vorster. 10. Jomo Kemyatta. 11. Daniel Arap Moi. 12. Menachem Begin. 13. Louise Brown. 14. Andrei Sakharov. 15. Ian Smith.

How much do you know about figures on the world scene? (9)

QUESTIONS.

1. What was the name of the Bulgarian defector, living in London, who died in 1978 after being stabbed with an umbrella with a poisoned tip?

2. Who was the London-born comic genius of silent films who died on Christmas day 1977?

3. Who was the leading black activist who died whilst in police custody in South Africa in September 1977?

4. What was the name of the German industrialist murdered by his terrorist abductors the Red Army Faction, in October 1977?

5. What was the name of the terrorist leader found shot dead in his police cell in October '77?

6. Who was the lyric soprano, U.S. born of Greek parentage, who excelled in all the great dramatic roles, dominating the operatic scene in the 1950's and 60's?

7. Who were the two Belfast women who were awarded the 1977 Nobel Peace Prize for starting the 'Ulster Peace Movement'?

8. Who was the German-born rocket scientist (the V.1 and V.2) who worked for NASA and invented the Saturn rocket that sent Apollo 12 to the moon in 1969?

9. Who was the Lebanese Muslim leader assassinated in March 1977?

10. What was the name of the Soviet dictator from 1924 until his death in 1953? In creating 'socialism in one country' his assassinations, purges, starvation and genocide wiped out an estimated 70 million people.

11, What was the name of Stalin's daughter who defected from the Soviet Union in 1966?

12. Who was the British Conservative politician and statesman, Foreign Secretary 1935-38; 1940-45 and 1951-55; Prime Minister 1955-1957, his supreme aim was world peace based on respect for law?

13. Who was the French statesman, a wartime colleague of de Gaulle, Prime Minister 1962-1968, and President 1969-74?

14. What was the name of Mao Tse-tung's widow, known as a radical communist?

15. With three close associates, they were known as .....what?

ANSWERS.
1. Georgi Markov. 2. Charlie Chaplin. 3. Steve Biko. 4. Hans Meyer Schleyer. 5. Andreas Baader. 6. Maria Callas. 7. Betty Williams and Mairead Corrigan. 8. Werner von Braun. 9. Kamal Jumblatt. 10. Josef Stalin. 11. Svetlana Alliluyeva. 12. Anthony Eden. 13. Georges Pompidou. 14. Jiang Qing. 15. 'The Gang of Four'.

How much do you know about figures on the world scene? (10)

QUESTIONS.

1. Who was the world's richest man at the time of his death June 6th 1976?

2. Who was the female leader of the Red Army Faction terrorist leader who committed suicide in prison in May 1976?

3. Who was the British Liberal politician, leader of the Liberal Party 1967-76, tried and acquitted on charges of conspiracy to murder a former homosexual lover?

4. Who was the Argentinian soldier and politician, took part in the 1943 army revolt and became virtual dictator of Argentina 1946-55, making a short-lived comeback 1973-74?

5. And what was the name of his first wife who became a powerful political influence in her own right, until her death in 1952

6. Who was the British Labour politician who became leader of the Party 1963, Prime Minister 1964-70 and 1974-76, knighted in 1976 and made a peer in 1983?

7. Who was the Marxist leader who became President of Angola after the departure of the Portuguese in 1974?

8. And who was the leader of the UNITA rebels who fought Neto's army until 1994?

9. Who succeeded the Spanish dictator Franco, after his death in November 1975?

10. Who was the Canadian-born theorist of communications who coined the phrase 'The Global Village' in his book 'The Gutenberg Galaxy' (1962)?

11. Who was the first Prime Minister of independent Malaya 1957-63, and of Malaysia 1963- 70?

12. Who is the Nigerian soldier/politician who seized power in a coup in 1966 and was Head of State until 1975 when he was deposed by another coup?

13. Who is the American palaeontologist and writer who proposed the theory of 'punctuated equilibrium', that the evolution of a species does not always proceed at a steady rate?

14. Who was the Greek-born shipping magnate who married Jacqueline Kennedy?

15. Who was the Russian writer whose books, especially 'The Gulag Archipelago' led to his exile by the Soviet authorities? Winner of the Nobel Prize for Literature 1970.

ANSWERS.
1. J. Paul Getty. 2. Ulrike Meinhof. 3. Jeremy Thorpe. 4. Juan Peron. 5. Eva Peron. 6. Harold Wilson. 7. Agostinho Neto. 8. Jonas Savimbi. 9. King Juan Carlos. 10. Marshall McLuhan. 11. Tunku Abdul Rahman. 12. Yakubu Gowon. 13. Stephen Jay Gould. 14. Aristotle Onassis. 15. Aleksandr Solzhenitsyn.

How much do you know about figures on the world scene? (11)

QUESTIONS.

1. Who was the 20th century Indian politician known as 'The Lion of Kashmir'?

2. Who was the leader of Bangladesh when it declared independence from Pakistan in March 1971?

3. Who was the Pakistani President 1969-71 whose mishandling of the Bangladesh separatist issue led to civil war, then war with India, and then to his resignation?

4. Who was the Chancellor of West Germany 1949-1963 who achieved the post-war reconciliation with France and strongly supported the Western bloc in Europe?

5. What was the name of the Field Marshal who commanded the Afrika Korps in the western desert of North Africa 1941-43?

6. Who was the Algerian politician who brought the nationalist leader Ben Bella to power in 1962, then removed him to take over power himself in 1965?

7. Who is the Albanian former communist leader, who took over as Head of State after the death of Enver Hoxha, and began to relax his predecessors Stalinist and isolationist policies?

8. Who was the English Field Marshal in WW1, who served in France before taking command in the Middle East where he defeated the Turkish forces at Megiddo in September 1918?

9. Who was the left-wing Chilean politician, elected President 1970, deposed by a military coup under General Pinochet in 1973?

10. Who was the last British Prime Minister to come from the ranks of the Liberal Party?

11. Who was the Ba'athist politician President of Syria from 1971 until his death in 2000?

12. Who was the French socialist who was first president of the Fourth Republic, 1947-54?

13. Who was the Nigerian soldier and politician who led a coup against President Buhari in 1985 and appointed himself president from 1985 until 1993?

14. Who was the British Prime Minister at the time of the abdication crisis in 1936?

15. Who was the British Foreign Secretary in 1915 who issued the declaration about a Jewish national homeland?

ANSWERS.

1. Abdullah Sheik Muhammad. 2. Sheikh Mujibur Rahman. 3. General Yahya Khan. 4. Konrad Adenauer. 5. Erwin Rommel. 6. Houari Boumedienne. 7. Ramiz Alia. 8. Viscount Allenby. 9. Salvador Allende. 10. Herbert Henry Asquith (1908-16). 11. Hafez al-Assad. 12. Vincent Auriol. 13. Ibrahim Babangida. 14. Stanley Baldwin 15. Arthur Balfour.

How much do you know about figures on the world scene? (12)

QUESTIONS.

1. Who became the first female Prime Minister of Bangladesh in February 1991?

2. Who was the first Prime Minister of a semi-independent Barbados in 1954?

3. Who was the NAZI officer granted the sobriquet of the 'Butcher of Lyon'? He was expelled from Bolivia in 1983, taken to France, tried and convicted of crimes against humanity.

4. Who was the first Prime Minister of Australia, 1901-03?

5. Who was the Cuban dictator who was deposed by Castro's 1959 revolution?

6. Who was the King of Belgium from 1951 until his death in 1993?

7. Who was the President of Peru 1963-68 and 1980-85?

8. Who became the first Prime Minister of an independent Belize in 1964?

9. Who was the first Prime Minister (1956) then first President of an independent Tunisia before being overthrown in a bloodless coup in 1987?

10. Who was the Czech nationalist leader who directed the revolutionary movement against the Austrians, serving three times as President of independent Czechoslovakia 1918-35?

11. Who was the Czech foreign minister of the government in exile 1940-45? He returned to Prague in 1945 but committed suicide under pressure from the Communists.

12. Who succeeded Tomas Masaryk in 1935, was driven out by the Germans in 1939, was head of the government in exile 1939-45, became President again in 1945 but was deposed by the communist coup in 1948?

13. Who was Israel's first Prime Minister 1948-53 and again 1955-63

14. Which hereditary title did Labour politician Tony Benn give up in order to stay in the House of Commons?

15. Who was the infamous Soviet minister of the interior and head of the secret police 1938-53 responsible for the imprisonment, transportation and liquidation of millions of Soviet citizens?

ANSWERS.
1. Begum Khaleda Zia. 2. Grantley Adams. 3. Klaus Barbie. 4. Edmund Barton. 5. Fulgencio Batista. 6. King Baudouin 7. Fernando Belaunde Terry. 8. George Price. 9. Habib ben Ali Bourguiba. 10. Tomas Masaryk. 11. Jan Masaryk. 12. Eduard Benes. 13. David Ben-Gurion. 14. Viscount Stansgate. 15. Lavrenti Beria.

How much do you know about figures on the world scene? (13)

QUESTIONS.

1. Who was the American Baptist missionary killed by Chinese communists in 1945 at the age of 27, after whom a U.S. right-wing society is now named?

2. Who became the first socialist Prime Minister of France in 1936?

3. Who was the German foreign minister who signed the Treaty of Rapallo in 1922, a treaty of friendship with the Soviet Union, for which he was assassinated by right-wing fanatics?

4. Who was the 20th century Spanish-Basque journalist, politician and Loyalist leader in the Civil War, spent the Franco years exiled in the USSR, was called by her admirers 'La Pasionaria'?

5. Who is the Zulu leader and politician, chief minister of KwaZulu black homeland and founder and president of the Inkatha political and paramilitary organisation?

6. Who was the 20th century professor of philosophy and literature who was also Venezuela's first democratically elected president in 1948, before being deposed by a military coup?

7. Who was the 20th century Argentinian general and president who in 1982 ordered the seizure of the Falkland Islands?

8. Who was the 20th century Burmese diplomat and secretary general of U.N. 1962-71?

9. Who was the South African surgeon who pioneered heart transplant surgery in 1967?

10. Who was the French designer who dominated the world of haute couture for many years, giving the world the 'little black dress' and 'No 5' perfume?

11. Who was military governor of Nigeria's eastern region who declared it an independent state of Biafra on May 30th 1967?

12. Who was the one-eyed Israeli Defence Minister who led the Israeli Army to such a comprehensive victory over Egyptian, Jordanian and Syrian forces in the 6 day war 1967?

13. Who was the Soviet politician, secretary general of the CPSU 1953-64, premier 1958-64 whose speech denouncing Stalin surprised the world?

14. Who was the charismatic French general, leader of the Free French in the 2nd World War who became President of the 5th Republic, 1958-69?

15. Who was the first President of Israel, 1948-52?

ANSWERS.
1. John Birch. 2. Leon Blum. 3. Walter Rathenau. 4. Dolores Ibarruri. 5. Chief Gatsha Buthelezi. 6. Romulo Gallegos. 7. Leopoldo Galtieri. 8. U Thant. 9. Prof. Christian Barnard. 10. 'Coco' Chanel. 11. Colonel Ojukwu. 12. Moshe Dayan. 13. Nikita Khrushchev. 14. Charles de Gaulle. 15. Chaim Weizman.

How much do you know about figures on the world scene? (14)

QUESTIONS.

1. Who was the Swedish-born Secretary-General of the United Nations who was killed in an air crash in Northern Rhodesia (now Zambia) in September, 1961?

2. Who was the 19th/20th century Austrian doctor who literally invented the field of psychoanalysis? He was called 'the Copernicus of the Mind'.

3. Who was the 19th/20th century Swiss psychiatrist who, from 1907 until 1913 was Freud's principal collaborator, leaving him to pursue his own ideas?

4. Who was the 19th/20th century Russian ballet dancer who became enormously and internationally famous for presenting new roles, such as 'L'Apres-midi d'un faune'?

5. Who was the politician who led Ghana to independence in the 1950's and was the moving spirit behind the 'Charter of African States'? He was overthrown by a military coup in 1966.

6. Who was the brilliant Russian ballet dancer who defected to the West during a visit to Paris in 1961? For many years he danced with the London Royal Ballet and Margot Fonteyn.

7. In 1962 the Nazi bureaucrat responsible for implementing 'the final solution' against the Jewish race, was executed for crimes against humanity. What was his name?

8. Who was the first black man to take his place as a student at the previously all-white University of Mississippi in September 1962?

9. What was the name of the Russian cosmonaut who was the first man in space in 1961?

10. Who captained the English football team when it won the World Cup in 1966?

11. Who was arrested for the murder of President John F. Kennedy in Dallas, Texas 1963?

12. And who murdered Oswald before he could be brought to trial?

13. What was the name of the Texas Governor who was slightly injured in the assassination?

14. Who was the highly unpopular President of South Vietnam, killed in a military coup '63?

15. Who was the West German chief economist during the Konrad Adenauer administration, architect of the 'economic miracle', successor to Adenauer as Chancellor?

ANSWERS.
1. Dag Hammarskjold. 2. Sigmund Freud. 3. Carl Jung. 4. Vaslav Nijinsky. 5. Kwame Nkrumah. 6. Rudolf Nuryev. 7. Adolf Eichmann. 8. James Meredith. 9. Yuri Gagarin. 10. Bobby Moore. 11. Lee Harvey Oswald. 12. Jack Ruby. 13. John B. Connally. 14. Ngo Dinh Diem. 15. Ludwig Erhard.

How much do you know about figures on the world scene? (15)

QUESTIONS.

1. Who was sworn in on January 20th 2001 as the 43rd President of the U.S.?

2. Who was obliged to resign from Tony Blair's cabinet for the second time in January '01?

3. What was the name of the British G.P. found guilty of murdering 15 of his patients?

4. Who was the young yachtswoman who completed the Vendee Globe race in February 2001, and although not the winner, her efforts captivated the imagination of the world?

5. Who was persuaded to be indiscreet in her conversation with a News of the World reporter disguised as an Arab Sheik, in April 2001?

6. What was the name of the Oklahoma City bomber, executed on May 16th 2001?

7. Who returned to Britain from Brazil and was promptly arrested?

8. What was the name of the Conservative leader who resigned after losing the elections to Labour in June 2001?

9. What was the name of the man found guilty of the murder of Jill Dando and sentenced to life imprisonment?

10. Who was sentenced to four years imprisonment for bribing and forging his way to a £500,000 libel victory over the Daily Star newspaper?

11. Who was the ecstatic winner of the Men's Singles Final at Wimbledon in July 2001?

12. Who said, in September 2001, 'Today we must firmly declare that the Cold War is over. The world is at a new stage'?

13. What was the name of the 'adviser' to the Secretary of State for Transport whose callous and cynical observations in a memo sent out on September 11th 2001 were; 'It is now a very good day to get out anything we want to bury. Councillors' expenses, anyone?'

14. Who was the Saudi-born leader of the al-Quaeda terrorist organisation who launched the September 11th attacks against America?

15. What is the name of the Mayor of New York who responded so magnificently?

ANSWERS.
1. George W. Bush. 2. Peter Mandelson. 3. Harold Shipman. 4. Ellen MacArthur. 5. Sophie Wessex. 6. Timothy McVeigh. 7. Ronnie Biggs. 8. William Hague. 9. Barry George. 10. Jeffrey Archer. 11. Goran Ivanisevic. 12. Vladimir Putin, President of Russia. 13. Jo Moore. 14. Osama bin-Laden. 15. Rudolph Giuliani.

Famous Dogs

How much do you know about famous dogs in fact and fiction?

QUESTIONS.

1. What is the name of the three-headed dog which guards the entrance to Hades?

2. What is the name of the most famous Beagle in the world, Charlie Brown's guide and mentor?

3. What was the name of the canine cosmonaut sent into space by the Russians?

4. What was the name of the collie which starred in a number of films, starting in the '40's?

5. But Lassie wasn't the first canine film star. Before her there had been an Alsatian who appeared in a whole series of silent movies. What was he called?=

6. And there was the wire-haired terrier to whom Nick and Nora Charles belonged in the 'Thin Man' series in the thirties. What was his name?

7. What was the name of the dog which accompanied the 'Three Men in a Boat' by Jerome K. Jerome?

8. England would never have won the World Cup in 19966 without the aid of a dog. The Cup was stolen and then thrown away by the nervous villain, and was then found by ......?

9. 'Blondie' of comic-strip fame has a dog who is frequently the most intelligent person in the strip. What is it's name?

10. What was the name of the fox terrier who posed for the logo for His Master's Voice?

11. What is the breed of the dog who starred in 'Beethoven' in 1992 and the sequel in '93?

12. What was the name of the famous terrier which kept a vigil on his master's grave for fourteen years?

13. What is the name of the dog which appears in public whenever and wherever Punch and Judy appear?

14. What is the name of Tintin's dog?

15. What was the name of Odysseus's dog, which recognised him and then died?

ANSWERS.
1. Cerberus. 2. Snoopy. 3. Laika. 4. Lassie. 5. Rin Tin Tin. 6. Asta. 7. Montmorency. 8. Pickles. 9. Daisy. 10. Nipper. 11. A St. Bernard. 12. Greyfriars Bobby. 13. Toby. 14. Snowy. 15. Argus.

Famous Horses

How much do you know about famous horses in fact and fiction?

QUESTIONS.

1. What was the name of Alexander the Great's famous war-horse?

2. What was the name of Don Quixote's horse in Cervante's epic story?

3. Dick Turpin was a fictitious highwayman. What was the name of his horse?

4. What was the name of the horse appointed Senator by his owner the Emperor Caligula?

5. What was the name of the favourite war-horse of the legendary Spanish knight El Cid?

6. What was the name of the beautiful white stallion ridden by the cowboy matinee idol, Roy Rogers?

7. What was the name of the horse which was the central character of the famous book for children by Anna Sewell?

8. What was the name of the Duke of Wellington's favourite war-horse?

9. What was the name of the winged horse beloved of the Gods, which was tamed by the Greek hero Bellerophon?

10. According to Greek legend Pegasus was fathered by Poseidon on Medusa, but he had already fathered another horse on the Goddess Demeter. What was that horse's name?

11. What was the name of the warhorse of the 'perfect knight' Orlando in the 16th century poem by Ariosto - 'Orlando Furioso'?

12. What was the name of the horse of the Lone Ranger of television fame?

13. Napoleon's favourite war-horse was named after one of his victories. What was it?

14. What was the name of Col. Harry Llewellyn's famous show jumper?

15. In the 'Twilight of the Gods', the last part of Wagner's trilogy 'The Ring of the Nibelung'. Brunnhilde rides her horse through the flames and onto Siegfried's funeral pyre. What is her horse's name?

ANSWERS.
1. Bucephalus. 2. Rosinante. 3. Black Bess. 4. Incitatus. 5. Babieca. 6. Trigger. 7. Black Beauty. 8. Copenhagen. 9. Pegasus. 10. Arion. 11. Brigliandoro. 12. Silver. 13. Marengo. 14. Foxhunter. 15. Grane.

9
SPORT

American football

How much do you know about American football? (1)

QUESTIONS.

What are the names of the teams from the following towns or states:

1. Denver?

2. Dallas?

3. Washington?

4. Kansas City?

5. Chicago?

6. Miami?

7. Carolina?

8. Baltimore?

9. New Orleans?

10. New York?

11. Detroit?

12. Atlanta?

13. Buffalo?

14. Cincinnati?

15. Minnesota?

ANSWERS.
1. Broncos. 2. Cowboys. 3. Redskins. 4. Chiefs. 5. Bears. 6. Dolphins. 7. Panthers. 8. Ravens. 9. Saints. 10. Giants. 11. Lions. 12. Falcons. 13. Bills. 14. Bengals. 15. Vikings.

How much do you know about American football? (2)

QUESTIONS.

What are the names of the teams from the following towns or states:

1. St. Louis?

2. San Diego?

3. Pittsburgh?

4. Arizona?

5. Indianapolis?

6. Jacksonville?

7. New England?

8. New York?

9. Oakland?

10. San Francisco?

11. Green Bay?

12. Philadelphia?

13. Phoenix?

14. Tampa Bay?

15. Tennessee?

ANSWERS.
1. Rams. 2. Chargers 3. Steelers. 4. Cardinals. 5. Colts. 6. Jaguars. 7. Patriots. 8. Jets. 9. Raiders. 10. '49'ers. 11. Packers. 12. Eagles. 13. Cardinals. 14. Buccaneers. 15. Oilers.

How much do you know about American football? (3)

QUESTIONS.

1. What is the shape of and what are the measurements of an American Football playing field?

2. 10 yards (9 metres) in from each end of the playing rectangle white lines called 'goal lines' bisect the full width of the field. What are the two areas thus marked out called?

3. The remaining 100 yards of the playing area is also bisected across it's width by white lines. What is the space between these lines?

4. Two rows of brief white lines run the length of the field indicating each yard. What are they called?

5. What is the weight of a football?

6. How many periods of play constitute a game of football, and what are they called?

7. How many players are there in each team?

8. How many officials supervise a professional football game?

9. Where did football begin in the US?

10. What is considered by football historians to be the birth-date of football in the US?

11. On that date a team from Rutgers University met a team from which other university for the first intercollegiate game?

12. What are the games which mark the climax of the College football season called?

13. This tradition began in 1902 when Stanford University invited the University of Michigan to a New Year's Day contest. What did this particular game evolve into?

14. In Dallas, Texas they play for the Cotton Bowl, in Miami Florida for the Orange Bowl. What do they play for in New Orleans, Louisiana?

15. Some outstanding student athletes became US sporting heroes. Joe Namath, for example, began his career at which institute of learning?

ANSWERS.
1. A rectangle, 120 yards (110 metres) long x 53.5 yards (48.9 metres) wide. 2. 'End Zones'. 3. Five yards (4.5 m). 4. 'Hash marks'. 5. 14-15 oz. (397-425 g). 6. Four quarters. 7. Eleven. 8. Seven. 9. In colleges and universities. 10. November 6th 1869. 11. Princeton. 12. College Bowl Games. 13. The 'Rose Bowl' game. 14. The 'Sugar Bowl'. 15. University of Alabama.

How much do you know about American football? (4)

QUESTIONS.

1. A team scores a 'touchdown' when they get the ball into the opposing team's 'end zone'. How many points is a touchdown worth?

2. How many points do you score with a running/passing 'conversion' or with a kicking conversion?

3. How many points do you score with a 'field goal'?

4. What is a 'touchback'?

5. What is a 'safety'?

6. How many points does the defensive team earn by a 'safety'?

7. In what year did the first professional football game in the US take place?

8. The two teams participating were Latrobe, Pennsylvania, and ...... which other?

9. The first league of professional footballers was formed in what year?

10. And was called ....What?

11. In 1922 this was changed to ......What?

12. In the 1960's there were two professional football leagues in the US. One, obviously, was the NFL. What was the other called?

13. In what year did the NFL and the AFL merge to become the only major professional football league in the US, retaining the name – NFL?

14. In 1967, before the merger, the best two teams from the two leagues met in a major contest to determine the best team in the country. After the merger this contest became a fixture, played in January it is the final match of the professional season, played by the best two teams from the two 'conferences' which constitute the NFL What is the contest called now?

15. In that first contest in 1967 the Green Bay Packers won by a score of 35-10. Who was the team that lost?

ANSWERS.
1. Six. 2. Two and one respectively. 3. Three. 4. A deliberate touchdown in the attacking team's own end zone. 5. An involuntary touchdown in the attacking team's own end zone, caused by the play of the defending team. 6. Two. 7. 1895. 8. Jeannette, Pennsylvania. 9. 1920. 10. American Professional Football Association. 11. National Football League (NFL). 12. American Football League (AFL). 13. 1970. 14. The 'Super Bowl'. 15. Kansas City Chiefs.

How much do you know about American football? (5)

QUESTIONS.

1. Who was the great football coach who is commemorated by the trophy awarded to the winner of the Super Bowl contest?

2. Who was the great player who is commemorated by the trophy awarded to the player voted Most Valuable Player of the year?

3. National League football is played according to what rules?

4. Which team won the Super Bowl in the year 2001?

5. Which team plays on a home ground called 'Three Rivers Stadium'?

6. Who coached Miami Dolphins in 1972 when they were the only professional team to complete the season undefeated with 17 wins, and in '73 and '74 when they won the Super Bowl ? He retired in 1996 with the highest record in the NFL of 347 wins over 33 seasons.

7. Who was the football defensive back and baseball outfielder who, in September 1989, scored a touchdown for the Atlanta Falcons and a home run for the New York Yankees in the same week?

8. Which team plays its home games in Arrowhead Stadium?

9. Who was the quarterback for the San Francisco '49ers who led them to victory in the Super Bowl in 1982-85-89-90? He was the NFL's first three-time winner of the MVP award, 82-83-90.

10. Which team plays its home games at Lambeau Field?

11. Who scored 5 touchdowns the first 5 times he carried the ball in a game for University of Illinois against Michigan, in 1924, earning himself the nickname 'The Galloping Ghost' and a professional career with the Chicago Bears?

12. Who was a student at Rutgers University when he was made the first black 'All-American? He went on to make a career in music, on the stage and in the cinema.

13. Which team plays its home games at Candlestick Park?

14. Who was the Miami Dolphin's quarterback who, in 1984, became the first quarterback to pass for more than 5,000 yards in a season, and broke the single-season record for touchdown passes?

15. What is the name of the Miami Dolphins home ground?

ANSWERS.
1. Vince Lombardi. 2. Jim Thorpe. 3. Harvard Rules. 4. Baltimore Ravens. 5. Pittsburgh Steelers. 6. Don Shula. 7. Deion Sanders. 8. Kansas City Chiefs. 9. Joe Montana. 10. Green Bay Packers 11. Red Grange. 12. Paul Robeson. 13. San Francisco '49ers. 14. Dan Marino. 15. Joe Robbie Stadium.

How much do you know about American football? (6)

QUESTIONS.

1. Which team won the Super Bowl in the year 2000?

2. Who was the New York Jets quarterback who led them to a famous victory over the defending champions, the Baltimore Colts, in the 1969 Super Bowl?

3. Which team's home ground is in the Hubert H. Humphrey Metrodome?

4. Who was the star receiver for the San Francisco '49ers, making such effective passing combinations with Joe Montana, and helping them to win the Super Bowl in 1989 and 1990?

5. Who was the great running back who went from the University of Pittsburgh to the Dallas Cowboys in 1979 and set an NFL record with a run of 99 yards against Minnesota Vikings in 1983? He had a career rushing total of 12,739 yards.

6. Which team won the Super Bowl in both 1998 and 1999?

7. Who was the Cleveland Brown's full back who led the NFL statistics for rushing yards 8 times in a 9 year (1957 – 1966) career?

8. Which team has its home ground at Rich Stadium, Orchard Park?

9. Who was the head football coach at Yale University who, in 1889, in collaboration with the editor Caspar W. Whitney, began honouring the best football players by nominating them to an 'All-American' team?

10. Which team won the Super Bowl in 1993, 1994 and 1996?

11. Who was the Norwegian born player and coach at the University of Notre Dame who revolutionised football strategy by the introduction of the forward pass? He led Notre Dame to 3 National Collegiate Championships (1924, 29 and 30), winning 105 games, losing 12 and drawing 5.

12. Who was the running back for the Chicago Bears who retired in 1987, the NFL's career leader with 3,838 rushing attempts; 16,726 rushing yards and 110 rushing touchdowns? His nickname was 'Sweetness'

13. Which team reached the Super Bowl four years in succession, 1991-92-93 and 94 , only to lose each time?

14. Which team plays its home games in the Riverfront Stadium?

15. Two teams have won the Super Bowl 5 times each. One is the San Francisco '49ers. What is the other?

ANSWERS.
1. St.Louis Rams. 2. Joe Namath. 3. Minnesota Vikings. 4. Jerry Rice. 5. Tony Dorsett. 6. Denver Broncos. 7. Jim Brown. 8. Buffalo Bills. 9. Walter Chauncey Camp. 10. Dallas Cowboys. 11. Knut Rockne. 12. Walter Jerry Paton. 13. Buffalo Bills. 14. Cincinnati Bengals. 15. Dallas Cowboys.

Major league baseball teams

How much do you know about major league baseball teams? (1)

QUESTIONS.

What are the names of the teams from the following towns or states:

1. Detroit?

2. Cincinnati?

3. Baltimore?

4. Anaheim?

5. Toronto?

6. Los Angeles?

7. Kansas City?

8. Montreal?

9. St. Louis?

10. Philadelphia?

11. Cleveland?

12. Boston?

13. Atlanta?

14. Chicago?

15. New York?

ANSWERS.
1.Tigers (AL). 2. Reds.)NL). 3. Orioles (AL). 4.Angels (AL). 5. Blue Jays (AL). 6.
Dodgers. (NL). 7. Royals (AL). 8. Expos (NL). 9. Cardinals (NL). 10. Phillies (NL) 11.
Indians (AL). 12. Red Sox (AL). 13. Braves (NL). 14. Cubs. (NL). 15. Mets (NL).

Leagues : NL = National League; AL = American League.

How much do you know about major league baseball teams? (2)

QUESTIONS.

What are the names of the teams from the following towns or states:

1. Chicago?

2. Colorado?

3. Florida?

4. Houston?

5. Milwaukee?

6. Minnesota?

7. New York?

8. Oakland?

9. Pittsburgh?

10. San Diego?

11. San Francisco?

12. Seattle?

13. Texas?

14. Washington? >1971

15. Boston? >1952

ANSWERS.
1. White Sox (AL). 2. Rockies (NL). 3. Marlins (NL). 4. Astros (NL). 5. Brewers (AL). 6. Twins (AL). 7. Yankees (AL). 8. Athletics (AL). 9. Pirates (NL). 10. Padres (NL). 11. Giants (NL). 12. Mariners (AL). 13. Rangers (AL). 14. Senators (AL). 15. Braves (NL).

Leagues: NL = National League; AL = American League. In the league up to the date shown.

How much do you know about major league baseball teams? (3)

QUESTIONS.

1. According to popular legend, who invented baseball in Cooperstown, New York in 1839?

2. The first organised baseball club was formed in 1842. What was its name?

3. Who was the principal organiser?

4. In which town did all this take place?

5. When did the first official modern baseball game take place?

6. What was the name of the other club, against which the Knickerbockers played?

7. What was the final score?

8. In 1862 the first fully enclosed baseball park was completed. Where was it?

9. In 1869 the first fully professional baseball team was launched. What it called?

10. In 1876 eight professional clubs formed the National League. In 1901 the American League was formed. Who was its founder?

11. In what year did teams from each league meet in the first World Series?

12. Which team was involved in a scandal in 1919, after losing the World Series to the Cincinnati Reds?

13. Who was the federal judge who became baseball's commissioner, establishing stricter rules and regulations?

14. What institution was opened in 1939 to display baseball memorabilia and to honour the game's greatest players?

15. Who was the major league's first black player, joining the Brooklyn Dodgers in 1947?

ANSWERS.
1. Abner Doubleday. 2. The 'Knickerbocker Base Ball Club'. 3. Alexander Cartwright. 4. New York. 5. June 19th, 1846. 6. The 'New York Club'. 7. NYC 23 – Knickerbockers 1. 8. Union Grounds, Brooklyn. 9. Cincinnati Red Stockings. 10. Ban Johnson. 11. 1903. 12. Chicago White Sox. 13. Kenesaw Mountain Landis. 14. National Baseball Hall of fame. 15. Jackie Robinson.

How much do you know about major league baseball teams? (4)

QUESTIONS.

1. What major innovation occurred to baseball during the 2nd World War?

2. In 1953 the Boston Braves relocated. Where did they go to?

3. In 1958 the Brooklyn Dodgers also relocated. Where to?

4. Also in 1958 the New York Giants also went West. Where to?

5. In September 1994 a very unusual situation presented itself, which lasted until May 1995. What was it?

6. What was the name of the American who introduced baseball to Japan in 1872?

7. How large is a baseball field?

8. A baseball field is divided into two areas: the first is the playing area; the second is all the rest. In baseball terminology what is the playing area called?

9. And what is all the rest?

10. The playing area (fair territory) is again divided into two areas. What are they called?

11. The infield is a square shaped plot. What is it called?

12. What does each side of the square measure?

13. One corner of the square (or diamond) is marked by a five-sided piece of rubber. What is this called?

14. How many players are there in each team?

15. How many umpires officiate at each major league baseball game?

ANSWERS.
1. Establishment of American Girls Professional Baseball League. 2. Milwaukee. 3. Los Angeles. 4. San Francisco. 5. Player's strike. 6. Horace Wilson. 7. About 2 acres (0.8 hectares) 8. Fair territory. 9. Foul territory. 10. Infield and outfield. 11. The 'diamond'. 12. 90 feet (27 metres). 13. The 'home plate'. 14. Nine. 15. Four.

How much do you know about major league baseball teams? (5)

QUESTIONS.

1. Who bats first? The home team or the visiting team?

2. What is the area into which the pitcher must throw the ball known as?

3. Pitches thrown into this area that the batter does not hit are known as …..what?

4. 'Strikes' also includes pitches that the batter swings at but misses and the first two times that a batter hits the ball out of the playing area (into foul territory). After how many 'strikes' is a batter given out by the umpire?

5. Pitches outside the 'strike zone' are called 'balls'. A batter can proceed to first base after a pitcher has thrown how many 'balls'?

6. What is this action called?

7. What is it called if a batter gets to first base after hitting the ball into the playing area?

8. What is it called if the batter gets to seconds base after hitting the ball?

9. What is it called if the batter gets to third base?

10. What is it called if the batter gets all the way round the four bases (including the 'home plate') on one hit?

11. What is it called if a batter scores a home run from a ball which remains inside the field of play (as opposed to a ball knocked over the outfield fence, the usual source of home runs)?

12. What is the play called if there are three runners, one at each base, preceding the batter who hits the 'home run', all of whom get home and all score runs?

13. How many professional teams are there in each of the National League and the American League?

14. How many divisions are there in each of the leagues?

15. What are the divisions called?

ANSWERS.
1. The visitors 2. The 'strike zone'. 3. 'Strikes'. 4. Three. 5. Four. 6. 'A walk'. 7. A 'base hit' 8. A 'double'. 9. A 'triple'. 10. A 'home run'. 11. An 'inside-the-park home run'. 12. A 'grand slam'. 13. Fourteen. 14. Three. 15. Eastern, Central and Western Divisions.

How much do you know about major league baseball teams? (6)

QUESTIONS.

1. The major league baseball season in North America lasts from April to October. How many games does each team play as part of their regular season (not counting play-offs and World Series)?

2. What are the 'play-offs'?

3. How many teams from each of the two leagues enter the first stage of the play-offs?

4. The final series in the play-offs determines which team wins the championship of each league. What prize are they awarded?

5. The winners of the league pennants then meet each other to decide who is the major league world champion. Which team won the World Series in 1998, 1999 and 2000?

6. What is the annual competition called which matches two teams of players drawn from clubs in each league which takes place during the mid-season break?

7. What was so extraordinary about the 1956 World Series between New York Yankees and Brooklyn Dodgers?

8. What was the name of the Pittsburgh Pirates' second baseman who hit a home run at the end of the ninth inning to defeat New York Yankees and give the Pirates their first championship title since 1925?

9. Which ex-Oakland Athletics ex Baltimore Orioles hitter became a star for New York Yankees in the 1977 championship by hitting four consecutive home runs off four different Brooklyn Dodger's pitchers in the fifth and sixth games?

10. Which club was the first club based outside the USA to win the World Series, which they did twice, in 1992 and 1993?

11. Who was the Boston Red Sox pitcher who, in1904, became the first player in major league history to pitch a perfect game, allowing no batters to reach first base? The award for the best pitcher of the year is named after him?

12. Which baseball team has its home ground in the Olympic Stadium, St Helene's Island?

13. Considered to be one of baseball's greatest catchers, he played for Philadelphia Athletics 1925-34, and was player-manager of Detroit Tigers 1934-38. What was his name?

ANSWERS.
1. 162. 2. Qualifying rounds for the World Series. 3. Four. (Three divisional winners and one wild card). 4. The League Pennant. 5. New York Yankees. 6. The 'All-Star Game'. 7. In one innings Yankee's Don Larsen got 27 Dodger's batters out, without score. The first World Series 'no-hitter'. 8. Bill Mazeroski. 9. Reggie Jackson. 10. Toronto Blue Jays. 11. Cy Young. 12. Montreal Expos. 13. Mickey Cochrane.

How much do you know about major league baseball teams? (7)

QUESTIONS.

1. He was the first black American to be appointed captain of a major league team the New York Giants, and the first player to hit 300 home runs and steal 300 bases, and first NL player to reach 600 home runs on his way to a career total of 660. Considered by many to have been the greatest baseball player of all time, his name was ......what?

2. In which city is the College World Series staged every year?

3. The Shea Stadium is home ground to which NL club?

4. He started as a left-handed pitcher for Baltimore and went on to become one of the greatest outfielders and batters the game has ever known, finishing his career with a total of 714 home runs. Who was he?

5. Which team has it's home ground in the Veterans Stadium?

6. Which team won the World Series in 1997?

7. Who was the Japanese batter who hit at least 30 home runs per season for 19 consecutive seasons, leading the Japanese Central League 15 times, retiring in 1980 with a career total of 868 home runs?

8. Who was the Seattle Mariners catcher, winner four years in succession (1990-93) of the Gold Glove, who was the first major league player to play in the same team with his father?

9. Who was the baseball player known as 'The Iron Horse'?

10. Who was the hard-throwing, right-handed pitcher whose fastball helped him win 251 major league games over 17 seasons (1959-75), all with St Louis Cardinals, and two of three World Series championships?

11. Which team plays its home games in the Jack Murphy Stadium?

12. He is considered to have been one of the greatest centre fielders and hitters of all time. He led the New York Yankees to 9 World Series titles. Who was he?

13. Which team plays it's home games in the Kingdome?

14. Who was nicknamed the 'Georgia Peach' and considered by many to have been the outstanding offensive player of all time?

15. Who was nicknamed 'The Hammer', who, at his retirement in 1976 could claim many batting records, including most home runs (755), times at bat (12,364), total bases (6,856) etc. etc?

ANSWERS.
1. Willie Howard Mays Jnr. 2. Omaha, Nebraska. 3. New York Mets. 4. Babe Ruth. 5. Philadelphia Phillies. 6. Florida Marlins. 7. Oh Sadaharu. 8. Ken Griffey Jnr. 9. Lou Gehrig. 10. Robert Gibson. 11. San Diego Padres. 12. Joe DiMaggio. 13. Seattle Mariners. 14. Ty Cobb. 15. Hank Aaron.

Major league basketball teams

How much do you know about American basketball teams? (1)

QUESTIONS.

What are the names of the teams from the following towns or states:

1. Los Angeles?
2. New York?
3. San Antonio?
4. Washington?
5. Chicago?
6. Sacramento?
7. New Jersey?
8. Houston?
9. Minnesota?
10. Orlando?
11. Indiana?
12. Detroit?
13. Atlanta?
14. Portland?
15. Golden State?

ANSWERS.
1. Lakers. 2. Knickerbockers. 3. Spurs. 4. Bullets. 5. Bulls. 6. Kings. 7. Nets. 8. Rockets. 9. Timberwolves. 10. Magic. 11. Pacers. 12. Pistons. 13. Hawks. 14. Trail Blazers. 15. Warriors.

How much do you know about American basketball teams? (2)

QUESTIONS.

What are the names of the teams from the following towns or states:

1. Boston?

2. Utah?

3. Seattle?

4. Charlotte?

5. Milwaukee?

6. Los Angeles?

7. Dallas?

8. Cleveland?

9. Denver?

10. Miami?

11. Phoenix?

12. Philadelphia?

13. Kansas City?>1985

14. San Diego?>1984

15. Baltimore?>1973

ANSWERS.
1. Celtics. 2. Jazz. 3. SuperSonics. 4. Hornets. 5. Bucks. 6. Clippers. 7. Mavericks. 8. Cavaliers. 9. Nuggets. 10. Heat. 11. Suns. 12. '76'ers. 13. Kings. 14. Clippers. 15. Bullets.

How much do you know about American basketball teams? (3)

QUESTIONS.

1. Who was the inventor of Basketball?

2. When did he invent it?

3. What was the name of the first professional basketball league?

4. When was it formed?

5. How long was it in existence?

6. What was the name of one of the first and greatest professional teams which was formed in New York about 1915?

7. What year was the Harlem Globetrotters formed?

8. The National Basketball League was formed for a second time in 1937 and the Basketball Association of America was formed in 1946. In 1949 they merged to become ......what?

9. What year was the first collegiate basketball game for women staged?

10. What shape and size is a basketball court?

11. At each end of the court is a backboard anchored firmly to a wall or ceiling. What size is a backboard?

12. What height above the court should the lower edge of the backboard be?

13. What height above the court should the baskets be?

14. What is the diameter of a basket?

15. What is the weight of a standard basketball?

ANSWERS.
1 James Naismith. 2. December 1891. 3. National Basketball League. 4. 1898. 5. About 5 years. 6. Original Celtics. 7. 1927. 8. The National Basketball Association. 9. 1893. 10. A rectangle, from 29m x 15m (94 ft x 50 ft) to 22m x 13m (74 ft x 52 ft). 11. About 2m x 1m (6 ft x 3 ft). 12. About 2.7 m (9 ft). 13. About 3m (10 ft). 14. About 46 cm (18 in). 15. 567 to 624 grams (20 to 22 oz)

How much do you know about American basketball teams? (4)

QUESTIONS.

1. What is the circumference of a standard basketball?

2. How many players are there in a conventional basketball team?

3. Two players are 'guards', two are 'forwards'. What position does the fifth man play?

4. What is the beginning of play called?

5. At the beginning of play, the two forwards stand in the half of the court containing the basket defended by the other team. What is this area called?

6. The guards stand in the half containing their own basket. What is this area called?

7. To walk or run with the ball without bouncing it (dribbling) is a violation. What is the violation called?

8. What is the violation called when illegal body contact is made?

9. The person fouled then typically is awarded one or two free throws. The 'foul line' is at what distance from the basket?

10. A player fouled in the act of scoring receives a free throw, even though he scored. What is this called?

11. In professional basketball, players are allowed to commit how many fouls before being ejected from the game?

12. What is interference with a ball about to drop through the basket called, when it is committed by a defender?

13. Scoring is usually done by using any one of four shots. There is the 'lay-up'; the 'jump shot', the 'dunk shot' and ......what is the fourth?

14. What is a pass called, that leads directly to a basket being scored?

15. What is the art of out-positioning opponents to gain possession of the ball off the backboard called?

ANSWERS.
1. About 76 cm (30 in). 2. Five. 3. 'Centre'. 4. 'Tip-off'. 5. 'The forecourt'. 6. 'The backcourt'. 7. 'Travelling'. 8. 'Personal foul'. 9. About 4m (15 ft). 10. 'A three point play'. 11. Six. 12. 'Goaltending'. 13. The 'hook shot'. 14. An 'assist'. 15. 'Rebounding'.

How much do you know about American basketball teams? (5)

QUESTIONS.

1. What is a high-speed attack over the full length of the court called?

2. In football there is a play called 'running interference'. What is the similar move in basketball called?

3. A change of hands of the ball from one team to another in play is called .....what?

4. What is the play called when the team with the ball is aggressively challenged the whole length of the court?

5. When was basketball introduced into the Olympic Games?

6. What is the name of the regulating association of amateur basketball?

7. In the US, the college basketball season runs from December to March. Two important post-season tournaments are then held. One is the National Invitation Tournament. What is the other?

8. When were the World Championships for men first held?

9. And the women's World Championships?

10. In what year were the European Championships (for national teams) first held?

11. In what year were the European Championships (for clubs) for men first held?

12. And the women's European Championship for clubs?

13. In the women's tournament, one team has dominated the European Championship. Which club?

14. In the US, how many games do the professional clubs play in their regular season?

15. How many games do the clubs in the National League in Great Britain play in their regular seasson?

ANSWERS.
1. 'A fast break'. 2. 'Setting a pick'. 3. 'A turnover'. 4. A 'full-court press'. 5. 1936. 6. Federation Internationale de Basketball Amateur (FIBA). 7. The National Collegiate Athletic Association (NCAA) tournament. 8. 1950. 9. 1953. 10. 1935. 11. 1958. 12. 1959. 13. Daugawa Riga (Latvia). 14. 82. 15. 36.

How much do you know about American basketball teams? (6)

QUESTIONS.

1. Which club won the NBA Championship 1991-92-93-96-97-98?

2. Who was the seven-time consecutive winner of the NBA scoring title from 1960 to 1966; second all-time leading scorer, and record scorer of 100 points in one game in 1962? Played for the Warriors in Philadelphia and San Fancisco, traded in '65 to the Philadelphia 76ers and to the Los Angeles Lakers in '68.

3. Which club plays its home games in the Market Square Arena?

4. He won Olympic gold in 1984, then joined the Chicago Bulls. He led the NBA in scoring for seven consecutive seasons, '87-93. He became the Bulls' all-time leading scorer with 21,541 points; won gold again in '92 . Retired from basketball in '94 to try baseball, but returned to basketball in '95. Who was he?

5. Which club has its home ground at the Memorial Coliseum?

6. At 6'9" tall, he is considered to be one of the greatest point-guards and playmakers of all time. He helped the Los Angeles Lakers to 5 NBA championships(1980-82-85-87-88) and was named MVP 3 times. He held the NBA record for 'assists' (9,921). His sporting career was derailed by illness. What was his name?

7. Which club has its home ground in the America West Arena?

8. Who was the 7'11" player, 6-time NBA champion and 6-time winner of the MVP award? When he retired in 1989 he was NBA all-time leader in points (38,387) and games played (1,560).

9. The National Basketball Hall of Fame (also known as the Naismith Memorial Hall of Fame),is located in which town in the US?

10. Who was the professional basketball player known to his fans as 'Sir Charles'?

11. Which club has its home ground at the Delta Center Arena?

12. To which media mogul do the Atlanta Hawks belong?

13. Who was the legendary coach of the Boston Celtics for 16 years, winning 9 NBA championships, eight of them consecutive? (1957, 59-66). He became the Celtics general manager and president.

14. Which club plays its home games in the Reunion Arena?

15. In which Olympic Games did the American 'Dream Team' play – and win gold?

ANSWERS.
1. Chicago Bulls. 2. Wilt Chamberlain. 3. Indiana Pacers. 4. Michael Jordan. 5. Portland Trailblazers. 6. Earvin 'Magic' Johnson. 7. Phoenix Suns. 8. Kareem Abdul-Jabbar. 9. Springfield, Massachusetts. 10. Charles Wade Barkley. 11. Utah Jazz. 12. Ted Turner. 13. Arnold 'Red' Auerbach. 14. Dallas Mavericks. 15. 1992.

Champions

How much do you know about world-class sporting champions? (1)

QUESTIONS.

1. Who was the US male swimmer who won two gold medals at the 1968 Olympics and seven at the 1972 Games, setting a new world record each time?

2. Who was the French motor racing driver won his first Grand Prix in 1981, was world champion four times ('85;'86;'89 and '93) and runner-up four times ('83;'84;'88 and '90)?

3. Who was the Soviet gymnast who in the 1972 Olympics at the age of 16, won a team gold medal plus two individual golds and one silver?

4. Who was the Irish rugby lock forward who played mainly with Ballymena, won 63 caps for Ireland and made a record 17 appearances for the British Lions on 5 tours?

5. Who was the English world snooker champion 1927-46 and billiards champion 1928-33? He was the first player to score a maximum break of 147 in a snooker match in 1955

6. Who was the Austrian-born Luxembourg skier, winner of overall World Cuptitle more times than anyone else, also 11 world championship medals and 2 Olympic silver medals?

7. Who was the Swedish tennis player, member of Davis Cup team at 15, Wimbledon junior champion at 16, winner of Wimbledon men's singles title in 5 successive years 1976-80?

8. Who was the US golfer, a brilliant amateur until 1955, won eight majors as a professional, captained the American Ryder Cup team twice?

9. Who was the Finnish athlete, known as the Flying Finn, won 9 gold medals over three Olympic Games, set world records at 3,000 m; 1 mile, 2 miles and 6 miles?

10. Who was the West Indies cricketer who in 93 Test Matches scored more than 8,000 runs (inc. 26 centuries), took 235 wickets as a bowler and 110 catches as a fielder? In a match in 1968, captaining Notts. against Glamorgan scored a maximum of 36 (6X6) off one over.

11. Who was the Belgian racing cyclist (nicknamed The Cannibal) the first to win the Tour de France 5 times; also 5 times winner of Tour of Italy and winner of all the classics?

12. Who is the only European golfer to win the US Masters three times?

ANSWERS.
1. Mark Spitz. 2. Alain Prost. 3. Olga Korbut. 4. Willie John McBride. 5. Joe Davis 6. Marc Girardelli. 7. Bjorn Borg. 8. Arnold Palmer. 9. Paavo Nurmi. 10. Garfield Sobers. 11. Eddy Merckx. 12. Nick Faldo.

How much do you know about world-class sporting champions? (2)

QUESTIONS.

1. Who was the South Africa golfer who won the South African Open 13 times; the Australian Open x 7; US Open x 1; US PGA x 2; US Masters x 3 and the British Open x 3?

2. Who was the Scots motor racing driver, world champion in 1969, '71 and '73?

3. Who was the Czech middle-distance runner, winner of Olympic gold in 1948 for the 10,000 metres and three golds, 5,000m; 10,000m and the marathon, in the Olympics of 1952?

4. Who was the Pakistani squash player winner of 3 world amateur titles; a record 6 World Open titles and 9 consecutive British Open titles?

5. Who was the US track athlete who dominated the 400 metres and to a slightly lesser degree, the 200 metres during the 1990''s?

6. Who was the English footballer who was capped a record 108 times, 90 of them as Captain, including the victorious World Cup side in 1966?

7. Who was the English medical practitioner who played cricket for Gloucester and England, scoring 54,896 runs, including 126 centuries, and taking 2,876 wickets?

8. Who was the Soviet cross-country woman skier who won 23 medals between 1974 and 1992, including a record of 10 Olympic skiing medals?

9. Who is the English All-England Badminton champion in seven successive years 1968-74?

10. Who was the Canadian ice-hockey player, played mainly in the US, voted NHL's most valuable player 9 times and retired in 1989 with a total of 2,857 points scored?

11. Who was the US tennis player, winner of 157 professional titles including 18 Grand Slam singles titles won between 1974 and 1986?

12. Who was the English rugby union player, the most capped wing – 85 caps from '85-96? Set a record with 49 tries in the 85 matches. Also capped for the British Lions.

13. Who was the French downhill skier who won 2 gold medals at the World Championships in Chile in 1996, and 3 golds at the Olympics 1968?

14. Who was the Spanish cyclist, only the fourth to win the Tour de France five times?

15. Who was the US heavyweight, undisputed world champion '90-'92; '93-'94 and '96-'97?

ANSWERS.
1. Gary Player. 2. Jackie Stewart. 3. Emil Zatopek. 4. Jahangir Khan. 5. Michael Johnson. 6. Bobby Moore. 7. W. G. Grace. 8. Raisa Smetanina. 9. Rudy Hartono. 10. Wayne Gretzky. 11. Chris Evert. 12. Rory Underwood. 13. Jean-Claude Killy. 14. Miguel Indurain. 15. Evander Holyfield.

How much do you know about world-class sporting champions? (3)

QUESTIONS.

1. Who was the Swedish skier who was World Master 1978 and 1982, Olympic gold in 1980; winner of a record 86 World Cup races between 1974 and 1989?

2. Who was the US golfer who, with Jack Nicklaus, dominated golf from the mid-'70's to the early '80's, winning US Open; 2 Masters and 5 British Opens? 6 times US Player of the Year.

3. Who was the French racing cyclist, 5 times winner of the Tour de France (1957; 1961-64), winner of the Tour of Spain (1963) and Tour of Italy (1964)?

4. Who was the Australian cricketer, world record holder for most test and one-day international appearances' and for runs scored in Test matches (10,161).

5. Who was New Zealand's most capped rugby player and the world's most capped hooker?

6. Who was the Scottish motor racer who won the Formula 1 World Championship with Lotus (1963 and 1965).? First non-American since 1916 to win Indianapolis 500 – 1965.

7. Who was the Prague-born US tennis player who won Wimbledon ladies singles a record of 9 times; US Open 4 times? Her 100-plus tournament wins include 2 Golden Grand Slams.

8. Who was the US athlete who won 4 golds at the 1984 Olympics; 2 in 1988; 2 in 1992 and 1 in 1996?

9. Who was the Indian cricketer , the most prolific run-scorer in Test cricket history, in 125 Test Matches he scored 10,122 runs, including 34 centuries?

10. Who was the first American golfer to win the British Open, which he did 4 times, winner of the US Open x 2; the US PGA x 5 (a record) and captained first 6 Ryder Cup teams?

11. Who was the Native American footballer and athlete who won the pentathlon and decathlonin the 1912 Olympics, and was considered to be the greatest all-round athlete ever?

12. Who was the US heavyweight world champion from 1937 until 1949 (a record)?

13. Who was the US jockey to be the first to ride 8,000 winners, retiring 1990 with 8,833?

14. Who was the second French cyclist to win the Tour de France five times?

15. Who was the Romanian gymnast who was the first ever to obtain a perfectscore of ten at the 1976 Olympic Games at the age of 14?

ANSWERS.
1. Ingemar Stenmark. 2. Tom Watson. 3. Jacques Anquetil. 4. Allan Border. 5. Sean Fitzpatrick. 6. Jim Clark. 7. Martina Navratilova. 8. Carl Lewis. 9. Sunil Gavaskar. 10. Walter Hagen. 11. Jim Thorpe. 12. Joe Louis. 13. Willy Shoemaker. 14. Bernard Hinault. 15. Nadia Comaneci

How much do you know about world-class sporting champions? (4)

QUESTIONS.

1. Who was the German tennis player who won the ladies singles title at the French Open x 5; the Australian Open x 4; the US Open x 5 and Wimbledon x 7; and retired at 30?

2. Who was the Scots rugby full-back who played three World Cups 1987/91/95, captaining Scotland for the first time in 1992-93 season?

3. Who was the Ukrainian athlete who dominated pole vaulting 1983-94, breaking 35 world records and setting a new world record of 6.14 metres in 1994?

4. Who was the English athlete, winner of Olympic gold at 1,500m and silver at 800m at both '80 and '84 games? Broke world record for 800m; 1,000m and mile in 1981.

5. Who was the Argentinian footballer of outstanding ability winning over 80 caps, whose name now always invokes the 'Hand of God' cheating incident in the 1990 World Cup semi-finals?

6. Who was the Austrian downhill skier, Olympic champion; World Champion 1975-8; & '83?

7. Who was the US athlete who won 4 gold medals at the 1936 Olympic Games in Berlin?

8. Who was the English jockey, voted Champion 11 times; rode 30 Classic winners including the Derby 9 times? Retired (for the 2nd time) in 1995 at 60 years of age.

9. Who was the US discus thrower who won the Gold medal at four consecutive Olympic Games, 1956-60-64-68, breaking the Olympic record each time?

10. Who was the Australian batsman whose batting average in Test Matches was 99.94 runs?

11. Who was the US swimmer, winner of 7 medals at 1986 World Championships; 7 medals at 1988 Olympics and 1 medal at the 1992 Olympics?

12. Who was the English snooker player, Worlds leading player during the 1980's and world champion 6 times - 1981-83-84-87-88-89?

13. Who was the US baseball player whose career 1936-51 was with the New York Yankees? He was renowned for batting safely, scoring in every one of 56 consecutive games.

14. Who was Northern Ireland's greatest footballing talent, Man U's leading scorer '67-8?

15 Who was the Welsh rugby player whose 53 consecutive caps are a Welsh record; Wales youngest ever captain also played in 10 British Lions Tests?

ANSWERS.
1. Steffi Graf. 2. Gavin Hastings. 3. Sergei Bubka. 4. Sebastian Coe. 5. Diego Maradona. 6. Franz Klammer. 7. Jesse Owens. 8. Lester Piggott. 9. Alfred Oerter. 10. Don Bradman. 11. Matt Biondi. 12. Steve Davis. 13. Joe DiMaggio. 14. George Best. 15. Gareth Edwards.

How much do you know about world-class sporting champions? (5)

QUESTIONS.

1. Who was the US woman sprinter, Olympic silver medallist 1984 and winner of 3 golds in the 1988 Olympics, died in 1998 at 29 years of age?

2. Who was the English footballer, long time associated with Manchester United, capped 106 times for England scoring 49 goals? In all played 754 games, scored 245 goals.

3. Who was the US heavyweight champion of the world 3 times, now a sporting icon considered by many to have been 'the Greatest'?

4. Who was the Moroccan athlete, Olympic champion 1984; Grand Prix winner 1986 and World Champion 1987, all distances from 1,500 metres to 5,000 metres?

5. Who was the US athlete who dominated the long-jump, his record set in 1968 of 8.90m remained until broken by Mike Powell in 1991?

6. Who was the English cricketer who scored 5,200 runs and took 383 wickets in 102 Test Matches? 4 times took ten wickets in amatch.

7. Who was the US tennis player, won men's singles title at Wimbledon x 2; US Open x 5; and Australian Open x 1? Partnered Ilie Nastase in winning men's doubles twice.

8. Who was the Scottish jockey, third in the all-time winners table; ridden 17 Cl;assic winners including the Derby twice, (1979 on Troy; 1980 on Henbit)?

9. Who was the US athlete, the greatest 400m hurdler ever? Olympic champion x 2 (1976/84), World champion x 4 .

10. Who was the Swiss skier, winner of a record number of victories in the downhill during the '80's and a total of 39 World Cup victories?

11. Who was the English rower, Commonwealth and World champion and winner of 5 consecutive Olympic gold medals?

12. Who was the US Baseball player considered by experts to be the greatest all-rounder ever?

13. Who was the Brazilian footballer, a legend in the game, played in 4 World Cups, winning 3; scored 1,281 goals in 1,363 first-class games?

14. Who was the most-capped French rugby player (111 caps) at centre?

15. Who was the US boxer who won 12 world title fights at 5 different weights?

ANSWERS.
1. Florence Griffith-Joyner. 2. Bobby Charlton. 3. Muhammad Ali. 4. Said Aouita. 5. Bob Beaman. 6. Ian Botham. 7. Jimmy Connors. 8. Willie Carson. 9. Edwin Moses. 10. Pirmin Zurbriggen. 11. Steve Redgrave. 12. Babe Ruth. 13. Edison Arantes do Nascimento (Pele). 14. Philippe Sella. 15. Sugar Ray Leonard.

Field Hockey

How much do you know about field hockey?

QUESTIONS.

1. What was the name of the first recorded Hockey Club?

2. What year was it founded?

3. In 1871 a second club was formed in another London borough. Which one?

4. In what year was the English Hockey Association founded?

5. In what year was Hockey introduced into the Olympic Games?

6. In what year was the Federation Internationale de Hockey (FIH) founded?

7. In what year was the FIH World Cup for men played?

8. And for women?

9. Which two national teams dominated the game in the first half of the 20th century, winning every Olympic Games from 1928 through to 1968?

10. What is the shape and what are the dimensions of a field hockey pitch?

11. How many players are there on each side?

12. How many umpires oversee a game?

13. Which nation won the men's World Championship in 1998?

14. Which nation won the women's World Championship in 1998?

15. Who was the British hockey player who played for East Grinstead; the South of England; England and Great Britain, being capped for the national team 70 times and winning two Olympic medals? He retired in 1990.

ANSWERS.
1. Blackheath, London. 2. 1861. 3. Teddington. 4. 1875. 5. 1908. 6. 1924. 7. 1971. 8. 1974. 9. India and Pakistan. 10. Rectangular. 100 yards (91.4m) x 60 yards (55m). 11. Eleven. 12. Two. 13. Netherlands. 14. Australia. 15. Richard Leman

Association football

How much do you know about Association football? (1)

QUESTIONS.

1. In what year was there a determined attempt to establish the first codified set of rules for the game of football?

2. Where did this take place?

3. Who were the main instigators of this action?

4. What was the name of the world's oldest football club?

5. In what year was it formed?

6. What is (still) the name of the world's oldest league club?

7. In what year did it come into existence?

8. When was the Football Association founded?

9. What was the name of the FA Secretary who, in 1871, proposed to organise a Football Association Challenge Cup tournament, to be played annually?

10. What was the name of the winning team of the first FA Cup, played in 1872?

11. Where were all the finals held up until 1893?

12. The first international match was played between England and Scotland. In what year?

13. What year was the English Football League formed?

14. In what year were the Netherlands FA and Danish FA formed?

15. In what year was the Italian FA formed?

ANSWERS.
1. 1843. 2. Cambridge. 3. J.C. Thring and H. de Winton. 4. Sheffield FC. 5. 1855. 6. Notts County. 7. 1862. 8. October 1863. 9. Charles Alcock. 10. Wanderers. 11. Kennington Oval. 12. 1872. 13. 1888. 14. 1889. 15. 1898.

How much do you know about Association football? (2)

QUESTIONS.

1. In what year were the Belgium and Swiss Football Associations formed?

2. In what year was the German FA formed?

3. In what year were the Czechoslovakian and Hungarian FA's formed?

4. In what year was the Norwegian FA formed?

5. In what year were the Swedish and Austrian FA's formed?

6. In what year was the Finnish FA formed?

7. In what year was the Luxembourg FA formed?

8. In what year was the Romanian FA formed?

9. In what year was the Spanish FA formed?

10. In what year was the Portuguese FA formed?

11. What was the name of the two English mill-owner brothers who introduced football to Russia in 1887?

12. What was the name of the Austrian, member of the Vienna Cricket and Football Club, the main force behind the 'Mitropa Cup', the forerunner of today's European club events?

13. In which Scandinavian capital was there an English Football Club in 1879?

14. What is the name of Italy's oldest league club?

15. And what was it's full name when it was founded by resident Englishmen in 1892?

ANSWERS.
1. 1895. 2. 1900. 3. 1901. 4. 1902. 5. 1904. 6. 1907. 7. 1908. 8. 1909. 9. 1913. 10. 1914.
11. Charnock. 12. Hugo Meisl. 13. Copenhagen. 14. Genoa. 15. Genoa Football and Cricket Club.

How much do you know about Association football? (3)

QUESTIONS.

1. What was the name of the English immigrant who was mainly responsible for introducing to Brazil?

2. What was the name of the first Brazilian club to be formed?

3. In what year was the Argentinian FA formed?

4. In what year was the Chilean FA formed?

5. In what year was the Football Association of Uruguay formed?

6. In what year was the Paraguayan FA formed?

7. In what year was the first Association football club formed in the USA?

8. What was it called?

9. What is the name of the world governing body?

10. When and where was it formed?

11. How many members (Association football playing nations) did it have as at 1997?

12. The English Football League is made up of how many clubs?

13. Every year all teams take part in two knockout tournaments, the FA Cup and the ....what?

14. In what year was the Scottish Football League formed?

15. The 1st Division, the Scottish FA Cup and the Scottish League Cup have been dominated since their inception by two clubs. One is Glasgow Rangers. What is the name of the other?

ANSWERS.
1. Charles Miller. 2. Associaciao Athletica Mackenzie College, Sao Paulo. 3. 1893. 4. 1895. 5. 1900. 6. 1906. 7. 1862. 8. The Oneida Club of Boston. 9. FIFA (Federation Internationale de Football Association). 10. 1904, Paris. 11. 200. 12. 92. 13. The Football League Cup. 14. 1890. 15. Glasgow Celtic.

How much do you know about Association football? (4)

1. In what year was the Irish Football Association formed?

2. In what year was the Welsh Football Association formed?

3. What is the London address of the Football Association?

4. What is the shape and what are the dimensions of an Association football pitch?

5. A goal consists of two uprights and a crossbar, backed by a net What are its dimensions?

6. What is the circumference of a football?

7. What is the weight of a football?

8. How many officials control a game of professional Association football?

9. What are their roles?

10. How long does a match normally last?

11. How many players are there in each team on the field at any one time?

12. By what name is the start of a match known?

13. How many substitutes are allowed in normal league and international matches?

14. What is it called when the whole of the ball passes between the goal posts, under the cross- bar, traversing the whole of the goal line?

15. How is play re-started after the ball has gone out of play over the white lines marking the width of the playing area?

ANSWERS.
1. 1880. 2. 1876. 3. Lancaster Gate. 4. Rectangular. 100 yards (91m) to 130 yards (119m) in length x 50 yards (45.5m) to 100 yards (91m) in width. 5. 8 yards (7.32m) wide and 8 feet (2.44m) high. 6. 27 to 28 ins. ((68 to 71 cm). 7. 14 to 16 oz. (396 to 453 grams). 8. Four. 9. One referee; two assistant referees (or linesmen) and a fourth official, who controls substitutions etc. 10. 90 minutes. (Two periods of 45 minutes each). 11. Eleven, maximum. 12. 'Kick-off'. 13. Three from five previously named substitutes. 14. A goal. 15. By a 'throw-in'.

How much do you know about Association football? (5)

QUESTIONS.

1. How is play re-started after the ball has gone out of play over the white lines marking the length of the playing area, when it was last touched by a member of the attacking team?

2. How is play re-started after the ball has gone out of play over the white lines marking the length of the playing area, when it was last touched by a member of the defending team?

3. What is the term for a serious offence committed in a careless or reckless manner or with the use of excessive force?

4. What will the referee award to the player on the receiving end of a foul?

5. What will the referee award to the attacking team if the foul is committed by a member of the defending team in his own penalty area?

6. How far must the opposing players be away from the ball when a free-kick is to be taken?

7. If a player continues to commit serious offences after having received a verbal warning, the referee will officially caution him with the aid of ....What?

8. If a player continues to offend after receiving a yellow card, or if he commits a really serious offence, the referee will send him from the field by showing him a ...... What?

9. Only two FA clubs have ever won the FA Challenge Cup three years in succession. One was Wanderers (1876-77-78), which was the other, who won it 1884-85-86?

10. Who was the first foreign player to captain an FA Cup winning team?

11. What was the last 'second division' club to win the FA Cup?

12. What year was the FA Cup final played at Wembley for the first time?

13. Which was the first club to do 'the double', winning the FA Cup final and leading the first division?

14. In 1903, Bury set the record for the winning margin in an FA Cup final, against Derby. What was the score?15. In what year did Arsenal beat Sheffield Wednesday in both the FA Cup final and the League Cup final?

15. In what year did Arsenal beat Sheffield Wednesday in both the FA Cup final and the League Cup final?

ANSWERS.

1. A 'goal-kick'. 2. A 'corner-kick'. 3. A 'foul'. 4. A 'direct free-kick'. 5. A 'penalty'. 6. 10 yards (9.15m). 7. A yellow card. 8. A red card. 9. Blackburn Rovers. 10. Eric Cantona (Man U 1996). 11. West Ham United (1980). 12. 1923. 13. Preston North End 1889. 14. 6-0. 15. 1993.

How much do you know about Association football? (6)

QUESTIONS.

1. Up to the end of 2001, only one English club has won the FA Cup 10 times. Which one?

2. Since the formation of the Football League in 1888, only one non-league side has won the FA Cup. Which club was it?

3. Only one non-English club side has ever won the FA Cup. Which one?

4. In two consecutive FA Cup finals play was interrupted when the ball burst. What years?

5. In what year did Stan Mortensen score a hat-trick in the FA Cup final?

6. Up to and including the 2001- 2002 season, which team has won the Scottish FA Cup final the most times?

7. How many times?

8. Which club is the runner-up, and how many times has it won the Cup?

9. In what year was the Cup withheld by the Scottish FA because Celtic and Rangers refused to participate in a third replay, after a riot had broken out in extra time of the second replay?

10. In what year was the first World Cup held?

11. Where was it staged and which national team was the winner?

12. What was the World Cup trophy called, at that time?

13. Who was Jules Rimet?

14. Which national team won the trophy outright after their third World Cup victory in 1970?

15. In 1934 the World Cup was staged in which country and which national team was the winner?

ANSWERS.
1. Manchester United. 2. Tottenham Hotspur in 1901. 3. Cardiff City in 1927. 4. 1946 and 1947. 5. 1953. 6. Glasgow Celtic. 7. 32. 8. Rangers – 29. 9. 1909. 10. 1930. 11. Uruguay/Uruguay. 12. The Jules Rimet Trophy. 13. Former President of FIFA. 14. Brazil. 15. Italy/Italy.

How much do you know about Association football? (7)

QUESTIONS.

1. In 1960 a new Association football tournament for nations was launched. What is it called?

2. It is held under the auspices of which organisation?

3. What is the name of the trophy which is contested?

4. Who was Henri Delaunay?

5. How often is the European Championship held?

6. How long is the 'lead-in' period, for the qualifying games?

7. In which country was it staged and which national team was the winner in 2000?

8. In which country was it staged and which national team was the winner in 1996?

9. In its 40 year history only one country has won the European Nations Championship three times. Which country?

10. In the 1955-56 season a major new club tournament was launched. What is it called?

11. The motive force behind it was the football editor of the French newspaper 'L'Equipe'. What was his name?

12. The European Cup was originally open to teams from all UEFA-affiliated countries, provided they had qualified as ......what?

13. In recent years it has been enlarged to include other teams from those countries with the highest UEFA points coefficient. Which other teams?

14. One team has won the European Cup eight times. Who is it?

15. Which French winner was subsequently stripped of the title following a bribery scandal?

ANSWERS.
1. The European Championship (previously the European Nations Cup). 2. UEFA, (The Union of European Football Associations). 3. The Henri Delaunay Cup. 4. The former general secretary of UEFA. 5. Every four years. 6. Two years. 7. Holland/ France. 8. England/Germany. 9. Germany. 10. The European Champion Clubs' Cup (usually called the European Cup). 11. Gabriel Hanot. 12. League Champions. 13. Those finishing the season in 2nd, 3rd and 4th places. 14. Real Madrid. 15. Marseilles (1993).

How much do you know about Association football? (8)

QUESTIONS.

1. In 1961 another European-wide club tournament was launched, open to winners of domestic senior cup competitions. What was it called?

2. What other teams qualified to participate, if the national cup winners were tied up with the European Cup?

3. This competition came to an end in 1999. Since then national cup winners have participated in which competition?

4. In which city was the last Cup Winners Cup staged, and which club was the last winner?

5. Which was the last English team to win the Cup Winners Cup?

6. In 1955 a tournament was established for European cities that sponsored international trade fairs, known as the International Industries Fairs Inter-Cities Cup (or Fairs Cup). What was this changed to in 1971?

7. The UEFA Cup is open to which teams?

8. Which team won the UEFA Cup in 2001?

9. Which team did Galatasaray defeat on penalties to win in 2000?

10. From the year 1972 to1999, the winners of the European Cup and the European Cup Winners' Cup (since 2000 the UEFA Cup), have met in a two-stage match to decide the winner of which competition?

11. Five English teams have won the European Super Cup: Chelsea (1998); Manchester United (1991); Aston Villa 1982; Liverpool (1977) and ....Who was the fourth?

12. What is the South American Club Champions cup known as?

13. Since 1960 the winners of the European Champions Clubs Cup and the winner of the Copa Libertadores have been meeting in ....what is the tournament known as?

14. Where was the World Club Cup played from 1980 to 1998?

15. And where has it been played since 1999?

ANSWERS.
1. European Cup Winners' Cup. 2. Their runners-up. 3. An expanded UEFA Cup tournament. 4. Birmingham/Lazio. 5. Chelsea (1998). 6. The UEFA Cup. 7. Leading teams not eligible for the other two principal European competitions. 8. Liverpool. 9. Arsenal. 10. European Super Cup. 11. Nottingham Forest (1979). 12. The Copa Libertadores. 13. The World Club Championship Cup. 14. Tokyo. 15. Brazil.

How much do you know about Association football? (9)

QUESTIONS.

1.   For what trophy do the South American nations battle it out every two years?

2.   Which nation won the South American Championship in 1997 and 1999?

3.   Since the South American Championship was inaugurated in 1910 through to the end of the 1999 season, it has been dominated by two national teams. One is Argentina with 15 wins. Who is the other, with 14 wins?

4.   Who were the winners of the Copa Libertadores in 2000?

5.   Which team won the Copa Libertadores four years in succession, 1972-73-74-75, also winning the World Club cup in '73?

6.   The African Nations Cup was born in 1957 and is now staged every two years. Which national team won it in 2000?

7.   Between 1957 and 2000, only one nation has won the African Nations Cup five times. Which one?

8.   The African Champions (club) Cup has been staged every year since 1964. Who were the winners in 2000?

9.   From 1964 to 2000 only one club has won the African Champions Cup four times. Who?

10. What is the African equivalent of UEFA and when was it formed?

11. In what year was the African Cup Winners Cup launched ?

12. Between 1956 and 1996 two national teams have won the Asian Cup three times. One was Saudi Arabia. Who was the other?

13. The Central American Championship was inaugurated in 1941. In 1991 it became the CONCACAF Gold Cup. What is it known as today?

14. Clubs from which country have been most successful in this competition?

15. What is the Central American, Caribbean and South American club championship trophy?

ANSWERS.
1. The Copa America. 2. Brazil. 3. Uruguay. 4. Boca Juniors, Argentina. 5. Independiente. Argentina. 6. Cameroon. 7. Ghana. 8. Hearts of Oato, Ghana. 9. Zamalek, Egypt. 10. CAF (Confederation of African Football) – 1957. 11. 1975. 12. Iran. 13. The American Airlines Cup. 14. Mexico. 15. The Inter-American Cup.

How much do you know about Association football? (10)

QUESTIONS.

1.   When was the first Women's World Cup staged?

2.   Where did the World Cup finals take place?

3.   Which nations provided the finalists?

4.   Who won, and what was the score?

5.   Who were the winners in 1995?

6.   Who were the winners in 1999?

7.   When was the first Women's European Championship staged?

8.   Who were the winners in 1989-91-95-97?

9.   Between 1961 and 2001 the English Football League Cup has been won six times by only one club. Which one?

10. In 1988 Arsenal were the losing finalists in the League Cup to Luton Town. To whom did they lose in 1969?

11. Which club did Leicester defeat in the 2000 finals?

12. Between 1947 and 2001 the Scottish League Cup has been won 21 times by only one club. Between 1892 and 2001 the same team has been crowned League Champions 48 times. Which one?

13. Which team was second with 10 wins and 35 championships?

14. Which was the first English team to use artificial turf?

15. Who was the first black player to win a cap for England?

ANSWERS.
1. 1991. 2. Guangzhou, China. 3. Norway and the USA. 4. USA. 2-1. 5. Norway. 6. USA.
7. 1983. 8. Germany. 9. Liverpool. 10. Swindon. 11. Tranmere Rovers. 12. Glasgow
Rangers. 13. Glasgow Celtic. 14. Queen's Park Rangers – 1981. 15. Viv Anderson.

How much do you know about Association football? (11)

QUESTIONS.

What are the nicknames of the following english league teams?

1. Derby County?

2. Aston Villa?

3. Arsenal?

4. Newcastle United?

5. Manchester United?

6. Leicester City?

7. Everton?

8. Ipswich?

9. Bradford City?

10. Tottenham Hotspur?

11. Sunderland?

12. Charlton Athletic?

13. Leeds?

14. Liverpool?

15. Chelsea?

ANSWERS.
1. The Rams. 2. The Villains. 3. The Gunners. 4. The Magpies. 5. The Red Devils. 6. The Foxes. 7. The Toffees. 8. The Tractor Boys. 9. The Bantams. 10. The Spurs. 11. The Rokerites. 12. The Addicks. 13. The Whites. 14. The Reds. 15. The Blues.

How much do you know about Association football? (12)

What are the nicknames of the following english league teams?

1.   West Ham?

2.   Manchester City?

3.   Bolton Wanderers?

4.   Burnley?

5.   Portsmouth?

6.   Watford?

7.   Stockport County?

8.   Wolverhampton Wanderers?

9.   Sheffield United?

10. Norwich City?

11. Preston North End?

12. Sheffield Wednesday?

13. West Bromwich Albion?

14. Huddersfield Town?

15. Crystal Palace?

ANSWERS.
1. The Hammers. 2. The Citizens. 3. The Trotters. 4. The Clarets. 5. Pompey. 6. The Hornets. 7. The Hatters. 8. The Wolves. 9. The Blades. 10. The Canaries. 11. The Lilywhites. 12. The Owls. 13. The Baggies. 14. The Terriers. 15. The Eagles.

How much do you know about Association football? (13)

QUESTIONS.

What are the nicknames of the following english league teams?

1. Crewe Alexander?

2. Fulham?

3. Grimsby Town?

4. Bournemouth?

5. Peterborough United?

6. Stoke City?

7. Bristol Rovers?

8. Bristol City?

9. Millwall?

10. Oldham Athletic?

11. Brentford?

12. Bury?

13. Northampton Town?

14. Port Vale?

15. Swansea Town?

ANSWERS.
1.The Railwaymen. 2.The Cottagers. 3.The Mariners. 4.The Cherries. 5. Posh. 6.The Potters. 7.The Pirates 8. .The Robins. 9.The Lions. 10.The Latics. 11.The Bees. 12. The Shakers. 13.The Cobblers. 14.The Valiants. 15.The Swans.

How much do you know about Association football? (14)

QUESTIONS.

What are the nicknames of the following english league teams?

1. Reading?
2. Wycombe Wanderers?
3. Walsall?
4. Rotherham United?
5. Blackpool?
6. Brighton & Hove Albion?
7. Macclesfield Town?
8. Plymouth Argyle?
9. Darlington?
10. Cardiff City?
11. Mansfield Town?
12. Exeter City?
13. Hull City?
14. Scunthorpe United?
15. Carlisle United?

ANSWERS.
1.The Royals. 2.The Chairboys. 3.The Saddlers. 4.The Merry Millers. 5.The Seasiders. 6.The Seagulls. 7.The Silkmen. 8.The Pilgrims. 9.The Quakers. 10.The Bluebirds. 11.The Stags. 12.The Grecians. 13.The Tigers. 14.The Irons. 15.The Cumbrians

How much do you know about Association football? (15)

QUESTIONS.

1. Which English Premier Division club plays its home games at The Stadium of Light?

2. What year were caps first awarded to English players chosen for international duty?

3. In 1894 one club supplied all eleven players for an England v Wales match. Which club?

4. England's first away defeat in an international came in 1929. Who was the opposition?

5. England's first home defeat in an international came in 1953. Who was the opposition?

6. Who was elected the first European Footballer of the year in 1956?

7. Which English League team play its home games at the Modejski Stadium?

8. Who was elected the first World Footballer of the year in 1991?

9. In 1998, 1999 and 2000 the Professional Footballers Association and the Football Writers agreed on their Player of the Year. In 2000 it was Roy Keane, in 1999 it was David Ginola. Who was it in 1998?

10. Which two teams qualify to play in the English Football Association's Charity Shield match?

11. Who was the first player to be sent off in an FA Cup final?

12. Who was the Manchester City goalkeeper who broke his neck in the 1956 FA Cup final?

13. Two non-league clubs have participated in every FA Cup competition since 1872. One is Maidenhead, What is the name of the other?

14. In which World Cup competition were England put out in the first round by the USA, 1-0?

15. In which country other than England and Scotland are there two league teams called Everton and Rangers?

ANSWERS.
1. Sunderland. 2. 1886. 3. Corinthians. 4. Spain. 5. Hungary. 6. Stanley Matthews. 7. Reading. 8. Lothar Matthaus. 9. Dennis Bergkamp. 10. FA Cup Winners v League Winners. 11. Kevin Moran (Man U 1985). 12. Bert Trautmann. 13. Marlow. 14. Mexico, 1950. 15. Chile.

Golf

How much do you know about golf?

QUESTIONS.

1. In what year was the British Open Golf Championship first staged?

2. In what year was the US Open Golf Championship first staged?

3. In what year was the US PGA Championship first staged?

4. In what year was the US Masters Championship first staged?

5. What is the name of the biennial tournament between teams of amateur male golfers from the US and the UK?

6. When was this competition inaugurated?

7. What is the name of the biennial tournament between teams of professional male golfers from the US and originally the UK, but since, 1979 Europe?

8. When was this competition inaugurated?

9. What is the name of the biennial tournament between teams of amateur female golfers from the US and Great Britain and Ireland?

10. When was this competition inaugurated?

11. What is the name of the biennial tournament between teams of professional female golfers from the US and Europe?

12. When was this competition inaugurated?

13. Who was the oldest winner of the US Masters?

14. Who was the first UK winner of the US Women's Open?

15. Father and son professional golfers have twice represented their nations in the Ryder Cup. Antonio and Ignacio Garrido were one, who were the second?

ANSWERS.
1. 1860. 2. 1895. 3. 1916. 4. 1934. 5. The Walker Cup. 6. 1922. 7. The Ryder Cup. 8. 1927. 9. The Curtis Cup. 10. 1932. 11. The Solheim Cup. 12. 1990. 13. Jack Nicklaus (46). 14. Laura Davies (1987). 15. Percy and Peter Alliss.

Horse racing

How much do you know about horse racing? (1)

QUESTIONS.

1. In what year was the first Arab stallion imported into England from Spain by King Henry I?

2. The first recorded horse races in England took place in the 12th century. Whereabouts?

3. Where was the first permanent race course created, in 1540?

4. What was its name?

5. What famous race was first staged in 1634?

6. The first race track in America was built in 1665. Whereabouts?

7. Between 1689 and 1724 three Arab stallions were imported into England. They became the ancestors of all modern thoroughbreds. They were the Byerly Turk; the Darley Arabian and ....What was the name of the third?

8. In what year was a descendant of the Darley Arabian sold to America?

9. In what year was the British stud book begun?

10. In what year was the American stud book begun?

11. Modern horse racing in France began about .....when?

12. And in Germany, about .....when?

13. And in Italy, about .....when?

14. Some races are for fillies only. What is a 'filly'?

15. And some are for colts. What is a 'colt'?

ANSWERS.
1. 1110, 2. Smithfield, London. 3. Chester. 4. The Roodee. 5. The Newmarket Gold Cup. 6. Long Island. 7. The Godolphin Barb. 8. About 1730 , 9. 1791. 10. 1873. 11. 1833. 12. 1867. 13. 1881. 14. A female horse less than 5 years old. 15. A male horse less than 5 years old.

How much do you know about horse racing? (2)

QUESTIONS.

1. Horse racing people talk about distances in miles and furlongs. How long is a furlong?

2. The 'Derby' is a major British flat race for three year old colts and fillies, run over 2 miles and 4 furlongs, every year in June at ....which racecourse?

3. It was created by Edward Stanley, 12th earl of Derby, after whom it is named. In what year?

4. Over the years it has become the generic term for important flat races of this kind. There are 'Derbys' in 13 European countries and many non-European. The most famous is the U.S.A.'s Kentucky Derby, staged every year in May, at ....which course?

5. What is the name of the French 'Derby'?

6. At which French race course is it run?

7. What is the name of the Russian 'Derby'?

8. What is the name of the Japanese 'Derby'?

9. The Kentucky Derby is one of three classic races for three year olds. What are these races called collectively?

10. What is the name of the second race in the Triple Crown?

11. Which is run ......where?

12. What is the name of the third race in the Triple Crown?

13. Which is run .....where?

14. What is the name of the oldest continuously held race in North America?

15. Which is run .....where?

ANSWERS.
1. 220 yards (200 metres). 2. Epsom Downs. 3. 1780. 4. Churchill Downs, Louisville, Kentucky. 5. 'Le Prix du Jockey Club'. 6. Chantilly. 7. The 'Bolshoi Vsiesoyuzny Priz. 8. The 'Tokyo Yushin Kyoso'. 9. The 'Triple Crown'. 10. The 'Preakness Stakes'. 11. Pimlico, Maryland. 12. The 'Belmont Stakes'. 13. Belmont Park, New York State. 14. 'The Queen's Plate'. 15. Woodbine, Toronto.

How much do you know about horse racing? (3)

QUESTIONS.

1. The English Derby is one of five major flat races for three year olds, known as
   ....what?

2. What is the oldest of the other four races, which is run over 1 mile, 6 furlongs
   and 132 yards at Doncaster?

3. What is the second oldest, a race for fillies only, which is run over 1 mile and 4
   furlongs at Epsom Downs?

4. In what year were these two races first run?

5. The Derby being the third oldest, what is the fourth oldest race, which is run
   over 1 mile at Newmarket?

6. In what year was this race first run?

7. What is the youngest of the five Classics, which is a race for fillies only, also run
   over 1 mile at Newmarket?

8. In what year was this race first run?

9. Ireland also has five races, the counterparts to the Classics, all run over the same
   distances. At which course?

10. France has six 'Classics', two of which are run at Chantilly. Where are the other
    four run?

11. New Zealand has the same number of Classics as England, with the same names.
    Australia however has its 'Triple Crown', constituted by ......which three races?

12. Canada also has its 'Triple Crown'. What are the two races called which
    constitute, with the Queen's Cup, the Canadian Triple Crown?

13. What is the name of the major 'classic' in South Africa?

14. What is the most lucrative 'quarter-horse' race called? Held in New Mexico in
    September.

15. Which horse was the first winner of the English Derby?

ANSWERS.
1. 'The Classics'. 2. The 'St Leger'. 3. The 'Oaks'. 4. 1779. 5. The '2,000 Guineas'. 6.
1809. 7. The '1,000 Guineas'. 8. 1814. 9. 'The Curragh', County Kildare. 10.
Longchamps, Paris. 11. The Melbourne Cup; the Sydney Cup and the Caulfield Cup.
12. The Prince of Wales Stakes and the Breeders Stakes. 13. 'The Cape of Good Hope
Derby'. 14. The 'All-American Futurity'. 15. 'Diomed'.

How much do you know about horse racing? (4)

QUESTIONS.

1. Who was the American champion jockey, youngest winner of the Triple Crown, who moved to Britain in 1979 and had similar success? The first jockey to win both the Epsom and the Kentucky Derbies.

2. Which English jockey, now retired, was the winner of the most British Classics?

3. Which English jockey was flat-racing champion the most times?

4. Which two races are referred to as the Spring Double?

5. Which two races are referred to as the Autumn Double?

6. The U.K. has three all-weather race courses. Lingfield, Wolverhampton and …..what is the name of the third?

7. Which horse won the Cheltenham Gold Cup in 5 successive years, and the Grand National in between?

8. Which horse won the 2001 Grand National?

9. Which horse won the 2001 Derby?

10. In which year was the Grand National first run?

11. Only two British jockeys have won the title 'Champion Jockey' 13 years in succession. One was E. Flatman (1840-52). Who was the other?

12. In which year did User Friendly win the Oaks and the St. Leger?

13. In which year did Nijinsky win the St Leger, The 2,000 Guineas and the Derby?

14. Which horse won the Grand National three times in five years?

15. What was the name of the horse that won the 1981 Derby by a record 10 lengths?

ANSWERS.
1. Steve Cauthen. 2. Lester Piggott (30). 3. Gordon Richards (26). 4. The Lincoln and the Grand National. 5. The Cesarewitch and the Cambridgeshire. 6. Southwell. 7. Golden Miller (1932-36). 8. Red Marauder. 9. Galileo. 10. 1837. 11. Fred Archer (1874-86). 12. 1992. 13. 1970. 14. Red Rum (1973-74-77). 15. Shergar.

Ice Hockey

How much do you know about ice hockey? (1)

QUESTIONS.

1. Ice Hockey is obviously related to Field Hockey, but there are various theories as to how it came to be developed. The first of these suggests that it grew out of an English game played in the 1700's . Which game?

2. Another hypothesis has it growing out of a game played by a tribe of Indians in Nova Scotia in the early part of the 19th century. Do you know which tribe?

3. The most popular theory is that it was developed by British soldiers stationed in Canada during which period?

4. The name 'hockey' appears to derive from the French word for a shepherd's stick. Which is?

5. Early games were played on frozen lakes with anything up to 30 players on each side. The goals were stones frozen into the ice. The first recorded use of a puck was in what year?

6. Where did that occur?

7. In what year did the first recorded game take place on an indoor rink?

8. Do you know where?

9. The antagonists were two teams of students from which Montreal University?

10. McGill formed the very first ice hockey club, in what year was that?

11. In what year did they publish the first Book of Rules, and limit the teams to 9 a side?

12. And in what year was the very first national hockey organisation, the Amateur Hockey Association (AHA) of Canada, formed in Montreal?

13. In the same year the first league was formed in Kingston with four teams. Do you know the name of the first championship game winners?

14. In what year was the Canadian Amateur Hockey League formed?

15. The first professional hockey team in the world was formed in 1903 in Houghton, Michigan, USA. What was the name of the team?

ANSWERS.
1. Bandy. 2. The Micmacs. 3. The 1850's. 4. Hoquet. 5. 1860. 6. Kingston Harbour, Ontario. 7. 1875. 8. The Victoria Skating Rink, Montreal. 9. McGill University. 10. 1877. 11. 1879. 12. 1885. 13. Queen's University. 14. 1899. 15. The 'Portage Lakes'.

How much do you know about ice hockey? (2)

QUESTIONS.

1. The 'Portage Lakes' was owned by a dentist who, in 1904, established the world's first professional ice hockey league, the Int'l Pro Hockey League. What was his name?

2. The Ontario Professional Hockey League, Canada's first, followed, in what year?

3. In what year was the National Hockey Association formed?

4. In 1911 a competitive organisation was launched. What was its name?

5. Who were the founders of the PCHA?

6. In what year did the NHA disband and reform itself as the National Hockey League?

7. The founder members of the NHL were five Canadian clubs. In 1924 the first US based club applied for membership, and was accepted. What was the name of the US club?

8. In 1925 two other US clubs joined the NHL. One was the New York Americans. What was the other?

9. In 1926 three more US based clubs joined, the New York Rangers, the Detroit Cougars (later called the Red Wings), and what was the name of the third?

10. From then on the NHL dominated North American Ice hockey. However, in 1972, a new 12 – team league was launched. What was it called?

11. In what year did the NHL take over the WHA, to become a 21-team league?

12. What year was the first amateur league in Europe (in England) formed?

13. What year was the International Ice Hockey Federation (IIHF) formed in Europe?

14. Which country won the first European championship, held in Switzerland in 1910?

15. Which country won the first Olympic Ice Hockey gold medal and the first IIHF world championship in 1920, then retaining both titles until 1936?

ANSWERS.
1. J. L. Gibson. 2. 1908. 3. 1910. 4. The Pacific Coast Hockey Association. 5. Joseph Patrick and his two sons, Lester and Frank. 6. 1917. 7. The Boston Bruins. 8. The Pittsburgh Pirates. 9. The Chicago Black Hawks. 10. The World Hockey Assoc. 11. 1979. 12. 1903. 13. 1908. 14. Great Britain. 15. Canada.

How much do you know about ice hockey? (3)

QUESTIONS.

1. Today Ice Hockey is played in about 30 different countries. In which country is it the national sport?

2. What is the shape and what are the dimensions of a standard NHL ice rink?

3. What are the dimensions of a U.S. college ice rink?

4. What are the dimensions of an international ice rink?

5. What is the minimum height of the board wall which encloses the playing area?

6. What are the dimensions of the goal cages, one at either end of the playing area?

7. What is the zone called immediately in front of each goal, 4 ft deep x 8 ft wide, marked by a red line into which no attacking player may enter, unless the puck is there?

8. The playing area is divided into three zones by two latitudinal blue lines. The zone nearest a team's goal is called the defence zone; the zone nearest the opponent's goal is called the attacking zone. What is the central zone called?

9. The playing area is also divided latitudinally by three red lines. Two mark the 'goal lines' behind which the goals are erected. What does the third line indicate?

10. The rink also has five red circles clearly marked, each with a radius of 15 ft (4.6m), two in each team's defence zone and one at centre ice. What are these circles called?

11. How many players are there in a team, on the ice at any one time?

12. How many officials control a game of NHL or international ice hockey?

13. A game is divided into three periods. How long is each period, in minutes?

14. With what action does play begin, and begin again after every stoppage?

15. Substitutions are permitted during play. What is a change of player during play called?

ANSWERS.
1. Canada. 2. A round-cornered rectangle. 200 ft (61m) long x 85 ft (25.5m) wide. 3. 200 ft (61 m) x 100 ft (30.5 m). 4. 184-200 ft (56-61 m) x 85-98 ft (26-30 m). 5. 4 ft (1.22m). 6. 4 ft (1.22m) high x 6 ft (1.83m) wide. 7. The 'Crease'. 8. The 'Neutral Zone'. 9. The centre of the playing area. 10. 'Face-off' circles. 11. Six. 12. One referee; two linesmen and five off-ice officials. 13. Twenty. 14. 'Face-off'. 15. A 'Line Change'.

How much do you know about ice hockey? (4)

QUESTIONS.

1. A goal is scored when a vulcanised rubber disk 1 in (2.5 cm) thick x 3 in (7.6 cm) in diameter, is driven into the opponent's goal. What is the 'disk' called?

2. How long is the shaft of a hockey stick?

3. What are the measurements of the blade of a hockey stick?

4. What is the ruling if a player makes or takes a pass that traverses both a red and a blue line?

5. What is the ruling if a player arrives in the attacking zone before the puck?

6. What is it called when a puck is shot from behind the centre line to behind the opponent's goal line?

7. What is the principal means of defence known as?

8. If the score is a draw at the end of three periods in an NHL game, how many extra minutes are allowed?

9. For a minor infraction of the rules, an offending player can be sent to the penalty box for two minutes. How long for a major infraction?

10. Is a goaltender ever sent off for an infraction?

11. How many points is a victory worth in the standings, in organised ice hockey?

12. And how many points is a draw worth?

13. The scorer of a goal is awarded an individual point for the statistics. Two other points may be awarded for the same goal. What term is applied to these other points?

14. There are three types of shot commonly used in ice hockey – the wrist shot, the backhander and ….. what is the third?

15. Which hockey institution was established in Toronto, Ontario in 1961

ANSWERS.
1. A 'puck'. 2. Maximum of 60 in (142 cm). 3. Maximum 12.6 in (32 cm) long x maximum 3 in (7.6 cm) wide. 4. 'Offside'. 5. 'Offside'. 6. 'Icing'. 7. 'Checking'. 8. Five. 9. Five. 10. No. Penalties incurred by a goalie are served by a team-mate. 11. Two. 12. One 13. An 'Assist'. 14. The 'Slap shot'. 15. The 'Hockey Hall of Fame'.

How much do you know about ice hockey? (5)

QUESTIONS.

1. What is the prize awarded to the best team in the National Hockey League every year?

2. This three foot high silver cup was first given to amateur champions. In what year?

3. The cup was presented by the then Governor - General of Canada, whose name was …?

4. From 1912 onwards it was presented to the professional champions. In what year did it pass into the permanent possession of the NHL?

5. What is the name of the trophy awarded annually to the best goaltender in the NHL?

6. What is the name of the trophy awarded annually to the goalie (or goalies) with the team which let in the fewest goals during the season?

7. The 'Rookie of the Year' wins which award?

8. What is awarded to the player elected 'Most Valuable Player of the Year'?

9. What is the name of the trophy awarded to the outstanding defense player of the year?

10. The top point scorer of the year receives which award?

11. The player who best combined skill and clean play is awarded what prize?

12. What is awarded to the outstanding performer during the play-offs (the qualifying rounds of the championship)?

13. The best defensive forward is awarded which prize?

14. What is the name of the award given to the best Coach of the year?

15. What is the award given to the player who best exemplifies perseverance, sportsmanship and dedication to the sport?

ANSWERS.
1. The Stanley Cup. 2. 1893-94. 3. Sir Frederick Arthur, 1st Baron Stanley of Preston. 4. 1926. 5. The Vezina Trophy. 6. The William M. Jennings Trophy. 7. The Calder Trophy. 8. The Hart Trophy. 9. The Norris Trophy. 10. The Art Ross Trophy. 11. The Lady Byng Trophy. 12. The Conn Smythe Trophy. 13. The Frank J. Selke Trophy. 14. The Jack Adams Award. 15. The Bill Masterton Memorial Trophy.

How much do you know about ice hockey? (6)

QUESTIONS.

1. What prize is awarded annually to the person judged to have been of outstanding service to the sport, in the United States?

2. At the end of each season, the Professional Hockey Writers Association chooses two teams from the outstanding players. What are they called?

3. What is the name of the organisation which, in collaboration with the U.S. Olympic Committee, chooses players to go the Olympic Games, and also is responsible for picking the national team to enter the world championships?

4. What is the name of the major U.S. collegiate championship?

5. What is the prize fought for by the senior Canadian amateur hockey clubs?

6. And for what prize do the junior (below 20 years of age) Canadian amateur hockey teams play?

7. Who were the two Canadian-born brothers who as players, managers, owners and league officials made an enormous contribution to the successful development of Ice Hockey?

8. Who was the Czech born goalminder for Buffalo Sabres, who won 4 Vezina trophies as best goalie; and consecutive Hart Memorial Trophies as MVP, and an Olympic Gold medal? His fans called him 'The Dominator'.

9. Which NHL team plays its home games in the Northlands Coliseum?

10. Who was the Russian coach who introduced aggressive Canadian-style play to his country, and led the Soviet national team to 11 European Championships and 10 World titles, including 3 Olympic Gold medals, in the '60's and '70's?

11. Who was the Boston Bruins goaltender who in the first weeks of a ten year career made a series of shut-outs, earning himself the nickname 'Mr Zero'? 8 times an All-Star.

12. Which team won the Stanley Cup in 1999?

13. Which national team won the World Championship in 1999?

14. What is the name of the British team which plays out of Nottingham?

15. Which NHL team has the Madison Square Garden for its home ground?

ANSWERS.
1. The Lester Patrick Trophy. 2. The 'All-Stars'. 3. The Amateur Hockey Association of the United States (AHAUS). 4. The National Collegiate Athletic Association (NCAA) Tournament. 5. The Allen Cup. 6. The Memorial Cup. 7. Lester and Frank Patrick. 8. Dominik Hasek. 9. Edmonton Oilers. 10. Anatoly Tarasov. 11. Frankie Brimsek. 12. Dallas Stars. 13. Czech Republic. 14. Panthers. 15. New York Rangers.

How much do you know about ice hockey? (7)

QUESTIONS.

1. Who was the brilliant but somewhat unorthodox French-Canadian goaltender who won many awards playing for several NHL teams in the 1950's, 60's and 70's? His fans called him 'Jake the Snake'.

2. Who was the player, coach, manager who organised the New York Rangers in 1927 and then went on to found the Toronto Maple Leafs?

3. The home ground of which team is called the 'Pacific Coliseum'?

4. Who was the Detroit Red Wings and Houston Aeros player and administrator who retired with a record 1,071 goals. 1,518 assists and 2,421 games played, a record which stood until Wayne Gretzky passed it?

5. Who was the Boston Bruins defenseman, the first to lead the NHL in scoring goals? He received 16 major awards in his highly successful career.

6. Which NHL team won the Stanley Cup in 1995?

7. Which national team won the World Championship in 1998?

8. Who was known as 'The Great One'? 9 times leader of the league in scoring; 9 times the league's MVP; 4 times Stanley Cup winner with the Edmonton Oilers.

9. Which team plays its home games in 'The Forum'?

10. Who led the Pittsburgh Penguins to the Stanley Cup championship title in 1991 and 92? He overtook Wayne Gretzky as the NHL's leading scorer.in 1987-88.

11. Who was the goaltender, one of the profession's finest, who made his career with the Red Wings, the Bruins, the Maple Leafs and the Rangers, from 1949 to 1970?

12. Who made the swinging 'slap-shot' famous?

13. Who played centre for the Montreal Canadiens for his entire career (1953-71), leading them to 10 Stanley Cup wins and becoming a vice president after his retirement.?

14. Which national team won the World Championship in 1995?

15. Which NHL team won the Stanley Cup in 1996?

ANSWERS.
1. Jacques Plante. 2. Conn Smythe. 3. Vancouver Canucks. 4. Gordie Howe 5. Bobby Orr. 6. New Jersey Devils. 7. Sweden. 8. Wayne Gretzky. 9. Montreal Canadiens. 10. Mario Lemieux. 11. Terry Sawchuk. 12. Bobby Hull. 13. Jean Beliveau. 14. Finland. 15. Colorado Avalanche.

How much do you know about ice hockey? (8)

QUESTIONS.

What are the names of the teams from the following towns or states:

1. New York?
2. Washington?
3. San Jose?
4. Montreal?
5. Boston?
6. Detroit?
7. Chicago?
8. Los Angeles?
9. Philadelphia?
10. Toronto?
11. Pittsburgh?
12. St Louis?
13. Buffalo?
14. Vancouver?
15. Edmonton?

ANSWERS.
1. Rangers. 2. Capitals. 3. Sharks. 4. Canadiens. 5. Bruins. 6. Red Wings. 7. Blackhawks
8. Kings. 9. Flyers. 10. Maple Leafs. 11. Penguins. 12. Blues. 13. Sabres. 14. Canucks.
15. Oilers

How much do you know about ice hockey? (9)

QUESTIONS.

What are the names of the teams from the following towns or states:

1. Calgary?

2. New Jersey?

3. Ottawa?

4. Tampa Bay?

5. Anaheim?

6. Dallas?

7. Florida?

8. Colorado?

9. Phoenix?

10. Carolina?

11. New York?

12. Minnesota? >1993

13. Quebec? >1995

14. Winnipeg? >1996

15. Hartford? >1997

ANSWERS.
1. Flames. 2. Devils. 3. Senators. 4. Lightning. 5. Mighty Ducks. 6. Stars. 7. Panthers. 8. Avalanche. 9. Coyotes. 10.Hurricanes. 11. Islanders. 12. North Stars. 13. Nordiques. 14. Jets. 15. Whalers. League members up to the date shown. .

Formula 1 motor racing

How much do you know about Formula 1 Motor Racing?

QUESTIONS.

1. What year did Formula 1 Motor Racing begin?

2. Who was the first Champion driver?

3. From 1950 to 2000 only one driver has been World Champion five times. Who?

4. Where is the Dutch Formula 1 racing circuit?

5. Between 1950 and 2000, which driver registered the most consecutive wins?

6. Which Formula 1 flag is used to indicate the end of the race?

7. Who was the first woman to drive in a Formula 1 race?

8. What kind of fuel is used in Formula 1 racing?

9. Where is the French Formula 1 racing circuit?

10. Who was the only driver to win the Monaco Grand Prix five times?

11. To win the World Championship in 1994 Michael Schumacher drove a Benetton-Ford. To win again in 1995 he drove a Benetton-Renault. What did he drive in 2000?

12. Where is the Luxembourg Grand Prix run?

13. Who was the French-born driver who was World Champion four times and also runner-up four times?

14. What colour is the flag used to indicate the premature end of the race?

15. Who was the British driver who was runner-up four years in succession, 1955-58, but never became World Champion?

ANSWERS.
1. 1950. 2. Giuseppe Farina. 3. Juan Manuel Fangio. 4. Zandvoort. 5. Alberto Ascari (9). 6. Black and white chequered. 7. Leila Lombardi (1975). 8. Nitro-methane. 9. Magny Cours, Dijon. 10. Graham Hill. 11. Ferrari. 12. Nurburgring, Germany. 13. Alain Prost. 14. Red. 15. Stirling Moss.

The Olympic Games

How much do you know about the Olympic Games? (1)

QUESTIONS.

1. The original Olympic Games were organised by the ancient Greeks on a four year cycle in honour of which of their Gods?

2. During which period did the original games run?

3. What was the name of the Roman Emperor who abolished the games?

4. In what year were the games revived?

5. Who was the French educationalist mainly responsible for their revival?

6. What is the name of the association which has the responsibility for organising every aspect of the games today?

7. What was the name of the American athlete and businessman who was closely associated with the development of the I.O.C. throughout the 20th century, until his death in 1975?

8. In the 20th century the Olympic Games were cancelled twice and postponed once. The cancellations were 1916 (Berlin) and 1940 (Tokyo). Where should the 1944 games have taken place had they not been postponed?

9. Only one country has taken part in every games, summer and winter, since 1896. Which?

10. The Olympic motto is 'Citius, Altius, Fortius'. What is that in English?

11. Medals are awarded to the winner(s) and to the 2nd and 3rd in each event. What is given to those who come in 4th to 8th?

12, What do the rings on the Olympic flag represent?

13. The Olympic flag is white with five rings in different colours: blue; yellow; black; and green. What is the colour of the 5th ring?

14. Which country always leads the opening parade?

15. Which country always terminates the opening parade?

ANSWERS.
1. Zeus. 2. From 776 BC to 393 AD. 3. Theodosius I. 4. 1896. 5. Baron Pierre de Coubertin. 6. The International Olympic Committee (IOC). 7. Avery Brundage. 8. London. 9. The United Kingdom. 10. 'Faster, Higher, Stronger'. 11. Diplomas. 12. The Five Continents. 13. Red. 14. Greece. 15. The host country.

How much do you know about the Olympic Games? (2)

QUESTIONS.

1. Only once in the modern games has an extra lap of a race been run by mistake. Which race and which games?

2. Where was the first winter Olympics held in 1924?

3. What is the name of the men's event which contains the following activities in this order: 100m Sprint; Long Jump; Shot Putt; High Jump; 400m; 110m Hurdles; Discus; Pole Vault; Javelin and 1,500m?

4. What was unusual about Abebe Bikila's win of the Marathon, Rome, 1960?

5. What is the exact distance of the Olympic Marathon?

6. What is the name of the women's event which contains the following activities in this order: 100m Hurdles; High Jump; Shot Putt; 200m Sprint; Long Jump; Javelin and 800m, all to be completed over two days?

7. Only one world record has never been broken at an Olympic Games. Which one?

8. The distance between hurdles in both the men's and the women's 400 metres hurdles is the same. What is it?

9. Where were the 1984 Winter Olympics held?

10. Who was the I.O.C. President from 1980 until 2001?

11. Who was the first woman gold medallist of the modern Olympic Games?

12. Which British gold medal winner (1956, Equestrian) escaped from Colditz P.O.W. camp during the 2nd World war?

13. Who was the first male athlete to swim 100 metres in under 1 minute?

14. Who was the first male athlete to go over 6 metres in the Pole Vault?

15. Who was the first male athlete to run 100 metres in under 10 seconds?

ANSWERS.
1. Steeplechase, Los Angeles, 1932. 2. Chamonix, France. 3. Decathlon. 4. He ran barefooted. 5. 26 miles and 385 yards. 6. Heptathlon. 7. Men's Discus. 8. 35 metres. 9. Sarajevo, Yugoslavia. 10. Juan Antonio Samaranch. 11. Charlotte Cooper, 1900. (Tennis Singles). 12. Frank Weldon. 13. Johnny Weismuller (1924). 14. Sergei Bubka (1985). 15. Armin Hary (1960).

How much do you know about the Olympic Games? (3)

QUESTIONS.

1. What year did sex testing at the Olympics begin?

2. In what discipline was Ulrike Mayfarth the youngest gold winner at 16 (Rome, 1960)and the oldest at 28 (Montreal, 1976)?

3. Who was the American woman who won gold in the 80 metre Hurdles and Javelin throw, and silver in the High Jump at Los Angeles, 1932?

4. Which summer Olympics were destroyed by the Black September terrorists killing Israeli athletes?

5. What is the weight and what are the measurements of the men's javelin?

6. How many times do the steeplechasers jump the water jump?

7. Which events were included in the ancient pentathlon?

8. Which events make up the modern men's pentathlon?

9. Which events make up the modern women's pentathlon?

10. Who was the first female athlete to pass 2 metres in the High Jump?

11. How high are the hurdles in the men's 110 m Hurdles?

12. How high are the hurdles in the women's 100 m Hurdles?

13. What is the name of the organisation which has the responsibility, amongst others, of ratifying world records?

14. What is the name of the U.K. organisation which started arranging track and field competitions in 1880, growing out of a club which was formed in 1866?

15. What is the name of its US counterpart?

ANSWERS.
1. 1968, Mexico. 2. High Jump. 3. Mildred Didrikson. 4. Munich, 1972. 5. 800 grams (1lb 12 oz) and minimum 260 cm long. 6. Seven. (Not jumped in first lap). 7. Running; Jumping; Discus; Javelin; Wrestling. 8. Riding; Fencing; Shooting; Swimming; Cross-country Running. 9. 200m; 100m Hurdles; Shot Putt; High Jump; Long Jump. 10. Rosie Ackerman (Germany). 11. 3'6" (106.7 cm). 12. 2'9" (83.8 cm). 13. International Amateur Athletics Federation. 14. Amateur Athletics Association. 15. Amateur Athletics Union.

Olympic Gold Medallists

How much do you know about the recent Olympic Gold Medallists? (1)

QUESTIONS.

1. Who won gold for the men's 100 metres in both 1984 and 1988?

2. Who won gold for both the men's 200 and 400 metres in 1996?

3. Who won gold for the men's 100 metres in 1992?

4. Who won gold for the men's 1,500 metres in both 1980 and 1984?

5. Who won gold for the men's 800 metres in 1996?

6. Who won gold for the men's 1,500 metres in 1996?

7. Who won gold for the men's 10,000 metres in 1996?

8. Who won gold for the men's 400 metres in 1992?

9. Who won gold for the men's 5,000 metres in 1996?

10. Who won gold for the men's marathon in 1996?

11. Who won gold for the men's 110 metre hurdles in 1992?

12. Who won gold for the men's 400 metre hurdles in 1996?

13. Who won gold for the men's 20 km walk in 1988?

14. Who won the gold for the men's hammer throw in 1996?

15. Who won the gold for the men's long jump in 1984-88-92-96?

ANSWERS.
1. Carl Lewis. 2. Michael Johnson. 3. Linford Christie. 4. Sebastian Coe. 5. Vebjorn Rodal. 6. Noureddine Morceli. 7. Haile Gebrselassie. 8. Quincy Watts. 9. Venuste Niyongabo. 10. Josia Thugwane. 11. Mark McKoy. 12. Derrick Adkins. 13. Josef Pribilinec. 14. Balazs Kiss. 15. Carl Lewis.

How much do you know about the recent Olympic Gold Medallists? (2)

QUESTIONS.

1. Who won gold for the women's 100 metres in both 1992 and 1996?

2. Who won gold for both the women's 100 and 200 metres in 1988?

3. Who won gold for the women's 200 metres in 1992?

4. Who won gold for the women's 400 metres in 1992?

5. Who won gold for both the women's 200 and 400 metres in 1996?

6. Who won gold for both the women's 800 and 1,500 metres in 1996?

7. Who won gold for the women's heptathlon in both 1988 and 1992?

8. Who won gold for the women's long jump in 1988?

9. Who won gold for the women's long jump in 1992?

10. Who won gold for the women's 400 metre hurdles in 1992?

11. Who won gold for the women's 10,000 metres in 1996?

12. Who won gold for the women's marathon in 1996?

13. Who won gold for the women's triple jump in 1996?

14. Who won the gold for the women's 400 metre hurdles in 1996?

15. Who won gold for the women's high jump in 1996?

ANSWERS.
1. Gail Devers. 2. Florence Griffith-Joyner. 3. Gwen Torrance. 4. Marie-Jose Perec. 5. Marie-Jose Perec. 6. Svetlana Masterkova. 7. Jackie Joyner-Kersee. 8. Jackie Joyner-Kersee. 9. Heike Drechsler. 10. Sally Gunnell. 11. Fernanda Ribeiro. 12. Fatuma Roba. 13. Inessa Kravets. 14. Deon Hemmings. 15. Stefka Kostadinova.

How much do you know about the recent Olympic Gold Medallists? (3)

QUESTIONS.

1. Who won gold for the men's 100 metres in 2000?

2. Who won gold for the men's 200 metres in 2000?

3. Who won gold for the men's 400 metres in 2000?

4. Who won gold for the men's 800 metres in 2000?

5. Who won gold for the men's 1,500 metres in 2000?

6. Who won gold for the men's 5,000 metres in 2000?

7. Who won gold for the men's 10,000 metres in 2000?

8. Who won gold for the men's marathon in 2000?

9. Who won gold for the men's 3,000 metre steeplechase in 2000?

10. Who won gold for the men's 110 metre hurdles in 2000?

11. Who won gold for the men's 400 metre hurdles in 2000?

12. Who won gold for the men's pole vault in 2000?

13. Who won gold for the men's high jump in 2000?

14. Who won gold for the men's long jump in 2000?

15. Who won gold for the men's triple jump in 2000?

ANSWERS.
1. Maurice Greene. 2. K. Kenteris. 3. Michael Johnson. 4. N. Schumann. 5. Noah Ngeny. 6. M. Wolde. 7. Haile Gebrselassie. 8. G. Abera. 9. R. Kosgei. 10. A. Garcia. 11. A. Taylor. 12. N. Hysong. 13. S. Kliugin. 14. I. Pedroso. 15. Jonathan Edwards.

How much do you know about the recent Olympic Gold Medallists? (4)

QUESTIONS.

1. Who won gold for the women's 100 metres in 2000?

2. Who won gold for the women's 200 metres in 2000?

3. Who won gold for the women's 400 metres in 2000?

4. Who won gold for the women's 800 metres in 2000?

5. Who won gold for the women's 1,500 metres in 2000?

6. Who won gold for the women's 5,000 metres in 2000?

7. Who won gold for the women's 10,000 metres in 2000?

8. Who won gold for the women's marathon in 2000?

9. Who won gold for the women's 100 metre hurdles in 2000?

10. Who won gold for the women's 400 metre hurdles in 2000?

11. Who won gold for the women's pole vault in 2000?

12. Who won gold for the women's high jump in 2000?

13. Who won gold for the women's long jump in 2000?

14. Who won gold for the women's triple jump in 2000?

15. Who won gold for the women's shot putt in 2000?

ANSWERS.
1. Marion Jones. 2. Marion Jones. 3. Cathy Freeman. 4. M. Mutola. 5. N. Merah-Benida. 6. Karolina Szabo. 7. D. Tulu. 8. N. Takahashi. 9. O. Shishigina. 10. I. Privalova. 11. Stacy Dragila. 12. Y. Yelesina/H. Cloete. 13. Heike Drechsler. 14. T. Marinova. 15. Y. Yorolchik.

How much do you know about the recent Olympic Gold Medallists? (5)

QUESTIONS.

1. Who won gold for the men's shot putt in 2000?

2. Who won gold for the men's discus throw in 2000?

3. Who won gold for the men's hammer throw in 2000?

4. Who won gold for the men's javelin throw in 2000?

5. Who won gold for the men's decathlon in 2000?

6. Who won gold for the men's 20 km walk in 2000?

7. Who won gold for the men's 50 km walk in 2000?

8. Who won gold for the men's 4 x 100 metres relay in 2000?

9. Who won gold for the men's 4 x 400 metres relay in 2000?

10. Who won gold for the women's discus throw in 2000?

11. Who won gold for the women's hammer throw in 2000?

12. Who won gold for the women's javelin throw in 2000?

13. Who won gold for the women's heptathlon in 2000?

14. Who won gold for the women's 4 x 100 metres relay in 2000?

15. Who won gold for the women's 4 x 400 metres relay in 2000?

ANSWERS.
1. A. Harju. 2. V. Alekna. 3. S. Ziolkowski.. 4. Jan Zelezny. 5. E. Nool. 6. R. Korzeniowski.
7. R. Korzeniowski. 8. USA. 9. USA. 10. E. Zvereva. 11. K. Skolimowska. 12. T. Hattestad.
13. Denise Lewis. 14. Bahamas. 15. USA.

Tennis

How much do you know about tennis? (1)

QUESTIONS.

1. The origins of Tennis can be traced to a 12th/13th century French handball game called ......what?

2. From those origins developed a complex racket and ball indoor game. What was this game called?

3. Still played today, what is it called in the US?

4. Where and when was the first known Tennis Club formed?

5. Who was the Welshman who produced the first book of rules in 1873 and patented the game in 1874?

6. What did he call his book?

7. Which organisation, at the time the governing body of real tennis, produced a new, standardised set of rules in 1875?

8. Who is believed to have owned the first lawn tennis set in the US?

9. In 1876 the All-England Croquet Club set aside one of its lawns for tennis. Where was this?

10. In what year were the very first Wimbledon Tennis Championships played?

11. It was a men's singles championship only. Who was the winner?

12. In what year were the women's singles and the men's doubles first played?

13. In what year was the US National Lawn Tennis Association (late the US Lawn Tennis Association and later still the US Tennis Association) formed?

14. An unofficial US men's championship had been held in 1880, but the first official tournament was held in 1881. The winner went on to hold the title for six more consecutive years. What was his name?

15. Where was the first official US men's tournament held?

ANSWERS.
1. 'Jeu de paume' 2. 'Real' (Royal) tennis. 3. 'Court tennis'. 4. Leamington, England. 1872. 5. Major Walter Wingfield. 6. 'Sphairistike, or Lawn Tennis'. 7. The MCC (Marylebone Cricket Club) 8. William Appleton of Nahant, Mass. 9. Wimbledon. 10. 1877. 11. Spencer Gore. 12. 1884. 13. 1881. 14. Richard Sears. 15. Newport, Rhode Island

How much do you know about tennis? (2)

QUESTIONS.

1. What year was the British Lawn Tennis Association (the LTA) formed, to replace the MCC and the All-England Club as the governing bodies?

2. In what year was the first Australian Open Tennis Championships held?

3. Again, at first it was a men's only competition. In what year did the women's championships make their first appearance?

4. In what year was the Lawn Tennis Association of Australasia (later just Australia) formed?

5. In New Zealand national championships were inaugurated in what year?

6. The first French Championships were held in 1891, but the tournament was not open to international competition until ....which year?

7. In what year was the French Federation of Lawn Tennis established?

8. In what year did the women's championships make their first appearance in the US Open?

9. In what year were the national championships inaugurated in Canada?

10. In what year were the national championships inaugurated in South Africa?

11. In what year were the national championships inaugurated in Spain?

12. In what year were the national championships inaugurated in Denmark?

13. In what year were the national championships inaugurated in Egypt?

14. In what year were the national championships inaugurated in Italy?

15. In what year were the national championships inaugurated in Sweden?

ANSWERS.
1. 1888. 2. 1905. 3. 1922. 4. 1904. 5. 1886. 6. 1925. 7. 1920. 8. 1887. 9. 1890. 10. 1891. 11. 1910. 12. 1921. 13. 1925. 14. 1930. 15. 1936. .

How much do you know about tennis? (3)

QUESTIONS.

1. What are the dimensions of the playing area of a tennis court, for singles?

2. What are the dimensions of the playing area of a tennis court, for doubles?

3. What is the height of the net at centre court?

4. What is the diameter of a tennis ball?

5. What is the weight of a tennis ball?

6. A tennis ball must have a bounce of how many inches when dropped on a concrete surface from 100 inches height?

7. What are the maximum dimensions of a tournament racket?

8. What are the maximum dimensions of the head of a tournament racket?

9. What year saw the foundation of the International Lawn Tennis Federation?

10. What year was tennis accepted into the Olympic Games?

11. If a player wins all four of the major open tournaments (Australia; France; England and the US) consecutively but not necessarily in the same year, what is it called?

12. What is the guild of male professional tennis players called?

13. What is the name of the women's professional tennis players guild?

14. What is the name of the Paris stadium in which the French Open is staged?

15. And where is the Australian Open played?

ANSWERS.
1. 78 feet (23.77 m) x 27 feet (8.23 m). 2. 78 feet (23.77 m) x 36 feet (10.97 m). 3. 3 feet (0.91 m) 4. 6 - 7 cm. 5. 57 - 58 grams. 6. 53 to 58 ins. 7. 32 ins (81.3 cm) x 12.5 ins (31.8 cm). 8. 15.5 ins (39.4 cm) x 11.5 ins (29.2 cm). 9. 1912. 10. 1988. 11. A 'Grand Slam'. 12. The Association of Tennis Professionals (ATP). 13. The Women's Tennis Association (WTA). 14. 'Roland Garros'. 15. Flinders Park, Melbourne.

Sporting terminology

How much do you know about terms used in different sports? (1)

QUESTIONS.

1. In cricket, what is the name given to a ball bowled directly at the feet of the batsman?

2. What is the name given to the action in dressage when the horse trots on the spot?

3. What, in downhill skiing, is the name given to the total skiing area?

4. What is a boxer who leads with his right hand called?

5. What, in curling, is the round target area of concentric circles called?

6. What, in golf, did a No. 5 iron used to be called?

7. What in fencing, is the padded, leather-covered breast-plate called?

8. What, in basketball, is the defensive technique of harassing a player into a hurried play called?

9. What is the vehicle used in harness racing (trotting) called?

10. What, in rugby, is another name for an up-and-under?

11. What, in ice-skating, is the name given to a full-turn jump from the inside back-edge of one skate to the outside back-edge of the other?

12. What, in trampolining, is a three-and-a-half twisting somersault called?

13. What is the area at the back of a badminton court called?

14. What is it called, in baseball, to let the ball hit the bat without swinging at it?

15. What is a playing period known as in polo?

ANSWERS.
1. A 'yorker'. 2. 'Piaffe'. 3. The 'piste'. 4. A 'southpaw'. 5. The 'house'. 6. A 'mashie'. 7. The 'plastron'. 8. 'Press' 9. A 'sulky'. 10. A 'garryowen'. 11. A 'salchow'. 12. An 'adolph'. 13. The 'back alley'. 14. A 'bunt'. 15. A 'chukka'.

How much do you know about terms used in different sports? (2)

QUESTIONS.

1. What, in kendo, is the end of the match?

2. What, in rugby, is a kick that is made by dropping the ball and kicking it before it reaches the ground?

3. What name is given, in ten-pin bowling, to the achievement of knocking all the pins down with one ball?

4. What is it called in baseball, when the batter swings but misses the ball completely?

5. What is the traditional technique of holding a table-tennis bat with fingers on the face called?

6. What, in American football, is a 'warner single wing'?

7. What is it called, in surfing, when the surfer is tumbled off his board, for example, by an unseen wave?

8. What, in ice-skating, is a 'rocker'?

9. What term is used in cycling for pedalling fast in a gear with no pressure asserted?

10. What name is given in cricket to the fielding position slightly wide of slips?

11. What term is used, in golf, for a score 3 under par on a particular hole?

12. What, in gymnastics, is a cartwheel with a quarter turn?

13. What is the playing stick called in the game of shinty?

14. What, in motor racing, is a sharp double-bend?

15. What is it called in dressage, when the horse raises and draws in its forelegs whilst balancing on its hind legs?

ANSWERS.
1. 'Shobu-ari'. 2. A 'punt'. 3. A 'strike'. 4. A 'strike'. 5. The 'western grip'. 6. An offensive formation. 7. A 'wipe-out'. 8. A skate with a curved blade. 9. 'Twiddling' or 'Spinning'. 10. 'Gully'. 11. An 'albatross'. 12. An 'Arab spring'. 13. A 'caman'. 14. A 'chicane'. 15. A 'levade'

How much do you know about terms used in different sports? (3)

QUESTIONS.

1. What in wrestling , is the one-handed throw whereby the arm is whipped back and forth forcing the opponent into a somersault in mid-air?

2. What is a front somersault with a half twist called in trampolining?

3. What in golf, is the short grass between fairway and approach to the green called?

4. What in cricket, is a ball bowled short and fast to force the batsman to take evasive action?

5. What in skiing, is the turn in which the skis are kept parallel, used for stopping short?

6. What is it called in squash, when a player loses a point on his service?

7. What, in American football, is each of a fixed number of attempts to advance the ball 10 yards?

8. What is the name given to a participant in a judo contest?9. What is it called in Association football, when a player passes the ball between the legs of an opponent, and then runs around him to collect it?

10. What is the large triangular sail carried forward or opposite the main sail in yacht racing?

11. What is it called, in rugby, when the ball is touched down behind the opponent's goal line?

12. What are the outer lines of a tennis court called?

13. What is the grand champion called in sumo wrestling?

14. What, in curling, is the heavy 'top' with a handle, which is aimed at the 'house'?

15. What is it called in basketball, when two opponents both have such a grip of the ball that neither can gain possession?

ANSWERS.
1. An 'Irish whip'. 2. A 'barani'. 3. The 'apron'. 4. A 'bouncer'. 5. A 'christie' or 'christiania'. 6. A 'hand-out'. 7. A 'down'. 8. A 'judoka'. 9. A 'nutmeg'. 10. The 'spinnaker'. 11. A 'try'. 12. The 'tram lines'. 13. The 'yokozuna'. 14. A 'stone'. 15. A 'held ball'.

How much do you know about terms used in different sports? (4)

QUESTIONS.

1. What, in golf, is the name given to a free shot awarded informally after a particularly poor shot e.g. an air shot (a miss)?

2. What, in cricket, is the term for an off-break ball bowled with an apparent leg-break action?

3. What, in yachting, is the triangular staysail stretched from the outer end of the jib-boom to the fore-topmast?

4. What is the throw used in wrestling, to pitch an opponent head first over one's hip?

5. What name is given, in canoeing, to a 360 degree roll, beginning and ending above water, but passing 180 degrees under water?

6. What, in rugby, is a ruck in which the ball remains off the ground?

7. What, in ice skating, is the jump called, in which the skater takes off from the outside back- edge of one skate, and lands, after full rotation, on the outside back edge of the other?

8. What, in volleyball, is the one-handed attacking shot from above and across the net called?

9. What do they call it in baseball, when the batting side advance safely to bases, without the striker hitting the ball?

10. What is the name, in curling, of the centre point of the house?

11. What is the title of the person in a cycling team, who is responsible for taking care of the physical and mental health and preparation of the cyclists?

12. What, in squash, is the lower line on the wall called, above which all shots must be played?

13. What, in American football, is a 'shotgun'?

14. What is a karate school called?

15. What, in judo, is the break of a hold called?

ANSWERS.
1. A 'Mulligan'. 2. A 'googly'. 3. The jib. 4. A 'cross-buttock'. 5. An Eskimo roll. 6. A maul. 7. A lutz. 8. A spike. 9. 'Stealing bases'. 10. The tee. 11. The 'soigneur'. 12. The tin. 13. An offensive formation. 14. A 'shukokai'. 15. 'Mata'.

How much do you know about terms used in different sports? (5)

1. What, in high jumping, is the name given to the technique (named after its inventor) whereby head and shoulders are thrown over the bar first, chest upwards and legs pulled back?

2. What, in wrestling, is the hold in which the arms are passed under the arms of the opponent and interlocked behind his neck, immobilising his upper body?

3. What, in American football, is an 'eagle'?

4. What, in fencing, is the act of stamping the foot, generally prior to an attack, called?

5. What, in baseball, is an illegal action by a pitcher called?

6. What is the name given, in curling, to the type of broom used to sweep the ice in front of the stone?

7. What in rugby, is the name given to the short side between scrum and touchline?

8. What is it called in dressage, when the horse jumps straight upwards with its forelegs drawn in under its body, kicking backwards horizontally with its hind legs?

9. What , in Association football, is the defensive formation called which incorporates a 'sweeper' behind the line of backs?

10. What name is given in golf to a score of 2 under par on a hole?

11. What, in cricket, is a run scored after the ball has touched any part of the batsman but his hand (or his bat)?

12. What in judo, is a hold which lasts between 10 and 20 seconds?

13. What is it called, in ten-pin bowling, to score a strike in each of three successive bowls?

14. What, in gymnastics, is a flat handspring over the vaulting horse called?

15. What in rowing, is the term used for getting an oar trapped underwater or missing the water with a stroke?

ANSWERS.
1. The 'Fosbury Flop'. (After Dick Fosbury). 2. The full-nelson. 3. A defensive formation. 4. An appel. 5. A baulk. 6. A besom. 7. The blind side. 8. A 'capriole'. 9. Catenaccio. 10. An eagle. 11. A leg-bye. 12. A koka. 13. A turkey. 14. A yamashita. 15. Catching a crab.

Sporting Trophies

How much do you know about sporting trophies? (1)

QUESTIONS.

1. In which sport do international teams compete for the Cowdray Park Gold Cup?

2. In which sport do Oxford and Cambridge compete annually for the Bowring Bowl?

3. What is the trophy awarded annually to the winner of the Indianapolis 500?

4. In which sport is the George Hearn Cup awarded to the most successful English exponent?

5. What trophy is awarded to the nation with the best results in the World Fencing Championships?

6. What trophy is given to the winners of the men's World Badminton Team Championship?

7. In which annual tournament do crews compete for the Wyfold Challenge Cup?

8. What trophy is awarded to the winners of the women's World Table Tennis Team Championships?

9. In which sport do clubs compete for the Britannia Shield?

10. What is the blue riband event in single sculling?

11. There is a biennial competition for the Eisenhower Trophy. In which sport?

12. What trophy is awarded annually by the Downtown Athletic Club of New York to the season's outstanding college football player?

13. The Iroquois Cup is awarded annually to the winners of the English Club Championship in which sport?

14. There is fierce competition between Scotland and Canada for the Strathcona Cup. Which sport does this concern?

15. In which sport will the winners of the USA-GB women's challenge match receive the Wolfe-Noel Cup?

ANSWERS.
1. Polo. 2. Rugby Union. 3. The Borg-Warner Trophy. 4. Diving. 5. The Prince Rainier Cup. 6. The Thomas Cup. 7. The Henley Regatta. 8. The Marcel Corbillon Cup. 9. Speedway Racing. 10. The Diamond Challenge. 11. Golf. 12. The Heisman Memorial Trophy. 13. Lacrosse. 14. Curling. 15. Squash.

How much do you know about sporting trophies? (2)

QUESTIONS.

1. In which sport is the Dewar Cup presented?

2. For which trophy do England and Scotland battle it out each year on the rugby union ground?

3. Which yachting trophy was originally called the 100 Guineas Cup?

4. In which sport at club competition level is the Baron Matsui Inter-Club Cup presented?

5. Which trophy is awarded to the shinty Champions of Scotland?

6. In which sport do the women's World Amateur Team Champions win the Federation Cup?

7. In which sport does the MacRobertson International Shield await the winner?

8. The winners of the World Cup in the sport of rugby union receive ....which trophy?

9. Which trophy is awarded to England's most successful swimming and water polo club?

10. The Gordon Bennett Trophy was the forerunner of the Grand Prix in ......which sport?

11. What does the most stylish boxer at the Olympic Games receive?

12. What trophy is awarded to the winners of the Women's World Badminton Team Championship?

13. The England v Australia test matches at cricket is all about winning ......what?

14. In which sport does the World Championship competition lead to the Volvo World Cup?

15. The South African Provincial cricket competition is for ......what prize?

ANSWERS.
1. Rifle Shooting. 2. The Calcutta Cup. 3. The America's Cup. 4. Judo. 5. The Camanachd Cup. 6. Tennis. 7. Croquet. 8. The Webb-Ellis Trophy. 9. The Henry Benjamin Trophy. 10. Motor Racing. 11. The Val Barker Trophy. 12. The Uber Cup. 13. The Ashes. 14. Show Jumping. 15. The Currie Cup.

How much do you know about sporting trophies? (3)

QUESTIONS.

1. 'The Cole Cup' is an award made in fencing. But in which particular discipline?

2. Which trophy is awarded to the winners of the National 12 foot Dinghy Championship?

3. In which sport do teams from Great Britain and the USA compete for the Westchester Cup?

4. Which trophy is awarded to the winner of the World Championship of Race Walking?

5. Male golfers from the USA compete against golfers from the Rest of the World to win which major trophy?

6. What is the prize of the Men's World Table Tennis Team Championships?

7. In which sport do competitors meet in the London Open Competition for the Goldberg-Vass Memorial Trophy?

8. The national Rugby Union teams of New Zealand and Australia fight it out for ......what?

9. What is the name of the famous sculling contest on the Thames for passenger skiffs?

10. In which sport is the Air Canada Silver Broom awarded?

11. What is the prize for the 'Derby' of coursing, dating back to 1836?

12. For which trophy do cricket teams from the West Indies and Australia compete?

13. Which rowing competition at Henley Regatta is for the Grand Challenge Cup?

14. The Women's International Show Jumping Competition, held each year at Hickstead, is for which prize?

15. What is the prize for the London Grammar Schools Rugby Fives Competition?

ANSWERS.
1. Men's sabre. 2. The Sir William Burton Trophy. 3. Polo. 4. The Lugano Trophy. 5. The Presidents Trophy. 6. The Swaythling Cup. 7. Judo. 8. The Bledisloe Cup. 9. Doggett's Coat and Badge. 10. Curling. 11. The Waterloo Cup. 12. The Worrell Trophy. 13. The Eights. 14. The Queen Elizabeth II Cup. 15. The Marchant Cup.

World record holders

How much do you know about world record-holders? (1)

QUESTIONS.

Who is the current holder of the world record, and what is the record in the following events:

1. Men's 100 metres?

2. Men's 200 metres?

3. Men's 400 metres?

4. Men's 800 metres?

5. Men's 1,000 metres?

6. Men's 1,500 metres?

7. Men's mile?

8. Men's 2,000 metres?

9. Men's 3,000 metres?

10. Men's 5,000 metres?

11. Men's 10,000 metres?

12. Men's 20,000 metres?

13. Men's 25,000 metres?

14. Men's 30,000 metres?

15. Men's decathlon?

ANSWERS.
1. Maurice Green, USA. 9.79 sec. 2. Michael Johnson, USA. 19.32 sec. 3. Michael Johnson, USA. 43.18 sec. 4. Wilson Kipteker, Denmark. 1 min. 41.11 sec. 5. Noah Ngeny, Kenya. 2 min 11.96 sec. 6. Hicham El Guerrouj, Morocco. 3 min 26 sec. 7. Hicham El Guerrouj, Morocco. 3 min 43.13 sec. 8. Hicham El Guerrouj, Morocco. 4 min 44.79 sec. 9. Daniel Komen, Kenya. 7 min 20.67 sec. 10. Haile Gebrselassie, Ethiopia. 12 min 39.36 sec. 11. Haile Gebrselassie, Ethiopia. 26 min 22.75 sec. 12. Arturo Barrios, Mexico. 56 min 55.6 sec. 13. Toshihiko Seko, Japan. 1 hr 13 min 55.8 sec. 14. Toshihiko Seko, Japan. 1 hr 29 min 18.8 sec. 15. Roman Sebrie, Czech Republic. 9,026 points.

PLease note - records standing as at 30 May 2001.

How much do you know about world record-holders? (2)

QUESTIONS.

Who is the current holder of the world record, and what is the record in the following events:

1. Men's 110 metre hurdles?

2. Men's 400 metre hurdles?

3. Men's 3,000 metres steeplechase?

4. Men's 4 x 100 metres relay?

5. Men's 4 x 400 metres relay?

6. Men's 4 x 800 metres relay?

7. Men's 4 x 1,500 metres relay?

8. Men's High Jump?

9. Men's Pole Vault?

10. Men's Long Jump?

11. Men's Triple Jump?

12. Shot putt?

13. Discus throw?

14. Hammer throw?

15. Javelin throw.?

ANSWERS.
1. .Colin Jackson, GB. 12.91 sec. 2. Kevin Young, USA. 46.78 sec. 3. Bernard Barmasai, Kenya. 7 min 55.72 sec. 4. USA. 37.40 sec. 5. USA. 2 min 54.20 sec. 6. GB. 7 min 03.89 sec. 7. Germany. 14 min 38.80 sec. 8. Javier Sotomayor, Cuba. 2.45 metres. 9. Sergei Bubka, Ukraine. 6.14 metres. 10. Mike Powell, USA. 8.95 metres. 11. Jonathan Edwards, GB. 18.29 metres. 12. Randy Barnes, USA. 23.12 metres. 13. Jurgen Schult, Germany. 74.08 metres. 14. Yuri Sedykh, CIS. 86.74 metres. 15. Jan Zelezny, Czech Republic. 98.48 metres.

PLease note - records standing as at 30 May 2001.

How much do you know about world record-holders? (3)

QUESTIONS.

Who is the current holder of the world record, and what is the record in the following events:

1. Men's marathon?

2. Women's 100 metres?

3. Women's 200 metres?

4. Women's 400 metres?

5. Women's 800 metres?

6. Women's 1,000 metres?

7. Women's 1,500 metres?

8. Women's mile?

9. Women's 2,000 metres?

10. Women's 3,000 metres?

11. Women's 5,000 metres?

12. Women's 10,000 metres?

13. Women's 25,000 metres?

14. Women's 30,000 metres?

15. Women's 100 metre hurdles?

ANSWERS.
1. Khalid Khannouchi, Morocco. 2 hr 5 min 42 sec. 2. Florence Griffith-Joyner, USA. 10.49 sec. 3. Florence Griffith-Joyner, USA. 21.34 sec. 4. Marita Koch, Germany. 47.60 sec. 5. Jarmila Kratochvilova, Czech Republic. 1 min 53.28 sec. 6. Svetlana Masterkova, Russia. 2 min 28.98 sec. 7. Qu Yunxia, China. 3 min 50.46 sec. 8. Svetlana Masterkova, Russia. 4 min 12.56 sec. 9. Sonia O'Sullivan, Ireland. 5 min 25.36 sec. 10. Wang Junxia, China. 8 min 06.11 sec. 11. Jiang Bo, China. 14 min 28.09 sec. 12. Wang Junxia, China. 29 min 31.78 sec. 13. Karolina Szabo, Hungary. 1 hr 29 min 29.2 sec. 14. Karolina Szabo, Hungary. 1 hr 49 min 5.6 sec. 15. Yordanka Donkova, Bulgaria. 12.21 sec.
PLease note - records standing as at 30 May 2001.

How much do you know about world record-holders? (4)

QUESTIONS.

Who is the current holder of the world record, and what is the record in the following events:

1. Women's 400 metre hurdles?

2. Women's 4 x 100 metre relay?

3. Women's 4 x 200 metre relay?

4. Women's 4 x 400 metre relay?

5. Women's high jump?

6. Women's pole vault?

7. Women's long jump?

8. Women's triple jump?

9. Women's shot putt?

10. Women's discus throw?

11. Women's hammer throw?

12. Women's javelin throw?

13. Women's heptathlon?

14. Women's marathon?

15. Women's 20, 000 metre?

ANSWERS.
1. Kim Batten, USA. 52.61 sec. 2. Germany. 41.37 sec. 3. Germany. 1 min 28.15 sec. 4. CIS. 3 min 15.17 sec. 5. Stefka Kostadinova, Bulgaria. 2.09 metres. 6. Stacy Dragila, USA. 4.63 metres. 7. Galina Chistiakova, Russia. 7.52 metres. 8. Inessa Kravets, Ukraine. 15.5 metres. 9. Natalya Lisovskaya, Russia. 22.63 metres. 10. Gaby Reinsch, Germany. 76.80 metres. 11. Michaela Melinte, Romania. 75.97 metres. 12. Pre-1999: Petra Felke, Germany. 80.00 metres. Post 1999: Trine Hattestad, Norway. 69.48 metres. 13. Jackie Joyner-Kersee, USA. 7,291 points. 14. Tegla Laroupe, Kenya. 2 hr 20 min 43 sec. 15. Tegla Laroupe, Kenya. 1 hr 05 min 26.06 sec.

PLease note - records standing as at 30 May 2001.

10

LANGUAGE

Adjectives

How much do you know about adjectives relating to animals? (1)

QUESTIONS.

1. What is the meaning of saurian?

2. What is the meaning of cervine?

3. What is the meaning of caprine?

4. What is the meaning of apian?

5. What is the meaning of leporine?

6. What is the meaning of taurine?

7. What is the meaning of leonine?

8. What is the meaning of piscine?

9. What is the meaning of ovine?

10. What is the meaning of anguine?

11. What is the meaning of simian?

12. What is the meaning of lupine?

13. What is the meaning of murine?

14. What is the meaning of passerine?

15. What is the meaning of ursine?

ANSWERS.
1. Lizard–like. 2. Deer-like. 3. Goat-like. 4. Bee-like. 5. Hare-like. 6. Bull-like. 7. Lion-like. 8. Fish-like. 9. Sheep-like. 10. Snake-like. 11. Ape-like. 12. Wolf-like 13. Mouse-like. 14. Sparrow-like. 15. Bear-like.

How much do you know about adjectives relating to animals? (2)

QUESTIONS.

1. What is the meaning of asinine?

2. What is the meaning of porcine?

3. What is the meaning of anserine?

4. What is the meaning of lyncean?

5. What is the meaning of bovine?

6. What is the meaning of corvine?

7. What is the meaning of equine?

8. What is the meaning of aquiline?

9. What is the meaning of turdoid?

10. What is the meaning of vulpine?

11. What is the meaning of feline?

12. What is the meaning of avian?

13. What is the meaning of canine?

14. What is the meaning of pavanine?

15. What is the meaning of psittacine?

ANSWERS.
1. Ass-like. 2. Pig-like. 3. Goose-like. 4. Lynx-like. 5. Ox-like. 6. Crow-like. 7. Horse-like. 8. Eagle-like. 9. Thrush-like. 10. Fox-like. 11. Cat-like. 12. Bird-like. 13. Dog-like. 14. Peacock-like. 15. Parrot-like.

How much do you know about adjectives relating to objects? (1)

QUESTIONS.

1.   What is the meaning of oviform?

2.   What is the meaning of annular?

3.   What is the meaning of cordate?

4.   What is the meaning of cuneal?

5.   What is the meaning of sagittate?

6.   What is the meaning of toroid?

7.   What is the meaning of verticillate?

8.   What is the meaning of alaric?

9.   What is the meaning of clavate?

10. What is the meaning of dentoid?

11. What is the meaning of falciform?

12. What is the meaning of xiphoid?

13. What is the meaning of stellate?

14. What is the meaning of navicular?

15. What is the meaning of reniform?

ANSWERS.
1. Egg-shaped. 2. Ring-shaped. 3. Heart-shaped. 4. Wedge-shaped. 5. Arrow-shaped. 6. Doughnut-shaped. 7. Whorl-shaped. 8. Wing-shaped. 9. Club-shaped. 10. Tooth-shaped. 11. Sickle-shaped. 12. Sword-shaped. 13. Star-shaped. 14. Boat-shaped. 15. Kidney-shaped.

How much do you know about adjectives relating to objects? (2)

QUESTIONS.

1. What is the meaning of acinaciform?

2. What is the meaning of trochal?

3. What is the meaning of dendroid?

4. What is the meaning of allantoic?

5. What is the meaning of scutate?

6. What is the meaning of unciform?

7. What is the meaning of linguiform?

8. What is the meaning of amygdaloid?

9. What is the meaning of lenticular?

10. What is the meaning of hastate?

11. What is the meaning of lunate?

12. What is the meaning of oculiform?

13. What is the meaning of palmate?

14. What is the meaning of decussate?

15. What is the meaning of arcuate?

ANSWERS.
1. Scimitar-shaped. 2. Wheel-shaped. 3. Tree-shaped. 4. Sausage-shaped. 5. Shield-shaped. 6. Hook-shaped. 7. Tongue-shaped. 8. Almond-shaped. 9. Lens-shaped. 10. Spear-shaped. 11. Crescent-shaped. 12. Eye-shaped. 13. Palm-shaped. 14. Cross-shaped. 15. Bow-shaped.

How much do you know about adjectives relating to objects? (3)

QUESTIONS.

1. What is the meaning of ligneous?

2. What is the meaning of acicular?

3. What is the meaning of cyprinoid?

4. What is the meaning of saponaceous?

5. What is the meaning of pyriform?

6. What is the meaning of marmoreal?

7. What is the meaning of pinnate?

8. What is the meaning of baculiform?

9. What is the meaning of crinoidal?

10. What is the meaning of aciniform?

11. What is the meaning of cancroid?

12. What is the meaning of ethmoid?

13. What is the meaning of ganoid?

14. What is the meaning of crenate?

15. What is the meaning of nervate?

ANSWERS.
1. Wood-like. 2. Needle-like. 3. Carp-like. 4. Soap-like. 5. Pear-like. 6. Marble-like. 7. Feather-like. 8. Rod-like. 9. Lily-like. 10. Grape-like. 11. Crab-like. 12. Sieve-like. 13. Scale-like. 14. Saw-like. 15. Leaf-like.

Americanisms

How much do you know about Americanisms? (1)

QUESTIONS.

What is the American equivalent for each of the following words:

1. Anorak?

2. Braces?

3. Car boot?

4. Caretaker?

5. Motorway?

6. Pushchair?

7. Swede (vegetable)?

8. Maize?

9. Lodger?

10. Undertaker?

11. Merry-go-round?

12. Aubergine?

13. Lift?

14. Sweets?

15. Waistcoat?

ANSWERS.
1. Parka. 2. Suspenders. 3. Trunk. 4. Janitor. 5. Expressway. 6. Stroller. 7. Rutabaga. 8. Corn. 9. Roomer. 10. Mortician. 11. Carousel. 12. Egg plant. 13. Elevator. 14. Candy. 15. Vest.

How much do you know about Americanisms? (2)

QUESTIONS.

What is the American equivalent for each of the following words:

1. Hire purchase?

2. Sweet potato?

3. Suitcase?

4. Autumn?

5. Courgette?

6. Drawing pin?

7. Drainpipe?

8. Curtains?

9. Dinner jacket?

10. Car bonnet?

11. Nappy?

12. Trilby?

13. Tram?

14. Lorry?

15. Flyover?

ANSWERS.
1. Instalment plan. 2. Yam. 3. Valise. 4. Fall. 5. Zucchini. 6. Thumb tack 7. Downspout. 8. Drapes. 9. Tuxedo. 10. Hood. 11. Diaper. 12. Fedora. 13. Street-car. 14. Truck. 15. Overpass.

How much do you know about Americanisms? (3)

QUESTIONS.

What is the American equivalent for each of the following words:

1. Pharmacy?

2. Solicitor?

3. Wallet?

4. Patience? (Card game)

5. Paraffin?

6. Petrol?

7. Frying pan?

8. Short-hand typist?

9. Saloon car?

10. Spanner?

11. Jug?

12. Draughts?

13. Cashier?

14. Music-hall?

15. Underground (tube)?

ANSWERS.
1. Drug-store. 2. Attorney. 3. Billfold. 4. Solitaire. 5. Kerosene. 6. Gas. 7. Skillet. 8. Stenographer. 9. Sedan. 10. Wrench. 11. Pitcher. 12. Checkers. 13. Teller. 14. Vaudeville. 15. Subway.

QUESTION 16 (for no extra points): Who was the literary giant who referred to England and America as 'two countries divided by the same language'?
ANSWER : George Bernard Shaw.

Etymology

How much do you know about the meaning of words? (1)

QUESTIONS.

1. What word means 'to be afflicted with difficulties'?

2. What word means 'to be lacking in moral restraint or self-discipline'?

3. What word means 'existing in a thing as a permanent quality'?

4. What word means 'to be the centre of attraction or admiration'?

5. What word means 'to be fond of or inclined to argument'?

6. In anatomy, what does the word 'genial' mean?

7. What word means 'of, or due to, motion'?

8. What word means 'to wall up, or shut up, in a confined space?

9. In biology, what does the word 'blastula' mean?

10. What word is used to denote a squirrel's nest?

11. What adjective is used to denote something made of earth or clay by a potter?

12. What does the word 'hebdomadal' mean?

13. What does the word 'pixilated' mean?

14. What word describes a sheep that has been shorn only once?

15. In geology what does the word 'surficial' mean?

ANSWERS.
1. Bedevilled. 2. Dissolute. 3. Inherent. 4. Cynosure. 5. Disputatious. 6. Of, or related to, the chin. 7. Kinetic. 8. Mure. 9. An animal embryo at an early stage of development when it is a hollow ball of cells. 10. Drey. 11. Fictile. 12. Weekly. 13. Bewildered, dazed. (Perhaps drunk). 14. Shearling. 15. Of, or relating to the earth's surface.

How much do you know about the meaning of words? (2)

QUESTIONS.

1. What is the meaning of the word 'toponym'?

2. In botany, what is a 'vasculum'?

3. What word means 'a military government'?

4. What word means 'a wicker or wooden basket of any form'?

5. What did the word 'refusenik' mean?

6. In zoology, what does the word 'ovibovine' mean.

7. What word is used to indicate 'low marshy unhealthy land near a seashore'?

8. What word means 'the quantity of motion of a moving body, measured as a product of it's mass and velocity'?

9. In zoology, what name is given to 'any aquatic animal able to swim and move independently'?

10. What word is used to indicate something that is 'showy but flimsy and worthless'?

11. What word means 'to put poison or bitterness into something or into someone's mind'?

12. In music, what word means 'harsh-toned, inharmonious'?

13. What word means 'a couplet or pair of verse lines'?

14. In botany, what word means 'arranged in two opposite vertical rows'?

15. What word means 'extremely distasteful'?

ANSWERS.
1. A descriptive place-name. 2. A collecting-case with a lengthwise opening.
3. Stratocracy. 4. Skep. 5. A Jew who was refused permission to emigrate to Israel from the former Soviet Union. 6. An animal having characteristics intermediate between an ox and a sheep. 7. Maremma. 8. Momentum. 9. A nekton. 10. Gimcrack. 11. Envenom. 12. Dissonant. 13. Distich. 14. Distichous. 15. Repugnant.

How much do you know about the meaning of words? (3)

QUESTIONS.

1. What word means 'an unprincipled person, probably of highly immoral character'?

2. What does the word 'splenology' mean?

3. What word means 'to isolate, seclude, set apart'?

4. What does the word 'serendipity' mean?

5. What does the word 'thalassic' mean?

6. What name is given to a wooden funnel used in brewing?

7. What noun do we use for 'a person of poor health, or unduly anxious about health'?

8. What does the word 'vivers' mean?

9. What word means 'corrupt dealing'?

10. What does the word 'histolysis' mean?

11. What does the word 'dashpot' mean?

12. What word describes the 'act of surrender'?

13. What word means 'having a sandy texture'?

14. What word means 'flatter, coax, cajole'?

15. What does the word 'exurb' mean?

ANSWERS.
1. Reprobate. 2. The scientific study of the spleen. 3. Sequester. 4. The faculty of making happy and unexpected discoveries. 5. Of the seas. 6. Tundish. 7. Valetudinarian. 8. Food, victuals. 9. Jobbery. 10. The breaking down of tissue. 11. A device for damping vibrations or shock. 12. Capitulation. 13. Arenaceous. 14. Blandish. 15. The area (generally prosperous) beyond the suburbs of a town or city. .

How much do you know about the meaning of words? (4)

QUESTIONS.

1. What name is given to waterside coal depot equipped for loading vessels?

2. What does the word ' tenebrous' mean?

3. What adjective indicates a direct line of descent or ancestry?

4. And what adjective relates to the sense of touch?

5. What word means cherry-coloured?

6. What is the hooked staff carried by a bishop as a symbol of his pastoral office called?

7. What is the adjective which indicates a connection to a river or rivers?

8. What is the adjective used to indicate that a vehicle chassis hangs lower than its wheels?

9. What is the meaning of the word 'scepsis'?

10. To what or whom would a Maori be referring if he used the word 'wahine'?

11. What, in the U.S., is a 'yardbird'?

12. What does the word 'tautophony' mean?

13. What does the word 'paronomasia' mean?

14. What does the word 'ogdoad' mean?

15. What name is given to a rope-walker?

ANSWERS.
1. Staithe. 2. Dark, gloomy. 3. Lineal. 4. Haptic. 5. Cerise. 6. A crosier. 7. Fluvial. 8. Underslung. 9. Philosophical doubt. 10. Woman or wife. 11. A convict. 12. Repetition of the same sound. 13. A play on words; a pun. 14. A group of eight. 15. Funambulist.

How much do you know about the meaning of words? (5)

QUESTIONS.

1. In anatomy, what is the word which means the base of a hollow organ, the part farthest from the opening?

2. What word means hard to understand, obscure, profound?

3. What word means to appease an offended person?

4. In anatomy and zoology, what is the word for the urinary bladder?

5. What word means the loss of will-power as a mental disorder?

6. What is the adjective which means away from or opposite the mouth?

7. What do we call a French idiom, especially one adopted into another language?

8. What is the name given to the white area at the base of a fingernail?

9. What is a young chicken bred for eating?

10. What is the word for a narrow passage, or alleyway, between houses?

11. What do we call a band placed round a horse's body to keep a pack in place?

12. What is the light-reflecting part of the choroid membrane of a cat's eye called?

13. What is the name given to the study of the flow and deformation of matter?

14. What is the transitive verb which means to change the order or arrangement of something?

15. What do we call the prediction of the future through communication (supposed) with the dead?

ANSWERS.
1. Fundus. 2. Abstruse. 3. Propitiate. 4. Vesica. 5. Aboulia. 6. Aboral. 7. Gallicism. 8. Lunula. 9. Poussin. 10. Snicket. 11. Surcingle. 12. Tapetum. 13. Rheology. 14. Permutate. 15. Necromancy.

Proverbs

How much do you know about proverbs? (1)

QUESTIONS.

According to collective wisdom:

1. Who makes the best gamekeeper?
2. To where do all roads lead?
3. What does nature abhor?
4. If you sing before breakfast, what will you do before supper?
5. What is the mother of good luck?
6. In what is the proof of the pudding?
7. Out of what can you not make a silk purse?
8. What is its own reward?
9. With what is the road to hell paved?
10. How do still waters run?
11. For what purpose should you save your breath?
12. A fair exchange is no what?
13. What is as good as a feast?
14. What should he have, that sups with the devil?
15. What is knowledge?

ANSWERS.
1. An old poacher. 2. Rome. 3. A vacuum. 4. Cry. 5. Diligence. 6. The eating. 7. A sow's ear. 8. Virtue. 9. Good intentions. 10. Deep. 11. To cool your porridge. 12. Robbery. 13. Enough. 14. A long spoon. 15. Power.

How much do you know about proverbs? (2)

QUESTIONS.

According to collective wisdom:

1. What is the mother of invention?

2. What is Monday's child?

3. What grow from little acorns?

4. If you go to bed with the lamb, you will rise with what?

5. What does every cloud have?

6. What will a drowning man clutch at?

7. What are all grey in the dark?

8. What butter no parsnips?

9. What will you catch, if you chase two hares?

10. What does one magpie stand for?

11. What did faint heart never win?

12. What does a heavy purse make?

13. How long does a wonder last?

14. Who will appear, when you talk of him?

15. What is better than cure?

ANSWERS.
1. Necessity. 2. Fair of face. 3. Mighty oaks. 4. The lark. 5. A silver lining. 6. A straw. 7. Cats. 8. Fair words. 9. Neither. 10. Sorrow. 11. Fair lady. 12. A light heart. 13. Nine days. 14. The devil. 15. Prevention.

How much do you know about proverbs? (3)

QUESTIONS.

According to collective wisdom:

1. What must be done to that which cannot be cured?
2. What is better than rent?
3. What is spoiled by sparing the rod?
4. What is the thief of time?
5. What is Tuesday's child?
6. Who must be above suspicion?
7. The folly of one man is the – what? – of another.
8. He was a bold man who first ate a …..what?
9. What or who comes in like a lion, but goes out like a lamb?
10. What kind of sky is never long dry?
11. What should you never trouble, until it troubles you?
12. What is the mistress of fools?
13. What do two magpies stand for?
14. What is the key to poverty?
15. Who says the least?

ANSWERS.
1. It must be endured. 2. Providence. 3. The child. 4. Procrastination. 5. Full of grace. 6. Caesar's wife. 7. Fortune. 8. An oyster. 9. March. 10. A mackerel sky. 11. Trouble. 12. Experience. 13. Mirth. 14. Sloth. 15. He who knows the most.

Foreign languages

How much do you know about French sayings? (1)

QUESTIONS.

1. What does 'A bon marche' mean?

2. What does 'A la carte' mean?

3. What does 'A la mode' mean?

4. What does 'A propos' mean?

5. What does 'Au revoir' mean?

6. What does ;Avant-garde' mean?

7. What is a 'Billet-doux'?

8. What does 'Bonhomie' mean?

9. What is a 'Bon mot'?

10. What does 'Bourgeois' mean?

11. What does 'Carte blanche' mean?

12. What does 'Cela va sans dire'?

13. What does 'C'est la vie' mean?

14. What is a 'Coup de grace'?

15. What is a 'Coup d'etat'?

ANSWERS.
1. Cheap. 2. According to the menu. 3. Fashionable. 4. To the purpose. 5. Until we see one another again. 6. In the vanguard. 7. Love letter. 8. Good nature. 9. A witty remark. 10. Middle-class person. 11. Free hand. 12. That goes without saying. 13. That's life. 14. A stroke of mercy. 15. Sudden, violent overthrow of a government or leader.

How much do you know about French sayings? (2)

QUESTIONS.

1. What does 'Cri de coeur' mean?

2. What is a 'Cul-de-sac'?

3. What does 'Déjà vu' mean?

4. What does 'De rigueur' mean?

5. What does 'Dernier cri' mean?

6. What does 'De trop' mean?

7. What does 'Dos-a-dos' mean?

8. What does 'Esprit de corps' mean?

9. What does 'Fait accompli' mean?

10. What is a 'Faux pas'?

11. What does 'Haute couture' mean?

12. What does 'Vis-à-vis' mean?

13. What does 'Tour-de-force' mean?

14. What is a 'Table d'hote'?

15. What is a 'Soupcon' ?

ANSWERS.
1.A cry from the heart. 2.A dead end. 3.Already seen. 4. Required by etiquette or good taste. 5.The very latest thing. 6. Over the top. 7. Back to back. 8.Team spirit. 9. An accomplished fact. 10.A social gaffe. 11. High fashion. 12. In relation to. 13. Display of power or strength. 14. Fixed price menu. 15.A grain of, a suspicion of.

How much do you know about French sayings? (3)

QUESTIONS.

1. What does 'Savoir faire' mean?

2. What does it mean, to be 'Sans souci'?

3. What does it mean, to have 'Sang-froid'

4. What does 'Rien-ne-va-plus' mean?

5. What does 'Raison d'etre' mean?

6. What does 'Pret-a-porter' mean?

7. What does 'Pis aller' mean?

8. What is a 'Patois'?

9. What is a 'Parvenu'?

10. What is a 'Nom de plume'?

11. What does 'Mot juste' mean?

12. What does 'Laissez-faire' mean?

13. What does 'Hors de combat' mean?

14. What is an 'Homme d'affaires'?

15. What does 'Joie de vivre' mean?

ANSWERS.
1. Know-how. 2. Without a care. 3. To be cool, composed. 4. No more bets. 5. Reason for being. 6. Ready to wear. 7. Last choice. 8. A dialect. 9. An upstart. 10. Pen-name. 11. Appropriate word. 12. Unrestricted trade. 13. Out of the battle. 14. A businessman. 15. Joy of living.

How much do you know about German sayings? (1)

QUESTIONS.

1. What does 'Achtung' mean?

2. What does 'Angst' mean?

3. What does 'Anschauung' mean?

4. What does 'Auf wiedersehen' mean?

5. What is a 'Doppelganger'?

6. What do we mean by 'Dummkopf'?

7. What does 'Ersatz' mean?

8. What is a 'Gastarbeiter'?

9. What do we mean by 'Jugendstil'?

10. What is 'Kitsch'?

11. What do we experience when we feel 'Schadenfreude'?

12. What is a 'Wunderkind'?

13. What did 'Wehrmacht' mean?

14. What is meant by 'Realpolitik'?

15. What does 'Ich dien' mean?

ANSWERS.
1. Attention! 2. Anxiety. 3. Viewpoint. 4. Until we see each other again. 5. A double. 6. Idiot. 7. Substitute. 8. Guest worker, foreign worker. 9. Art nouveau. 10. Cheap, vulgar, worthless art. 11. Joy in another's misfortune. 12. Wonder child. 13. Defence forces. 14. A totally realistic and opportunistic approach to politics. 15. I serve.

How much do you know about German sayings? (2)

QUESTIONS.

1. What is the 'Deutsche Aktien Index (commonly known as DAX) ?

2. What is a 'Briefmarke'?

3. What is a 'Schloss'?

4. What is a 'Personenkraftwagen' (commonly known as a PKW) ?

5. Who is the 'Bundeskanzler'?

6. What is a 'Bahnhof'?

7. What does 'Guten Tag' mean?

8. What does 'Gruss Gott' mean?

9. What is a 'Brauerei'?

10. What is a 'U-Bahn'?

11. What does 'Rundfunk' mean?

12. What is 'Lebensversicherung'?

13. What does 'Ausgang' mean?

14. What is a 'Fernseher'?

15. What does 'Strand' mean?

ANSWERS.

1. German Shares Index. 2. A postage stamp. 3. A castle. 4. A motor car. 5. The Chancellor (Germany's equivalent of the Prime Minister). 6. A railway station. 7. Good-day. 8. 'Guten Tag' in Southern Germany. 9. A brewery. 10. Underground railway 11. Radio. 12. Life insurance. 13. Way Out. 14. A TV set. 15. Beach.

How much do you know about German sayings? (3)

QUESTIONS.

1. What are we talking about when we refer to the 'Wirtschaftswunder'?

2. Who is a 'Burgermeister'?

3. What is the 'Bundesbank'?

4. What is a 'Flughafen'?

5. What is a 'Europapokalsieger'?

6. What, in football, is an 'Elfmeter'?

7. If you were in the 'Schwarzwald', where would you be?

8. If you were studying 'Naturwissenschaften', of what would you be a student?

9. And if you were receiving 'Arbeitslosenunterstutzung', what would you be getting?

10. What is a 'Junggeselle'?

11. If you needed the services of a 'Rechtsanwalt', who would you be looking for?

12. If you were in a 'Selstbedienungsrestaurant', where would you be?

13. What is an 'Abschleppwagen'?

14. What is a Schonheitkonigin'?

15. If you were watching the 'Fussballweltmeisterschaft' what would you be looking at?

ANSWERS.
1.The German economic regeneration of the 1950's and '60's. 2.Town Mayor. 3. Germany's central bank. 4.An airport. 5.A European Cup Winner. 6.A penalty. 7.The Black Forest. 8. Science. 9. Unemployment benefit. 10.A bachelor. 11.A lawyer. 12. In a cafeteria. 13. Breakdown van. 14. Beauty Queen. 15.The world cup.

How much do you know about Latin sayings? (1)

QUESTIONS.

1. What does the famous Roman maxim 'Divide et impera' mean?

2. What does the motto of the U.S.A. 'E pluribus unum' mean?

3. What does 'Ab initio' mean?

4. What does 'Ad astra' mean?

5. So what does the motto of the R.A.F. 'Per ardua ad astra' mean?

6. What does 'bona fide' mean?

7. What does 'cui bono?' mean?

8. What does 'Non compos mentis' mean?

9. What does 'Carpe diem' mean?

10. What doe 'Caveat emptor' mean?

11. What does 'De profundis' mean?

12. What does 'Nota bene' mean?

13. What does 'In vino, veritas' mean?

14. What does 'Inter alia' mean?

15. What does 'Quid pro quo' mean?

ANSWERS.
1. Divide, and rule. 2. From many, one. 3. From the beginning. 4. To the stars. 5. Through adversity to the stars. 6. In good faith. 7. To whose good? 8. Not of sound mind. 9. Seize the day. 10. Let the buyer beware. 11. Out of the depths. 12. Note well. 13. In wine, truth. 14. Among other things. 15. One thing for another.

How much do you know about Latin sayings? (2)

QUESTIONS.

1. What does 'Nil desperandum' mean?

2. What does 'Tempus fugit' mean?

3. What does 'Vox populi' mean?

4. What does 'Sub rosa' mean?

5. What does 'Tabula rasa' mean?

6. What does 'Viva voce' mean?

7. What does 'Sine qua non' mean?

8. What does 'Obiter dictum' mean?

9. What does 'Non sequitur' mean?

10. What does 'Hic jacet' mean?

11. What does 'Hic et nunc' mean?

12. What does 'Ipso facto' mean?

13. What does 'In flagrante delecto' mean?

14. What does 'Nec plus ultra' mean?

15. What does 'Modus operandi' mean?

ANSWERS.
1. Never despair. 2. Time flies. 3. The voice of the people. 4. In secret. 5. Clean slate. 6. Orally. 7. An essential condition. 8. Said in passing 9. Irrelevant. 10. Here lies. 11. Here and now. 12. By the fact itself. 13. In the act of the crime. 14. Perfection. 15. Method of working

How much do you know about Latin sayings? (3)

QUESTIONS.

1. What does 'Ad hoc' mean?

2. What does 'Alma Mater' mean?

3. What does 'Annus mirabilis' mean?

4. What does 'Ex officio' mean?

5. What does 'Floreat' mean?

6. What does 'Fidei Defensor' mean?

7. What does 'Persona non grata' mean?

8. What does 'Per se' mean?

9. What does 'Quod erat demonstrandum' (usually seen as just qed) mean?

10. What does 'A priori' mean?

11. What does 'Corpus delecti' mean?

12. What does 'Cum grano salis' mean?

13. What does 'Infra dig' mean?

14. What does 'Curriculum vitae' mean?

15. What does 'Lapsus liguae' mean?

ANSWERS.
1. To this (particular purpose). 2. Fostering mother. 3. Wonderful year. 4. By virtue of his office. 5. May it flourish. 6. Defender of the faith. 7. An unacceptable person. 8. In itself. 9. Which was to be demonstrated. 10. From cause to effect. 11. The body, or substance of a crime. 12. With a grain of salt. 13. Below one's dignity. 14. The course of a life. 15. A slip of the tongue.

How much do you know about collective nouns? (1)

QUESTIONS.

What are the collective nouns for the following subjects:

1. Budgerigars ?
2. Falcons?
3. Bees?
4. Chickens?
5. Eagles?
6. Foresters?
7. Donkeys?
8. Cats?
9. Boys?
10. Rooks?
11. Rhinoceroses?
12. Partridges?
13. Harpists?
14. Parrots?
15. Penguins?

ANSWERS.
1.A chatter. 2.A cast. 3.A swarm. 4.A brood. 5.A convocation. 6.A stalk. 7.A drove. 8. A clowder. 9.A blush. 10.A clamour. 11.A crash. 12.A covey 13.A melody. 14.A company. 15.A colony or rookery

How much do you know about collective nouns? (2)

QUESTIONS.

What are the collective nouns for the following subjects:

1. Starlings?

2. Peacocks?

3. Monkeys?

4. Ravens?

5. Tigers?

6. Lions?

7. Nightingales?

8. Quail?

9. Thrushes?

10. Trout?

11. Sandpipers?

12. Guillemots?

13. Hermits?

14. Hunting dogs?

15. Turkeys?

ANSWERS.
1. A murmuration. 2. A muster. 3. A troop. 4. An unkindness. 5. An ambush. 6. A pride.
7. A watch. 8. A bevy. 9. A mutation. 10. A hover. 11. A fling. 12. A bazaar. 13. An
observance. 14. A cry. 15. A rafter.

How much do you know about collective nouns? (3)

QUESTIONS.

What are the collective nouns for the following subjects:

1. Owls?

2. Spiders?

3. Kittens?

4. Snipe?

5. Roes?

6. Porpoises?

7. Whales?

8. Wild cats?

9. Turtle doves?

10. Goldfish?

11. Bloodhounds?

12. Toads?

13. Woodpeckers?

14. Pheasants?

15. Jellyfish?

ANSWERS.
1.A parliament. 2.A clutter. 3.A kindle. 4.A wisp. 5.A bevy. 6.A school. 7.A pod. 8.A dout. 9.A pitying. 10.A troubling. 11.A sute. 12.A knot or kneb. 13.A descent. 14.A nye. 15.A smuck.